GLOBAL  STUDIES

AFRICA

SEVENTH EDITION

Dr. F. Jeffress Ramsay

Dushkin/McGraw-Hill
Sluice Dock, Guilford, Connecticut 06437

Visit us on the Internet—http://www.dushkin.com/

Africa

OTHER BOOKS IN THE GLOBAL STUDIES SERIES

- China
- India and South Asia
- Japan and the Pacific Rim
- Latin America
- The Middle East
- Russia, the Eurasian Republics, and Central/Eastern Europe
- Western Europe

Cataloging in Publication Data
Main Entry under title: Global Studies: Africa. 7th ed.
        1. Africa—History—1960–. I. Title: Africa. II. Ramsay, Jeffress F., *comp.*
ISBN 0–697–37422–X   960.3   91–71258

Seventh Edition

Printed in the United States of America

Africa

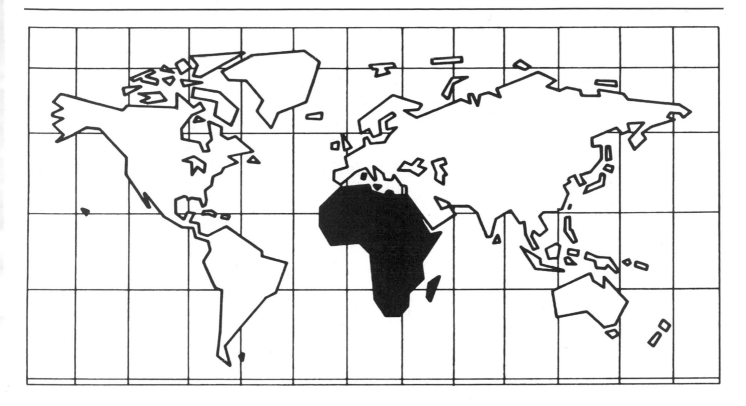

AUTHOR/EDITOR

Dr. F. Jeffress Ramsay

Dr. F. Jeffress ("Jeff") Ramsay, the author/editor of *Global Studies: Africa,* obtained his Ph.D. in African history from Boston University. He has extensive experience in both secondary and tertiary education in the United States and in Botswana, where he is currently the principal of Legae Academy in Gaborone. Dr. Ramsay regularly writes for Botswana newspapers, as well as popular and academic periodicals; he is the vice-chairman of the Botswana Chapter of the Media Institute of Southern Africa; secretary of the Botswana Society; and he has been involved in the development of regional museums. He recently received Botswana's Presidential Order of Honour for his varied contributions to the country. Along with Barry Morton and Themba Mgadla, he is the coauthor of *Building a Nation, a History of Botswana from 1800–1910* (Longman Botswana, 1996); he is the coeditor with Fred Morton of *Birth of Botswana, a History of the Bechuanaland Protectorate from 1910–1966* (Longman Botswana, 1987); the coauthor of *A Historical Dictionary of Botswana* (Scarecrow Press, 3rd ed., 1997), with Barry Morton and Fred Morton; he collaborated with Barry Morton on *The Making of a President, Sir Ketumile Masire's Early Years* (Pula Press, 1996); and, along with Lucey Clarke, he coauthored *New Three Year I. C. Social Studies Revision Notes* (Tasalls, 1997).

SERIES CONSULTANT

H. Thomas Collins
PROJECT LINKS
George Washington University

STAFF

Ian A. Nielsen	Publisher
Brenda S. Filley	Production Manager
Lisa M. Clyde	Developmental Editor
Roberta Moncao	Editor
Charles Vitelli	Designer
Cheryl Greenleaf	Permissions Coordinator
Shawn Callahan	Graphics
Lara M. Johnson	Graphics
Laura Levine	Graphics
Michael Campbell	Graphics
Joseph Offredi	Graphics
Juliana Arbo	Typesetting Supervisor

Selected World Wide Web Sites for Africa

GENERAL SITES

CNN Online Page—**http://www.cnn.com/**—U.S. 24-hour video news channel. News, updated every few hours, includes text, pictures, and film. Good external links.

C-SPAN ONLINE—**http://www.c-span.org/**—See especially C-SPAN International on the Web for International Programming Highlights and archived C-Span programs.

International Network Information Center at University of Texas—**http://inic.utexas.edu/**—Gateway has pointers to international sites, including Africa, as well as African Studies Resources.

Political Science RESOURCES—**http://www.keele.ac.uk:80/depts/po/psr.htm/**—Dynamic gateway to sources available via European addresses. Listed by country name.

ReliefWeb—**http://www.reliefweb.int/**—UN's Department of Humanitarian Affairs clearinghouse for international humanitarian emergencies. Has daily updates, including Reuters, VOA, PANA.

Social Science Information Gateway (SOSIG)—**http://sosig.esrc.bris.ac.uk/**—Project of the Economic and Social Research Council (ESRC). It catalogs 22 subjects and lists developing countries' URL addresses.

United Nations System—**http://www.unsystem.org/**—This is the official Web site for the United Nations system of organizations. Everything is listed alphabetically. Offers: UNICC; Food and Agriculture Organization.

UN Development Programme (UNDP)—**http://www.undp.org/**—Publications and current information on world poverty, Mission Statement, UN Development Fund for Women, and more. Be sure to see Poverty Clock.

U.S. Agency for International Development (USAID)—**http://www.info.usaid.gov/**—U.S. policy regarding assistance to African countries is available at this site.

U.S. Central Intelligence Agency Home Page—**http://www.odci.gov/cia/**—This site includes publications of the CIA, such as the 1996 World Fact Book, 1995 Fact Book on Intelligence, Handbook of International Economic Statistics, 1996, and CIA maps.

U.S. Department of State Home Page—**http://www.state.gov/index.html/**—Organized by categories: Hot Topics (i.e., 1996 Country Reports on Human Rights Practices), International Policy, Business Services.

World Bank Group—**www.worldbank.org/html/Welcome.html/**—News (i.e., press releases, summary of new projects, speeches), publications, topics in development, countries and regions. Links to other financial organizations.

World Health Organization (WHO)—**http://www.who.ch/**—Maintained by WHO's headquarters in Geneva, Switzerland, uses Excite search engine to conduct keyword searches.

World Trade Organization—**http://www.wto.org/**—Topics include foundation of world trade systems, data on textiles, intellectual property rights, legal frameworks, trade and environmental policies, recent agreements, etc.

AFRICAN SITES

Africa News Web Site: Crisis in the Great Lakes Region—**http://www.africanews.org/greatlakes.html/**—African News Web Site on Great Lakes (i.e., Rwanda, Burundi, Zaire, and Kenya, Tanzania, Uganda). Frequent updates, good links to other sites. Can order e-mail crisis updates here.

African Policy Information Center (APIC)/—**http://www.igc.apc.org/apic/index.shtml/**—Developed by Washington Office on Africa to widen policy debate in the United States on African issues. Includes special topic briefs, regular reports, and documents on African politics.

Africa: South of the Sahara—**http://www-sul.stanford.edu/depts/ssrg/africa/guide.html/**—Link headings, Topics and Regions, will lead to a wealth of information.

African Studies WWW (U.Penn)—**http://www.sas.upenn.edu/African_Studies/AS.html/**—This excellent site will lead you to facts about each African country: news, statistics, and links to other Web sites.

Great Horn Information Exchange—**http://www.info.usaid.gov/HORN)/**—You will find information about African problems and humanitarian efforts to solve them, compiled by the U.S. Agency for International Development.

Library of Congress Country Studies—**http://lcweb2.loc.gov/frd/cs/cshome.html#toc/**—There are 71 countries that are covered in the continuing series of books available at this Web site. At least a dozen of them are in Africa.

South African Government Index—**http://www.polity.org.za/gnuindex.html/**—Official site included links to government agencies. Provides information on structures of government and links to detailed documents.

Weekly Mail & Guardian (Johannesburg)—**http://www.mg.co.za/mg/**—Free electronic daily South African newspaper (see especially What's New on Web). Includes archived back issues of newspapers. Good links to other links related to Africa.

COUNTRIES

Additional individual-country information can be located at the following sites:

Eritrea—**http://www.cs.indiana.edu/hyplan/dmulholl/eritrea/eritrea.html/**

Kenya—**http://www.AfricaOnline.co.kc/**

Nigeria—**http://www.coe.uncc.edu/~ecodili/nigeria.html/**

South Africa—**http://www.ananzi.co.za/catalog/**

Sudan—**http://lcweb2.loc.gov/frd/cs/sutoc.html/**

Contents

Global Studies: Africa, Seventh Edition

North Africa   Page 11

West Africa   Page 47

Central Africa   Page 73

East Africa   Page 111

Southern Africa   Page 164

Introduction

THE GLOBAL AGE

As we approach the end of the twentieth century, it is clear that the future we face will be considerably more international in nature than was ever believed possible in the past. Each day, print and broadcast journalists make us aware that our world is becoming increasingly smaller and substantially more interdependent.

The environmental crisis, world food shortages, nuclear weaponry, and regional conflicts that threaten to involve us all make it clear that the distinctions between domestic and foreign problems are all too often artificial, that many seemingly domestic problems no longer stop at national boundaries. As Rene Dubos, the 1969 Pulitzer Prize recipient, stated: "[I]t becomes obvious that each [of us] has two countries, [our] own and planet Earth." As global interdependence has become a reality, it has become vital for the citizens of this world to develop literacy in global matters.

THE GLOBAL STUDIES SERIES

It is the aim of this Global Studies series to help readers acquire a basic knowledge and understanding of the regions and countries in the world. Each volume provides a foundation of information—geographic, cultural, economic, political, historical, artistic, and religious—that will allow readers to better understand the current and future problems within these countries and regions and to comprehend how events there might affect their own well-being. In short, these volumes attempt to provide the background information necessary to respond to the realities of our global age.

Author/Editor
Each of the volumes in the Global Studies series is crafted under the careful direction of an author/editor—an expert in the area under study. The author/editors teach and conduct research and have traveled extensively through the regions about which they are writing.

The author/editor for each volume has written the umbrella essay introducing the area. For the seventh edition of *Global Studies: Africa*, the author/editor has extensively revised and updated the regional essays and country reports. In addition, he has overseen the gathering of statistical information for each country and has been instrumental in the selection of the world press articles that appear at the end of the book.

Contents and Features
The Global Studies volumes are organized to provide concise information and current world press articles on the regions and countries within those areas under study.

Area and Regional Essays
Global Studies: Africa covers North Africa, West Africa, Central Africa, East Africa, and Southern Africa. Each of these regions is discussed in a regional essay focusing on the geographical, cultural, sociopolitical and economic aspects of the countries and people of that area. The purpose of the regional essays is to provide the reader with a sense of the diversity of the area as well as an understanding of its common cultural and historical backgrounds. Accompanying each of the regional narratives is a full-page map showing the political boundaries of the countries within the region. In addition to these regional essays, the author/editor has provided a narrative essay on the African continent as a whole. This area essay examines a number of broad themes in an attempt to define what constitutes "Africa."

A Special Note on the Regions of Africa
The countries of Africa do not fall into clear-cut regions. Many of the political divisions that exist today are the product of Africa's colonial heritage, and often they do not reflect cultural, religious, or historical connections. This has created tensions within and among nations, and it makes abstract divisions somewhat arbitrary. Nations that share geographical aspects with one group of countries may share a cultural history with a different group. The regional essays provide explanations for how countries have been grouped in this volume. Readers may encounter different arrangements in other sources. The regional essays should be read carefully to understand why the author/editor chose the divisions made here.

North Africa
North Africa is a special case in relation to the rest of the African continent. Culturally, geopolitically, and economically, the Muslim countries of North Africa are often major players on the Middle Eastern stage as well as on the African scene. For this reason, we have included a regional essay for North Africa in this volume, but the individual country reports and the world press articles for that region appear as part of the expanded coverage of North Africa in *The Middle East* volume of the Global Studies series.

Country Reports
Concise reports on each of the regions with the exception of North Africa follow the regional essays. These reports are the heart of each Global Studies volume. *Global Studies: Africa, Seventh Edition*, contains 48 country reports.

The country reports are composed of six standard elements. Each report contains a small, semidetailed map visually positioning the country among its neighboring states; a detailed summary of statistical information; a brief "wild card" highlighting an important or informative aspect of the country; a current essay providing important historical, geographical, political, cultural, and economic information; a historical timeline offering a convenient visual survey of some key historical events; and, at the end of each report, four graphic indicators with summary statements about the country in terms of development, freedom, health/welfare, and achievements.

A Note on the Statistical Summaries
The statistical information provided for each country has been drawn from a wide range of sources. (The most frequently referenced are listed on page 264.) Every effort has been made to provide the most current and accurate information available. However, occasionally the information cited by sources differs to some extent; and, all too often, the most current information available for some countries happens to be dated. Aside from these difficulties, the statistical summary of each country is generally quite complete and up to date. Care should be taken in using these statistics—or, for that matter, any published statistics—when making hard comparisons among countries. However, as a point of reference, we have also provided comparable statistics for Canada and the United States, which follow on the next two pages.

World Press Articles
Within each Global Studies volume is reprinted a number of articles carefully selected by our editorial staff and the author/editor from a broad range of international periodicals and newspapers. The articles have been chosen for currency, interest, and their differing perspectives on the subject countries. There are 20 articles in this edition of *Global Studies: Africa*.

The articles section is preceded by an annotated table of contents as well as a topic guide. The annotated table of contents offers a brief summary of each article, while the topic guide indicates the main theme(s) of each article. Thus, readers wishing to focus on a particular theme, say, religion, may refer to the topic guide to find those articles.

Spelling
In many instances, articles may use forms of spelling that are different from the American style. In order to retain the flavor of the articles and to make the point that our system is not the only one, spellings have not been altered to conform to the U.S. system.

WWW Sites, Glossary, Bibliography, Index
An annotated list of selected World Wide Web sites can be found on page v in this edition of *Global Studies: Africa*.

At the back of each Global Studies volume, readers will find a glossary of terms and abbreviations, which provides a quick reference to the specialized vocabulary of the area under study and to the standard acronyms (IMF, OAU, ANC, etc.) used throughout the volume.

Following the glossary is a bibliography. The bibliography is organized into general-reference volumes, national and regional histories, novels in translation, current events publications, and periodicals that provide regular coverage on Africa.

The index at the end of the volume is an accurate reference to the contents of the volume. Readers seeking specific information and citations should consult this standard index.

Currency and Usefulness
This seventh edition of *Global Studies: Africa* is intended to provide the most current and useful information available necessary to understanding the events that are shaping the cultures of Africa today.

We plan to revise this volume on a continuing basis. The statistics will be updated, regional essays rewritten, country reports revised, and articles replaced as new and current information becomes available. In order to accomplish this task, we will turn to our author/editor, and—hopefully—to you, the users of this volume. Your comments are more than welcome. If you have an idea that you think will make the volume more useful, an article or bit of information that will make it more current, or a general comment on its organization, content, or features that you would like to share with us, please send it in for serious consideration for the next edition.

(Oxfam photo)
We must understand the hopes, problems, and cultures of the people of other nations in order to understand our own future.

Canada

GEOGRAPHY

Area in Square Kilometers (Miles):
9,976,140 (3,850,790) (slightly larger
than the United States)
Capital (Population): Ottawa
(980,000)
Climate: from temperate in south to
subarctic and arctic in north

PEOPLE

Population
Total: 28,820,670
Annual Growth Rate: 1.09%
Rural/Urban Population Ratio: 23/77
Major Languages: English; French
Ethnic Makeup: 40% British Isles
origin; 27% French origin; 20% other
European; 1.5% indigenous Indian
and Eskimo; 11.5% mixed

Health
Life Expectancy at Birth: 76 years
(male); 83 years (female)
Infant Mortality Rate (Ratio):
6.8/1,000
Average Caloric Intake: 127% of
FAO minimum
Physicians Available (Ratio): 1/464

Religions
46% Roman Catholic; 16% United
Church; 10% Anglican; 28% others

Education
Adult Literacy Rate: 97%

COMMUNICATION

Telephones: 18,000,000
Newspapers: 96 in English; 11 in
French

TRANSPORTATION

Highways—Kilometers (Miles):
849,404 (530,028)
Railroads—Kilometers (Miles):
78,148 (48,764)
Usable Airfields: 1,386

GOVERNMENT

Type: confederation with
parliamentary democracy
Independence Date: July 1, 1867
Head of State/Government: Queen
Elizabeth II; Prime Minister Jean
Chrétien
Political Parties: Progressive
Conservative Party; Liberal Party;
New Democratic Party; Reform

Party; Bloc Québécois
Suffrage: universal at 18

MILITARY

Number of Armed Forces: 88,000
*Military Expenditures (% of Central
Government Expenditures):* 1.6%
Current Hostilities: none

ECONOMY

Currency ($U.S. Equivalent): 1.35
Canadian dollars = $1
Per Capita Income/GDP:
$22,760/$639.8 billion
Inflation Rate: 0.2%
Natural Resources: petroleum; natural
gas; fish; minerals; cement; forestry
products; fur
Agriculture: grains; livestock; dairy
products; potatoes; hogs; poultry and
eggs; tobacco
Industry: oil production and refining;
natural-gas development; fish
products; wood and paper products;
chemicals; transportation equipment

FOREIGN TRADE

Exports: $164.3 billion
Imports: $151.5 billion

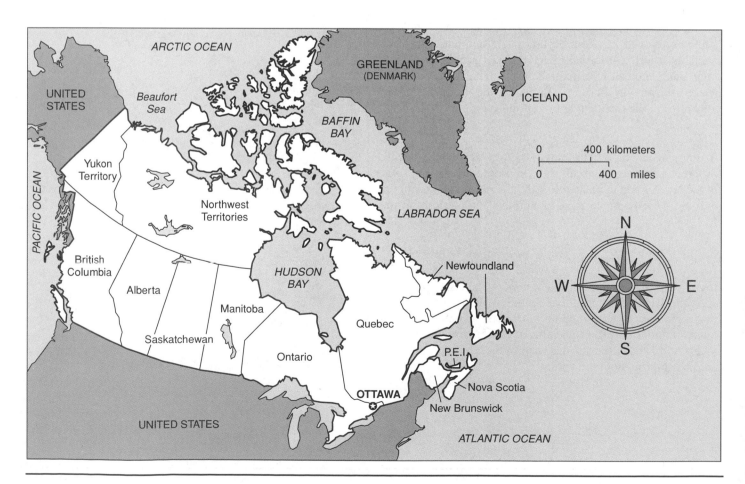

The United States

GEOGRAPHY

Area in Square Kilometers (Miles):
9,578,626 (3,618,770)
Capital (Population): Washington,
D.C. (567,100)
Climate: temperate

PEOPLE

Population
Total: 265,562,700
Annual Growth Rate: 1.02%
Rural/Urban Population Ratio: 25/75
Major Languages: English; Spanish;
others
Ethnic Makeup: 80% white; 12%
black; 6% Hispanic; 2% Asian,
Pacific Islander, American Indian,
Eskimo, and Aleut

Health
Life Expectancy at Birth: 73 years
(male); 80 years (female)
Infant Mortality Rate (Ratio):
7.8/1,000
Average Caloric Intake: 138% of
FAO minimum
Physicians Available (Ratio): 1/391

Religions
55% Protestant; 36% Roman
Catholic; 4% Jewish; 5% Muslim
and others

Education
Adult Literacy Rate: 97.9% (official)
(estimates vary widely)

COMMUNICATION

Telephones: 182,558,000
Newspapers: 1,679 dailies;
approximately 63,000,000 circulation

TRANSPORTATION

Highways—Kilometers (Miles):
6,243,163 (3,895,733)
Railroads—Kilometers (Miles):
240,000 (149,161)
Usable Airfields: 15,032

GOVERNMENT

Type: federal republic
Independence Date: July 4, 1776
Head of State: President William
("Bill") Jefferson Clinton
Political Parties: Democratic Party;
Republican Party; others of minor
political significance
Suffrage: universal at 18

MILITARY

Number of Armed Forces: 1,807,177
*Military Expenditures (% of Central
Government Expenditures):* 4.2%
Current Hostilities: none

ECONOMY

Per Capita Income/GDP:
$25,800/$6.738 trillion
Inflation Rate: 2.6%
Natural Resources: metallic and
nonmetallic minerals; petroleum;
arable land
Agriculture: food grains; feed crops;
oil-bearing crops; livestock; dairy
products
Industry: diversified in both capital-
and consumer-goods industries

FOREIGN TRADE

Exports: $513 billion
Imports: $664 billion

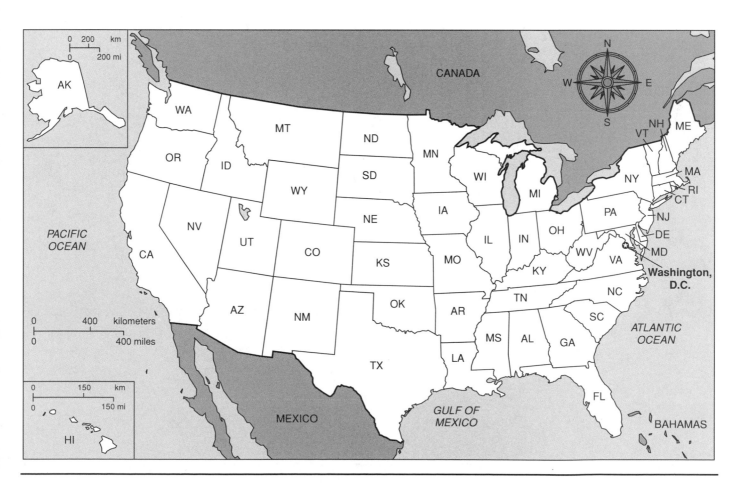

This map of the world highlights the nations of Africa that are discussed in this volume. Regional essays and country reports are written from a cultural perspective in order to give a frame of reference to the current events in that region. All of the essays are designed to present the most current and useful information available today. Other volumes in the Global Studies series cover different areas of the globe and examine the current state of affairs of the countries within those regions.

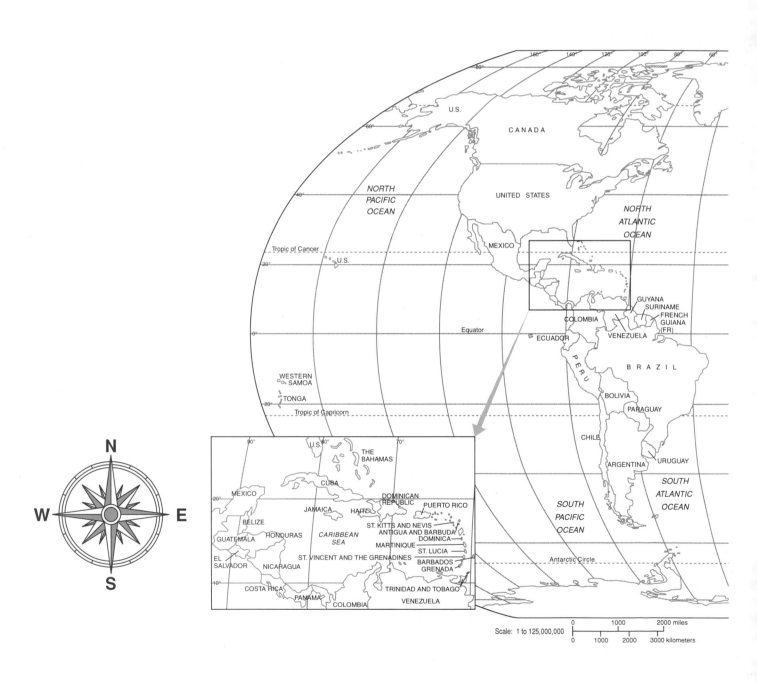

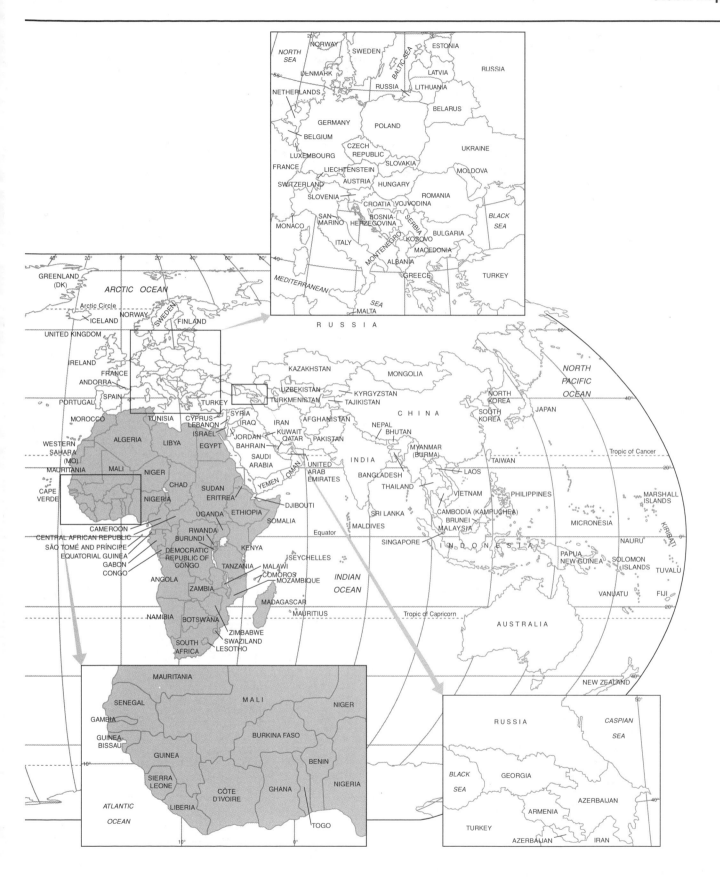

Africa

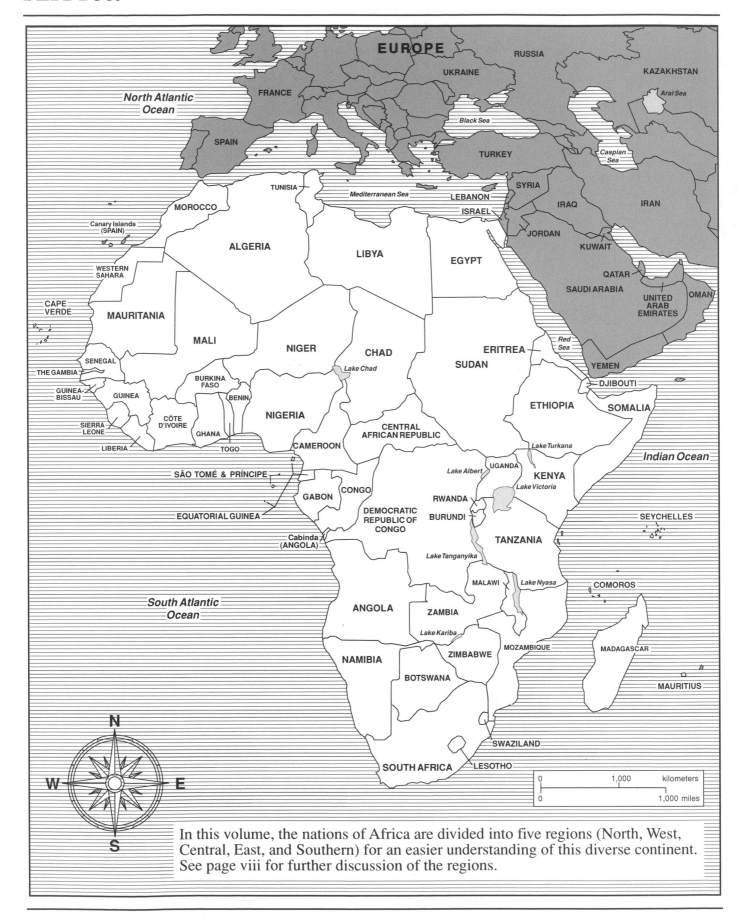

In this volume, the nations of Africa are divided into five regions (North, West, Central, East, and Southern) for an easier understanding of this diverse continent. See page viii for further discussion of the regions.

Africa: The Struggle for Development

Seventeen African nations gained their independence in 1960, liberating most of the continent of colonial rule. The times were electric. In country after country, the flags of Great Britain, Belgium, France, and the United Nations were replaced by the banners of new states, whose leaders offered idealistic promises to remake the continent and thus the world. Hopes were high, and the most ambitious of goals seemed obtainable. Even non-Africans spoke of the resource-rich continent as being on the verge of a developmental takeoff. Some of the old, racist myths about Africa were at last being questioned.

Yet today, nearly 4 decades after the great freedom year, conditions throughout Africa are sobering rather than euphoric. For most Africans, independence has been more of a desperate struggle for survival rather than an exhilarating path to development. Now Africa is often described in the global media as a "continent in crisis," a "region in turmoil," "on a precipice," and "suffering"—phrases that echo the sensationalist writings of nineteenth-century missionaries eager to convince others of the continent's need for "salva-tion." But the modern headlines are far more accurate than the mission tracts of yesteryear. Today millions of Africans are indeed seeking some form of salvation—but now from the grinding poverty, pestilence, and, in many areas, wars that afflict their lives. Perhaps this hunger is why contemporary African evangelists are so much more successful in swelling their congregations than were their counterparts in the past. It is certainly not for lack of competition; Africa is a continent of many, often overlapping, faiths. In addition to Islam and other spiritual paths, Africans have embraced a myriad of secular ideologies: Marxism, African socialism, people's capitalism, structural adjustment, pan-Africanism, authenticity, nonracialism, the one-party state, and the multiparty state. The list is endless, but salvation seems ever more distant.

Africa's current circumstances are indeed difficult, yet it is also true that the years have brought progress as well as problems. The goals so optimistically pronounced at independence have, for the most part, not been abandoned. Even when the states have faltered, the societies that they encompass have remained dynamic and adaptable to shifting opportunities. The support of strong families continues to allow most Africans to overcome enormous adversity. Today there are starving children in Africa, but there are also many more in school uniforms studying to make their future dreams a reality.

A DIVERSE CONTINENT

Africa, which is almost 4 times the size of the United States (excluding Alaska), ranks just below Asia as the world's biggest continent. Well over one quarter of the membership of the United Nations consists of African states—more than 50 in all. Such facts are worth noting, for even educated outsiders often lose sight of Africa's continental scope when they discuss its problems and prospects.

Not only is the African continent vast but, archaeology tells us, it was also the cradle of human civilization. It should therefore not be surprising that the 700 million or so contemporary Africans maintain extraordinarily diverse ways of life. They speak more than 1,000 languages and live their lives according to a rich variety of household arrangements, kinship systems, and religious beliefs. The art and music styles of the continent are as varied as its people.

Given its diversity, it is not easy to generalize about Africa. For each statement, there is an exception. However, one aspect that is constant to all African societies is that they have always been changing, albeit in modern times at an ever-increasing rate. Cities have grown and people have moved back and forth between village and town, giving rise to new social groups, institutions, occupations, religions, and forms of communication that have made their mark in the countryside as well as in the urban centers. All Africans, whether they be urban computer programmers or hunter-gatherers living in the remote corners of the Kalahari Desert, have taken on new practices, interests, and burdens, yet have retained their African identity. Uniquely

(World Bank photo by Pamela Johnson)
This is an electrical transformer at the Volta Aluminum Company in Terna, Ghana. Modern technology and new sources of power are among the factors that contribute to economic development in Africa.

WOULD YOU BELIEVE?

The following countries [region] could fit within Africa:

China	3,705,390	sq. mi.
U.S.A.	3,618,770	*
India	1,266,595	
[Europe]	1,905,000	**
Argentina	1,065,189	
New Zealand	103,736	
	11,664,680	sq. mi.

The area of Africa is
	11,700,000	sq. mi.

Source of Data: *The 1990 World Almanac and Book of Facts.*

* Total, land and water, 50 states

** *1989 Information Please Almanac.* Includes Iceland. Excludes the former European Soviet Union and European Turkey.

Available as a wall poster from World Eagle, Inc., 64 Washburn Avenue, D1, Wellesley, MA 02181.

African institutions, values, and histories underlie contemporary lifestyles throughout the continent.

Memories of past civilizations are a source of pride and community. The medieval Mali and Ghana Empires, the glory of Pharaonic Egypt, the Fulani Caliphate of northern Nigeria, the knights of Kanem and Bornu, the Great Zimbabwe, and the Kingdom of the Kongo, among others, are all remembered. The past is connected to the present through the generations and by ties to the land. In a continent where the majority of people are still farmers, land remains "the mother that never dies." It is valued for its fruits and because it is the place to which the ancestors came and were buried.

The art of personal relationships continues to be important. People typically live in large families. Children are considered precious, and large families are still desired for social as well as economic reasons. Elders are an important part of a household; nursing homes and retirement communities generally do not exist. People are not supposed to be loners. "I am because we are" remains a valued precept. In this age of nation-states, the "we" may refer to one's ethnic community, while obligations to one's extended family often take precedence over other loyalties.

Most Africans, like the majority of other peoples, believe in a spiritual as well as material world. The continent contains a rich variety of indigenous belief systems, which often coexist with the larger religions of Islam and various Christian sects. Many families believe that their lives are influenced by their ancestors. Africans from all walks of life will seek the services of professional "traditional" healers to explain an illness or suggest remedies for such things as sterility or bad fortune. But this common pattern of behavior does not preclude one from turning to scientific medicine; all African governments face strong popular demands for better access to modern health facilities.

Islam has long been a strong force in Africa. Today the religion rivals Christianity as the fastest-growing faith on the continent. The followers of both religions often adapt their faiths to accommodate local traditions and values. Some people also join new religious movements and churches, such as the Brotherhood of the Cross and Star in Nigeria or the Church of Simon Kimbangu in Zaire, that link Christian and indigenous beliefs with new ideas and rituals. Like other institutions in the towns and cities, the churches and mosques provide their followers with social networks.

Local art, like local religion, often reflects the influence of the changing world. An airplane is featured on a Nigerian gelede mask, the Apollo space mission inspires a Burkinabe carver, and a Ndebele dance wand is a beaded electric pole.

THE TROUBLED PRESENT

Some of the crises in Africa today threaten its peoples' traditional resiliency. The facts are grim: In material terms, the average African is poorer today than at independence, and it is predicted that poverty will only increase in the immediate future. Drought conditions over the last 2 decades have led to food shortages across the continent. In the 1980s, widespread famine occurred in 22 African nations; the Food and Agriculture Organization (FAO) of the United Nations estimated that 70 percent of all Africans did not have enough to eat. An outpouring of assistance and relief efforts at the time saved as many as 35 million lives. Overall per capita food production in Africa dropped by 12 percent between 1961 and 1995. One factor in the decline has been the tendency of agricultural planners to ignore the fact that up to 70 percent of Africa's food crops are grown by women. It has also been estimated that up to 40 percent of the continent's food crops go uneaten due to poor transport. Although agricultural production has risen modestly in the 1990s, the food crisis continues. In 1994, large parts of East Africa, in particular, faced the prospect of renewed hunger. Other areas have become dependent on outside food aid. Marginal advances in agricultural production, through better incentives to farmers, have often been counterbalanced by declining commodity prices on world markets, explosive population growth, and recurring drought and locust infestations. Problems of climate irregularity, transport, obtaining needed goods and supplies, and storage require continued assistance and long-range planning.

Wood, the average person's source of energy, grows scarcer every year, and most governments have had to contend with the rising cost of imported fuels. Meanwhile, diseases that once were believed to have been conquered have reappeared: Rinderpest has been discovered among cattle, and cholera has been found among populations where they have not been seen for generations. The spread of Acquired Immune Deficiency Syndrome (AIDS) also threatens lives and long-term productivity.

Armed conflicts have devastated portions of Africa. The current carnage in Angola, Djibouti, Liberia, Rwanda, Sierra Leone, Somalia, Sudan, and Zaire due to internal strife encouraged to greater or lesser degrees by outside forces, place them in a distinct class of suffering—a class that until recently (and that may yet again) also included Chad, Eritrea, Ethiopia, Mozambique, and Uganda. More than 2 million people have died in these countries over the past decade, while millions more have become refugees. Except for scattered enclaves, normal economic activities have been greatly disrupted or ceased altogether.

Almost all African governments are in debt. In 1991, the foreign debt owed by all the sub-Saharan African countries except South Africa stood at about $175 billion. Although it is smaller in its absolute amount than that of Latin America, as a percentage of its economic output, the continent's debt is the highest in the world and is rising swiftly. The combined gross national product (GNP) for the same countries, whose total populations are in excess of 500 million, was less than $150 billion, a figure that represents only 1.2 percent of the global GNP and is about equal to the GNP of Belgium, a country of 10 million people. In Zambia, an extreme exam-

Measuring Misery

United Nations Human Development Index,* 1993

Country	Rank	Country	Rank
Mauritius	54	Central African Rep.	148
Seychelles	60	Mauritania	149
Boswana	71	Madagascar	150
South Africa	100	Rwanda	152
Swaziland	110	Senegal	153
Namibia	116	Benin	154
Gabon	120	Uganda	155
Cape Verde	122	Malawi	157
Zimbabwe	124	Liberia	158
Congo	125	Guinea	160
Cameroon	127	Guinea-Bissau	161
Kenya	128	Gambia	162
Ghana	129	Chad	163
Lesotho	130	Djibouti	164
Equatorial Guinea	131	Angola	165
São Tomé & Príncipe	132	Burundi	166
Zambia	136	Mozambique	167
Nigeria	137	Ethiopia	168
Comoros	139	Burkina Faso	170
Togo	140	Mali	171
Zaire	141	Somalia	172
Tanzania	144	Sierra Leone	173
Sudan	146	Niger	174
Côte D'Ivoire	147		

Source: UNDP

*Standings in a league of 174 countries

THE EVOLUTION OF AFRICA'S ECONOMIES

Africa has seldom been rich, although it has vast resources and some rulers and elites have become very wealthy. In earlier centuries, the horror of the slave trade greatly contributed to limiting economic development in many African regions. During the period of European exploration and colonialism, Africa's involvement in the world economy greatly increased with the emergence of new forms of "legitimate" commerce. But colonial-era policies and practices assured that this development was of little long-term benefit to most of the continent's peoples.

During the 70 or so years of European colonial rule throughout most of Africa, its nations' economies were shaped to the advantage of the imperialists. Cash crops such as cocoa, coffee, and rubber began to be grown for the European market. Some African farmers benefited from these crops, but the cash-crop economy also involved large foreign-run plantations. It also encouraged the trends toward use of migrant labor and the decline in food production. Many people became dependent for their livelihood on the forces of the world market, which, like the weather, were beyond their immediate control.

Mining also increased during colonial times, again for the benefit of the colonial rulers. The ores were extracted from African soil by European companies. African labor was employed, but the machinery came from abroad. The copper, diamonds, gold, iron ore, and uranium were shipped overseas to be processed and marketed in the Western economies. Upon independence, African governments received a varying percentage of the take through taxation and consortium agreements. But mining remained an enclave industry, sometimes described as a "state within a state" because such industries were run by outsiders who established communities that used imported machinery and technicians and exported the products to industrialized countries.

Inflationary conditions in other parts of the world have had adverse effects on Africa. Today the raw materials that Africans produce often receive low prices on the world market, while the manufactured goods that African countries import are expensive. Local African industries lack spare parts and machinery, and farmers frequently cannot afford to transport crops to market. As a result, the whole economy slows down. Thus, Africa, because of the policies of former colonial powers and current independent governments, is tied into the world economy in ways that do not always serve its peoples' best interests.

THE PROBLEMS OF GOVERNMENT

Outside forces are not the only cause of Africa's current crises. In general, Africa is a misgoverned continent. After independence, the idealism that characterized various nationalist movements, with their promises of popular self-determi-

ple, the per capita foreign debt theoretically owed by each of its citizens is nearly $1,000, while its annual per capita income is well below that.

A factor that helps to account for Africa's relative poverty is the low levels of industrial output of all but a few of its countries. The decline of many commodity prices on the world market has further reduced national incomes. As a result, the foreign exchange needed to import food, machinery, fuel, and other goods is very limited in most African countries. The continent's economy in 1987 grew by only 0.8 percent, far below its annual population growth rate of about 3.2 percent. In the same year, cereal production declined 8 percent and overall agricultural production grew by only 0.5 percent. There has been some modest improvement in subsequent years. But more recent estimates put the economic growth rate at 1.5 percent, still the world's lowest and far below that of the population growth rate.

In order to obtain money to meet debts and pay for their running expenses, many African governments have been obliged to accept the stringent terms of global lending agencies, most notably the World Bank and the International Monetary Fund (IMF). These terms have led to great popular hardship, especially in the urban areas, through austerity measures such as the abandonment of price controls on basic foodstuffs and the freezing of wages. African governments and some experts are questioning both the justice and practicality of these terms.

(This photo is available as a wall poster from World Eagle, Inc., 64 Washburn Avenue, D1, Wellesley, MA 02181.)

African families treasure their children.

nation, gave way in most states to cynical authoritarian regimes. By 1989, only Botswana, Mauritius, soon-to-be-independent Namibia, and, arguably, The Gambia and Senegal could reasonably claim that their governments were elected in genuinely free and fair elections.

The government of Robert Mugabe in Zimbabwe, in Southern Africa, undoubtedly enjoyed majority support, but political life in that country had been seriously marred by violence and intimidation aimed mostly at the opposition. Past multiparty contests in the North African nations of Egypt, Morocco, and Tunisia, as well as in the West African state of Liberia, had been manipulated to assure that the ruling establishments remained unchallenged. Elsewhere, the continent was divided between military and/or one-party regimes, which often combined the seemingly contradictory characteristics of weakness and absolutism at the top. While a few of the one-party states, most notably Tanzania, then offered

people genuine, if limited, choices of leadership, most have, to a greater or lesser degree, been simply vehicles of personal rule.

But since 1990 there has been a democratic reawakening in Africa, which has toppled the political status quo in some areas and threatened its survival throughout the continent. Whereas in 1989 some 35 nations were governed as single-party states, by 1994 there were none, though Swaziland and Uganda were experimenting with no-party systems. In a number of countries—Benin, Cape Verde, Central African Republic, Congo, Madagascar, Mali, Malawi, Niger, São Tomé and Príncipe, South Africa, and Zambia—ruling parties were decisively rejected in multiparty elections, while elections in other areas led to a greater sharing of power between the old regimes and their formerly suppressed oppositions. In many countries, the democratic transformation is still ongoing and remains fragile. There have been accusations of manipulation and voting fraud by those in power in a number of countries, but so far, only in Algeria and Nigeria has the will of the electorate been overtly overridden through military coups.

Military regimes have not been immune to the winds of change sweeping the continent. In Nigeria, Africa's most populous country, a military attempt to foster a "guided democracy" in which only two government-created (and government-defined), parties were allowed to compete for power has ended as a complete farce, with the army still clinging onto power amid the powerful opposition of key trade unions. In The Gambia, 3 decades of multiparty rule have been disrupted by the country's Nigerian-trained army.

Events in Benin have most closely paralleled the recent changes of Central/Eastern Europe. Benin's military-based, Marxist-Leninist regime of Mathieu Kérékou was pressured into relinquishing power to a transitional civilian government made up of technocrats and former dissidents. (Television broadcasts of this "civilian coup" enjoyed large audiences in neighboring countries.) In several other countries, such as Equatorial Guinea, Gabon, and Togo, mounting opposition has resulted in the semblance without the substance of free elections by long-ruling military autocrats. Moves toward multiparty reform in Zaire have given way to an almost complete collapse of authority. Many people fear that these countries may soon experience turmoil similar to that which has engulfed Ethiopia, Liberia, Rwanda, Somalia, and Uganda, where military autocrats have been overthrown by armed rebels.

Why did most postcolonial African governments, until recently, take on autocratic forms? And why are these forms now being so widely challenged? There are no definitive answers to either of these questions. One common explanation for authoritarianism in Africa has been the weakness of the states themselves. Most African governments have faced the difficult task of maintaining national unity with diverse, ethnically divided citizenries. Although the states of Africa may overlay and overlap historic kingdoms, most are products of colonialism. Their boundaries were fashioned during the late-nineteenth-century European partition of the continent, which divided and joined ethnic groups by lines drawn in Europe. The successful leaders of African independence movements worked within the colonial boundaries; and when they joined together in the Organization of African Unity (OAU), they agreed to respect the territorial status quo.

While the need to stem interethnic and regional conflict has been one justification for placing limits on popular self-determination, another explanation can be found in the administrative systems that the nationalist leaderships inherited. All the European colonies in Africa functioned as police states. Not only were various forms of opposition curtailed, but intrusive security establishments were created to watch over and control the indigenous populations. Although headed by Europeans, most colonial security services employed local staff members who were prepared to assume leadership roles at independence. A wave of military coups swept across West Africa during the 1960s; elsewhere, aspiring dictators like so-called life president Ngwazi Hastings Banda of Malawi were quick to appreciate the value of the inherited instruments of control.

Africa's economic difficulties have also frequently been cited as contributing to its political underdevelopment. On one hand, Nigeria's last civilian government, for example, was certainly undermined in part by the economic crisis that engulfed it due to falling oil revenues. On the other hand, in a pattern reminiscent of recent changes in Latin America, current economic difficulties resulting in high rates of inflation and indebtedness seem to be tempting some African militaries, such as Benin's, to return to the barracks and allow civilian politicians to assume responsibility for the implementation of inevitably harsh austerity programs.

External powers have long sustained African dictatorships through their grants of military and economic aid and, on occasion, direct intervention. For example, a local attempt in 1964 to restore constitutional rule in Gabon was thwarted by French paratroopers, while Joseph Desiré Mobutu's kleptocratic hold over Zaire relied from the very beginning on overt and covert assistance from the United States and other Western states. The former Soviet bloc and China also helped in the past to support their share of unsavory African allies, in places like Ethiopia, Equatorial Guinea, and Burundi. But the end of the cold war has led to a reduced desire on the part of outside powers to prop up their unpopular African allies. At the same time, the major international lending agencies have increasingly concerned themselves with the perceived need to adjust the political as well as economic structures of debtor nations. This new emphasis is justified in part by the alleged linkage between political unaccountability and economic corruption and mismanagement.

The ongoing decline of socialism on the continent is also having a significant political effect. Some regimes have professed a Marxist orientation, while others have felt that a special African socialism could be built on the communal and cooperative traditions of their societies. In countries such as Guinea-Bissau and Mozambique, a revolutionary socialist orientation was introduced at the grass-roots level during the struggles for independence, within areas liberated from colonialism. The various socialist governments have not been free of personality cults, nor from corruption and oppressive measures. And many governments that have eschewed the socialist label have, nonetheless, developed public corporations and central-planning methods similar to those governments that openly profess Marxism. In recent years, virtually all of Africa's governments, partly in line with IMF and World Bank requirements but also because of the inefficiency and losses of many of their public corporations, have placed greater emphasis on private-sector development.

REASONS FOR OPTIMISM

Although the problems facing African countries have grown since independence, so have the countries' achievements. The number of people who can read and write in local languages as well as English, French, or Portuguese has increased enormously. More people can peruse newspapers, follow instructions for fertilizers, and read the labels on medicine bottles. Professionals trained in modern technology who, for example, plan electrification schemes, organize large office staffs, or develop medical facilities are more available because of the large number of African universities that have developed since the end of colonialism. Health care has also expanded and improved in most areas. Outside of the areas that have been ravaged by war, life expectancy has generally increased and infant mortality rates have declined.

Despite the terrible wars that are being waged in a few nations, mostly in the form of civil wars, postcolonial African governments have been notably successful in avoiding armed conflict with one another. But South Africa's recent transformation into a nonracial democracy, which has been accompanied by its emergence as the leading member of the Southern African Development Community, has brought an end to its previous policy of regional destabilization.

Another positive development is the increasing attention that African governments and intra-African agencies are giving to women, as was exemplified in the 1994 global population summit held in Cairo, Egypt. The pivotal role of women in agriculture and other activities is now being recognized and supported. In many countries, prenatal and hospital care for mothers and their babies have increased, conditions for women workers in factories have improved, and new cooperatives for women's activities have been developed. Women have also played an increasingly prominent role in the political life of many African countries.

The advances that have been made in Africa are important ones, but they could be undercut by continued economic decline. Africa needs debt relief and outside aid just to maintain the gains that have been made. Yet, as the African proverb observes, "someone else's legs will do you no good in traveling." Africa, as the individual country reports in this volume observe, is a continent of many and varied resources. There are mineral riches and a vast agricultural potential. However, the continent's people, the youths who make up more than half the population and the elders whose wisdom is revered, are its greatest resource. The rest of the world, which has benefited from the continent's material resources, can also learn from the social strengths of African families and communities.

North Africa

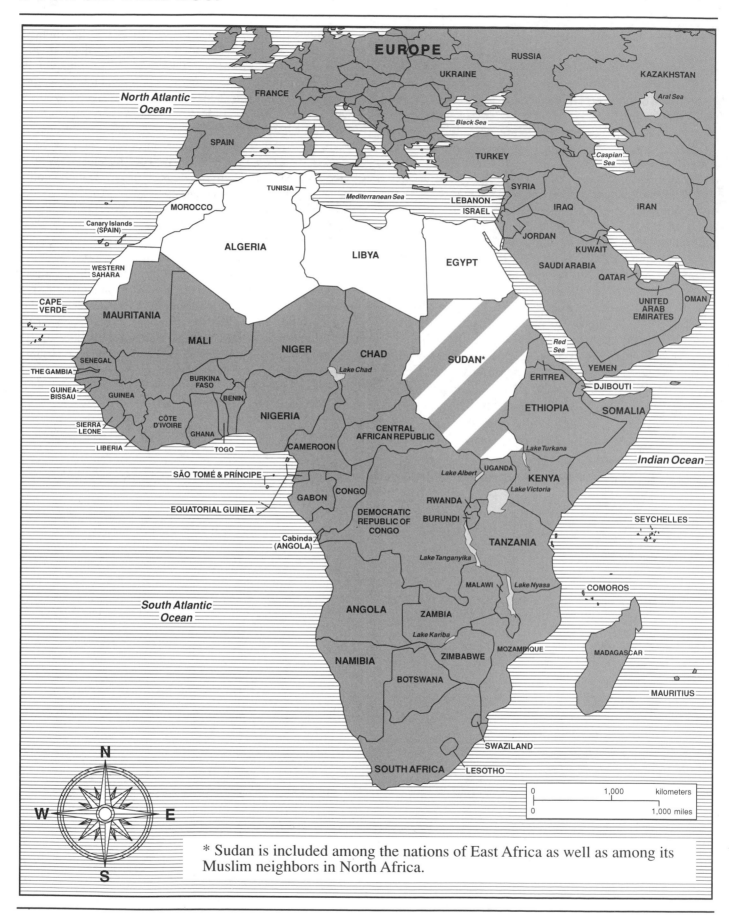

North Africa: The Crossroads of the Continent

Located at the geographical and cultural crossroads between Europe, Asia, and the rest of the Africa, North Africa has served since ancient times as a link between the civilizations of sub-Saharan Africa and the rest of the world. Traders historically carried the continent's products northward, either across the Sahara Desert or up the Nile River and Red Sea, to the great port cities of the region's Mediterranean coast. Goods also flowed southward. In addition, the trade networks carried ideas: Islam, for example, spread from coastal North Africa across much of the rest of the continent to become the religion of at least one third of all Africans.

North Africa's role as the continent's principal window to the world gradually declined after the year A.D. 1500, as the trans-Atlantic trade increased. (The history of East Africa's participation in Indian Ocean trade goes back much further.) However, the countries of North Africa have continued to play an important role in the greater continent's development.

The countries of North Africa—Morocco, Algeria, Tunisia, Libya, and Egypt—and their millions of people differ from one another, but they share a predominant, overarching Arab-Islamic culture that both distinguishes them from the rest of Africa and unites them with the Arabic-speaking nations of the Middle East. To begin to understand the societies of North Africa and their role in the rest of the continent, it is helpful to examine the area's geography. The region's diverse environment has long encouraged its inhabitants to engage in a broad variety of economic activities: pastoralism, agriculture, trading, crafts, and, later, industry.

GEOGRAPHY AND POPULATION

Except for Tunisia, which is relatively small, the countries of North Africa are sprawling nations. Algeria, Libya, and Egypt are among the biggest countries on the continent, and Morocco is not far behind. Their size can be misleading, for much of their territories are encompassed by the largely barren Sahara Desert. The approximate populations of the five states today range from Egypt's 55 million people to Libya's 4 million; Morocco has 26 million, Algeria 26 million, and Tunisia 8 million citizens. All these populations are increasing at a rapid rate; indeed, well over half the region's citizens are under age 21.

Due to its scarcity, water is the region's most precious resource, so most people live either in valleys near the Mediterranean coast or along the Nile. The latter courses through the desert for thousands of miles, creating a narrow green ribbon that is the home of the 95 percent of Egypt's population who live within 12 miles of its banks. More than 90 percent of the people of Algeria, Libya, Morocco, and Tunisia live within 200 miles of either the Mediterranean or, in the case of Morocco, the Atlantic coast.

(United Nations photo)

Geography has been less of a barrier to regional cohesiveness in North Africa than have politics and ideology.

Besides determining where people live, the temperate, if often too dry, climate of North Africa has always influenced local economies and lifestyles. There is intensive agriculture along the coasts and rivers. Algeria, Morocco, and Tunisia are well known for their tree and vine crops, notably citrus fruits, olives, and wine grapes. The intensively irrigated Nile Valley has, since the time of the American Civil War, which temporarily removed U.S.–produced fiber from the world market, been a leading source of high-quality cotton as well as locally consumed foodstuffs. In the oases that dot the Sahara Desert, date palms are grown for their sweet fruits, which are almost a regional staple. Throughout the steppe lands, between the fertile coasts and the desert, pastoralists follow flocks of sheep and goats or herds of cattle and camels in constant search of pasture. Although now few in number, it was these nomads who in the past developed the trans-Saharan trade. As paved roads and airports have replaced their caravan routes,

(United Nations photo by Y. Nagata)
Oil and gas discoveries in North Africa produced wide-ranging economic effects.

long-distance nomadism has declined. But the traditions it bred, including a love of independence, remain an important part of North Africa's cultural heritage.

Urban culture has flourished in North Africa since the ancient times of the Egyptian pharaohs and the mercantilist rulers of Carthage. Supported by trade and local industries, the region's medieval cities, such as Cairo, Fez, and Kairouan, were the administrative centers of great Islamic empires, whose civilizations shined during Europe's dark ages. In the modern era, the urban areas are bustling industrial centers, ports, and political capitals.

Geography—or, more precisely, geology—has helped to fuel economic growth in recent decades. Although agriculture continues to provide employment in Algeria and Libya for as much as a third of the labor force, discoveries of oil and natural gas in the 1950s dramatically altered these two nations' economic structures. Between 1960 and 1980, Libya's annual per capita income jumped from $50 to almost $10,000, transforming it from among the poorest to among the richest countries in the world. Today, Libya is the richest country in Africa. Algeria has also greatly benefited from the exploitation of hydrocarbons, although less dramatically than Libya. Egypt and Tunisia havedeveloped much smaller oil industries, which nonetheless provide for their domestic energy needs and generate much needed foreign exchange. The decline in oil prices during the 1980s, however, reduced revenues, increased unemployment, and contributed to unrest, especially in Algeria. While it has no oil, Morocco profits from its possession of much of the world's phosphate production.

CULTURAL AND POLITICAL HERITAGES

The vast majority of the inhabitants of North Africa are Arabic-speaking Muslims. Islam and Arabic both became established in the region between the seventh and eleventh centuries A.D. Thus, by the time of the Crusades in the eastern Mediterranean, the societies of North Africa were thoroughly incorporated into the Muslim world, even though the area had earlier been the home of many early Christian scholars, such as St. Augustine. Except for Egypt, where about 5 percent of the population remain loyal to the Coptic Church, there is virtually no Christianity among modern North Africans. Until recently, important Jewish communities existed in all the region's countries, but their numbers have dwindled as a result of mass immigration to Israel.

With Islam came Arabic, the language of the Koran. Today, Egypt and Libya are almost exclusively Arabic-speaking. In Algeria, Morocco, and Tunisia, Arabic coexists with various local minority languages, which are collectively known as Berber (from which the term "Barbary," as in Barbary Coast, was derived). As many as a third of the Moroccans speak a form of Berber as their first language. Centuries of interaction between the Arabs and Berbers as well as their common adherence to Islam have promoted a sense of cultural unity between the two communities, although ethnic disputes have developed in Algeria and Morocco over demands that Berber be included in local school curriculums. As was the case almost everywhere else on the continent, the linguistic situation in North Africa was further complicated by the introduction of European languages during the colonial era. Today, French is particularly important as a language of technology and administration in Algeria, Morocco, and Tunisia.

Early in the nineteenth century, all the countries of North Africa, except Morocco, were autonomous provinces of the Ottoman Empire, which was based in present-day Turkey and also incorporated most of the Middle East. Morocco was an independent state; indeed, it was one of the earliest to recognize the independence of the United States from England. From 1830, the European powers gradually encroached upon the Ottoman Empire's North African realm. Thus, like most of their sub-Saharan counterparts, all the states of North Africa fell under European imperial control. Algeria's conquest by the French began in 1830 but took decades to accomplish, due to fierce local resistance. France also seized Tunisia in 1881 and, along with Spain, partitioned Morocco in 1912. Britain occupied Egypt in 1882, and Italy invaded Libya in 1911, although anti-Italian resistance continued until World War II, when the area was liberated by Allied troops.

The differing natures of their European occupations have influenced the political and social characters of each North African state. Algeria, which was directly incorporated into France as a province for 120 years, did not win its independence until 1962, after a protracted and violent revolution. Morocco, by contrast, was accorded independence in 1956, after only 44 years of Franco–Spanish administration, during which the local monarchy continued to reign. Tunisia's 75 years of French rule also ended in 1956, as a strong nationalist party took the reins of power. Egypt, although formally independent of Great Britain, did not win genuine self-determination until 1952, when a group of nationalist army officers came to power by overthrowing the British-supported monarchy. Libya became a temporary ward of the United Nations after Italy was deprived of its colonial empire during World War II. The nation was granted independence by the United Nations in 1951, under a monarch whose religious followers had led much of the anti-Italian resistance.

NATIONAL POLITICS

Egypt

Egypt reemerged as an important actor on the world stage soon after Gamal Abdel Nasser came to power, in the aftermath of the overthrow of the monarchy. One of the major figures in the post-World War II Non-aligned Movement, Nasser gave voice to the aspirations of millions in the Arab world and Africa, through his championing of pan-Arab and pan-African anti-imperialist sentiments. Faced with the problems of his nation's burgeoning population and limited natural resources, Nasser nonetheless refused to let his government become dependent on a single foreign power. Domestically, he adopted a policy of developmental socialism.

Because of mounting debts, spurred by enormous military spending, and increasing economic problems, many Egyptians had already begun to reassess some aspects of Nasser's policies by the time of his death in 1970. His successor, Anwar al-Sadat, reopened Egypt to foreign investment in hopes of attracting much-needed capital and technology. In 1979, Sadat drew Egypt closer to the United States by signing the Camp David Accords, which ended more than 3 decades

(United Nations photo by Y. Nagata)
The Egyptian president, Hosni Mubarak, continues the legacy of his predecessor, Anwar al-Sadat.

of war with Israel. Egypt has since been one of the largest recipients of U.S. economic and military aid.

Sadat's increasingly authoritarian rule, as well as his abandonment of socialism and foreign policy initiatives, made him a target of domestic discontent, and in 1981, he was assassinated. His successor, Hosni Mubarak, has modestly liberalized Egyptian politics and pursued what are essentially moderate internal and external policies. While maintaining peace with Israel, Mubarak has succeeded in reconciling Egypt with other Arab countries, which had strongly objected to the Camp David agreement. In 1990–1991, he took a leading role among the majority of Arab leaders opposed to Iraq's seizure of Kuwait. However, rapid urbanization, declining per capita revenues, debt, and unemployment, all linked to explosive population growth, have continued to strain the Egyptian economy and fuel popular discontent. Some of this discontent has in recent years been channeled into violence by extremist Islamic groups, which now threaten to destroy the traditional tolerence that has existed between Egypt's Muslim majority and Christian minority.

Libya
Libya was ruled for years by a pious, autocratic king whose domestic legitimacy was always in question. After 1963, the nation came under the heavy influence of foreign oil companies, which discovered and produced the country's only substantial resource. In 1969, members of the military, led by Colonel Muammar al-Qadhafi, overthrew the monarchy. Be-

(United Nations photo by Bill Graham)

Nomadic traditions, including loyalty to family and love of independence, are still integral to the cultures of North Africa.

lieved to be about age 27 at the time of the coup, Qadhafi was an ardent admirer of Nasser's vision of pan-Arab nationalism and antiimperialism. Qadhafi invested billions of dollars, earned from oil, in ambitious domestic development projects, successfully ensuring universal health care, housing, and education for his people by the end of the 1970s. He also spent billions more on military equipment and aid to what he deemed "nationalist movements" throughout the world. Considered a maverick, he came into conflict with many African and Arab rulers as well as with outside powers like the United States. Despite Qadhafi's persistent efforts to forge regional alliances, political differences, economic pressures, and the expulsion of expatriate workers (due to declining oil revenues) have increased tensions between Libya and its neighbors as well as between the country's own military and middle class.

Strained relations between Libya and the United States over Qadhafi's activist foreign policy and support for international terrorists culminated in a U.S. air raid on Tripoli in 1986. In that year, the United States required American businesses and citizens to leave Libya and since then has sought other ways to undermine Qadhafi's ambitions. With the support of the United States and other powers, the Hissène Habré government of Chad was able in 1987 to expel the Libyan military from its northern provinces. In 1991, Libya came under greater international pressure when the UN Security Council backed American and British demands for the extradition of two alleged Libyan agents suspected of complicity in the 1987 blowing up of a Pan Am passenger jet over Lockerbie, Scotland. The Qadhafi government's failure to submit to this decision led to the imposition of international sanctions barring other countries from maintaining air links with or selling arms to Libya.

Tunisia

Although having the fewest natural resources of the North African countries, Tunisia enjoyed a high degree of political stability and economic development during the first 3 decades that followed the restoration of its independence, in 1956. Habib Bourguiba, leader of the local nationalist party known as the Neo-Destour, led the country to independence while retaining cordial economic and political ties with France as well as other Western countries. Bourguiba's government was a model of pragmatic approaches to both economic growth and foreign policy. A mixed economy was developed, and education's contribution to development was emphasized. The nation's Mediterranean coast was transformed into a vacation spot for European tourists.

However, in the 1980s, amid economic recession and after 30 years of single-party rule, Tunisians became increasingly impatient with their aging leader's refusal to recognize opposition political parties. Strikes, demonstrations, and opposition from Muslim fundamentalists as well as underground secular movements were the context for Bourguiba's forced

retirement in 1987. He was succeeded by his prime minister, Zine al-Abidine ben Ali, whose efforts in 1988 to release jailed Muslim activists and to open political dialogue led to a period of optimism and widespread support. By the middle of that year, he had replaced most of the cabinet ministers who had served under Bourguiba. Multiparty elections were held in 1989, but they were marred by opposition charges of fraud. There is growing unemployment among Tunisia's youthful, rapidly expanding population.

Algeria

Algeria, wracked by the long and destructive revolution that preceded independence in 1962, was long ruled by a coalition of military and civilian leaders who rose to power as revolutionary partisans of the National Liberation Front (FNL) during the war. Although FNL leaders have differed over what policies and programs to emphasize, in the past they were able to forge a governing consensus in favor of secularism (but with respect for Islam's special status), a socialist domestic economy, and a foreign policy based on nonalignment. The country's substantial oil and gas revenues were invested in large-scale industrial projects, which were carried out by the state sector. But by the end of the 1970s, serious declines in agricultural productivity and growing urban unemployment, partially due to the country's high overall rate of population growth, sent hundreds of thousands of Algerian workers to France in search of jobs. As a result, cautious encouragement began to be given to private-sector development.

In 1988, rising bread prices led to severe rioting, which left more than 100 people dead. In the aftermath, the FNL's long period of one-party rule came to an end, with the legalization of opposition parties. In the 1990 local elections, the Islamic Salvation Front (FIS), a coalition group of Muslim fundamentalists, managed to take control of about 80 percent of the country's municipal and departmental councils. This triumph was followed by FIS success in the first round of voting for a new National Assembly in December 1991; the Front captured 187 out of 230 seats. But, just before a second round of voting could be held, in January 1992, the military seized power in a coup. A state of emergency was declared, and thousands of FIS supporters and other opponents of the new regime were detained. In response, some turned to armed resistance. In June 1992, the political temperature was raised further by the mysterious assassination of Mohamed Boudiaf, a veteran nationalist who had been installed by the military's High State Committee as the president. In 1993 elements of the Islamic resistance began an increasingly effective campaign of isolating Algeria internationally by assassinating foreign expatriates residing in the country. In 1995, Liamine Zeroual was elected president in a poll boycotted by the FIS and other major opposition parties. He cited the relatively high voter turnout as a mandate for a peaceful settlement based on dialogue. But the nation remains polarized by civil war.

Internationally, Algeria has been known for its troubleshooting role in difficult diplomatic negotiations. In 1980 it mediated the release of the U.S. hostages held in Iran. After years of tension, largely over the war in Western Sahara, Algeria resumed diplomatic relations with its western neighbor, Morocco, in 1988.

Morocco

Morocco is ruled by King Hassan II, who came to power in 1961, when his highly respected father, King Muhammad V, died. The political parties that developed during the struggle against French rule have continued to contest elections. However, Hassan has rarely permitted them to have a genuine influence in policy making, preferring to reserve the role for himself and his advisers. As in Tunisia, Moroccan agricultural development has been based on technological innovations rather than on land reform. (The latter, while it could raise productivity, would also likely anger the propertied supporters of the king. Elites also oppose business-tax reforms, yet the government needs revenues to repay its multibillion-dollar debt.) Much of the country's economic development has been left to the private sector. High birth rates and unemployment have led many Moroccans to join the Algerians and Tunisians in seeking employment in Europe.

By the mid-1990s, Morocco's 3-decade-long war to retain control of the phosphate-rich Western Sahara—a former Spanish colony whose independence is being fought for by a local nationalist movement known as Polisario—had become an unsettled stalemate, with Morocco controlling most of the Western Sahara. By the late 1980s, Moroccan forces had become increasingly effective in frustrating the infiltration of Polisario guerrillas in the main centers of the territory by enclosing them behind a network of security walls. These walls have also effectively shut out some 120,000 refugees (the number is bitterly disputed by the contestants) living in Polisario-controlled camps in Algeria. A UN peace plan calling for a referendum over the territory's future was agreed to by both sides in 1990. But, though the two parties have generally maintained a cease-fire since 1991, other provisions of the plan have not been implemented, largely as a result of continued Moroccan intransigence. In 1995, Polisario formally renounced the agreement. But, with waning international support and the Moroccan forces now well dug in, Polisario's short-term prospects of making either a political or a military breakthrough appear unpromising.

REGIONAL AND CONTINENTAL LINKS

There have been many calls for greater regional integration in North Africa since the 1950s. Under Nasser, Egypt was the leader of the pan-Arab movement; it even joined Syria in a brief political union, from 1958 to 1961. Others have attempted to create a union of the countries of the Maghrib (Arabic for "west") region—that is, Algeria, Morocco, and

(United Nations photo by Saw Lwin)

Morocco's King Hassan II is a leader whose influence is often pivotal in North African regional planning.

Tunisia. Recently, these three countries, along with the adjacent states of Libya and Mauritania, agreed to work toward an economic community, but they continue to be politically divided. At one time or another, Qadhafi has been accused of subverting all the region's governments; Algeria and Morocco have disagreed over the disposition of the Western Sahara; and each country has at one point or another closed its borders to its neighbors' citizens. Still, the logic of closer political and economic links and the example of increasing European unity on the other side of the Mediterranean will likely keep the issue of regional unity alive.

Both as members of the Organization of African Unity (OAU) and as individual states, the North African countries have had strong diplomatic and political ties to the rest of the continent. They are, however, also deeply involved in regional affairs outside Africa, particularly those of the Arab and Mediterranean worlds. There have also been some modest tensions across the Sahara. Requests by the North African nations that other OAU countries break diplomatic relations with Israel were promptly met in the

(United Nations photo by J. Slaughter)

Creating economic and political integration has been a goal of North African countries for a number of years. Economic unification would have the benefits of wider markets, diversified products, and expanded employment; political unification, however, is more problematic, due to the historical and cultural diversity of the area. The Moroccan port of Casablanca, pictured above, is clearly an economic asset to the region.

aftermath of the 1974 Arab–Israeli War. Many sub-Saharan countries hoped that, in return for their solidarity, the Arab nations would extend development aid to help them, in particular to cope with rising oil prices. Although some aid was forthcoming (mostly from the Persian Gulf countries rather than the North African oil producers), it was less generous than many had expected. During the 1980s, a number of sub-Saharan countries resumed diplomatic relations with Israel.

Border disputes, ideological differences, and internal conflicts have caused additional tensions. The Polisario cause in Western Sahara, for example, badly divided the OAU. When the OAU recognized the Polisario's exiled government in 1984, Morocco, along with Zaire, withdrew from membership in the body. However, the OAU has also had significant regional successes. In 1974, for example, its mediation led to a settlement of a long-standing border dispute between Algeria and Morocco.

West Africa

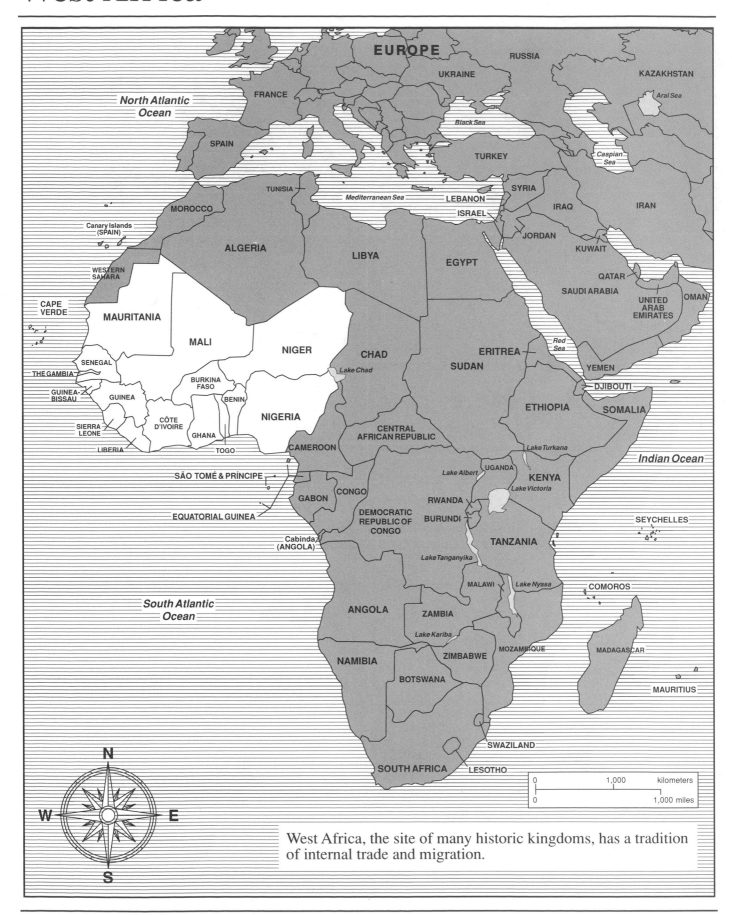

West Africa, the site of many historic kingdoms, has a tradition of internal trade and migration.

West Africa: Seeking Unity in Diversity

Anyone looking at a map of Africa will identify West Africa as the great bulge on the western coast of the continent. It is a region bound by the Sahara Desert to the north, the Atlantic Ocean to the south and west, and, in part, by the Cameroonian Mountains to the east. Each of these boundaries has historically been a bridge rather than a barrier, in that the region has long been linked through trade to the rest of the world.

At first glance, West Africa's great variety is more striking than any of its unifying features. It contains the environmental extremes of desert and rain forest. While most of its people rely on agriculture, every type of occupation can be found, from herders to factory workers. Hundreds of different languages are spoken; some are as different from one another as English is from Arabic or Japanese. Local cultural traditions and the societies that practice them are also myriad.

Yet the more one examines West Africa, the more one is impressed with the features that give the nations of the region a degree of coherence and unity. Some of the common characteristics and cross-cutting features of West Africa as a whole include the vegetation belts that stretch across the region from west to east, creating a similar environmental mix among the region's polities; the constant movement of peoples across local and national boundaries; and efforts being made by West African governments toward greater integration in the region, primarily through economic organizations. West Africans also share elements of a common history.

With the exception of Liberia, all the contemporary states of West Africa were the creations of competing European colonial powers—France, Germany, Great Britain, and Portugal—that divided most of the area during the late nineteenth century. Before this partition, however, much of the region was linked by the spread of Islam and patterns of trade, including the legacy of intensive involvement between the sixteenth and nineteenth centuries in the trans-Atlantic slave trade. From ancient times, great kingdoms expanded and contracted across the West African savanna and forest, giving rise to sophisticated civilizations.

WEST AFRICAN VEGETATION AND CLIMATE ZONES

Traveling north from the coastlines of such states as Nigeria, Ghana, and Côte d'Ivoire, one encounters tropical rain forests, which give way first to woodland savanna and then to more arid, more open plains. In Mali, Niger, and other landlocked countries to the north, the savanna gives way to the still drier Sahel environment, between the savanna and the Sahara Desert, and finally to the desert itself.

Whatever their ethnicity or nationality, the peoples living within each of these vegetation zones generally share the benefits and problems of similar livelihoods. For instance, cocoa, coffee, yams, and cassava are among the cash and food crops planted in the cleared forest and woodland zones, which stretch from Guinea to Nigeria. Groundnuts, sorghum, and millet are commonly harvested in the savanna belt that runs from Senegal to northern Nigeria. Herders in the Sahel, who historically could not go too far south with their cattle because of the presence of the deadly tsetse fly in the forest, continue to cross state boundaries in search of pasture.

People throughout West African have periodically suffered from drought. The effects of drought have often been aggravated in recent years by population pressures on the land. These factors have contributed to environmental changes and degradation. The condition of the Sahel in particular has deteriorated through a process of desertification, leading to large-scale relocations among many of its inhabitants. The eight Sahelian countries—Cape Verde, The Gambia, Burkina Faso, Mali, Senegal, Niger, Chad (in Central Africa), and Mauritania—have consequently formed a coordinating Committee for Struggle Against Drought in the Sahel (CILSS).

Farther to the south, large areas of woodland savanna have turned into grasslands as their forests have been cut down by land-hungry farmers. Drought has also periodically resulted in widespread brushfires in Ghana, Côte d'Ivoire, Togo, and Benin, which have transformed forests into savannas and savannas into deserts. Due to the depletion of forest, the Harmattan, a dry wind that blows in from the Sahara during January and February, now reaches many parts of the coast that in the recent past did not feel its breath. Its dust and haze have become a sign of the new year—and of new agricultural problems—throughout much of West Africa.

The great rivers of West Africa, such as The Gambia, Niger, Senegal, and Volta, along with their tributaries, have become increasingly important both as avenues of travel and trade and for the water they provide. Countries have joined together in large-scale projects designed to harness their waters for irrigation and hydroelectric power through regional organizations, like the Mano River grouping of Guinea, Liberia, and Sierra Leone and the Organization for the Development of the Senegal River, composed of Mali, Mauritania, and Senegal.

THE LINKS OF HISTORY AND TRADE

The peoples of West Africa have never been united as members of a single political unit. Yet some of the precolonial kingdoms that expanded across the region have great symbolic importance for those seeking to enhance interstate cooperation. The Mali empire of the thirteenth to fifteenth centuries, the Songhai empire of the sixteenth century, and the nineteenth-century Fulani caliphate of Sokoto, all based in the savanna, are widely remembered as examples of past supranational glory. The kingdoms of the southern forests, such as the Asante Confederation, the Dahomey kingdom, and the Yoruba city-states, were smaller than the great savanna empires to their north. Although generally later in origin and different in character from the northern states, the forest kingdoms are, nonetheless, sources of greater regional identity.

The precolonial states of West Africa gave rise to great urban centers, interlinked through extensive trade networks. This development was probably the result of the area's agricultural productivity, which supported a relatively high population density from early times. Many modern settlements have long histories. Present-day Timbuctu and Gao, in Mali, were important centers of learning and commerce in medieval times. Some other examples include Ouagadougou, Ibadan, Benin, and Kumasi, all in the forest zone. These southern centers prospered in the past by sending gold, kola, leather goods, cloth—and slaves—to the northern savanna and southern coast.

The cities of the savannas linked West Africa to North Africa. Beginning in the eleventh century, the ruling groups of the savanna increasingly turned to the universal vision of Islam. While Islam also spread to the forests, the southernmost areas were ultimately more strongly influenced by Christianity, which was introduced by Europeans, who became active along the West African coast in the fifteenth century. For centuries, the major commercial link among Europe, the Americas, and West Africa was the trans-Atlantic slave trade; during the nineteenth century, however, so-called legitimate commerce in palm oil and other tropical products replaced it. New centers such as Dakar, Accra, and Freetown emerged as a result either of the slave trade or its subsequent suppression.

THE MOVEMENT OF PEOPLES

Despite the (incorrect) view of many who see Africa as being a continent made up of isolated groups, one constant characteristic of West Africa has been the transregional migration of its people. Herders have moved east and west across the savanna and south into the forests. Since colonial times, many professionals as well as laborers have sought employment outside their home areas.

Some of the peoples of West Africa, such as the Malinke, Fulani, Hausa, and Mossi, have developed especially well-established heritages of mobility. In the past, the Malinke journeyed from their early center in Mali to the coastal areas in Guinea, Senegal, and The Gambia. Other Malinke traders made their way to Burkina Faso, Liberia, and Sierra Leone, where they came to be known as Mandingoes.

The Fulani have developed their own patterns of seasonal movement. They herd their cattle south across the savanna during the dry season and return to the north during the rainy season. Urbanized Fulani groups have historically journeyed from west to east, often serving as agents of Islamization as well as promoters of trade. More recently, many Fulani have been forced to move southward as a result of the deterioration of their grazing lands. The Hausa, who mostly live in northern

(IFC/World Bank photo by Ray Witkin)

A worker cuts cloth at a textile mill in Côte d'Ivoire. The patterns are similar to traditional regional patterns. Most of the cloth made in Côte d'Ivoire is exported.

Nigeria and Niger, are found throughout much of West Africa. Indeed, their trading presence is so widespread that some have suggested that the Hausa language be promoted as a lingua franca, or common language, for West Africa.

Millions of migrant laborers are regularly attracted to Côte d'Ivoire and Ghana from the poorer inland states of Burkina Faso, Mali, and Niger, thus promoting economic interdependence between these states. Similar large-scale migrations also occur elsewhere. The drastic expulsion of aliens by the Nigerian government in 1983 was startling to the outside world, in part because few had realized that so many Ghanaians, Nigeriens, Togolese, Beninois, and Cameroonians had taken up residence in Nigeria. Such immigration is not new, though its scale into Nigeria was greatly increased by that country's oil boom. Peoples such as the Yoruba, Ewe, and Vai, who were divided by colonialism, have often ignored modern state boundaries in order to maintain their ethnic ties. Other migrations also have roots in the colonial past. Sierra Leonians worked as clerks and craftspeople throughout the coastal areas of British West Africa, while Igbo were recruited to serve in northern Nigeria. Similarly, Beninois became the assistants of French administrators in other parts of French West Africa, while Cape Verdians occupied intermediate positions in Portugal's mainland colonies.

THE PROGRESS OF WEST AFRICAN INTEGRATION

Many West Africans recognize the weaknesses inherent in the region's national divisions. The peoples of the region would benefit from greater multilateral political cooperation and economic integration. Yet there are many obstacles blocking the growth of pan-regional development. National identity is probably even stronger today than it was in the days when Kwame Nkrumah, the charismatic Ghanaian leader, pushed for African unity but was frustrated by parochial interests. The larger and more prosperous states, such as Nigeria and Côte d'Ivoire, are reluctant to share their relative wealth with smaller countries, which, in turn, fear being swallowed.

One-party rule and more overt forms of dictatorship have recently been abandoned throughout West Africa. However, for the moment, the region is still politically divided between those states that have made the transition to multiparty constitutional systems of government and those that are still under effective military control. Overlapping ethnicity is also sometimes more a source of suspicion rather than unity between states. Because the countries were under the rule of different colonial powers, French, English, and Portuguese serve today as official languages of the different nations, which also inherited different administrative traditions. Moreover, during colonial times, independent infrastructures were developed in each country; these continue to orient economic activities toward the coast and Europe rather than encouraging links among West African countries.

Political changes also affect regional cooperation and domestic development. Senegambia, the now-defunct confederation of Senegal and The Gambia, was dominated by Senegal and resented by many Gambians. The civil war in Liberia has also led to division between the supporters and opponents of the intervention of a multinational peacekeeping force.

Despite the many roadblocks to unity, multinational organizations have developed in West Africa, stimulated in large part by the severity of the common problems that the countries face. The West African countries have a good record of cooperating in the avoidance of armed conflict and the settlement of their occasional border disputes. In addition to the multilateral agencies that are coordinating the struggle against drought and the development of various river basins, there are also a number of regional commodity cartels, such as the five-member Groundnut Council. The West African Examinations Council standardizes secondary-school examinations in most of the countries where English is an official language, and most of the Francophonic states have the same currency.

The most ambitious and encompassing organization in the region is the Economic Organization of West African States (ECOWAS), which includes all the states incorporated in the West African section of this text. Established in 1975 by the Treaty of Lagos, ECOWAS aims to promote trade, cooperation, and self-reliance. The progress of the organization in these areas has thus far been limited. But ECOWAS can point to some significant achievements. Several joint ventures have been developed; steps toward tariff reduction are being taken; competition between ECOWAS and the Economic Community of West Africa (CEAO), an economic organization of former French colonies, has been lessened by limiting CEAO; and ECOWAS members have agreed in principle to establish a common currency. Some members of ECOWAS are currently seeking to have the organization play a political role in settling the bloody Liberian conflict, but their efforts to date have been unsuccessful. Nonetheless, there remains hope that ECOWAS will become more effective in developing West African solutions to the problems of the region's fragmented economies.

Benin (People's Republic of Benin)

GEOGRAPHY
Area in Square Kilometers (Miles): 112,620 (43,483) (slightly smaller than Pennsylvania)
Capital (Population): official: Porto-Novo (330,000); de facto: Cotonou (487,000)
Climate: tropical

PEOPLE

Population
Total: 5,522,700
Annual Growth Rate: 3.33%
Rural/Urban Population Ratio: 62/38
Major Languages: French; Fon; Yoruba; Adja; Bariba; others
Ethnic Makeup: 99% African (most important groupings being Fon, Adja, Yoruba, and Bariba); 1% European

Health
Life Expectancy at Birth: 50 years (male); 54 years (female)
Infant Mortality Rate (Ratio): 107.6/1,000
Average Caloric Intake: 100% of FAO minimum
Physicians Available (Ratio): 1/11,306

THE DAHOMEY KINGDOM

The Dahomey kingdom, established in the early eighteenth century by the Fon people, was a highly organized state. The kings had a standing army, which included women; a centralized administration, whose officers kept census and tax records and organized the slave trade and, later, the oil trade; and a sophisticated artistic tradition. Benin, like Togo, has important links with Brazil that date back to the time of the Dahomey kingdom. Some present-day Beninois families—such as the da Souzas, the da Silvas, and the Rodriguezes—are descendants of Brazilians who settled on the coast in the mid-nineteenth century. Some were descended from slaves who may have been taken from Dahomey long before. They became the first teachers in Western-oriented public schools and continued in higher education themselves. Yoruba religious cults, which developed from those of the Yoruba in Benin and Nigeria, have become increasingly popular in Brazil in recent years.

Religions
70% traditional indigenous, including Voodoo; 15% Muslim; 15% Christian

Education
Adult Literacy Rate: 23%

COMMUNICATION
Telephones: 8,650
Newspapers: 31

TRANSPORTATION
Highways—Kilometers (Miles): 8,435 (5,238)
Railroads—Kilometers (Miles): 579 (360)
Usable Airports: 7

GOVERNMENT
Type: pluralist democracy
Independence Date: August 1, 1960
Head of State: President Mathieu Kérékou
Political Parties: about 60 parties, including: Alliance of the Democratic Union for the Forces of Progress; Movement for Democracy and Social Progress; Union for Liberty and Development; Alliance of the National Party for Democracy and Development and the Democratic Renewal Party; National Rally for Democracy; others
Suffrage: universal at 18

MILITARY
Number of Armed Forces: 4,350
Military Expenditures (% of Central Government Expenditures): 3.2%
Current Hostilities: none

ECONOMY
Currency ($ U.S. Equivalent): 529.43 CFA francs = $1
Per Capita Income/GDP: $1,260/$6.7 billion
Inflation Rate: 35%
Natural Resources: none known in commercial quantities
Agriculture: palm products; cotton; corn; yams; cassava; cocoa; coffee; groundnuts
Industry: shoes; beer; textiles; cement; processed palm oil

FOREIGN TRADE
Exports: $332 million
Imports: $571 million

BENIN

In March 1996, former president Mathieu Kérékou returned to power with 52 percent of the vote, defeating incumbent Nicephore Soglo in Benin's second ballot since the 1990 restoration of multiparty democracy. Five years earlier, Soglo had defeated Kérékou, who had ruled the country as a virtual dictator for 17 years before agreeing to a democratic transition. In the past, Kérékou styled himself as a Marxist-Leninist and presided over a one-party state. Today, he presents himself as Christian Democrat, affirming that there can be no turning back to the old order. In Parliament, his Popular Revolutionary Party of Benin (PRPB) shares power with other groupings whose existence is primarily a reflection of ethnoregional rather than ideological divisions.

It is unlikely that Kérékou's restoration will result in any significant moves away from his predecessor's economic reforms, which had resulted in a modest rise in gross domestic product, increased investment, reduced inflation, and an easing of the country's debt burden. He will be under pressure, however, to raise the living standards of Benin's impoverished masses, who have so far not benefited from the reforms.

THE OLD ORDER FALLS

Kérékou's first reign began to unravel in late 1989. Unable to pay its bills, his government found itself increasingly vulnerable to mounting internal opposition and, to a lesser extent, to external pressure to institute sweeping political and economic reforms.

A wave of strikes and mass demonstrations swept through Cotonou, the country's largest city, in December 1989. This upsurge in prodemocracy agitation was partially inspired by the overthrow of Central/Eastern Europe's Marxist-Leninist regimes; ironically, the Stalinist underground Communist Party of Dahomey (PCD) also played a role in organizing much of the unrest. Attempts to quell the demonstrations with force only increased public anger toward the authorities.

In an attempt to defuse the crisis, the PRPB's state structures were forced to give up their monopoly of power by allowing a representative gathering to convene with the task of drawing up a new constitution. For 10 days in February 1990, the Beninois gathered around their television sets and radios to listen to live broadcasts of the National Conference of Active Forces of the Nation. The conference quickly turned into a public trial of Kérékou and his PRPB. With the eyes and ears of the nation tuned

in, critics of the regime, who had until recently been exiled, were able to pressure Kérékou into handing over effective power to a transitional government. The major task of this new, civilian administration was to prepare Benin for multiparty elections while trying to stabilize the deteriorating economy.

The political success of Benin's "civilian coup d'etat" placed the nation in the forefront of the democratization process then sweeping Africa. But liberating a nation from poverty is a much more difficult process.

A COUNTRY OF MIGRANTS

Benin is one of the least developed countries in the world. Having for decades experienced only limited economic growth, in recent years, the nation's real gross domestic product has actually declined.

Emigration has become a way of life for many. The migration of Beninois in search of opportunities in neighboring states is not a new phenomenon. Before 1960, educated people from the then-French colony of Dahomey (as Benin was called until 1975) were prominent in junior administrative positions throughout other parts of French West Africa. But as the region's newly independent states be-

(United Nations photo)

Benin is one of the least developed countries in the world. Beninois must often fend for themselves in innovative ways. The peddlar pictured above moves among the lake dwellings of a fishing village, selling cigarettes, spices, rice, and other commodities.

| The kingdom of Dahomey is established **1625** | The French conquer Dahomey and declare it a French protectorate **1892** | Dahomey becomes independent **1960** | Mathieu Kérékou comes to power in the sixth attempted military coup since independence **1972** | The name of Dahomey is changed to Benin **1975** | An attempted coup involves exiles and mercenaries and implicates Gabon, Morocco, and France **1977** |

1990s

Kérékou announces the abandonment of Marxism-Leninism as Benin's guiding ideology

Unrest, strikes, and escapes by political prisoners lead to the promise of multiparty elections

Multiparty elections are held; Kérékou loses power to Nicephore Soglo; Kérékou is reelected 5 years later

gan to localize their civil-service staffs, most of the Beninois expatriates lost their jobs. Their return increased bureaucratic competition within Benin, which, in turn, led to heightened political rivalry among ethnic and regional groups. Such local antagonisms contributed to a series of military coups between 1963 and 1972. These culminated in Kérékou's seizure of power.

While Beninois professionals can be found in many parts of West Africa, the destination of most recent emigrants has been Nigeria. The movement from Benin to Nigeria is facilitated by the close links that exist among the large Yoruba-speaking communities on both sides of the border. After Nigeria, the most popular destination has been Côte d'Ivoire. This may change, however, as economic recession in both of these states has led to heightened hostility against the migrants.

THE ECONOMY

Nigeria's urban areas have also been major markets for food. This has encouraged Beninois farmers to switch from cash crops (such as cotton, palm oil, cocoa, and coffee) to food crops (such as yams and cassava), which are smuggled across the border to Nigeria. The emergence of this parallel export economy has been encouraged by the former regime's practice of paying its farmers among the lowest official produce prices in the region. Given that agriculture, in terms of both employment and income generation, forms the largest sector of the Beninois economy, the rise in smuggling activities has inevitably contributed to a growth of graft and corruption.

Benin's small industrial sector is primarily geared toward processing primary products, such as palm oil and cotton, for export. It has thus been adversely affected by the shift away from producing these cash crops for the local market. Small-scale manufacturing has centered around the production of basic consumer goods and construction materials. The biggest enterprises are state-owned cement plants. One source of hope is that with privatization and new exploration, the country's small oil industry will undergo expansion.

Transport and trade are another important activity. Many Beninois find legal as well as illegal employment carrying goods. Due to the relative absence of rain forest (an impediment to travel), Benin's territory has historically served as a trade corridor between the coastal and inland savanna regions of West Africa. Today the nation's roads are comparatively well developed, and the railroad carries goods from the port at Cotonou to northern areas of the country. An extension of the railroad will reach Niamey, the capital of Niger. The government has also tried, with little success, to attract tourists in recent years, through such gambits as selling itself as the "home of Voodoo."

POLITICS AND RELIGION

Kérékou's narrow victory margin in 1996 amid charges and countercharges of electoral fraud underscored the continuing north–south division of Beninois politics and society. Although he is now a self-proclaimed Christian, Kérékou's political base remains the mainly Muslim north, while Soglo enjoyed majority support in the more Christianized south. Religious allegiance in Benin is complicated, however, by the prominence of the indigenous belief system known as Voodoo. Having originated in Benin, belief in Voodoo spirits has taken root in the Americas, especially Haiti, as well as elsewhere in West Africa. During his first presidency, Kérékou's sought to suppress Voodoo, which he branded as "witchcraft." Soglo, on the other hand, publicly embraced Voodoo, which was credited with helping him recover from a serious illness in 1992. On the eve of the 1996 election, Soglo recognized Voodoo as an official religion, proclaiming January 10 as "Voodoo National Day." (This move may have politically backfired, however, as it was condemned by the influential Catholic archbishop of Cotonou.)

A more decisive factor in Soglo's fall was the failure of his free-market reforms to revive the Beninois economy. Modest initial growth was seriously undermined in 1994 by the massive devaluation of the CFA franc, while privatization led to the retrenchment of 10,000 public workers. It is unlikely, however, that Kérékou's will be tempted to return to his own failed policies of "Marxist-Beninism."

DEVELOPMENT

Palm-oil plantations were established in Benin by Africans in the mid-nineteenth century. They have continued to be African-owned and capitalist-oriented. Today, there are some 30 million trees in Benin, and palm-oil products are a major export used for cooking, lighting, soap, margarine, and lubricants.

FREEDOM

Since 1990, political restrictions have been lifted and prisoners of conscience freed. Recently, however, a number of people have been arrested for supposedly inciting people against the government and encouraging them not to pay taxes.

HEALTH/WELFARE

One third of the national budget of Benin goes to education, and the number of students receiving primary education has risen to 50% of the school-age population. College graduates serve as temporary teachers through the National Service System, but more teachers and higher salaries are needed.

ACHIEVEMENTS

Fon appliquéd cloths have been described as "one of the gayest and liveliest of the contemporary African art forms." Formerly these cloths were made and used by Dahomeyan kings. Now they are sold to tourists, but they still portray the motifs and symbols of past rulers and the society they ruled.

Burkina Faso

GEOGRAPHY

Area in Square Kilometers (Miles):
274,500 (106,000) (about the size of
Colorado)
Capital (Population): Ouagadougou
(442,000)
Climate: tropical to arid

PEOPLE

Population
Total: 10,423,000
Annual Growth Rate: 2.79%
Rural/Urban Population Ratio: 79/21
ajor Languages: French; Mossi;
Senufo; Fula; Bobo; Mande;
Gurunsi; Lobi
Ethnic Makeup: Mossi; Gurunsi;
Senufo; Lobi; Bobo; Mande; Fulani

Health
Life Expectancy at Birth: 46 years
(male); 48 years (female)
Infant Mortality Rate (Ratio): 117/1,000
Average Caloric Intake: 100% of
FAO minimum
Physicians Available (Ratio): 1/29,914

Religions
50% Muslim; 40% traditional
indigenous; 10% Christian

DR. OUEDRAOGO AND THE NAAM MOVEMENT

In 1989, Dr. Bernard Ledea Ouedraogo was awarded the Hunger
Project's third annual Africa Prize for Leadership for the Sustainable
End of Hunger, an honor bestowed in recognition of his important
contribution in raising rural living standards throughout West Africa.
During the 1960s, Ouedraogo became disillusioned with the top-down
methods then employed by the Burkinabe government and international
aid groups when trying to mobilize local peasants for development
projects. His response was to organize the Naam movement, originally
as a support network for the *naam,* the traditional Burkinabe village
cooperatives. The movement assisted the *naam* in establishing their
own development projects. *Naam* has since grown to become the largest
peasant movement in Africa, with more than 4,000 affiliated grassroots
groups in Chad, The Gambia, Guinea-Bissau, Mali, Mauritania, Niger,
Senegal, and Togo, as well as in Burkina Faso.

Education
Adult Literacy Rate: 18%

COMMUNICATION

Telephones: 14,000
Newspapers: 4

TRANSPORTATION

Highways—Kilometers (Miles):
16,500 (10,230)
Railroads—Kilometers (Miles): 622
(385)
Usable Airfields: 48

GOVERNMENT

Type: republic under control of a
military council
Independence Date: August 5, 1960
Head of State/Government: President
Blaise Compaore; Prime Minister
Roch Kabore
Political Parties: Popular Democratic
Organization–Workers Movement;
dozens of opposition parties
Suffrage: none

MILITARY

Number of Armed Forces: 7,200
*Military Expenditures (% of Central
Government Expenditures):* 4.3%
Current Hostilities: none

ECONOMY

Currency ($ U.S. Equivalent): 529.43
CFA francs = $1
Per Capita Income/GDP: $660/$6.5
billion
Inflation Rate: –0.6%
Natural Resources: manganese;
limestone; marble; gold; uranium;
bauxite; copper
Agriculture: millet; sorghum; corn;
rice; livestock; peanuts; shea nuts;
sugarcane; cotton; sesame
Industry: agricultural processing;
brewing; light industry

FOREIGN TRADE

Exports: $273 million
Imports: $636 million

BURKINA FASO

In February 1995, Burkina Faso held its second contested elections since the 1991 reintroduction of multiparty democracy. With the opposition vote divided among 19 parties, President Blaise Compaore's ruling Popular Democratic Organization–Worker's Movement (ODP–MT) captured 26 of the 33 seats. Despite the options, the majority of Burkinabe failed to vote. Since 1987, real power has remained in the hands of Compaore, who has proved to be a master of the art of political survival. Local indifference to the polls may also stem from popular cynicism about any government's ability to rescue the national from its chronic poverty. In 1993, the United Nations' Human Development Index listed Burkina Faso an abysmal 170 out of 174 countries.

Compaore rose to power through a series of coups, the last of which resulted in the overthrow and assassination of the charismatic and controversial Thomas Sankara. A man of immense populist appeal, Sankara's radical leadership had become by 1987 the focus of a great deal of internal and external opposition as well as support.

Of the three men responsible for Sankara's toppling, two—Boukari Lingani and Henri Zongo—were executed following a power struggle with the third, Compaore. Such sanguinary competition has aggravated the severe economic and social difficulties of the Burkinabe. (For decades, successive military and civilian regimes have faced a daunting task in trying to cope with the challenge of developing the nation's fragile, underdeveloped economy.) It also has called into question the government's commitment to political pluralism.

DEBILITATING DROUGHTS

At the time of its independence from France, in 1960, the landlocked country then known as the "Republic of Upper Volta" inherited little in the way of colonial infrastructure. Since independence, progress has been hampered by prolonged periods of severe drought. As a result, much of the country has been forced at times to depend on international food aid. To counteract some of the negative effects of this circumstance, efforts have been made to integrate relief donations into local development schemes. Of particular note have been projects instituted by the traditional rural cooperatives known as *naam,* which have been responsible for such small-scale but often invaluable local improvements as new wells and pumps, better grinding mills, and distribution tools and medical supplies.

Despite such community action, the effects of drought have been devastating. Particularly hard-hit has been pastoral production, which has long been a mainstay of the local economy, especially in the north. It is estimated that the most recent drought destroyed about 90 percent of the livestock in Burkina Faso.

(United Nations photo by John Isaac)

Since Burkina Faso gained its independence from France, its progress has been hampered by prolonged periods of drought. Local cooperatives have been responsible for small-scale improvements such as the construction of the water barrage or barricade pictured above. Despite such community action, the effects of drought have been devastating.

	The French finally overcome Mossi resistance and claim Upper Volta	Upper Volta is divided among adjoining French colonies			Lieutenant Colonel Laminzana succeeds Yameogo, who resigns following rioting in the country	Captain Thomas Sankara seizes power and changes the country's name to Burkina (Mossi for "land of honest men") Faso (Dioula for "democratic republic")	Sankara is assassinated in a coup; Blaise Compaore succeeds as head of state
The first Mossi kingdom is founded 1313	1896	1932	Upper Volta is reconstituted as a colony 1947	Independence under President Maurice Yameogo 1960	1966		1980s

1990s

Compaore introduces multipartyism, but his critics call the reforms a "shamocracy"

Compaore retains control of Burkina Faso

Most Burkinabe continue to survive as agriculturalists and herders, but many are dependent on wage labor. In the urban centers, there exists a significant working-class population that supports the nation's politically powerful trade union movement. The division between this urban community and rural population is not absolute, for it is common for individuals to combine wage labor with farming activities. Another population category—whose numbers exceed those of the local wage-labor force—are individuals who seek employment outside of the country. At least 1 million work as migrant laborers in other parts of West Africa. This is part of a pattern that dates back to the early twentieth century. Approximately 700,000 of these workers regularly migrate to Côte d'Ivoire. Returning workers have infused the rural areas with consumer goods and a working-class consciousness.

UNIONS FORCE CHANGE

As is the case in much of Africa, it is the salaried urban population who (at least, next to the army), have exercised the greatest influence over successive Burkinabe regimes. Trade-union leaders representing these workers have been instrumental in forcing changes in government. They have spoken out vigorously against government efforts to ban strikes and restrain unions. They have also demanded that they be shielded from downturns in the local economy. Although many unionists have championed various shades of Marxist-Leninist ideology, they, along with their natural allies in the civil

service, arguably constitute a conservative element within the local society. During the mid-1980s, they became increasingly concerned about the dynamic Sankara's efforts to promote a nationwide network of grass-roots Committees for the Defense of the Revolution (CDRs) as vehicles for empowering the nation's largely rural masses.

To many unionists, the mobilization and arming of the CDRs was perceived as a direct challenge to their own status. This threat seemed all the more apparent when Sankara began to cut urban salaries, in the name of a more equitable flow of revenue to the rural areas. When several union leaders challenged this move, they were arrested on charges of sedition. Sankara's subsequent overthrow thus had strong backing from within organized labor and the civil service. These groups, along with the military, remain the principal supporters of Compaore's ODP–MT and its policy of "national rectification." Yet, despite this support base, the government has moved to restructure the until recently all-encompassing public sector of the economy by reducing its wage bill. This effort has impressed international creditors.

Beyond its core of support, ODP–MT government has generally been met with sentiments ranging from hostility to indifference. While Compaore claimed—with some justification—that Sankara's rule had become too arbitrary and that he had resisted forming a party with a set of rules, many people mourned the fallen leader's death. In the aftermath of the coup, the widespread use of a new cloth pattern, known locally as "homage to Sankara," became an informal barometer of popular dissatisfaction. Compaore has also been challenged by the high regard

that has been accorded Sankara outside Burkina Faso, as a symbol of a new generation of African radicalism.

Although Compaore, like Sankara, has sometimes turned to sharp anti-imperialist rhetoric, his government has generally sought to cultivate good relations with France and the major international financial institutions. But he has alienated himself from many of his fellow West African leaders as well as from the Euro–American diplomatic consensus, through his aggressive support of Charles Taylor's National Patriotic Front in Liberia. Compaore admits to sending troops to Liberia to help topple leader Samuel Doe—"It was a moral duty to save Liberians from the wrath of a ruthless dictator"—but claims that such support ended in April 1991. (Others in the region are skeptical of this claim.) In 1992, Compaore was also accused of harboring Gambian dissidents, a charge he denies. To many outsiders, as well as Burkinabe people themselves, the course of Compaore's government remains ambiguous.

DEVELOPMENT

Despite political turbulence, Burkina Faso's economy has recorded positive, albeit modest, annual growth rates for more than a decade. Most of the growth has been in agriculture. New hydroelectric projects should reduce the country's dependence on imported energy.

FREEDOM

There has been a surprisingly strong tradition of pluralism despite the circumscribed nature of human rights under successive military regimes. Freedom of speech and association are still curtailed, and political detentions are common. The Burkinabe Movement for Human Rights has challenged the government.

HEALTH/WELFARE

The inadequacy of the country's public health measures is reflected in the low Burkinabe life expectancy. Mass immunization campaigns have been successfully carried out, but in an era of structural adjustment, the prospects for a dramatic improvement in health appear bleak.

ACHIEVEMENTS

The biannual Pan-African Film Festival is held in Ouagadougou. This festival has contributed significantly to the development of the film industry in Africa. Burkina Faso has nationalized its movie houses, and the government has encouraged the showing of films by African filmmakers.

Cape Verde (Republic of Cape Verde)

GEOGRAPHY

Area in Square Kilometers (Miles): 4,033 (1,557) (a bit larger than Rhode Island)
Capital (Population): Praia (37,670)
Climate: temperate

PEOPLE

Population
Total: 436,000
Annual Growth Rate: 3%
Rural/Urban Population Ratio: 56/44
Major Languages: Portuguese and Kriolu
Ethnic Makeup: 71% Creole (mixed); 28% African; 1% European

Health
Life Expectancy at Birth: 61 years (male); 65 years (female)
Infant Mortality Rate (Ratio): 56/1,000
Average Caloric Intake: 133% of FAO minimum
Physicians Available (Ratio): 1/4,208

CAPE VERDEAN AMERICANS

Large-scale immigration of Cape Verdeans to the United States began in the nineteenth century. Today, the Cape Verdean-American community is larger than the population of Cape Verde itself; it is concentrated in southern New England. The 1980 U.S. Census was the first to count Cape Verdeans as a separate ethnic group.

Most early immigrants arrived in the region aboard whaling and packet ships. The community has, on the whole, prospered, and is currently better educated than the national American norm. Cape Verdeans in the United States maintain close ties with their homeland, assisting in local development projects.

Religions
80% Catholic; 20% traditional indigenous

Education
Adult Literacy Rate: 66%

COMMUNICATION

Telephones: 1,700
Newspapers: 7 weeklies

TRANSPORTATION

Highways—Kilometers (Miles): 1,100 (686)
Railroads—Kilometers (Miles): none
Usable Airfields: 6

GOVERNMENT

Type: republic
Independence Date: July 5, 1975
Head of State/Government: President Antonio Mascarenhas Monteiro; Prime Minister Carlos Alberto Wahnonde Carvacho Veiga
Political Parties: Movement for Democracy; African Party for the Independence of Cape Verde
Suffrage: universal at 18

MILITARY

Number of Armed Forces: 1,325
Military Expenditures (% of Central Government Expenditures): 11%
Current Hostilities: none

ECONOMY

Currency ($ U.S. Equivalent): 85.53 escudos = $1
Per Capita Income/GDP: $1,000/$410 million
Inflation Rate: 7.0%
Natural Resources: fish; agricultural land; salt deposits
Agriculture: corn; beans; manioc; sweet potatoes; bananas
Industry: fishing; flour mills; salt

FOREIGN TRADE

Exports: $4.4 million
Imports: $173 million

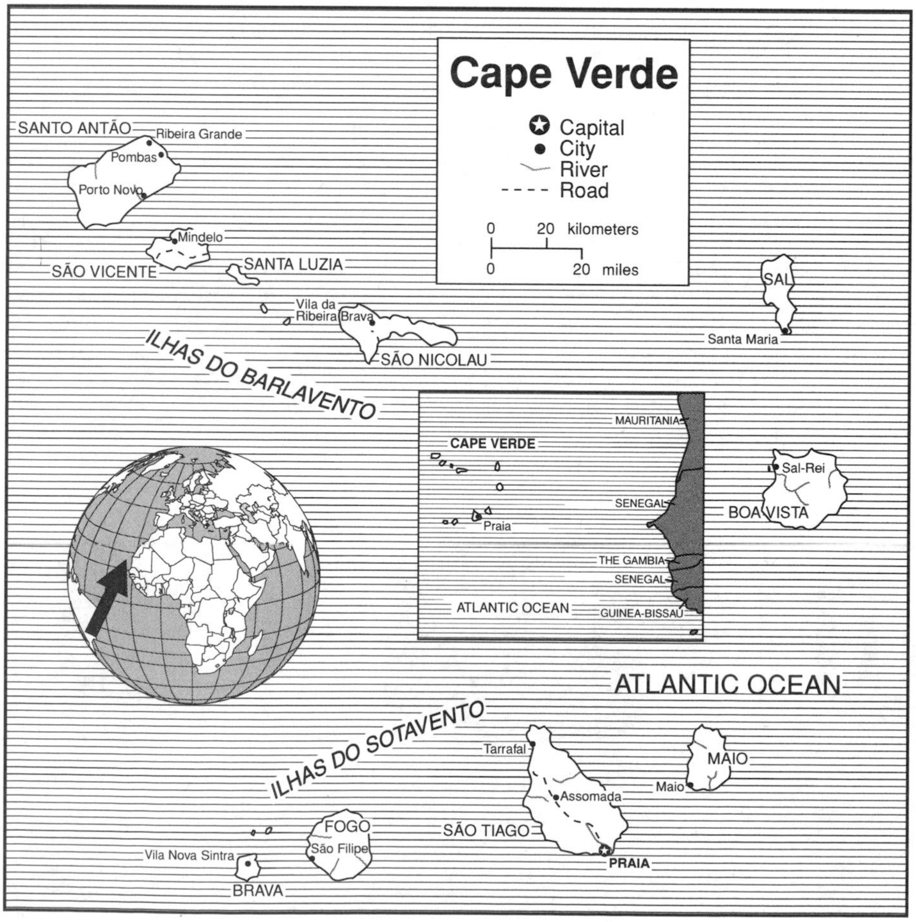

Cape Verde
Capital
City
River
Road
0 20 kilometers
0 20 miles
SANTO ANTÃO
Ribeira Grande
Pombas
Porto Novo
Mindelo
SÃO VICENTE
SANTA LUZIA
Vila da Ribeira Brava
SÃO NICOLAU
SAL
Santa Maria
ILHAS DO BARLAVENTO
MAURITANIA
CAPE VERDE
Praia
SENEGAL
THE GAMBIA
SENEGAL
ATLANTIC OCEAN
GUINEA-BISSAU
Sal-Rei
BOA VISTA
ATLANTIC OCEAN
ILHAS DO SOTAVENTO
Tarrafal
Assomada
MAIO
Maio
FOGO
São Filipe
SÃO TIAGO
Vila Nova Sintra
PRAIA
BRAVA

Cape Verdean settlement begins 1462	Slavery is abolished 1869	Thousands of Cape Verdeans die of starvation during World War II 1940s	The PAIGC is founded 1956	Warfare begins in Guinea-Bissau; Amilcar Cabral is assassinated 1973	A coup in Lisbon initiates the Portuguese decolonization process 1974	Independence 1975

1990s

The PAICV is defeated by the MPD in the country's first multiparty elections

Antonio Mascarenhas Monteiro defeats Aristides Pereira to become Cape Verde's second president

Cape Verde adopts a new Constitution; Monteiro is reelected in an unopposed election

THE REPUBLIC OF CAPE VERDE

In 1992, Cape Verde adopted a new flag and Constitution, consolidating the island's transition to political pluralism. After 15 years of single-party rule by the African Party for the Independence of Cape Verde (PAICV), rising agitation led to the legalization of opposition groups in 1990. In January 1991, a quickly assembled antigovernment coalition, the Movement for Democracy (MPD), stunned the political establishment by gaining 68 percent of the votes and 56 out of 79 National Assembly seats. A month later, the MPD candidate, Antonio Mascarenhas Monteiro, defeated the long-serving incumbent, Aristides Pereira, in the presidential election. It is a credit to both the outgoing administration and its opponents that this dramatic political transformation occurred without significant violence or rancor. Parliamentary elections in December 1995 resulted in the MPD retaining power with a reduced majority.

The Republic of Cape Verde is an archipelago located about 400 miles west of the Senegalese Cape Verde, or "Green Cape," after which it is named. Unfortunately, green is a color that is often absent in the lives of the islands' citizens. Throughout its history, Cape Verde has suffered from periods of prolonged drought, which before the twentieth century were often accompanied by extremely high mortality rates (up to 50 percent). The last severe drought lasted from 1968 to 1984. Even in normal years, though, rainfall is often inadequate.

When the country gained independence, in 1975, there was little in the way of non-agricultural production. As a result, the new nation had to rely for its survival on foreign aid and the remittances of Cape Verdeans working abroad, but the post-independence period has been marked by a genuine improvement in the lives of most Cape Verdeans.

Cape Verde was ruled by Portugal for nearly 500 years. Most of the islanders are the descendants of Portuguese colonists, many of whom arrived as convicts, and African slaves who began to settle on the islands shortly after their discovery by Portuguese mariners in 1456. The merging of these two groups gave rise to the distinct Cape Verdean Kriolu language (which is also spoken in Guinea-Bissau). Under Portuguese rule, Cape Verdeans were generally treated as second-class citizens, although a few rose to positions of prominence in other parts of the Portuguese colonial empire. Economic stagnation, exacerbated by cycles of severe drought, caused many islanders to emigrate elsewhere in Africa, Western Europe, and the Americas.

In 1956, the African Party for the Independence of Guinea-Bissau and Cape Verde (PAIGC) was formed under the dynamic leadership of Amilcar Cabral, a Cape Verdean revolutionary who, with his followers, hoped to see the two Portuguese colonies form a united nation. Between 1963 and 1974, PAIGC waged a successful war of liberation in Guinea-Bissau and led to the independence of both territories. Although Cabral was assassinated by the Portuguese in 1973, his vision was preserved during the late 1970s by his successors, who, while ruling the two countries separately, maintained the unity of the PAIGC. This arrangement, however, began to break down in the aftermath of a 1980 coup in Guinea-Bissau and resulted in the party's division along national lines. In 1981, the Cape Verdean PAIGC formally renounced its Guinean links, becoming the PAICV.

After independence, the PAIGC/CV government was challenged by the colonial legacy of economic underdevelopment, exacerbated by drought. In contemporary times, massive famine has been warded off through a reliance on imported foodstuffs, mostly received as aid. The government attempted to strengthen local food production and assist the 70 percent of the local population engaged in subsistence agriculture. Its efforts took the forms of drilling for underground water, terracing, irrigating, and building a water-desalinization plant with U.S. assistance. Major efforts also were devoted to tree-planting schemes as a way to cut back on erosion and eventually make the country self-sufficient in wood fuel.

With no more than 15 percent of the islands' territory potentially suitable for cultivation, the prospect of Cape Verde developing self-sufficiency in food appears remote. The few factories that exist on Cape Verde are small-scale operations catering to local needs. Only textiles have enjoyed modest success as an export. Another promising area is fishing.

DEVELOPMENT

In a move designed to attract greater investment from overseas, especially from Cape Verdean Americans, the country has joined the International Finance Corporation. Efforts are under way to promote the islands as an offshore banking center for the West African (ECOWAS) region.

FREEDOM

The new Constitution should entrench the country's recent political liberalization. Opposition publications have emerged to complement the state- and Catholic Church-sponsored media.

HEALTH/WELFARE

Greater access to health facilities has resulted in a sharp drop in infant mortality and a rise in life expectancy. Clinics have begun to encourage family planning. Since independence, great progress has taken place in social services. Nutrition levels have been raised, and basic health care is now provided to the entire population.

ACHIEVEMENTS

Cape Verdean Kriolu culture has a rich literary and musical tradition. With emigrant support, Cape Verde bands have acquired modest followings in Western Europe, Lusophone Africa, Brazil, and the United States. Local drama, poetry, and music are showcased on the national television service.

Côte d'Ivoire (Republic of Côte d'Ivoire)

GEOGRAPHY

Area in Square Kilometers (Miles):
323,750 (124,503) (slightly larger
than New Mexico)
Capital (Population): Abidjan
(economic) (1,850,000);
Yamoussoukro (political) (120,000)
Climate: tropical

PEOPLE

Population
Total: 14,791,000
Annual Growth Rate: 3.38%
Rural/Urban Population Ratio: 61/39
Major Languages: French; Dioula;
Agni; Baoulé; Kru; Senufo;
Mandinka; others
Ethnic Makeup: 23% Baoule; 18%
Bete; 15% Senoufou; 11% Malinke;
33% others

Health
Life Expectancy at Birth: 47 years
(male); 51 years (female)
Infant Mortality Rate (Ratio):
93/1,000
Average Caloric Intake: 112% of

FAO minimum
Physicians Available (Ratio): 1/24,696

Religions
60% Muslim; 28% traditional
indigenous; 12% Christian

Education
Adult Literacy Rate: 54%

COMMUNICATION

Telephones: 87,700
Newspapers: 1

THE ARTS OF CÔTE d'IVOIRE

The arts of Côte d'Ivoire, including music, weaving, dance, and sculpture,
have flourished. The wood carvings of the Senufo, Dan, and Baoulé peoples
are famous the world over for their beauty and intricate design. Masks are
particularly valued and admired by outsiders, but many collectors have
never met the Ivoirian people, for whom the art has social and religious
significance. The Dan mask, for example, is not only beautiful—it also
performs a spiritual function. When worn as part of a masquerade performance, it represents religious authority, settling of disputes, enforcing the
laws of the community, and respect for tradition.

TRANSPORTATION

Highways—Kilometers (Miles):
46,600 (28,892)
Railroads—Kilometers (Miles): 657
(408)
Usable Airfields: 40

GOVERNMENT

Type: republic
Independence Date: August 7, 1960
Head of State/Government: President
Henri Konan Bedie; Prime Minister
Daniel Kablan Duncan
Political Parties: Democratic Party
of Côte d'Ivoire; opposition groups,
including the Ivoirian Popular Front
Suffrage: universal at 21

MILITARY

Number of Armed Forces: 14,900
*Military Expenditures (% of Central
Government Expenditures):* 1.4%
Current Hostilities: none

ECONOMY

Currency ($ U.S. Equivalent):
529.43 CFA francs = $1
Per Capita Income/GDP:
$1,430/$20.5 billion
Inflation Rate: 1.0%
Natural Resources: agricultural lands;
timber
Agriculture: coffee; cocoa; bananas;
pineapples; palm oil; corn; millet;
cotton; rubber
Industry: food and lumber
processing; oil refinery; textiles;
soap; automobile assembly

FOREIGN TRADE

Exports: $2.7 billion
Imports: $1.6 billion

Côte d'Ivoire
⊗ Capital
● City
〜 River
--- Road

0   100   kilometers
0   100 miles

CÔTE d'IVOIRE

Since the death in 1993 of its unifying first president Félix Houphouët-Boigny, politics and society in Côte d'Ivoire (French for "Ivory Coast") have become increasingly polarized. In October 1995, Houphouët-Boigny's successor, Henri Konan Bedie, retained power in an election boycotted by the supporters of his main rival, Allassane Ouattera, who was banned from running due to a new law mandating that both parents of presidential candidates must be born in Côte d'Ivoire. While the turnout remains a matter of dispute, it is clear that the boycott enjoyed widespread support in the predominantly Muslim north, which is Ouattera's home area. For the first time since independence, immigrants, who make up 40 percent of the population, were banned from voting. Violent protests before the poll were accompanied by increased governmental repression of the people.

Africa's longest-serving leader, for more than half a century Houphouët-Boigny had been a dominant figure not only in Côte d'Ivoire but throughout Francophonic Africa. A pioneering pan-Africanist, he had served for 3 years as a French cabinet minister before leading his country to independence, in 1960. Under him, Ivoirians had enjoyed stability and economic growth that was the envy of their neighbours. But his paternalistic autocracy, exercised through his Democratic Party of Côte d'Ivoire (PDCI), had started to break down before his death. Since 1990, Ivoirian politics has fluctuated between reform and repression. There is as yet little sign that Bedie is prepared to meet popular demands for a democratic transformation of society.

REFORM AND REPRESSION

After 3 decades of PDCI single-party rule, the political life of Côte d'Ivoire entered a new phase in 1990. Months of mounting prodemocracy protests and labor unrest led to the legalization of previously banned opposition parties as well as to the emergence within the PDCI itself of a strong progressive wing seemingly committed to liberalization. Although the first multiparty presidential and, especially, legislative elections in October 1990 were widely regarded as having been less than free and fair by outside observers and the opposition, many nevertheless believed that the path was open for further reform. Houphouët-Boigny garnered 82 percent of the vote against a challenger named Lauret Gbagbo, while the PDCI captured 163 out of 175 National Assembly seats. In November 1990, the outgoing National Assembly passed a constitutional amendment to allow its speaker to take over the presidency in the event of a vacancy. This move brought about premature speculation that Houphouët-Boigny was preparing to step aside in favor of Bedie. Another amendment provided for the naming of a prime minister, a post that was subsequently filled by Ouattara, an able technocrat. But the octogenarian president refused to give up power. As his health declined, resulting in extended stays in France, his actions became more erratic. The reform process was probably further paralyzed by a power struggle between Bedie and Ouattara. So far, Bedie has clearly come out ahead: In 1994, Ouattara lost his position.

In February 1992, a mass demonstration called by the main opposition party, Gbagbo's Ivoirian Popular Front (FPI), and the Ivoirian Human Rights League turned into a riot. The violence provided the government with a pretext to jail Gbagbo, along with the Human Rights League head Degny Segui and dozens of other prominent political and community leaders, including members of another opposition movement, the Ivoirian Workers Party (PIT), as well as journalists and students. Gbagbo, Segui, and 10 others were subsequently convicted of being "responsible" for "acts of violence," although state prosecutors acknowledged that they had not been personally involved in any criminal activity. Others were imprisoned on charges ranging from "harboring criminals" to putting forward "outrageous arguments." Denouncing what was characterized as an "undeclared state of siege," the FPI temporarily withdrew from National Assembly, making it once more the sole preserve of the PDCI.

ECONOMIC DOWNTURN

Reform and repression have been taking place against the backdrop of a prolonged deterioration in Côte d'Ivoire's once-vibrant economy. The primary explanation for this downturn is the decline in revenue from cocoa and coffee, which have long been the country's principal export earners. This has led to mounting state debt, which in turn has pressured the government to adopt unpopular austerity measures. The economy's current problems and prospects are best understood in the context of its past performance.

During its first 2 decades of independence, Côte d'Ivoire enjoyed one of the highest economic growth rates in the world. This growth was all the more notable in that, in contrast to many other developing-world "success stories" during the same period, it had been fueled by the expansion of commercial agriculture. The nation became the world's leading producer of cocoa and the third-largest producer of coffee. Although prosperity gave way to recession during the 1980s, the average per capita income of the country is still one of Africa's highest. Statistics also indicate that, on average, Ivoirians live longer and better than people in many neighboring states. But the creation of a productive, market-oriented economy has not eliminated the harsh reality of widespread poverty, leading some to question whether the majority of Ivoirians have derived reasonable benefit from their nation's wealth. To the dismay of many young Ivoirians struggling to enter the country's tight job market, much of the political and economic life of Côte d'Ivoire is controlled by its large expatriate population, largely comprised of French and Lebanese. The size of these communities has multiplied since independence.

Commercial farmers, who include millions of medium- and small-scale producers, also have prospered. About two thirds of the workforce are employed in agriculture, with coffee alone being the principal source of income for some 2.5 million people, including those who provide services for the industry. In addition to cocoa and coffee, Ivoirian planters grow bananas, pineapples, sugar, cotton, palm oil, and other cash crops for export. While some of these farmers are quite wealthy, most have only modest incomes.

In recent years, the circumstance of Ivoirian coffee and cocoa planters has become much more precarious, due to fluctuations in commodities prices. In this respect, the growers, along with their colleagues elsewhere, are to some extent victims of their own success. Their productivity, in response to international demand, has been a factor in depressing prices through increased supply. In 1988, Houphouët-Boigny held cocoa in storage in an attempt to force a price rise, but the effort failed, aggravating the nation's economic downturn. As a result, the government took a new approach, scrapping plans for future expansion in cocoa production in favor of promoting food crops such as yams, corn, and plantains, for which there is a regional as well as a domestic market.

Ivoirian planters often hire low-paid laborers from other West African countries. There are about 2 million migrant laborers in Côte d'Ivoire, employed throughout the economy. Their presence is not a new phenomenon but goes back to colonial times. Many laborers come from Burkina Faso which was once a part of Côte d'Ivoire. Today Burkinabe as well as citizens of other former colonies of French West Africa have the advantage of being paid in a re-

Agni and Baoulé
peoples migrate
to the Ivory
Coast from
the East
1700s

The Ivory Coast
officially
becomes a
French colony
1893

Samori Touré, a
Malinke Muslim
leader and an
empire builder, is
defeated by the
French
1898

The final French
pacification of
the country takes
place
1915

Côte d'Ivoire
becomes
independent
under Félix
Houphouët-Boigny's
leadership
1960

The PDCI
approves a plan to
move the capital
from Abidjan to
Houphouët-Boigny's
home village of
Yamoussoukro
1980s

1990s

Prodemocracy
demonstrations
lead to multiparty
elections

Houphouët-Boigny
dies; Henri
Konan Bedie
becomes the new
president

Bedie wins a
controversial
presidential
election amid
growing social
unrest

gional currency, the CFA franc, as well as sharing the colonial vernacular. A good road system and the Ivoirian railroad (which extends to the Burkinabe capital of Ouagadougou) facilitate the travel of migrant workers to rural as well as urban areas.

DEBT AND DISCONTENT

Other factors may determine how much an Ivoirian benefits from the country's development. Residents of Abidjan, the capital, and its environs near the coast receive more services than do citizens of interior areas. Professionals in the cities make better salaries than do laborers on farms or in small industries. Yet persistent inflation and recession have made daily life difficult for the middle class as well as poorer peasants and workers. This has led to rising discontent. In 1983, teachers went on strike to protest the discontinuance of their housing subsidies. The government refused to yield and banned the teachers' union; the teachers went back to work. The ban has since been lifted, but the causes of discontent remain, for no teacher can afford the high rents in the cities. Moreover, teachers deeply resent the fact that other civil servants, ministers, and French cooperants (helpers on the Peace Corps model) did not have their subsidies cut back, and they demand a more even "distribution of sacrifices." In 1987, teachers' leaders were detained by the government.

The nonagricultural sectors of the national economy have also been experiencing difficulties. Many state industries are unable to make a profit due to their heavy indebtedness. Serious brush fires, mismanagement, and the clearing of forests for cash-crop plantations have put the nation's once-sizable timber industry in jeopardy. Out of a former total of 12 million hectares of forest, 10½ million have been lost. Plans for expansion of offshore oil and natural-gas production were delayed due to an inability to raise needed investment capital. In March 1994, however, significant new discoveries were announced, which should allow for fuel self-sufficiency in coming years.

Difficulty in raising capital for oil and gas development is a reflection of the debt crisis that has plagued the country since the collapse of its cocoa and coffee earnings. Finding itself in the desperate situation of being forced to borrow to pay interest on its previous loans, the government suspended most debt repayments in 1987. Subsequent rescheduling negotiations with international creditors resulted in a Structural Adjustment Plan, approved by the World Bank and International Monetary Fund. This plan has resulted in a reduction in the prices paid to Ivoirian farmers and a drastic curtailment in public spending, leading to severe salary cuts for public and parastatal workers. Recent pressure on the part of the lending agencies for the Ivoirian government to cut back further on its commitment to cash crops is particularly ironic, given the praise that they bestowed on the same policies in the not-too-distant past.

THE SEARCH FOR STABILITY

The government's ability to gain popular acceptance for its austerity measures has been compromised by corruption and extravagance at the top. A notorious example of the latter is the basilica that was recently constructed at Yamoussoukro, the home village of Houphouët-Boigny, which is to become the nation's new capital city. This air-conditioned structure, patterned after the papal seat of St. Peter's in Rome, is the largest Christian church building in the world. Supposedly a personal gift from Houphouët-Boigny to the Vatican (a most reluctant recipient), its construction is believed to have cost hundreds of millions of dollars.

Côte d'Ivoire's current period of political upheaval comes after decades of stability. Houphouët-Boigny had been adept at striking a balance between the country's various regional and ethnic groups. Despite his authoritarianism, he had also generally preferred to deal with internal opponents by emphasizing the carrot rather than the stick. By contrast, Bedie has sought to suppress dissent, arresting more than 40 journalists in the first 2 years of his presidency. His government remains vulnerable, however, in the face of widespread opposition. It is too early to say whether Houphouët-Boigny's passing will result in greater democracy or dictatorship at the top.

DEVELOPMENT

It has been said that Côte d'Ivoire is "power hungry." The Soubre Dam, being developed on the Sassandra River, is the sixth and largest hydroelectric project in Côte d'Ivoire. It will serve the eastern area of the country. Another dam is planned for the Cavalla River, between Côte d'Ivoire and Liberia.

FREEDOM

Thus far, President Konan Bedie has shown little tolerance for dissent within either the PDCI or society as a whole. Journalists have been jailed for writing "insulting" articles.

HEALTH/WELFARE

Côte d'Ivoire has one of the lowest soldier-to-teacher ratios in Africa. Education absorbs about 40% of the national budget. The National Commission to Combat AIDS has reported significant success in its campaign to promote condom use, by targeting especially vulnerable groups.

ACHIEVEMENTS

Ivoirian textiles are varied and prized. Block printing and dyeing produce brilliant designs; woven cloths made strip by strip and sewn together include the white Korhogo tapestries, covered with Ivoirian figures, birds, and symbols drawn in black. The Ivoirian singer Alpha Blondy has become an international superstar as the leading exponent of West African reggae.

The Gambia (Republic of The Gambia)

GEOGRAPHY

Area in Square Kilometers (Miles): 11,295 (4,361) (smaller than Connecticut)
Capital (Population): Banjul (49,200)
Climate: subtropical

PEOPLE

Population
Total: 989,300
Annual Growth Rate: 3.08%
Rural/Urban Population Ratio: 74/26
Major Languages: English; Mandinka; Wolof; Fula; Sarakola; Diula; others
Ethnic Makeup: 42% Mandinka; 18% Fula; 16% Wolof; 24% others

Health
Life Expectancy at Birth: 48 years (male); 53 years (female)
Infant Mortality Rate (Ratio): 121/1,000
Average Caloric Intake: 97% of FAO minimum
Physicians Available (Ratio): 1/14,536

Religions
90% Muslim; 9% Christian; 1% traditional indigenous

Education
Adult Literacy Rate: 27%

COMMUNICATION

Telephones: 3,500
Newspapers: 6

TRANSPORTATION

Highways—Kilometers (Miles): 3,083 (1,911)

Railroads—Kilometers (Miles): none
Usable Airfields: 1

GOVERNMENT

Type: military
Independence Date: February 18, 1965
Head of State: President (Lieutenant) Yahya Jammeh
Political Parties: Alliance for Patriotic Reorientation and Construction (APRC); United Democratic Party; others banned, boycotting, or defunct
Suffrage: universal at 21

MILITARY

Number of Armed Forces: 870
Military Expenditures (% of Central Government Expenditures): 3.8%
Current Hostilities: internal conflicts

HALEY'S *ROOTS*

"Kambay Bolong" and "Kunte Kinte" were two of the terms that Alex Haley's grandmother repeated as she told him of their "furthest back" ancestor, the African. When Haley, an American, started the search for his roots, he consulted linguists as well as Africans about these words. "Kambay Bolong" was identified as The Gambia River and "Kinte" as one of the major Mandinka lineages or large families. Thus began Haley's association with The Gambia, which culminated in his visit to the town of Juffure in Gambia's interior. There Haley heard the history of the Kinte clan from a *griot,* or bard, and identified his past ancestor. Haley told his story in his well-known book *Roots.* He died in 1992.

ECONOMY

Currency ($ U.S. Equivalent): 9.56 dalasis = $1
Per Capita Income/GDP: $1,050/$1.0 billion
Inflation Rate: 6.5%
Natural Resources: fish; ilmenite; zircon; rutile
Agriculture: peanuts; rice; cotton; millet; sorghum; fish; palm kernels; livestock; rutile
Industry: peanuts; brewing; soft drinks; agricultural machinery assembly; wood- and metalworking; clothing; tourism

FOREIGN TRADE

Exports: $81 million
Imports: $154 million

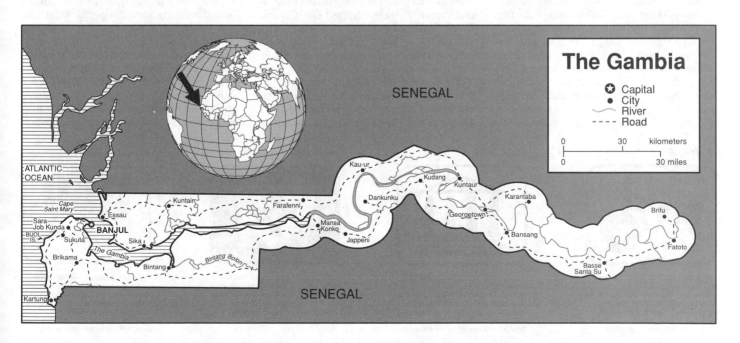

The British build
Fort James at the
current site of
Banjul, on the
Gambia River
1618

The Gambia is
ruled by the
United Kingdom
through Sierra
Leone
1807

Independence
1965

Dawda Jawara
comes to power
1970

An attempted
coup against
President Dawda
Jawara
1980s

The rise and fall
of the
Senegambia
Confederation

1990s

Jawara is
overthrown by a
military coup

Yahya Jammeh
becomes head of
state

THE GAMBIA

In July 1994, The Gambia's armed forces overthrew the government of Sir Dawda Jawara, bringing to an abrupt end what had been postcolonial West Africa's only example of uninterrupted multiparty democracy. Under international pressure, the new military ruler, Yahya Jammeh, agreed after many delays to hold elections under a new Constitution, in 1996. But this process has been marred by his regime's intolerance of genuine opposition. Since the failure of an alleged coup attempt in January 1995, critical voices have been largely silenced by an increasingly powerful National Intelligence Agency. Meanwhile, The Gambia's already weak economy has suffered from reduced revenues from tourism and foreign donors.

The Gambia is Africa's smallest noninsular nation. Except for a small seacoast, it is entirely surrounded by its much larger neighbor, Senegal. The two nations' separate existence is rooted in the activities of British slave traders who, in 1618, established a fort at the mouth of The Gambia River, from which they gradually spread their commercial and, later, political dominance upstream. Gambians have much in common with Senegalese. The Gambia's three major ethnolinguistic groups—Mandinka, Wolof, and Fula (or Peul)—are found on both sides of the border. The Wolof language serves as a lingua franca in both the Gambian capital of Banjul and the urban areas of Senegal. Islam is the major religion of both countries, while each also has a substantial Christian minority. The economies of the two countries are also similar, with each being heavily reliant on the cultivation of groundnuts as a cash crop.

In 1981, the Senegalese and Gambian governments were drawn closer together by an attempted coup in Banjul. While Jawara was in London, dissident elements within his Paramilitary Field Force joined in a coup attempt with members of two small, self-styled revolutionary parties. Based on a 1965 mutual-defense agreement, Jawara received assistance from Senegal in putting down the rebels. Constitutional rule was restored, but the killing of 400 to 500 people during the uprising and the subsequent mass arrest of suspected accomplices left Gambians bitter and divided.

In the immediate aftermath of the coup, The Gambia agreed to join Senegal in a loose confederation, which some hoped would lead to a full political union. But from the beginning, the Senegambia Confederation was marred by the circumstances of its formation. The continued presence of Senegalese soldiers in their country led Gambians to speak of a "shotgun wedding." Beyond fears of losing their local identity, many believed that proposals for closer economic integration, through a proposed monetary and customs union, would be to The Gambia's disadvantage. Underlying this concern was the role played by Gambian traders in providing imports to Senegal's market. Other squabbles, such as a long-standing dispute over the financing of a bridge across The Gambia River, finally led to the Confederation's formal demise in 1989. But the two countries still recognize a need to develop alternative forms of cooperation.

The Gambia was modestly successful in rebuilding its politics in the aftermath of the 1981 coup attempt. Whereas the 1982 elections were arguably compromised by the detention of the main opposition leader, Sherif Mustapha Dibba, on later-dismissed charges of complicity in the revolt, the 1987 and 1992 polls restored most people's confidence in Gambian democracy. In both elections, opposition parties significantly increased their share of the vote, while Jawara's People's Progressive Party retained majority support.

Instances of official corruption had compromised the Jawara government's ability to use its electoral mandate to implement an Economic Recovery Program, which included austerity measures. The Gambia has always been a poor country. During the 1980s, conditions worsened as a result of bad harvests and falling prices for groundnuts, which usually account for some 50 percent of the nation's export earnings. The tourist industry was also disrupted by the 1981 coup attempt. Faced with a mounting debt, the government submitted to International Monetary Fund pressure by cutting back its civil service and drastically devaluing the local currency. The latter step initially led to high inflation, but prices have become more stable in recent years, while the economy as a whole has begun to enjoy a gross domestic product growth rate of about 5 percent per year. As elsewhere, the negative impact of structural adjustment has proved especially burdensome to urban dwellers.

DEVELOPMENT

Since independence, The Gambia has developed a tourist industry. Whereas in 1966 only 300 individuals were recorded as having visited the country, the figure for 1988–1989 was over 112,000. Tourism is now the second-biggest sector of the economy.

FREEDOM

Despite the imposition of martial law in the aftermath of the 1981 coup attempt, The Gambia has had a strong record of respect for individual liberty and human rights. Under its current military regime, the Gambia has forfeited its model record of respect for freedom of speech and association.

HEALTH/WELFARE

Forty percent of Gambian children remain outside the primary-school setup. Economic Recovery Program austerity has made it harder for the government to achieve its goal of education for all.

ACHIEVEMENTS

Gambian *griots*—hereditary bards and musicians such as Banna and Dembo Kanute—have maintained a traditional art. Formerly, griots were attached to ruling families; now, they perform over Radio Gambia and are popular throughout West Africa.

Ghana (Republic of Ghana)

GEOGRAPHY

Area in Square Kilometers (Miles):
238,538 (92,100) (slightly smaller
than Oregon)
Capital (Population): Accra (965,000)
Climate: tropical to semiarid

PEOPLE

Population

Total: 17,763,000
Annual Growth Rate: 3.06%
Rural/Urban Population Ratio: 66/34
Major Languages: English; Akan
(including Fanti, Asante, Twi); Ewe;
Ga; Hausa; others
Ethnic Makeup: 44% Akan; 16%
Moshi-Dagomba; 13% Ewe; 8% Ga;
19% others

Health

Life Expectancy at Birth: 54 years
(male); 58 years (female)
Infant Mortality Rate (Ratio): 82/1,000
Average Caloric Intake: 100% of
FAO minimum
Physicians Available (Ratio): 1/22,452

Religions

38% traditional indigenous; 30%
Muslim; 24% Christian; 8% others

THE KING OF HIGHLIFE

E. T. Mensah is widely credited with having been the creator of modern
Highlife, the popular music style, which, during his 5-decade career, he
helped spread from Ghana to the rest of Africa and the world. During the
1930s, Mensah's band, The Tempos, began to experiment with the then-
popular dance music of big-band jazz by introducing Ghanaian rhythms
and indigenous instruments and lyrics into their repertoire. A new sound
quickly emerged, which, while drawing inspiration from the traditional
rural environment, reflected the fast pace and sophistication of Ghana's
emerging urban centers. Recording contracts and tours allowed the so-
called King of Highlife to spread his reign across West Africa in the 1940s.
Soon the music had become identified with the nationalist struggle. During
the 1960s, Mensah often accompanied Nkrumah on foreign visits, becoming known as the "Musical Ambassador of Ghana." His death in July 1996
was mourned throughout Africa.

Education

Adult Literacy Rate: 60%

COMMUNICATION

Telephones: 42,300
Newspapers: 3

TRANSPORTATION

Highways—Kilometers (Miles):
32,250 (20,027)
Railroads—Kilometers (Miles): 953
(592)
Usable Airfields: 12

GOVERNMENT

Type: constitutional democracy
Independence Date: March 6, 1957
Head of State: President Jerry John
Rawlings
Political Parties: National
Democratic Congress; New Patriotic
Party; Convention People's Party;
others
Suffrage: universal at 18

MILITARY

Number of Armed Forces: 6,850
*Military Expenditures (% of Central
Government Expenditures):* 1.5%
Current Hostilities: internal conflicts

ECONOMY

Currency ($ U.S. Equivalent):
1,046.74 cedis = $1
Per Capita Income/GDP:
$1,310/$22.6 billion
Inflation Rate: 25%
Natural Resources: gold; diamonds;
bauxite; manganese; fish; timber; oil
Agriculture: cocoa; coconuts; coffee;
subsistence crops; rubber
Industry: mining, lumber; light
manufacturing; fishing; aluminum

FOREIGN TRADE

Exports: $1.0 billion
Imports: $1.7 billion

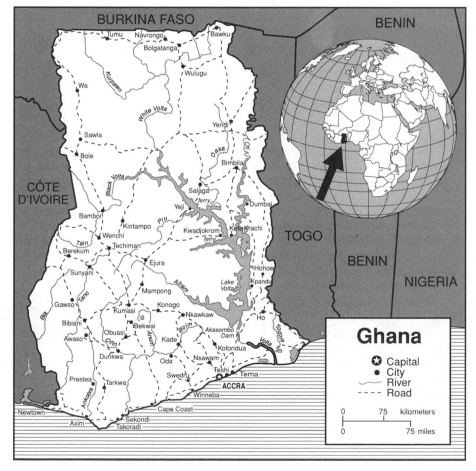

Ghana

✪ Capital
● City
～ River
--- Road

0 — 75 kilometers
0 — 75 miles

GHANA

In recent years, after decades of decline, Ghana has made gradual but steady progress in rebuilding its economy and political culture. The country has achieved sustained gross domestic product growth while implementing a comprehensive, socially painful, World Bank/IMF–sponsored Economic Recovery Program (ERP). Yet, when it is adjusted for inflation, per capita income is still below the level that existed in 1957, when Ghana became the first colony in sub-Saharan Africa to obtain independence.

The country is also overcoming a legacy of political instability brought about by revolving-door military coups. In March 1992, Ghana's current head of state, Flight Lieutenant Jerry Rawlings, marked the 35th anniversary of independence by announcing an accelerated return to multiparty rule. Eight months later, he was elected by a large majority as the president of what has been hailed as Ghana's "Fourth Republic." Although the election received the qualified endorsement of international monitors, its result was rejected by the main opposition New Patriotic Party (NPP). The NPP subsequently boycotted parliamentary elections, allowing an easy victory for Rawlings' National Democratic Congress (NDC), which captured 189 out of 200 seats, with a voter turnout of just under 30 percent. After months of bitter standoff, the political climate has eased since December 1993, when the NPP agreed to enter into a dialogue with the government about its basic demand that the interests of the ruling party be more clearly separated from those of the state.

Ghana's political transformation has been a triumph for Rawlings, who has ruled since 1981, when he and other junior military officers seized power as the Provisional National Defense Council (PNDC). In the name of ending corruption, they overthrew Ghana's previous freely elected government after it had been in office for less than 2 years. Rawlings was then dismissive of elections: "What does it mean to stuff bits of paper into boxes?" But success seems to have altered his opinion.

At its independence, Ghana assumed a leadership role in the struggle against colonial rule elsewhere on the continent. Both its citizens and many outside observers were optimistic about the country's future. As compared to many other former colonies, the country seemed to have a sound infrastructure for future progress. Unfortunately, economic development and political democracy have since proved to be elusive goals.

The "First Republic," led by the charismatic Kwame Nkrumah, degenerated into a bankrupt and an increasingly authoritarian one-party state. Nkrumah had pinned his hopes on an ambitious policy of industrial development. When substantial overseas investment failed to materialize, he turned to socialism. His efforts led to a modest rise in local manufacturing, but the sector's productivity was compromised by inefficient planning, limited resources, expensive inputs, and mounting government corruption. The new state enterprises ended up being financed largely from the export earnings of cocoa, which had emerged as Ghana's principal cash crop during the colonial period.

(United Nations photo)

The sea is important to the Ghanaian economy. The form of fishing shown in this photograph demands both power and skill; the men in the surf have to throw the weighted net far out in the water.

A Portuguese fort is built at Elmina
1482

The establishment of the Asante Confederation under Osei Tutu
1690s

The "Bonds" of 1844 signed by British officials and Fante chiefs as equals
1844

The British finally conquer the Asante, a final step in British control of the region
1901

Ghana is the first of the colonial territories in sub-Saharan Africa to become independent
1957

Nkrumah is overthrown by a military coup
1966

The first coup of Flight Lieutenant Rawlings
1979

The second coup by Rawlings; the PNDC is formed
1980s

1990s

Rawlings accepts World Bank and IMF austerity measures

Prodemocracy agitation leads to a transition to multiparty rule

Two thousand flee ethnic clashes in northern Ghana between Nanumbas and Konkombas

Following colonial precedent, Nkrumah resorted to paying local cocoa farmers well below the world market price for their output in an attempt to expand state revenues.

Nkrumah was overthrown by the military in 1966. Despite his regime's shortcomings, he is still revered by many as the leading pan-African nationalist of his generation. His warnings about the dangers of neo-imperialism have proved prophetic.

Since Nkrumah's fall, the army has been Ghana's dominant political institution, although there were brief returns to civilian control in 1969–1972 and again in 1979–1981. Both the military and the civilian governments abandoned much of Nkrumah's socialist commitment, but for years they continued his policy of squeezing the cocoa farmers, with the long-term result of encouraging planters both to cut back on their production and to attempt to circumvent the official prices through smuggling. This situation, coupled with falling cocoa prices on the world market and rising import costs, helped to push Ghana into a state of severe economic depression during the 1970s. During that period, real wages fell by some 80 percent. Ghana's crisis was then aggravated by an unwillingness on the part of successive governments to devalue the country's currency, the cedi, which encouraged black-market trading.

RAWLINGS'S RENEWAL

By 1981, many Ghanaians welcomed the PNDC, seeing in Rawlings's populist rhetoric the promise of change after years of corruption and stagnation. The PNDC initially tried to rule through People's De-

fense Committees, which were formed throughout the country to act as both official watchdogs and instruments of mass mobilization. Motivated by a combination of idealism and frustration with the status quo, the vigilantism of these institutions threatened the country with anarchy until, in 1983, they were reined in. Also in 1983, the country faced a new crisis, when the Nigerian government suddenly expelled nearly 1 million Ghanaian expatriates, who had to be resettled quickly.

Faced with an increasingly desperate situation, the PNDC, in a move that surprised many, given its leftist leanings, began to implement the Economic Recovery Program. Some 100,000 public and parastatal employees were retrenched, the cedi was progressively devalued, and wages and prices began to reflect more nearly their market value. These steps have led to some economic growth while annually attracting $500 million in foreign aid and soft loans and perhaps double that amount in cash remittances from the more than 1 million Ghanaians living abroad.

The human costs of ERP have been a source of criticism. Many ordinary Ghanaians, especially urban salary-earners, have suffered from falling wages coupled with rising inflation. Unemployment has also increased in many areas. Yet a recent survey found surprisingly strong support among "urban lower income groups" for ERP and the government in general. In the countryside farmers have benefited from higher crop prices and investments in rural infrastructure, while there has been a countrywide boom in legitimate retailing.

While ERP continues to have its critics, it now enjoys substantial support from

politicians aligned with Ghana's three principal political tendencies: the Nkrumahists, loyal to the first president's pan-African socialist vision; the Danquah-Busia grouping, named after two past statesmen who struggled against Nkrumah for more liberal economic and political policies; and those loyal to the PNDC. In the November 1992 presidential election, the NPP emerged as the main voice of the Danquah-Busia camp, while Rawlings' NDC attracted substantial support from Nkrumists as well as those sympathetic to his own legacy. There is also a body of opinion that was critical of all three historic tendencies, characterizing the NPP and NDC as fronts for power-hungry men fighting yesterday's battles. During the April 1992 referendum to approve the new Constitution, more than half the registered voters (many Ghanaians have complained that they have been denied registration) failed to participate, despite the government and opposition's joint call for a large "Yes" vote. Many also boycotted the November presidential poll. In December 1996, in a poll widely judged to have been fair, Rawlings was reelected. He narrowly defeated his former vice president, John Kufuor, who enjoyed the backing of both the New Patriotic Party and the Convention People's Party.

DEVELOPMENT

In the 1960s, Ghana invested heavily in schooling, resulting in perhaps the best-educated population in Africa. Today, hundreds of thousands of professionals who began their schooling under Nkrumah work overseas, annually remitting an estimated $1 billion to the Ghanaian economy.

FREEDOM

The move to multipartyism has promoted freedom of speech and assembly. Dozens of independent periodicals have emerged. But government opponents claim harassment and arbitrary arrests, especially by progovernment paramilitary groups in rural areas.

HEALTH/WELFARE

In 1991, the African Commission of Health and Human Rights Promoters established a branch in Accra to help rehabilitate victims of human-rights violations from throughout Anglophone Africa. The staff deals with both the psychological and physiological aftereffects of abused ex-detainees.

ACHIEVEMENTS

In 1993, Ghana celebrated the 30th anniversary of the School of the Performing Arts at the University of Legon. Integrating the world of dance, drama, and music, the school has trained a generation of artists committed to perpetuating Ghanaian, African, and international traditions in the arts.

Guinea (Republic of Guinea)

GEOGRAPHY

Area in Square Kilometers (Miles):
246,048 (95,000) (slightly larger than
Oregon)
Capital (Population): Conakry
(705,000)
Climate: tropical

PEOPLE

Population
Total: 6,550,000
Annual Growth Rate: 2.45%
Rural/Urban Population Ratio: 74/26
Major Languages: French; Fula;
Mandinka; Susu; Malinke
Ethnic Makeup: 35% Fulani; 30%
Malinke; 20% Soussou; 15% others

Health
Life Expectancy at Birth: 42 years
(male); 47 years (female)
Infant Mortality Rate (Ratio):
136.6/1,000
Average Caloric Intake: 100% of
FAO minimum
Physicians Available (Ratio): 1/9,732

Religions
85% Muslim; 8% Christian; 7%
traditional indigenous

Education
Adult Literacy Rate: 24%

COMMUNICATION

Telephones: 15,000
Newspapers: 3

SAMORI TOURÉ

In the late nineteenth century, Malinke leader Samori Touré established
a powerful state in the interior of present-day Guinea and Côte d'Ivoire.
Samori, called "the Napoleon of the Sudan," was a Muslim who
converted many of the areas that he conquered. His state was based on
modern military organization and tactics; this enabled him to resist the
European conquest longer and more effectively than any other West
African leader. Through alliances, sieges, control of the arms trade, and,
ultimately, manufacture of guns and ammunition, Samori fought the
French and resisted conquest throughout the 1890s. Manipulating Af-
rican competition and people's fear of Samori, the French allied with
African leaders and prevented a unified resistance to their rule.

TRANSPORTATION

Highways—Kilometers (Miles):
30,100 (10,662)
Railroads—Kilometers (Miles): 1,045
(648)
Usable Airfields: 15

GOVERNMENT

Type: republic
Independence Date: October 2, 1958
Head of State: President (General)
Lansana Conté
Political Parties: Party for Unity and
Progress; Union for a New Republic;
Party for Renewal and Progress;
others
Suffrage: universal at 18

MILITARY

Number of Armed Forces: 9,300
*Military Expenditures (% of Central
Government Expenditures):* 1.6%
Current Hostilities: none

ECONOMY

Currency ($ U.S. Equivalent):
810.94 francs =$1
Per Capita Income/GDP: $980/$6.3
billion
Inflation Rate: 16.6%
Natural Resources: bauxite; iron ore;
diamonds; gold; water power
Agriculture: rice; cassava; millet;
corn; coffee; bananas; palm products;
pineapples
Industry: bauxite; alumina; light
manufacturing and processing

FOREIGN TRADE

Exports: $622 million
Imports: $768 million

Guinea

⊗ Capital
● City
River
- - - Road

0 ——— 100 kilometers
0 ——— 100 miles

A major Islamic kingdom is established in the Futa Djalon
1700s

Samori Touré is defeated by the French
1898

Led by Sekou Touré, Guineans reject continued membership In the French Community; an independent republic is formed
1958

French president Giscard d'Estaing visits Guinea: the beginning of a reconciliation between France and Guinea
1978

Sekou Touré's death is followed by a military coup
1980s

The introduction of SAP leads to urban unrest

1990s

President Lansana Conté begins to establish a multiparty democracy

Multiparty elections are held for the presidency; Conté claims victory

Soldiers riot when their pay is withheld

GUINEA

In February 1996, some 2,000 soldiers rioted for 2 days in the streets of Conakry after failing to receive their pay. Although order was restored, the incident underscored the continuing political uncertainty afflicting Guinea since its transition to multiparty politics in 1992. With a weak economy and half a million refugees crowding in from Sierra Leone and Liberia, the challenge facing any Guinean government is formidable.

Since 1984, the country has been governed by Lansana Conté, who has proved more adept at surviving challenges to his authority than at charting a progressive course for his country. In April 1992, Conté announced that a new Constitution guaranteeing freedom of association would take immediate effect. Within a month, more than 30 political parties had been formed. Conté's initiative was a political second chance for a nation whose potential had for decades been mismanaged under the dictatorial rule of its first president, Sekou Touré.

From his early years as a radical trade-union activist in the late 1940s until his death in office in 1984, Sekou Touré was Guinea's dominant personality. A descendent of the nineteenth-century Malinke hero Samori Touré, who fiercely resisted the imposition of French rule, Sekou Touré was a charismatic but repressive leader. In 1958, he inspired Guineans to vote for immediate independence from France. At the time, Guinea was the only territory to opt out of Charles de Gaulle's newly established French Community. The French reacted spitefully, withdrawing all aid, personnel, and equipment from the new nation, an event that influenced Guinea's postindependence path. The ability of Touré's Democratic Party of Guinea (PDG) to step into the administrative vacuum was the basis for the quick transformation into the continent's first one-party socialist state, a process that was encouraged by the then–Soviet bloc.

Touré's rule was characterized by economic mismanagement and the widespread abuse of human rights. It is estimated that some 2 million people—at the time about one out of every four Guineans—fled the country during his rule. At least 2,900 individuals disappeared under detention.

By the late 1970s, Touré, pressured by rising discontent and his own apparent realization of his country's poor economic performance, began to modify both his domestic and foreign policies. This shift led to better relations with Western countries but little improvement in the lives of his people. In 1982, Amnesty International publicized the Touré regime's dismal record of political killings, detentions, and torture, but the world remained largely indifferent.

On April 3, 1984, a week after Touré's death, the army stepped in, claiming that it wished to end all vestiges of the late president's dictatorial regime. The bloodless coup was well received by Guineans. Hundreds of political prisoners were released; and the once-powerful Democratic Party of Guinea, which during the Touré years had been reduced from a mass party into a hollow shell, was disbanded. A new government was formed, under the leadership of then-colonel Conté, and a 10-point program for national recovery was set forth, including the restoration of human rights and the renovation of the economy.

Faced with an empty treasury, the new government committed itself to a severe Structural Adjustment Program (SAP). This has led to a dismantling of many of the socialist structures that had been established by the previous government. While international financiers have generally praised it, the government has had to weather periodic unrest and coup attempts. In spite of these challenges, however, it has remained committed to SAP.

Guinea is blessed with mineral resources, which could lead to a more prosperous future. The country is rich in bauxite and has substantial reserves of iron and diamonds. New mining agreements, leading to a flow of foreign investment, have already led to a modest boom in bauxite and diamond exports. Small-scale gold mining is also being developed.

Guinea's greatest economic failing has been the poor performance of its agricultural sector. Unlike many of its neighbors, the country enjoys a favorable climate and soils. But, although some 80 percent of Guineans are engaged in subsistence farming, only 3 percent of the land is cultivated, and foodstuffs remain a major import. Blame for this situation largely falls on the Touré regime's legacy of an inefficient, state-controlled system of marketing and distribution. In 1987, the government initiated an ambitious plan of road rehabilitation, which, along with better produce prices, has begun to encourage farmers to produce more for the domestic market.

DEVELOPMENT

A measure of economic growth in Guinea is reflected in the rising traffic in Conakry harbor, whose volume rose 415% over a 4-year period. Plans are being made to improve the port's infrastructure.

FREEDOM

Guineans approved a new Constitution, which includes recognition of freedom of speech, assembly, and association as well as human-rights guarantees. But a complementary culture of political tolerance has yet to take hold. In September 1993, troops fired on opposition demonstrators.

HEALTH/WELFARE

The life expectancy of Guineans is among the lowest in the world, reflecting the stagnation of the nation's health service during the Sekou Touré years.

ACHIEVEMENTS

More than 80% of the programming broadcast by Guinea's television service is locally produced. This output has included more than 3,000 movies. A network of rural radio stations is currently being installed.

Guinea-Bissau (Republic of Guinea-Bissau)

GEOGRAPHY

Area in Square Kilometers (Miles): 36,125 (13,948) (about the size of Indiana)
Capital (Population): Bissau (200,000)
Climate: tropical

PEOPLE

Population
Total: 1,151,300
Annual Growth Rate: 2.36%
Rural/Urban Population Ratio: n/a
Major Languages: Portuguese; Kriolo; Fula; Mandinka; Manjaca; Balanta; others
Ethnic Makeup: 30% Balanta; 20% Fula; 14% Manjaca; 13% Mandinka; 23% others

Health
Life Expectancy at Birth: 46 years (male); 50 years (female)
Infant Mortality Rate (Ratio): 117.9/1,000
Average Caloric Intake: 74% of FAO minimum
Physicians Available (Ratio): 1/9,477

Religions
65% traditional indigenous; 30% Muslim; 5% Christian

Education
Adult Literacy Rate: 36%

COMMUNICATION

Telephones: 3,000
Newspapers: 1

AMILCAR CABRAL

Amilcar Cabral (1924–1973), born in Cape Verde and raised in Guinea-Bissau, was an idealist who developed plans for his country's liberation and an activist who worked to put these plans into action. He was a friend of Agostinho Neto of Angola, a founding member of Angola's current ruling party, MPLA, and he worked in Angola. Cabral worked for an African system of government, a change in structures that would mean "a reorganization of the country on new lines." He believed that a revolution could not result from leadership alone; rather, all must fight a mental battle and know their goals before taking up arms. Cabral's work with peasants from 1952 to 1954, while carrying out an agricultural census, helped him to understand and reach rural peoples who were to be the crucial force in the development of Guinea-Bissau's independence from Portugal.

TRANSPORTATION

Highways—Kilometers (Miles): 3,218 (2,008)
Railroads—Kilometers (Miles): none
Usable Airfields: 32

GOVERNMENT

Type: republic; overseen by Revolutionary Council
Independence Date: September 10, 1974
Head of State: President (Major) João Bernardo Vieira
Political Parties: African Party for the Independence of Guinea-Bissau and Cape Verde (PAIGC); Democratic Social Front; Democratic Front; others
Suffrage: universal at 15

MILITARY

Number of Armed Forces: 9,200
Military Expenditures (% of Central Government Expenditures): 5%–6%
Current Hostilities: recent border clashes with Senegal

ECONOMY

Currency ($ U.S. Equivalent): 14,482 pesos = $1
Per Capita Income/GDP: $840/$900 million
Inflation Rate: 55%
Natural Resources: bauxite; timber; shrimp; fish
Agriculture: peanuts; rice; palm kernels; groundnuts
Industry: agricultural processing; hides and skins; beer; soft drinks

FOREIGN TRADE

Exports: $19.0 million
Imports: $56.0 million

Guinea-Bissau

⊛ Capital
• City
〜 River
- - - Road

0   50   kilometers
0   50 miles

GUINEA-BISSAU

Guinea-Bissau, a small country wedged between Senegal and Guinea on the west coast of Africa, has an unenviable claim to being perhaps the poorest country in the world. To many outsiders, the nation is better known for the liberation struggle waged by its people against Portuguese colonial rule between 1962 and 1974. Mobilized by the African Party for the Independence of Guinea-Bissau and Cape Verde (PAIGC), Guinea-Bissau played a major role in the overthrow of Fascist rule within Portugal and the liberation of its other African colonies. The movement's effectiveness has led many to view its struggle as a model of anti-imperialist resistance.

The origins of Portuguese rule in Guinea-Bissau go back to the late 1400s. For centuries, the area was raided as a source of slaves, who were shipped to Portugal and its colonies of Cape Verde and Brazil. With the nineteenth-century abolition of slave trading, the Portuguese began to impose forced labor within Guinea-Bissau itself. During the twentieth century, the Fascist government in Lisbon rationalized its repression by extending limited civil rights to only those educated Africans who were officially judged to have assimilated Portuguese culture—the *assimilados*. In Guinea-Bissau, only 0.3 percent of the local population were ever recognized as assimilados. Many within this select group were migrants from Cape Verde, who, in contrast to mainland Africans, automatically enjoyed the status.

In 1956, six assimilados, led by Amilcar Cabral, founded the PAIGC as a vehicle for the liberation of Cape Verde as well as Guinea-Bissau. From the beginning, many Cape Verdeans, such as Cabral, played a prominent role within the PAIGC. But the group's largest following and main center of activity were in Guinea-Bissau. In 1963, the PAIGC turned to armed resistance and began organizing itself as an alternative government. By the end of the decade, the movement had gained a mass following and was in control of two thirds of the countryside.

(FAO photo by F. Mattioli)

With the implementation of 200-mile Exclusive Economic Zones (EEZs), the fishing industry of West African nations has increased in overall terms. Previously, a large majority of the region's fish stocks were harvested by foreign vessels from the former Soviet Union, Poland, Spain, South Korea, and France; EEZs have effectively given countries like Guinea-Bissau a much-needed boost in food production.

Portuguese ships arrive; claimed as Portuguese Guinea; slave trading develops
1446

Portugal gains effective control over most of the region
1915

The African Party for the Independence of Guinea-Bissau and Cape Verde is formed
1956

Liberation struggle in Guinea-Bissau under the leadership of the PAIGC and Amilcar Cabral
1963–1973

Amilcar Cabral is assassinated; the PAIGC declares Guinea-Bissau independent
1973

Revolution in Portugal leads to Portugal's recognition of Guinea-Bissau's independence and the end of war
1974

João Vieira comes to power through a military coup, ousting Guinea-Bissau's first president, Luis Cabral
1980

1990s

The country moves toward multipartyism

An alleged coup attempt

Voters keep Vieira in power

In its liberated areas, the PAIGC was notably successful in establishing its own marketing, judicial, and educational as well as political institutions. Widespread participation throughout Guinea-Bissau in the 1973 election of a National Assembly encouraged a number of countries formally to recognize the PAIGC declaration of state sovereignty. This development also helped to convince leading Portuguese officers that the fight to maintain their African empire was futile. By then, many of them had also begun to sympathize with their "enemy," in part through their clandestine exposure to the writings of Cabral and other revolutionaries. In 1974, the military seized power in Lisbon and moved quickly to recognize Guinea-Bissau's independence.

CHALLENGES OF INDEPENDENCE

Since 1974, the leaders of Guinea-Bissau have tried to confront the problems of independence while maintaining the idealism of their liberation struggle. Their nation's weak economy has limited their success. Guinea-Bissau has little in the way of mining or manufacturing, although explorations have revealed potentially exploitable reserves of oil, bauxite, and phosphates. More than 80 percent of the population are engaged in agriculture, but urban populations depend on imported foodstuffs. This situation has been generally attributed to the poor infrastructure and a lack of incentives for farmers to grow surpluses. Efforts to improve the rural economy during the early years of independence were further marred by severe

drought. Only 8 percent of the small country's land is currently cultivated.

Under financial pressure, the government adopted a Structural Adjustment Program (SAP) in 1987. The peso was devalued, civil servants were dismissed, and various subsidies were reduced. The effects of these SAP reforms on urban workers were cushioned somewhat by external aid.

In 1988, in a desperate move, the government signed an agreement with the Intercontract Company, allowing the firm to use its territory for 5 years as a major dump site for toxic waste from Great Britain, Switzerland, and the United States. In return, the government was to earn up to $800 million, a figure 50 times greater than the annual value of the nation's exports. But the deal was revoked after it was exposed by members of the country's exiled opposition. It is believed that a major environmental catastrophe would have resulted had the deal gone through. The incident underscores the vulnerability of Guinea-Bissau's economy.

POLITICAL DEVELOPMENT

Following the assassination of Amilcar Cabral, in 1973, his brother, Luis Cabral, succeeded him as the leader of the PAICG, thereafter becoming Guinea-Bissau's first president. Before 1980, both Guinea-Bissau and Cape Verde were separately governed by a united PAIGC, which had as its ultimate goal the forging of a political union between the two territories. But in 1980, Luis Cabral was overthrown by the military, which accused him of governing through a "Cape Verdean clique." João Vieira, a popular commander during the

liberation war who had also served as prime minister, was appointed as the new head of state. As a result, relations between Cape Verde and Guinea-Bissau deteriorated, leading to a breakup in the political links between the two nations.

The PAIGC under Vieira continued to rule Guinea-Bissau as a one-party state for 10 years. The system's grass-roots democracy, which had been fostered in its liberated zones during the war, gave way to a centralization of power around Vieira and other members of his military dominated Council of State. Several coup attempts resulted in increased authoritarianism.

But in 1990, the government reversed course. Vieira went so far as to denounce in a speech single-party rule as inherently undemocratic, elitist, and repressive. In April 1991, the country formally embraced multipartyism. But progress has been slow. An alleged coup attempt in March 1993 led to the detention and subsequent trial of a leading opposition figure, João da Costa, on charges of plotting the government's overthrow. Elections finally occurred in July 1994. The vote resulted in a narrow second-round victory for Vieira against a very divided opposition.

DEVELOPMENT

With help from the UN Development Program, the Guinea-Bissau government has improved the tourist infrastructure of the 40-island Bijagos Archipelago. The increased flow of visitors has led to plans for an airline.

FREEDOM

Recent moves toward multiparty democracy in Guinea-Bissau have been accompanied by an opening up of public debate. Exiles have been allowed to return to the country to take part in politics.

HEALTH/WELFARE

Despite genuine efforts on the part of the government and international aid agencies to improve health conditions in the country, Guinea-Bissau's health statistics remain appalling: an overall 47-year life expectancy, 12% infant mortality, and more than 90% of the population infected with malaria.

ACHIEVEMENTS

With Portuguese assistance, a new fiber-optic digital telephone system is being established in Guinea-Bissau, which will help to improve communications in the country.

Liberia (Republic of Liberia)

GEOGRAPHY

Area in Square Kilometers (Miles):
111,370 (43,000) (somewhat larger than Pennsylvania)
Capital (Population): Monrovia (1,000,000)
Climate: tropical

PEOPLE

Population
Total: 2,109,789
Annual Growth Rate: 3.32%
Rural/Urban Population Ratio: 56/44
Major Languages: official: English; others spoken: Kpelle, Bassa, Dan, Vai, Wee, Loma, Kru, Glebo, Mano, Gola, Mandinka
Ethnic Makeup: 95% indigenous groups; 5% Americo-Liberian

Health
Life Expectancy at Birth: 56 years (male); 61 years (female)
Infant Mortality Rate (Ratio): 110.6/1,000
Average Caloric Intake: 114% of FAO minimum
Physicians Available (Ratio): 1/11,185

Religions
70% traditional indigenous; 20% Muslim; 10% Christian

Education
Adult Literacy Rate: 40%

COMMUNICATION

Telephones: 5,820
Newspapers: 4

KING GEORGE

Amidst the divisive terror of civil war, Liberians have been able to unite over the last several years around the exploits of their national soccer team and its superstar, George Ousmanu Oppong Weah. In 1996, "King George" Weah became the first person on Earth to be proclaimed by FIFA, the sport's international governing body, as the African, European, and world's best player of the year. Weah earned this distinction by dividing his time between the Italian club AC Milan and the Liberian team, which he led to the African Nations Cup finals in January 1996. Weah is the principal sponsor as well as leader of the latter team. "I have committed my personal funds to the team because I want Liberia's international image, badly dented by the brutal civil war, to be repaired through football," he said.

TRANSPORTATION

Highways—Kilometers (Miles): 10,087 (6,783)
Railroads—Kilometers (Miles): 490 (306)
Usable Airfields: 59

GOVERNMENT

Type: republic
Independence Date: July 26, 1847
Head of State: President Ruth Sandra Perry
Political Parties: National Democratic Party of Liberia; Liberian Action Party; Liberian People's Party (banned); Liberian Unification Party; National Patriotic Party; Unity Party; United People's Party
Suffrage: universal at 18

MILITARY

Number of Armed Forces: n/a
Military Expenditures (% of Central Government Expenditures): n/a
Current Hostilities: civil war

ECONOMY

Currency ($ U.S. Equivalent): 1 Liberian dollar = $1
Per Capita Income/GDP: $770/$2.3 billion
Inflation Rate: 12%
Natural Resources: iron ore; rubber; timber; diamonds
Agriculture: rubber; rice; palm oil; cassava; coffee; cocoa; sugar
Industry: iron and diamond mining; rubber processing; food processing; lumber milling

FOREIGN TRADE

Exports: $505 million
Imports: $394 million

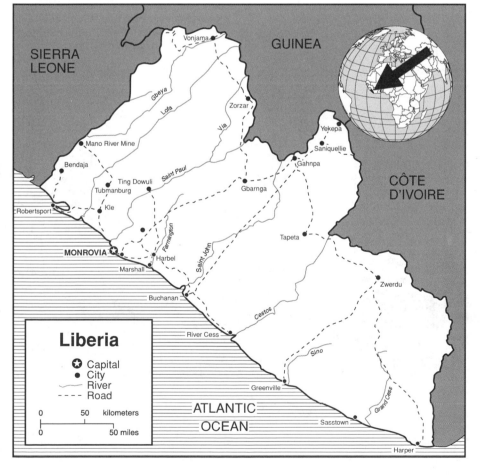

Liberia
- ✪ Capital
- ● City
- River
- --- Road

0   50   kilometers
0   50 miles

LIBERIA

In September 1996, Ruth Sandra Perry was sworn in as Liberia's first female head of state, as part of the 13th peace accord designed to end the Liberian Civil War. Since December 1989, the country has been stuck in a quagmire of self-destruction that has claimed some 200,000 lives out of a total population of about 2 million. As part of a permanent settlement, elections are now scheduled for May 1997, but it is too early to tell whether or not peace will soon be restored in Africa's oldest republic. Despite the presence of a West African peacekeeping force (ECO-MOG), and a smaller UN contingent (UNOMIL), the last agreement collapsed in an orgy of violence. In April 1996, thousands were killed in the capital city, Monrovia, when an attempt was made to arrest Roosevelt Johnson, a powerful warlord who remains excluded from the current agreement.

AFRICAN-AMERICAN-AFRICANS

Among the African states, Liberia shares with Ethiopia the distinction of having avoided European rule. Between 1847 and 1980, Liberia was governed by an elite made up primarily of descendants of African Americans who had begun settling along its coastline 2 decades earlier. These "Americo-Liberians" make up only 5 percent of the population. But for decades, they dominated politics through their control of the governing True Whig Party (TWP). Although the republic's Constitution was ostensibly democratic, the TWP rigged the electoral process.

Most Liberians belong to indigenous ethnolinguistic groups, such as the Kpelle, Bassa, Gio, Kru, Krahn, and Vai, who were conquered by the Americo-Liberians during the 1800s and early 1900s. Some individuals from these subjugated communities accepted Americo-Liberian norms. Yet book learning, Christianity, and an ability to speak English helped an indigenous person to advance within the state only if he or she accepted its social hierarchy by becoming a "client" of an Americo-Liberian "patron." In a special category were the important interior "chiefs," who were able to maintain their local authority as long as they remained loyal to the republic.

During the twentieth century, Liberia's economy was transformed by vast Firestone rubber plantations, iron-ore mining, and urbanization. President William Tubman (1944–1971) proclaimed a Unification Policy, to promote national integration, and an Open-Door Policy, to encourage outside investment in Liberia. However, most of the profits that resulted from the modest external investment that did occur left the country, while the wealth that remained was concentrated in the hands of the TWP elite.

During the administration of Tubman's successor, William Tolbert (1971–1980), Liberians became more conscious of the inability of the TWP to address the inequities of the status quo. Educated youths from all ethnic backgrounds began to join dissident associations rather than the regime's patronage system.

As economic conditions worsened, the top 4 percent of the population came to control 60 percent of the wealth. Rural stagnation drove many to the capital city of Monrovia (named after U.S. president James Monroe), where they suffered from high unemployment and inflation. The inevitable explosion occurred in 1979, when the government announced a 50 percent price increase for rice, the national food staple. Police fired on demonstrators, killing and wounding hundreds. Rioting, which resulted in great property damage, led the government to appeal to neighboring Guinea for troops. It was clear that the TWP was losing its grip. Thus Sergeant Samuel Doe enjoyed widespread support when, in 1980, he led a successful coup.

DOE DOESN'T DO

Doe came to power as Liberia's first indigenous president, a symbolically important event that many believed would herald major substantive changes. Some institutions of the old order, such as the TWP and the Masonic Temple (looked upon as Liberia's secret government) were disbanded. The House of Representatives and Senate were suspended. Offices changed hands, but the old administrative system persisted. Many of those who came to power were members of Doe's own ethnic group, the Krahn, who had long been prominent in the lower ranks of the army.

Doe declared a narrow victory for himself in the October 1985 elections, but there was widespread evidence of ballot tampering. A month later, exiled General Thomas Quiwonkpa led an abortive coup attempt. During and after the uprising, thousands of people were killed, mostly civilians belonging to Quiwonkpa's Gio group who were slaughtered by loyalist (largely Krahn) troops. Doe was inaugurated, but opposition-party members refused to take their seats in the National Assembly. Some, fearing for their lives, went into exile.

During the late 1980s, Doe became increasingly dictatorial. Many called on the U.S. government, in particular, to withhold aid until detainees were freed and new elections held. The U.S. Congress criticized the regime but authorized more than $500 million in financial and military support. Meanwhile, Liberia suffered from a shrinking economy and a growing foreign debt, which by 1987 had reached $1.6 billion.

(United Nations photo by N. van Praag)

The chaos that has afflicted Liberia in recent years has left the country destitute. Political anarchy has destroyed much of the infrastructure, economy, and culture.

| The Vai move onto the Liberian coast from the interior **1500s** | The first African-American settlers arrive from the United States **1822** | The first coup exchanges one Americo-Liberian government for another **1871** | The League of Nations investigates forced labor charges **1931** | President William Tubman comes to office **1944** | William Tolbert becomes president **1972** | The first riots in contemporary Liberian history occur when the price of rice is raised **1979** | William Tolbert is assassinated; a military coup brings Samuel Doe to power **1980s** |

1990s

| Civil war leads to the execution of Doe, anarchy, and foreign intervention | The violence and chaos in Liberia are perceived as a regional threat | Violent factionalism proliferates |

Doe's government was not entirely to blame for Liberia's financial condition. When Doe came to power, the Liberian treasury was already empty, in large part due to the vast expenditure incurred by the previous administration in hosting the 1979 Organization of African Unity Conference. The rising cost of oil and decline in world prices for natural rubber, iron ore, and sugar further crippled the economy. Government corruption and instability under Doe made a bad situation worse.

DOE'S DOWNFALL

Liberia's descent into violent anarchy began on December 24, 1989, when a small group of insurgents, led by Charles Taylor, who had earlier fled the country amid corruption charges, began a campaign to overthrow Doe. As Taylor's National Patriotic Front of Liberia (NPFL) rebels gained ground, the war developed into an increasingly vicious interethnic struggle among groups who had been either victimized by or associated with the regime. Thousands of civilians were thus massacred by ill-disciplined gunmen on both sides; hundreds of thousands began to flee for their lives. By June 1990, with the rump of Doe's forces besieged in Monrovia, a small but efficient breakaway armed faction of the NPFL, under the ruthless leadership of a former soldier named Prince Johnson, emerged as a deadly third force.

By August, with the United States unwilling to do more than evacuate foreign nationals from Monrovia (the troops of Doe, Johnson, and Taylor had begun kidnapping expatriates and violating diplomatic immunity), members of the Economic Community of West African States decided to establish a framework for peace by installing an interim government, with the support of a regional peacekeeping force known as ECOMOG: the ECOWAS Monitoring Group. The predominantly Nigerian force, which also included contingents from Ghana, Guinea, Sierra Leone, The Gambia, and, later, Senegal, landed in Monrovia in late August. This coincided with the nomination, by a broad-based but NPFL-boycotted National Conference, of Amos Sawyer, a respected academic, as the head of the proposed interim administration.

Initial hopes that ECOMOG's presence would end the fighting proved to be naïve. On September 9, 1990, Johnson captured Doe by shooting his way into ECOMOG headquarters. The following day, Doe's gruesome torture and execution were videotaped by his captors. This "outrage for an outrage" did not end the suffering. Protected by a reinforced ECOMOG, Sawyer was able to establish his interim authority over most of Monrovia, but the rest of the country remained in the hands of the NPFL or of local thugs.

Repeated attempts to get Johnson and Taylor to cooperate with Sawyer in establishing an environment conducive to holding elections have so far proved fruitless. While most neighboring states have supported ECOMOG's mediation efforts, some have provided support (and, in the case of Burkina Faso, troops) to the NPFL, which has encouraged Taylor in his on-again, off-again approach toward national reconciliation.

In September 1991, a new, fiercely anti-NPLF force, the United Liberation Movement of Liberia (ULIMO), emerged from bases in Sierra Leone. The group is identified with former Doe supporters. Subsequent clashes between ULIMO and NPFL on both sides of the Liberian–Sierra Leonean border contributed to the April 1992 overthrow of the Sierra Leonean government as well as the failure of an October 1991 peace accord brokered by the Côte d'Ivoire's late president Félix Houphouët-Boigny.

In October 1992, ECOWAS agreed to impose sanctions on the NPFL for blocking Monrovia. ECOMOG then joined ULIMO and remnants of the Armed Forces of Liberia (AFL) in a counteroffensive. In 1993, yet another armed faction, the Liberia Peace Council (LPC), emerged to challenge Taylor for control of southeastern Liberia. In March 1994, an all-party interim State Council, agreed to in principle 8 months earlier, was finally sworn in. But it quickly collapsed, while a violent split in ULIMO contributed to further anarchy. With Guinean as well as Sierra Leonean border villages coming under occasional attack, and some Nigerians beginning to speak of "our Vietnam," Liberia's ongoing disintegration has become a threat to the entire West African region.

DEVELOPMENT

Liberia's economic and social infrastructure has been devastated by the war. People are surviving through informal-sector trading, which is controlled by those with guns.

FREEDOM

Many Liberians remain committed to the ideal of establishing a genuine democracy with freedom of association, belief, and speech. But, under current conditions, there are no guarantors of human rights.

HEALTH/WELFARE

Outside aid and local self-help were mobilized against famine in Liberia in 1990–1991. But the Civil War continues to take a dreadful toll. Orphans have reportedly been used as human shields.

ACHIEVEMENTS

Through a shrewd policy of diplomacy, Liberia managed to maintain its independence when Great Britain and France conquered neighboring areas during the late nineteenth century. It espoused African causes during the colonial period; for instance, Liberia brought the case of Namibia to the World Court in the 1950s.

Mali (Republic of Mali)

GEOGRAPHY

Area in Square Kilometers (Miles):
1,240,142 (478,819) (about the size
of Texas and California combined)
Capital (Population): Bamako
(894,000)
Climate: tropical to arid

PEOPLE

Population

Total: 9,375,000
Annual Growth Rate: 2.89%
Rural/Urban Population Ratio: 74/26
Major Languages: official: French;
others spoken: Bamanankan,
Mandinka, Voltaic, Tamacheg
(Tuareg), Dogon, Fulde, Songhai,
Malinké
Ethnic Makeup: 50% Mande; 17%
Peul; 12% Voltaic; 6% Songhai; 10%
Tuareg and Moor; 5% others

Health

Life Expectancy at Birth: 45 years
(male); 48 years (female)
Infant Mortality Rate (Ratio):
104.5/1,000
Average Caloric Intake: 83% of FAO
minimum
Physicians Available (Ratio): 1/12,652

Religions
90% Muslim; 9% traditional
indigenous; 1% Christian

Education
Adult Literacy Rate: 19%

COMMUNICATION

Telephones: 11,000
Newspapers: 2

JAMANA

Mali's president Dr. Alpha Konare is the founder of Jamana, a highly
successful cultural cooperative, which has sponsored forums, festivals,
publications, and literacy programs since 1983. It has also established
museum-documentation centers, crafts workshops, a printing and publishing company, and Mali's first private radio station. Mali's rich
cultural diversity, which Jamana has sought to promote, is exemplified
by such aspects as the popular singing of epic praise poems, local Kora
music, which has evolved popular and classical styles, sophisticated
carvings, and often-satirical puppet theaters. Although rooted in traditional esthetics, each of these arts reflects upon contemporary society:
Under the former dictatorship, the dynamism of their indigenous culture
provided Malians with avenues of sociopolitical criticism and debate.

TRANSPORTATION

Highways—Kilometers (Miles):
15,700 (9,756)
Railroads—Kilometers (Miles): 642
(400)
Usable Airfields: 33

GOVERNMENT

Type: republic
Independence Date: September 22,
1960
Head of State: President Alpha
Konare
Political Parties: Association for
Democracy; National Congress for
Democratic Initiative; Sudanese
Union/African Democratic Rally;
others
Suffrage: universal at 21

MILITARY

Number of Armed Forces: 7,350
*Military Expenditures (% of Central
Government Expenditures):* 2.2%
Current Hostilities: none

ECONOMY

Currency ($ U.S. Equivalent):
529.43 CFA francs = $1
Per Capita Income/GDP: $600/$5.4
billion
Inflation Rate: 35%
Natural Resources: bauxite; iron ore;
manganese; lithium; phosphate;
kaolin; salt; limestone; gold
Agriculture: millet; sorghum; corn;
rice; sugar; cotton; peanuts; livestock
Industry: food processing; textiles;
cigarettes; fishing; construction;
mining

FOREIGN TRADE

Exports: $415 million
Imports: $842 million

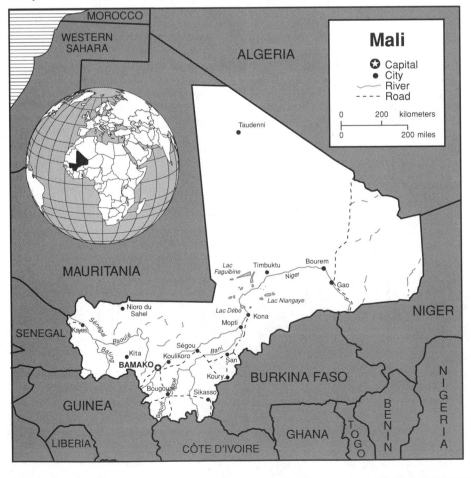

MALI

In 1992, Malians elected a new president and national Legislature in the country's first multiparty elections since independence, in 1960. The new government was inaugurated a year after a coup ended the authoritarian regime of Moussa Traoré. Like his predecessor, Modibo Keita, the first president of Mali, Traoré had governed Mali as a single-party state. True to their word, the young officers who seized power in 1991 following bloody antigovernment riots presided over a quick transition to civilian rule. The new president, Dr. Alpha Konare, is an activist scholar who, like many Malians, finds political inspiration in his country's rich heritage.

Konare's efforts to rebuild Mali have been hampered by a weak economy, aggravated by the 1994 collapse in value of the CFA franc. In 1994 and 1995, violence occurred between security forces and university students protesting against economic hardship. The plight of Malian economic refugees in France gained international attention in 1996, when a number sought sanctuary in a Parisian church and went on a hunger strike in protest against attempts to deport them. The government has enjoyed greater success in reaching a (still fragile) settlement with Tuareg rebels in the country's far north. In June 1995, the government signed a "national pact" with the rebel Islamic Arab Front of Azaouad, building upon an earlier peace accord with the larger Tuareg Movement for the Union of Azaouad (MFUA).

AN IMPERIAL PAST

The published epic of Sundiata Keita, the thirteenth-century A.D. founder of the great Mali empire, is recognized throughout the world as a masterpiece of classical African literature. In Mali itself, the story and deeds of the legendary hero-king can still be heard from the lips of the *griots,* or bards, who sing at public gatherings and over the radio. Sundiata remains a source of national pride and unity.

Sundiata's state was one of three great West African empires whose centers lay in modern Mali. Between the fourth and thirteenth centuries, the area was the site of ancient Ghana, which prospered through its export of gold to Asia, Europe, and the rest of Africa (the modern state of Ghana, whose territory was never part of the earlier empire, adopted its name at independence as a symbol of Pan-African rather than local grandeur). The Malian empire was superseded by that of Songhai, which was conquered by the Moroccans at the end of the sixteenth century. All these empires were in fact confedera-

(United Nations photo by John Isaac)

Countries in the Sahel, a band of land on the southern edge of the Sahara, are still affected by a crisis of alarming proportions. In Mali, drought and famine, which have manifested themselves since the late 1960s, continue. It is hoped that President Alpha Konare will be able to bring about a measure of political and economic stability.

The Mali Empire
extends over
much of the
upper regions of
West Africa
1250–1400s

The Songhai
empire controls
the region
**late 1400s–
late 1500s**

The French
establish control
over Mali
1890

Mali gains
independence as
part of the Mali
Confederation;
Senegal secedes
from the
confederation
months later
1960

A military coup
brings Moussa
Traoré and
the Military
Committee
for National
Liberation
to power
1968

The Democratic
Union of the
Malian People is
the single ruling
party; Traoré is
the secretary
general
1979

School
strikes and
demonstrations;
teachers and
students are
detained
1979–1980

1990s

The country's
first multiparty
elections are
held

Alpha Konare
becomes
president

Economic
problems stir
civic unrest

tions. Although they encompassed vast areas united under a single supreme ruler, local communities generally enjoyed a great deal of autonomy.

From the 1890s until 1960, another form of imperial unity was imposed over Mali (then called the French Sudan) and the adjacent territories of French West Africa. The legacy of broader colonial and precolonial unity as well as its landlocked position have inspired Mali's postcolonial leaders to seek closer ties with neighboring countries.

Mali formed a brief confederation with Senegal during the transition period to independence. This initial union broke down after only a few months, but since then, the two countries have cooperated in the Organization for the Development of the Senegal River and other regional groupings. The Senegalese port of Dakar, which is linked by rail to Mali's capital city, Bamako, remains the major outlet for Malian exports.

Mali has also sought to strengthen its ties with nearby Guinea. In 1983, the two countries signed an agreement to harmonize policies and structures. Sekou Touré, the late president of Guinea, then spoke of "the reconstitution on the basis of an egalitarian and democratic state, of the ancient Mali Empire" as a political entity that could eventually embrace all the states in the region. But this lofty goal remains a distant dream.

ENVIRONMENTAL CHALLENGES

In terms of its per capita gross national product, Mali is one of the poorest countries in the world. More than 85 percent

of the people are employed in (mostly subsistence) agriculture, but the government usually has to rely on international aid to make up for local food deficits. Most of the country lies within either the expanding Sahara Desert or the semiarid region known as the Sahel, which has become drier as a result of recurrent drought. Much of the best land lies along the Senegal and Niger Rivers, which support most of the nation's agropastoral production. In earlier centuries, the Niger was able to sustain great trading cities such as Timbuctu and Djenne, but today, most of its banks do not support crops. Efforts to increase cultivation, through expanded irrigation and various crop schemes, have so far been met with limited overall success.

Mali's frequent inability to feed itself has been largely blamed on environmental constraints, namely, locust infestation, drought, and desertification. The inefficient state-run marketing and distribution system, however, has also had a negative impact. Low official produce prices have encouraged farmers either to engage in subsistence agriculture or to sell their crops on the black market. Thus, while some regions of the country remain dependent on international food donations, crops continue to be smuggled across Mali's borders. New policy commitments to liberalize agricultural trading, as part of an International Monetary Fund (IMF)–approved Structural Adjustment Program, have yet to take hold.

In contrast to agriculture, Mali's mining sector has experienced promising growth. The nation exports modest amounts of gold, phosphates, marble, and uranium. Potentially exploitable deposits of bauxite,

manganese, iron, tin, and diamonds exist. Small-scale manufacturing is concentrated in Bamako.

For decades, Mali was officially committed to state socialism. Its first president, Keita, a descendant of Sundiata, established a command economy and one-party state during the 1960s. His attempt to go it alone outside the French-sponsored African Financial Community (CFA Franc Zone) proved to be a major failure. Under Traoré, socialist structures were modified but not abandoned. Agreements with the IMF ended some government monopolies, and the country adopted the CFA franc as its currency. But the lack of a significant class of private entrepreneurs and the role of otherwise unprofitable public enterprises in providing employment discouraged radical privatization. The economic direction of Konare's government still remains to be seen.

DEVELOPMENT

In 1989 the government received international financial backing for ongoing efforts to overhaul its energy infrastructure. A new oil-storage depot is to be built, and the country's hydroelectric capacity is to be expanded. The UN Human Development Index lists Mali as a low 171 out of 174 countries.

FREEDOM

The introduction of multipartyism has allowed for freedom of expression and association in Mali. However, unrest among the Tuaregs has led to human-rights violations.

HEALTH/WELFARE

About a third of Mali's budget is devoted to education. A special literacy program in Mali teaches rural people how to read and write and helps them with the practical problems of daily life by using booklets that concern fertilizers, measles, and measuring fields.

ACHIEVEMENTS

For centuries, the ancient Malian city of Timbuctu was a leading center of Islamic learning and culture. Chronicles published by its scholars of the Middle Ages still enrich local culture. Modern Malian culture enjoys a favorable international reputation due to the popularity of musical artists such as Salif Keita.

Mauritania (Islamic Republic of Mauritania)

GEOGRAPHY

Area in Square Kilometers (Miles):
1,030,700 (398,000) (about the size
of Texas and California combined)
Capital (Population): Nouakchott
(480,400)
Climate: arid to semiarid

PEOPLE

Population
Total: 2,337,000
Annual Growth Rate: 3.17%
Rural/Urban Population Ratio: 61/39
Major Languages: official: Arabic,
French; others: Hasanya,
Bamanankan, Fulde, Sarakole, Wolof,
Berber languages
Ethnic Makeup: 40% mixed
Maur/black; perhaps 30% Maur
(estimates vary widely); 30% black

Health
Life Expectancy at Birth: 46 years
(male); 52 years (female)
Infant Mortality Rate (Ratio):
83.5/1,000
Average Caloric Intake: 94% of FAO
minimum
Physicians Available (Ratio): 1/13,167

SLAVERY IN MAURITANIA

Mauritania has been one of the few regions in the world where the
widespread practice of slavery continues to this day. In 1980, slavery
was formally abolished, but there have been several reports of its
persistence. A 1984 UN report, like the reports of past French colonial
administrators, noted that slavery had still to be eliminated in isolated
areas. However, the human-rights organization Africa Watch more
recently accused successive Mauritanian regimes of passing antislavery
legislation simply to appease world opinion, while pursuing policies
that ensure the institution's survival. Africa Watch estimates that there
are at least 100,000 black slaves (more than 5 percent of the nation's
population) serving Maurish masters in the country.

Religions
More than 99% Sunni Muslim

Education
Adult Literacy Rate: 35%

COMMUNICATION

Telephones: 8,168
Newspapers: 1

TRANSPORTATION

Highways—Kilometers (Miles): 7,525
(4,696)

Railroads—Kilometers (Miles): 690
(430)
Usable Airfields: 28

GOVERNMENT

Type: Islamic republic
Independence Date: November 28,
1960
Head of State: President Maauia
Ould Sidi Ahmed Taya
Political Parties: emerging parties
include Democratic and Social
Republican Party; Union of
Democratic Forces—New Era;
Assembly for Democracy and Unity;
Popular Social and Democratic
Union; Mauritanian Party for
Renewal; National Avant-Garde
Party; Mauritanian Party of the
Democratic Center.
Suffrage: universal at 18

MILITARY

Number of Armed Forces: 15,600
*Military Expenditures (% of Central
Government Expenditures):* 2.7%
Current Hostilities: internal conflicts

ECONOMY

Currency ($ U.S. Equivalent):
125.91 ouguiyas = $1
Per Capita Income/GDP: $1,110/$2.4
billion
Inflation Rate: 10%
Natural Resources: iron ore; gypsum;
fish; copper; phosphate
Agriculture: livestock; millet;
sorghum; wheat; dates; rice; peanuts;
root crops
Industry: iron-ore and gypsum
mining; fish processing

FOREIGN TRADE

Exports: $401 million
Imports: $378 million

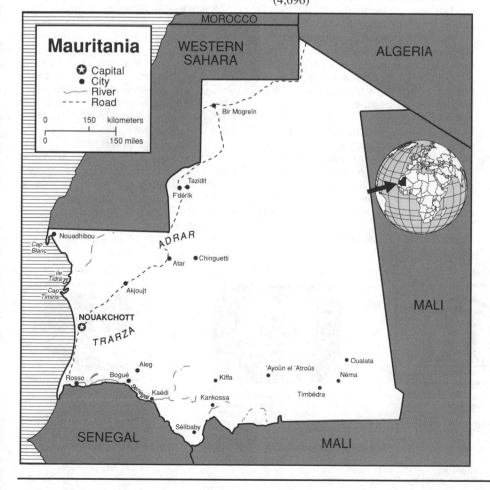

Mauritania

⊛ Capital
● City
～ River
--- Road

0   150   kilometers
0   150   miles

MOROCCO
WESTERN SAHARA
ALGERIA
Bir Mogreïn
Tazidit
F'dérïk
Nouadhibou
Cap Blanc
ADRAR
Atar
Chinguetti
Ile Tidra
Cap Timiris
Akjoujt
NOUAKCHOTT
TRARZA
MALI
Aleg
Bogué
'Ayoûn el 'Atroûs
Oualata
Néma
Rosso
Kiffa
Kaédi
Kankossa
Timbédra
Sélibaby
SENEGAL
MALI

The Almoravids spread Islam in the Western Sahara areas through conquest
1035–1055

The Mauritanian area becomes a French colony
1920

Mauritania becomes independent under President Moktar Ould Daddah
1960

A military coup brings Khouma Ould Haidalla and the Military Committee for National Recovery to power
1978

The Algiers Agreement: Mauritania makes peace with Polisario and abandons claims to Western Sahara
1979

Slavery is formally abolished
1980

1990s

Multiparty elections are boycotted by the opposition

Tensions continue between Mauritania and Senegal

Desertification

MAURITANIA

In 1992, for the first time in decades, Mauritania held multiparty elections, electing incumbent President Ould Taya and his newly formed Republican Social Democratic Party (PRDS) with large majorities. But, after the first round of voting, the polls were boycotted by the leading opposition grouping, the Union of Democratic Forces (UFD), which alleged that voting fraud and continued repression had turned the exercise into a farce. Mauritania's move to multipartyism thus appeared unlikely to resolve the country's severe social and economic problems.

For decades, Mauritania has grown progressively drier. Today, about 75 percent of the country is covered by sand. Less than 1 percent of the land is suitable for cultivation, 10 percent for grazing. To make matters worse, the surviving arable and pastoral areas have been plagued by grasshoppers and locusts.

In the face of natural disaster, people have moved. Since the mid-1960s, the percentage of urban dwellers has swelled, from less than 10 percent to 39 percent, while the nomadic population during the same period has dropped, from more than 80 percent to about 20 percent. In Nouakchott, the capital city, vast shantytowns now house nearly a quarter of the population. As the capital has grown, from a few thousand to more than half a million in a single generation, its poverty—and that of the nation as a whole—has become more obvious. People seek new ways to make a living away from the land, but there are few jobs.

Mauritania's faltering economy has coincided with an increase in racial and ethnic tensions. Since independence, the government has been dominated by the Maurs, or Moors, who speak Hassaniya Arabic. This community has historically been divided between the aristocrats and commoners, of Arab and Berber origin, and their black African slaves who have been assimilated into Maurish culture but remain socially segregated as "Haratine." Together the Maurs account for anywhere from 30 to 60 percent of the citizenry (the government has refused to release comprehensive data from the last two censuses).

The other half of Mauritania's population is composed of the "blacks," who are mostly Pulaar, Soninke, and Wolof speakers. Like the Maurs, all these groups are Muslim. Thus Mauritania's rulers have stressed Islam as a source of national unity. The country proclaimed itself an Islamic republic at independence, and since 1980 the Shari'a, the Islamic penal code, has been the law of the land.

Muslim brotherhood has not been able to overcome the divisions between the northern Maurs and southern blacks. One major source of friction has been official Arabization efforts, which are opposed by most southerners. In recent years, the country's desertification has created new sources of tension. As their pastures turned to sand, many of the Maurish nomads who did not find refuge in the urban areas moved southward. There, with state support, they began in the 1980s to deprive southerners of their land.

Growing oppression of blacks has been met with resistance from the underground Front for the Liberation of Africans in Mauritania (FLAM). Black grievances were also linked to an unsuccessful coup attempt in 1987. In 1989, interethnic hostility exploded when a border dispute with Senegal led to race riots that left several hundred "Senegalese" dead in Nouckchott. In response, the "Moorish" trading community in Senegal became the target of reprisals. Mauritania claimed that 10,000 Maurs were killed, but other sources put the number at about 70. Following this bloodshed, more than 100,000 refugees were repatriated across both sides of the border. Mass deportations of "Mauritanians of Senegalese origin" have fueled charges that the Nouckchott regime is trying to eliminate its non-Maurish population.

Despite international mediation efforts, a state of belligerence persists between Senegal and Mauritania. Deported black Mauritanians have organized cross-border raids, often hoping to regain property. At the same time, Mauritania's military regime has sent conflicting signals about its willingness to accommodate its black population and ease tensions with Senegal. The government has legalized opposition parties but has also stepped up its Arabization program, and it has been selectively arming Maur militias. The army has also been greatly expanded, with assistance from Iraq and Libya.

DEVELOPMENT

Mauritania's coastal waters are among the richest in the world. During the 1980s, the local fishing industry grew at an average annual rate of more than 10%. Many now believe that the annual catch has reached the upper levels of its sustainable potential.

FREEDOM

Most freedoms are restricted, and there have been reports of the perpetuation of chattel slavery. Mauritania's prison at Oualata, where many black activists have been detained, is notorious for its particularly brutal conditions of incarceration.

HEALTH/WELFARE

There have been some modest improvements in the areas of health and education since the country's independence, but conditions remain poor. Mauritania has received low marks regarding its commitment to human development.

ACHIEVEMENTS

There is a current project to restore ancient Mauritanian cities, such as Chinguette, which are located on traditional routes from North Africa to Sudan. These centers of trade and Islamic learning were points of origin for the pilgrimage to Mecca and were well known in the Middle East.

Niger (Republic of Niger)

GEOGRAPHY

Area in Square Kilometers (Miles):
1,267,000 (489,191) (almost 3 times the size of California)
Capital (Population): Niamey (398,000)
Climate: arid to semiarid

PEOPLE

Population
Total: 9,113,000
Annual Growth Rate: 2.9%
Rural/Urban Population Ratio: 85/15
Major Languages: French; Hausa; Zarma/Songhai; Kanuri; Fulde; Tamacheg (Tuareg); others
Ethnic Makeup: 56% Hausa; 22% Djerma; 8% Fula; 8% Tuareg; 5% others

Health
Life Expectancy at Birth: 43 years (male); 47 years (female)
Infant Mortality Rate (Ratio): 109.3/1,000
Average Caloric Intake: 91% of FAO minimum
Physicians Available (Ratio): 1/54,444

MATERNAL-LANGUAGE SCHOOLS

In Niger, more and more primary-school pupils are attending classes conducted in their maternal languages. These "maternal-language schools," as they are called, have been developed over a number of years through careful planning and experimentation and are based on the idea that the mastery of basic concepts is achieved most successfully in one's first language. These schools also work to foster and reinforce values of the community through a curriculum that reflects the cultural heritage of the pupils. Niger's maternal-language schools are dedicated to providing students with strong foundations in reading, writing, and arithmetic as well as to encouraging individuals' strong sense of their own cultural identities.

Religions
80% Muslim; 20% traditional indigenous and Christian

Education
Adult Literacy Rate: 14%

COMMUNICATION

Telephones: 14,260
Newspapers: 1

TRANSPORTATION

Highways—Kilometers (Miles):
39,970 (24,781)

Railroads—Kilometers (Miles): none
Usable Airfields: 29

GOVERNMENT

Type: republic, administered by the Supreme Military Council
Independence Date: August 3, 1960
Head of State: President (Colonel) Ibrahim Bare Mainassara
Political Parties: National Movement for the Development of Society; Democratic and Social Convention—Rahama; Nigerien Party for Democracy and Socialism; Nigerien Alliance for Democracy and Progress-Zamanlahia; Union of Patriots, Democrats, and Progressives; Niger Progressive Party-African Democratic Rally; Niger Social Democrat Party; Union for Democracy and Social Progress
Suffrage: universal at 18

MILITARY

Number of Armed Forces: 5,300
Military Expenditures (% of Central Government Expenditures): 1.3%
Current Hostilities: civil strife

ECONOMY

Currency ($ U.S. Equivalent):
529.43 CFA francs = $1
Per Capita Income/GDP: $550/$4.6 billion
Inflation Rate: n/a
Natural Resources: uranium; coal; iron; tin; phosphates
Agriculture: millet; sorghum; peanuts; beans; cotton; cowpeas
Industry: mining; textiles; cement; agricultural products; construction

FOREIGN TRADE

Exports: $246 million
Imports: $286 million

Niger

⊛ Capital
● City
River
Road

0   150 kilometers
0   150 miles

LIBYA
ALGERIA
Madama
Djado
Arhli
MALI
Bilma
Agadez
Tahoua   Bouza   Vallée d'Elik
seasonal high water
Tillabéri   Ouallam   Filingué   Madaoua   Nguigmi   CHAD
Téra   Baléyara   Dogondouchi   Zinder   Gouré
Maradi
NIAMEY
Tamou   Dosso
BURKINA FASO
Gâya
BENIN
GHANA
TOGO
NIGERIA
CAMEROON

NIGER

In recent years, Niger's farmers have produced a modest surplus in cereals. Although boosted by a temporary return of adequate rains, the good harvests are primarily an outgrowth of determined efforts to promote local agricultural productivity. As former president Ali Saibou said, "No Nigerien will die of hunger and thirst, even if it means devoting the entire budget to it." Niger's spending on agriculture as a percentage of the national budget has been among the highest in the world.

DROUGHT AND DESERTIFICATION

Farming is especially difficult in Niger. Less than 10 percent of the nation's vast territory is suitable for cultivation even during the best of times. Most of the cultivable land lies along the banks of the Niger River. Unfortunately, much of the past 2 decades has been the worst of times. Nigeriens have been constantly challenged by recurrent drought and an ongoing process of desertification.

Drought had an especially catastrophic effect during the 1970s. Most Nigeriens were reduced to dependency on foreign food aid, while about 60 percent of their livestock perished. Some people believe that the ecological disaster that afflicted Africa's Sahel region, which includes southern Niger, during that period was of such severity as to disrupt the delicate long-term balance between desert and savanna. Others, however, have concluded that the intensified desertification of recent years is primarily rooted in human, rather than natural, causes, which can be reversed. In particular, many attribute environmental degradation to the introduction of inappropriate forms of cultivation, overgrazing, deforestation, and new patterns of human settlement.

Ironically, much of the debate on people's negative impact on the Sahel environment has been focused on some of the agricultural development schemes that once were conceived as the region's salvation. In their attempts to boost local food production, international aid agencies often promoted so-called green revolution programs. These were designed to increase per acre yields, typically through the intensive planting of new, higher-yielding seeds and reliance on imported fertilizers and pesticides. Such projects often led to higher initial local outputs that proved unsustainable, largely due to expensive overhead. In addition, many experts promoting the new agricultural techniques failed to appreciate the value of traditional technologies and forms of

(United Nations photo)

Drought and desertification in Niger have been amplified by inappropriate forms of cultivation, overgrazing, deforestation, and human settlement. Attempted "improvements" to increase local food production have discouraged the traditional nomadic pattern of life in Niger and, in consequence, have upset the delicate long-term balance between desert and savanna.

The Mali Empire includes territories and peoples of current Niger areas **1200s–1400s**	Hausa states develop in the south of present-day Niger **1400s**	The area is influenced by the Fulani Empire, centered at Sokoto, now in Nigeria **1800s**	France consolidates rule over Niger **1906**	Niger becomes independent **1960**	A military coup brings Colonel Seyni Kountché and a Supreme Military Council to power **1974**	President Kountché dies and is replaced by Ali Saibou **1987**

1990s

A French DC-10 on a flight between Brazzaville and Paris is blown up by terrorists over Niger, killing 172; France implicates Libya

The Nigerien National Conference adopts multipartyism

social organization in limiting desertification while allowing people to cope with drought. It is now appreciated that patterns of cultivation long championed by Nigerien farmers allowed for soil conservation and reduced the risks associated with pests and poor climate.

The government's recent emphasis has been on helping Niger's farmers to help themselves through the extension of credit, better guaranteed minimum prices, and improved communications. Vigorous efforts have been made in certain regions to halt the spread of desert sands by supporting village tree-planting campaigns. Given the local inevitability of drought, the government has also increased its commitment to the stockpiling of food in granaries. But, for social and political as much as economic reasons, government policy has continued to discourage the flexible, nomadic pattern of life that is characteristic of many Nigerien communities.

The Nigerien government's emphasis on agriculture has, in part, been motivated by the realization that the nation could not rely on its immense uranium deposits for future development. The opening of uranium mines in the 1970s resulted in the country becoming the world's fifth-largest producer. By the end of that decade, uranium exports accounted for some 90 percent of Niger's foreign-exchange earnings. Depressed international demand throughout the 1980s, however, resulted in substantially reduced prices and output. Although uranium still accounts for 75 percent of foreign-exchange earnings, its revenue contribution in recent years is only about a third of what it was prior to the slump.

MILITARY RULE

For nearly half of its existence since its independence, Niger was governed by a civilian administration, under President Hamani Diori. In 1974, during the height of drought, Lieutenant Colonel (later, Major General) Seyni Kountché took power in a bloodless coup. Kountché ruled as the leader of a Supreme Military Council, which met behind closed doors. Ministerial portfolios, appointed by the president, were filled by civilians as well as military personnel. In 1987, Kountché died of natural causes and was succeeded by Colonel Ali Saibou.

A National Movement for the Development of Society (MNSD) was established in 1989 as the country's sole political party, after a constitutional referendum in which less than 4 percent of the electorate participated. But, as was the case in many other countries in Africa, 1990 saw a groundswell of local support for a return to multipartyism. In Niger, this prodemocracy agitation was spearheaded by the nation's labor confederation, which organized a widely observed 48-hour general strike. Having earlier rejected the strikers "as a handful of demagogues," in 1991, President Saibou agreed to the formation of a National Conference to prepare a new constitution.

The conference ended its deliberations with the appointment of an interim government, headed by Amadou Cheffou, which led the country to multiparty elections in February–March 1993. After two rounds of voting, the presidential contest was won by Mahamane Ousmane. Ousmane's Alliance of Forces for Change (AFC) opposition captured 50 seats in the new 83-seat National Assembly, while the MNSD became the major opposition party, with 29 seats.

Ousmane's government made a promising start by reaching peace agreements with the rebel movements the Tuareg Front for the Liberation of Air and Azaouad and the Organization of Army Resistance. But the nation's economic crisis deepened with the 1994 devaluation of the CFA franc. In February 1995, the opposition coalition led by Hama Amadou gained control of the National Assembly, resulting in an uneasy government of "cohabitation." Serious student unrest was followed by a military coup in January 1996, which resulted in the installation of Colonel Ibrahim Bare Mainassara as president. Under international pressure, Mainassara agreed to the holding of new elections in July 1996, in which he claimed victory with 52 percent of the vote in a disputed result.

The political turn is likely to further poison interethnic relations in Niger. Since independence, members of the Zarma group have been especially prominent in the government, MNSD, and military. The deposed Ousmane has been Niger's first Hausa leader (the Hausa constitute the country's largest ethnolinguistic group).

DEVELOPMENT

Nigerien village cooperatives, especially marketing cooperatives, pre-date independence and have grown in size and importance in recent years. They have successfully competed with well-to-do private traders for control of the grain market.

FREEDOM

The election of the AFC government has improved the human-rights situation in Niger. But continuing civil strife involving the Tuareg community and rising tensions between Islamic militants and moderates continue to threaten social peace.

HEALTH/WELFARE

A national conference on educational reform stimulated a program to use Nigerien languages in primary education and integrated the adult literacy program into the rural development efforts. The National Training Center for Literacy Agents is crucial to literacy efforts.

ACHIEVEMENTS

Niger has consistently demonstrated a strong commitment to the preservation and development of its national cultures through its media and educational institutions, the National Museum, and events such as the annual youth festival at Agades.

Nigeria (Federal Republic of Nigeria)

GEOGRAPHY

Area in Square Kilometers (Miles):
923,768 (356,669) (twice the size of California)
Capital (Population): Abuja (339,100)
Climate: tropical to arid

PEOPLE

Population
Total: 103,913,000
Annual Growth Rate: 3.16%
Rural/Urban Population Ratio: 84/16
Major Languages: English; Hausa; Yoruba; Ibo; Fulani; others (250 languages are recognized by the government)
Ethnic Makeup: 21% Hausa; 20% Yoruba; 17% Ibo; 9% Fulani, 33% others

Health
Life Expectancy at Birth: 55 years (male); 57 years (female)
Infant Mortality Rate (Ratio): 72.6/1,000 est.
Average Caloric Intake: 91% of FAO minimum
Physicians Available (Ratio): 1/4,692

Religions
50% Muslim; 40% Christian; 10% traditional indigenous

Education
Adult Literacy Rate: 51%

COMMUNICATION
Telephones: 389,185
Newspapers: 48

CULTURAL GIANTS

Nigeria is renowned for its arts. Contemporary giants include Wole Solyinka, who received the Nobel Prize for Literature for his work—plays such as "The Trials of Brother Jero" and "The Road," novels such as *The Interpreters,* and poems and nonfiction works. Two other literary giants are Chinua Achebe, author of *Things Fall Apart, A Man of the People,* and *Anthills of the Savannah,* and the feminist writer Buchi Emecheta, whose works include *The Joy of Motherhood.* The legendary Fela Anikulado Kuti's "Afro-Beat" sound and critical lyrics have made him a local hero and international music megastar. Also prominent is "King" Sunny Ade, who has brought Nigeria's distinctive Juju music to international audiences.

TRANSPORTATION
Highways—Kilometers (Miles): 107,990 (67,104)
Railroads—Kilometers (Miles): 3,567 (2,226)
Usable Airfields: 80

GOVERNMENT
Type: transitional under military rule
Independence Date: October 1, 1960
Head of State: President Sani Abacha
Political Parties: two-party system suspended after coup of November 17, 1993
Suffrage: universal at 21

MILITARY
Number of Armed Forces: 77,100
Military Expenditures (% of Central Government Expenditures): 1%
Current Hostilities: civil strife

ECONOMY
Currency ($ U.S. Equivalent): 21.99 naira = $1
Per Capita Income/GDP: $1,250 (est.)/$122.6 billion
Inflation Rate: 53%
Natural Resources: oil; minerals
Agriculture: cotton; cocoa; rubber; yams; cassava; sorghum; palm kernels; millet; corn; rice; livestock
Industry: mining; crude oil; natural gas; coal; tin; columbite; processing: palm oil, cotton, rubber, petroleum; manufacturing: textiles, cement, building materials, chemicals, beer brewing

FOREIGN TRADE
Exports: $11.9 billion
Imports: $8.3 billion

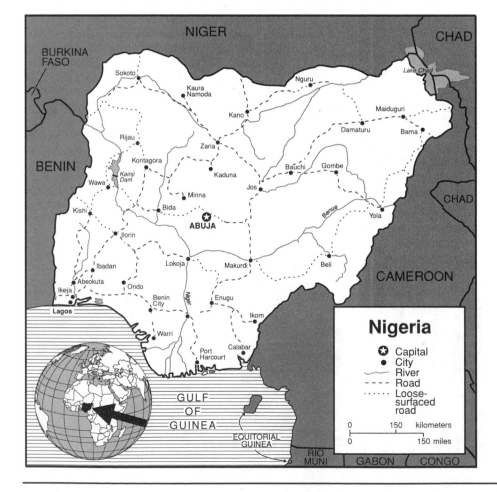

Nigeria
- ⭐ Capital
- ● City
- — River
- --- Road
- ...... Loose-surfaced road

0 ——— 150 kilometers
0 ——— 150 miles

NIGERIA

In November 1995, the Nigerian government became the target of international condemnation following its execution of Ken Saro Wiwa, a prominent writer and human-rights activist. In June 1996, the world's attention was once more focused on Nigeria by the assassination of Kudirat Abiola, the wife of the detained winner of the country's last—aborted—election, Mashood Abiola. These two incidents reflect Nigeria's continued decline under dictatorship. The current strongman, General Sani Abacha, is widely seen as the most brutally incompetent of a series of military rulers who have misruled Nigeria throughout most of its independence. Along with corrupt civilian politicians, they have reduced Nigeria from the status of a country of continental leadership to an impoverished pariah nation.

Since Nigeria's independence, in 1960, its citizens have been through an emotional, political, and material rollercoaster ride. It has been a period marred by interethnic violence, economic downturns, and mostly military rule. But there have also been impressive levels of economic growth, cultural achievement, and human development. To some people, this land of great extremes thus typifies both the hopes and frustrations of its continent.

With the elephant as a symbol, many Nigerians like to think of their country as the giant of Africa. In 1992, its status as Africa's most populous country was confirmed by the first seemingly successful census since 1963. With a 1994 population of 98 million, Nigeria still far outranks second-place Egypt's 52 million. But the country is far less crowded than had been suggested by commonly quoted precensus estimates of 120 million or more.

Nigeria's hard-working population is also responsible for Africa's second-largest economy, as measured by gross domestic product (GDP), which stands at $95 billion, as compared to South Africa's GDP of $115 billion. But per capita income is still estimated at only $600 per year (about the same as per capita debt), which is about average for the globe's most impoverished continent but way down from Nigeria's estimated 1980 per capita income of $1,500. A decade ago, it was common to equate Nigeria's wealth with its status as Africa's leading oil producer, but oil earnings have since plummeted. Although hydrocarbons still account for about 90 percent of the country's export earnings and 75 percent of its government revenue, the sector's current contribution to total GDP is a more modest 20 percent.

NIGERIA'S ROOTS

For centuries, the river Niger, which cuts across much of Nigeria, has facilitated long-distance communication among various communities of West Africa's forest and savanna regions. This fact helps to account for the rich variety of cultures that have emerged within the territory of Nigeria over the past millennium. Archaeologists and historians have illuminated the rise and fall of many states whose cultural legacies continue to define the nation.

Precolonial Nigeria produced a wide range of craft goods, including leather, glass, and metalware. The cultivation of cotton and indigo supported the growth of a local textiles industry. During the mid-nineteenth century, southern Nigeria prospered through palm-oil exports, which lubricated the wheels of Europe's industrial revolution. Earlier, much of the country was disrupted through its participation in the slave trade. Most African Americans have Nigerian roots.

Today, more than 250 languages are spoken in Nigeria. Pidgin, which combines an English-based vocabulary with local grammar, is widely used as a lingua franca in the cities and towns. Roughly two thirds of Nigerians speak either Hausa, Yoruba, or Igbo as a home language. During and after the colonial era, the leaders of these three major ethnolinguistic groups clashed politically from their separate regional bases.

The British, who conquered Nigeria in the late nineteenth and early twentieth centuries, administered the country through a policy of divide-and-rule. In the predominantly Muslim, Hausa-speaking north, they co-opted the old ruling class while virtually excluding Christian missionaries. But in the south, the missionaries, along with their schools, were encouraged, and Christianity and education spread rapidly. Many Yoruba farmers of the southwest profited through their cultivation of cocoa. Although most remained as farmers, many of the Igbo of the southeast became prominent in nonagricultural pursuits, such as state employees, artisans, wage workers, and traders. As a result, the Igbo tended to migrate in relatively large numbers to other parts of the colony.

REGIONAL CONFLICTS

At independence, the Federal Republic of Nigeria was composed of three states: the Northern Region, dominated by Hausa speakers; the Western Region, of the Yoruba; and the predominantly Igbo Eastern Region. National politics quickly deteriorated into conflict between these three regions. At one time or another, politicians in each of the areas threatened to secede from the federation. In 1966, this strained situation turned into a crisis following the overthrow by the military of the first civilian government.

In the coup's aftermath, the army itself was divided along ethnic lines; its ranks soon became embroiled in an increasingly violent power struggle. The unleashed tensions culminated in the massacre of up to 30,000 Igbos living in the north. In response, the Eastern Region declared its independence, as the Republic of Biafra. The ensuing civil war between Biafran partisans and federal forces lasted for 3 years, claiming an estimated 2 million lives. During this time, much of the outside world's attention became focused on the conflict through visual images of the mass starvation that was occurring in rebel-controlled areas under federal blockade. Despite the extent of the war's tragedy, the collapse of Biafran resistance was followed by a largely successful process of national reconciliation. The military government of Yakubu Gowon (1966–1975) succeeded in diffusing ethnic politics, through a restructured federal system based on the creation of new states. The oil boom, which began soon after the conflict, helped the nation-building process by concentrating vast resources in the hands of the federal government in Lagos.

CIVILIAN POLITICS

Thirteen years of military rule ended in 1979. A new Constitution was implemented, which abandoned the British parliamentary model and instead adopted a modified version of the American balance-of-powers system. In order to encourage a national outlook, Nigerian presidential candidates needed to win a plurality that included at least one fourth of the vote in two thirds of the states.

Five political parties competed in the 1979 elections. They all had similar platforms, promising social welfare for the masses, support for Nigerian business, and a foreign policy based on nonalignment and anti-imperialism. Ideological differences tended to exist within the parties as much as among them, although the People's Redemption Party (PRP) of Aminu Kano became the political home for many Socialists. The most successful party was the somewhat right-of-center National Party of Nigeria (NPN), whose candidate, Shehu Shagari, won the presidency.

New national elections took place in August and September 1983, in which Shagari received more than 12 million of 25.5 million votes. However, the reelected government did not survive long. On December 31,

1983, there was a military coup, led by Major General Muhammad Buhari. The 1979 Constitution was suspended, Shagari and others were arrested, and a federal military government was reestablished. Although no referendum was ever taken on the matter, it is clear that many Nigerians welcomed the coup: this initial response was a reflection of widespread disillusionment with the Second (civilian) Republic.

The political picture seemed very bright in the early 1980s. A commitment to national unity was well established. Although marred by incidents of political violence, two elections had successfully taken place. Due process of law, judicial independence, and press freedom—never entirely eliminated under previous military rulers—had been extended and were seemingly entrenched. But the state was increasingly seen as an instrument of the privileged that offered little to the impoverished masses, with an electoral system that, while balancing the interests of the elite in different sections of the country, failed to empower ordinary citizens. A major reason for this failing was pervasive corruption. People lost confidence as certain officials and their cronies became overnight-millionaires. Transparent abuses of power had also occurred under the previous military regime. Conspicuous kleptocracy (rule by thieves) had been tolerated during the oil-boom years of the 1970s, but it became the focus of popular anger as Nigeria's economy contracted during the 1980s.

OIL BOOM—AND BUST

Nigeria, as a leading member of the Organization of Petroleum Exporting Countries, experienced a period of rapid social and economic change during the 1970s. The recovery of oil production after the Civil War and the subsequent hike in its prices led to a massive increase in government revenue. This allowed for the expansion of certain types of social services. Universal primary education was introduced, and the number of universities increased from five (in 1970) to 21 (in 1983). A few Nigerians became very wealthy, while a growing middle class was able to afford what previously had been luxuries.

Oil revenues had already begun to fall off when the NPN government embarked upon a dream list of new prestige projects, most notably the construction of a new federal capital at Abuja, in the center of the country. While such expenditures provided lucrative opportunities for many businesspeople and politicians, they did little to promote local production.

Agriculture, burdened by inflationary costs and low prices, entered a period of crisis, leaving the rapidly growing cities dependent on foreign food. Nonpetroleum exports, once the mainstay of the economy, either virtually disappeared or declined drastically.

While gross indicators appeared to report impressive industrial growth in Nigeria, most of the new industry depended heavily on foreign inputs and was geared toward direct consumption rather than the production of machines or spare parts. Selective import bans led merely to the growth of smuggling.

The golden years of the 1970s were also banner years for inappropriate expenditures, corruption, and waste. For a while, given the scale of incoming revenues, it looked as if these were manageable problems. But GDP fell drastically in the 1980s, with the collapse of oil prices. As the economy worsened, populist resentment grew.

In 1980, an Islamic movement condemning corruption, wealth, and private property defied authorities in the northern metropolis of Kano. The army was called in, killing nearly 4,000. Similar riots subsequently occurred in the cities of Maiduguri, Yola, and Gombe. Attempts by the government to control organized labor by reorganizing the union movement into one centralized federation sparked unofficial strikes (including a general strike in 1981). In an attempt to placate the growing number of unemployed Nigerians, more than 1 million expatriate West Africans, mostly Ghanaians, were suddenly expelled, a domestically popular but essentially futile gesture.

REFORM OR RETRIBUTION?

Buhari justified the military's return to power on the basis of the need to take drastic steps to rescue the economy, whose poor performance he blamed almost exclusively on official corruption. A "War Against Indiscipline" was declared, which initially resulted in the trial of a number of political leaders, some of whose economic crimes were indeed staggering. The discovery of large private caches of naira, the Nigerian currency, and foreign exchange fueled public outrage (and added modestly to the country's treasury). Tribunals sentenced former politicians to long jail terms. In its zeal, the government looked for more and more culprits, while jailing journalists and others who questioned aspects of its program. In 1985, Major General Ibrahim Babanguida led a successful military coup, charging Buhari with human-rights abuses, autocracy, and economic mismanagement.

Babanguida released political detainees. In a clever strategy, he also encouraged all Nigerians to participate in national forums on the benefits of an International Monetary Fund (IMF) loan and Structural Adjustment Program (SAP). The government turned down the loan but used the consultations to legitimize the implementation of "homegrown" austerity measures consistent with IMF and World Bank prescriptions.

The 1986 budget signaled the beginning of SAP. The naira was devalued, budgets were restricted, and the privatization of many state-run industries was planned. Because salaries remained the same while prices rose, the cost of basic goods rose dramatically, with painful consequences for middle- and working-class Nigerians as well as for the poor.

Although the international price of oil improved somewhat in the late 1980s, there was no immediate return to prosperity. Continued budgetary excesses on the part of the government (which heaped perks on its officer corps and created more state governments to soak up public coffers), coupled with instability, undermined SAP sacrifices.

(United Nations photo)

Nigeria experienced a tremendous influx of money when its oil industry took advantage of the 1970s' worldwide oil panics. The huge increase in cash resources led to the growth of a middle class and a flurry of expensive new projects. One such project was the Kainji Dam, shown above, which supplies a significant amount of energy to agriculture, industry, and the populace.

Ancient life flourishes
1100–1400

The beginning of Usuman dan Fodio's Islamic jihad (struggle)
1804

The first British protectorate is established at Lagos
1851

A protectorate is proclaimed over the north
1900

Nigeria becomes independent as a unified federal state
1960

Military seizure of power; proclamation of Biafra; civil war
1966–1970

An oil-price hike inaugurates the oil boom
1973

Elections · restore civilian government
1979

Muhammed Buhari's military coup ends the Second Republic; later Buhari is toppled by Ibrahim Babanguida
1980s

Lean times; austerity measures provoke protests and strikes

1990s

Babanguida resigns and installs an ill-fated interim government

President (General) Sani Abacha takes the reins

Civil unrest and violence intensify

In 1988, the government attempted a moderate reduction in local fuel subsidies. But when, as a result, some transport owners raised fares by 50 to 100 percent, students and workers protested, and bank staff and other workers went on strike. Police killed demonstrators in Jos. Domestic fuel prices have since remained among the lowest in the world, encouraging a massive smuggling of petroleum to neighboring states. This has recently led to the ironic situation of a severe local petroleum shortage.

The Babanguida government faced additional internal challenges while seeking to project an image of stability to foreign investors. Coup attempts were foiled in 1985 and 1991, while chronic student unrest led to the repeated closure of university campuses. Religious riots between Christians and Muslims became endemic in many areas, leading to hundreds, if not thousands, of deaths.

In 1986, Babanguida promised a phased return to full civilian control. But his program of guided democratization degenerated into a farce. Local nonparty elections were held in 1987, and a (mostly elected) Constituent Assembly subsequently met and approved modifications to Nigeria's 1979 Constitution. Despite the trappings of electoral involvement, the Transitional Program was tightly controlled. Many politicians were banned as Babanguida tried to impose a two-party system on what traditionally had been a multiparty political culture. When none of 13 potential parties gained his approval, the general decided to create two new parties of

his own: the "a little to the left" Social Democratic Party (SDP) and the "a little to the right" National Republican Convention (NRC).

Doubts about the military in general and Babanguida's grasp on power in particular were raised in April 1990, when a group of dissident officers launched yet another coup. In radio broadcasts, the insurrectionists announced the expulsion of five northern states from the federal republic, thus raising the specter of a return to interethnic civil war. The uprising was crushed.

A series of national elections were held in 1992 between the two officially sponsored parties. But public indifference and/or fear of intimidation, institutionalized by the replacement of the (ideally, secret) ballot with a procedure of publicly lining up for one's candidate, compromised the results. Allegations of gross irregularities led to the voiding of first-round presidential primary elections and the banning of all the candidates. After additional delays, accompanied by a serious antigovernment rioting in Lagos and other urban areas, escalating intercommunal violence, and further clampdowns on dissent, a presidential poll was finally held in June 1993 between two government-approved candidates: Mashood Abiola and Bashir Tofa. The result was a convincing 58 percent victory for the SDP's Abiola, though an estimated 70 percent of the electorate refused to participate in the charade.

Babanguida annulled the results before they had been officially counted (the final results were released by local officials in de-

fiance of Banbanguida's regime). Instead, in August 1992, he resigned and installed an interim government led by an ineffectual businessman, Ernest Shonekan. Growing unrest—aggravated by an overnight 600 percent increase in domestic fuel prices and a dramatic airline hijacking by a group calling itself the Movement for the Advancement of Democracy (MAD)—led to the interim regime's rapid collapse. In November, the defense minister, General Sani Abacha, reimposed full military rule.

Resistance to military rule steadily increased throughout 1994. Abiola was arrested in June after proclaiming himself president. His detention touched off nationwide strikes, which shut down the oil industry and other key sectors of the economy. In August, Abacha suspended the unions, but workers refused to call off their campaign. While gaining momentum, agitation to install Abiola has become increasingly colored by ethnicity. Support for Abiola has been strongest in the south, especially among his fellow Yoruba, and relatively weak in the Hausa–Fulani north, home of most of Nigeria's military rulers. With rising violence and a sinking economy, the Nigerian rollercoaster may be about to crash.

DEVELOPMENT

Nigeria hopes to mobilize its human and natural resources to encourage labor-intensive production and self-sufficient agriculture. Recent bans on food imports will increase local production, and restrictions on imported raw materials should encourage research and local input for industry.

FREEDOM

Nigeria has one of the world's worst human-rights records. Its current regime is intolerant of genuine dissent and rules through a combination of political detention, torture, judicial murder, assassination, and communal massacre.

HEALTH/WELFARE

Nigeria's infant mortality rate is now believed to have dropped to about 73 per 1,000. (Some estimate it to be as high as 150 per 1,000.) While social services grew rapidly during the 1970s, Nigeria's strained economy since then has led to cutbacks in health and education.

ACHIEVEMENTS

With many of its leading writers, artists, and intellectuals now in exile and its once-lively press suppressed, Nigerians have found some solace in the success of their athletes. At the 1996 Atlanta Summer Olympic Games, Nigeria's female track and field team distinguished itself, winning five medals, while its football team, the Super Eagles, beat Argentina in the finals. The Super Eagles are now a strong contender to become the first African team to capture the World Cup.

Senegal (Republic of Senegal)

GEOGRAPHY

Area in Square Kilometers (Miles):
196,840 (76,000) (about the size of
South Dakota)
Capital (Population): Dakar
(1,730,000)
Climate: tropical

PEOPLE

Population
Total: 9,093,000
Annual Growth Rate: 3.1%
Rural/Urban Population Ratio: 57/43
Major Languages: French; Wolof;
Fulde; Oyola; Mandinka; Sarakole;
Serer
Ethnic Makeup: 36% Wolof; 17%
Fulani; 17% Serer; 9% Toucouleur;
9% Diola; 9% Mandingo; 3%
European, Lebanese, and others

Health
Life Expectancy at Birth: 56 years
(male); 59 years (female)
Infant Mortality Rate (Ratio):
73.6/1,000
Average Caloric Intake: 100% of
FAO minimum
Physicians Available (Ratio): 1/14,817

GORÉE ISLAND

The tiny, rocky island of Gorée, opposite Dakar on the Senegalese
mainland, has a tragic history. Gorée was occupied by European traders
beginning in the seventeenth century as an easily defensible slave
entrepôt. For more than 200 years, the French, Dutch, and English used
Gorée as a collection and distribution center for the Atlantic slave trade.
Slaves from the Senegalese interior and many other parts of West Africa
were housed and examined in cramped slave quarters before walking
the narrow passageway to the sea and transport to the Americas. The
Senegalese government has preserved the site as a reminder of the slave
trade's horrors. Gorée attracts visitors from around the world, including
many African Americans.

Religions
92% Muslim; 6% traditional
indigenous; 2% Christian

Education
Adult Literacy Rate: 27%

COMMUNICATION

Telephones: 73,925
Newspapers: 3

TRANSPORTATION

Highways—Kilometers (Miles):
14,007 (8,740)
Railroads—Kilometers (Miles): 905
(565)
Usable Airfields: 20

GOVERNMENT

Type: republic under multiparty
democratic rule
Independence Date: April 4, 1960
Head of State: President Abdou Diouf
Political Parties: Socialist Party;
Senegalese Democratic Party;
Democratic League-Labor Party
Movement; Independent Labor Party;
Senegalese Democratic
Union-Renewal; other small,
uninfluential parties
Suffrage: universal at 18

MILITARY

Number of Armed Forces: 13,350
*Military Expenditures (% of Central
Government Expenditures):* 2.1%
Current Hostilities: skirmishes with
Guinea-Bissau and Mauritania

ECONOMY

Currency ($ U.S. Equivalent):
529.43 CFA francs = $1
Per Capita Income/GDP:
$1,450/$12.3 billion
Inflation Rate: 1.8%
Natural Resources: fish; phosphates;
iron ore
Agriculture: millet; sorghum; manioc;
rice; cotton; groundnuts
Industry: fishing; food processing;
light manufacturing

FOREIGN TRADE

Exports: $904 million
Imports: $1.2 billion

SENEGAL

While most African states have recently moved away from systems of authoritarian control, Senegal has struggled for decades to build a tolerant, multiparty system of government. This genuine, if imperfectly realized, commitment has not been easy. A heterogeneous mix of indigenous, Islamic, and European influences, Senegal's multiethnic society has maintained its balance in the face of economic adversity, regional separatism, external disputes, and sectarian pressures.

THE IMPACT OF ISLAM

The vast majority of Senegalese are Muslim. Islam was introduced into the region by the eleventh century A.D. and was spread through trade, evangelism, and the establishment of a series of theocratic Islamic states from the 1600s to the 1800s.

Today, most Muslims are associated with one or another of the Islamic Brotherhoods. The leaders of these Brotherhoods, known as marabouts, often act as rural spokespeople as well as the spiritual directors of their followers. Abdou Diouf, the current president of Senegal, has relied on the political support of prominent marabouts in his election campaigns. The Brotherhoods also play an important economic role. For example, the members of Mouride Brotherhood, who number about 700,000, cooperate in the growing of groundnuts, the nation's principal exported cash crop.

FRENCH INFLUENCE

In the 1600s, French merchants established coastal bases to facilitate their trade in slaves and gum. As a result, the coastal communities have been influenced by French culture for generations. More territory in the interior gradually fell under French political control.

Although Wolof is used by many as a lingua franca, French continues to be the common language of the country, and the educational system maintains a French character. Many Senegalese migrate to France, usually to work as low-paid laborers. The French maintain a military force near the capital, Dakar, and are major investors in the Senegalese economy. Senegal's judiciary and bureaucracy are also modeled after those of France.

(United Nations photo by Purcell/AB)

The potential for drought is an ongoing concern in the Sahel zone of Senegal. It is an ever-present factor in any agricultural program. The young herder shown above with his starving cattle is an all-too-familiar image.

The French occupy present-day St. Louis and, later, Gorée Island
1659

The Jolof kingdom controls much of the region
1700s

All Africans in four towns of the coast vote for a representative to the French Parliament
1848

Interior areas are added to the French colonial territory
1889

Senegal becomes independent as part of the Mali Confederation; shortly afterward, it breaks from the Confederation
1960

President Leopold Senghor retires and is replaced by Abdou Diouf
1980s

Senegalese political leaders unite in the face of threats from Mauritania

1990s

Serious rioting breaks out in Dakar protesting the devaluation of the CFA franc

Tensions escalate between Senegal and Guinea-Bissau

Senegal and Mauritania try to improve relations

POLITICS

Under Diouf, Senegal has strengthened its commitment to multipartyism. After succeeding Leopold Senghor, the nation's scholarly first president, Diouf liberalized the political process by allowing an increased number of opposition parties effectively to compete against his own ruling Socialist Party (PS). He also restructured his administration in ways that were credited with making it less corrupt and more efficient. Some say that these moves have not gone far enough, but the reformist Diouf has had to struggle against reactionary elements within his own party.

In national elections in 1988, Diouf won 77 percent of the vote and the Socialists took 103 out of 120 seats. Outside observers believed that the election had been plagued by fewer irregularities than in the past. However, opposition protests against alleged fraud touched off serious rioting in Dakar. As a result, the city was placed under a 3-month state of emergency. Diouf's principal opponent, Maitre Abdoulaye Wade of the Democratic Party, was among those arrested and tried for incitement. But subsequent meetings between Diouf and Wade resulted in an easing of tensions. Indeed, in April 1991, Wade shocked many by accepting the post of minister of state in Diouf's cabinet. Subsequent elections in 1993 were less controversial, with Diouf being reelected with 58 percent of the vote. PS representation dropped to 84 seats.

In March 1995, a new multiparty government of national unity was formed, which has survived despite the defection of one of its members, the Independent Labor Party, in September 1996. But interparty tension is growing in the face of Diouf's failure to appoint an independent elections commission in preparation for elections in November 1996.

THE ECONOMY

Many believe that the Sopi (Wolof for "change") riots of 1988 were primarily motivated by popular frustration with Senegal's weak economy, especially among its youth (about half the population are under age 21), who face an uncertain future. Senegal's relatively large (38 percent) urban population has suffered from rising rates of unemployment and inflation, which have been aggravated by the country's attempt to implement an International Monetary Fund–approved Structural Adjustment Program. In recent years, the economy has grown modestly but has so far failed to attract the investment needed to meet ambitious privatization goals. Among rural dwellers, drought and locusts have also made life difficult. Fluctuating world market prices and disease as well as drought have undermined groundnut exports.

Senegal has also been beset by difficulties in its relations with neighboring states. The Senegambia Confederation, which many hoped would lead to greater cooperation with The Gambia, was dissolved in September 1989. Relations with Guinea-Bissau are strained as a result of that nation's failure to recognize the result of international arbitration over disputed, potentially oil-rich waters. Senegalese further suspect that individuals in Guinea-Bissau may be linked to separatist unrest in Senegal's southern region of Casamance. There some 1,000 people died in an insurgency campaign between the Senegalese Army and the guerrillas of the Movement of Democratic Forces of Casamance. In July 1993, the rebels agreed to a cease-fire, but progress toward a final political settlement has been slow. The cease-fire collapsed in 1995. Senegalese peacekeeping troops have been attacked in Liberia by the National Patriotic Front of Liberia.

A small contingent of Senegalese also participated in the Persian Gulf War against Iraq.

But the major source of cross-border tension has been Mauritania. In 1989, long-standing border disputes between the two countries led to a massacre of Senegalese in Mauritania, setting off widespread revenge attacks against Mauritanians in Senegal. More than 200,000 Senegalese and Mauritanians were repatriated. Relations between the two countries have remained tense, in large part due to the persecution of Mauritania's "black" communities by its Maur-dominated military government. Many Mauritanians belonging to the persecuted groups have been pushed into Senegal, leading to calls for war, but in April 1992, the two countries agreed to restore diplomatic, air, and postal links.

DEVELOPMENT

The recently built Diama and Manantali Dams will allow for the irrigation of many thousands of acres for domestic rice production. At the moment, large amounts of rice are imported to Senegal, mostly to feed the urban population.

FREEDOM

Senegal's generally favorable human-rights record is marred by persistent violence in its southern region, Casamance, where rebels are continuing to right for independence. A 2-year cease-fire broke down in 1995 after an army offensive was launched against the rebel Movement of Democratic Forces of Casamance.

HEALTH/WELFARE

Like other Sahel countries, Senegal has a high infant mortality rate and a low life expectancy rate. Health facilities are considered to be below average, even for a country of Senegal's modest income, but recent child-immunization campaigns have been fairly successful.

ACHIEVEMENTS

Dakar, sometimes described as the "Paris of West Africa," has long been a major cultural center for the region. Senegalese writers such as former president Leopold Senghor were founders of the Francophonic African tradition of Negritude.

Sierra Leone (Republic of Sierra Leone)

GEOGRAPHY

Area in Square Kilometers (Miles):
72,325 (27,925) (slightly smaller than South Carolina)
Capital (Population): Freetown (469,000)
Climate: tropical

PEOPLE

Population
Total: 4,793,100
Annual Growth Rate: 2.6%
Rural/Urban Population Ratio: 65/35
Major Languages: English, Krio, Temne, Mende, Vai, Kru, Fulde, Mandinka, others
Ethnic Makeup: 30% Temne; 30% Mende; 5% Krio; 35% others

Health
Life Expectancy at Birth: 44 years (male); 50 years (female)
Infant Mortality Rate (Ratio): 139/1,000
Average Caloric Intake: 85% of FAO minimum
Physicians Available (Ratio): 1/13,150

Religions
60% traditional indigenous; 30% Muslim; 10% Christian

Education
Adult Literacy Rate: 21%

COMMUNICATION

Telephones: 23,650
Newspapers: 1

FOURAH BAY COLLEGE

Fourah Bay College, an important educational institution for all of West Africa, was founded in Sierra Leone in 1814 as a Christian school. By 1827, it was a training institution for teachers and missionaries, and in 1876, it was affiliated with the University of Durham in Great Britain. As the only option for higher education on the African continent before 1918, Fourah Bay College trained many early nationalists and coastal elites during the colonial period. These graduates formed a significant network of Western-educated African leaders throughout West Africa.

TRANSPORTATION

Highways—Kilometers (Miles): 7,400 (4,617)
Railroads—Kilometers (Miles): 84 (52)
Usable Airfields: 11

GOVERNMENT

Type: military rule
Independence Date: April 27, 1961
Head of State: President Ahmad Tejan Kabbah
Political Parties: status unknown since coup of April 29, 1992
Suffrage: universal at 18

MILITARY

Number of Armed Forces: 6,200
Military Expenditures (% of Central Government Expenditures): 2.6%
Current Hostilities: none

ECONOMY

Currency ($ U.S. Equivalent): 618 leones = $1
Per Capita Income/GDP: $1,000/$4.5 billion
Inflation Rate: more than 22%
Natural Resources: diamonds; bauxite; gold; chromite; iron ore
Agriculture: coffee; cocoa; ginger; rice; piassava
Industry: mining; beverages; cigarettes; construction materials

FOREIGN TRADE

Exports: $149 million
Imports: $149 million

Early inhabitants arrive from Africa's interior 1400–1750	Settlement by people from the New World and recaptured slave ships 1787	Sierra Leone is a Crown colony 1801	Mende peoples unsuccessfully resist the British in the Hut Tax War 1898	Independence 1961	The new Constitution makes Sierra Leone a one-party state 1978	President Siaka Stevens steps down; Joseph Momoh, the sole candidate, is elected 1985

1990s

Debt-servicing cost mounts; SAP is introduced

Liberian rebels destabilize Sierra Leone; Momoh is overthrown in a coup

Ahmed Kabbah wins a contested election; in May 1997 rebel soldiers staged coup to oust Kabbah; fighting continues

SIERRA LEONE

In February–March 1996, against popular expectations, Sierra Leoneans went to the polls to elect a new government, headed by Ahmed Tejan Kabbah. Despite a pre-election coup and violent attempts to intimidate voters by groups allegedly associated with both the Sierra Leone military and rebel Revolutionary United Front (RUF), observers declared the election result to be a fair reflection of the popular will. In April 1996, Kabbah met with the RUF leader Foday Sankoh, giving hope that a peaceful settlement may be possible, ending years of political turmoil.

Sierra Leone's period of political instability began in April 1992, when Captain Valentine Strasser announced the overthrow of the long-governing All People's Congress (APC). The coup was initially welcomed, as the APC governments of the deposed president Joseph Momoh and his predecessor Siaka Stevens had been renowned for their institutionalized corruption and economic incompetence.

But, disillusionment grew as the Strasser-led National Provisional Ruling Council postponed holding multiparty elections while sinking into its own pattern of corruption. The emergence of the RUF insurgency brought further misery, with both the rebels and army being accused of atrocities.

Sierra Leone is the product of a unique colonial history. Its capital city, Freetown, was founded by waves of black settlers who were brought there by the British. The first to arrive were the so-called Black Poor, a group of 400 people sent from England in 1787. Shortly thereafter, former slaves from Jamaica and Nova Scotia

arrived. The latter group had gained their freedom by fighting with the British, against their American masters, in the U.S. War of Independence. About 40,000 Africans who were liberated by the British and others from slave ships captured along the West African coast were also settled in Freetown and the surrounding areas in the first half of the nineteenth century. The descendants of Sierra Leone's various black settlers blended African and British ways into a distinctive *Krio,* or Creole, culture. Besides speaking English, they developed their own Krio language, which has become the nation's lingua franca. Today, the Krio make up only about 5 percent of Sierra Leone's multiethnic population.

As more people were given the vote in the 1950s, the indigenous communities ended Krio domination in local politics. The first party to win broad national support was the Sierra Leone People's Party (SLPP), under Sir Milton Margai, which led the country to independence in 1961. During the 1967 national elections, the SLPP was narrowly defeated by Stevens' APC. From 1968 to 1985, Stevens presided over a steady erosion of Sierra Leone's economy and civil society.

In 1978, the APC, through a blatantly rigged referendum, elevated itself as the sole political party. Elections thereafter became meaningless. In 1985, Stevens, then 80 years old, stepped down in favor of his chosen successor, Major General Momoh, whose promotion to the presidency underscored the military's stake in the regime.

The APC's increasingly authoritarian control coincided with the country's economic decline. Although rich in its human as well as natural resources at inde-

pendence, today Sierra Leone is one of the world's poorest countries. Revenues from diamonds, which formed the basis for prosperity during the 1950s, and gold have steadily fallen due to the depletion of old diggings and massive smuggling.

The two thirds of Sierra Leone's labor force employed in agriculture have suffered the most from the nation's faltering economy. Poor producer prices, coupled with an international slump in demand for cocoa and robusta coffee, have cut into rural incomes. Momoh's promise to improve producer prices as part of a "green-revolution" program was largely unfulfilled. Like its minerals, much of Sierra Leone's agricultural production has been smuggled out of the country. In 1989, the cost of servicing Sierra Leone's foreign debt was estimated to have amounted to 130 percent of the total value of its exports. This grim figure led to the introduction of an International Monetary Fund–supported Structural Adjustment Program (SAP), whose austerity measures have made life even more difficult for urban dwellers. Like the previous military regime, the newly elected government will face difficulties in continuing with SAP. It will also be challenged in its attempts to reach a final settlement with the RUF, which is currently maintaining an uneasy cease-fire.

DEVELOPMENT

The recently relaunched Bumbuna hydroelectric project should reduce Sierra Leone's dependence on foreign oil, which has accounted for nearly a third of its imports. In response to threats of boycotting, the country's Lungi International Airport was upgraded. Inflation and unemployment are taking a severe toll on the country's people.

FREEDOM

Human rights in Sierra Leone have been severely compromised by the Civil War, which has reduced hundreds of thousands of its citizens to refugee status both inside and outside the country.

HEALTH/WELFARE

Life expectancy for both males and females in Sierra Leone is only in the 40s, while the infant mortality rate, 139 per 1,000, remains appalling. In 1990, hundreds, possibly thousands, of Sierra Leone children were reported to have been exported to Lebanon on what amounted to slave contracts.

ACHIEVEMENTS

The Sande Society, a women's organization that trains young Mende women for adult responsibilities, has contributed positively to life in Sierra Leone. Beautifully carved wooden helmet masks are worn by women leaders in the society's rituals. Ninety-five percent of Mende women join the society.

Togo (Republic of Togo)

GEOGRAPHY

Area in Square Kilometers (Miles):
56,600 (21,853) (slightly smaller than
West Virginia)
Capital (Population): Lomé (513,000)
Climate: tropical

PEOPLE

Population

Total: 4,570,500
Annual Growth Rate: 3.6%
Rural/Urban Population Ratio: 70/30
Major Languages: French; Ewe;
Mina; Dagomba; Kabye
Ethnic Makeup: Ewe; Mina; Kabye;
many others

Health

Life Expectancy at Birth: 55 years
(male); 60 years (female)
Infant Mortality Rate (Ratio):
86.5/1,000
Average Caloric Intake: 92% of FAO
minimum
Physicians Available (Ratio): 1/11,270

Religions

70% traditional indigenous; 20%
Christian; 10% Muslim

Education

Adult Literacy Rate: 43%

COMMUNICATION

Telephones: 19,616
Newspapers: 1

TRANSPORTATION

Highways—Kilometers (Miles): 6,462
(4,032)
Railroads—Kilometers (Miles): 532
(352)
Usable Airfields: 9

GOVERNMENT

Type: republic under transition to
democratic multiparty rule
Independence Date: April 27, 1960
Head of State/Government: President
Gnassingbé Eyadéma; Prime Minister
Kwassi Klutse
Political Parties: Rally of the
Togolese People; Coordination des
Forces Nouvelles; Togolese Union for
Democracy; Action Committee for
Renewal; Union for Democracy and
Solidarity; Pan-African
Sociodemocrats Group (an alliance of
three radical parties); Union of
Forces for Change
Suffrage: universal for adults

MILITARY

Number of Armed Forces: 6,950
*Military Expenditures (% of Central
Government Expenditures):* 2.9%
Current Hostilities: internal civil
unrest

ECONOMY

Currency ($ U.S. Equivalent): 529.43
CFA francs = $1
Per Capita Income/GDP: $800/$3.3
billion
Inflation Rate: 0.5%
Natural Resources: phosphates;
limestone; marble
Agriculture: yams; manioc; millet;
sorghum; cocoa; coffee; rice
Industry: phosphates; textiles;
agricultural products; tourism

FOREIGN TRADE

Exports: $221 million
Imports: $292 million

"THE GUIDE"

For years, President Gnassingbé Eyadéma has tried to make himself the focus of a cult of personality in Togo. His public picture—sometimes enhanced with angel wings—have been omnipresent as state icons. Official publications, including a comic book, have further extolled his supposedly heroic accomplishments as "The Guide"—"accomplishments" that once included taking personal credit for the murder of his predecessor. And a failed assassination attempt against Eyadéma was annually commemorated as "the Feast of Victory Over Forces of Evil." Until recently, Eyadéma and his foreign backers justified his personal rule as a necessary burden to encourage national unity among Togo's more than 40 ethnic groups. But the dictator has made sure that his fellow Kabye account for up to 90 percent of the country's military and security forces.

TOGO

In the 1990s, Togo has become a prime example of the fragility of prodemocracy forces in the face of determined resistance by a ruling clique with a strong ethnic support base. Togo's army set a sad regional precedent in 1963 by assassinating the nation's first president, Sylvanus Olympio. After a subsequent period of instability, power was seized by Gnassingbé Eyadéma. In 1969, Eyadéma institutionalized his increasingly dictatorial regime as a one-party state. All Togolese have been required to belong to his Coalition of the Togolese People (RPT). But in 1991, faced with mass prodemocracy demonstrations in Lomé, the capital city, Eyadéma acquiesced to opposition calls for a National Conference that would end the RPT's monopoly of power. Since then, Eyadéma has survived Togo's turbulent return to multiparty politics with characteristic ruthlessness, skillfully taking advantage of the weakness of his divided opponents.

DEMOCRACY VS. DICTATORSHIP

Meeting in July–August 1991, the National Conference turned into a public trial of the abuses of the ruling regime. Resisting the president's attempts to dissolve it, the Conference appointed Kokou Koffigoh as the head of an interim government, charged with preparing the country for multiparty elections. The RPT was to be disbanded, and Eyadéma himself was barred from standing in for reelection.

In November–December 1991, however, soldiers loyal to Eyadéma launched a bloody attack on Koffigoh's residence. The French, whose troops had intervened in the past to keep Eyadéma in power, refused Koffigoh's plea for help. Instead, the coup attempt ended with the now-almost-irrelevant Koffigoh and Eyadéma agreeing to maintain their uneasy cohabitation. Elections were now to include the RPT. Despite the "compromise," there was an upsurge in political violence in 1992, which included the May shooting of Gilchrist Olympio (the son of Sylvanus) and other Eyadéma opponents. In September, "rebel" soldiers once more held the government hostage.

A January 1993 massacre of the prodemocracy demonstrators pushed the country even further to the brink. Some 300,000 southern Togolese, mostly Ewe speakers, fled the country, fearing "ethnic cleansing" by the largely northern, Kabyespeaking army. In 1993–1994, exiled anti-Eyadéma militants—many of whom coalesced as the Front of the National

Committee for the Liberation of the Togolese People (FNCL)—began to fight back. The army chief of staff was among those killed during a daring raid on the main military headquarters in Lomé, in which grenades were also thrown into Eyadéma's bedroom.

In July 1993, Eyadéma and his more moderate opponents signed a peace accord in Burkina Faso, pledging renewed movement toward election. A month later, however, the opposition boycotted a snap presidential poll. Thereafter, Eyadéma gave ground, agreeing to internationally supervised legislative elections in February 1994. After two rounds of voting, amid escalating violence, Eyadéma's RPT and the main opposition—Action Committee for Renewal (CAR), led by Yaovi Agboyibor—each controlled about 35

seats in the 75-seat Assembly. (The situation was clouded by judicial reviews of the results in five constituencies). The balance of power rested with former Organization of African unit secretary general Edem Kodjo's Togo Union for Democracy (UTD), which had entered the election allied with CAR. But in May, Kodjo became prime minister, with Eyadéma's backing. The failure of the moderate opposition to capitalize on its apparent victory in undoubtedly flawed elections has strengthened the determination of the militants to carry on by other means.

STRUCTURAL ADJUSTMENT

Togo's political crisis has taken place against a backdrop of economic restructuring. In 1979, Togo adopted an economic-

(United Nations photo by Anthony Fisher)

The water that these children are drawing is not universally available in Togo. While food production in Togo is officially said to be adequate, outside observers contend that the drought-prone north is uncomfortably reliant on the more agriculturally productive southern areas.

Germany occupies Togo **1884**	Togo is mandated to the United Kingdom and France by the League of Nations following Germany's defeat in World War I **1919**	UN plebiscites result in the independence of French Togo and incorporation of British Togo into Ghana **1956–1957**	Independence is achieved **1960**	Murder of President Sylvanus Olympio; a new civilian government is organized after the coup **1963**	The coup of Colonel Etienne Eyadéma, now President Gnassingbé Eyadéma **1967**	The Coalition of the Togolese People (RPT) becomes the only legal party in Togo **1969**

1990s

Prodemocracy demonstrations lead to interim government and the promise of multiparty elections

Eyadéma survives escalating violence and controversial elections

recovery strategy that many consider to have been a forerunner of other Structural Adjustment Programs (SAPs) introduced throughout most of the rest of Africa. Faced with mounting debts as a result of falling export revenue, the government began to loosen the state's grip over the local economy. Since 1982 a more rigorous International Monetary Fund/World Bank–supported program of privatization and other market-oriented reforms has been pursued. Given this chronology, Togo's economic prospects have become a focus of attention for those looking for lessons about the possible effects of SAPs elsewhere. Both proponents and opponents of SAP have grounds for debate.

Supporters of Togo's SAP point out that, since 1985, the country has enjoyed an average growth in gross domestic product of 3.3 percent per year. While this statistic is an improvement over the 1.7 percent rate recorded between 1973 and 1980, however, it is well below the 7.2 percent growth that prevailed from 1965 to 1972. During the late 1980s, there was also a rise in private consumption, 7.6 percent per year, and a drop in inflation, from about 13 percent in 1980 to an estimated 2 percent in 1989. In 1996, a still low inflation rate (0.5 percent) was estimated.

The livelihoods of certain segments of the Togolese population have also materially improved during the past decade. Beneficiaries include some of the more than two thirds of the workforce employed in agriculture. Encouraged by increased official purchase prices, cash-crop farmers have expanded their outputs of cotton and coffee. This is especially true in the case of cotton production, which tripled between 1983 and 1989. Nearly half the nation's small farmers now grow the crop.

Balanced against the growth of cotton has been a decline in cocoa, which emerged as the country's principal cash crop under colonialism. Despite better producer prices during the mid-1980s, output fell as a result of past decisions not to plant new trees. Given the continuing uncertainty of cocoa prices, this earlier shift may prove to have been opportune. The long-term prospects of coffee are also in doubt, due to a growing global preference for the arabica beans of Latin America over the robusta beans that thrive throughout much of West Africa. As a result, the government had to reverse course in 1988, drastically reducing its prices for both coffee and cocoa, a move that it hopes will prove to be only temporary.

Eyadéma's regime has claimed great success in food production, but its critics have long countered official reports of food self-sufficiency by citing the importation of large quantities of rice, a decline in food production in the cotton-growing regions, and widespread childhood malnutrition. The country's food situation is complicated by an imbalance between the drought-prone northern areas and the more productive south. In 1992, famine threatened 250,000 Togolese, mostly northerners.

There have been improvements in transport and telecommunications. The national highway system, largely built by the European Development Fund, has allowed the port of Lomé to develop as a transshipment center for exports from neighboring states as well as Togo's interior. At the same time, there has been modest progress in cutting the budget deficit. But it

is in precisely this area that the cost of Togo's SAP is most apparent. Public expenditure in health and education declined by about 50 percent between 1982 and 1985. Whereas school enrollment rose from 40 percent to more than 70 percent during the 1970s, it has slipped back below 60 percent in recent years.

The ultimate justification for SAP has been a desire to attract overseas capital investment. In addition to sweeping privatization, a Free Trade Zone has been established. But overseas investment in Togo has always been modest. There have also been complaints that many foreign investors have simply bought former state industries on the cheap rather than starting up new enterprises. Furthermore, privatization and austerity measures are blamed for unemployment and wage cuts among urban workers. One third of the state-divested enterprises have been liquidated.

Whatever the long-term merits of SAP, it is clear that it has so far resulted in neither a clear pattern of sustainable growth nor an improved standard of living for most Togolese. For the foreseeable future, the health of Togo's economy will continue to be tied to export earnings derived from three commodities—phosphates, coffee, and cocoa—whose price fluctuations have been responsible for the nation's previous cycles of boom and bust.

DEVELOPMENT

Much hope for the future of Togo is riding on the recently created Free Trade Zone at Lomé. Firms within the zone are promised a 10-year tax holiday if they export at least three quarters of their output. The project is backed by the U.S. Overseas Private Investment Corporation.

FREEDOM

Human rights in Togo continue to be violated by pro-Eyadéma security forces. Since 1992, there has been a serious rise in political killings and interethnic violence, leading to major population displacements.

HEALTH/WELFARE

The nation's health service has declined as a result of austerity measures. Juvenile mortality is 15%. Self-induced abortion now causes 17% of the deaths among Togolese women of child-bearing age. School attendance has dropped in recent years.

ACHIEVEMENTS

The name of Togo's capital, Lomé, is well known in international circles for its association with the Lomé Convention, a periodically renegotiated accord through which products from various African, Caribbean, and Pacific countries are given favorable access to European markets.

Central Africa

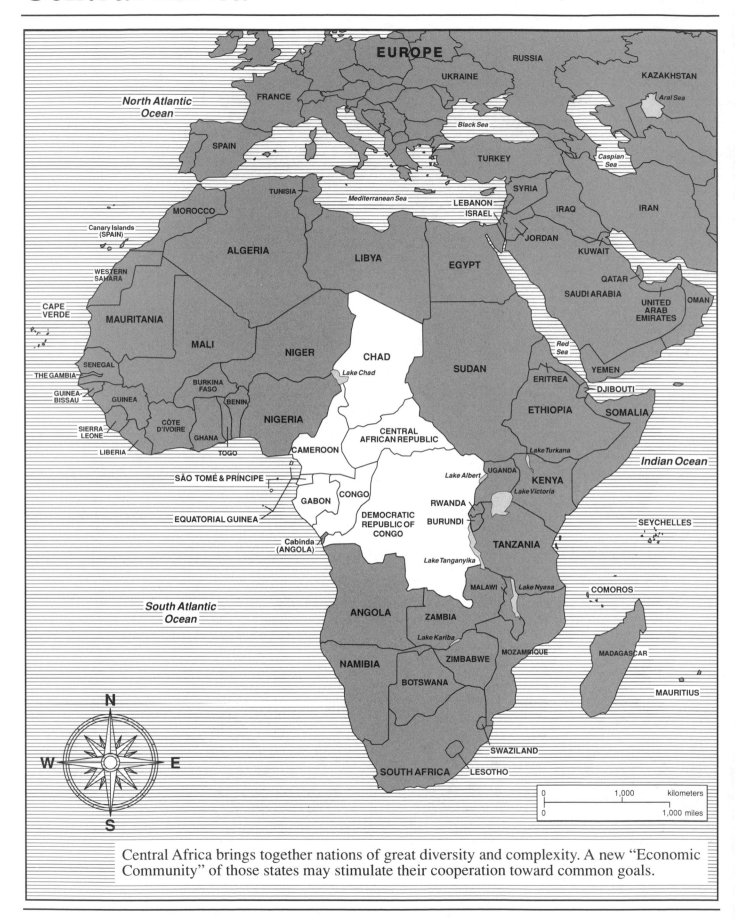

Central Africa brings together nations of great diversity and complexity. A new "Economic Community" of those states may stimulate their cooperation toward common goals.

Central Africa: Possibilities for Cooperation

The Central African region, as defined in this book, brings together countries that have not shared a common past, nor do they necessarily seem destined for a common future. Cameroon, Chad, Central African Republic, Congo, Democratic Republic of Congo (formerly Zaire), Equatorial Guinea, Gabon, and São Tomé and Príncipe are not always grouped together as one region. Indeed, users of this volume who are familiar with the continent may also associate the label "Central Africa" with other states such as Angola and Zambia rather than with some of the states mentioned here. Geographically, Chad is more closely associated with the Sahelian nations of West Africa than with the heavily forested regions of Central Africa to its south. Similarly, southern former Zaire has long-standing cultural and economic links with Angola and Zambia, which in this text are associated with the states of Southern Africa, largely because of their political involvements.

Yet, despite its seemingly arbitrary nature, the eight states that are designated here as belonging to Central Africa have much in common. French is a predominant language in all the states except Equatorial Guinea and São Tomé and Príncipe. All the states except São Tomé and Príncipe and former Zaire share a common currency, the CFA franc. And while Chad's current economic prospects appear to be exceptionally poor, the natural wealth found throughout the rest of Central Africa makes the region as a whole one of enormous potential. Finally, in the postcolonial era, all the Central African governments have made some progress in better realizing their developmental possibilities through greater regional cooperation.

The countries of Central Africa incorporate a variety of peoples and cultures, resources, environments, systems of government, and national goals. Most of the modern nations overlay both societies that were village-based and localized and societies that were once part of extensive state formations. Islam has had little influence in the region, outside of Chad and in northern Cameroon. In most areas, Christianity coexists with indigenous systems of belief.

Sophisticated wooden sculptures are one of the great cultural achievements associated with most Central African societies. To many people, the carvings are only material manifestations of the spiritual potential of complex local cosmologies. However, the art forms are myriad and distinctive, and their diversity is as striking as the common features that they share.

On a surface level, the postcolonial political orders of Central Africa have ranged from the conservative regimes in Gabon and former Zaire to the Marxist-Leninist states of Congo or São Tomé and Príncipe. More fundamentally, all the states have fallen under the rule of unelected autocracies, whose continued existence has been dependent on military force, sometimes external. But in recent years, this authoritarian status quo has begun to collapse. In Congo, Central African Republic, and São Tomé and Príncipe, the introduction of multiparty democracy has resulted in the peaceful

(United Nations photo)

In Africa, cooperative work groups such as the one pictured above often take on jobs that would be done by machinery in industrialized countries.

election of new governments. Opposition politics has also been legalized in the region's other states, though their old regimes are still tenuously holding on to power.

GEOGRAPHIC DISTINCTIVENESS

All the states of the Central African region except Chad encompass equatorial rain forests. Citizens who live in these regions must cope with a climate that is hot and moist while facing the challenges of utilizing (and, in some cases, clearing) the great equatorial forests. The problems of living in these heavily forested areas account, in part, for the relatively low, albeit growing, population densities of most of the states. The difficulty of establishing roads and railroads impedes communication and thus economic development. The peoples of the rain-forest areas tend to cluster along riverbanks

(Photo from World Bank by Alain Prott)

In Central Africa, the rain forests are a rich source of lumber. All of the countries in the region, except for Chad and São Tomé and Príncipe, export lumber and other forest products. Environmentalists are warning that the forests are being depleted at an alarming rate.

and existing rail lines. In modern times, largely because of the extensive development of minerals, many inhabitants have moved to the cities, accounting for a comparatively high urban population in all the states.

Central Africa's rivers have long been its lifelines. The watershed in Cameroon between the Niger and Zaire Rivers provides a natural divide between the West and Central African regions. The Congo, or Zaire, River is the largest in the region, but the Oubangi, Chari, Ogooue, and other rivers are important also for the communication and trading opportunities they offer. The rivers flow to the Atlantic Ocean, a fact that has encouraged the orientation of Central Africa's external trade toward Europe and the Americas.

Many of the countries of the region have similar sources of wealth. The rivers are capable of generating enormous amounts of hydroelectric power. The rain forests are also rich in lumber, which is a major export of every country except Chad and São Tomé and Príncipe. Other forest products, such as rubber and palm oil, are widely marketed. Yet lumbering and clearing activities for agriculture have created worldwide concern about the depletion of the rain forests. As a result, in recent years, there have been some organized boycotts in Europe of the region's hardwood exports, although far more trees are felled to process plywood.

As one might expect, Central Africa as a whole is one of the areas least affected by the drought conditions that peri-

odically plague much of Africa. Nevertheless, serious drought is a well-known visitor in Chad, Central African Republic, and the northern regions of Cameroon, where it contributes to local food shortages. Savanna lands are found to the north and the south (in southern former Zaire) of the forests. Whereas rain forests have often inhibited travel, the savannas have long been transitional areas, great avenues of migration linking the regions of Africa, while providing agricultural and pastoral opportunities for their residents.

Besides the products of the forest, the Central African countries share other resources. Cameroon, Congo, and Gabon derive considerable revenues from their petroleum reserves. Other important minerals include diamonds, copper, gold, manganese, and uranium. The processes involved in the exploitation of these commodities, as well as the demand for them in the world market, are issues of common concern among the producing nations. Many of the states also share an interest in exported cash crops such as coffee, cocoa, and cotton, whose international prices are subject to sharp fluctuations. The similarity of their environments and products provides an economic incentive for Central African cooperation.

LINKS TO FRANCE

Many of the different ethnic groups in Central Africa overlap national boundaries. Examples include the Fang, who are

(WFP photo by F. Mattioli)

Central Africa is generally not affected by drought, but Chad, Central African Republic, and certain parts of Cameroon have all faced food shortages due to the lack of rain. In these countries, care must be taken to maximize food supplies. These women are winnowing sesame seeds near the town of N'Djamena in Chad to ensure a seed bank for the next planting season.

found in Cameroon, Equatorial Guinea, and Gabon; the Bateke of Congo and Gabon; and the Kongo, who are concentrated in Angola as well as in Congo and former Zaire. Such cross-border ethnic ties are less important as sources of regional unity than the European colonial systems that the countries inherited. While Equatorial Guinea was controlled by Spain, São Tomé and Príncipe by Portugal, and Zaire by Belgium, the predominant external power in the region remains France. Central African Republic, Chad, Congo, and Gabon were all once part of French Equatorial Africa. Most of Cameroon was also governed by the French, who were awarded the bulk of the former German colony of the Kamerun as a "trust territory" in the aftermath of World War I. French administration provided the five states with similar colonial experiences.

Early colonial development in the former French colonies and Zaire were affected by European concessions companies,

institutions that were sold extensive rights (often 99-year leases granting political as well as economic powers) to exploit such local products as ivory and rubber. At the beginning of the twentieth century, just 41 companies controlled 70 percent of the territory of contemporary Central African Republic, Congo, and Gabon. Mining operations as well as large plantations were established that often relied on forced labor. Individual production by Africans was also encouraged, often through coercion rather than economic incentives. While the colonial companies encouraged production and trade, they did little to aid the growth of infrastructure or long-term development. Only in Zaire was industry promoted to any great extent.

In general, French colonial rule, along with that of the Belgians, Portuguese, and Spanish and the activities of the companies, offered few opportunities for Africans to gain training and education. There was also little encouragement of local entrepreneurship. An important exception to this pattern was the policies pursued by Felix Eboue, a black man from French Guiana (in South America) who served as a senior administrator in the Free French administration of French Equatorial Africa during the 1940s. Eboue increased opportunities for the urban elite in Central African Republic, Congo, and Gabon. He also played an important role in the Brazzaville Conference of 1944, which, recognizing the important role that the people of the French colonies had played in World War II, abolished forced labor and granted citizenship to all. Yet political progress toward self-government was uneven. Because of the lack of local labor development, there were too few people at independence who were qualified to shoulder the bureaucratic and administrative tasks of the regimes that took power. People who could handle the economic institutions for the countries' benefit were equally scarce. And in any case, the nations' economies remained for the most part securely in outside—largely French—hands.

The Spanish on the Equatorial Guinea island of Fernando Po and the Portuguese of São Tomé and Príncipe also profited from the exploitation of forced labor. Political opportunities in these territories were even more limited than on the African mainland. Neither country gained independence until fairly recently: Equatorial Guinea in 1968, São Tomé and Príncipe in 1975.

In the years since independence, most of the countries of Central Africa have been influenced, pressured, and supported by France and the other former colonial powers. French firms in Central African Republic, Congo, and Gabon continue to dominate the exploitation of local resources. Most of these companies are only slightly encumbered by the regulations of the independent states in which they operate, and all are geared toward European markets and needs. Financial institutions are generally branches of French institutions, and all the former French colonies as well as Equatorial Guinea are members of the Central African Franc Zone. French expatriates occupy senior positions in local civil service establishments and in companies; many more of them are resident in the region today than was true 30 years ago. In addition, French troops are stationed in Central African Republic, Chad, and Gabon, regimes that owe their very existence to past French military interventions. Besides being a major trading partner, France has contributed significantly to the budgets of its former possessions, especially the poorer states of Central African Republic and Chad.

Despite having been under Belgian rule, former Zaire is an active member of the Francophonic bloc in Africa. In 1977, French troops put down a rebellion in southeastern Zaire. Zaire, in turn, has sent its troops to serve beside those of France in Chad and Togo. Since playing a role in the 1979 coup that brought the current regime to power, France has also had a predominant influence in Equatorial Guinea.

(World Bank/CIRC photo by Alain Prott)

Regional cooperation will be necessary to utilize the natural resources of Central African countries without destroying their fragile environment.

EFFORTS AT COOPERATION

Although many Africans in Central Africa recognize that closer links among their countries would be beneficial, there have been fewer initiatives toward political unity or economic integration in this region than in East, West, or Southern Africa. In the years before independence, Barthelemy Boganda, of what is now Central African Republic, espoused and publicized the idea of a "United States of Latin Africa," which was to include contemporary Angola and Zaire as well as the territories of French Equatorial Africa, but he was frustrated by Paris as well as by local politicians. When France offered independence to its colonies in 1960, soon after Boganda's death, the possibility of forming a federation was discussed. But Gabon, which was wealthier than the other countries, declined to participate. Central African Republic, Chad, and Congo drafted an agreement that would have created a federal legislature and executive branch governing all three countries, but local jealousies defeated this plan.

There have been some formal efforts at economic integration among the former French states. The Customs and Eco-

(World Bank photo by Ivan Albert Andrews)

This palm-oil processing mill was financed by the World Bank as part of a development project in Cameroon.

nomic Union of the Central African States (UDEAC) was established in 1964, but its membership has been unstable. Chad and Central African Republic withdrew to join Zaire in an alternate organization. (Central African Republic later returned, bringing the number of members to six.) The East and Central African states together planned an "Economic Community" in 1967, but it never materialized.

Only in recent years have there been new and hopeful signs of progress toward greater economic cooperation. Urged on by the United Nations Economic Commission on Africa, and with the stimulus of the 1980 Lagos Plan of Action, representatives of the Central African states met in 1982 to prepare for a new economic grouping. In 1983, all the Central African states as well as Rwanda and Burundi in East Africa signed a treaty establishing the Economic Community of Central African States (ECCA) to promote economic and industrial cooperation. Some have criticized ECCA as a duplicate of UDEAC, but its goals are broader than a customs union

(though it does urge cooperation in that area). Members hoped that the union would stimulate industrial activity, increase markets, and reduce the dependence on France and other countries for trade and capital. But, with dues often unpaid and meetings postponed, ECCA has so far failed to meet its potential.

Central African states, while sharing a rich environment, have suffered more than other regions in Africa from the neglect and exploitation of their former colonial powers. They have not found common ways to develop mineral and forest resources and to deal with outside companies. Little implementation has resulted from former unions. As a Swahili proverb says, "The toughness of the hoe is tested in the garden." Many hope that ECCA will lead to a pragmatic Central African market, thus fulfilling the need for a harmonization of trade and industrial policies and, perhaps, becoming a building block for greater continental as well as Central African unity.

Cameroon (United Republic of Cameroon)

GEOGRAPHY

Area in Square Kilometers (Miles):
475,400 (183,568) (somewhat larger than California)
Capital (Population): Yaoundé (649,000)
Climate: tropical to semiarid

PEOPLE

Population

Total: 14,262,000
Annual Growth Rate: 2.92%
Rural/Urban Population Ratio: 60/41
Major Languages: English; French; Fulde; Ewondo; Duala; Bamelke; Bassa; Bali; others
Ethnic Makeup: 31% Cameroonian Highlander; 19% Equatorial Bantu; 11% Kirdi; 10% Fulani; 29% others

Health

Life Expectancy at Birth: 55 years (male); 60 years (female)
Infant Mortality Rate (Ratio): 75.4/1,000
Average Caloric Intake: 106% of FAO minimum
Physicians Available (Ratio): 1/11,848

THE KORUP FOREST

"Do not call the forest that shelters you a jungle" is an African proverb. The primary rain forests in Cameroon and other parts of Central Africa are the homes of plants and animals that have developed in this environment over thousands of years and that serve humanity.

Korup is one Cameroon rain forest that is to be designated a national park. A recent survey discovered more than 42,000 trees and climbers in Korup, including 17 tree species never described before. An international campaign has been launched to preserve such rain forests, under the auspices of the World Wildlife Fund and the International Union for the Conservation of Nature and Natural Resources. Korup is the subject of a film that is being shown to raise funds for its preservation and that of other rain forests.

Religions

51% traditional indigenous; 33% Christian; 16% Muslim

Education

Adult Literacy Rate: 55%

COMMUNICATION

Telephones: 26,000
Newspapers: 1

TRANSPORTATION

Highways—Kilometers (Miles): 65,000 (40,560)
Railroads—Kilometers (Miles): 1,111 (693)
Usable Airfields: 60

GOVERNMENT

Type: republic
Independence Date: January 1, 1960
Head of State: President Paul Biya
Political Parties: Cameroon People's Democratic Movement; Union for National Democracy and Progress; Social Democratic Front; Cameroonian Democratic Union; Union of Cameroonian Populations; Movement for the Defence of the Republic
Suffrage: universal at 20

MILITARY

Number of Armed Forces: 23,600
Military Expenditures (% of Central Government Expenditures): 2.1%
Current Hostilities: border conflicts with Nigeria

ECONOMY

Currency ($ U.S. Equivalent): 529.43 CFA francs = $1
Per Capita Income/GDP: $1,200/$15.7 billion
Inflation Rate: −0.8%
Natural Resources: timber; oil; bauxite; iron ore; rubber
Agriculture: coffee; cocoa; food crops; cotton; bananas; peanuts; tobacco; tea
Industry: small manufacturing; consumer goods; aluminum

FOREIGN TRADE

Exports: $1.6 billion
Imports: $1.9 billion

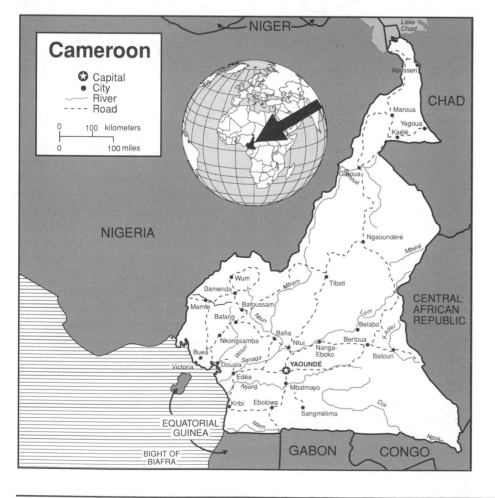

CAMEROON

In 1994, Cameroonians were united by at least two things: support for their football team's second World Cup appearance and condemnation for neighboring Nigeria's occupation of the disputed Bakassi Peninsula. But politically, Cameroonians remain deeply divided. In March 1992, the country held its first multiparty elections in a quarter century, ending the ruling People's Democratic Party (CPDM) monopoly of power. The results gave the CPDM a plurality of 88 out of 180 seats in the new National Assembly, allowing it to form a coalition government with the Movement for the Defense of the Republic (MDR), which won 6 seats. The Union for Progress and Democracy (UNDP) captured 68 seats, while the Union of the Cameroonian People (UPC) won 18.

But many have since rejected the legitimacy of the new government. Most of the opposition parties—most notably including the Social Democratic Front (SDF), the Democratic Union (CDU), and a faction of the UPC—boycotted the polls, allowing the CPDM to win numerous constituencies by default. The situation was aggravated in October 1992 when the incumbent CPDM president, Paul Biya, was declared the victor in a snap election accompanied by opposition allegations of vote-rigging. In March 1993, most of the opposition parties formed a new coalition. Under pressure from better-coordinated opposition, Biya agreed in June 1993 to revise the Constitution. But subsequent progress has been slow, and Cameroon's politics remains in turmoil.

Cameroon's fractious politics is a reflection of its diversity. In geographical terms, the land is divided between the tropical forests in the south, the drier savanna of the north-central region, and the mountainous country along its western border, which forms a natural division between West and Central Africa. In terms of religion, the country has many Christians, Muslims, and followers of indigenous belief systems. More than a dozen major languages, with numerous dialects, are spoken. The languages of southern Cameroon are linguistically classified Bantu. The "Bantu line" that runs across the country, roughly following the course of the Sanaga River, forms a boundary between the Bantu languages of Central, East, and Southern Africa and the non-Bantu tongues of North and West Africa. Many scholars believe that the roots of the Bantu language tree are buried in Cameroonian soil. Cameroon is also unique among the continental African states in sharing two European languages, English and French, as its official mediums. This circumstance is a product of the country's unique colonial heritage.

Three European powers have ruled over Cameroon. The Germans were the first. From 1884 to 1916, they laid the foundation of much of the country's communications infrastructure and, primarily through the establishment of European-run plantations, export agriculture. During World War I, the area was divided between the British and French, who subsequently ruled their respective zones as League of Nations (later the United Nations) mandates. French "Cameroun" included the eastern four fifths of the former German colony, while British "Cameroons" consisted of two narrow strips of territory that were administered as part of its Nigerian territory.

In the 1950s, Cameroonians in both the British and French zones began to agitate for unity and independence. At the core of their nationalist vision was the "Kamerun Idea," a belief that the period of German rule had given rise to a pan-Cameroonian identity. The largest and most radical of the nationalist movements in the French zone was the Union of the Cameroonian People, which turned to armed struggle. Between 1955 and 1963, when most of the UPC guerrillas had been defeated, some 10,000 to 15,000 people were killed. Most of the victims belonged to the Bamileke and Bassa ethnic groups

(United Nations photo by Shaw McCutcheon)

Cameroon has experienced political unrest in recent years as various factions have moved to establish a stable form of government. At the heart of this political turmoil is the need to raise the living standards of the population through an increase in agricultural production. These farmers with their cattle herds are one part of this movement.

The establishment of the German Kamerun Protectorate **1884**	The partition of Cameroon; separate British and French mandates are established under the League of Nations **1916**	The UPC is formed **1948**	The UPC is outlawed for launching revolts in the cities **1955**	The Independent Cameroon Republic is established with Ahmadou Ahidjo as the first president **1960**	The Cameroon Federal Republic reunites French Cameroon with British Cameroon after a UN-supervised referendum **1961**	The new Constitution creates a unitary state **1972**	Ahidjo resigns and is replaced by Paul Biya **1980s**	Lake Nyos releases lethal volcanic gases, killing an estimated 2,000 people

1990s

Nationwide agitation for a restoration of multiparty democracy

Biya retains presidency in elections, though the results are widely disputed

New clashes on the Bakassi Peninsula as the border dispute goes before the International Court of Justice

of southwestern Cameroon, which continues to be the core area of UPC support. (Some sources refer to the UPC uprising as the Bamileke Rebellion.)

To counter the UPC revolt, the French adopted a dual policy of repression against the guerrillas' supporters and the devolution of political power to local non-UPC politicians. Most of these "moderate" leaders, who enjoyed core followings in both the heavily Christianized southeast and the Muslim north, coalesced as the Cameroonian Union, whose leader was Ahmadou Ahidjo, a northerner. In pre-independence elections, Ahidjo's party won just 51 out of the 100 seats. Ahidjo thus led a divided, war-torn state to independence in 1960.

In 1961, the southern section of British Cameroons voted to join Ahidjo's republic. The northern section opted to remain part of Nigeria. The principal party in the south was the Kamerun National Democratic Party, whose leader, John Foncha, became the vice president of the Cameroon republic, while Ahidjo served as president. The former British and French zones initially maintained their separate local parliaments, but the increasingly authoritarian Ahidjo pushed for a unified form of government. In 1966, all of Cameroon's legal political groups were dissolved into Ahidjo's new Cameroon National Union (CNU), creating a de facto one-party state. Trade unions and other mass organizations were also brought under CNU control. In 1972, Ahidjo proposed the abolition of the federation and the creation of a constitution for a unified Cameroon. This was approved by a suspiciously lopsided vote of 3,217,058 to 158.

In 1982, Ahidjo, believing that his health was graver than was actually the case, suddenly resigned. His handpicked successor was Paul Biya. To the surprise of many, the heretofore self-effacing Biya quickly proved to be his own man. He brought young technocrats into the ministries and initially called for a more open and democratic society. But as he pressed forward, Biya came into increasing conflict with Ahidjo, who tried to reassert his authority as CNU chairperson. The ensuing power struggle took on overtones of an ethnic conflict between Biya's largely southern Christian supporters and Ahidjo's core following of northern Muslims. In 1983, Ahidjo lost and went into exile. The next year, he was tried and convicted, in absentia, for allegedly plotting Biya's overthrow.

In April 1984, only 2 months after the conviction, Ahidjo's supporters in the Presidential Guard attempted to overthrow Biya. The revolt was put down, but up to 1,000 people were killed. In the coup's aftermath, Biya combined repression with attempts to restructure the ruling apparatus. In 1985, the CNU was overhauled as the Cameroon People's Democratic Movement. However, President Biya became increasingly reliant on the support of his own Beti group.

An upsurge of prodemocracy agitation began in 1990. In March, the Social Democratic Front was formed in Bamenda, the main town of the Anglophonic west, over government objections. In May, as many as 40,000 people from the vicinity of Bamenda, out of a total population of about 100,000, attended an SDF rally. Government troops opened fire on school children returning from the demonstration. This action led to a wave of unrest, which spread to the capital city of Yaoundé. The government media tried to portray the SDF as a subversive movement of "English speakers," but it attracted significant support in Francophonic areas. Dozens of additional opposition groups, including the UNDP (which is loyal to the now deceased Ahidjo's legacy) and the long-underground UPC, joined forces with the SDF in calling for a transition government, a new constitution, and multiparty elections.

Throughout much of 1991, Cameroon's already depressed economy was further crippled by opposition mass action, dubbed the Ghost Town campaign. A series of concessions by Biya culminated in a November agreement between Biya and most of the opposition (the SDF being among the holdouts) to formulate a new constitution and prepare for elections. In this context, the government's decision to hold early elections (on March 1) was rejected by most of its opponents, although some reluctantly participated. The CPDM's subsequent failure to gain a majority of the vote, despite the partial opposition boycott and the CPDM's control of the election process, left the government weak.

DEVELOPMENT

The Cameroon Development Corporation coordinates more than half of the agricultural exports and, after the government, employs the most people. Cocoa and coffee comprise more than 50% of Cameroon's exports. Lower prices for these commodities have reduced the country's income.

FREEDOM

While Cameroon's human-rights record has improved since its return to multipartyism, political detentions and harassment continue. Amnesty International has drawn attention to the alleged starvation of detainees at the notorious Tchollire prison.

HEALTH/WELFARE

The *overall* literacy rate in Cameroon, about 76%, is among the highest in Africa. There exist, however, great divergences in regional figures. In addition to public schools, the government devotes a large proportion of its budget to subsidizing private schools.

ACHIEVEMENTS

The strong showing by Cameroon's national soccer team, the Indomitable Lions, in the 1990 and 1994 World Cup competitions is a source of pride for sports fans throughout Africa. Their success, along with the record numbers of medals won by African athletes in the 1988 and 1992 Olympics, is symbolic of the continent's coming of age in international sports competitions.

Central African Republic

GEOGRAPHY

Area in Square Kilometers (Miles):
622,436 (240,324) (slighty smaller than Texas)
Capital (Population): Bangui (452,000)
Climate: tropical to semiarid

PEOPLE

Population
Total: 3,274,400
Annual Growth Rate: 2.1%
Rural/Urban Population Ratio: 61/39
Major Languages: French; Sangho; Arabic; others
Ethnic Makeup: 27% Banda; 34% Baya; 21% Mandja; 10% Sara; 8% others

Health
Life Expectancy at Birth: 41 years (male); 44 years (female)
Infant Mortality Rate (Ratio): 136/1,000
Average Caloric Intake: 92% of FAO minimum
Physicians Available (Ratio): 1/18,660

Religions
24% traditional indigenous; 25% Protestant; 25% Roman Catholic; 15% Muslim; 11% others

Education
Adult Literacy Rate: 38%

COMMUNICATION
Telephones: 7,600
Newspapers: 2

THE BREAKUP OF FRENCH EQUATORIAL AFRICA

In 1959, as Central African Republic (C.A.R.) moved toward independence, Barthelemy Boganda, the leader of the territory's nationalist movement, did not share the sense of euphoria exhibited by many of his colleagues. To him, the French path to independence had become a trap. Where there once had been a united French Equatorial Africa (A.E.F.) there were now five separate states, each struggling toward its own nationhood. Boganda, as president of the Grand Council of the A.E.F., had led the struggle to transform the territory into a true Central African Republic. But in 1958, French president Charles de Gaulle overruled all objections in forcing the breakup of the A.E.F. Boganda believed that, thus balkanized, the Central African states would each be too weak to achieve true independence, but he still hoped that A.E.F. reunification might prove possible after independence.

TRANSPORTATION
Highways—Kilometers (Miles): 22,000 (13,728)
Railroads—Kilometers (Miles): none
Usable Airfields: 61

GOVERNMENT
Type: republic; under military rule
Independence Date: August 13, 1960
Head of State/Government: President Ange-Félix Patassé; Prime Minister Jean-Paul Ngopaude
Political Parties: Movement for the Liberation of the Central African People; Central African Democratic Assembly; Movement for Democracy and Development; others
Suffrage: universal at 21

MILITARY
Number of Armed Forces: 4,950
Military Expenditures (% of Central Government Expenditures): 2.3%
Current Hostilities: none

ECONOMY
Currency ($ U.S. Equivalent): 529.43 CFA francs = $1
Per Capita Income/GDP: $700/$2.2 billion
Inflation Rate: −40%
Natural Resources: diamonds; uranium; timber
Agriculture: coffee; cotton; peanuts; food crops; livestock
Industry: timber; textiles; soap; cigarettes; processed food; diamond mining

FOREIGN TRADE
Exports: $123.5 million
Imports: $165.1 million

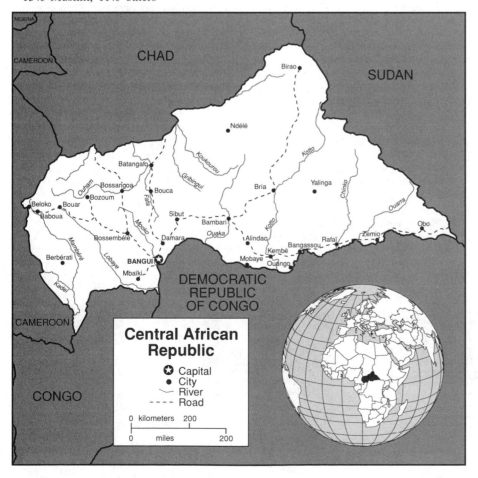

Central African Republic
⊗ Capital
● City
River
--- Road
0 kilometers 200
0 miles 200

Separate French administration of the Oubangui-Chàri colony is established
1904

Gold and diamonds are discovered
1912–1913

Barthelemy Boganda sets up MESAN, which gains wide support
1949

Boganda dies; David Dacko, his successor, becomes president at independence
1960

Jean-Bedel Bokassa takes power after the first general strike
1966

Bokassa declares himself emperor
1976

Bokassa is involved in the massacre of schoolchildren; Dacko is returned as head of state
1979

André Kolingba takes power from Dacko
1981

1990s

Bokassa returns to C.A.R. and is tried for murder, embezzlement, and other abuses; he is released in 1993

Ange-Félix Patassé wins the presidency in multiparty elections

Patassé requires French intervention to overcome an army mutiny

CENTRAL AFRICAN REPUBLIC

In April–May 1996, the French military rescued the government of Central African Republic (C.A.R.) president Ange-Félix Patassé from an army mutiny. The intervention, which left 43 dead and 238 wounded, underscored the fragile hold of Patassé's government, which came to power in a French-sponsored election in September 1993, after 3 decades of military dictatorship. Hopes that the transition from single-party military rule to multiparty civilian rule would be accompanied by economic progress in the C.A.R. have so far been unrealized.

Although it gained its independence from France in 1960, French political, economic, and military presence in C.A.R. has remained pervasive. At the same time, the country's resources—as well as French largess—have been dissipated. Yet with diamonds, timber, and a resilient peasantry, the country is better endowed than many of its neighbors. C.A.R.'s population has traditionally been divided between the so-called river peoples and savanna peoples, but most of the population as a whole are united by the Songo language. What the country has lacked is a leadership committed to national development rather than to internationally sanctioned waste.

The independence movement was led by Barthelemy Boganda, a former priest who, in 1949, founded the Popular Movement for the Social Evolution of Black Africa (MESAN). While Boganda was a pragmatist willing to use moderate means in his struggle, his vision was radical, for he hoped to unite French, Belgian, and Portuguese territories into an independent republic. His movement succeeded in gaining a local following among the peasantry as well as intellectuals. In 1958, Boganda led the territory to self-government, but he died in a mysterious plane crash just before independence.

Boganda's successors have failed to live up to his stature. At independence, the country was led by David Dacko, a nephew of Boganda's, who succeeded to the leadership of MESAN but also cultivated the political support of local French settlers who had seen Boganda as an agitator. Dacko's MESAN became the vehicle of the wealthy elite.

A general strike in December 1965 was followed by a military coup on New Year's Eve, which put Dacko's cousin, Army Commander Jean-Bedel Bokassa, in power. Dacko's overthrow was justified by the need to launch political and economic reforms. But more likely motives for the coup were French concern about Dacko's growing ties with China and Bokassa's own budding megalomania.

The country suffered greatly under Bokassa's eccentric rule. He was often portrayed, alongside Idi Amin of Uganda, as an archetype of African leadership at its worst. It was more the sensational nature—such as public torture and dismemberment of prisoners—rather than the scale of his brutality that captured headlines. In 1972, he made himself president-for-life. Unsatisfied with this position, he went a step further in 1976 and proclaimed himself emperor, in the image of his hero Napoleon Bonaparte. The $22 million spent on his coronation ceremony, which attracted widespread coverage in the global media, was underwritten by the French government.

In 1979, reports surfaced that Bokassa himself had participated in the beating to death of schoolchildren who had protested his decree that they purchase new uniforms bearing his portrait. The French government finally decided that its ally had become a liability. While Bokassa was away on a state visit to Libya, French paratroopers returned Dacko to power. In 1981, Dacko was once more toppled, in a coup that installed prime minister General André Kolingba. In 1985, Kolingba's provisional military regime was transformed into a one-party state. But in 1991, under a combination of local and French pressure, he agreed to the legalization of opposition parties.

Pressure for multiparty politics had increased as the government sank deeper into debt, despite financial intervention on the part of France, the World Bank, and the International Monetary Fund. Landlocked C.A.R.'s economy has long been constrained by high transport costs. But a perhaps greater burden has been the smuggling of its diamonds and other resources, including poached ivory, by high government officials.

DEVELOPMENT

C.A.R.'s timber industry has suffered from corruption and environmentally destructive forms of exploitation. However, the nation has considerable forestry potential, with dozens of commercially viable and renewable species.

FREEDOM

The human-rights situation in Central African Republic has steadily improved since the 1991 introduction of multiparty politics. Political prisoners have been released.

HEALTH/WELFARE

The literacy rate is very low in Central African Republic. Teacher training is currently being emphasized, especially for primary-school teachers.

ACHIEVEMENTS

Despite recurrent drought, a poor infrastructure, and inefficient official marketing, the farmers of Central African Republic have generally been able to meet most of the nation's basic food needs.

Chad (Republic of Chad)

GEOGRAPHY

Area in Square Kilometers (Miles):
1,284,634 (496,000) (four fifths the
size of Alaska)
Capital (Population): N'Djamena
(531,000)
Climate: arid to semiarid

PEOPLE

Population
Total: 6,977,000
Annual Growth Rate: 2.18%
Rural/Urban Population Ratio: 78/22
Major Languages: French; Arabic;
Fulde; Hausa; Kotoko; Kanembou;
Sara Maba; others
Ethnic Makeup: 200 distinct groups

Health
Life Expectancy at Birth: 40 years
(male); 42 years (female)
Infant Mortality Rate (Ratio):
129.7/1,000
Average Caloric Intake: 72% of FAO
minimum
Physicians Available (Ratio): n/a

Religions
50% Muslim; 25% Christian; 25%
traditional indigenous

Education
Adult Literacy Rate: 30%

COMMUNICATION

Telephones: 5,325
Newspapers: 4

THE KNIGHTS OF KANEM-BORNU

Between the ninth and nineteenth centuries A.D., much of modern Chad prospered under the rulers of Kanem and Bornu. The sultans of these two states, which were usually united, established great trading empires, linking the Mediterranean coast of North Africa with the Central African interior. As was the case in medieval Europe and Japan, the leading element in the sultans' armies was heavily armored cavalry. Despite the local introduction of firearms by the sixteenth century, the tradition of armored knighthood survived until the arrival of the French colonialists. Kanem–Bornu armored costume is distinctive, being designed for the hot Sahelien climate.

TRANSPORTATION

Highways—Kilometers (Miles):
31,322 (19,544)
Railroads—Kilometers (Miles): none
Usable Airfields: 66

GOVERNMENT

Type: republic
Independence Date: August 11, 1960
Head of State/Government: President
Idriss Déby; Prime Minister Koibla
Djimasta
Political Parties: Patriotic Salvation
Movement
Suffrage: n/a

MILITARY

Number of Armed Forces: 30,350
(including paramilitary force)
*Military Expenditures (% of Central
Government Expenditures):* 11.1%
Current Hostilities: ongoing civil war

ECONOMY

Currency ($ U.S. Equivalent):
529.43 CFA francs = $1
Per Capita Income/GDP: $530/$2.8
billion
Inflation Rate: −4.1%
Natural Resources: petroleum;
uranium; natron; kaolin
Agriculture: subsistence crops;
cotton; cattle; fish; sugar
Industry: livestock products; beer;
bicycle and radio assembly; textiles;
cigarettes

FOREIGN TRADE

Exports: $190 million
Imports: $261 million

Chad

- ⊛ Capital
- ● City
- ⌇ River
- - - - Road

0   200   kilometers
0   200 miles

CHAD

In June 1996, Chad held its first genuinely contested presidential elections since independence, in 1960. The result was a (disputed) second-round victory of 67.5 percent for the incumbent Idriss Déby, who, like most of his predecessors, originally came to power (in 1990) by armed force. Since then, Déby's government has made gradual progress toward rebuilding Chad, which in the 1980s was described as the "Lebanon of Africa." While his success in defeating, marginalizing, and/or reconciling with rival armed factions has restored a semblance of statehood to Chad, Déby presides over a bankrupt government whose control over much of the countryside remains tenuous. His opting for a unitary rather than a federal state, which is favored by most southerners, is also divisive.

CIVIL WAR

Chad's conflicts are partially rooted in the country's ethnic and religious divisions. It has been common for outsiders to portray the struggle as being between Arab-oriented Muslim northerners and black Christian southerners, but Chad's regional and ethnic allegiances are much more complex. Geographically, the country is better divided into three zones: the northern Sahara, a middle Sahel region, and the southern savanna. Within each of these ecological areas live peoples who speak different languages and engage in a variety of economic activities. Wider ethnoregional and religious loyalties have emerged as a result of the Civil War, but such aggregates have tended to be fragile, and their allegiances shifting.

At Chad's independence, France turned over power to François Tombalbaye, a Sara-speaking Christian southerner. Tombalbaye ruled with a combination of repression, ethnic favoritism, and incompetence, which quickly alienated his regime from broad sectors of the population. A northern-based coalition of armed groups, the National Liberation Front, or Frolinat, launched an increasingly successful insurgency. The

intervention of French troops on Tombalbaye's behalf failed to stem the rebellion. In 1975, the army, tired of the war and upset by the president's increasingly conspicuous brutality, overthrew Tombalbaye and established a military regime, headed by Felix Malloum.

Malloum's government was also unable to defeat Frolinat; so, in 1978, it agreed to share power with the largest of the Frolinat groups, the Armed Forces of the North (FAN), led by Hissène Habré. This agreement broke down in 1979, resulting in fighting in N'Djamena. FAN came out ahead, while Malloum's men withdrew to the south. The triumph of the "northerners" immediately led to further fighting among various factions—some allied to Habré, others loyal to his main rival within the Frolinat, Goukkouni Oueddie. Earlier Habré had split from Oueddie, whom he accused of indifference toward Libya's unilateral annexation in 1976 of the Aouzou Strip, along Chad's northern frontier. At the time, Libya was the principal foreign backer of Frolinat.

(United Nations photo by John Isaac)

Thousands upon thousands of Chadians have died as a result of the Chadian Civil War. Compounding the civil strife in the 1980s was severe drought, which caused a great deal of internal migration. Migrating families such as that shown above became the rule rather than the exception.

Independence is
achieved under
President
François
Tombalbaye
1960
●

Revolt breaks out
among peasant
groups;
FROLINAT
is formed
1965–1966
●

Establishment of
a Transitional
Government of
National Unity
(GUNT) with
Hissène Habré
and Goukkouni
Oueddie
1978
●

Habré seizes
power and
reunites the
country in a
U.S.–supported
war against Libya
1980s
●

1990s

Habré is
overthrown by
Idriss Déby; the
United States
evacuates a
force of
anti-Qadhafi
Libyans

Déby promises
to create a
multiparty
democracy, but
conditions
remain anarchic

Déby retains
presidency in
disputed
second-round
election victory

In 1980, shortly after the last French forces withdrew from Chad, the Libyan army invaded the country, at the invitation of Oueddie. Oueddie was then proclaimed the leader in a Transitional Government of National Unity (GUNT), which was established in N'Djamena. Nigeria and other neighboring states, joined by France and the United States, pressed for the withdrawal of Libyan forces. This pressure grew in 1981 after Libyan leader Muammar al-Qadhafi announced the merger of Chad and Libya. Following a period of intense multinational negotiations, the Libyan military presence was reduced at Oueddie's request.

The removal of the Libyan forces from most of Chad was accompanied by revived fighting between GUNT and FAN, with the latter receiving substantial U.S. support, via Egypt and Sudan. A peacekeeping force assembled by the Organization of African Unity proved ineffectual. The collapse of GUNT in 1982 led to a second major Libyan invasion. The Libyan offensive was countered by the return of French forces, assisted by Zairian troops and by smaller contingents from several other Francophonic African countries. Between 1983 and 1987, the country was virtually partitioned along the 16th Parallel, with Habré's French-backed, FAN-led coalition in the south and the Libyan-backed remnants of GUNT in the north.

A political and military breakthrough occurred in 1987. Habré's efforts to unite the country led to a reconciliation with Malloum's followers and with elements within GUNT. Oueddie himself was apparently placed under house arrest in Libya. Emboldened, Habré launched a major offensive north of the 16th Parallel that rolled back the better-equipped Libyan forces, who by now included a substantial number of Lebanese mercenaries. A factor in the Libyan defeat was U.S.-supplied Stinger missiles, which allowed Habré's forces to neutralize Libya's powerful air force (Habré's government lacked significant air power of its own). A cease-fire was declared after the Libyans had been driven out of all of northern Chad with the exception of a portion of the disputed Aouzou Strip.

In 1988, Qadhafi announced that he would recognize the Habré government and pay compensation to Chad. The announcement was welcomed—with some skepticism—by Chadian and other African leaders, although no mention was made of the conflicting claims to the Aouzou Strip.

The long-running struggle for Chad took another turn in November 1990, with the sudden collapse of Habré's regime in the face of a three-week offensive by guerrillas loyal to his former army commander, Idriss Déby. Despite substantial Libyan (and Sudanese) backing for his seizure of power, Déby has the support of France, Nigeria, and the United States (Habré had supported Iraq's annexation of Kuwait). A 1,200-man French force began assisting Déby against rebels loyal to Habré and other faction leaders.

Between January and April 1993, Déby's hand was strengthened by the successful holding of a National Convention, in which a number of formerly hostile groups agreed to cooperate with the government in drawing up a new constitution. In April 1994, his government was further boosted by Qadhafi's unexpected decision to withdraw his troops from the Aouzou Strip, leaving Chad in undisputed control of the territory. The move followed an International Court of Justice ruling in Chad's favor.

A BETTER FUTURE?

The long, drawn-out conflict in Chad has led to immense suffering. Up to a half a million people—the equivalent of 10 percent of the total population—have been killed in the fighting.

Even if peace could be restored, the overall prospects for national development are bleak. The country has potential mineral wealth, but its geographic isolation and current world prices are disincentives to investors. Local food self-sufficiency should be obtainable despite the possibility of recurrent drought, but geography limits the potential of export crops. Chad thus appears to be an extreme case of the more general African need for a radical transformation of prevailing regional and global economic interrelationships. Had outside powers devoted half the resources to Chad's development over the past decades as they provided to its civil conflicts, perhaps the country's future would appear brighter.

DEVELOPMENT

Chad has potential petroleum and mineral wealth that can help the economy if stable central government can be created. Deposits of chromium, tungsten, titanium, gold, uranium, and tin as well as oil are known to exist.

FREEDOM

For many years, Chad was ruled by gunmen, with armed political factions and outright criminal gangs struggling for spoils. The reestablishment of state structures has led to a modest improvement in human rights. Parliamentary elections scheduled for November 1996 will hopefully lead to a further consolidation of law and order.

HEALTH/WELFARE

In 1992, there were reports of catastrophic famine in the countryside. Limited human services were provided by external aid agencies.

ACHIEVEMENTS

In precolonial times, the town of Kanem was a leading regional center of commerce and culture. Since independence in 1960, perhaps Chad's major achievement has been the resiliency of its people under the harshest of circumstances. The holding of truly contested elections is also a significant accomplishment.

Congo (Republic of the Congo)

GEOGRAPHY

Area in Square Kilometers (Miles):
349,650 (132,000) (slightly smaller than Montana)
Capital (Population): Brazzaville (938,000)
Climate: tropical

PEOPLE

Population
Total: 2,527,000
Annual Growth Rate: 2.23%
Rural/Urban Population Ratio: 59/41
Major Languages: French; Lingala; Kikongo; Teke; Sangha; M'Bochi; others
Ethnic Makeup: 48% Kongo; 20% Sangha; 17% Teke; 14% others

Health
Life Expectancy at Birth: 45 years (male); 49 years (female)
Infant Mortality Rate (Ratio): 109/1,000
Average Caloric Intake: 99% of FAO minimum
Physicians Available (Ratio): 1/3,873

Religions
50% Christian; 48% traditional indigenous; 2% Muslim

Education
Adult Literacy Rate: 57%

COMMUNICATION

Telephones: 18,100
Newspapers: 3

RELIGIOUS LIFE

Many different religions have gained followings among peoples of Congo in recent times. There is a Tenrikyo Shinto center from Japan in the country. Many people claim affiliation with Christian faiths; one third are Roman Catholic. Swedish evangelical missionaries came to Congo in the early twentieth century, and the Salvation Army and Jehovah's Witnesses gained followers in the pre-independence period. Many new religious movements developed in Congo after World War I, often centered around figures who were considered messiahs, such as Simon Kimbangu, who founded a Christian church that is now a member of the World Council of Churches; and André Matsoua, an early nationalist. Until the 1950s, the only secondary schools in the country were the two seminaries preparing priests for the Roman Catholic Church.

TRANSPORTATION

Highways—Kilometers (Miles): 11,960 (7,463)
Railroads—Kilometers (Miles): 797 (494)
Usable Airfields: 41

GOVERNMENT

Type: republic
Independence Date: August 15, 1960
Head of State/Government: President Pascal Lissouba; Prime Minister Jacques Joachim Yuombi-Opango
Political Parties: Congolese Labor Party; Pan-African Union for Social Development; Association for Democracy and Development; Congolese Movement for Democracy and Integral Development; others
Suffrage: universal at 18

MILITARY

Number of Armed Forces: 10,900
Military Expenditures (% of Central Government Expenditures): 3.8%
Current Hostilities: civil conflicts

ECONOMY

Currency ($ U.S. Equivalent): 529.43 CFA francs = $1
Per Capita Income/GDP: $2,820/$6.7 billion
Inflation Rate: 2.2%
Natural Resources: wood; potash; petroleum; natural gas
Agriculture: cocoa; coffee; tobacco; palm kernels; sugarcane; rice; peanuts
Industry: processed agricultural and forestry goods; cement; textiles

FOREIGN TRADE

Exports: $1.1 billion
Imports: $472 million

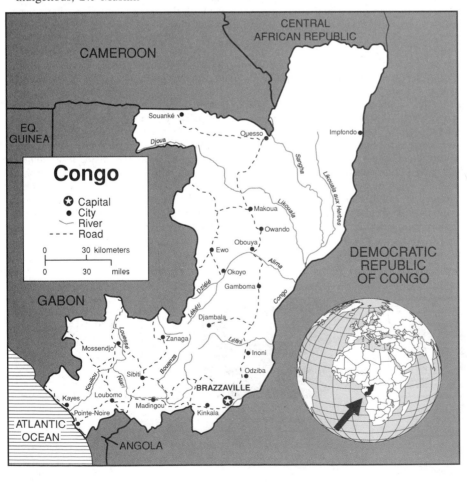

A TIME OF TRANSITION

In January 1995, a Government of National Unity was formed in Congo, bringing at least a temporary end to political-faction fighting, which had threatened to tear the nation apart. In November 1993, large sections of Brazzaville, Congo's capital city, had been a battleground between troops loyal to the elected Pan-African Union of Social Democracy (UPADS) government of President Pascal Lissouba and the so-called Ninjas—or armed supporters of opposition leader Bernard Kolelas's Union for the Renewal of Democracy (URD). After several weeks of fighting, peace was finally restored, with the intervention of an Organization of African Unity mediator. The crisis underscored the continuing fragility of Congo's difficult political transition into a multiparty democracy.

For more than 2 decades, Congo had been ruled as a self-proclaimed Marxist-Leninist one-party state. But in 1990, the ruling Congolese Workers Party (PCT) agreed to abandon both its past ideology and its monopoly of power. In 1991, a 4-month-long National Conference met to pave the way for a new constitutional order. An interim government, headed by Andre Milongo, was appointed pending elections, while the former regime's strongman, President Denis Sassou-Nguesso, was stripped of all but ceremonial authority. In the face of coup attempts by elements of the old order and a deteriorating economy, legislative and executive elections were finally held in the second half of 1992, resulting in Lissouba's election and a divided National Assembly.

A new National Assembly election in 1993 resulted in a decisive UPADS victory over a URD–PCT alliance, but the losers rejected the results for 5 months. With the economy experiencing a prolonged depression, political tensions remained high.

CONGO

The Republic of the Congo takes its name from the river that forms its southeastern border, with the Democratic Republic of Congo (formerly Zaire). Because forme sr Zaire prior to 1971 also called itself the Congo, the two countries are sometimes confused. Close historical and ethnic ties do in fact exist between the nations. The BaKongo are the largest ethnolinguistic group in Congo and western former Zaire as well as in northern Angola. During the fifteenth and sixteenth centuries, this group was united under a powerful Kingdom of the Kongo, which ruled over much

(United Nations photo by Sean Sprague)

Since Congo achieved its independence in 1960, it has made enormous educational strides. Almost all children in the country now attend school, which has had a tremendous effect on helping to realize the potential of the country's natural resources.

Middle Congo
becomes part
of French
Equatorial Africa
1910

Conference
establishes
French Union;
Felix Eboue
establishes
positive policies
for African
advancement
1944

Independence is
achieved, with
Abbe Fulbert
Youlou as the
first president
1960

A general strike
brings the army
and a more radical
government
(National
Revolutionary
Movement)
to power
1963

A new military
government
under Marien
Ngouabi takes
over; the
Congolese
Workers' Party
is formed
1968–1969

Ngouabi is
assassinated;
Colonel
Yhombi-Opango
rules
1977

Denis
Sassou-Nguesso
becomes
president
1979

1990s

The ruling
PCT
abandons
Marxism and
its monopoly
of power

National
Conference

Pascal
Lissouba is
elected
president

of Central Africa while establishing commercial and diplomatic ties with Europe. But the kingdom had virtually disappeared by the late nineteenth century, when the territory along the northwest bank of the Congo River, the modern republic, was annexed by France, while the southeast bank, Zaire, was placed under the rule of King Leopold of Belgium.

Despite the establishment of this political division, cultural ties between Congo and former Zaire, the former French and Belgium Congos, remained strong. Brazzaville, the Congolese capital, sits across the river from the Zairian capital of Kinshasha. The metropolitan region formed by these two centers has, through such figures as the late Congolese artist Franco, given rise to *soukous,* a musical style that is now popular in such places as Tokyo and Paris as well as throughout much of Africa.

ECONOMIC DEVELOPMENT

Brazzaville, which today houses more than one quarter of Congo's population, was established during the colonial era as the administrative headquarters of French Equatorial Africa, a vast territory that included the modern states of Chad, Central African Republic, Gabon, and Congo. As a result, the city expanded, and the area around it developed as an imperial crossroads. Congolese paid a heavy price for this growth. Thousands died while working under brutal conditions to build the Congo-Ocean Railroad, which linked Brazzaville with Pointe-Noire on the coast. Many more suffered as forced laborers for foreign concessionaires during the early decades of the twentieth century.

While the economies of many African states stagnated or declined during the 1970s and 1980s, Congo generally experienced growth, a result of its oil wealth. Hydrocarbons account for 90 percent of the total value of the nation's exports. But the danger of this dependence has been apparent since 1986, when falling oil prices led to a sharp decline in gross domestic product. An even greater threat to the nation's economic health is its mounting debt. As a result of heavy borrowing during the oil-boom years, by 1989 the total debt was estimated to be 50 percent greater than the value of the country's annual economic output. The annual cost of servicing the debt was almost equal to domestic expenditure.

The debt led to International Monetary Fund pressure on Congo's rulers to introduce austerity measures as part of a Structural Adjustment Program. The PCT regime and its interim successor were willing to move away from the country's emphasis on central planning toward a greater reliance on market economics. But after an initial round of severe budgetary cutbacks, both administrations found it difficult to reduce their spending further on such things as food subsidies and state-sector employment.

With more than half of Congo's population now urbanized, there has been deep concern about the social and political consequences of introducing harsher austerity measures. Many urbanites are already either unemployed or underemployed; even those with steady formal-sector jobs have already been squeezed by wages that fail to keep up with the inflation rate. The country's powerful trade unions, which

are hostile to SAP, have been in the forefront of the democratization process.

Although most Congolese appear to be facing tough times in the immediate future, the economy's long-term prospects remain hopeful. Besides oil, the country is endowed with a wide variety of mineral reserves: iron, zinc, gold, potash, copper, lead, bauxite, and phosphates. Timber has long been a major industry. Congolese forests, along with those of neighboring Gabon, are the world's main source of okoume logs, which are a preferred material for manufacturing plywood. And after years of neglect, the agricultural sector is growing. The goal of a return to food self-sufficiency appears achievable. Despite their currently low commodity prices, cocoa, coffee, tobacco, and sugar are major cash crops, while palm-oil estates are being rehabilitated.

The small but well-established Congolese manufacturing sector also has much potential. Congo's urbanized population is relatively skilled, thanks to the enormous educational strides that have been made since independence. Almost all children in Congo now attend school. The infrastructure serving Brazzaville and Pointe-Noire, coupled with the government's new emphasis on private-sector growth, should prove attractive to outside investors as well as local entrepreneurs.

DEVELOPMENT

Congo's Niari Valley has become the nation's leading agricultural area, due to its rich alluvial soils. The government has been encouraging food-processing plants to locate in the region.

FREEDOM

Until 1990, political opposition groups, along with Jehovah's Witnesses and certain other religious sects, were vigorously suppressed. The new Constitution provides for basic freedoms of association, belief, and speech.

HEALTH/WELFARE

Almost all Congolese between ages 6 and 16 currently attend school. Adult-literacy programs have also proved successful, giving the country one of the highest literacy rates in Africa. However, 30% of Congolese children under age 5 are reported to suffer from chronic malnutrition.

ACHIEVEMENTS

There are a number of Congolese poets and novelists who combine their creative efforts with teaching and public service. Tchicaya U'Tam'si, who died in 1988, wrote poetry and novels and worked for many years for UNESCO.

Democratic Republic of Congo (Formerly Republic of Zaire)

GEOGRAPHY

Area in Square Kilometers (Miles): 2,300,000 (905,063) (one-quarter the size of the United States)
Capital (Population): Kinshasa (4,700,000)
Climate: equatorial

PEOPLE

Population
Total: 46,499,000
Annual Growth Rate: 3.18%
Rural/Urban Population Ratio: 60/40
Major Languages: French; Swahili; Lingala; Azande; Luba; Chokwe; Songo; many others
Ethnic Makeup: Bantu majority; more than 200 African groups

Health
Life Expectancy at Birth: 46 years (male); 50 years (female)
Infant Mortality Rate (Ratio): 108.7/1,000
Average Caloric Intake: 94% of FAO minimum
Physicians Available (Ratio): 1/15,584

Religions
70% Christian; 20% traditional indigenous; 10% Muslim

Education
Adult Literacy Rate: 72%

COMMUNICATION

Telephones: 31,850
Newspapers: 4

TRANSPORTATION

Highways—Kilometers (Miles): 146,500 (90,830)

Railroads—Kilometers (Miles): 5,138 (3,206)
Usable Airfields: 270

GOVERNMENT

Type: republic; strong presidential authority
Independence Date: June 30, 1960
Head of State/Government: President Laurent Kabila
Political Parties: Alliance of Democratic Forces for the Liberation of Congo-Zaire; Popular Movement of the Revolution; Democratic Social Christian Party; Union for Democracy and Social Progress; others
Suffrage: universal at 18

MILITARY

Number of Armed Forces: 67,100
Military Expenditures (% of Central Government Expenditures): 0.8%
Current Hostilities: low-intensity insurgency

ECONOMY

Currency ($ U.S. Equivalent): 3,275 new Zaires = $1
Per Capita Income/GDP: $125/$18.8 billion
Inflation Rate: 35%–40% per month
Natural Resources: copper; cobalt; zinc; diamonds; manganese; tin; gold; rare metals; bauxite; iron; coal; hydroelectric potential; timber
Agriculture: coffee; palm oil; rubber; tea; cotton; cocoa; manioc; bananas; plantains; corn; rice; sugar
Industry: mineral mining; consumer products; food processing; cement

FOREIGN TRADE

Exports: $362 million
Imports: $356 million

A SCENE FROM KING LEOPOLD'S GENOCIDE

Look inside the hostage house, staggering back as you enter from odours which belch forth in poisonous fumes. As your eyes get accustomed to the half-light, they will not rest on those skeleton-like forms—bones held together by black skin—but upon the faces. . . . A woman, her pendulous, pear shaped breasts hanging like withered parchment against her sides, where ribs seem bursting from its covering, holds in her emaciated arms a small object more pink than black. You stoop to touch it—a new born babe, twenty-four hours old, assuredly not more. It is dead but the mother clasps it still. She herself is almost past speech, and will soon join her babe in the great Unknown. The horror of it the unspeakable horror of it.

—An excerpt from E. D. Morel's *Red Rubber* (p. 97).

Democratic Republic of Congo
- ✪ Capital
- ● City
- River
- - - - Road

0   250   kilometers
0   250   miles

DEMOCRATIC REPUBLIC OF CONGO (formerly Zaire)

In the final months of 1996, rebels of the Alliance of Democratic Forces for the Liberation of Congo-Zaire, led by Lauret Kabila, swept across eastern Zaire. In early May 1997, the rebels closed down the capital, Kinshasa, in an attempt to oust long-reigning dictator Mobutu Seso Seko. By the middle of May, ailing Mobutu headed into exile and Kabila took over. He then renamed the country the Democratic Republic of Congo.

Meanwhile, the country's already decayed social and economic infrastructure continues to disintegrate. In theory, annual per capita gross domestic product declined from $220 in 1990 to $125 in 1995, a figure that fails to take into account the informal sector that now dominates the local economy. In the process, national unity is being challenged by the reemergence of secessionist tendencies in the mineral-rich provinces of Katanga (Shaba) and Kasai. Western and eastern former Zaire has been inundated by an influx of some 2 million refugees from the killing fields of Rwanda and Burundi. A vast country of potentially great wealth, former Zaire's fate will ultimately affect the future of neighboring states as well as its own citizens. As the new Kabila government takes over, plans are being made to address the economic problems.

Geographically, former Zaire is the hub of Africa. Located at Africa's center, it encompasses the entire Congo, or Zaire, River Basin, whose waters are the potential source of 13 percent of the world's hydroelectric power. This immense area, about one quarter the size of the United States, encompasses a variety of land forms. It contains good agricultural possibilities and a wide range of natural resources, some of which have been intensively exploited for decades.

Former Zaire links Africa from west to east. Its very narrow coastline faces the Atlantic. Eastern former Zaire has long been influenced by forces from the East African coast, however. In the mid-nineteenth century, Swahili, Arab, and Nyamwezi traders from Tanzania established their hegemony over much of southeastern Zaire, pillaging the countryside for ivory and slaves. While the slave trade has left bitter memories, the Swahili language has spread to become a lingua franca throughout the eastern third of the country.

The 46.5 million people of the Democratic Republic of Congo belong to more than 200 different ethnic groups, speak nearly 700 languages and dialects, and have varied lifestyles. Boundaries established in the late nineteenth century hemmed in portions of the Azande, Konga, Chokwe, and Songye peoples, yet they maintain contact with their kin in other countries.

Many important precolonial states were centered in Zaire, including the Luba, Kuba, and Lunda kingdoms, the latter of which, in earlier centuries, exploited the salt and copper of southeast Zaire. The kingdom of Kongo, located at the mouth of the Congo River, flourished during the fifteenth and sixteenth centuries, establishing important diplomatic and commercial relations with Portugal. The elaborate political systems of these kingdoms are an important heritage for the former Zaire.

LEOPOLD'S GENOCIDE

The European impact, like the Swahili and Arab influences from the east, had deeply destructive results. The Congo Basin was explored and exploited by private individuals before it came under Belgian domination. King Leopold of Belgium, as a private citizen, sponsored H. M. Stanley's expeditions to explore the basin. In 1879, Leopold used Stanley's "treaties" as a justification for setting up the "Congo Independent State" over the whole region. This state was actually a private proprietary colony. To turn a profit on his vast enterprise, Leopold acted under the assumption that the people and resources in the territory were his personal property. His commercial agents and various concessionaires, to whom he leased portions of his colony, began brutally to coerce the local African population into providing

(United Nations photo by Caracciolo/Banoun)

The Democratic Republic of Congo is the geographical hub of Africa. On the west, the Congo (or Zaire) River Basin empties into the South Atlantic, where a small fishing industry exists.

Refugee children line up for medical treatment at a field hospital near Goma in eastern former Zaire. Most refugees in eastern former Zaire are from Rwanda.

ivory, wild rubber, and other commodities. The armed militias sent out to collect quotas of rubber and other goods committed numerous atrocities against the people, including destroying whole villages.

No one knows for sure how many Africans perished in Congo Independent State as a result of the brutalities of Leopold's agents. Some critics estimate that the territory's population was reduced by 10 million people over a period of 20 years. Many were starved to death as forced laborers. Others were massacred in order to induce survivors to produce more rubber. Women and children suffocated in "hostage houses" while their men did their masters' bidding. Thousands fled to neighboring territories.

For years, the Congo regime was able to keep information of its crimes from leaking overseas, but eventually, tales from missionaries and others did emerge. Accounts such as E. D. Morel's *Red Rubber* and Mark Twain's caustic *King Leopold's Soliloquy,* as well as gruesome pictures of men, women, and children whose hands had been severed by troops (who were expected to produce the hands for their officers as evidence of their diligence), stirred public opinion. Joseph Conrad's fictionalized account of his experiences, *The Heart of Darkness,* became a popular literary classic. Finally even the European imperialists, during an era when

their racial arrogance was at its height, could no longer stomach Leopold, called by some "the king with ten million murders on his soul."

During the years of Belgian rule, 1908 to 1960, foreign domination was less genocidal, but a tradition of abuse had nevertheless been established. The colonial authorities still used armed forces for "pacification" campaigns, tax collection, and labor recruitment. Local collaborators were turned into chiefs and given arbitrary powers that they would not have had under indigenous political systems. Concessionary companies continued to use force to recruit labor for their plantations and mines. The colonial regime encouraged the work of Catholic missionaries. Health facilities as well as a paternalistic system of education were developed. A strong elementary-school system was part of the colonial program, but the Belgians never instituted a major secondary-school system, and there was no institution of higher learning. By independence, only 16 Congolese had been able to earn university degrees, all but two in non-Belgian institutions. A small group of high-school–educated Congolese, known as *évolués* ("evolved ones"), served the needs of an administration that never intended nor planned for Zaire's independence.

In the 1950s, the Congolese, especially townspeople, were affected by the independence movements that were emerging

throughout Africa. The Belgians began to recognize the need to prepare for a different future. Small initiatives were allowed; in 1955, nationalist associations were first permitted and a 30-year timetable for independence was proposed. This sparked heated debate. Some *évolués* agreed with the Belgians' proposal. Others, including the members of the Alliance of the Ba-Kongo (ABAKO), an ethnic association in Kinshasa, and the National Congolese Movement (MNC), led by then–prime minister Patrice Lumumba, rejected it.

A serious clash at an ABAKO demonstration in 1959 resulted in some 50 deaths. In the face of mounting unrest, further encouraged by the imminent independence of French Congo (the Republic of the Congo), the Belgians conceded a rapid transition to independence. A constitutional conference in January 1960 established a federal-government system for the future independent state. But there was no real preparation for this far-reaching political change.

THE CONGO CRISIS

The Democratic Republic of the Congo became independent on June 30, 1960, under the leadership of President Joseph Kasavubu and Prime Minister Patrice Lumumba. Within a week, an army mutiny had stimulated widespread disorder. The scars of

Congo's uniquely bitter colonial experience showed. Unlike in Africa's other postcolonial states, hatred of the white former masters turned to violence in Congo, resulting in the hurried flight of the majority of its large European community. Ethnic and regional bloodshed took a much greater toll among the African population. The wealthy Katanga Province (now Shaba) and South Kasai seceded.

Lumumba called upon the United Nations for assistance, and troops came from a variety of countries to serve in the UN force. Later, as a result of a dispute with President Kasavubu, Lumumba sought Soviet aid. Congo could have become a cold war battlefield, but the army, under Lumumba's former confidant, Joseph Desiré Mobutu, intervened. Lumumba was arrested and turned over to the Katanga rebels; he was later assassinated. Western interests and, in particular, the U.S. Central Intelligence Agency (CIA) played a substantial if not fully revealed role in the downfall of the idealistic Lumumba and the rise of his cynical successor, Mobutu. Rebellions by Lumumbists in the northeast and Katanga secessionists, supported by foreign mercenaries, continued through 1967.

MOBUTUISM

Mobutu seized full power in 1965, ousting Kasavubu in a military coup. With ruthless energy, he eliminated the rival political factions within the central government and crushed the regional rebellions. Mobutu banned party politics. In 1971, he established the Second Republic as a one-party state in which all power was centralized around the "Founding President." Every citizen, at birth, was legally expected to be a disciplined member of Mobutu's Popular Revolutionary Movement (MPR). With the exception of some religious organizations, virtually all social institutions were to function as MPR organs. The official ideology of the MPR republic became "Mobutuism"—the words, deeds, and decrees of "the Guide" Mobutu. All citizens were required to sing his praises daily at the workplace, at schools, and at social gatherings. In hymns and prayers, the name Mobutu was often substituted for that of Jesus. A principal slogan of Mobutuism was "authenticity." Supposedly this meant a rejection of European values and norms for African ones.

But it was Mobutu alone who defined what was authentic. He added to his own name the title "Sese Seko" ("the all powerful") while declaring all European personal names illegal. He also established a national dress code; ties were outlawed, men were expected to wear his abacost suit, and women were obliged to wear the *paigne,* or wrapper. (The former Zaire was perhaps the only place in the world where the necktie was a symbol of political resistance.) The name of the country was changed from Congo to *Zaire,* derived from sixteenth-century Portuguese mispronunciation of the (Ki)Kongo word for "river."

Outside of Zaire, some took Mobutu's protestations of authenticity at face value, while a few other African dictators, such as Togo's Gnassingbé Eyadéma, emulated aspects of his Fascist methodology. But the majority of Zairians grew to loathe his "cultural revolution."

Authenticity was briefly accompanied by a program of nationalization. Union Minière and other corporations were placed under government control. In 1973 and 1974, plantations, commercial institutions, and other businesses were also taken over, in a "radicalizing of the Zairian Revolution."

But the expropriated businesses simply enriched a small elite. In many cases, Mobutu gave them away to his cronies, who often simply sold off the assets. Consequently, the economy suffered. Industries and businesses were mismanaged or ravaged. Some individuals became extraordinarily wealthy, while the population as a whole became progressively poorer with each passing year. Mobutu allegedly has become the wealthiest person in Africa, with a fortune estimated in excess of $5 billion (about equal to Zaire's national debt), most of which is invested and spent outside of Africa. He and his relatives own mansions all over the world.

Until recently, no opposition to Mobutu was allowed. Those critical of the regime faced imprisonment, torture, or death. The Roman Catholic Church and the Kimbanguist Church of Jesus Christ Upon This Earth were the only institutions able to speak out. Strikes were not allowed. In 1977 and 1978, new revolts in the Shaba Province were crushed by U.S.–backed Moroccan, French, and Belgian military interventions. In 1997 rebels, under leader Laurent Kabila, ousted ailing Mobutu and renamed the country the Democratic Republic of Congo.

ECONOMIC DISASTER

The former Zaire's economic potential was developed by and for the Belgians, but by 1960, that development had gone further than in most other African colonial territories. I
t started with a good economic base, but the chaos of the early 1960s brought development to a standstill, and the Mobutu years were marked by regression. Development projects have been initiated, but often without careful planning. World economic conditions, including falling copper and cobalt prices, have contributed to Zaire's difficulties.

But the main obstacle to any sort of economic progress was the rampant corruption of Mobutu and those around him. The governing system in Zaire was characterized as a kleptocracy (rule by thieves). A well-organized system of graft transfers wealth from ordinary citizens to officials and other elites. With Mobutu stealing billions and those closest to him stealing millions, the entire society operated on an invisible tax system; citizens had to, for example, bribe nurses for medical care, bureaucrats for documents, principals for school admission, and police to stay out of jail. For most civil servants, who are paid little or nothing, accepting bribes was a necessary activity. This fundamental fact also applied to most soldiers, who thus survive by living off the civilian population. Recently, the U.S. military learned this lesson first-hand when it conducted joint military exercises with former Zairian paratroopers. When a number of American troops' parachutes got caught in trees, the soldiers were robbed of their possessions by former Zairian troops, who then deserted into the forest.

Ordinary people suffer. By 1990, real wages of urban workers in former Zaire were only 2 percent of what they were in 1960. Rural incomes had also deteriorated. The official 1990 price paid to coffee farmers, for example, was only one fifth of what it was in 1954 under the exploitive Belgian regime. The situation has worsened since, due to hyperinflation.

Much of the state's coffee and other cash crops have long been smuggled, more often than not through the connivance of senior government officials. Thus, although former Zaire's agriculture has great economic potential, the returns from this sector continue to shrink. Despite its immense size and plentiful rainfall, Zaire must import about 60 percent of its food requirements. Rural people move to the city or, for lack of employment, move back to the country and take up subsistence agriculture, rather than cash-crop farming, in order to ensure their own survival. The deterioration of roads and bridges has led to the decline of all trade.

In 1983, the government adopted International Monetary Fund (IMF) austerity measures, but this has only cut public expenditures. It has had no effect on the endemic corruption, nor has it increased taxes on the rich. Under Bobutu's regime, more than 30 percent of former Zaire's budget went for debt servicing.

Leopold sets up
the Congo
Independent
State as his
private kingdom
1879

Congo becomes
a Belgian colony
1906

Congo gains
independence;
civil war begins;
a UN force is
involved; Patrice
Lumumba is
murdered
1960

Joseph Desiré
Mobutu takes
command in a
bloodless coup
1965

The name of the
state is changed
to Zaire
1971

1990s

Tens of
thousands of
foreigners flee
Zaire as central
authority
crumbles

Millions of
Rwandan and
Burundian
refugees flood
into Zaire

The National
Conference
extends its power

In June 1997, Kabila announced short-term economic priorities that include job creation, road and hospital rebuilding, and a national fuel supply pipeline. But it is unclear where the money will come from to implement these plans.

U.S. SUPPORT FOR MOBUTU

Mobutu's regime was able to sidestep its financial crises and maintain power through the support of foreign powers, especially Belgium, France, Germany, and the United States. A U.S. intelligence report prepared in the mid-1950s concluded that the then–Belgian Congo was indeed the hub of Africa and thus vital to America's strategic interests. U.S. policy has thus been first to promote and then to perpetuate Mobutu as a pro-Western source of stability in the region. Mobutu himself skillfully cultivated this image.

Mobutu collaborated with the United States in opposing the Marxist-oriented Popular Movement for the Liberation of Angola. By so doing, he not only set himself up as an important cold war ally but also was able to pursue regional objectives of his own. The National Front for the Liberation of Angola, long championed by the CIA as a counterforce to the MPLA, was led by an in-law of Mobutu, Holden Roberto. Mobutu also long coveted Angola's oil-rich enclave of Cabinda and thus sought CIA and South African assistance for the "independence" movement there. In recent years, millions of U.S. dollars have been spent upgrading the airstrip at Kamina in Shaba Province, used by the CIA to supply the guerrillas of the National Union for the Total Independence

of Angola, another faction opposed to the MPLA government. In 1989, Mobutu attempted to set himself up as a mediator between the government and the UNITA rebels, but even the latter have grown to distrust him.

The United States has long known of Mobutu's human-rights violations and of the oppression and corruption that characterize his regime; high-level defectors as well as victims have publicized its abuses. Since 1987, Mobutu responded with heavily financed public relations efforts aimed at lobbying U.S. legislators. U.S. support for Mobutu continued, but the recent collapse of his authority has led Washington belatedly to search for alternatives.

Mobutu also allied himself with other conservative forces in Africa and the Middle East. Moroccan troops came to his aid during the revolts in Shaba Province in 1977 and 1978. For his part, Mobutu has been a leading African supporter of Morocco's stand with regard to the Western Sahara dispute. The former Zaire has been an active member of the Francophonic African bloc. In 1983, Mobutu dispatched 2,000 Zairian troops to Chad in support of the government of Hissène Habré, then under attack from Libya, while in 1986, his men again joined French forces in propping up the Eyadéma regime in Togo. He also maintained and strengthened his ties with South Africa; today, the former Zaire imports almost half its food from that state. In 1982, former Zaire renewed the diplomatic ties with Israel that had been broken after the Arab–Israeli War of 1973. Israelis have since joined French and Belgians as senior advisers and trainers working within the former Zairian

Army. In 1990, the outbreak of violent unrest in Kinshasha once more led to the intervention of French and Belgian troops.

Despite Mobutu's cultivation of foreign assistance to prop up his dictatorship, internal opposition grew. In 1990, he tried to head off his critics both at home and abroad by promising to set up a new Third Republic, based on multiparty democracy. Despite this step, repression intensified.

In October 1996, while Mobutu was in Europe recovering from cancer surgery, rebel troops under the leadership of Laurent Kabila seized their first major town, Uvira. Thousands of Rwandan Hutu refugees were forced to flee back to Rwanda. When Mobuto returned home in April 1997, he declared a nationwide state of emergency. Kabila's supporters then closed down Kinshasa as part of the campaign to oust Mobutu. Following negotiations with South Africa's Mandela, Mobutu leaves Kinshasa and heads into exile. Kabila then takes over as head of state in May 1997, and he renames the country the Democratic Republic of Congo. Kabila has promised a new constitution followed by elections in two years. However, as the new government assumes power, some expect that resistance will emerge from former Zairean military and ex-Rwandan Hutu soliders.

DEVELOPMENT

Western aid and development assistance were drastically reduced in 1992, but new aid was pledged in 1994 as a reward for Mobutu's cooperation in dealing with the Rwandan conflict. An agreement was signed with Egypt for the long-term development of Zaire's hydroelectric power.

FREEDOM

Zaire has shown little respect for human rights. One Amnesty International report concluded that all political prisoners are tortured. Death squads are active.

HEALTH/WELFARE

In 1978, more than 5 million students were registered for primary schools and 35,000 for college. However, the level of education is declining. Many teachers were laid off in the 1980s, though nonexistent "ghost teachers" remained on the payroll. The few innovative educational programs that do manage to exist are outside of the state system.

ACHIEVEMENTS

Kinshasha has been called the dance-music capital of Africa. The most popular sound is *souskous*, or "Congo rumba." The grand old man of the style, Rochereau Tabu Ley, is still going strong, while other artists, like Papa Wemba, Pablo Lubidika, and Sandoka, have joined him in spreading its rhythms internationally.

Equatorial Guinea (Republic of Equatorial Guinea)

GEOGRAPHY

Area in Square Kilometers (Miles):
28,023 (10,820) (about the size of
Maryland)
Capital (Population): Malabo (58,000)
Climate: equatorial

PEOPLE

Population

Total: 431,300
Annual Growth Rate: 2.6%
Rural/Urban Population Ratio: n/a
Major Languages: Spanish; Fang;
Benge; Combe; Bujeba; Balengue;
Fernandino; Bubi
Ethnic Makeup: 80% Fang;
15% Bubi; 5% others

Health

Life Expectancy at Birth: 50 years
(male); 55 years (female)
Infant Mortality Rate (Ratio):
100/1,000
Average Caloric Intake: n/a
Physicians Available (Ratio): 1/3,532

Religions

60% Catholic; 40% Protestant or
traditional indigenous

Education

Adult Literacy Rate: 50%

COMMUNICATION

Telephones: 2,000
Newspapers: 2

TRANSPORTATION

Highways—Kilometers (Miles): 2,760
(1,714)
Railroads—Kilometers (Miles): none
Usable Airfields: 3

GOVERNMENT

Type: republic in transition to
multiparty democracy
Independence Date: October 12, 1968
Head of State/Government: President
(Brigadier General) Teodoro Obiang
Nguema Mbasogo; Prime Minister
Silvestre Siale Bileka
Political Parties: Democratic Party
for Equatorial Guinea; Progressive
Democratic Alliance; Popular Action
of Equatorial Guinea; Liberal
Democratic Convention; Convergence
for Social Democracy; others
Suffrage: universal for adults

MILITARY

Number of Armed Forces: 1,220
*Military Expenditures (% of Central
Government Expenditures):* n/a
Current Hostilities: none

ECONOMY

Currency ($ U.S. Equivalent):
529.43 CFA francs = $1
Per Capita Income/GDP: $700/$280
million
Inflation Rate: 1.6%
Natural Resources: wood
Agriculture: cocoa; coffee; timber;
rice; yams; bananas
Industry: fishing; sawmilling;
palm-oil processing

FOREIGN TRADE

Exports: $56 million
Imports: $62 million

AID ATROCITIES

Since 1979, Obiang Nguema and his relatives have maintained their grip
over Equatorial Guinea by taking advantage of competition between France
and Spain for neocolonial influence. Foreign aid accounts for approximately
70 percent of the economy; Spain and France are the principal donors.

The former Spanish colony has recently associated itself with its Francophonic neighbors and with France by joining the Central African Franc
Zone. The use of the French language within governing circles is increasing,
especially among the French-trained security forces. But Madrid recently
financed a Spanish television service, and Spain remains the major trading
partner. Equatorial Guinea has also sought closer relations with the United
States, via the Hispanic states of Latin America, by becoming the only
African state with observer status in the Organization of American States.
U.S. assistance is increasing, in line with growing U.S. corporate involvement in local oil and gas.

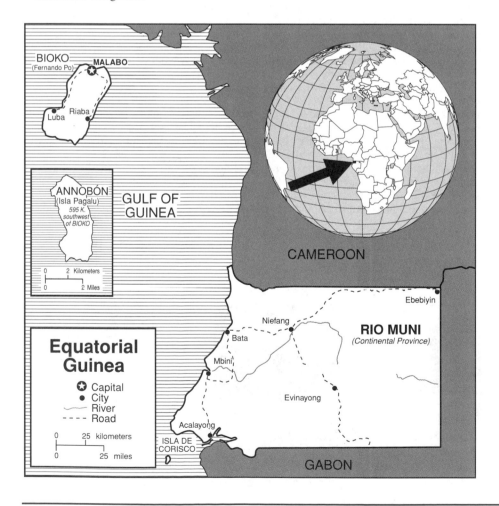

Europeans
explore modern
Equatorial Guinea
1500s

The Dutch
establish
slave-trading
stations
1641

Spain claims
the area of
Equatorial
Guinea; de facto
control is not
completed
until 1926
1778

The League
of Nations
investigates
charges of
slavery on
Fernando Po
1930

The murder of
nationalist leader
Acacio Mane
leads to the
founding of
political parties
1958

Local autonomy
is granted
1963

Independence;
Macias Nguema
begins his reign
1968

A coup ends the
dictatorial regime
of Macias
Nguema; Obiang
Nguema
becomes the
new ruler
1979

1990s

A shift to
multipartyism is
accompanied by
wave of political
detentions

Opposition
groups boycott
the 1993
presidential
election

Nguema claims
an overwhelming
win in the 1996
election

EQUATORIAL GUINEA

Few countries have been more consistently misruled than Equatorial Guinea. Having been traumatized during its first decade of independence by the sadistic Macias Nguema (1968–1979), the country continues to decay under his nephew and former security chief, Obiang Nguema. In 1992, Obiang officially transformed his regime into a multiparty democracy. But this gesture has been widely dismissed as a thinly disguised sham for the benefit of the French, Spanish, and Americans who provide assistance to his regime. And in the end, the move may have backfired. As a result of the government's failure to honor its commitments under a March 1993 multiparty national election, all the significant opposition groups boycotted the November 1993 election, describing it as a farce. Subsequent opposition attempts to come to an accommodation with the government were set back in April 1995, when the leader of the Party of Progress, Severo Moto, was arrested. (He was later released as a result of international pressure.) In February 1996, Obiang claimed 97.85% of the vote in a new presidential poll.

Equatorial Guinea's current suffering contrasts with the mood of optimism that characterized the country when it gained its independence from Spain in 1968. Confidence was then buoyed by a strong and growing gross domestic product, potential mineral riches, and exceptionally good soil.

The republic is comprised of two small islands, Fernando Po (now officially known as Bioko) and Annobón, and the larger and more populous coastal enclave of Rio Muni. Before the two islands and the enclave were united, during the 1800s,

as Spain's only colony in sub-Saharan Africa, all three areas were victimized by their intense involvement in the slave trade.

Spain's major colonial concern was the prosperity of the large cocoa and coffee plantations that were established on the islands, particularly on Fernando Po. Because of local resistance from the local Bubi, labor for these estates was imported from elsewhere in West Africa. Coercive recruitment and poor working conditions led to frequent charges of slavery.

Despite early evidence of its potential riches, Rio Muni was largely neglected by the Spanish, who did not occupy its interior until 1926. In the 1930s and 1940s, much of the enclave was under the political control of the Elar-ayong, a nationalist movement that sought to unite the Fang, Rio Muni's principal ethnic group, against both the Spanish and the French rulers in neighboring Cameroon and Gabon. The territory has remained one of the world's least developed areas.

In 1968, then–Fascist-ruled Spain entrusted local power to Macias Nguema, who had risen through the ranks of the security service. Under his increasingly deranged misrule, virtually all public and private enterprise collapsed; indeed, between 1974 and 1979, the country had no budget. One third of the nation's population went into exile; tens of thousands of others were either murdered or allowed to die of disease and starvation. Many of the survivors were put to forced labor, and the rest were left to subsist off the land. Killings were carried out by boys conscripted between the ages of 7 and 14.

Although no community in Equatorial Guinea was left unscarred by Macias's

tyranny, the greatest disruption occurred on the islands. By 1976, the entire resident-alien population had left, along with most surviving members of the educated class. On Annobón, the government blocked all international efforts to stem a severe cholera epidemic in 1973. The near-total depopulation of the island was completed in 1976, when all able-bodied men on Annobón, along with another 20,000 from Rio Muni, were drafted for forced labor on Fernando Po.

If Equatorial Guinea's first decade of independence was hell, the years since have at best been purgatory. No sector of the economy is free of corruption. Uncontrolled—and in theory illegal—logging is destroying Rio Muni's environment, while in Malabo, the police routinely engage in theft. Food is imported and malnutrition commonplace. It has been reported that the remaining population of Annobón is being systematically starved while Obiang collects huge payments from international companies that use the island as a toxic-waste dump.

At least one fifth of the Equato-Guinean population continue to live in exile, mostly in Cameroon and Gabon. This community has fostered a number of opposition groups. The government relies financially on French and Spanish aid. But Madrid's commitment has been strained by criticism from the Spanish press, which has been virtually alone in publicizing Equatorial Guinea's continued suffering.

DEVELOPMENT

The exploitation of oil and gas by U.S., French, and Spanish companies should soon greatly increase government revenues. The U.S. company Walter International recently finished work on a gas-separation plant.

FREEDOM

People continue to be detained, tortured, and disappear for such crimes as "Disrespect to the President." The local media are government-controlled, and there are few foreign periodicals. Possession of the clandestine antigovernment paper *The Truth* is a serious offense.

HEALTH

At independence, Equatorial Guinea had one of the best doctor-to-population ratios in Africa, but Macias's rule left it with the lowest. Health care is gradually reviving, however, with major assistance coming from public and private sources.

ACHIEVEMENTS

At independence, 90% of all children attended school, but the schools were closed under Macias. Since 1979, primary education has revived and now incorporates most children. Major assistance currently comes from the World Bank and from Spanish missionaries.

Gabon (Gabonese Republic)

GEOGRAPHY

Area in Square Kilometers (Miles):
264,180 (102,317) (about the size of
Colorado)
Capital (Population): Libreville (419,000)
Climate: tropical

PEOPLE

Population
Total: 1,193,000
Annual Growth Rate: 1.46%
Rural/Urban Population Ratio: 54/46
Major Languages: French; Fang;
Eshira; Bopounou; Bateke; Okande;
others
Ethnic Makeup: 25% Fang; 10%
Bapounon; 65% others

Health
Life Expectancy at Birth: 52 years
(male); 58 years (female)
Infant Mortality Rate (Ratio): 92.4/1,000
Average Caloric Intake: 102% of
FAO minimum
Physicians Available (Ratio): 1/2,337

Religions
55%–75% Christian; less than 1%
Muslim; remainder traditional
indigenous

Education
Adult Literacy Rate: 61%

COMMUNICATION

Telephones: 15,000
Newspapers: 2

ALBERT SCHWEITZER AT LAMBARENE

Lambarene, a town of about 7,000 residents on the Ogooue River in Gabon's interior, is the site of the mission hospital that Albert Schweitzer built
and in which he practiced medicine. Schweitzer, born in Alsace-Lorraine,
then a part of Germany, was a philosopher, theologian, organist, and specialist on Bach as well as a medical missionary. At age 38 he came to
Lambarene, where he lived and worked for 52 years. The hospital that he
built was like an African village, consisting of numerous simple dwellings.
It accommodated many patients and their relatives and operated without all
of the necessities of hospitals in Europe. In later times, innovative changes
were not always accepted by the authoritarian Schweitzer and his staff, but
their work at Lambarene saved lives and cured thousands. Schweitzer was
awarded the Nobel Peace Prize for his efforts for "the Brotherhood of Nations." Yet he shared the distorted images of Africans so deeply ingrained
among Westerners, and he did not believe that Africans could advance in
Western ways.

TRANSPORTATION

Highways—Kilometers (Miles): 7,500
(4,650)
Railroads—Kilometers (Miles): 649
(402)
Usable Airfields: 69

GOVERNMENT

Type: republic; multiparty presidential
regime
Independence Date: August 17, 1960
Head of State/Government: President
Omar Bongo; Prime Minister Paulin
Obame Nguema
Political Parties: Gabonese
Democratic party; National Recovery
Movement—Lumberjacks; Gabonese
Party for Progress; National
Recovery Movement; Coordination of
Democratic Opposition; others
Suffrage: universal at 21

MILITARY

Number of Armed Forces: 6,750
*Military Expenditures (% of Central
Government Expenditures):* 2.4%
Current Hostilities: none

ECONOMY

Currency ($ U.S. Equivalent): 529.43
CFA francs = $1
Per Capita Income/GDP: $4,900/$5.6
billion
Inflation Rate: 35%
Natural Resources: timber;
petroleum; iron ore; manganese;
uranium; gold; zinc
Agriculture: cocoa; coffee; palm oil
Industry: petroleum; lumber; minerals

FOREIGN TRADE

Exports: $2.1 billion
Imports: $832 million

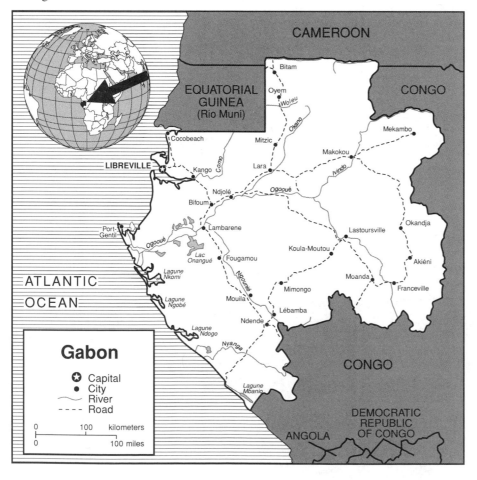

Gabon
✪ Capital
• City
〜 River
- - - - Road

0   100   kilometers
0   100   miles

Libreville is
founded by the
French as a
settlement for
freed slaves
1849

Gabon becomes
a colony within
French
Equatorial Africa
1910

The Free French
in Brazzaville
seize Gabon
from the
pro-Vichy
government
1940

Independence is
gained; Leon
M'ba becomes
president
1960

Omar Bongo
becomes
Gabon's second
president after
M'ba's death
1967

The Gabonese
Democratic Party
(PDG) becomes
the only party of
the state
1968

1990s

Bongo agrees to
multiparty
elections but
seeks to put
limits on the
opposition

Riots in
Port-Gentil lead
to French military
intervention

The PDG
narrowly wins
elections, amid
charges of fraud

GABON

Since independence, Gabon has achieved one of the highest per capita gross domestic products in Africa due to exploitation of the country's natural riches, especially its oil. But there is a wide gap between such statistical wealth and the real poverty that still shapes the lives of most Gabonese.

At the top of the local governing elite is President Omar Bongo, whose main palace, built at a reported cost of $300 million, symbolizes his penchant for grandeur. Shortly after taking office, in 1967, Bongo institutionalized his personal rule as the head of a one-party state. Until recently, his Democratic Party of Gabon (PDG) held a legal monopoly of power. But, although the PDG's Constitution restricted the presidency to the "Founder President," it has been Gabon's former colonial master, France, not the ruling party's by-laws, that has upheld the Bongo regime.

The French colonial presence in Gabon dates back to 1843. Between 1898 and 1930, many Gabonese were subject to long periods of forced labor, cutting timber for French concessions companies. World War II coincided with a period of political liberalization in the territory under the Free French government of Felix Emboue, a black man born in French Guiana. Educated Gabonese were promoted for the first time to important positions in the local administration. In the 1950s, two major political parties emerged to compete in local politics: the Social Democratic Union of Gabon (UDSG), led by Jean-Hilaire Aubame, and the Gabonese Democratic Bloc (BDG) of Indjenjet Gondjout and Leon M'ba.

In the 1957 elections, the USDG received 60 percent of the popular vote but gained only 19 seats in the 40-seat Assembly. M'ba,

who had the support of French logging interests, was elected leader by 21 BDG and independent deputies. As a result, it was M'ba who was at the helm when Gabon gained its independence, in 1960. This birth coincided with M'ba's declaration giving himself emergency powers, provoking a period of prolonged constitutional crisis.

In January 1964, M'ba dissolved the Assembly over its members' continued refusal to accept a one-party state under his leadership. In February, the president himself was forced to resign by a group of army officers. Power was transferred to a civilian Provisional Government, headed by Aubame, which also included BDG politicians such as Grondjout and several prominent, unaffiliated citizens. However, no sooner had the Provisional Government been installed than Gabon was invaded by French troops. Local military units were massacred in the surprise attack, which returned M'ba to office. Upon his death, M'ba was succeeded by his hand-picked successor, Bongo.

It has been suggested that France's 1964 invasion was motivated primarily by a desire to maintain absolute control over Gabon's uranium deposits, which were vital to France's nuclear weapons program. Many Gabonese have believed that their country has remained a de facto French possession. France has maintained its military presence, and the Gabonese Army is outgunned by the Presidential Guard, mainly officered by Moroccan and French mercenaries. France dominates Gabon's resource-rich economy.

Gabon's status quo has been challenged by its increasingly urbanized population. Although Bongo was able to co-opt or exile many of the figures who had once opposed M'ba, a new generation of opposition has

emerged both at home and in exile. The leading opposition group for the past decade has been the underground Movement for National Recovery (MORENA). In 1989, Bongo began talks with some elements within MORENA, which led to a division within its ranks. But the breakup of MORENA failed to stem the emergence of new groups calling for a return to multiparty democracy.

Demonstrations and strikes at the beginning of 1990 led to the legalization of opposition parties. But the murder of a prominent opposition leader in May led to serious rioting at Port-Gentil, Gabon's second city. In response, France sent troops into the area. Multiparty elections for the National Assembly, in September–October 1990, resulted in a narrow victory for the PDG, amid allegations of widespread fraud. In 1992, most opposition groups united as the Coordination of Democratic Opposition. Bongo's victory claim in the December 1993 presidential election was widely disbelieved. In September 1994, he agreed to the formation of a coalition Transitional Government and the drafting of a new Constitution, which was approved by 96% of the voters in July 1995.

In new elections in December 1996, Bongo and the PDG maintained power through a combination of patronage and manipulation.

DEVELOPMENT

The Trans-Gabonais Railway is one of the largest construction projects in Africa. Work began in 1974 and, after some delays, most of the line is now complete. The railway has opened up much of Gabon's interior to commercial development.

FREEDOM

Since 1967 Bongo has maintained power through a combination of repression and the deft use of patronage. The current transition to a multiparty process has led to an improvement in human rights.

HEALTH/WELFARE

The government claims to have instituted universal, compulsory education for Gabonese up to age 16. Independent observers doubt the government's claim but concur that major progress has been made. Health services have also expanded greatly.

ACHIEVEMENTS

Gabon will soon have a second private television station, funded by a French cable station. Profits will be used to fund films that will be shown on other African stations. Gabon's first private station is funded by Swiss and Gabonese capital.

SãoTomé and Príncipe
(Democratic Republic of São Tomé and Príncipe)

GEOGRAPHY

Area in Square Kilometers (Miles): 1,001 (387) (slightly larger than New York City)
Capital (Population): São Tomé (43,000)
Climate: tropical

PEOPLE

Population
Total: 144,000
Annual Growth Rate: 2.6%
Rural/Urban Population Ratio: n/a
Major Languages: Portuguese; Fang; Kriolu
Ethnic Makeup: Portuguese-African mixture; African minority

Health
Life Expectancy at Birth: 62 years (male); 66 years (female)
Infant Mortality Rate (Ratio): 62/1,000
Average Caloric Intake: 78% of FAO minimum
Physicians Available (Ratio): 1/1,881

THE SÃOTOMÉANS

The current inhabitants of São Tomé and Príncipe are primarily of mixed African and European descent. During the colonial period, the society was stratified along racial lines. At the top were the Europeans—mostly Portuguese. Just below them were the *mesticos* or *filhos da terra*, the mixed-blood descendants of slaves. Descendants of slaves who arrived later were known as *forros*. Contract workers were labeled as *servicais*, while their children became known as *tongas*. Still another category was the *angolares*, who reportedly were the descendants of shipwrecked slaves. All of these colonial categories were used to divide and rule the local population; the distinctions have begun to diminish, however, as an important sociological factor on the islands.

Religions
80% Christian; 20% traditional indigenous

Education
Adult Literacy Rate: 57%

COMMUNICATION

Telephones: 2,200
Newspapers: 2 weeklies

TRANSPORTATION

Highways—Kilometers (Miles): 300 (186)
Railroads—Kilometers (Miles): none
Usable Airfields: 2

GOVERNMENT

Type: republic
Independence Date: July 12, 1975
Head of State/Government: President Miguel Trovoada; Prime Minister Carlos da Graca
Political Parties: Party of Democratic Convergence-Group of Reflection; Liberation Movement of São Tomé and Príncipe–Social Democratic Party; Christian Democratic Front; Democratic Opposition Coalition; others
Suffrage: universal at 18

MILITARY

Number of Armed Forces: n/a
Military Expenditures (% of Central Government Expenditures): n/a
Current Hostilities: none

ECONOMY

Currency ($ U.S. Equivalent): 130 dobras = $1
Per Capita Income/GDP: $1,000/$133 million
Inflation Rate: 27%
Natural Resources: fish
Agriculture: cacao; coconut palms; coffee; bananas; palm kernels
Industry: beer; soft drinks; palm oil; copra; tourism; manufacturing; construction

FOREIGN TRADE

Exports: $5.5 million
Imports: $31.5 million

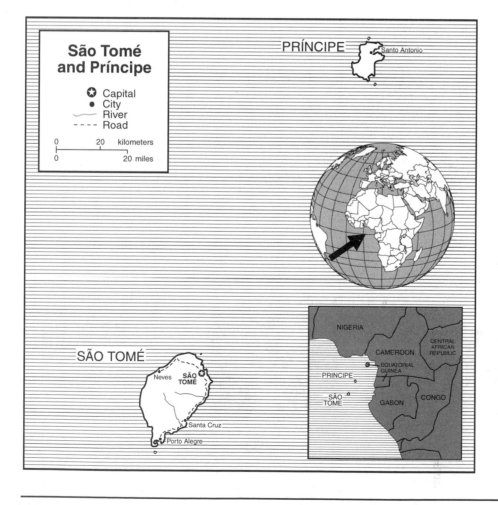

The Portuguese settle São Tomé and Príncipe
1500s

Slavery is abolished, but forced labor continues
1876

The Portuguese massacre hundreds of islanders
1953

Factions within the liberation movement unite to form the MLSTP in Gabon
1972

Independence
1975

Manuel Pinto da Costa deposes and exiles Miguel Trovoada, the premier and former number-two man in the MLSTP
1979

1990s

Economic and political liberalization

Multiparty elections lead to the defeat of the MLSTP–PSD and the election to the presidency of Trovoada

Trovoada maintains an uneasy hold on power following July 1996 elections

SÃO TOMÉ AND PRÍNCIPE

In August 1995, soldiers in the small island nation of São Tomé and Príncipe briefly deposed Miguel Trovoada, the country's first democratically elected president. The coup quickly collapsed, however, in the face of domestic and international opposition. While the country's new democracy survived, it remains vulnerable to a weak economy, which shows little prospect of improvement.

The islands had held their first multiparty elections in January 1991. The elections resulted in the defeat of the former ruling party, the Liberation Movement of São Tomé and Príncipe–Social Democratic Party (MLSTP–PSD), by Trovoada's Party of Democratic Convergence–Group of Reflection (PDC–GR). Subsequent elections in December 1992, however, reversed the PDC–GR advantage in Parliament, leading to an uneasy division of power.

São Tomé and Príncipe gained its independence in 1975, after a half-millennium of Portuguese rule. During the colonial era, economic life centered around the interests of a few thousand Portuguese settlers, particularly a handful of large-plantation owners who controlled more than 80 percent of the land. After independence, most of the Portuguese fled, taking their skills and capital and leaving the economy in disarray. But production on the plantations has since been revived.

The Portuguese began the first permanent settlement of São Tomé and Príncipe in the late 1400s. Through slave labor, the islands developed rapidly as one of the world's leading exporters of sugar. Only a small fraction of the profits from this boom were consumed locally; and high mortality rates, caused by brutal working conditions, led to an almost insatiable demand for more slaves. Profits from sugar declined after the mid-1500s due to competition from Brazil and the Caribbean. A period of prolonged depression set in.

In the early 1800s, a second economic boom swept the islands, when they became leading exporters of coffee, and, more importantly, cocoa. São Tomé and Príncipe's position in the world market has since declined, yet these two cash crops, along with copra, have continued to be economic mainstays. Although slavery was officially abolished during the nineteenth century, forced labor was maintained by the Portuguese into modern times. Involuntary contract workers, known as *serviçais*, were imported to labor on the islands' plantations, which had notoriously high mortality rates. Sporadic labor unrest and occasional incidents of international outrage led to some improvement in working conditions, but fundamental reforms came about only after independence. A historical turning point for the islands was the Batepa Massacre in 1953, when several hundred African laborers were killed following local resistance to labor conditions.

Between 1975 and 1991, São Tomé and Príncipe was ruled by the MLSTP–PSD, which had emerged in exile as the island's leading anticolonial movement, as a one-party state initially committed to Marxist-Leninism. But in 1990, a new policy of *abertura,* or political and economic "opening," resulted in the legalization of opposition parties and the introduction of direct elections with secret balloting. Press restrictions were also lifted, and the nation's security police were purged. The democratization process was welcomed by previously exiled opposition groups, most of which united as the DCP–GR. The changed political climate has also been reflected in the establishment of an independent labor movement. Previously, strikes were forbidden .

The move toward multiparty politics was accompanied by an evolution to a market economy by the former socialist government. Since 1985, a Free Trade Zone has been established, state farms have been privatized, and private capital has been attracted to build up a tourist industry. These moves have been accompanied by a major expansion of Western loans and assistance to the islands, an inflow of capital that now accounts for nearly half of the gross domestic product.

The government has also focused its development efforts on fishing. In 1978, a 200-mile maritime zone was declared over the tuna-rich waters around the islands. The state-owned fishing company, Empesca, is upgrading the local fleet, which still consists mostly of canoes using old-fashioned nets. The influx of aid and investment has resulted in several years of sustained economic growth.

DEVELOPMENT

Local food production has been significantly boosted by a French-funded scheme. Japan is assisting in fishery development. There is concern that tourist fishermen may adversely affect the local fishing industry.

FREEDOM

Before 1987, human rights were circumscribed in São Tomé and Príncipe. Gradual liberalization has now given way to a commitment to political pluralism.

HEALTH/WELFARE

Since independence, the government has had enormous progress in expanding health care and education. The Sãotoméan infant mortality rate is now among the lowest in Africa and average life expectancy is among the highest. About 65% of the population between 6 and 19 years of age are now in school.

ACHIEVEMENTS

São Tomé and Príncipe shares in a rich Luso-African artistic tradition. The country is particularly renowned for poets such as Jose de Almeida and Francisco Tenriero, who were among the first to express in the Portuguese language the experiences and pride of Africans.

East Africa

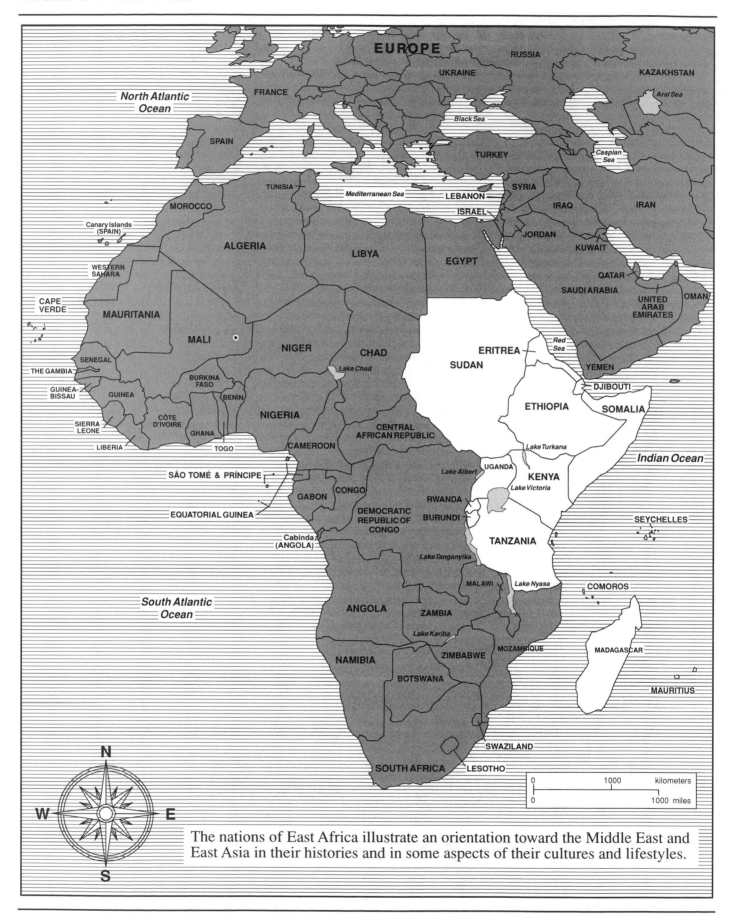

The nations of East Africa illustrate an orientation toward the Middle East and East Asia in their histories and in some aspects of their cultures and lifestyles.

East Africa: A Mixed Inheritance

The vast East African region, ranging from Sudan in the north to Tanzania and the Indian Ocean islands in the south, is an area of great diversity. Although the islands are the homes of distinctive civilizations with ties to Asia, their interactions with the African mainland give their inclusion here validity. Ecological features, such as the Great Rift Valley, the prevalence of cattle-herding lifestyles, and long-standing participation in the Indian Ocean trading networks are some of the region's unifying aspects.

CATTLE-HERDING SOCIETIES

A long-horned cow would be an appropriate symbol for East Africa. Most of the region's rural inhabitants, who make up the majority of people from the Horn, to Lake Malawi, to Madagascar, value cattle for their social as well as economic importance. The Nuer of Sudan, the Somali near the Red Sea (who, like many other peoples of the Horn, herd camels as well as cattle, goats, and sheep), and the Maasai of Tanzania and Kenya are among the pastoral peoples whose herds are their livelihoods. Farming communities such as the Kikuyu of Kenya, the Baganda of Uganda, and the Malagasey of Madagascar also prize cattle.

Much of the East African landmass is well suited for herding. Whereas the rain forests of West and Central Africa are generally infested with tsetse flies, whose bite is fatal to livestock, most of East Africa is made up of belts of tropical and temperate savanna, which are ideal for grazing. Thus pastoralism has long been predominant in the savanna zones of West and Southern, as well as East, Africa. Tropical rain forests are found in East Africa only on the east coast of Madagascar and scattered along the mainland's coast. Much of the East African interior is dominated by the Great Rift Valley, which stretches from the Red Sea as far south as Malawi. This geological formation is characterized by mountains as well as valleys, and it features the region's great lakes, such as Lake Albert, Lake Tangan-yika, and Lake Malawi.

People have been moving into and through the East African region since the existence of humankind; indeed, most of the earliest human fossils have been unearthed in this region. Today, almost all the mainland inhabitants speak languages that belong to either the Bantu or Nilotic linguistic families. There has been much historical speculation about the past migration of these peoples, but current archaeology indicates that both linguistic groups have probably been established in the area for a long time, although oral traditions and other forms of historical evidence indicate locally important shifts in settlement patterns into the contemporary period. Iron working and, in at least a few cases, small-scale steel production have been a part of the regional economy for more than 2,000 years. Long-distance trade and the production of various crafts have also existed since ancient times.

The inhabitants of the region have had to confront insufficient and unreliable rainfall. Drought and famine in the Horn and in areas of Kenya and Tanzania have in recent years changed lifestyles and dislocated many people.

ISLAMIC INFLUENCE

Many of the areas of East Africa have been influenced—since at least as far back as Roman times and perhaps much further— by the Middle East and other parts of Asia. Over the past thousand years, most parts of East Africa, including the Christian highlands of Ethiopia and the inland interlake states such as Buganda, Burundi, and Rwanda, became familiar to the Muslim Arab traders of the Swahili and Red Sea coasts and the Sudanese interior. Somalia, Djibouti, and Sudan, which border the Red Sea and are close to the Arabian Peninsula, have been the most influenced by Arab Islamic culture. Mogadishu, the capital of Somalia, began as an Islamic trading post in the tenth century. The Islamic faith, its various sects or brotherhoods, the Koran, and the Shari'a (the Islamic legal code) are predominant throughout the Horn, except in the Ethiopian and Eritrean highlands and southern Sudan. In recent years, many Somali, Sudanese, and others have migrated to the oil-rich states of Arabia to work.

Farther south, in the communities and cultures on the perimeters of the east coast, Arabs and local Bantu-speaking Africans combined, from as early as the ninth century, but especially during the 1200s to 1400s, to form the culture and the language that we now call Swahili. In the first half of the nineteenth century, Seyyid Said, the sultan of Oman, transferred his capital to Zanzibar, in recognition of the outpost's economic importance. Motivated by the rapid expansion of trade in ivory and slaves, many Arab–Swahili traders began to establish themselves and build settlements as far inland as the forests of eastern Zaire. As a result, some of the noncoastal peoples also adopted Islam, while Swahili developed into a regional lingua franca.

The whole region from the Horn to Tanzania continued to be affected by the slave trade through much of the nineteenth century. Slaves were sent north from Uganda and southern Sudan to Egypt and the Middle East, and from Ethiopia across the Red Sea. Others were taken to the coast by Arab, Swahili, or African traders, either to work on the plantations in Zanzibar or to be transported to the Persian Gulf and the Indian Ocean islands.

In the late 1800s and early 1900s, South Asian laborers from what was then British India were brought in by the British to build the East African railroad. South Asian traders already resided in Zanzibar; others now came and settled in Kenya and Tanzania, becoming shopkeepers and bankers in inland centers, such as Kampala and Nairobi, as well as on the coast, in Mombasa and Dar es Salaam or in smaller stops along the railroad. South Asian laborers were also sent in large numbers to work on the sugar plantations of Mauritius; their descendants there now make up about two thirds of that island's population.

The subregions of East Africa include the following: the countries of the Horn, East Africa proper, and the islands. The Horn includes Djibouti, Ethiopia, Eritrea, Somalia, and Sudan, which are associated here with one another not so much because of a common heritage or on account of any compatibility of their governments (indeed, they are often hostile to one another), but because of the movements of peoples across borders in recent times. East Africa proper is comprised of Kenya, Tanzania, and Uganda, which do have underlying cultural ties and a history of economic relations, in which Rwanda and Burundi have also shared. The Indian Ocean islands include the Comoros, Madagascar, Mauritius, and Seychelles, which, notwithstanding the expanses of ocean that separate them, have certain cultural aspects and current interests in common.

THE HORN

Ethiopia traditionally has had a distinct, semi-isolated history that has separated the nation from its neighbors. This early Christian civilization, which was periodically united by a strong dynasty but at other times was disunited, was centered in the highlands of the interior, surrounded by often hostile lowland peoples. Before the nineteenth century, it was in infrequent contact with other Christian societies. During the 1800s, however, a series of strong rulers reunified the highlands and went on to conquer surrounding peoples such as the Afar, Oromo, and Somali. In the process, the state expanded to its current boundaries. While the empire's expansion helped it to preserve its independence during Africa's colonial partition, sectarian and ethnic divisions, a legacy of the imperial state-building process, now threaten to tear the polity apart.

Ethiopia and the other contemporary nations of the Horn have been influenced by outside powers, whose interests in the region have been primarily rooted in its strategic location. In the nineteenth century, both Great Britain and France became interested in the Horn, because the Red Sea was the link between their countries and the markets of Asia. This was especially true after the completion of the Suez Canal in 1869. Both of the imperial powers occupied ports on the Red Sea at the time. They then began to compete over the upper Nile in modern Sudan. In the 1890s, French forces, led by Captain Jean Baptiste Marchand, literally raced from the present-day area of Congo to reach the center of Sudan before the arrival of a larger British expeditionary force, which had invaded the region from Egypt. Ultimately, the British were able to consolidate their control over the entire Sudan.

Italian ambitions in the Horn were initially encouraged by the British, in order to counter the French. Italy's defeat by the Ethiopians at the Battle of Adowa in 1896 did not deter its efforts to dominate the coastal areas of Eritrea and southeastern Somalia. Later, Italy, under Benito Mussolini, briefly (1936–1942) occupied Ethiopia itself.

(United Nations photo by Ray Witlin)

In the drought-affected areas of East Africa, people must devote considerable time and energy to the search for water.

During the cold war, great-power competition for control of the Red Sea and the Gulf of Aden, which are strategically located near the oil fields of the Middle East as well as along the Suez shipping routes, continued between the United States and the Soviet Union. Local events sometimes led to shifts in alignments. Before 1977, for instance, the United States was closely allied with Ethiopia, and the Soviet Union with Somalia. However, in 1977–1978, Ethiopia, having come under a self-proclaimed Marxist-Leninist government, allied itself with the Soviet Union, receiving in return the support of Cuban troops and billions of dollars' worth of Socialist bloc military aid, on loan, for use in its battles against Eritrean and Somali rebels. The latter group, living in Ethiopia's Ogaden region, were seeking to become part of a greater Somalia. In this irredentist adventure, they had the direct support of invading Somalia troops. Although the United States refused to counter the Soviets by in turn backing the irredentists, it subsequently established relations with the Somali government at a level that allowed it virtually to take over the former Soviet military facility at Berbera.

Discord and Drought

The countries of the Horn, unlike the East African states farther south or the island states, are alienated from one another, and there are no prospects for a regional community among them in the foreseeable future. Although the end of the cold war greatly reduced superpower competition, local animosities continue to wreak havoc in the region. Today, the Horn is bound together and torn apart by its millions of refugees, who continue to flee civil wars in all of the Horn's states except Eritrea. Over the past 2 decades, Ethiopia, Somalia, and Sudan have suffered under vicious authoritarian regimes, which engaged in genocide against dissident segments of their populations. Although the old regimes have recently been overthrown in Ethiopia and Somalia, peace has yet to come to either society. Having gained its independence only in 1993, Africa's newest nation, Eritrea, is struggling to overcome the devastating legacy of its 30-year liberation struggle against Ethiopia. Djibouti, long a regional enclave of tranquillity, is now also being undermined by political violence.

The horrible effects of these wars have been magnified by recurrent droughts. Hundreds of thousands of people have starved to death in the past decade, while many more have survived only because of international aid efforts.

Ethiopians leave their homes for Djibouti, Somalia, and Sudan for relief from war and famine. Sudanese and Somali flee to Ethiopia for the same reasons. Today, every country harbors not only refugees but also dissidents from neighboring lands and has a citizenry related to those who live in adjoining countries. Peoples such as the Afar minority in Djibouti often seek support from their kin in Eritrea and Ethiopia. Many Somali guerrilla groups have used Ethiopia as a base, while Somali factions have continued to give aid

(WHO photo)

East African peoples, especially along the coast, blend heritages from Asia, the Middle East, and Africa.

(United Nations photo by Milton Grant)
Of the millions of refugees who have been displaced by civil wars in Ethiopia, Somalia, and Sudan, fully 60 percent are children.

and comfort to Ethiopia's rebellious Ogaden population. Ethiopian factions allegedly continue to assist southern rebels against the government of Sudan, which had long supported the Tigray and Eritrean rebel movements of northern Ethiopia.

At times, the states of the region have reached agreements among themselves to curb their interference in one another's affairs. But they have made almost no progress in the more fundamental task of establishing internal peace, thus assuring that the region's violent downward spiral continues.

THE SOUTHERN STATES OF EAST AFRICA

The peoples of Kenya, Tanzania, and Uganda as well as Burundi and Rwanda have underlying connections rooted in the past. The kingdoms of the Lakes region of Uganda,

Rwanda, and Burundi, though they have been politically superseded in the postcolonial era, have left their legacies. For example, myths about a heroic dynasty of rulers, the Chwezi, who ruled over an early Ugandan-based kingdom, are widespread. Archaeological evidence attests to the actual existence of the Chwezi, probably in the sixteenth century. Peoples in western Kenya and Tanzania, who have lived under less centralized systems of governance but nonetheless have rituals similar to those of the Ugandan kingdoms, also share the traditions of the Chwezi dynasty, which have become associated with a spirit cult.

The precolonial kingdoms of Rwanda and Burundi, both of which came under German and, later, Belgian control during the colonial era, were socially divided between a ruling warrior class, the Tutsi, and a much larger peasant class, the Hutu. Although both states are now independent republics, their societies remain bitterly divided along these ethnoclass lines. In Rwanda, the feudal hegemony of the Tutsi was overthrown in a bloody civil conflict in 1959, which led to the flight of many Tutsi. But in 1994, the sons of these Tutsi exiles came to power, after elements in the former Hutu-dominated regime organized a genocidal campaign against all Tutsi. In the belief that the Tutsi were back on top, millions of Hutu then fled the country. In Burundi, Tutsi rule was maintained for decades through a repressive police state, which in 1972 and 1988 resorted to the mass murder of Hutu. Elections in 1993 resulted in the country's first Hutu president at the head of a government that included members of both groups, but he was murdered by the predominantly Tutsi army. Since then, the country has been teetering on the brink of yet another crisis, as some of its politicians try to promote reconciliation.

Kenya and Uganda were taken over by the British in the late nineteenth century, while Tanzania, originally conquered by Germany, became a British colony after World War I. In Kenya the British encouraged the growth of a settler community. Although never much more than 1 percent of the colony's resident population, the settlers were given the best agricultural lands in the rich highlands region around Nairobi; and, throughout most of the colonial era, they were allowed to exert their political and economic hegemony over the local Africans. The settler populations in Tanzania and Uganda were smaller and less powerful. While the settler presence in Kenya led to land alienation and consequent immiseration for many Africans, it also fostered a fair amount of colonial investment in infrastructure. As a result, Kenya had a relatively sophisticated economy at the time of its independence, a fact that was to complicate proposals for its economic integration with Tanzania and Uganda.

In the 1950s, the British established the East African Common Services Organization to promote greater economic cooperation among its Kenyan, Tanganyikan (Tanzanian), and Ugandan territories. By the early 1960s, the links among the states were so close that President Julius Nyerere of Tanzania proposed that his country delay its independence until Kenya also gained its freedom, in hopes that the two countries would then join together. This did not occur.

In 1967, the Common Services Organization was transformed by its three (now independent) members into a full-fledged "common market," known as the East African Community (EAC). The EAC collectively managed the railway system, development of harbors, and international air, postal, and telecommunication facilities. It also maintained a common currency, development bank, and other economic, cultural, and scientific services. Peoples moved freely across the borders of the three EAC states. However, the EAC soon began to unravel, as conflicts over its operations grew. It finally collapsed in 1977. The countries disputed the benefits of the association, which seemed to have been garnered primarily by Kenya. The ideologies and personalities of its leaders at the time—Nyerere, Jomo Kenyatta of Kenya, and Idi Amin of Uganda—differed greatly. Relations between Kenya and Tanzania deteriorated to the point that the border between them was closed for several years.

In 1983, Kenya, Tanzania, and Uganda agreed on the division of the assets of the old Community; Kenya experienced the largest losses. Tanzania and Kenya opened their borders and began rebuilding their relationship. The economic strains that all three countries currently face in their dealings with the world economy make clear the value of the defunct EAC. But political factors continue to complicate the quest for greater regional cooperation. Kenyatta was succeeded by his vice president, Daniel arap Moi, whose regime over the past decade has become increasingly repressive in the face of mounting opposition. Uganda still suffers from years of warfare and instability, the legacies of the brutal regimes of Amin and Milton Obote, whose second administration was overthrown in a 1985 coup. Uganda's current president, Yoweri Museveni, maintains an uneasy control over a country still plagued by violence. Although the governments of Kenya, Rwanda, Sudan, Tanzania, and Zaire pledged in 1986 to prevent exiles from using asylum to destabilize their homelands, tensions in the region have continued. Relations between Uganda and Kenya have been strained over allegations that each has harbored the other's dissidents.

A number of joint projects may contribute to the rebirth of some form of East African community. A "Preferential Trade Area" of 19 East and Southern African nations was established in 1981. Burundi, Rwanda, Tanzania, and Uganda are sharing in the construction of a hydroelectric project on the Kagera River. Uganda has established cooperative military links with both Kenya and Tanzania. The governments of Burundi, Rwanda, Tanzania, and Zaire have met to discuss security, trade, and cultural exchange in the region. Rwanda and Burundi are members of the Economic Community of Central African States, but their economic ties with East African states have led the UN Economic Commission on Africa, as well as other multinational organizations, to include them in the East African regional groupings.

There has been much talk of improving relations. "Think East Africa," *The Standard* of Kenya wrote, commenting on the cultural links that existed in the area before colonialism. Salim Salim, a Tanzanian statesman, noted, "You can choose a friend, but you cannot choose a brother. . . . In this case Kenyans and Ugandans are our brothers."

THE ISLANDS

The Comoros, Madagascar, Mauritius, and Seychelles each has its own special characteristics. Nonetheless, they have some important traits in common. All four island nations have been strongly influenced historically by contacts with Asia as well as with mainland Africa and Europe. Madagascar and the Comoros have populations that originated in Indonesia and the Middle East as well as in Africa; the Malagasey language is related to Indonesian Malay. The citizens of Mauritius and Seychelles are of European as well as African and Asian origin.

All four island groups have also been influenced by France. Mauritius and Seychelles were not permanently inhabited until the 1770s, when French settlers arrived with their African slaves. The British subsequently took control of these two island groups and, during the 1830s, abolished slavery. Thereafter the British encouraged migration from South Asia and, to a lesser extent, from China to make up for labor shortages on the islands' plantations. Local French-based creoles remain the major languages on the islands.

In 1978, all the islands, along with opposition groups from the French possession of Réunion, formed the Indian Ocean Commission. Originally a body with a Socialist orientation, the commission campaigned for the independence of Réunion and the return of the island of Diego Garcia by Britain to Mauritius, as well as the dismantling of the U.S. naval base located there. By the end of the 1980s, however, the export-oriented growth of Mauritius and the continuing prosperity of Seychelles' tourist-based economy were helping to push all nations toward a greater emphasis on market economics in their multilateral, as well as internal, policy initiatives. Madagascar and the Comoros have recently offered investment incentives for Mauritius-based private firms. Mauritians have also played prominent roles in the development of tourism in the Comoros.

In addition to their growing economic ties, the Comoros and Mauritius, and to a somewhat lesser extent, Madagascar and Seychelles, have created linkages with South Africa. In 1995, Mauritius followed South Africa's lead to become the 12th member of the Southern African Development Community.

Burundi (Republic of Burundi)

GEOGRAPHY

Area in Square Kilometers (Miles):
27,834 (10,759) (about the size of Maryland)
Capital (Population): Bujumbura (240,000)
Climate: tropical to temperate

PEOPLE

Population
Total: 6,262,500
Annual Growth Rate: 2.18%
Rural/Urban Population Ratio: 94/6
Major Languages: Kirundi; French; Kiswahili; others
Ethnic Makeup: 83% Hutu; 15% Tutsi; 2% Twa and others

Health
Life Expectancy at Birth: 38 years (male); 42 years (female)
Infant Mortality Rate (Ratio): 112/1,000
Average Caloric Intake: 99% of FAO minimum
Physicians Available (Ratio): 1/31,777

Religions
67% Christian; 32% traditional indigenous; 1% Muslim

Education
Adult Literacy Rate: 50%

COMMUNICATION

Telephones: 8,000
Newspapers: 1 daily

THE BUTLER–OBIOZOR REPORT

"The Burundian Affair," a report drafted by William Butler and George Obiozor, issued in 1972 by the International Commission of Jurists and the International League of the Rights of Man, was an early indictment of the role of the Burundi government in its ongoing atrocities against the Hutu population. It concluded that the government was guilty of genocidal acts, defining *genocide* as "a denial of the right of existence of entire human groups" and/or the "systematic killing of people based on their race or ethnic origin, creed or color." The report served as the major evidence for introducing the situation in Burundi as a case for consideration by the UN Commission on Human Rights. However, the Commission dropped the case in 1975, without having undertaken any action.

TRANSPORTATION

Highways—Kilometers (Miles): 5,900 (3,682)
Railroads—Kilometers (Miles): none
Usable Airfields: 4

GOVERNMENT

Type: republic
Independence Date: July 1, 1962
Head of State/Government: President (General) Pierre Buyoyo; Prime Minister Sylvestre Kanyenkiko
Political Parties: Union National Progress; Burundi Democratic Front; Organization of the People of Burundi; Socialist Party of Burundi; People's Reconciliation Party
Suffrage: universal over 19

MILITARY

Number of Armed Forces: 7,150
Military Expenditures (% of Central Government Expenditures): 2.6%
Current Hostilities: internal conflict

ECONOMY

Currency ($ U.S. Equivalent): 248.5 Burundi francs = $1
Per Capita Income/GDP: $600/$3.7 billion
Inflation Rate: 10%
Natural Resources: nickel; uranium; cobalt; copper; platinum
Agriculture: coffee; tea; cotton; food crops
Industry: light consumer goods; beer brewing

FOREIGN TRADE

Exports: $68 million
Imports: $203 million

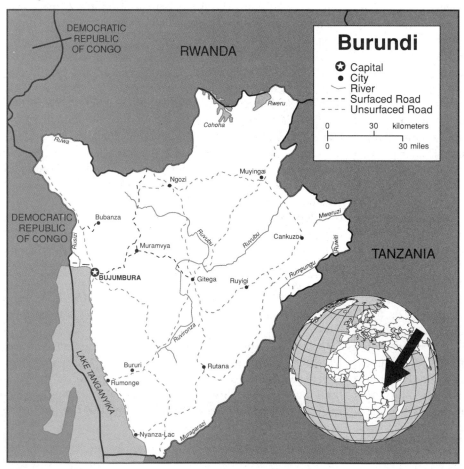

BURUNDI

Burundi is a small, beautiful, and crowded country whose people are deeply divided. Since the 1993 murder of the country's only democratically elected president, Melchior Ndadye, more than 150,000 Burundians have been killed in interethnic violence. In 1972 and again in 1988, tens of thousands perished in the nation's killing fields. There are now fears of even greater mass killings.

In the past, the violence was initiated by members of the Tutsi governing elite seeking to maintain their privileged status through brutal military control. Today, the army's hold on the countryside is being increasingly challenged by an armed movement, Forces for the Defense of Democracy (FDD), which is spreading counterterror in the name of the country's Hutu majority. What *has* remained the same over the years is the general indifference of the outside world to Burundi's horrific record of genocide.

The successful holding of democratic elections in July 1993 had given rise to cautious optimism about the dawning of a new era of national reconciliation in Burundi. Ndadye was a Hutu who formed an interethnic coalition government of national unity. His death, followed by the April 1994 assassination of his successor, Cyprien Ntaryamira, sparked a wave of ethnic cleansing. The capital city, Bujumbura, has been emptied of its Hutu majority, while ordinary Tutsi have had to abandon much of the countryside. In July 1996, the army overthrew what was left of civilian authority under President Sylveste Ntibantunganya, a Hutu, bringing back to power the Tutsi general Pierre Buyoyo, who had ruled the country from 1987 to 1993.

A DIVIDED SOCIETY

Burundi's population is ethnosocially divided into three distinctive groups. At the bottom of the social hierarchy are the Twa, commonly stereotyped as "pygmies." Believed to be the earliest inhabitants of the country, today the Twa account for only about 1 percent of the population. The largest group, constituting 83 percent of the population, are the Hutu, most of whom subsist as farmers. The dominant group are the Tutsi, who comprise some 15 percent of the population. Among the Tutsi, who are subdivided into clans, status has long been associated with cattle-keeping. Leading Tutsi continue to form an aristocratic ruling class over the whole of Burundi society. Until 1966, the leader of Burundi's Tutsi aristocracy was the Mwami, or king.

The Burundi kingdom goes back at least as far as the sixteenth century. By the late nineteenth century, when the kingdom was incorporated into German East Africa, the Tutsi had subordinated the Hutu, who became clients of local Tutsi aristocrats, herding their cattle and rendering other services. The Germans and subsequently the Belgians, who assumed paramount authority over the kingdom after World War I, were content to rule through Burundi's established social hierarchy. But many Hutu as well as Tutsi were educated by Christian missionaries.

In the late 1950s, Prince Louis Rwagazore, a Tutsi, tried to accommodate Hutu as well as Tutsi aspirations by establishing a nationalist reform movement known as the Union for National Progress (UPRONA). Rwagazore was assassinated before independence, but UPRONA led the country to independence in 1962, with King Mwambutsa IV retaining considerable power as head of state. The Tutsi elite remained dominant, but the UPRONA cabinets contained representation from the two major groups. This attempt to balance the interests of the Tutsi and Hutu broke down in 1965, when Hutu politicians within both UPRONA and the rival People's Party won 80 percent of the vote and the majority of the seats in both houses of the bicameral Legislature. In response, the king abolished the Legislature before it could convene. A group of Hutu army officers then attempted to overthrow the government. Mwambutsa fled the country, but the revolt was crushed in a countercoup by Tutsi officers, led by Michel Micombero.

In the aftermath of the uprising, Micombero took power amid a campaign of reprisals in which, it is believed, some 5,000 Hutu were killed. He deposed Mwambutsa's son, Ntare V, from kingship and set up a "Government of Public Safety," which set about purging Hutu members from the government and the army. Political struggle involved interclan competition among the Tutsi as well as the maintenance of their hegemony over the Hutu.

Under Micombero, Burundi continued to be marred by interethnic violence, occasional coup attempts, and promonarchist agitation. A major purge of influential Hutu was carried out in 1969. In 1972, Ntare V was lured to Uganda by Idi Amin, who turned him over to Micombero. Ntare was placed under arrest upon his arrival and was subsequently murdered by his guards.

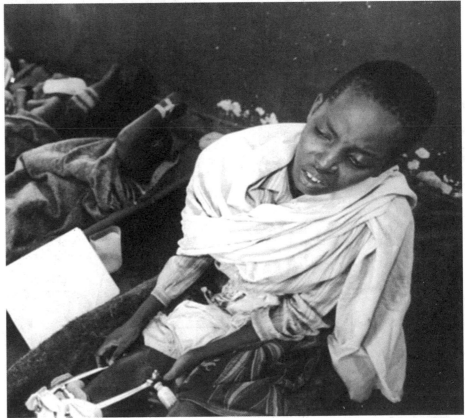

(AP photo by Jean-Marc Bosju)

The fallout from the war between the Hutu and Tutsi generated a horrible genocide and left the population wounded, displaced, and in chaos. The urgent need for medical assistance far outstripped the available resources.

A declaration of martial law then set off an explosion of violence. In response to an alleged uprising involving the deaths of up to 2,000 Tutsi, government supporters began to massacre large numbers of Hutu. Educated Hutu were especially targeted in a 2-month campaign of selective genocide, which is generally estimated to have claimed 200,000 victims (estimates range from 80,000 to 500,000 deaths for the entire period, with additional atrocities being reported through 1973). More than 100,000 Hutu fled to Uganda, Rwanda, Zaire, and Tanzania. Among the governments of the world, only Tanzania and Rwanda showed any deep concern for the course of events. China, France, and Libya used the crisis to upgrade their military aid to the Burundi regime significantly.

In 1974, Micombero formally transformed Burundi into a single-party state under UPRONA. Although Micombero was replaced 2 years later in a military coup by Colonel Jean-Baptiste Bagaza, power remained effectively in the hands of members of the Tutsi elite who controlled UPRONA, the civil service, and the army. In 1985, Bagaza widened existing state persecution of Seventh Day Adventists and Jehovah's Witnesses to include the Catholic Church, to which two thirds of Burundi's population belong, suspecting it of fostering seditious—that is, pro-Hutu—sympathies. (The overthrow of Bagaza by Pierre Buyoyo, in a 1987 military coup, led to a lifting of the anti-Catholic campaign.)

Ethnic violence erupted again in 1988. Apparently some Tutsi were killed by Hutu in northern Burundi, in response to rumors of another massacre of Hutu. In retaliation, the army massacred between 5,000 and 25,000 Hutu. Another 60,000 Hutu took temporary refuge in Rwanda, while more than 100,000 were left homeless. In 1991, the revolutionary Party for the Liberation of the Hutu People, or Palipehutu, launched its own attacks on Tutsi soldiers and civilians, leading to further killing on all sides.

LAND ISSUES

Burundi remains one of the poorest countries in the world, despite its rich volcanic soils and generous international development assistance (it has consistently been one of the highest per capita aid recipients on the continent). In addition to the dislocations caused by cycles of interethnic violence, the nation's development prospects are seriously compromised by geographic isolation and population pressure on the land. About 25 percent of Burundi is under cultivation, generally by individual farmers trying to subsist on plots of no more than 3 acres. Another 60 percent of the country is devoted to pasture for mostly Tutsi livestock. Hutu farmers continue to be tied by patron–client relationships to Tutsi overlords. In recent years, the government has tied its rural development efforts to an unpopular villagization scheme.

This issue has complicated ongoing attempts to reach some kind of accommodation between the Tutsi elite and Hutu masses. Having cautiously increased Hutu participation in his government, while reserving ultimate power in the hands of all Tutsi Military Committee of National Salvation, Buyoyo agreed to the restoration of multiparty politics in 1991. A new Constitution was approved in March 1992; it allowed competition between approved, ethnically balanced, parties. In the resulting July 1993 election, Buyoyo's UPRONA was defeated by the Front for Democracy in Burundi (FRODEBU). FRODEBU's Ndadaye was sworn in as Burundi's first Hutu leader at the head of a joint FRODEBU–UPRONA government. His subsequent assassination by Tutsi hard-liners in the military set off a new wave of interethnic killings. The firm stand against the coup by Buyoyo and the Tutsi/UPRONA prime minister, Sylvie Kinigi, helped to calm the situation, but attempts to make a fresh start collapsed when a plane carrying Ntaraymira and his Rwandan counterpart was shot down over Rwanda. The latest coup followed UPRONA's withdrawal from the government following the massacre of more than 300 Tutsi by FDD, who by September 1996 were attempting to besiege the capital.

During a four-week period from late October to November 1996, the Tutsi-led Burundian military massacred at least 1,000 civilians. The government forces fought with Hutu rebels, as some 50,000 Hutus returned from camps that had been closed in Zaire. The Tutsi-dominated military set up more than a dozen "protection zones" for Hutu civilians while soldiers continued battling Hutu rebels. Strife continued as an estimated 200,000 Burundians were living in refugee camps in Tanzania.

DEVELOPMENT

Burundi's sources of wealth are limited. There is no active development of mineral resources, although sources of nickel have been located and may be mined soon. There is little industry, and the coffee crop, which contributes 75% to 90% of export earnings, has declined.

FREEDOM

Beset by ongoing genocide, there is currently no genuine freedom in Burundi, for either its ethnic majority or minority populations. Tens of thousands continue to flee the country.

HEALTH/WELFARE

Much of the educational system has been in private hands, especially the Roman Catholic Church. Burundi lost many educated and trained people during the Hutu massacres in the 1970s and '80s.

ACHIEVEMENTS

Burundians were briefly united in July 1996 by the victory of their countryman Venuste Niyongabo in the men's 5000-meter race at the Atlanta Summer Olympic Games. He dedicated his gold medal (the first for a Burundi citizen) to the hope of national reconciliation.

Comoros (Comoros Federal Islamic Republic)

GEOGRAPHY

Area in Square Kilometers (Miles): 2,171 (838) (about the size of Delaware)
Capital (Population): Moroni (30,000)
Climate: tropical; marine

PEOPLE

Population
Total: 569,300
Annual Growth Rate: 3.55%
Rural/Urban Population Ratio: n/a
Major Languages: Shaafi-Islam; Swahili; French; Arabic
Ethnic Makeup: Arab; African; East Indian

Health
Life Expectancy at Birth: 56 years (male); 61 years (female)
Infant Mortality Rate (Ratio): 77.3/1,000
Average Caloric Intake: 102% of FAO minimum
Physicians Available (Ratio): 1/23,009

Religions
86% Sunni Muslim; 14% Roman Catholic

Education
Adult Literacy Rate: 48%

COMMUNICATION

Telephones: 1,800
Newspapers: n/a

MAYOTTE ISLAND

In 1974, when the other Comoran islands voted overwhelmingly for independence, Mayotte opted to remain French, by a two-to-one margin. Since then, the French have continued to administer the island, with the support of the local population—more than 95 percent of whom have, in recent years, voted in favor of becoming an overseas department of France. Unlike the other Comoran islands, Mayotte is predominantly Christian. Historically, it has been greatly influenced by Malagasy and French culture. Comoran claims to the island are supported by the Organization of African Unity; and in the United Nations, only France voted against a resolution calling for its inclusion in the Comoros. Despite the location of its naval base on the island, France may be eager to withdraw from Mayotte but is reluctant to do so against the wishes of Mayotte and domestic opinion.

TRANSPORTATION

Highways—Kilometers (Miles): 750 (465)
Railroads—Kilometers (Miles): none
Usable Airfields: 4

GOVERNMENT

Type: Islamic republic
Independence Date: July 6, 1975
Head of State/Government: President Mohamed Taki; Prime Minister Halifa Houmadi
Political Parties: Comoran Union for Progress; Islands' Fraternity and Unity Party; Comoran Party for Democracy and Progress; Realizing Freedom's Capability; Democratic Front of the Comoros; others
Suffrage: universal at 18

MILITARY

Number of Armed Forces: 900
Military Expenditures (% of Central Government Expenditures): 3%
Current Hostilities: none

ECONOMY

Currency ($ U.S. Equivalent): 297 Comoran francs = $1
Per Capita Income/GDP: $700/$370 million
Inflation Rate: 15%
Natural Resources: agricultural land
Agriculture: perfume essences; copra; coconuts; cloves; vanilla; cinnamon; yams; rice
Industry: perfume distillation; tourism

FOREIGN TRADE

Exports: $13.7 million
Imports: $40.9 million

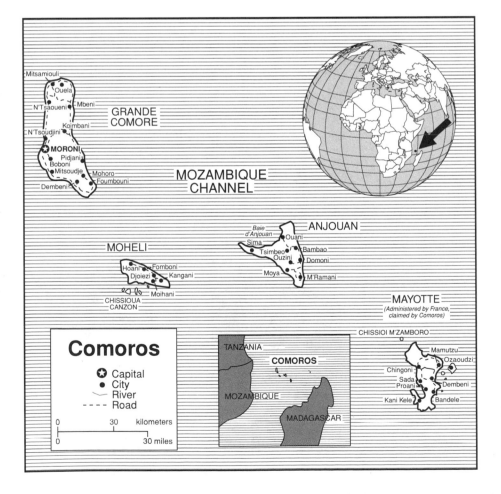

Comoros
- ⊛ Capital
- ● City
- ⌇ River
- ---- Road

0   30   kilometers
0   30 miles

Various groups settle in the islands, which become part of a Swahili trading network
1500s

French rule over Mayotte is established
1843

A French protectorate over the remaining Comoro islands is proclaimed
1886

The islands are ruled as part of the French colony of Madagascar
1914–1946

Independence is followed by a mercenary coup, which installs Ali Soilih
1975

Ali Soilih is overthrown by mercenaries; Ahmed Abdullah is restored
1978

Abdullah proclaims a one-party state; real power remains in the hands of mercenary leader Bob Denard
1980s

Comoros is linked to the South African supply of Renamo rebels in Mozambique

1990s

The assassination of Abdullah leads to the removal of Denard and to multiparty elections

A hijacked Ethiopian Air jet crashes off the Comoros

Mohamed Taki becomes president

COMOROS

At the time of its unilateral declaration of independence from France, in 1975, the Comoros was listed by the United Nations as one of the world's least developed nations. The succeeding years have not been especially kind to the Comorans; their lives have been made even more difficult by natural disaster, eccentric and authoritarian leadership, and external intervention. The 1990 restoration of a multiparty democracy has yet to provide a basis for political stability. Elections in 1992 and 1993 failed to produce a government with a clear mandate, while a rebellion on the island of Moroni was put down by force. Meanwhile, the islands remain impoverished. With 80 percent of Comorans underemployed as subsistence farmers, half the country's food must still be imported.

The Comoros archipelago was populated by a number of Indian Ocean peoples, who—by the time of the arrival of Europeans during the early 1500s—had combined to form the predominantly Muslim, Swahili-speaking society found on the islands today. In 1886, the French proclaimed a protectorate over the three main islands that currently constitute the Comoros Federal Islamic Republic. Throughout the colonial period, the Comoros were especially valued by the French, for strategic reasons. A local elite of large landholders prospered from the production of cash crops. Life for most Comorans, however, remained one of extreme poverty.

A month after independence, the first Comoran government, led by Ahmed Abdullah Abderemane, was overthrown by mercenaries, who installed Ali Soilih in power. He promised a socialist transformation of the nation and began to implement land reform but rapidly lost support both at home and abroad: Under his leadership, gangs of undisciplined youths terrorized society while the basic institutions and services of government all but disappeared. In 1977, the situation was made even worse by a major volcanic eruption, which left 20,000 people homeless, and by the arrival of 16,000 Comoran refugees following massacres in neighboring Madagascar.

In 1978, another band of mercenaries—this time led by the notorious Bob Denard, whose previous exploits in Zaire, Togo, and elsewhere had made his name infamous throughout Africa—overthrew Soilih and restored Abdullah to power. Denard, however, remained the true power behind the throne.

The Denard–Abdullah government enjoyed close ties with influential right-wing elements in France and South Africa. Connections with Pretoria were manifested through the use of the Comoros as a major conduit for South African supplies to the Renamo rebels in Mozambique. Economic ties with South Africa, especially in tourism and sanctions-busting, also grew. The government also established good relations with Saudi Arabia, Kuwait, and other conservative Arab governments while attracting significant additional aid from the international donor agencies.

In 1982, the country legally became a one-party state. Attempted coups in 1985 and 1987 aggravated political tensions. Many Comorans particularly resented the overbearing influence of Denard and his men. By November 1989, this group included President Abdullah himself. With the personal backing of President François Mitterand of France and President F. W. de Klerk of South Africa, Abdullah moved to replace Denard's mercenaries with a French-approved security unit. But before this move could be implemented, Abdullah was murdered following a meeting with Denard.

The head of the Supreme Court, Said Mohamed Djohar, was appointed interim president in the wake of the assassination. After a period of some confusion, during which popular protests against Denard swelled, Djohar quietly sought French intervention to oust the mercenaries. With both Paris and Pretoria united against him, Denard agreed to relinquish power, in exchange for safe passage to South Africa. The removal of Denard and temporary stationing of a French peacekeeping force was accompanied by the lifting of political restrictions in preparation for presidential elections. In 1990, a runoff resulted in a 55 percent electoral mandate for Djohar.

In September 1995, Denard's men returned to overthrow Djohar. But the mercenaries were soon forced to surrender to French forces, who installed Caambi el Yachourtu, rather than Djohar, as acting president. At the end of 1996, Mohamed Taki replaced Yachourtu.

DEVELOPMENT

One of the major projects undertaken since independence has been the ongoing expansion of the port at Mutsamundu, which will allow large ships to visit the islands. Vessels of up to 25,000 tons can now dock at the harbor. In recent years, there has been a significant expansion of tourism.

FREEDOM

Freedom was abridged after independence under both Ahmed Abdullah and Ali Soilih. The government elected in 1990 ended abuses.

HEALTH/WELFARE

Health statistics improved during the 1980s. A recent World Health Organization survey estimated that 10% of Comoran children ages 3 to 6 years are seriously malnourished and another 37% are moderately malnourished.

ACHIEVEMENTS

Comoros has long been the world's leading exporter of ylang-ylang, an essence used to make perfume. It is also the second-leading producer of vanilla and a major grower of cloves. Together, these cash crops account for more than 95% of export earnings. Unfortunately, the international prices of these crops have been low for the past 2 decades.

Djibouti (Republic of Djibouti)

GEOGRAPHY

Area in Square Kilometers (Miles):
23,200 (8,960) (about the size of
New Hampshire)
Capital (Population): Djibouti
(383,000) (est.)
Climate: arid to semiarid

PEOPLE

Population
Total: 427,700
Annual Growth Rate: 1.48%
Rural/Urban Population Ratio: 23/77
Major Languages: French; Arabic;
Somali; Saho-Afar
Ethnic Makeup: Somali; Afar

Health
Life Expectancy at Birth: 48 years
(male); 52 years (female)
Infant Mortality Rate (Ratio):
108.8/1,000
Average Caloric Intake: n/a
Physicians Available (Ratio): 1/3,790

Religions
94% Muslim; 6% Christian

Education
Adult Literacy Rate: 48%

DJIBOUTI POLITICS

Local politics in Djibouti has been dominated since independence by
the aging President Hassan Gouled Aptidon. No clear-cut successor
currently exists. Since the creation of a one-party state, a number of
underground movements have emerged in opposition to the continued
domination of the president's Popular Rally for Progress. One group
that surfaced in 1989, the Movement for Unity and Democracy, poses
a potential threat through its alleged association with the Somali National Movement, which is currently waging an armed struggle in
northern Somalia against that country's government. In 1990, two other
dissident movements, one Afar-oriented and the other Issa-oriented,
combined forces as the Union of Movements for Democracy. Another
important nonparty political force is the Ugaz, or sultan, of the Issa
Somali, who is based in the Ethiopian town of Dire Diwa. It is said that
the Ugaz and his council confirmed Gouled Aptidon as the political
leader of Djibouti's Issa in 1975. Other Afar and Somali clan heads,
living on both sides of the border, are also influential.

COMMUNICATION

Telephones: 7,300
Newspapers: 3 weeklies

TRANSPORTATION

Highways—Kilometers (Miles): 2,906
(1,801)
Railroads—Kilometers (Miles): 97
(60)
Usable Airfields: 13

GOVERNMENT

Type: republic
Independence Date: June 27, 1977
Head of State/Government: President
Hassan Gouled Aptidon; Prime
Minister Barkat Gourad Hamadou
Political Parties: People's
Progressive Assembly; Democratic
Renewal Party; Democratic National
Party; others
Suffrage: universal for adults

MILITARY

Number of Armed Forces: 6,600
*Military Expenditures (% of Central
Government Expenditures):* n/a
Current Hostilities: civil war; border
clashes with Eritrea

ECONOMY

Currency ($ U.S. Equivalent): 177.7
Djibouti francs = $1
Per Capita Income/GDP:
$1,200/$500 million
Inflation Rate: 6%
Natural Resources: none
Agriculture: goats; sheep; camels;
cattle; coffee
Industry: port and maritime support;
construction

FOREIGN TRADE

Exports: $184 million
Imports: $384 million

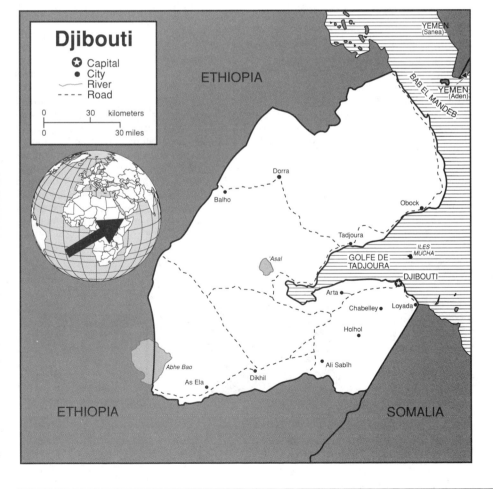

France buys the
port of Obock
1862

France acquires
the port of Djibouti
1888

The Addis
Ababa-Djibouti
Railroad is
completed
1917

Djibouti votes to
remain part of
Overseas France
1958

Independence;
the Ogaden War
1977

The underground
Union of
Movements for
Democracy is
formed as an
interethnic
antigovernment
coalition
1980s

1990s

Famine and
warfare in
Somalia and
Ethiopia lead to a
massive flow of
refugees to
Djibouti

Civil war rends
the country

President Hassan
Gouled Aptidon is
reelected; in 1996,
he returns home
after spending 3
months in a
French hospital

DJIBOUTI

Since 1992, Djibouti, once a small zone of peace in the troubled Horn of Africa, has been increasingly torn apart by civil war. An ethnic power struggle between Afar- and Somali-speaking groups has emerged, with predominantly Afar rebels of the Front for the Restoration of Unity (FRUD) holding northern areas of the country. This ongoing conflict has overshadowed cautious efforts by President Hassan Gouled Aptidon's mildly authoritarian government to introduce greater democracy. Aptidon was reelected in May 1993, and his Issa-Somali–dominated Popular Rally for Progress (RPP) party won all 65 seats in the December 1992 National Assembly elections. But both ballots were boycotted by major, predominantly Afar and non-Issa Somali opposition groups, resulting in less than half of the electorate voting. Djibouti's transformation from a one-party state to a multiparty democracy has thus far only underscored the country's ethnic divisions.

Since achieving its independence from France, Djibouti has had to strike a cautious balance between the competing interests of its larger neighbors, Ethiopia and Somalia. Most of the nation's population are divided between Afar- and Somali-speakers. In the past, Somalia has claimed ownership of the territory, based on the numerical preponderance of Djibouti's Somali population, variously estimated at 50 to 70 percent. However, local Somali as well as Afars also have strong ties to communities in Ethiopia. Furthermore, Djibouti's location at the crossroads of Africa and Eurasia has made it a focus of continuing strategic concern to nonregional powers, particularly France, which

maintains a large military presence in the country.

Modern Djibouti's colonial genesis is a product of mid-nineteenth-century European rivalry over control of the Red Sea. In 1862, France occupied the town of Obock, across the harbor from Djibouti city. This move was taken in anticipation of the 1869 opening of the Suez Canal, which transformed the Red Sea into the major shipping route between Asia, East Africa, and Europe. In 1888, Paris, having acquired Djibouti city and its hinterland, proclaimed its authority over French Somaliland, the modern territory of Djibouti.

The independence of France's other mainland African colonies by 1960, along with the formation in that year of the Somali Democratic Republic, led to local agitation for an end to French rule. To counter the effects of Somali nationalism, the French began to favor the Afar minority in local politics and employment. French president Charles de Gaulle's 1966 visit was accompanied by large, mainly Somali, pro-independence demonstrations. As a result, a referendum on the question of independence was held. Colonial control of voter registration assured a predominantly Afar electorate who, motivated by fears of Somali domination, opted for continued French rule. French Somaliland was then transformed into the self-governing Territory of Afars and Issas. The name reflected a continuing colonial policy of divide and rule; members of the Issas clan constituted just over half of the area's Somali speakers.

By the 1970s, neither Ethiopia nor France was opposed to Djibouti's independence but, for their own strategic reasons, both backed the Afar community in its desire for

assurances that the territory would not be incorporated into Somalia. An ethnic power-sharing arrangement was established that in effect acknowledged local Somali preponderance. The empowerment of local Somali, in particular the Issa, was accompanied by diminished pan-Somali sentiment. On June 27, 1977, the Republic of Djibouti became independent. French troops remained in the country, supposedly as a guarantee of its sovereignty. Internally, political power was divided by means of ethnically balanced cabinets, with the prime minister always being an Afar. The presidency has remained in the hands of Aptidon, an Issa-Somali.

War broke out between Ethiopia and Somalia a few months after Djibouti's independence. Djibouti remained neutral, but ethnic tensions mounted with the arrival of Somali refugees. In 1981, the Afar-dominated Djiboutian Popular Movement was outlawed. The Issa-dominated Popular Rally for Progress (RPP) then became the country's sole legal party.

Refugees have poured into Djibouti for years now, fleeing conflict and famine in Ethiopia, Somalia, and Sudan. The influx has swelled the country's population by about one third. This increase has deepened Djibouti's dependence on external food aid. Massive unemployment among Djibouti's largely urbanized population remains a critical problem.

DEVELOPMENT

Recent discoveries of gas reserves could result in a surplus for export. A number of small-scale irrigation schemes have been established. There is also a growing, though still quite small, fishing industry.

FREEDOM

Freedom of speech, association, and other rights are restricted. However, the government has not been associated with acts of arbitrary repression or gross violations of human rights.

HEALTH/WELFARE

Progress has been made in reducing infant mortality, but health services are strained. School enrollment has expanded by nearly one third since 1987.

ACHIEVEMENTS

Besides feeding its own refugees, the government of Djibouti has played a major role in assisting international efforts to relieve the recurrent famines in Ethiopia, Somalia, and Sudan.

Eritrea (State of Eritrea)

GEOGRAPHY

Area in Square Kilometers (Miles):
121,320 (46,829) (slightly larger than
Pennsylvania)
Capital (Population): Asmara
(400,000)
Climate: Hot, dry desert on seacoast;
cooler and wetter in central highlands

PEOPLE

Population
Total: 3,909,700
Annual Growth Rate: 9.04%
Rural/Urban Population Ratio: 85/15
Major Languages: various, including
Tigrinya and Amharic
Ethnic Makeup: 50% ethnic Tigrays;
40% Tigre and Kunama; 4% Afar;
3% Saho (Red Sea coast dwellers);
3% other

Health
Life Expectancy at Birth: 48 years
(male); 52 years (female)
Infant Mortality Rate (Ratio):
120.6/1,000
Average Caloric Intake: 78% of FAO
minimum
Physicians Available (Ratio): 1/95,856

Religions
Muslim; Coptic Christian; Roman
Catholic; Protestant

Education
Adult Literacy Rate: 24%

COMMUNICATION

Telephones: n/a
Newspapers: n/a

PRIVATE SOCIALIST ENTERPRISE

Red Sea Trading Corporation (RSTC) is a prime example of how many self-
reliant, cooperative efforts promoted during Eritrea's liberation war have been
carried over into its budding peacetime market economy. The Corporation was
formed in 1984 by a group of Eritrean Popular Liberation Front (EPLF) fighters
to supply their liberated zone in northern Eritrea with basic necessities. At the
time, the area was being strangled by an Ethiopian army economic blockade.
Raising 40,000 birr (the local currency) from existing EPLF cooperatives,
RSTC agents began bringing goods across the Red Sea in small boats, which
were then smuggled through enemy lines. Today the RSTC is a 150-million-birr
enterprise, with annual profits of more than 10 million. As a public service,
however, the Corporation deliberately keeps its profits low—5 percent for foodstuffs, 10 to 20 percent for other goods. As a result, the RSTC has become an
unofficial market regulator of Eritrea's retail sector.

TRANSPORTATION

Highways—Kilometers (Miles): 3,845
(2,890)
Railroads—Kilometers (Miles): 307 (191)
Usable Airfields: 20

GOVERNMENT

Type: transitional
Independence Date: May 24, 1993
Head of State: President Issaias
Aferweki
Political Parties: People's Front for
Democracy and Justice; Eritrean
People's Liberation Front; Eritrean
Liberation Front; Eritrean Liberation
Front–United Organization; Eritrean
Liberation Front–Revolutionary
Council; Eritrean Islamic Jihad;
Islamic Militant Group
Suffrage: n/a

MILITARY

Number of Armed Forces: 80,000
*Military Expenditures (% of Central
Government Expenditures):* n/a
Current Hostilities: border clashes
with Djibouti and Yemen

ECONOMY

Currency ($ U.S. Equivalent): 5.95
birr = $1 (currently the Ethiopian
currency is being used)
Per Capita Income/GDP: $500/$1.8
billion
Inflation Rate: n/a
Natural Resources: gold; copper; iron
ore; potash
Agriculture: sorghum; livestock; fish;
lentils; vegetables; maize; cotton;
tobacco; coffee; sisal
Industry: food processing; beverages;
clothing and textiles

FOREIGN TRADE

Exports: n/a
Imports: n/a

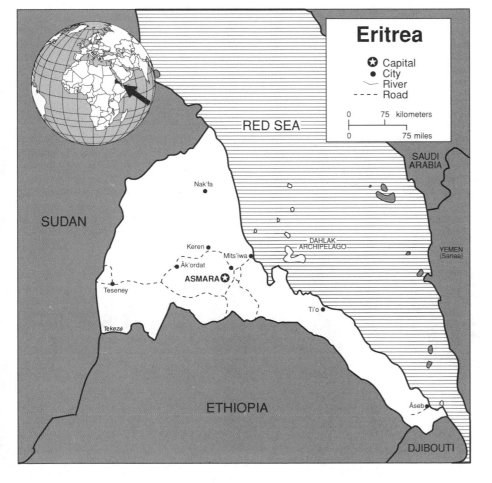

Italians occupy
the Eritrean port
of Assab
1869

Italians occupy
all of Eritrea
1889

Italians use
Eritrea as a
springboard for
conquest of
Ethiopia
1935–1936

Great Britain
occupies Eritrea
1941–1952

Eritrea is
federated with
Ethiopia
1952

The ELF begins
the liberation
struggle
1961

Federation is
ended; Eritrea is
incorporated as a
province of
Ethiopia
1962

1990s

The EPLF takes
over all of Eritrea;
the new Ethiopian
government
agrees to allow a
referendum on the
question of
independence

99.8% vote yes
for Eritrea's
independence;
Issaias Aferweki
becomes the
nation's first
president

Eritrea is involved
in border clashes
with Djibouti and
Yemen, hosts
armed Sudanese
opposition

ERITREA

Just after midnight on May 24, 1993, Eritrea became Africa's newest nation, ending 41 years of union with Ethiopia. However, Eritrea's true separation from Ethiopia began in September 1961, when a small group of armed men calling themselves the Eritrean Liberation Front (ELF) began a bitter, 3-decade-long anticolonial struggle.

Between 60,000 and 70,000 people perished as a result of that war, while another 700,000—then about one fifth of the total population—went into exile. What had been one of the continent's most sophisticated light-industrial infrastructures was largely reduced to ruins. Yet the war has also left a positive legacy, in the spirit of unity, self-reliance, and sacrifice that it engendered among Eritreans.

There is no clear-cut reason why a nationalist sentiment should have emerged in Eritrea. Like most African countries, the boundaries of Eritrea are an artificial product of the late nineteenth-century European scramble for colonies. Between 1869 and 1889, the territory fell under the rule of Italy. Italian influence survives today, especially in the overcrowded but elegant capital city of Asmara, which was developed as a showcase of neo-Roman imperialism. Italian rule came to an abrupt end in 1941, when British troops occupied the territory in World War II. The British withdrew only in 1952. In accordance with the wishes of the United Nations Security Council, the territory was then federated as an autonomous state within the "Empire of Ethiopia."

The federation did not come about through the wishes of the Eritreans. It was, rather, based on the dubious Ethiopian claim that Eritrea was an integral part of the Empire that had been alienated by the Italians. Among the Christians, there were historic cultural ties with their Ethiopian coreligionists, though the Tigrinya-speaking Copts of Eritrea were ethnically distinct from the Empire's then–politically dominant Amharic-speakers. The Muslim lowland areas had never been under any form of Ethiopian control. But, perhaps more important, developments under Italian rule had laid the basis for a sense that Eritrea had its own identity.

In the face of growing dissatisfaction inside the territory, Ethiopia's emperor, Haile Selassie, ended Eritrea's autonomous status in 1962. Fighting intensified in the early 1970s, after a faction ultimately known as the Eritrean Popular Liberation Front (EPLF) split from the ELF. The 1974 overthrow of Selassie briefly brought hopes of a peaceful settlement. But Ethiopia's new military rulers, known as the Dergue, committed themselves to securing the area by force. The ELF faded as the EPLF became increasingly effective in pinning down larger numbers of Ethiopian troops. In a major break with tradition, a large proportion of the EPLF's "Liberation Army," including many in command positions, was made up of women. In areas liberated by the EPLF, women were given the right to own land and choose their husbands, while the practice of female circumcision was discouraged.

Had it not been for the massive military support that the Dergue received from the Soviet Union and its allies, the conflict would have ended sooner. In the late 1980s, the EPLF began to work more closely with other groups inside Ethiopia proper that had taken up arms against their government. This resulted in an alliance between the EPLF and the Ethiopian People's Revolutionary Democratic Front (EPRDF), which was facilitated by the fact that leading members of both groups spoke Tigrinya. In May 1991, the Dergue collapsed, with the EPLF taking Asmara in the same month that EPRDF troops entered the Ethiopian capital of Addis Ababa. In July, the new EPRDF government agreed in principle to Eritrea's right to self-determination.

Eritrea's current Transitional Government was formed a few days after independence. It is scheduled to remain in power until 1997, when elections are to be held in accordance with a new Constitution. The head of state is former EPLF leader Issaias Aferweki. While the EPLF has in theory dissolved, a new People's Front for Democracy and Justice has emerged to take its place. A number of smaller parties, including remnants of the ELF, have joined the new Front as junior partners in the Transitional Government.

DEVELOPMENT

Since liberation, the Transitional Government has concentrated its efforts on restoring agricultural and communications infrastructure. The railway and ports of Assab and Massawa are being rehabilitated. In 1991, 80% of the country was dependent on food aid, but good rains in 1992–1993 helped boost crop production.

FREEDOM

The Transitional Government is pledged to uphold a bill of rights. While the government is dominated by the former EPLF, other parties and organizations participate in the 105-seat Provisional Council. Multiparty elections are scheduled for 1997.

HEALTH/WELFARE

A major challenge for the government has been the repatriation of 700,000 war refugees, mostly from neighboring Sudan. Rebuilding efforts are being spearheaded by ex-combatants of the Liberation Army, who have continued to work for virtually no pay. The EPLF had established its own medical and educational services during the war.

ACHIEVEMENTS

Eritrea's independence struggle and ongoing national development efforts have been carried out against overwhelming odds, with very little external support. During the war, self-reliance was manifested in the fact that most weapons and ammunition used by the EPLF were captured from Ethiopian forces.

Ethiopia (People's Democratic Republic of Ethiopia)

GEOGRAPHY

Area in Square Kilometers (Miles):
1,221,900 (471,800) (about four-fifths
the size of Alaska)
Capital (Population): Addis Ababa
(2,200,000)
Climate: temperate in highlands; arid
to semiarid in lowlands

PEOPLE

Population
Total: 57,172,000
Annual Growth Rate: 3.09%
Rural/Urban Population Ratio: 85/15
Major Languages: Amharic; Tigrinya;
Oromo; Somali; Arabic; Italian;
English
Ethnic Makeup: 40% Oromo; 32%
Amhara and Tigre; 9% Sidamo; 19%
others

Health
Life Expectancy at Birth: 48 years
(male); 52 years (female)
Infant Mortality Rate (Ratio):
120.6/1,000
Average Caloric Intake: 78% of FAO
minimum in areas not severely

affected by drought
Physicians Available (Ratio): 1/36,600

Religions
45%–50% Muslim; 35%–40%
Ethiopian Orthodox Christian;
remainder animist and others

Education
Adult Literacy Rate: 24%

COMMUNICATION

Telephones: 162,000
Newspapers: 4

KING LABILA

In the 1100s and 1200s, the Ethiopian state, having declined since the days of the Axumites, was revived under the Zagwe dynasty. The best known of the Zagwe rulers is Labila, who is remembered for his architectural legacy. He built an impressive palace, which stands to this day, at his capital of Roha. More famous, however, are the churches that he had carved out of solid rock, reportedly to fulfill a heavenly injunction that he received in his sleep. The churches survive as centers of worship, attracting pilgrims from throughout Coptic Ethiopia.

TRANSPORTATION

Highways—Kilometers (Miles):
24,127 (14,983)
Railroads—Kilometers (Miles): 681
(425)
Usable Airfields: 98

GOVERNMENT

Type: transitional government
Independence Date: oldest
independent country in Africa
Head of State/Government: President
Ngesso Giadada; Prime Minister
Meles Zenawi
Political Parties: Ethiopian People's
Revolutionary Democratic Front;
Oromo People's Democratic
Organization; Oromo Liberation
Front; Ethiopian People's
Revolutionary Party; numerous others
Suffrage: universal at 18

MILITARY

Number of Armed Forces: 106,500
*Military Expenditures (% of Central
Government Expenditures):* 4.1%
Current Hostilities: border disputes
with Somalia

ECONOMY

Currency ($ U.S. Equivalent): 5.95
birrs = $1
Per Capita Income/GDP: $380/$20.3
billion
Inflation Rate: 10%
Natural Resources: potash; salt; gold;
copper; platinum
Agriculture: cereals; coffee; pulses;
oil seeds; livestock
Industry: processed food; textiles;
cement; building materials;
hydroelectric power

FOREIGN TRADE

Exports: $219.8 million
Imports: $1.04 billion

ETHIOPIA

In August 1995, Ngesso Giadada was inaugurated as president and Meles Zenawi as prime minister of Ethiopia under a new Constitution that formally ended 5 years of transitional rule by the Ethiopian People's Revolutionary Democratic Front (EPRDF). But with overwhelming, if controversial, victories in elections held in 1994 and 1995, the EPRDF, under Zenawi's leadership, remains the country's dominant political force. Its hold on power, however, continues to be violently contested in a number of regions; several opposition movements boycotted the elections. Since coming to power, the EPRDF has faced a wide spectrum of opponents. Some critics see its transformation of Ethipoia into a multiethnic federation of 14 self-governing regions as a threat to national unity. Others contend that its devolutionary structures are a sham designed to obscure its own determination to rule from the center as a virtual one-party state. International as well as domestic supporters, however, see the new Constitution as a bold experiment in institutionalizing a new model of multiethnic statehood.

The EPRDF had emerged in the 1980s as an umbrella movement fighting to liberate Ethiopia from the repressive misrule by the Provisional Military Administrative Council, popularly known as the Dergue (Amharic for "Committee"). The Dergue had come to power through a popular uprising against the country's former imperial order. Time will tell whether Ethiopia's second revolution in 2 decades will succeed where its first one failed.

Political instability has reduced Ethiopia from a developing breadbasket to a famine-ridden basket case. Interethnic conflict among an increasingly desperate population, many of whom have long had better access to arms and ammunition than to food and medicine, could lead to the state's ultimate disintegration.

IMPERIAL PAST

Ethiopia rivals Egypt as Africa's oldest country. For centuries, its kings claimed direct descent from the biblical King Solomon and the Queen of Sheba. Whether Ethiopia was the site of Sheba is uncertain, as is the local claim that, prior to the birth of Christ, the country became the final resting place of the Ark of the Covenant holding the original Ten Commandments given to Moses (the Ark is said to survive in a local monastery).

Local history is better established from the time of the Axum empire, which prospered from the first century. During the fourth century, the Axumite court adopted the Coptic Christian faith, which has remained central to the culture of Ethiopia's highland region. The Church still uses the Geez, the ancient Axumite tongue from which the modern Ethiopian languages of Amharic and Tigrinya are derived, in its services.

From the eighth century, much of the area surrounding the highlands fell under Muslim control, all but cutting off the Copts from their European coreligionists. (Today, most Muslim Ethiopians live in the lowlands.) For many centuries, Ethiopia's history was characterized by struggles among the groups inhabiting these two regions and religions. Occasionally a powerful ruler would succeed in making himself truly "King of Kings" by uniting the Christian highlands and expanding into the lowlands. At other times, the mountains would be divided into weak polities that were vulnerable to the raids of both Muslim and non-Muslim lowlanders.

Modern Ethiopian history began in the nineteenth century, when the highlands became politically reunited by a series of kings, culminating in Menilik II, who built up power by importing European armaments. Once the Coptic core of his kingdom was intact, Menilik began to spread his authority across the lowlands, thus uniting most of contemporary Ethiopia. In 1889 and 1896, Menilik also defeated invading Italian armies, thus preserving his empire's independence during the European partition of Africa.

From 1916 to 1974, Ethiopia was ruled by Ras Tafari (from which is derived the term *Rasta,* or *Rastafarian*), who, in 1930, was crowned Emperor Haile Selassie. The late Selassie remains a controversial figure. For many decades, he was seen both at home and abroad as a reformer who was modernizing his state. In 1936, after his kingdom had been occupied by Benito Mussolini, he made a memorable speech before the League of Nations, warning the world of the price it would inevitably pay for appeasing Fascist aggression. At the time, many African-Americans and Africans outside of Ethiopia saw Selassie as a great hero in the struggle of black peoples everywhere for dignity and empowerment. Selassie returned to his throne in 1941 and thereafter served as an elder statesman to the African nationalists of the 1950s and 1960s. However, by the latter decade, his own domestic authority was being increasingly questioned.

In his later years, Selassie could not, or would not, move against the forces that

(United Nations photo by Muldoon)

From 1916 to 1974, Ethiopia was ruled by Haile Selassie, also known as Ras Tafari (from which today's term Rastafarian is derived). He is pictured above, on the left, shaking hands with the infamous Idi Amin, past president of Uganda.

were undermining his empire. Despite its trappings of progress, the Ethiopian state remained quasi-feudal in character. Many of the best lands were controlled by the nobility and the Church, whose leading members lived privileged lives at the expense of the peasantry. Many educated people grew disenchanted with what they perceived as a reactionary monarchy and social order. Urban workers resented being paid low wages by often foreign owners. Within the junior ranks of the army and civil service, there was also great dissatisfaction with the way in which their superiors were able to siphon off state revenues for personal enrichment. But the empire's greatest weakness was its inability to accommodate the aspirations of the various ethnic, regional, and sectarian groupings living within its borders.

Ethiopia is a multiethnic state. Since the time of Menilik the dominant group has been the Coptic Amhara speakers, whose preeminence has been resented by their Tigrinya coreligionists as well as by predominantly non-Coptic groups such as the Afars, Gurages, Oromo, and Somalis. In recent years, movements fighting for ethnoregional autonomy have emerged among the Tigrinya of Tigray, the Oromo, and, to a lesser extent, the Afars, while many Somalis in Ethiopia's Ogaden region have long struggled for union with neighboring Somalia. Somali irredentism led to open warfare between the two principal Horn of Africa states in 1963–1964 and again in 1977–1978.

The former northern coastal province of Eritrea was a special case. From the late nineteenth century until World War II, it was an Italian colony. After the war, it was integrated into Selassie's empire. Thereafter, a local independence movement, largely united as the Eritrean People's Liberation Front (EPLF), waged a successful armed struggle, which led to Eritrea's full independence in 1993.

REVOLUTION AND REPRESSION

In 1974, Haile Selassie was overthrown by the military, after months of mounting unrest throughout the country. A major factor triggering the coup was the government's inaction in 1972–1974, when famine swept across the northern provinces, claiming 200,000 lives. Some accused the Amhara government of using the famine as a way of weakening the predominantly Tigrinya areas of the empire. Others saw the tragedy simply as proof of the venal incompetence of Selassie's administration.

The overthrow of the old order was welcomed by most Ethiopians. Unfortunately, what began as a promising revolutionary

transformation quickly degenerated into a repressive dictatorship, which pushed the nation into chronic instability and distress. By the end of 1974, after the first in a series of bloody purges within its ranks, the Dergue had embraced Marxism as its guiding philosophy. Revolutionary measures followed. Companies and lands were nationalized. Students were sent into the countryside to assist in land reforms and to teach literacy. Peasants and workers were organized into cooperative associations, called kebeles. Initial steps were also taken to end Amhara hegemony within the state.

Progressive aspects of the Ethiopian revolution were offset by the murderous nature of the regime. Power struggles within the Dergue, as well as its determination to eliminate all alternatives to its authority, contributed to periods of "red terror," during which thousands of supporters of the revolution as well as those associated with the old regime were killed. By 1977, the Dergue itself had been transformed from a collective decision-making body to a small clique loyal to Colonel Mengistu Haile Mariam, who became a presidential dictator.

Mengistu sought for years to legitimize his rule through a commitment to Marxist-Leninism. He formally presided over a

Commission for Organizing the Party of the Working People of Ethiopia, which, in 1984, announced the formation of a single-party state, led by the new Workers' Party. But real power remained in the hands of Mengistu's Dergue.

CIVIL WAR

From 1974 to 1991, Ethiopia suffered through civil war. In the face of oppressive central authority, ethnic-based resistance movements became increasingly effective in their struggles throughout much of the country. In the late 1970s, the Mengistu regime began to receive massive military aid from the Soviet bloc in its campaigns against the Eritreans and Somalis. Some 17,000 Cuban troops and thousands of other military personnel from the Warsaw Pact countries allowed the government temporarily to gain the upper hand in the fighting. The Ethiopian Army grew to more than 300,000 men under arms at any given time, the largest military force on the continent. Throughout the 1980s, military expenditures claimed more than half of the national budget.

Despite the massive domestic and international commitment on the side of the Mengistu regime, the rebels gradually gained the upper hand. Before 1991, al-

(United Nations photo by John Isaac)

Ethiopians experienced a brutal civil war from 1974 to 1991. The continuous fighting displaced millions of people. The problem of this forced migration was compounded by drought and starvation. The drought victims pictured above are gathered at one of the many relief camps.

							Tigray and Eritrean struggles intensify; many are killed; cities are captured and recaptured

Emperor Tewodros begins the conquest and development of modern Ethiopia
1855

Ethiopia defeats Italian invaders at the Battle of Adowa
1896

Fascist Italy invades Ethiopia and rules until 1941
1936

The Eritrean liberation struggle begins
1961

Famines in Tigray and Welo provinces result in up to 200,000 deaths
1972–1973

Emperor Haile Selassie is overthrown; the PMAC is established
1974

Diplomatic realignment and a new arms agreement with the Soviet Union
1977

Massive famine, resulting from both drought and warfare
1980s

1990s

The Mengistu regime is overthrown by ERPDF rebels

Interethnic political tensions continue

Eritrea achieves independence of Ethiopia

most all of northern Eritrea, except its besieged capital city of Asmara, had fallen to the EPLF, which had built up its own powerful arsenal, largely from captured government equipment. Local rebels had also liberated the province of Tigray and, as part of the EPRDF coalition, pushed south toward Ethiopia's capital city of Addis Ababa. In the south, independent Oromo and Somali rebels challenged government authority. There was also resistance to Mengistu from within the ranks of the national army. A major rebellion against his authority in 1989 was crushed, devastating military morale in the process. The regime was further undermined by the withdrawal of remaining Cuban and Soviet bloc support.

Ethiopians have paid a terrible price for their nation's conflicts. Tens of thousands have been killed in combat, while many more have died from the side effects of war. In 1984–1985, the conscience of the world was moved by the images of mass starvation in the northern war zone. (At the time, however, the global media and concerned groups like Band Aid paid relatively little attention to the nonenvironmental factors that contributed to the crisis.) Up to 1 million lives were lost before adequate relief supplies reached the famine areas. Although drought and other environmental factors, such as soil erosion, contributed to the catastrophe, the fact that people continued to starve despite the availability of international relief can be attributed only to the use of food as a weapon of war.

There were other political constraints on local crop production. Having seized the lands of the old ruling class, the Mengistu regime, in accordance with its Marxist-Leninist precepts, invested most of its agricultural inputs in large state farms, whose productivity was abysmal. Peasant production also fell in nondrought areas, due to insecure tenure, poor producer prices, lack of credit, and an absence of consumer goods. Ethiopia's rural areas were further disrupted by the government's heavy-handed villagization and relocation schemes. In 1984–1985, thousands died when the government moved some 600,000 northerners to what were supposedly more fertile regions in the southwest. Many considered the scheme to be part of the central government's war effort against local communities resistant to its authority. By the same token, villagization has long been associated with counterinsurgency efforts; concentrated settlements allow occupying armies to exert greater control over potentially hostile populations.

UNCERTAIN PROSPECTS

The Dergue's demise has not as yet been accompanied by national reconciliation. Opposition to the EPRDF's attempt to transform Ethiopia into a multiethnic federation has been especially strong among Amharas, many of whom support the All Amhara People's Organization. Others accuse the EPRDF—or, more especially, former Stalinists within the Tigrean People's Liberation Front (TPLF), which has been its predominant element—of trying to create its own monopoly of power.

In 1992, fighting broke out between the EPRDF and the forces of its former rebel partner, the Oromo Liberation Front (OLF), which claims to represent Ethiopia's largest ethnic group (Oromos constitute 40 percent of the population). The OLF was prominent among those who boycotted June 1992 local-government elections, which were further marred by allegations of vote-rigging and intimidation on behalf of the EPRDF. In December 1993, the OLF joined a number of other movements in a Council of Alternative Forces for Peace and Democracy (CAFPD). At its inaugural meeting, seven CAFPD delegates were detained for allegedly advocating the armed overthrow of the government. In April, another antigovernment coalition, the Ethiopian National Democratic party, was formed. Both movements called for an election boycott.

Another source of resistance to the EPRDF was the Ogadeni National Liberation Front (ONLF), which won strong support from Ogademi Somalis in the June 1992 elections. In April, the Transitional Government removed ONLF's Hassan Jireh from power as the Ogaden region's elected administrator; in May, he was arrested. As a result, clashes occurred between the ONLF and EPRDF in the area, with the former boycotting the subsequent polls. Smaller uprisings and acts of terror, such as a January 1996 bombing of an Addis Ababa hotel, have posed further challenges for the government, which has also had to cope with drought. But, while the extent of its electoral mandate is disputed, the EPRDF has demonstrated that it retains strong popular support, while its opposition is divided.

DEVELOPMENT

There has been some progress in the country's industrial sector in recent years, after a sharp decline during the 1970s. Soviet bloc investment resulted in the establishment of new enterprises in such areas as cement, textiles, and farm machinery.

FREEDOM

Despite its public commitment to freedom of speech and association, the ERPDF government has resorted to authoritarian measures against its critics; in 1995, Ethiopia had the highest number of jailed journalists in Africa. Basic freedoms are also compromised.

HEALTH/WELFARE

Progress in spreading literacy during the 1970s was undermined by the dislocations of the 1980s. By 1991, Ethiopia had some 500 government soldiers for every teacher.

ACHIEVEMENTS

With a history spanning 2 millennia, the cultural achievements of Ethiopia are vast. Addis Ababa is the headquarters of the Organization of African Unity. Ethiopia's Kefe Province is the home of the coffee plant, from whence it takes its name.

Kenya (Republic of Kenya)

GEOGRAPHY

Area in Square Kilometers (Miles):
582,488 (224,900) (slightly smaller
than Texas)
Capital (Population): Nairobi
(2,000,000)
Climate: tropical to arid

PEOPLE

Population
Total: 28,817,000
Annual Growth Rate: 3% (est.)
Rural/Urban Population Ratio: 75/25
Major Languages: English;
Kiswahili; Kikuyu Luo; Kamba;
Kipsigi; Maasai; Luhya; others
Ethnic Makeup: 21% Kikuyu; 14%
Luhya; 13% Luo; 11% Kalenjin; 11%
Kamba; 30% others

Health
Life Expectancy at Birth: 51 years
(male); 54 years (female)
Infant Mortality Rate (Ratio):
73.5/1,000
Average Caloric Intake: 88% of FAO
minimum
Physicians Available (Ratio): 1/7,410

Religions
38% Protestant; 28% traditional
indigenous; 28% Catholic; 6% Muslim

Education
Adult Literacy Rate: 69%

COMMUNICATION

Telephones: 260,000
Newspapers: 4

CULTURE AND POLITICS IN KENYA

In the past as well as today, cultural activities in Kenya have been closely connected to politics, encouraging nationalism and revealing inequities. Events at the Kamriitha Community Educational and Cultural Center illustrate this statement. The center was built by community efforts in Kamriithu, a town of 10,000 people. A literacy committee organized a literacy study course, and the community organized dramas that illustrated the people's experiences and ideas. Ngugi wa Thiong'o was commissioned to write the first play, about the townspeople's own lives, and they discussed and criticized it as well as performed it in a theater that the town had built. The production was highly successful, but it was banned because the authorities thought that it encouraged class conflict. Its potential for organizing peasants was a threat to the government. Ngugi was detained (he is now in exile). The center was later closed and the theater destroyed.

TRANSPORTATION

Highways—Kilometers (Miles):
64,590 (40,046)
Railroads—Kilometers (Miles): 2,650
(1,654)
Usable Airfields: 213

GOVERNMENT

Type: republic
Independence Date: December 12, 1963
Head of State: President Daniel arap
Moi
Political Parties: Kenya African
National Union; Forum for the
Restoration of Democracy;
Democratic Party of Kenya; Kenya
National Congress; others
Suffrage: universal at 18

MILITARY

Number of Armed Forces: 24,400
*Military Expenditures (% of Central
Government Expenditures):* 1.9%
Current Hostilities: border conflict
with Uganda; civil unrest and
interethnic violence

ECONOMY

Currency ($ U.S. Equivalent): 44.48
Kenya shillings = $1
Per Capita Income/GDP:
$1,170/$33.1 billion
Inflation Rate: 55%
Natural Resources: wildlife; land;
soda ash; wattle
Agriculture: corn; wheat; rice;
sugarcane; coffee; tea; sisal;
pyrethrum; livestock
Industry: petroleum products; cement;
beer; automobile assembly; food
processing; tourism

FOREIGN TRADE

Exports: $1.45 billion
Imports: $1.85 billion

Kenya

- ✪ Capital
- ● City
- ── River
- - - - Road

0   75 kilometers
0   75 miles

KENYA

Years of economic growth have helped to make Kenya the commercial center of East Africa. But today, $3\frac{1}{2}$ decades after independence, most Kenyans remain the impoverished citizens of a state struggling to develop as a nation. And the recent restoration of multiparty politics has so far served only to intensify interethnic conflict without diminishing the positions of those in the ruling Kenya African National Union (KANU) party who have plundered Kenya's wealth through their abuse of state power.

In the precolonial past, Kenyan communities belonged to relatively small-scale, but economically interlinked, societies. Predominantly pastoral groups, such as the Maasai and Turkana, exchanged cattle for the crops of the Kalinjin, Kamba, Kikuyu, Luo, and others. Swahili city-states developed on the coast. In the nineteenth century, caravans of Arab as well as Swahili traders stimulated economic and political changes. However, the outsiders who had the greatest modern impact on the Kenyan interior were European settlers, who began to arrive in the first decade of the twentieth century. By the 1930s, much of the temperate hill country around Nairobi, Kenya's capital city, had become the "White Highlands." More than 6 million acres of land—Maasai pasture and Kikuyu and Kamba farms—were stolen. African communities were often displaced to increasingly overcrowded reserves. Laborers, mostly Kikuyu migrants from the reserves, worked for the new European owners, sometimes on lands that they had once farmed for themselves.

By the 1950s, African grievances had been heightened by increased European settlement and the growing removal of African "squatters" from their estates. There were also growing class and ideological differences among Africans, leading to tensions between educated Christians with middle-class aspirations and displaced members of the rural underclass. Many members of the latter group, in particular, began to mobilize themselves in largely Kikuyu oathing societies, which coalesced into the Mau Mau movement.

Armed resistance by Mau Mau guerrillas began in 1951, with isolated attacks on white settlers. In response, the British proclaimed a state of emergency, which lasted for 10 years. Without any outside support, the Mau Mau held out for years by making effective use of the highland forests as sanctuaries. Nonetheless, by 1955, the uprising had largely been crushed. Although the name Mau Mau became for many outsiders synonymous with antiwhite terrorism, only 32

European civilians actually lost their lives during the rebellion. In contrast, at least 13,000 Kikuyu were killed. Another 80,000 Africans were detained by the colonial authorities, and more than 1 million were resettled in controlled villages. While the Mau Mau were overwhelmed by often ruthless counterinsurgency measures, they achieved an important victory: The British realized that the preservation of Kenya as a white-settler-dominated colony was militarily and politically untenable.

In the aftermath of the emergency, the person who emerged as the charismatic leader of Kenya's nationalist movement was Jomo Kenyatta, who had been detained and accused by the British—without any evidence—of leading the resistance movement. At independence, in 1963, he became the president. He held the office until his death in 1978.

To many, the situation in Kenya under Kenyatta looked promising. His government encouraged racial harmony, and the slogan *Harambee* (Swahili for "Pull together") became a call for people of all ethnic groups and races to work together for development. Land reforms provided plots to 1.5 million farmers. A policy of Africanization created business opportunities for local entrepreneurs, and industry grew. Although the Kenya African National Union was supposedly guided by a policy of "African Socialism," the nation was seen by many as a showcase of capitalist development.

POLITICAL DEVELOPMENT

Kenyatta's Kenya quickly became a de facto one-party state. In 1966, the country's first vice president, Oginga Odinga, resigned to form an opposition party, the Kenyan People's Union (KPU). Three years later, however, the party was banned and its leaders, including Odinga, were imprisoned. Thereafter KANU became the focus of political competition, and voters were allowed to remove sitting Members of Parliament, including cabinet ministers. But politics was marred by intimidation and violence, including the assassinations of prominent critics within government, most notably Economic Development Minister Tom Mboya, in 1969, and Foreign Affairs Minister J. M. Kariuki, in 1975. Constraints on freedom of association were justified in the interest of preventing ethnic conflict—much of the KPU support came from the Luo group. However, ethnicity has always been important in shaping struggles within KANU itself.

Under Daniel arap Moi, Kenyatta's successor, the political climate grew steadily more repressive. In 1982, his government was badly shaken by a failed coup at-

tempt, in which about 250 persons died and approximately 1,500 others were detained. The old air force was disbanded and the university, whose students came out in support of the coup-makers, was temporarily closed.

In the aftermath of the coup, all parties other than KANU were formally outlawed. Moi followed this step by declaring, in 1986, that KANU was above the government, the Parliament, and the judiciary. Press restrictions, detentions, and blatant acts of intimidation became common. Those Members of Parliament brave enough to be critical of Moi's imperial presidency were removed from KANU and thus Parliament. Political tensions were blamed on the local agents of an ever-growing list of outside forces, including Christian missionaries and Muslim fundamentalists, foreign academics and the news media, and Libyan and U.S. meddlers.

A number of underground opposition groups emerged during the mid-1980s, most notably the socialist-oriented Mwakenya movement, whose ranks included such prominent exiles as the writer Ngugi wa Thiong'o. In 1987, many of these groups came together to form the United Movement for Democracy, or UMOJA (Swahili for "unity"). But in the immediate aftermath of the 1989 KANU elections, which in many areas were blatantly rigged, Moi's grip on power appeared strong.

The early months of 1990, however, witnessed an upsurge in antigovernment unrest. In February, the murder of Foreign Minister Robert Ouko touched off rioting in Nairobi and his home city of Kisumu. Another riot occurred when squatters were forcibly evicted from the Nairobi shantytown of Muoroto. Growing calls for the restoration of multiparty democracy fueled a cycle of unrest and repression. The detention in July of two former cabinet ministers, Kenneth Matiba and Charles Rubia, for their part in the democracy agitation sparked nationwide rioting, which left at least 28 people dead and 1,000 arrested. Opposition movements, most notably the Forum for the Restoration of Democracy (FORD), began to emerge in defiance of the government's ban on their activities.

Under mounting external pressure from Western donor countries as well as from his internal opponents, Moi, in December 1991, finally agreed to the legalization of opposition parties. Unfortunately, this move failed to diffuse Kenya's increasingly violent political, social, and ethnic tensions.

Continued police harassment of the opposition triggered renewed rioting throughout the country. There was also a rise in interethnic clashes in both the rural and urban areas, which many, even within KANU, at-

The British East African Protectorate is proclaimed **1895**	British colonists begin to settle in the Highlands area **1900–1910**	Mau Mau, a predominately Kikuyu movement, resists colonial rule **1952**	Kenya gains independence under the leadership of Jomo Kenyatta **1963**	Daniel arap Moi becomes president upon the death of Kenyatta **1978**	A coup attempt by members of the Kenyan Air Force is crushed; political repression grows **1980s**

1990s

Prodemocracy agitation leads to a return of multiparty politics	An upsurge in interethnic violence in the Rift Valley threatens democratic transition	According to Amnesty International, Kenya had Africa's worst record of torture in 1995

tributed to government incitement. In the Rift Valley, armed members of Moi's own Kalinjin grouping attacked other groups for supposedly settling on their land. Hundreds were killed and thousands injured and displaced in the worst violence since the Mau Mau era. In the face of the government's cynical resort to divide-and-rule tactics, the fledgling opposition movement betrayed the hopes of many of its supporters by becoming hopelessly splintered. New groups, such as the Islamic Party of Kenya, openly appealed for support along ethnoreligious lines. More significantly, a leadership struggle in the main FORD grouping between Matiba and the veteran Odinga split the party into two, while a proposed alliance with Mwai Kibaki's Democratic Party failed to materialize. Although motivated as much by personal ambitions and lingering mistrust between KANU defectors and long-term KANU opponents, the FORD split soon took on an ethnic dimension, with many Kikuyu backing Matiba, while Luo remained solidly loyal to Odinga.

Taking skillful advantage of his opponents' disarray, Moi called elections in December 1992, which resulted in his plurality victory, with 36 percent of the vote. KANU was able to capture 95 of the 188 parliamentary seats that were up for grabs. The two FORD factions won 31 seats each, while the Democratic Party captured 23 seats. Notwithstanding voting irregularities, most independent observers blamed the divided opposition for sowing the seeds of its

own defeat. The death of the widely respected Odinga in January 1994 coincided with renewed attempts to form a united opposition to KANU. In 1996, a group of opposition Members of Parliament was established, with a secretariat headed by the internationally renowned anthropologist and conservationist Richard Leakey. Genuine unity, however, remains elusive.

Kenya's politics reflects class as well as ethnic divisions. The top 10 percent of the population own an estimated 40 percent of the wealth, while the bottom 30 percent own only 10 percent. Past economic growth has failed to alleviate poverty. Kenya's relatively large middle class has grown resentful of increased repression and the evident corruption at the very top, but it is also fearful about perceived anarchy from below.

Although its rate of growth declined during much of the 1980s, the Kenyan economy has, until the current crisis, consistently expanded since independence. Kenya is the most industrialized country of East Africa. Foreign capital has played an important role in industrial development, but the largest share of investment has come from the government and the local private sector.

The bulk of Kenya's foreign-exchange earnings has come from agriculture. A wide variety of cash crops is exported, a diversity that has buffered the nation's economy to some degree from the uncertainties associated with single-commodity dependence. While large plantations—

now often owned by wealthy Kenyans—have survived from the colonial era, much of the commercial production is carried out by small landholders.

Tourism has accounted for about 20 percent of Kenya's foreign-exchange earnings, but its immediate prospects are not good. The sector has suffered from a combination of increased competition from other African destinations, widely publicized attacks on visitors, the current political unrest, fears about AIDS, and a declining wildlife population.

Another major challenge to Kenya's well-being has been its rapidly expanding population. Although there are some hopeful signs that women are beginning to plan for fewer children than in the past, the nation has been plagued with one of the highest population growth rates in the world, approximately 3 percent per year. More than half of all Kenyans are under age 15. Pressure on arable land is enormous. It will be difficult to create nonagricultural employment for the burgeoning rural-turned-urban workforce, even in the context of democratic stability and renewed economic growth.

DEVELOPMENT

The Kenyan Wildlife Service has cracked down on poachers while placing itself at the forefront of the global campaign to ban ivory trading. Wildlife populations have rebounded. However, the 1994 resignation of its respected director, Richard Leakey, following criticism by KANU politicians, has shaken confidence in the future of the Service.

FREEDOM

The limits of freedom under Kenya's new multiparty order were demonstrated in 1995 by the government's persecution of Richard Leakey and others for trying to launch a new party known as Safina ("the Ark"). With its fresh faces and unifying message, the party was seen as a serious threat by some to Kenya's old-style politicians. The party has been refused registration.

HEALTH/WELFARE

Kenya's social infrastructure has been burdened by the influx of some 300,000 refugees from the neighboring states of Ethiopia, Somalia, and Sudan. In addition to mounting relief efforts to feed and settle the new arrivals, the government has had to combat growing lawlessness in its border regions.

ACHIEVEMENTS

Kenya annually devotes about half its government expenditures to education. Most Kenyan students can now expect 12 years of schooling. Tertiary education is also expanding.

Madagascar (Democratic Republic of Madagascar)

GEOGRAPHY

Area in Square Kilometers (Miles): 587,041 (226,658) (slightly smaller than Texas)
Capital (Population): Antananarivo (1,100,000)
Climate: tropical and moderate

PEOPLE

Population

Total: 13,671,000
Annual Growth Rate: 3.19%
Rural/Urban Population Ratio: 78/22
Major Languages: Malagasy; French
Ethnic Makeup: Malayo-Indonesian; Cotiers; French; Indian; Creole; Comoran

Health

Life Expectancy at Birth: 52 years (male); 56 years (female)
Infant Mortality Rate (Ratio): 87/1,000
Average Caloric Intake: 111% of FAO minimum
Physicians Available (Ratio): 1/8,628

Religions

52% traditional indigenous; 41% Christian; 7% Muslim

Education

Adult Literacy Rate: 80%

COMMUNICATION

Telephones: 38,200
Newspapers: 7

TRANSPORTATION

Highways—Kilometers (Miles): 40,000 (24,800)
Railroads—Kilometers (Miles): 1,020 (632)
Usable Airfields: 138

GOVERNMENT

Type: republic; authority held by Supreme Revolutionary Council
Independence Date: June 26, 1960
Head of State/Government: President Didier Ratsiraka; Prime Minister Francisque Ravony
Political Parties: Committee of Living Forces; Militant Party for the Development of Madagascar; Confederation of Civil Societies for Development; Association of United Malagasys; Rally for Social Democracy
Suffrage: universal at 18

MILITARY

Number of Armed Forces: 21,000
Military Expenditures (% of Central Government Expenditures): 1.3%
Current Hostilities: none

ECONOMY

Currency ($ U.S. Equivalent): 3,718 Malagasy francs = $1
Per Capita Income/GDP: $790/$10.6 billion
Inflation Rate: 35%
Natural Resources: graphite; chrome; coal; bauxite; ilmenite; tar sands; semiprecious stones; timber; mica; nickel
Agriculture: rice; livestock; coffee; vanilla; sugar; cloves; cotton; sisal; peanuts; tobacco
Industry: food processing; textiles; mining; paper; petroleum refining; automobile assembly; construction; cement; farming

FOREIGN TRADE

Exports: $240 million
Imports: $510 million

A TRADITION OF POETRY

What invisible rat
comes from the walls of night
gnaws at the milky cake of the moon?

Thus begins one of the poems of Jean-Joseph Rabearivelo (1901–1937), one of Madagascar's greatest twentieth-century poets. Like the poets who followed him, such as Jean Jacques Rebemananjara and Jacques Flavien Ranaivo, Rabearivelo wrote in French and was deeply affected by French poets, literature, and culture. Yet all of these poets were attached to local Malagasy forms and rhythms and were inspired by the *hainteny* form, which was characteristic of the popular songs of the island. Several of the poems of Rabearivelo and Ranaivo are reprinted in *A Book of African Verse*, edited by J. Reed and C. Wake.

Madagascar

⊗ Capital
● City
〜 River
- - - Road

0   100 kilometers
0   100 miles

MADAGASCAR

Madagascar has been called the "smallest continent"; indeed, many geologists believe that it once formed the core of a larger landmass, whose other principal remnants are the Indian subcontinent and Australia. The world's fourth-largest island remains a world unto itself in other ways. Botanists and zoologists know it as the home of flora and fauna not found elsewhere. The island's culture is also distinctive. The Malagasy language, which with dialectical variations is spoken throughout the island, is related to the Malay tongues of Indonesia. But, despite their geographic separation and Asiatic roots, the Malagasy are very aware of their African identity.

While the early history of Madagascar is the subject of much scholarly debate, it is clear that, by the year A.D. 500, the island was being settled by Malay-speaking peoples who may have migrated via the East African coast rather than directly from Indonesia. The cultural imprint of Southeast Asia is also evident in such aspects as local architecture, music, cosmology, and agricultural practices. African

influences are equally apparent. During the precolonial period, the peoples of Madagascar were in communication with communities on the African mainland. Waves of migration across the Mozambique channel contributed to the island's modern ethnic diversity.

During the early nineteenth century, most of Madagascar was united by the rulers of Merina. In seeking to build up their realm and preserve the island's independence, the Merina kings and queens welcomed European (mostly English) missionaries, who helped introduce new ideas and technologies. As a result, many Malagasy, including the royalty, adopted Christianity. The kingdom had established diplomatic relations with the United States and various European powers and was thus a recognized member of the international community. Foreign businesspeople were attracted to invest in the island's growing economy, while the rapid spread of schools and medical services, increasingly staffed by Malagasy, brought profound changes to the society.

The Merina court hoped that its "Christian civilization" and modernizing army

would deter European aggression. But the French were determined to rule the island. The 1884–1885 Franco–Malagasy War ended in a stalemate, but a French invasion in 1895 led to the kingdom's destruction. It was not an easy conquest. The Malagasy army, with its artillery and modern fortifications, held out for many months; eventually, however, it was outgunned by the invaders. French sovereignty was proclaimed in 1896, but "pacification" campaigns continued for another decade.

French rule reduced what had been a prospering state into a colonial backwater. The pace of development slowed as the local economy was restructured to serve the interests of French settlers, whose numbers had swelled to 60,000 by the time of World War II. Probably the most important French contribution to Madagascar was the encouragement their misrule gave to the growth of local nationalism. By the 1940s, a strong sense of Malagasy identity had been forged through common hatred of the colonialists.

The local overthrow of Vichy power by the British in 1943 created an opening for Malagasy nationalists to organize them-

(United Nations photo by L. Rajaonina)

Madagascar has a unique ethnic diversity, influenced by migrations from the African mainland and Southeast Asia. The varied ethnic makeup of the population can be seen in the faces of these schoolchildren.

| Merina rulers gain sovereignty over other peoples of the island 1828 | The French complete the conquest of the island 1904 | A revolt is suppressed by the French, with great loss of life 1947–1948 | Independence from France; Philibert Tsiranana becomes the first president 1960 | A coup leads to the fall of the First Malagasy Republic 1972 | Didier Ratsiraka becomes president by military appointment 1975 | Economic problems intensify 1980s | 1990s |

Elections in 1989–1990 strengthen multiparty democracy; a short-lived coup attempt takes place

A mass-action campaign by opponents of Ratsiraka leads to the appointment of an interim government

President Albert Zafy is approved by voters but later impeached; Ratsiraka becomes president

selves into mass parties, the most prominent of which was the Malagasy Movement for Democratic Renewal (MRDM). In 1946, the MRDM elected two overseas deputies to the French National Assembly, on the basis of its call for immediate independence. France responded by instructing its administrators to "fight the MRDM by every means." Arrests led to resistance. In March 1947, a general insurrection began. Peasant rebels, using whatever weapons they could find, liberated large areas from French control. French troops countered by destroying crops and blockading rebel areas, in an effort to starve the insurrectionists into surrendering. Thousands of Malagasy were massacred. By the end of the year, the rebellion had been largely crushed, although a state of siege was maintained until 1956. No one knows precisely how many Malagasy lost their lives in the uprising, but contemporary estimates indicate about 90,000.

INDEPENDENCE AND REVOLUTION

Madagascar gained its independence in 1960. However, many viewed the new government, led by Philibert Tsiranana of the Social Democratic Party (PSD), as a vehicle for continuing French influence; memories of 1947 were still strong. Lack of economic and social reform led to a peasant uprising in 1971. This Maoist-inspired rebellion was suppressed, but the government was left weakened. In 1972, new unrest, this time spearheaded by students and workers in the towns, led to Tsiranana's overthrow by the military. Af-

ter a period of confusion, radical forces consolidated power around Lieutenant Commander Didier Ratsiraka, who assumed the presidency in 1975.

Under Ratsiraka, a new Constitution was adopted that allowed for a controlled process of multiparty competition, in which all parties were grouped within the National Front. Within this framework, the largest party was Ratsiraka's Vanguard of the Malagasy Revolution (AREMA). Initially, all parties were expected to support the president's Charter of the Malagasy Revolution, which called for a Marxist-oriented socialist transformation. In accordance with the Charter, foreign-owned banks and financial institutions were nationalized. A series of state enterprises were also established to promote industrial development, but few proved viable.

Although 80 percent of the Malagasy were employed in agriculture, rural investment was modest. The government attempted to work through *fokonolas* (indigenous village management bodies). State farms and collectives were also established on land expropriated from French settlers. While these efforts led to some improvements, such as increased mechanization, state marketing monopolies and planning constraints contributed to shortfalls. Efforts to keep consumer prices low were blamed for a drop in rice production, the Malagasy staple, while cash-crop production, primarily coffee, vanilla, and cloves, suffered from falling world prices.

Since 1980, Madagascar has experienced great economic difficulties, which have given rise to political instability. Food shortages in towns had led to rioting,

while frustrated peasants have abandoned their fields. By the late 1980s, Ratsiraka's government had turned increasingly from socialism for a greater reliance on market economics. But the economy remained impoverished.

In 1985, having abandoned attempts to make the National Front into a vehicle for a single-party state, Ratsiraka presided over a loosening of his once-authoritarian control. In February 1990, most remaining restrictions on multiparty politics were lifted. But the regime's opponents, including a revived PSD, became militant in their demands for a new constitution. After 6 months of crippling strikes and protests, Ratsiraka formally ceded many of his powers to a transitional government, headed by Albert Zafy, in November 1991. In February 1993, Zafy won the presidency by a large margin. But subsequent divisions with Parliament over his rejection of an International Monetary Fund austerity plan, accompanied by allegations of financial irregularities, led to his impeachment in August 1996. In elections held at the end of the year, Ratsiraka made a comeback, narrowly defeating Zafy. Over half of the population, however, stayed away from the polls.

DEVELOPMENT

In 1989, "Export Processing Zones" were established to attract foreign investment through tax and currency incentives. The government especially hopes to attract business from neighboring Mauritius, whose success with such zones has led to labor shortages and a shift toward more value-added production.

FREEDOM

The consolidation of a liberal constitutional order has led to a respect for basic human freedoms in Madagascar. Political violence has declined since the 1993 elections.

HEALTH/WELFARE

Primary-school enrollment is now universal. Thirty-six percent of the appropriate age group attend secondary school, while 5% of those ages 20 to 24 are in tertiary institutions. Malaria remains a major health challenge.

ACHIEVEMENTS

A new wildlife preserve will allow the unique animals of Madagascar to survive and develop. Sixty-six species of land animals are found nowhere else on earth, including the aye-aye, a nocturnal lemur that has bat ears, beaver teeth, and an elongated clawed finger, all of which serve the aye-aye in finding food.

Mauritius (Republic of Mauritius)

GEOGRAPHY

Area in Square Kilometers (Miles): 1,865 (720) (about the size of Rhode Island)
Capital (Population): Port Louis (142,000)
Climate: subtropical; marine

PEOPLE

Population

Total: 1,140,300
Annual Growth Rate: 0.86%
Rural/Urban Population Ratio: 61/39
Major Languages: English; French; Creole; Hindi; Urdu
Ethnic Makeup: Indo-Mauritian Creole; others

Health

Life Expectancy at Birth: 67 years (male); 75 years (female)
Infant Mortality Rate (Ratio): 17.8/1,000
Average Caloric Intake: 122% of FAO minimum
Physicians Available (Ratio): 1/1,098

Religions

52% Hindu; 28% Christian; 17% Muslim; 3% others

Education

Adult Literacy Rate: 80%

COMMUNICATION

Telephones: 48,460
Newspapers: 7

DIEGO GARCIA

On the eve of the nation's independence, secret negotiations between British and Mauritian representatives resulted in Mauritius's sale of the island of Diego Garcia and neighboring atolls to the British, for the small sum of $7 million. The wishes of the inhabitants of Diego Garcia were completely ignored; moreover, they were subsequently moved to Mauritius in order to make room for a U.S. military base (thereby increasing the militarization of the Indian Ocean). The people of Mauritius have demanded the island's return. Great Britain and the United States have offered more money to former inhabitants of the island and have agreed to their eventual return in an unspecified, but distant, future. The first National Congress of the ruling Militant Socialist Movement in 1986 called for the restoration of Mauritian sovereignty over Diego Garcia, "currently occupied by the American Army." Mauritian claims enjoy widespread support from the international community, but the issue is still unresolved.

TRANSPORTATION

Highways—Kilometers (Miles): 1,801 (1,116)
Railroads—Kilometers (Miles): none
Usable Airfields: 5

GOVERNMENT

Type: parliamentary democracy
Independence Date: March 12, 1968
Head of State: Prime Minister Navin Ramgoolam
Political Parties: Mauritian Labor Party; Mauritian Militant Movement; Militant Socialist Movement; Mauritian Labor Party; others
Suffrage: universal at 18

MILITARY

Number of Armed Forces: 7,260
Military Expenditures (% of Central Government Expenditures): 0.4%
Current Hostilities: none

ECONOMY

Currency ($ U.S. Equivalent): 17.75 rupees = $1
Per Capita Income/GDP: $8,600/$9.3 billion
Inflation Rate: 4.6%
Natural Resources: agricultural land
Agriculture: sugar; tea; tobacco
Industry: sugar production; consumer goods; labor-intensive goods for export; tourism

FOREIGN TRADE

Exports: $1.32 billion
Imports: $1.70 billion

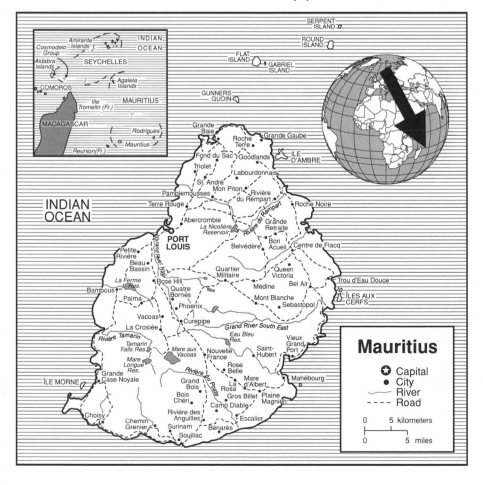

Mauritius
⊛ Capital
● City
～ River
--- Road

0   5 kilometers
0   5 miles

The Dutch claim, but abandon Mauritius
1600s

French settlers and slaves arrive
1722

The Treaty of Paris formally cedes Mauritius to the British
1814

Slavery is abolished; South Asians arrive
1835

Rioting on sugar estates shakes the political control of the Franco-Mauritian elite
1937

An expanded franchise allows greater democracy
1948

Independence
1968

Labor unrest leads to the detention of MMM leaders
1971

A cyclone destroys homes as well as much of the sugar crop
1979

Aneerood Jugnauth replaces Seewoosagur Ramgoolam as prime minister
1982

1990s

Mauritius becomes a republic

Cassam Uteem becomes president

Mauritius becomes the 12th member of the SADC

MAURITIUS

Although it was not permanently settled until 1722, today Mauritius is the home of more than 1 million people of South Asian, Euro-African, Chinese, and other origins. Out of this human diversity has emerged a society that in recent decades has become a model of democratic stability and economic growth as well as ethnic, racial, and sectarian tolerance.

Mauritius was first settled by the French, some of whom achieved great wealth by setting up sugar plantations. From the beginning, the plantations prospered through their exploitation of slave labor imported from the African mainland. Over time, the European and African communities merged into a common Creole culture; that membership currently accounts for one quarter of the Mauritian population. A small number also claim pure French descent. For decades, members of this latter group have formed an economic and social elite. More than half the sugar acreage remains the property of 21 large Franco–Mauritian plantations; the rest is divided among nearly 28,000 small landholdings. French cultural influence remains strong. Most of the newspapers on the island are published in French, which shares official-language status with English. Most Mauritians also speak a local, French-influenced, Creole language. Most Creoles are Roman Catholics.

In 1810, Mauritius was occupied by the British; they ruled the island until 1968. (After years of debate, in 1992, the country cut its ties with Great Britain to become a republic.) When the British abolished slavery, in 1835, the plantation owners turned to large-scale use of indentured labor from what was then British India. Today nearly two thirds of the population are of South Asian descent and have maintained their home languages. Most are Hindu, but a substantial minority are Muslim. Other faiths, such as Buddhism, are also represented.

Although the majority of Mauritians gained the right to vote after World War II, the island has maintained an uninterrupted record of parliamentary rule since 1886. Ethnic divisions have long been important in shaping political allegiances. But ethnic constituency-building has not led, in recent years, to communal polarization. Other factors—such as class, ideology, and opportunism—have also been been influential. All postindependence governments have been multiethnic coalitions.

After 13 years in power, in which he presided over shifting coalitions, Prime Minister Sir Aneerood Jugnauth lost power in a snap December 1995 election. A new governing coalition is now headed by Navin Ramgoolam, whose father, Seewoosagur Ramgoolam, had been prime minister for 3 decades before losing to Jugnauth in 1982. Although most major political parties historically have embraced various shades of socialism, Mauritius's economic success in recent years has created a strong consensus in favor or market economics.

Until the 1970s, the Mauritian economy was almost entirely dependent on sugar. While 45 percent of the island's total landmass continues to be planted with the crop, sugar now ranks below textiles and tourism in its contribution to export earnings and gross domestic product. The transformation of Mauritius from mono-crop dependency into a fledging industrial state with a strong service sector has made it one of the major economic success stories of the developing world. Mauritian growth has been built on a foundation of export-oriented manufacturing. At the core of the Mauritian take-off is its island-wide Export Processing Zone (EPZ), which has attracted industrial investment through a combination of low wages, tax breaks, and other financial incentives. Although most of the EPZ output has been in the field of cheap textiles, the economy has begun to diversify into more capital- and skill-intensive production. In 1989 Mauritius also entered the international financial services market by launching Africa's first offshore banking center.

The success of the Mauritian economy is measured in relative terms. Mauritius is still considered a middle-income country. In reality, however, there are, as with most developing societies, great disparities in the distribution of wealth. Nonetheless, quality-of-life indicators confirm a rising standard of living for the population as a whole. While great progress has been made toward eliminating poverty and disease, concern has also grown about the environmental capacity of the small, crowded country to sustain its current rate of development. There is also a general recognition that Mauritian prosperity is—and will for the foreseeable future remain—extremely vulnerable to global market forces.

DEVELOPMENT	FREEDOM	HEALTH/WELFARE	ACHIEVEMENTS

DEVELOPMENT

The success of the Mauritian EPZ along with the export-led growth of various Asian economies has encouraged a growing number of other African countries, such as Botswana, Cape Verde, and Madagascar, to launch their own export zones.

FREEDOM

Political pluralism and human rights are respected on Mauritius. The nation has more than 30 political parties, of which about a half dozen are important at any given time. The Mauritian labor movement is one of the strongest in all of Africa.

HEALTH/WELFARE

Medical and most educational expenses are free. Food prices are heavily subsidized. Rising government deficits, however, threaten future social spending. Mauritius has a high life expectancy rate and a low infant mortality rate.

ACHIEVEMENTS

Perhaps Mauritius's most important modern achievement has been its successful efforts to reduce its birth rate. This has been brought about by government-backed family planning as well as by increased economic opportunities for women.

Rwanda (Republic of Rwanda)*

GEOGRAPHY
Area in Square Kilometers (Miles):
26,338 (10,169) (about the size of Maryland)
Capital (Population): Kigali (257,000)
Climate: temperate

PEOPLE

Population
Total: 6,853,000
Annual Growth Rate: 2.7%
Rural/Urban Population Ratio: 95/5
Major Languages: Kinyarwanda; French; Kiswahili; English
Ethnic Makeup: 89% Hutu; 10% Tutsi; 1% Twa

Health
Life Expectancy at Birth: 39 years (male); 40 years (female)
Infant Mortality Rate (Ratio): 118/1,000
Average Caloric Intake: 94% of FAO minimum
Physicians Available (Ratio): 1/24,697

Religions
65% Roman Catholic; 25% traditional indigenous; 9% Protestant; 1% Muslim

Education
Adult Literacy Rate: 50%

COMMUNICATION
Telephones: 6,600
Newspapers: 1

TRANSPORTATION
Highways—Kilometers (Miles): 4,885 (3,069)
Railroads—Kilometers (Miles): none
Usable Airfields: 7

GOVERNMENT
Type: republic
Independence Date: July 1, 1962
Head of State/Government: President Pasteur Bizimungu; Prime Minister Faustin Twagiramungu
Political Parties: Rwandan Patriotic Front; Republican National Movement for Democracy and Development; Democratic Republican Movement; Liberal Party; Democratic and Socialist Party; others
Suffrage: universal for adults

MILITARY
Number of Armed Forces: 5,200
Military Expenditures (% of Central Government Expenditures): 1.6%
Current Hostilities: civil war

ECONOMY
Currency ($ U.S. Equivalent): 145 Rwanda francs = $1
Per Capita Income/GDP: $800/$6.8 billion
Inflation Rate: 9.5%
Natural Resources: tungsten; tin; cassiterite
Agriculture: coffee; tea; pyrethrum; beans; potatoes
Industry: food processing; mining; light consumer goods

FOREIGN TRADE
Exports: $66.6 million
Imports: $259.5 million

*Many of these statistics reflect conditions in Rwanda before the war that has destroyed much of the country and decimated its population.

THE RWANDAN PATRIOTIC FRONT

The Rwandan Patriotic Front (RPF), which now controls most of Rwanda, was formed in Uganda by Tutsi who grew up as second-generation exiles. While its commander, Paul Kagame, was 2 years old when his family fled Rwanda in 1959, many of his colleagues were born in Uganda as the children of refugees. For decades, they lived in miserable refugee camps, being denied citizenship by both their host country and their homeland. In the early 1980s, these "forgotten ones" become caught up in the rebellion against Milton Obote. Eventually, they became an important element in the National Resistance Army (NRA), led by fellow (Ugandan) Tutsi Yoweri Museveni. Kagame became the NRA's military-intelligence director. After the NRA triumph, a network of its exiled Tutsi veterans formed the RPF, with the goal of returning home. Like the NRA, the RPF immediately impressed outsiders with its military discipline. While French, along with Kinyarwanda, is an official language of Rwanda, having grown up in exile, many senior RPF speak English as a second language.

Rwanda
- ✪ Capital
- ● City
- River
- --- Road
- ⋯⋯ Unsurfaced road

0   150   kilometers
0   150 miles

RWANDA

The 1994 genocide in Rwanda is one of this century's greatest tragedies. A small country, only about the size of Maryland, Rwanda had 8 million inhabitants early in 1994, making it continental Africa's most densely populated state. This population was divided into three groups: the Hutu majority (89 percent); the Tutsi (10 percent); and the Twa, commonly stereotyped as "pygmies" (1 percent). By September 1994, civil war involving genocidal conflict between Hutu and Tutsi had nearly halved the country's resident population while radically altering its group demography.

THE 1994 GENOCIDE

The genocide began within a half-hour of the April 6, 1994, death of the country's democratizing dictator, President Juvenal Habyarimana. Along with the president of neighboring Burundi, Cyprien Ntaryamira, Habyarimana was killed when his plane was shot down. While the identity of the culprits remains a matter of speculation, Belgian troops reported that rockets were fired from Kanombe military base, which was then controlled by the country's Presidential Guard, known locally as the Akuza. In broadcasts over the independent Radio Libre Mille Collins, Hutu extremists then openly called for the destruction of the Tutsi—"The graves are only half full, who will help us fill them up?" Because the tirades were in idiomatic Kinyarwanda, the national language, they initially escaped the attention of most international journalists on the spot. Meanwhile, Akuza and regular army units set up roadblocks and began systematically to massacre Tutsi citizens in the capital, Kigali. Even greater numbers perished in the countryside, because their names appeared on death lists that had been prepared with the help of local Hutu chiefs.

By July, more than 500,000 people had been murdered. While most were Tutsi, Hutu who had supported moves toward ethnic reconciliation and democratization had also been targeted. In addition to elements within the Hutu-dominated military, the killings were carried out by youth-wing militias of the ruling party, the National Revolutionary Movement for Development (MRND) and the Coalition for Defense of Freedom (CDR). Known respectively as the Interahamwe and Impuzamugambi, the ranks of these two all-Hutu militias had mushroomed in the aftermath of an August 1993 agreement designed to return the country to multi-party rule. The extent of the killings was apparent in neighboring Tanzania, where thousands of corpses were televised being carried downstream by the Kagara River. At a rate of 80 an hour, they entered Lake Victoria, more than 100 miles from the Rwandan border.

SYSTEMATIC PLANS FOR MASS MURDER

Preparations for the genocide had been going on for months. According to Amnesty International, Hutu "Zero Network" death squads had already murdered some 2,300 people in the months leading up to the crisis. Although this information was the subject of press reports, no action was taken by the 2,500 peacekeeping troops who had been stationed in the country since June 1993 as the United Nations Assistance Mission to Rwanda (UNAMIR). Once the crisis began, most of UNAMIR's personnel were hastily withdrawn. French and Belgian paratroopers arrived for a brief time to evacuate their nationals.

Rwanda's genocide did not end with the destruction of a third or more of the Tutsi minority. Enraged by the massacres of their brethren, the 14,000-man Tutsi-dominated Rwanda Patriotic Front (RPF), which had been waging an armed struggle against the Habyarimana regime since October, launched a massive offensive. The 35,000-man regular army, along with the militias, crumbled. In July 1994, the RPF took full control of Kigali and drove the remnants of the government and its army eastward into Zaire. About 2 million panic-stricken Hutu civilians also fled across the border. By then, about 1 million Rwandans were already exiled. Another 2.5 million people were crowded into a "safe zone" created by the French military. As the French prepared to pull out, the fate of these refugees was uncertain.

In depopulated Kigali, the RPF set up a "Provisional Government" with a Hutu president, Pasteur Bizimungu, and prime minister, Faustin Twagiramungu. Its most powerful figure, however, was the RPF commander, Major General Paul Kagame, who became vice president and minister of defense.

HUTU AND TUTSI

The roots of Hutu–Tutsi animosity in Rwanda (as well as Burundi) run deep. Yet it is not easy for an outsider to differentiate between the two groups. Their members both speak Kinyarwanda and look the same physically, notwithstanding the stereotypes of the Tutsi being exceptionally tall; intermarriage between the two groups has taken place for centuries. By some accounts, the Tutsi arrived as northern Nilotic conquerors, perhaps in the fifteenth century. But others believe that the two groups have always been defined by class or caste rather than by ethnicity.

In the beginning, according to one epic Kinyarwanda poem, the godlike ruler Kigwa fashioned a test to choose his successor. He gave each of his sons a bowl of milk to guard during the night. His son Gatwa drank the milk. Yahutu slept and spilled the milk. Only Gatutsi guarded it well. The myth justifies the old Rwandan social order, in which the Twa were the outcasts, the Hutu servants, and the Tutsi aristocrats. Historically, Hutu serfs herded cattle and performed various other services for their Tutsi "protectors." At the top of the hierarchy was the Mwami, or king.

THE COLONIAL ERA: HUTU AND TUTSI ANIMOSITIES CONTINUE

Rwanda's feudal system survived into the colonial era. German and, later, Belgian administrators opted to rule through the existing order. But the social order was subtly destabilized by the new ideas emanating from the Catholic mission schools and by the colonialists' encouragement of the predominantly Hutu peasantry to grow cash crops, especially coffee. Discontent grew also due to the ever-increasing pressure of people and herds on already crowded lands.

In the late 1950s, under UN pressure, Belgium began to devolve political power to Rwandans. The death of the Mwami in 1959 sparked a bloody Hutu uprising against the Tutsi aristocracy. Tens of thousands, if not hundreds of thousands, were killed. Against this violent backdrop, pre-independence elections were held in 1961. These resulted in a victory for the first president, Gregoire Kayibanda's, Hutu Emancipation Movement, better known as Parmehutu. Thus, at independence, in 1962, Rwanda's traditionally Tutsi-dominated society was suddenly under a Hutu-dominated government.

In 1963 and 1964, continued interethnic competition for power exploded into more violence, which resulted in the flight of hundreds of thousands of ethnic Tutsi to neighboring Burundi, Tanzania, and Uganda. Along with their descendants, this refugee population today numbers about 1 million. Successive Hutu-dominated governments have barred their return, questioning their citizenship and citing extreme land pressure as barriers to their reabsorption. But the implied hope that the refugees would integrate into their host societies has failed to materialize. The RPF was originally formed in Uganda

Mwami Kigeri Rwabugiri expands and consolidates the kingdom **1860–1895**	Belgium rules Rwanda as a mandate of the League of Nations **1916**	The Hutu rebellion **1959**	Rwanda becomes independent; Gregoire Kayibana is president **1962**	Juvenal Habyarimana seizes power **1973**	The National Revolutionary Movement for Development is formed **1975**	A new Constitution is approved in a nationwide referendum; Habyarimana is reelected president **1978**

1990s

RPF rebels invade from Uganda; massacres of Tutsi by government forces are reported

French military "advisers" assist the government; rebels agree to a cease-fire; genocidal conflict results in a dramatic drop in the country's resident population; millions are killed or displaced

French relief workers withdraw from Rwanda; Tutsi massacre of Hutu at Kibeho refugee camp

by Tutsi exiles, many of whom were hardened veterans of that country's past conflicts. The repatriation of all Rwandan Tutsi has been a key RPF demand.

HABYARIMANA TAKES POWER

Major General Juvenal Habyarimana, a Hutu from the north, seized power in a military coup in 1973. Two years later, he institutionalized his still army-dominated regime as a one-party state under the MRND, in the name of overcoming ethnic divisions. Yet hostility between the Hutu and Tutsi remained. Inside the country, a system of ethnic quotas was introduced, which formally limited the remaining Tutsi minority to a maximum of 14 percent of the positions in schools and at the workplace. In reality, the Tutsi were often allocated less, while the MRND's critics maintained that the best opportunities were reserved for Hutu from Habyarimana's northern home area of Kisenyi.

POPULAR DISCONTENT

In the 1980s, many Hutu, as well as Tutsi, grew impatient with their government's corrupt authoritarianism. The post-1987 international collapse of coffee prices, Rwanda's major export-earner, led to an economic decline, further fueling popular discontent. Even before the armed challenge of the RPF, the MRND had agreed to give up its monopoly of power, though

this pledge was compromised by continued repression. Prominent among the new parties that then emerged were the Democratic Republic Movement (MDR), the Social Democrats (PSD), and the Liberals (PL). The PL and PSD were able to attract both Hutu and Tusi support. As a result, many of their Hutu as well as Tutsi members were killed in 1994. The MDR was associated with southern-regional Hutu resentment at the MRND's supposed northern bias.

A political breakthrough occurred in March 1992 with the formation of a Transitional Coalition Government, headed by the MDR's Dismas Nsengiyaremye, which also included MRND, PSD, and PL ministers. Habyarimana remained as president. With French military assistance, including the participation of several hundred French "advisers," Habyarimana's interim government of national unity was able to halt the RPF's advance in 1992. A series of cease-fires was negotiated with the RPF, leading up to the promise of (now aborted) UN-supervised elections in 1994. But from the beginning, progress toward national reconciliation was compromised by hard-line Hutu within the ruling military/MRND establishment and the extremist CDR. Ironically, these elements, who conspired to carry out the anti-Tutsi genocide in order to maintain control, were pushed out of the country by the RPF. These Hutu officials, soldiers, and militarymen, thought to

be responsible for massacring hundreds of thousands of Tutsis and moderate Hutu during the 1994 civil war, were exiled to camps in Zaire and Tanzania. Soon these militants returned and began a two-month wave of killings in Western Rwanda in an apparent attempt to stop the Tutsis from testifying at genocide trials being conducted by the Rwandan government and the U.N.

As Rwanda civil unrest intensified, refugees continued to flow into strife-torn Zaire. Estimates are that between 100,000 and 350,000 Hutu citizens are still in camps in Zaire. In March 1997, some 70,000 Rwandan Hutu refugees had gathered in Ubunda, a town 80 miles south of Kisangani on the Zaire River. But civil war in Zaire has caused these people to be pushed back into Rwanda, where they are faced with the chaotic unrest in their home country.

DEVELOPMENT

Hydroelectric stations meet much of the country's energy needs. Before the 1994 genocide, plans were being made to exploit methane gas reserves under Lake Kivu.

FREEDOM

In August 1996, the Africa Rights monitoring group reported continued killings, mostly by armed Hutu extremists who have specifically targeted people giving testimony before the War Crimes Commission, which began its deliberations in 1996.

HEALTH/WELFARE

The health system has collapsed. International relief agencies in Rwanda and neighboring countries are attempting to feed and care for the population. Diseases, like cholera have spread rapidly, to deadly effect.

ACHIEVEMENTS

Abbé Alexis Kagame, a Rwandan Roman Catholic churchman and scholar, has written studies of traditional Rwanda poetry and has written poetry about many of the traditions and rituals. Some of his works have been composed in Kinyarwanda, an official language of Rwanda, and translated into French. He has gained an international reputation among scholars.

Seychelles (Republic of the Seychelles)

GEOGRAPHY

Area in Square Kilometers (Miles):
435 (175) (about twice the size of
Washington, D.C.)
Capital (Population): Victoria
(25,000)
Climate: subtropical; marine

PEOPLE

Population
Total: 77,600
Annual Growth Rate: 0.81%
Rural/Urban Population Ratio: 50/50
Major Languages: English; French;
Creole
Ethnic Makeup: Seychellois (mixture
of Asians Africans, and French)
predominate

Health
Life Expectancy at Birth: 67 years
(male); 74 years (female)
Infant Mortality Rate (Ratio):
11.4/1,000
Average Caloric Intake: n/a
Physicians Available (Ratio): 1/947

Religions
98% Christian; 2% other

Education
Adult Literacy Rate: 58%

COMMUNICATION

Telephones: 13,000
Newspapers: 1

COCO DE MER

To botanists around the world, Seychelles has long been famous as the
home of the exotic coco de mer palm. The fruit of this tree, the *coco de
mer* ("sea coconut") is both the largest and heaviest of all seeds, taking
7 years to mature and weighing between 30 and 40 pounds. For
centuries, these nuts, which were carried by Indian Ocean currents to
distant shores, were worth more than their weight in gold. Their sensual
shape, like that of a female pelvis, made them highly valued as an
aphrodisiac; indeed, ancient legend held that the *coco de mer* was the
forbidden fruit of the biblical Garden of Eden. The source of the nuts
remained a mystery until 1768, when a Frenchman discovered the
palms.

TRANSPORTATION

Highways—Kilometers (Miles): 259
(160)
Railroads—Kilometers (Miles): none
Usable Airfields: 14

GOVERNMENT

Type: republic
Independence Date: June 29, 1976
Head of State: President France
Albert René
Political Parties: Seychelles People's
Progressive Front; Democratic Party;
United Opposition
Suffrage: universal at 17

MILITARY

Number of Armed Forces: 1,100
*Military Expenditures (% of Central
Government Expenditures):* 4.0%
Current Hostilities: none

ECONOMY

Currency ($ U.S. Equivalent): 4.94
rupees = $1
Per Capita Income/GDP:
$6,000/$430 million
Inflation Rate: 3.9%
Natural Resources: agricultural land;
fish
Agriculture: vanilla; coconuts;
cinnamon
Industry: tourism; copra and vanilla
processing; coconut oil; construction

FOREIGN TRADE

Exports: $50 million
Imports: $261 million

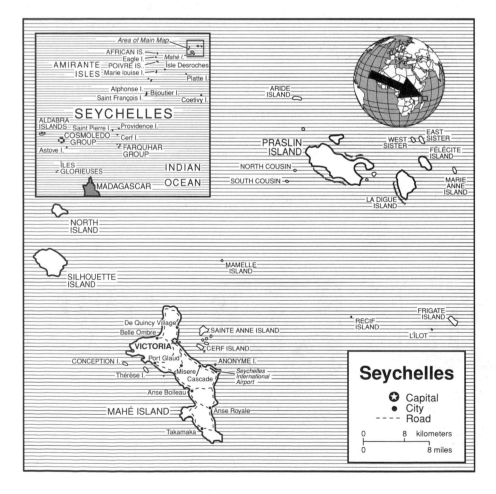

An Amnesty International report alleges government fabrication of drug-possession cases for political reasons
1980s

French settlement begins **1771**

British rule is established **1814**

The British end slavery **1830**

Seychelles is detached from Mauritius by the British and made a Crown colony **1903**

Legislative Council with qualified suffrage is introduced **1948**

Universal suffrage **1967**

Independence **1976**

A coup of Albert René against James Mancham **1977**

1990s

René agrees to a multiparty system

René and his party are approved by a solid majority in presidential and parliamentary elections

THE SEYCHELLES

Africa's smallest country, in terms of both size and population, the Republic of the Seychelles consists of a number of widely scattered archipelagos off the coast of East Africa. Over the last quarter-century, Seychellois have enjoyed enormous economic and social progress. But for an equally long time, the country's politics was bitterly polarized between supporters of President James Mancham and his successor, Albert René. The holding of multiparty elections in 1992 and 1993, after 15 years of single-party rule under René, was accompanied by a significant degree of reconciliation between the partisans of these two long-time rivals.

The roots of Seychelles' modern political economy go back to 1963, when Mancham's Democratic Party and René's People's United Party were established. The former originally favored private enterprise and the retention of the British imperial connection, while the latter advocated an independent socialist state. Electoral victories in 1970 and 1974 allowed Mancham to pursue his dream of turning Seychelles into a tourist paradise and a financial and trading center by aggressively seeking outside investment. Tourism began to flourish following the opening of an international airport on the main island of Mahe in 1971, fueling an economic boom. Between 1970 and 1980, per capita income rose from nearly $150 to $1,700 (today it is about $6,000).

In 1974, Mancham, in an about-face, joined René in advocating the islands' independence. The Democratic Party, despite its modest electoral and overwhelming parliamentary majority, set up a coalition government with the People's United Party. On June 29, 1976, Seychelles became independent, with Mancham as president and René as prime minister.

On June 5, 1977, with Mancham out of the country, René's supporters, with Tanzanian assistance, staged a successful coup in which several people were killed. Thereafter René assumed the presidency and suspended the Constitution. A period of rule by decree gave way in 1979, without the benefit of referendum, to a new constitutional framework in which the People's Progressive Front, successor to the People's United Party, was recognized as the nation's sole political voice. The first years of one-party government were characterized by continued economic growth, which allowed for an impressive expansion of social-welfare programs.

Political power since the coup remained largely concentrated in the hands of René. The early years of his regime, however, were marked by unrest. In 1978, the first in a series of unsuccessful countercoups was followed, several months later, by violent protests against the government's attempts to impose a compulsory National Youth Service, which would have removed the nation's 16- and 17-year-olds from their families in order to foster their sociopolitical indoctrination in accordance with the René government's socialist ideals. Another major incident occurred in 1981, when a group of international mercenaries, who had the backing of authorities in Kenya and South Africa as well as exiled Seychellois, were forced to flee in a hijacked jet after an airport shootout with local security forces. Following this attempt, Tanzanian troops were sent to the islands. A year later, the Tanzanians were instrumental in crushing a mutiny of Seychellois soldiers.

Despite its success in creating a model welfare state, which undoubtedly strengthened its popular acceptance, for years René continued to govern in a repressive manner. Internal opposition was not tolerated, and exiled activists were largely neutralized. About one fifth of the islands' population now live overseas; not all of these people left, however, for political reasons.

In 1991, René gave in to rising internal and external pressure for a return to multiparty democracy. In July 1992, his party won 58 percent of the vote for a commission to rewrite the Constitution. Mancham's Democrats received just over a third of the vote. But in November 1992, voters heeded Mancham's call, rejecting the revised constitution proposed by the pro-René commission. Faced with a possible deadlock, the two parties reached consensus on new proposals, which were ratified in a June 1993 referendum. Presidential and parliamentary elections held the following month confirmed majority support for René's party. The president was reelected with 60 percent of the vote; his party, the Seychelles People's Progressive Front, took 27 out of 32 parliamentary seats. A new coalition, the United Opposition, trailed well behind the Mancham's Democrats.

DEVELOPMENT

Seychelles has declared an Exclusive Economic Zone of 200 miles around all of its islands in order to promote the local fishing industry. Most of the zone's catch is harvested by foreign boats, which are supposed to pay licensing fees to the Seychelles government. Canned tuna is now the island's leading export-earner.

FREEDOM

Since the restoration of multiparty democracy, there has been greater political freedom in Seychelles. The opposition nonetheless continues to complain of police harassment and to protest about the government's control over the broadcast media.

HEALTH/WELFARE

A national health program has been established; private practice has been abolished. Free lunch programs have raised nutritional levels among the young. Education is also free up to age 14.

ACHIEVEMENTS

Under its current government, Seychelles has become a world leader in wildlife preservation. An important aspect of the nation's conservation efforts has been the designation of one island as an international wildlife refuge.

Somalia* (Somali Democratic Republic)

GEOGRAPHY

Area in Square Kilometers (Miles): 638,000 (246,331) (slightly smaller than Texas)
Capital (Population): Mogadishu (900,000)
Climate: arid to semiarid

PEOPLE

Population
Total: 9,639,000
Annual Growth Rate: 3.24%
Rural/Urban Population Ratio: 76/24
Major Languages: Somali; Arabic; Oromo; Italian; English
Ethnic Makeup: predominantly Somali

Health
Life Expectancy at Birth: 55 years (male); 56 years (female)
Infant Mortality Rate (Ratio): 119/1,000
Average Caloric Intake: 100% of FAO minimum
Physicians Available (Ratio): 1/19,071

Religions
99% Sunni Muslim; 1% others

Education
Adult Literacy Rate: 24%

REFUGEES IN AND OUT OF SOMALIA

Before its most recent crisis, life in Somalia had periodically been disrupted by large influxes of refugees. Drought in 1974–1975 led to the relocation of some 150,000 nomadic people into the arable regions of the country. War in the Ogaden region during the late 1970s led to a further migration of at least 700,000 Ethiopian Somalis. Although some returned to Ethiopia, drought and warfare there have led to new influxes since 1986. Today there are still perhaps 1 million Ogadeni refugees in Somalia; they have formed their own armed factions to fight on both sides of the border. Warfare within Somalia has also led to a reverse flow of some 1 million Somalis into Ethiopia and Kenya. Even before the recent famine, the refugee situation has been responsible for the injection of outside relief aid, which in 1990 constituted up to one third of the national budget.

COMMUNICATION

Telephones: 7,000
Newspapers: 2

TRANSPORTATION

Highways—Kilometers (Miles): 22,500 (13,972)
Railroads—Kilometers (Miles): —
Usable Airfields: 76

GOVERNMENT

Type: no functioning government
Independence Date: July 1, 1960
Head of State: none
Political Parties: none; various armed factions
Suffrage: universal at 18

MILITARY

Number of Armed Forces: —
Military Expenditures (% of Central Government Expenditures): n/a
Current Hostilities: border disputes with Ethiopia; conflicts with Ethiopian-backed Somali rebels; internal disputes

ECONOMY

Currency ($ U.S. Equivalent): 5,000 Somali shillings = $1
Per Capita Income/GDP: $500/$3.3 billion
Inflation Rate: 210%
Natural Resources: uranium; timber; fish
Agriculture: livestock; bananas; sugarcane; cotton; cereals
Industry: sugar refining; tuna and beef canning; textiles; iron-rod plants; petroleum refining

FOREIGN TRADE

Exports: $58 million
Imports: $249 million

*Note: The breakdown of government in Somalia has made the accurate gathering of statistics impossible. The figures listed on this page are only estimates.

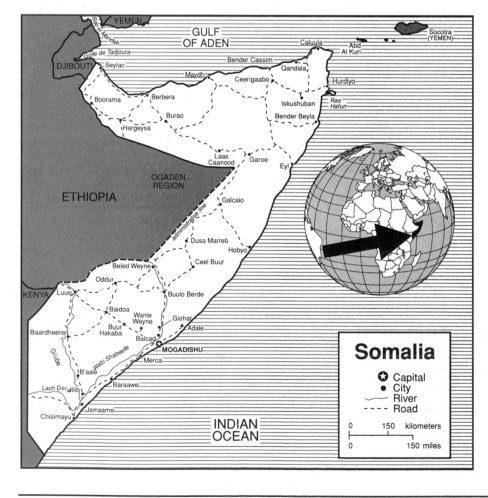

Somalia
- ✪ Capital
- ● City
- ~ River
- --- Road

0   150   kilometers
0   150 miles

SOMALIA

For much of the outside world, Somalia has become a symbol of failure of both international peacekeeping operations and the postcolonial African state. For the Somalis themselves, Somalia is now an ideal that has ceased to exist—but may yet be re-created. Since the January 1991 overthrow of the dictatorial regime of Mohammed Siad Barre, the country has been without any effective central government or formal economy. The territory is now divided by dozens of armed factions, organized on the basis of local clan loyalties, that are obedient only to the law of the gun and their warlords' own self-interests.

Literally hundreds of thousands of Somalis starved to death in 1991–1992 before a massive U.S.–led United Nations intervention—officially known as UNITAF but labeled "Operation Restore Hope" by the Americans—assured the delivery of relief supplies. The 1994 withdrawal of most UN forces (the last token units left in March 1995), following UNITAF's failure to disarm local militias while supporting the creation of a Transitional National Council, led to the termination of relief efforts in many areas, but widespread famine was averted in 1994–1995. Meanwhile, repeated attempts to reach a settlement between the various armed factions have ended in failure. The death in August 1996 of Somalia's most powerful warlord, General Mohammed Farah Aideed, may create new opportunities for negotiation, but prospects for national reconciliation in the near future remain dim.

SOMALI SOCIETY

The roots of Somalia's suffering run deep. Somalis have lived with the threat of famine for centuries, as Somalia is arid even in good years. Traditionally, most Somalis were nomadic pastoralists, but in recent years, this way of life has declined dramatically. Prior to the 1990s crisis, about half the population were still almost entirely reliant on livestock. Somali herds have sometimes been quite big: In the early 1980s, more than 1 million animals, mostly goats and sheep, were exported annually. Large numbers of cattle and camels have also been kept. But hundreds of thousands of animals were lost due to lack of rain during the mid-1980s; and since 1983, reports of rinderpest led to a sharp drop in exports, due to the closing of the once-lucrative Saudi Arabian market to East African animals.

A quarter of the Somali population have long combined livestock-keeping with agriculture. Cultivation is possible in the area between the Juba and Shebelle Rivers and in portions of the north. Although up to 15 percent of the country is potentially arable, only about 1 percent of the land has been put to plow at any given time. Bananas, cotton, and frankincense have been major cash crops, while maize and sorghum are subsistence crops. Like Somali pastoralists, Somali farmers walk a thin line between abundance and scarcity, for locusts as well as drought are common visitors.

The delicate nature of Somali agriculture helps to explain recent urbanization. One out of every four Somalis lives in the large towns and cities. The principal center is the capital, Mogadishu, which, despite being divided by war, still houses some 700,000 people. Unfortunately, as Somalis have migrated in from the countryside, they have found little employment. Even before the recent collapse, the country's manufacturing and service sectors were small. By 1990, more than 100,000 Somalis had become migrant workers in the Arab Gulf states. But in 1990–1991, many were repatriated as a result of the conflict over Kuwait.

Until recently, many outsiders assumed that Somalia possessed a greater degree of national coherence than most other African states. Somalis do share a common language and a sense of cultural identity. Islam is also a binding feature. However, competing clan and subclan allegiances have long played a divisive political role in the society. Membership in all the current armed factions is congruent with blood loyalties. Traditionally, the clans were governed by experienced, wise men. But the authority of these elders has now largely given way to the power of younger men with a surplus of guns and a surfeit of education and a lack of moral decency.

Past appeals to greater Somali nationalism have also been a source of conflict by encouraging irredentist sentiments against Somalia's neighbors. During the colonial era, contemporary Somalia was divided. For about 75 years, the northern region was governed by the British, while the southern portion was subject to Italian rule. These colonial legacies have complicated efforts at nation-building. Many northerners feel that their region has been neglected and would benefit from greater political autonomy or independence.

Somalia became independent on July 1, 1960, when the new national flag, a white, five-pointed star on a blue field, was raised in the former British and Italian territories. The star symbolized the five supposed branches of the Somali nation—that is, the now-united peoples of British and Italian Somalilands and the Somalis still living in French Somaliland (modern Djibouti), Ethiopia, and Kenya.

THE RISE AND FALL OF SIAD BARRE

Siad Barre came to power in 1969, through a coup promising radical change. As chairperson of the military's Supreme Revolutionary Council, Barre combined Somali nationalism and Islam with a commitment to "scientific socialism." Some genuine efforts were made to restructure society through the development of new local councils and worker management committees. New civil and labor codes were written. The Somali Revolutionary Socialist Party was developed as the sole legal political party.

Initially, the new order seemed to be making progress. The Somali language was alphabetized in a modified form of Roman script, which allowed the government to launch mass-literacy campaigns. Various rural-development projects were also implemented. In particular, roads were built, breaking down isolation among regions.

The promise of Barre's early years in office gradually faded. Little was done to follow through the developments of the early 1970s, as Barre increasingly bypassed the participatory institutions that he had helped to create. His government became one of personal rule; he took on emergency powers, relieved members of the governing council of their duties, surrounded himself with members of his own Marehan branch of the Darod clan, and isolated himself from the public. Barre also isolated Somalia from the rest of Africa by pursuing irredentist policies that would unite the other points of the Somali star under his rule. To accomplish this task, he began to encourage local guerrilla movements among the ethnic Somalis living in Kenya and Ethiopia.

In 1977, Barre sent his forces into the Ogaden region to assist the local rebels of the Western Somali Liberation Front. The invaders achieved initial military success against the Ethiopians, whose forces had been weakened by revolutionary strife and battles with Eritrean rebels. However, the intervention of some 17,000 Cuban troops and other Soviet bloc personnel on the side of the Ethiopians quickly turned the tide of battle. At the same time, the Somali incursion was condemned by all members of the Organization of African Unity.

The intervention of the Soviet bloc on the side of the Ethiopians was a bitter disappointment to Barre, who had enjoyed Soviet support for his military buildup. In exchange, he had allowed the Soviets to

The British take
control of
northern regions
of present-day
Somalia
1886–1887

Italy establishes
a protectorate in
the eastern areas
of present-day
Somalia
1889

The Somalia
Youth League is
founded; it
becomes a
nationalist party
1943

Somalia is
formed through a
merger of former
British and Italian
colonies under
UN Trusteeship
1960

Siad Barre
comes to power
through an army
coup; the
Supreme
Revolutionary
Council is
established
1969

The Ogaden war
in Ethiopia
results in
Somalia's defeat
1977–1978

SNM rebels escalate
their campaign in the
north; government
forces respond with
genocidal attacks on
the local Issaq
population
1980s

1990s

The fall of Barre
leaves Somalia
without an
effective central
government

U.S.– led UN
intervention
feeds millions
while attempting
to restore order

In the face of
mounting losses,
troops from the
United States
and elsewhere
pull out of
Somalia, leaving
behind chaos

establish a secret base at the strategic northern port of Berbera. However, in 1977, the Soviets decided to shift their allegiances decisively to the then–newly established revolutionary government in Ethiopia. Barre in turn tried to attract U.S. support with offers of basing rights at Berbera, but the Carter administration was unwilling to jeopardize its interests in either Ethiopia or Kenya by backing Barre's irredentist adventure. American–Somali relations became closer during the Reagan administration, which signed a 10-year pact giving U.S. forces access to air and naval facilities at Berbera, for which the United States increased its aid to Somalia, including limited arms supplies.

In 1988, Barre met with Ethiopian leader Mengistu Mariam. Together they pledged to respect their mutual border. This understanding came about in the context of growing internal resistance to both regimes. By 1990, numerous clan-based armed resistance movements—the Somali Salvation Democratic Front (SSDF), the Somalia Democratic Movement (SDM), the Somali National Movement (SNM), the Somalia Patriotic Movement (SPM), the United Somali Front (USF), the United Somali Party (USP), and the 16-faction United Somali Congress (USC)—were enjoying success against Barre.

Growing resistance was accompanied by massive atrocities on the part of government forces. Human-rights concerns were cited by the U.S. and other governments in ending their assistance to Somalia. In March 1990, Barre called for national dialogue and spoke of a possible end to one-party rule. But continuing atrocities, including the killing of more

than 100 protesters at the national stadium, fueled further armed resistance.

In January 1991, Barre fled Mogadishu, which was seized by USC forces. The USC set up an interim administration, but its authority was not recognized by other groups. By the end of the year, the USC itself had split into two warring factions. A 12-faction "Manifesto Group" recognized Ali Mahdi as the country's president. But Mahdi's authority was repudiated by the four-faction Somali National Alliance (SNA), led by Farah Aideed. Much of Mogadishu was destroyed in inconclusive fighting between the two groupings. Other militias, including forces still loyal to Barre (that is, the Somali National Front, or SNF), have also continued to fight one another. In the north, the Somali National Movement declared its zone's sovereign independence as "Somaliland."

Continued fighting coincided with drought. As failed crops and dying livestock resulted in countrywide famine, international relief efforts were unable to supply sufficient quantities of outside food to those most in need, due to the prevailing state of lawlessness. By mid-1992, the International Red Cross estimated that, of southern Somalia's 4.5 million people, 1.5 million were in danger of starvation. Another 500,000 or so had fled the country. More than 300,000 children under age 5 were reported to have perished.

As Somalia's suffering grew and became publicized in the Western media, many observers suggested the need for the United Nations to intervene. A small UN presence, known as UNISOM, was established in August 1992, but its attempts to police the delivery of relief supplies

proved to be ineffectual. Conceived as a massive U.S.–led military operation, initially consisting of 30,000 troops (22,000 Americans), UNITAF (Operation Restore Hope) averted catastrophe by assuring the delivery of food and medical supplies to Somalia's starving millions.

In March 1993, a UN–sponsored agreement was reached among most of the southern Somali factions to form a "Transitional National Council." But subsequent UNITAF attempts to enforce the agreement by disarming the militias ended in total failure. A bloody clash between Aideed's SNA militia and Pakistani troops in Mogadishu led to full-scale armed conflict. Efforts by UNITAF forces to capture Aideed and neutralize his men were unsuccessful. After a U.S. helicopter was shot down in October 1993, President Bill Clinton decided to end American involvement in UNITAF by March 1994, thus undermining the peacemaking effort. By then, much higher losses had been suffered by several other nations participating in the UNITAF–UNISOM coalition, causing them also to reassess their commitments. Outgunned and demoralized, the remaining UN forces (officially labeled UNISOM II) remained largely confined to their compounds until their withdrawal.

DEVELOPMENT

Most development projects have ended. Somalia's material infrastructure has largely been destroyed by war and neglect, though some local rebuilding efforts are under way, especially in the more peaceful central and northern parts of the country.

FREEDOM

Plagued by hunger and internal violence, and with the continuing threat of governance by the anarchic greed of the warlords, the living have no true freedom in Somalia.

HEALTH/WELFARE

Somalia's small 1990 health service has almost completely disappeared, leaving the country reliant on a handful of international health teams. By 1986, education's share of the national budget had fallen to 2%. Somalia had 525 troops per teacher, the highest such ratio in Africa.

ACHIEVEMENTS

Somalia has been described as a "nation of poets." Many scholars attribute the strength of the Somali poetic tradition not only to the nomadic way of life, which encourages oral arts, but to the role of poetry as a local social and political medium.

Sudan (Democratic Republic of the Sudan)

GEOGRAPHY

Area in Square Kilometers (Miles):
2,504,530 (967,500) (about one fourth the size of the United States)
Capital (Population): Khartoum (924,500)
Climate: desert in north to tropical in south

PEOPLE

Population
Total: 31,065,000
Annual Growth Rate: 2.35%
Rural/Urban Population Ratio: 77/23
Major Languages: Arabic; Nuer; Dinka; Shilluki; Masalatis; Fur; Nubian; English; others
Ethnic Makeup: 52% black; 39% Arab; 6% Beja; 3% others

Health
Life Expectancy at Birth: 54 years (male); 56 years (female)
Infant Mortality Rate (Ratio): 80/1,000
Average Caloric Intake: 99% of FAO minimum
Physicians Available (Ratio): 1/9,439

Religions
Sunni Muslim, especially in north; traditional indigenous; Christian

Education
Adult Literacy Rate: 27%

THE OPPRESSION OF WOMEN IN SUDAN

Since coming to power in 1989, the Sudanese military government has instituted a sweeping policy aimed at radically redefining the role of women in society. Traditionally, both Muslim and non-Muslim women in Sudan had enjoyed such basic freedoms as access to higher education, professional employment, the right to engage in trade, and freedom of movement; all these freedoms are now being curtailed in the name of Islamic propriety. Women are being systematically removed from the Sudanese civil service and from many fields of tertiary education. It has been suggested that, in the future, women will be free to be nurses and primary-school teachers. Women in Sudan are no longer free to travel without a male escort. And thousands of women, mostly non-Muslim, are the principal victims of enslavement by local militias.

COMMUNICATION
Telephones: 73,400
Newspapers: 2

TRANSPORTATION
Highways—Kilometers (Miles): 20,703 (12,877)
Railroads—Kilometers (Miles): 5,516 (3,425)
Usable Airfields: 66

GOVERNMENT
Type: military-ruled
Independence Date: January 1, 1956
Head of State: Prime Minister Omar Hasan Ahmad al-Bashir
Political Parties: banned
Suffrage: none

MILITARY
Number of Armed Forces: 112,500
Military Expenditures (% of Central Government Expenditures): 7.3%
Current Hostilities: civil war; clashes with Egypt, Eritrea, and Uganda

ECONOMY
Currency ($ U.S. Equivalent): 434.8 Sudanese pounds = $1
Per Capita Income/GDP: $870/$23.7 billion
Inflation Rate: 112%
Natural Resources: oil; iron ore; copper; chrome; other industrial metals
Agriculture: cotton; peanuts; sesame; gum arabic; sorghum; wheat
Industry: textiles; cement; cotton ginning; edible oils; distilling; pharmaceuticals

FOREIGN TRADE
Exports: $419 million
Imports: $1.7 billion

SUDAN

Sudan is Africa's largest country. Its tremendous size as well as its great ethnic and religious diversity have frustrated the efforts of successive postindependence governments to build a lasting sense of national unity. Since the takeover of the state in 1989 by a repressive military clique allied to the fundamentalist National Islamic Front (NIF), the polarization of Sudanese society has deepened to an unprecedented extent. At the moment, there is little hope for unity and reconciliation in this vast, suffering land of enormous potential.

HISTORY

Sudan, like its northern neighbor Egypt, is a gift of the Nile. The river and its various branches snake across the country, providing water to most of the 80 percent of Sudanese who survive by farming. From ancient times, the upper Nile region of northern Sudan has been the site of a series of civilizations, whose histories are closely intertwined with those of Egypt. There has been constant human interaction between the two zones. Some groups, such as the Nubians, expanded northward into the Egyptian lower Nile.

The last ruler to unite the Nile Valley politically was the nineteenth-century Turko–Egyptian ruler Muhammad Ali. After absorbing the by-then predominantly Arabized Muslim, northern Sudan into his Egyptian state, Ali gradually expanded his authority to the south and west over non-Arabic and, in many cases, non-Muslim groups. This process, which was largely motivated by a desire for slave labor, united for the first time the diverse regions that today make up Sudan. In the 1880s, much of Sudan fell under the theocratic rule of the Mahdists, a local anti-Egyptian Islamic movement. The Mahdists were defeated by an Anglo–Egyptian force in 1898. Thereafter, the British dominated Sudan until its independence, in 1956.

Sudanese society has remained divided ever since. There has been strong Pan-Arab sentiment in the north, but 60 percent of Sudanese, concentrated in the south and west, are non-Arab. Between 30 and 40 percent of Sudanese, especially in the south, are also non-Muslim. Despite this fact, many, but by no means all, Sudanese Muslims have favored the creation of an Islamic state. Ideological divisions among various Socialist- and non-Socialist-oriented factions have also been important. Sudan has long had a strong Communist Party (whether legal or not),

drawing on the support of organized labor, and an influential middle class.

The division between northern and southern Sudan has been especially deep. A mutiny by southern soldiers prior to independence escalated into a 17-year rebellion by southerners against what they perceived to be the hegemony of Muslim Arabs. Some 500,000 southerners perished before the Anya Nya rebels and the government reached a compromise settlement, recognizing southern autonomy in 1972.

In northern Sudan, the first 14 years of independence saw the rule of 7 different civilian coalitions and 6 years of military rule. Despite this chronic instability, a tradition of liberal tolerance among political factions was generally maintained. Government became increasingly authoritarian during the administration of Jaafar Nimeiri, who came to power in a 1969 military coup.

Nimeiri quickly moved to consolidate his power by eliminating challenges to his government from the Islamic right and the Communist left. His greatest success was ending the Anya Nya revolt, but his subsequent tampering with the provisions of the peace agreement led to renewed resistance. In 1983, Nimeiri decided to impose Islamic law throughout Sudanese society. This led to the growth of the Sudanese People's Liberation Army (SPLA), under

(United Nations photo by Milton Grant)

Millions of Sudanese have been displaced by warfare and drought. The effect on the population has been devastating, and even the best efforts of the international community have met with only limited success.

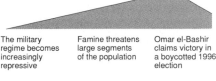

| Egypt invades northern Sudan **1820** | The Mahdist Revolt begins **1881** | Independence **1956** | Jaafar Nimeiri comes to power **1969** | Hostilities end in southern Sudan **1972** | Islamic law replaces the former penal code; renewed civil war in the south **1980s** | Nimeiri is overthrown in a popular coup; an elected government is installed | A military coup installs a hard-line Islamic fundamentalist regime **1989** |

1990s

The military regime becomes increasingly repressive

Famine threatens large segments of the population

Omar el-Bashir claims victory in a boycotted 1996 election

the leadership of John Garang, which quickly seized control of much of the southern Sudanese countryside. Opposition to Nimeiri had also been growing in the north, as more people became alienated by the regime's increasingly heavy-handed ways and inability to manage the declining economy. Finally, in 1985, he was toppled in a coup.

The holding of multiparty elections in 1986 seemed to presage a restoration of Sudan's tradition of pluralism. With the SPLA preventing voting in much of the south, the two largest parties were the northern-based Umma and Democratic Union (DUP). The third-largest vote-getter was the NIF, with eight other parties plus a number of independents gaining parliamentary seats. The major challenge facing the new coalition government, led by Umma, was reconciliation with the SPLA. Because the SPLA, unlike the earlier Anya Nya, was committed to national unity, the task did not appear insurmountable. However, arguments within the government over meeting key SPLA demands, such as the repeal of Islamic law, caused the war to drag on. A hard-line faction within Umma and the NIF sought to resist a return to secularism. In March 1989, a new government, made up of Umma and DUP, committed itself to accommodating the SPLA. However, a month later, on the day the cabinet was to ratify an agreement with the rebels, there was a coup by pro-NIF officers.

Besides leading to a breakdown in all efforts to end the SPLA rebellion, the NIF/military regime has been responsible for establishing the most intolerant, repressive government in Sudan's modern history. Extrajudicial executions have be-

come commonplace. Instances of pillaging and enslavement of non-Muslim communities by government-linked militias have increased. NIF-affiliated security groups have become a law unto themselves, striking out at their perceived enemies and intimidating Muslims and non-Muslims alike to conform to their fundamentalist norms. Islamic norms are also being invoked to justify a radical campaign to undermine the status of women.

In 1990, most of the now-banned political parties, including Umma, DUP, and the Communists, aligned themselves with the SPLA as the National Democratic Alliance. But opposition by the northern-based parties proved ineffectual, leading to the formation of a new, Eritrean-based armed movement—the Sudan Alliance of Forces, headed by Abdul Azizi Khalid.

Beginning in 1991, the SPLA was weakened by a series of splits. Two factions—Kerubino Kuanyin Bol's SPLA–Bahr al-Ghazal group and Riek Macher's Southern Sudan Independence Army (SSIA)—accepted a goverment peace plan in April 1996. But the plan was rejected by John Garang's SPLA (Torit faction), which remains the most powerful southern group. After a number of years of being on the defensive, Garang's forces began making significant advances in 1996, partially as a result of increased support from neighboring countries that have come to look upon the Khartoum regime as a regional threat. In June 1995, the regime was implicated in an attempt to assassinate Egyptian president Hosni Mubarak in Ethiopia, which resulted in the imposition of UN anti-terrorism sanctions. Border clashes have since occurred with Eritrea and Uganda as well as Egypt.

There is no immediate prospect of an end to the internal fighting, which has been accompanied by atrocities on all sides, including by a number of regional militias with shifting loyalties. By 1994, estimates of casualties in the conflict ranged from 1 million to 1.5 million.

ECONOMIC PROSPECTS

Although it has great potential, political conflict has left the Sudan one of the poorest nations in the world. The country's under-utilized water resources have led to talk of creating the "breadbasket of the Arab world," while untapped oil reserves in the south could transform the country from an energy importer to an exporter. However, persistent warfare and lack of financing are blocking needed infrastructural improvements. Sudan's unwillingness to pay its foreign debt has led to calls for its expulsion from the International Monetary Fund.

Nearly 7 million Sudanese (out of a total population then of 23 million) had been displaced by 1988—more than 4 million by warfare, with drought and desertification contributing to the remainder. Sudan has been a major recipient of international emergency food aid for years, but warfare, corruption, and genocidal indifference have often blocked help from reaching the needy. In 1994, the United Nations estimated that 700,000 southern Sudanese faced the prospect of starvation.

DEVELOPMENT

Many ambitious development plans have been launched since independence, but progress has been limited by political instability. The periodic introduction and redefinition of "Islamic" financial procedures have complicated long-term planning.

FREEDOM

The current regime rules through massive repression. In 1992, Africa Watch accused it of practicing genocide against the Nuba people. Elsewhere, tales of massacres, forced relocations, enslavement, torture, and starvation are commonplace.

HEALTH/WELFARE

Civil strife and declining government expenditures have resulted in rising rates of infant mortality. Warfare has also prevented famine relief from reaching needy populations, resulting in instances of mass starvation.

ACHIEVEMENTS

Although his music is banned in his own country, Mohammed Wardi is probably Sudan's most popular musician. Now living in exile, he has been imprisoned and tortured for his songs against injustice, which also appeal to a large international audience, especially in North Africa and the Middle East.

Tanzania (United Republic of Tanzania)

GEOGRAPHY

Area in Square Kilometers (Miles):
939,652 (363,950) (more than twice
the size of California)
Capital (Population): Dar es Salaam
(1,400,000); Dodoma (new national
capital) (1,238,000)
Climate: tropical; arid; temperate

PEOPLE

Population

Total: 19,058,500
Annual Growth Rate: 2.5%
Rural/Urban Population Ratio: 79/21
Major Languages: Iswahili; Chagga;
Gogo; Ha; Haya; Luo; Maasai;
English; others
Ethnic Makeup: African

Health

Life Expectancy at Birth: 41 years
(male); 44 years (female)
Infant Mortality Rate (Ratio):
110/1,000
Average Caloric Intake: 87% of FAO
minimum
Physicians Available (Ratio): 1/20,300

Religions

traditional indigenous; Muslim;
Christian; Zanzibar is predominantly
Muslim

Education

Adult Literacy Rate: 46%

COMMUNICATION

Telephones: 103,800
Newspapers: 5

THE SWAHILI COAST

A trading coastal culture, African-based with Arabian influence, developed over hundreds of years on the East African coast. For 2,000 years, merchants from the Mediterranean and the Middle East traded along the coast of East Africa. The mingling of Bantu-speaking peoples with Arab culture eventually created the Swahili, an Afro–Arab people with their own African-based language. Based in cities on islands and along the coast, they traded with Arabia, Persia, India, and China, and eventually with the interior of present-day Kenya and Tanzania. Converted to Islam and also Arabic-speaking, these cosmopolitan peoples traded interior produce for porcelain, spices, and textiles from all over the world and created an impressive written and oral literature. They still play an important role in the political and commercial life of Tanzania.

TRANSPORTATION

Highways—Kilometers (Miles):
81,900 (50,778)
Railroads—Kilometers (Miles): 2,600
(1,622)
Usable Airfields: 108

GOVERNMENT

Type: republic
Independence Date: December 9, 1961
Head of State/Government: President
Ben Mkapa; Prime Minister Cleopa
David Msoya
Political Parties: Chama Cha
Mapinduzi (Revolutionary Party);
National Committee for Constitutional
Reform; Civic United Front; Union for
Multiparty Democracy
Suffrage: universal at 18

MILITARY

Number of Armed Forces: 58,500
*Military Expenditures (% of Central
Government Expenditures):* 3.9%
Current Hostilities: none

ECONOMY

Currency ($ U.S. Equivalent): 523.4
Tanzanian shillings = $1
Per Capita Income/GDP: $750/$21
billion
Inflation Rate: 25%
Natural Resources: hydroelectric
potential; unexploited iron and coal;
gemstones; gold; natural gas
Agriculture: cotton; coffee; sisal; tea;
tobacco; wheat; cashews; livestock;
cloves
Industry: agricultural processing;
diamond mining; oil refining; shoes;
cement; textiles; wood products

FOREIGN TRADE

Exports: $462 million
Imports: $1.4 billion

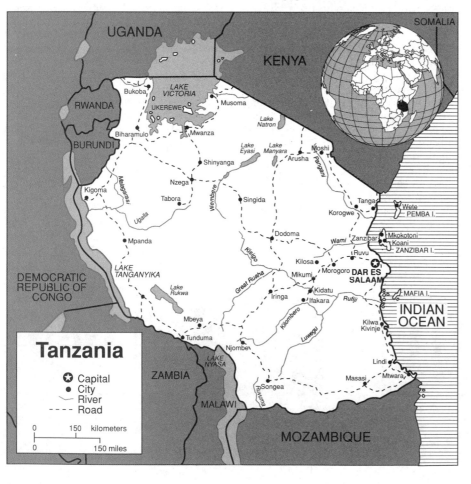

Tanzania
⊛ Capital
● City
⌇ River
- - - Road

0   150   kilometers
0   150 miles

TANZANIA

After a period of harsh German rule followed by paternalistic British trusteeship, the Tanzanian mainland gained its independence, as Tanganyika, in 1961. In 1964, it merged with the small island state of Zanzibar, which had been a British protectorate, to form the "United Republic of Tanzania." Political activity in Tanzania was restricted to the ruling Revolutionary or Chama Cha Mapinduzi (CCM) Party, which joined the former Tanganyika African National Union with its Zanzibar partner, the Afro-Shirazi Party.

In February 1992, the CCM agreed to compete with other "national parties"—provided they did not "divide the people along tribal, religious or racial lines." Multiparty elections were held in October–December 1995, with the CCM claiming victory over a divided opposition in a poll characterized by massive irregularities. The disputed official results were CCM, 60 percent of the vote and 187 Members of Parliament (MPs), including 128 seats where the results were still

being legally contested months later; the National Committee for Constitutional Reform (NCCR), 25 percent of the vote and 15 MPs; and the Civic United Front, 24 MPs but only a small percentage of the vote, concentrated in Zanzibar and Pemba Islands. The new CCM leader, Ben Mkapa, replaced as president Ali Hassan Mwinyi, who was forced to step down after having served two terms. The dominant personality in the CCM, however, remained former president Julius Nyerere.

By 1967, the CCM's predecessors had already eliminated legal opposition, when they proclaimed their commitment to the Arusha Declaration, a blueprint for "African Socialism." At the time, Tanzania was one of the least developed countries in the world. It has remained so. Beyond this fact, there is much controversy over the degree to which the goals of the Declaration have been achieved. To some critics, the Arusha experiment has been responsible for reducing a potentially well-off country to ruin. Supporters often counter that it has led to a stable society in which major strides have been made toward

greater democracy, equality, and human development. Both sides exaggerate.

Like many African states, Tanzania has a primarily agrarian economy that is constrained by a less than optimal environment. Although some 90 percent of the population are employed in agriculture, only 8 percent of the land is under cultivation. Rainfall for most of the country is low and erratic, and soil erosion and deforestation are critical problems in many areas. But geography and environmental problems are only one facet of Tanzania's low agricultural productivity. There has also been instability in world-market demand for the nation's principal cash crops: coffee, cotton, cloves, sisal, and tobacco. The cost of imported fuel, fertilizers, and other inputs has risen simultaneously.

Government policies have also led to underdevelopment. Perhaps the greatest policy disaster was the program of villagization. Tanzania hoped to relocate its rural and unemployed urban populations into *ujaama* (Swahili for "familyhood") villages, which were to become the basis for

(UN photo by Ray Witlin)

The economy of Tanzania is primarily agrarian. However, rainfall for most of the country is sporadic. This, coupled with wide swings in world-market demand for its cash crops, has led to economic pressures affecting food crops. These men in the village of Lumeji are receiving seed grains needed to develop Tanzania's food production.

agrarian progress. In the early 1970s, coercive measures were adopted to force the pace of resettlement. Agricultural production is estimated to have fallen as much as 50 percent during the initial period of *ujaama* dislocation, transforming the nation from a grain exporter to a grain importer.

Another policy constraint was the exceedingly low official produce prices paid by the government to farmers. Many peasants withdrew from the official market, while others turned to black-market sales. Since 1985, the official market has been liberalized and prices have risen. This has been accompanied by a modest rise in production, yet the lack of consumer goods in rural areas is widely seen as a disincentive to greater progress.

All sectors of the Tanzanian economy have suffered from deteriorating infrastructure. Here again there are both external and internal causes. Balanced against rising imported-energy and equipment costs have been inefficiencies caused by poor planning, barriers to capital investment, and a relative neglect of communications and transport. Even when crops or goods are available, they often cannot reach their destination. Tanzania's few bituminized roads have long been in a chronic state of disrepair, and there have been frequent shutdowns of its railways. In particular, much of the southern third of the country is isolated from access to even inferior transport services.

Manufacturing declined from 10 to 4 percent of gross domestic product in the 1980s, with most sectors operating at less than half of their capacity. Inefficiencies also grew in the nation's mining sector.

Diamonds, gold, iron, coal, and other minerals are exploited, but production has been generally falling and now accounts for less than 1 percent of GDP. Lack of capital investment has led to a deterioration of existing operations and an inability to open up new deposits.

As with agriculture, the Tanzanian government has in recent years increasingly abandoned socialism in favor of market economics, in its efforts to rehabilitate and expand the industrial and service sectors of the economy. A number of state enterprises are being privatized, and better opportunities are being offered to outside investors. Tourism is being promoted, after decades of neglect.

Tanzania has made real progress in extending health, education, and other social services to its population since independence, though the statistical evidence is inadequate and official claims exaggerated. Some 1,700 health centers and dispensaries have been built since 1961, but they have long been plagued by shortages of medicines, equipment, and even basic supplies such as bandages and syringes. Although the country has a national health service, patients often end up paying for material costs.

Much of the progress that has been made in human services is a function of outside donations. Despite the Arusha Declaration's emphasis on self-reliance, Tanzania has been either at or near the top of the list of African countries in its per capita receipt of international aid for decades. By 1987, aid, primarily from Western countries, accounted for more than one third of the gross national product.

Even before the recent opening to multipartyism, Tanzania's politics was in a state of transition. Political life has been dominated since the 1950s by Julius Nyerere, who was the driving personality behind the Arusha experiment. However, in 1985, he gave up the presidency in favor of Ali Hassan Mwinyi and, in 1990, Nyerere resigned as chairperson of the CCM, without having to give up his leading influence in the party.

The move to multiparty politics is complicated by the omnipresent CCM. The party has sought to control all organized social activity outside of religion. A network of community and workplace cells has assured that all Tanzanians have at least one party official responsible for monitoring their affairs.

In 1993, a dozen new opposition parties were registered, though others, notably the Democratic Party of Reverend Christopher Mtikila, remain banned. Opposition disunity contributed to subsequent CCM election victories. In addition, the CCM still enjoys a near media monopoly, occasionally invoking the National Security Act to harass independent journalists. Overt political repression has been most notable on Zanzibar and Pemba Islands, where the CCM claimed a narrow 50.2 percent victory over CUP in October 1996, amid allegations of electoral fraud. Resulting civil unrest on the islands led to a government crackdown, with some 600 arrests.

DEVELOPMENT

In April 1990, the World Bank approved a $200 million loan to assist Tanzania in the radical restructuring of its agricultural marketing system. Unprofitable state farms were to be sold off, the cereal marketing board was to be abolished, and the role of cash-crop marketing boards was to be reduced.

FREEDOM

Despite the return of multiparty democracy, the persecution of dissidents persists in Tanzania, while freedom of association, assembly, and speech continue to be heavily regulated. In 1992, the leader of the outlawed Democratic Party, Reverend Christopher Mtikila, was jailed for 9 months. He was rearrested in 1994 while attempting to campaign.

HEALTH/WELFARE

The Tanzanian Development Plan calls for the government to give priority to health and education in its expenditures. This reflects a recognition that early progress in these areas has been undermined to some extent in recent years. Malnutrition remains a critical problem.

ACHIEVEMENTS

The government has had enormous success in its program of promoting the use of Swahili as the national language throughout society. Mass literacy in Swahili has facilitated the rise of a national culture, helping to make Tanzania one of the more cohesive African states.

Uganda (Republic of Uganda)

GEOGRAPHY

Area in Square Kilometers (Miles):
235,885 (91,076) (slightly smaller than Oregon)
Capital (Population): Kampala (773,000)
Climate: tropical to semiarid

PEOPLE

Population
Total: 20,158,000
Annual Growth Rate: 2.25%
Rural/Urban Population Ratio: 89/11
Major Languages: English; Kiswahili; Luganda; Iteso; Soga; Acholi; Lugbara; Nyakole; Nyoro; others
Ethnic Makeup: Bantu; Nilotic; Nilo-Hamitic; Sudanic

Health
Life Expectancy at Birth: 36 years (male); 37 years (female)
Infant Mortality Rate (Ratio): 112/1,000
Average Caloric Intake: 83% of FAO minimum
Physicians Available (Ratio): 1/20,700

Religions
66% Christian; 18% traditional indigenous; 16% Muslim

Education
Adult Literacy Rate: 48%

COMMUNICATION

Telephones: 54,900
Newspapers: 22

TROUBLED WATERS

Lake Victoria, which borders southeastern Uganda, is the world's second-biggest body of fresh water. Millions of Ugandans depend on its fish. But environmental change is threatening their future. Rapidly rising levels of algae in the lake's lower depths are reducing oxygen levels in the water, killing off fish stocks. Most researchers now believe that the principal factor behind this shift was the introduction more than 3 decades ago of the Nile perch by local fishery officials. The motive for introducing this new species was its size (up to 200 pounds) and the quality of its meat. Since the early 1980s, the Nile perch has significantly boosted the value of local catches. But it has also greatly reduced the number of local haplochromines, some 400 species of small fish that have kept algae levels down. Now there are fears that fishing in Lake Victoria could soon collapse as more of its biomass dies of asphyxiation, destroying its natural food chain.

TRANSPORTATION

Highways—Kilometers (Miles): 26,200 (16,244)
Railroads—Kilometers (Miles): 1,300 (807)
Usable Airfields: 29

GOVERNMENT

Type: republic; under control of the National Resistance Council
Independence Date: October 9, 1962
Head of State/Government: President Yoweri Kaguta Museveni; Prime Minister Kintu Musoke
Political Parties: National Resistance Movement (only party allowed public political activities); Nationalist Liberal Party; Democratic Party; Conservative Party; Uganda People's Congress
Suffrage: universal at 18

MILITARY

Number of Armed Forces: 60,000
Military Expenditures (% of Central Government Expenditures): 1.7%
Current Hostilities: civil strife in the northeast

ECONOMY

Currency ($ U.S. Equivalent): 1,165 Uganda shillings = $1
Per Capita Income/GDP: $850/$16.2 billion
Inflation Rate: 5%
Natural Resources: copper; other minerals
Agriculture: coffee; tea; cotton
Industry: processed agricultural goods; copper; cement; shoes; fertilizer; steel; beverages

FOREIGN TRADE

Exports: $237 million
Imports: $696 million

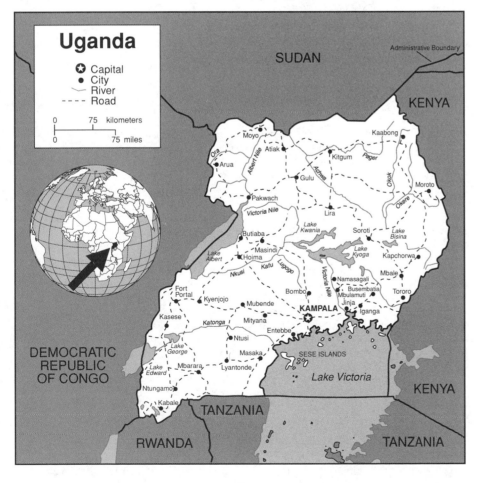

UGANDA

After years of repressive rule accompanied by massive interethnic violence, Uganda is still struggling for peace and reconciliation. A land rich in natural and human resources, Uganda suffered dreadfully during the despotic regimes of Milton Obote (1962–1971, 1980–1985) and Idi Amin (1971–1979). Under these two dictators, hundreds of thousands of Ugandans were murdered by the state.

The country had reached a state of general social and political collapse by 1986, when the forces of the National Resistance Movement (NRM) established the current administration, led by Yoweri Museveni. This government has made considerable progress in restoring a sense of normalcy throughout most of the country. Its hold on the north, however, has continued to be contested by armed factions, the most notable in recent years calling itself the Lord's Resistance Army. In May 1996, Museveni officially received 74 percent of the vote in a contested presidential poll. Despite charges of fraud by his closest rival Paul Ssemogerere, most independent observers accepted the poll as an endorsement of Museveni's leadership, including his view that politics should remain organized on a nonparty basis.

HISTORIC GEOGRAPHY

The breakdown of Uganda is an extreme example of the disruptive role of ethnic and sectarian competition, which was fostered by policies of both its colonial and postcolonial governments. Uganda consists of two major zones: the plains of the northeast and the southern highlands. It has been said that you can drop anything into the rich volcanic soils of the well-watered south and it will grow. Until the 1960s, the area was divided into four kingdoms—Buganda, Bunyoro, Ankole, and Toro—populated by peoples using related Bantu languages.

The histories of these four states stretch back to the fifteenth century. European visitors of the nineteenth century were impressed by their sophisticated social orders, which the Europeans equated with the feudal monarchies of medieval Europe. When the British took over, they integrated the ruling class of the southern highlands into a system of "indirect rule." By then, missionaries had already succeeded in converting many southerners to Christianity; indeed, civil war among Protestants, Catholics, and Muslims within Buganda had been the British pretext for establishing their overrule.

The Acholi, Langi, Karamojang, Teso, Madi, and Kakwa peoples, who are pre-

(UN photo by T. Chen)

Uganda is a land rich in natural and human resources, with tremendous potential for economic growth and improved quality of life. A major problem has been overcoming the abuses of Uganda's despotic regimes. Idi Amin, above, was dictator from 1971 to 1979. Under his infamously repressive rule, hundreds of thousands of Ugandans were murdered by the state.

dominant in the northeast, lack the political heritage of hierarchical state-building found in the south. These groups are also linguistically separate, speaking either Nilotic or Nilo-Hametic languages. The two regions were united by the British as the Uganda Protectorate during the 1890s (the name "Uganda," which is a corruption of "Buganda," has since become the accepted term for the larger entity). But the zones developed separately under colonial rule.

Cash-crop farming, especially of cotton, by local peasants spurred an economic boom in the south. The Bugandan ruling class benefited in particular. Increasing levels of education and wealth led to the European stereotype of the "progressive" Bugandans as the "Japanese of Africa." A growing class of Asian entrepreneurs also played an important role in the local economy, although its prosperity, as well as that of the Bugandan elite, suffered from subordination to resident British interests.

The south's growing economy stood in sharp contrast to the relative neglect of the northeast. Forced to earn money to pay taxes, many northeasterners became migrant workers in the south. They were also recruited, almost exclusively, to serve in the colonial security forces.

As independence approached, many Bugandans feared that their interests would be compromised by other groups. Under the leadership of their king, Mutesa II, they sought to uphold their separate status. Other groups feared that Bugandan wealth and educational levels could lead to their dominance. A compromise federal structure was agreed to for the new state.

Establishment of the oldest Ugandan kingdom, Bunyoro, followed by the formation of Buganda and other kingdoms **1500**

A British protectorate over Uganda is proclaimed **1893**

Uganda becomes independent **1962**

Milton Obote introduces a new unitary Constitution and forces Bugandan compliance **1966**

Idi Amin seizes power **1971**

Amin invades Tanzania **1978**

Tanzania invades Uganda and overturns Amin's government **1979**

The rise and fall of the second Obote regime leaves 300,000 dead **1980s**

The NRM takes power under Yoweri Museveni

1990s

Recovery produces slow gains; unrest continues in the northeast

AIDS emerges as a crisis in Uganda

Museveni retains power

At independence, the southern kingdoms retained their autonomous status within the "United Kingdom of Uganda." The first government was made up of Mutesa's royalist party and the United People's Congress (UPC), a largely non-Bugandan coalition, led by Milton Obote, a Langi. Mutesa was elected president and Obote prime minister.

THE REIGN OF TERROR

In 1966, the delicate balance of ethnic interests was upset when Obote used the army—still dominated by fellow northeasterners—to overthrow Mutesa and the Constitution. In the name of abolishing "tribalism," Obote established a one-party state and ruled in an increasingly dictatorial fashion. However, in 1971, he was overthrown by his army chief, Idi Amin. Amin began his regime with widespread public support but alienated himself by favoring fellow Muslims and Kakwa. He expelled the 40,000-member Asian community and distributed their property to his cronies. The Langi, suspected of being pro-Obote, were also early targets of his persecution, but his attacks soon spread to other members of Uganda's Christian community, at the time about 80 percent of the total population. Educated people in particular were purged. The number of Ugandans murdered by Amin's death squads is unknown; the most commonly cited figure is 300,000, but estimates range from 50,000 to 1 million. Many others went into exile. Throughout the world, Amin's name became synonymous with despotic rule.

A Ugandan military incursion into Tanzania led to war between the two countries in 1979. Many Ugandans joined with the Tanzanians in defeating Amin's army and its Libyan allies. Unfortunately, the overthrow of Amin, who fled into exile, did not lead to better times.

In 1980, Obote was returned to power, through a fraudulent vote count. His second administration was characterized by a continuation of the violence of the Amin years. An estimated 300,000 people, mostly southerners, were massacred by Obote's security forces; an equal number fled the country. Much of the killing occurred in the Bugandan area known as the Luwero triangle, which was completely depopulated; its fields are still full of skeletons today. As the killings escalated, so did the resistance of Museveni's NRM guerrillas, who had taken to the bush in the aftermath of the failed election. In 1985, a split between Ancholi and Langi officers led to Obote's overthrow and yet another pattern of interethnic recrimination. Finally, in 1986, the NRM gained the upper hand.

THE STRUGGLE CONTINUES

Museveni's National Resistance Movement administration has faced enormous challenges in trying to bring about national reconstruction. The task has been complicated by continued warfare in the northeast by armed factions representing elements of the former regimes, independent Karamojong communities, and followers of prophetic religious movements. In 1987, an uprising of the Holy Spirit rebels of Alice Lakwena was crushed, at the cost of some 15,000 lives.

Currently, there is cause for both hope and despair in Uganda. A sense of civil society has been returning to much of the country. Since 1990, the level of insurgency has been low. With peace has come economic growth, which has made up for some of the past decline.

While rebuilding their shattered country, Ugandans have had to cope with an especially severe outbreak of AIDS. Thousands have died of the disease in the last decade; it is believed that literally hundreds of thousands of Ugandans are HIV-positive. The government's bold acknowledgment of the seriousness of the crisis has given rise to (mostly internal) criticism as well as praise.

A new political order is emerging. Museveni has consistently advocated a "no party government," resisting agitation for a restoration of multiparty democracy. His position was strengthened in March 1994 when elections to a Constituent Assembly, which will endorse a new constitution, resulted in his supporters' capturing at least 150 of the 214 seats. In another controversial initiative, Museveni has allowed the restoration of traditional offices, including Bugandan kingship.

DEVELOPMENT

At least 15% of public spending goes toward supporting one of Africa's biggest militaries. This economic legacy of past conflicts hinders Uganda's development. Official figures show 13 million out of 19 million Ugandans living below the poverty line.

FREEDOM

The human-rights situation has improved greatly under Uganda's NRM government, but detentions without trial, massacres of civilians, and other abuses have been carried out by the current government as well as its opponents. Freedom of speech and association are curtailed.

HEALTH/WELFARE

Uganda's traditionally strong school system was damaged but not completely destroyed under Amin and Obote. In 1986, some 70% of primary-school children attended classes. The killing and exiling of teachers have resulted in a serious drop of standards at all levels of the education system, but progress is under way.

ACHIEVEMENTS

The Ugandan government was one of the first countries in Africa (and the world) to acknowledge the seriousness of the AIDS epidemic within its borders. It has instituted public information campaigns and welcomed outside support. In urban areas, the seropositive rate is 25%.

Southern Africa

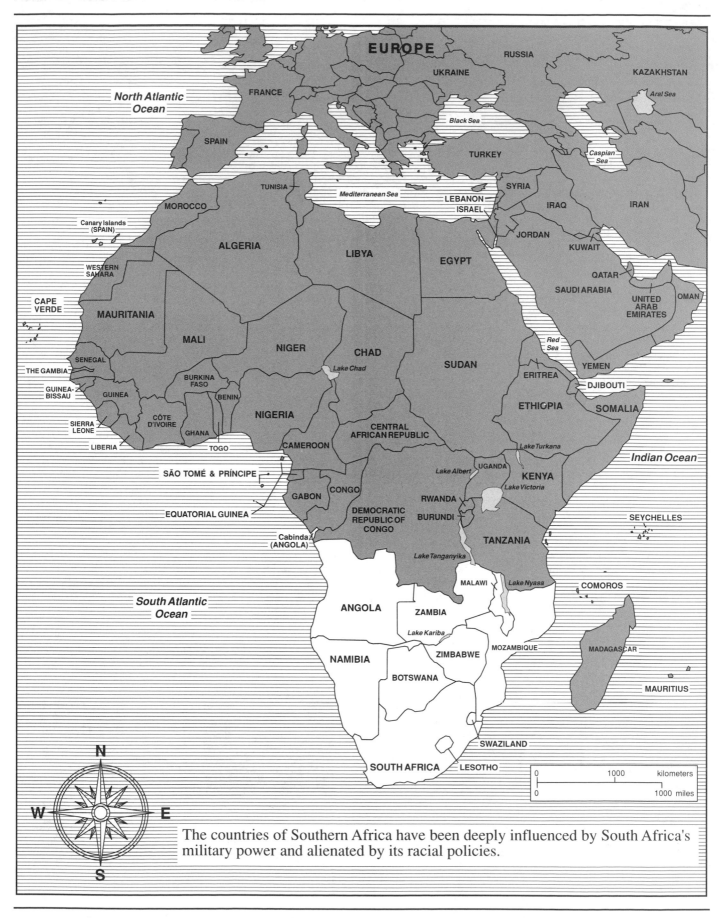

EUROPE

RUSSIA

UKRAINE

KAZAKHSTAN

North Atlantic Ocean

FRANCE

Aral Sea

Black Sea

TURKEY

Caspian Sea

SPAIN

Mediterranean Sea

TUNISIA

LEBANON

SYRIA

ISRAEL

IRAQ

IRAN

MOROCCO

JORDAN

KUWAIT

Canary Islands (SPAIN)

ALGERIA

LIBYA

EGYPT

QATAR

WESTERN SAHARA

SAUDI ARABIA

UNITED ARAB EMIRATES

OMAN

CAPE VERDE

MAURITANIA

MALI

NIGER

CHAD

SUDAN

Red Sea

YEMEN

Lake Chad

ERITREA

DJIBOUTI

SENEGAL

THE GAMBIA

BURKINA FASO

ETHIOPIA

SOMALIA

GUINEA-BISSAU

GUINEA

BENIN

NIGERIA

CENTRAL AFRICAN REPUBLIC

Lake Turkana

SIERRA LEONE

CÔTE D'IVOIRE

GHANA

CAMEROON

Indian Ocean

LIBERIA

TOGO

UGANDA

KENYA

Lake Albert

Lake Victoria

SÃO TOMÉ & PRÍNCIPE

CONGO

RWANDA

GABON

DEMOCRATIC REPUBLIC OF CONGO

BURUNDI

SEYCHELLES

EQUATORIAL GUINEA

Cabinda (ANGOLA)

TANZANIA

Lake Tanganyika

MALAWI

Lake Nyasa

COMOROS

South Atlantic Ocean

ANGOLA

ZAMBIA

Lake Kariba

MOZAMBIQUE

MADAGASCAR

NAMIBIA

ZIMBABWE

BOTSWANA

MAURITIUS

SWAZILAND

SOUTH AFRICA

LESOTHO

N

W E

S

0 1000 kilometers

0 1000 miles

The countries of Southern Africa have been deeply influenced by South Africa's military power and alienated by its racial policies.

Southern Africa:
The Continuing Struggle for Self-Determination

Southern Africa, which includes the nations of Angola, Botswana, Lesotho, Malawi, Mozambique, Namibia, South Africa, Swaziland, Zambia, and Zimbabwe, is a diverse region made up of savannas and forest, snow-topped mountains and desert, temperate Mediterranean and torrid tropical climates. Southern African identity is, however, as much defined by the region's peoples and their past and present interactions as by its geographic features. An appreciation of local history is crucial to understanding the forces that both divide and unite the region today.

EUROPEAN MIGRATION AND DOMINANCE

A dominant theme in the modern history of Southern Africa has been the evolving struggle of the region's indigenous black African majority to free itself of the racial hegemony of white settlers from Europe and their descendants. By the eighth century A.D., but probably earlier, the southernmost regions of the continent were populated by a variety of black African ethnic groups who spoke languages belonging to the Bantu as well as the Khoisan linguistic classifications. Members of these two groupings practiced both agriculture and pastoralism; archaeological evidence indicates that livestock keeping pre-dates the time of Christ. Some, such as the Kongo of northern Angola and the Shona peoples of the Zimbabwean plateaux, had, by the fifteenth century, organized strong states, while others, like most Nguni speakers prior to the early nineteenth century, lived in smaller communities. Trade networks existed throughout the region, linking various local peoples not only to one another but also to the markets of the Indian Ocean and beyond. In the grounds of the Great Zimbabwe, for example, a stone-walled settlement that flourished in the fifteenth century, porcelains from China have been unearthed.

In the sixteenth century, small numbers of Portuguese began settling along the coasts of Angola and Mozambique. A century later, in 1652, the Dutch established a settlement at Africa's southernmost tip, the Cape of Good Hope. While the Portuguese flag generally remained confined to coastal enclaves until the late nineteenth century, the Dutch colony expanded steadily into the interior throughout the eighteenth century, seizing the land of local Khoisan communities. Unlike the colonial footholds of the Portuguese and other Europeans on the continent, which prior to the nineteenth century were mostly centers for the export of slaves, the Dutch Cape Colony imported slaves from Asia as well as from elsewhere in Africa. Although not legally enslaved, conquered Khoisan were also reduced to servitude. In the process, a new society evolved at the Cape. Much like the American South before the Civil War, it was racially divided between free white settlers and subordinated peoples of mixed African and Afro-Asian descent.

Countries throughout Southern Africa are developing projects to employ laborers who might otherwise migrate to urban centers in South Africa—a pattern established in colonial times. These workers are building a highway in Lesotho.

During the Napoleonic Wars, Great Britain took over the Cape Colony. Shortly thereafter, in 1820, significant numbers of English-speaking colonists began arriving in the region. The arrival of the British coincided with a period of political realignment throughout much of Southern Africa that is commonly referred to as the *Mfecane*. Until recently, the historical literature has generally attributed this upheaval to dislocations caused by the rise of the Zulu state, under the great warrior prince Shaka. However, more recent scholarship has focused on the disruptive effects of increased traffic in contraband slaves from the interior to the Cape and the Portuguese stations of Mozambique, following the international ban on slave trading.

In the 1830s, the British abolished slavery throughout their empire and extended limited civil rights to nonwhites at the Cape. In response, a large number of white Dutch-descended Boers, or Afrikaners, moved into the interior, where they founded two republics that were free of British control. This migration, known as the Great Trek, did not lead the white settlers into an empty land. Many African groups lost their farms and pastures to the superior firepower of the early Afrikaners, who often coerced local communities into sup-

plying corvee labor for their farms and public works. But a few African polities, like Lesotho and the western Botswana kingdoms, were able to preserve their independence by acquiring their own firearms.

In the second half of the nineteenth century, white migration and dominance spread throughout the rest of Southern Africa. The discovery of diamonds and gold in northeastern South Africa encouraged white exploration and subsequent occupation farther north. In the 1890s, Cecil Rhodes's British South Africa Company occupied modern Zambia and Zimbabwe, which then became known as the Rhodesias. British traders, missionaries, and settlers also invaded the area now known as Malawi. Meanwhile, the Germans seized Namibia, while the Portuguese began to expand inland from their coastal enclaves. Thus, by 1900, the entire region had fallen under white colonial control.

With the exception of Lesotho and Botswana, which were occupied as British "protectorates," all the European colonies in Southern Africa had significant populations of white settlers, who in each case played a predominant political and economic role in their respective territories. Throughout the region, this white supremacy was fostered and maintained

(United Nations photo by J. P. Laffont)

Angolan youths celebrated when the nation became independent in 1974.

through racially discriminatory policies of land alienation, labor regulation, and the denial of full civil rights to non-whites. In South Africa, where the largest and longest-settled white population resided, the Afrikaners and English-speaking settlers were granted full self-government in 1910—with a Constitution that left the country's black majority virtually powerless.

BLACK NATIONALISM AND SOUTH AFRICAN DESTABILIZATION

After World War II, new movements advocating black self-determination gradually gained ascendancy throughout the region. However, the progress of these struggles for majority rule and independence was gradual. By 1968, the countries of Botswana, Lesotho, Malawi, Swaziland, and Zambia had gained their independence. The area was then polarized between liberated and nonliberated nations. In 1974, a military uprising in Portugal brought statehood to Angola and Mozambique, after long armed struggles by liberation forces in the two territories. Wars of liberation also led to the overthrow of white-settler rule in Zimbabwe, in 1980, and the independence of Namibia, in 1990. Finally, in 1994, South Africa completed a negotiated transition to a nonracial government.

South Africa's liberation has serious implications for the entire Southern African subcontinent as well as the country's own historically oppressed masses. Since the late nineteenth century, it has been the region's economic hub. Today, it accounts for about 80 percent of the total Southern African gross domestic product. Most of the subcontinent's roads and rails also run through South Africa. For generations, South Africa has recruited expatriate as well as local black African workers for its industries and mines. Today, it is the most economically developed country on the continent, with manufactured goods and agricultural surpluses that are in high demand elsewhere. By the late 1980s, when the imposition of economic sanctions against the then-apartheid regime was at its height, some 46 African countries were importing South African products. With sanctions now lifted, South Africa's economic role on the continent is likely to increase substantially.

A significant milestone was South Africa's August 1994 admittance as the 11th member of the Southern African Development Community (SADC). This organization's ultimate goal is to emulate the European Union (formerly the European Community) by promoting the economic integration and political coordination among Southern Africa's states (including Tanzania). While South Africa is expected to be at the center of the Community, SADC's roots lie in past efforts by its other members to reduce their ties to that country. The organization grew out of the Southern African Development Coordination Conference (SADCC), which was created by the region's then–black-ruled states in 1980 to lessen their dependency on white-ruled South Africa. Each SADCC government assumed responsibility for research and planning in a specific developmental area: Angola for energy, Mozambique for transport and communication, Tanzania for industry, and so on.

In its first decade, SADCC succeeded in attracting considerable outside aid for building and rehabilitating its member states' infrastructure. The organization's greatest success was the Beira corridor project, which enabled the Mozambican port to serve once more as a major regional transit point. Other successes included telecommunications independence of South Africa, new regional power grids, and the upgrading of Tanzanian roads to carry Malawian goods to the port of Dar es Salaam. In 1992, with South Africa's liberation on the horizon, the potential for a more ambitious and inclusive SADC grouping became possible.

In 1996, South African president Nelson Mandela replaced Botswana's president, Sir Ketumile Masire, as SADC chairperson, while Pretoria became the headquarters of a new SADC "Organ for Politics Defense and Security." The new South Africa's role as security coordinator within SADC is especially ironic: Before 1990, it had been the violent destabilizing policies of South Africa's military that had sabotaged efforts toward building greater regional cooperation. SADCC members, especially those that were further linked as the so-called Frontline States (Angola, Botswana, Mozambique, Tanzania, Zambia, and Zimbabwe), were then hostile to South Africa's racial policies. To varying degrees, they provided havens for those oppressed by these policies. South Africa responded by striking out against its exiled opponents through overt and covert military operations, while encouraging insurgent movements among some of its neighbors, most notably in Angola and Mozambique.

In Angola, South Africa (along with the United States) backed the rebel movement UNITA, while in Mozambique, it assisted RENAMO. Both of these movements resorted to the destruction of the railways and roads in their operational areas, a tactic that greatly increased the dependence on South African communications of the landlocked states of Botswana, Malawi, Zambia, and Zimbabwe. It is estimated that in the 1980s, the overall monetary cost to the Frontline States of South Africa's destabilization campaign was about $60 billion. (The same countries' combined annual gross national product was only about $25 billion in 1989.) The human costs were even greater: Hundreds of thousands of people were killed; at least equal numbers were maimed; and in Mozambique alone, more than 1 million people became refugees.

In the Southern African context, South Africa remains a military superpower. Despite the imposition of a mandatory United Nations arms embargo between 1977 and 1994, the country's military establishment was able to secure both the arms and sophisticated technology needed to develop its own military/industrial complex. Now a global arms exporter, South Africa is nearly self-sufficient in basic munitions, with a vast and advanced arsenal of weapons. Whereas in 1978 it imported 75 percent of its weapons, today that figure is less than 5 percent. By the 1980s, the country had also developed a nuclear arsenal, which it now claims to have dismantled. However, the former embargo was not entirely ineffective—while South African industry produced many sophisticated weapons systems, it found it increasingly difficult to maintain its regional superiority in such high-technology fields as fighter aircraft. By 1989, the increasing edge of Angolan pilots and air-defense systems was a significant factor in the former South African regime's decision to disengage from the Angolan Civil War. The economic costs of South African militarization were also steep. In addition to draining some 20 percent of its total budget outlays, the destabilization campaign contributed to increased international economic sanctions, which between 1985 and 1990 cost its own economy at least $20 billion. Today, both South Africa and its neighbors hope to benefit from a "peace dividend." But after a generation of militarization, progress in shifting resources from lethal to peaceful pursuits will be gradual.

Throughout the 1980s, South Africa justified its acts of aggression by claiming that it was engaged in counterinsurgency operations against guerrillas of the African National Congress (ANC) and Pan Africanist Congress (PAC), which were then struggling for the regime's overthrow. In fact, the various Frontline States took a cautious attitude toward the activities of South African political refugees, generally forbidding them from launching armed attacks from across their borders. In 1984, both Angola and Mozambique formally signed agreements of mutual noninterference with South Africa. But within a year, these accords had repeatedly and blatantly been violated by South Africa.

Over the past decade, drought, along with continued warfare, has resulted in recurrent food shortages in much of Southern Africa, again especially in Angola and Mozambique. The early 1980s' drought in Southern Africa neither lasted as long as nor was as widely publicized as those of West Africa and the Horn, yet it was as destructive. Although some countries, such as Botswana, Mozambique, and Zimbabwe, as well as areas of South Africa, suffered more from nature than others, the main features of the crisis were the same: water reserves were depleted; cattle and game died; and crop production declined, often by 50 percent or more.

Maize and cereal production suffered everywhere. South Africa and Zimbabwe, which are usually grain exporters, had to import food. The countries of Angola, Botswana, and Lesotho each had more than ½ million people who were affected by the shortfalls, while some 2 million were malnourished in Mozambique. But in 1988, the rains returned to the region, raising cereal production by 40 percent. Zimbabwe was able not only to export but also to provide food aid to other African countries. However, South African desta-

(United Nations photo by Jerry Frank)

South Africa's economic and military dominance overshadows the region's planning. Pictured above is the South African city of Cape Town, the chief port and legislative capital of the country.

bilization contributed to continuing food scarcities in many parts of Angola and Mozambique.

In 1991–1992, the entire region was once more pushed toward catastrophe, with the onset of the worst single drought year in at least a century. Although most of the region experienced improved rainfall in 1993–1994, many areas are still afflicted by food shortages, while the entire region remains vulnerable to famine. Up to 4.5 million people remain at risk of starvation in Mozambique, and another 3 million in Angola, while Malawi has had to struggle to feed hundreds of thousands of Mozambican refugees along with its own population.

A NEW ERA

Recent events in the region have given rise to hopes for a new era of peace and progress. In 1988, Angola, Cuba, and South Africa reached an agreement, with U.S. and Soviet support that led to South Africa's withdrawal from Namibia and the removal of Cuban troops from Angola, where they had been supporting government forces. In 1990, Namibia gained its independence under the elected leadership of SWAPO, the liberation movement that had fought against local South African occupation for more than a quarter of a century. In Zambia and Malawi, multiparty democracy was restored, resulting in the electoral defeat of long-serving authoritarian rulers. The most significant development in the region, however, has been South Africa's transformation. There, the 1990 release of prominent political prisoners, particularly Nelson Mandela, the unbanning of the ANC and PAC, and the lifting of internal state-of-emergency restrictions resulted in extended negotiations that led to an end to white-minority rule.

Southern Africa has also experienced some reversals. After an on-again/off-again start, direct negotiations between the Angolan government and UNITA rebels led in 1991 to a UN-supervised peace process based on multiparty elections. But this agreement collapsed in 1992, when UNITA rejected the election results. Although external support for UNITA is now minimal, casualties in the renewed fighting are as high as ever. Lesotho is also being rocked by (less violent) political turmoil as a result of continuing military opposition to the 1993 emergence of the nation's first freely elected government in 2 decades. In light of the Angolan reversal, observers are cautious in their optimism about the current UN-supervised peace process in Mozambique.

Having finally come to the end of its epoch of struggle against white-minority rule, Southern Africa as a whole may be on the threshold of sustained growth. Besides their now-shared commitment to nonracialism, cooperation among the state is being facilitated by their new-found, yet still tenuous,

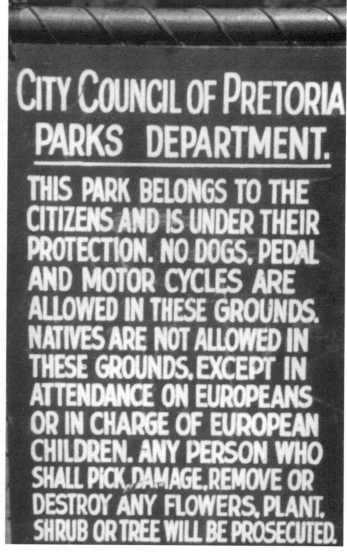

(United Nations photo)
This sign, once displayed in a park in Pretoria, South Africa, reflected the restrictions of apartheid, formerly the South African government's official policy of racial discrimination.

commitment to democracy. Economic thinking within the region has also converged toward a consensus favorable to the growth of market economies. While Angola, Mozambique, Tanzania, Zambia, and Zimbabwe have all moved away from past commitments to various shades of state-centered socialism, the South African economy is being freed from the statist distortions of apartheid. While reconstruction will take time, its resource base and human as well as physical infrastructure could make Southern Africa a major global nexus in the twenty-first century.

Angola (Republic of Angola)

GEOGRAPHY

Area in Square Kilometers (Miles):
1,246,699 (481,351) (larger than
Texas and California combined)
Capital (Population): Luanda
(2,000,000)
Climate: tropical and subtropical

PEOPLE

Population

Total: 10,343,000
Annual Growth Rate: 2.68%
Rural/Urban Population Ratio: 72/28
Major Languages: Portuguese;
Ovimbundu; Kimbundu; Kongo
Ethnic Makeup: 37% Ovimbundu;
25% Kimbundu; 13% Bakongo; 25%
others

Health

Life Expectancy at Birth: 44 years
(male); 49 years (female)
Infant Mortality Rate (Ratio):
142.1/1,000
Average Caloric Intake: 83% of FAO
minimum
Physicians Available (Ratio): 1/15,136

Religions

47% traditional indigenous; 38%
Roman Catholic; 15% Protestant

CABINDA

The tiny enclave of Cabinda, separated from the rest of Angola by a
25-mile strip of Zairian territory, is home to about 85,000 people. It is
also the location of most of Angola's current petroleum output, which
accounts for 86 percent of the nation's export earnings. Most of the oil
is pumped from offshore fields by the Gulf Oil Corporation, whose
royalty payments are the Angolan government's leading source of
income. Ironically, in the 1980s, this American company's installations
were guarded by Cuban troops against attacks from UNITA rebels, who
in turn were backed by the U.S. CIA. Peace within the enclave continues
to be threatened by various factions of the Front for the Liberation of
the Cabinda State, a local secessionist movement that was sponsored
by Zaire in the past.

Education

Adult Literacy Rate: 42%

COMMUNICATION

Telephones: 40,300
Newspapers: 2

TRANSPORTATION

Highways—Kilometers (Miles):
73,828 (45,877)

Railroads—Kilometers (Miles): 3,189
(1,982)
Usable Airfields: 289

GOVERNMENT

Type: transitional multiparty
democracy
Independence Date: November 11,
1975
Head of State/Government: President
José Edouardo dos Santos; Prime
Minister Marcolino José Carlos Moco
Political Parties: Popular Movement
for the Liberation of Angola;
National Front for the Liberation of
Angola; National Union for the Total
Independence of Angola; others
Suffrage: universal at 18

MILITARY

Number of Armed Forces: 127,500
*Military Expenditures (% of Central
Government Expenditures):* 31%
Current Hostilities: renewed civil war

ECONOMY

Currency ($ U.S. Equivalent):
900,000 kwanzas = $1
Per Capita Income/GDP: $620/$6.1
billion
Inflation Rate: 20% per month
Natural Resources: oil; diamonds;
manganese; gold; uranium
Agriculture: coffee; sisal; corn;
cotton; sugar; manioc; tobacco;
bananas; plantains
Industry: oil; diamond mining; fish
processing; brewing; tobacco; sugar
processing; textiles; cement; food
processing; construction

FOREIGN TRADE

Exports: $3.0 billion
Imports: $1.6 billion

ANGOLA

Since the resumption of direct talks in May 1995 between the Angolan government and the rebel Union for the Total Independence of Angola (UNITA), there have been cautious hopes that a lasting peace might end the more tran 2 decades of devasting civil war. In 1996, UNITA agreed in principal to join the governing Popular Movement for the Liberation of Angola (MPLA) in forming a government of national unity, but implementation was delayed. Since 1975, more than ½ million Angolans have perished as a result of fighting between the two movements, including many passive victims of land mines. Up to 1 million others fled the country, while another 1 million or so have been internally displaced. According to a report by the human-rights organization Africa Watch, tens of thousands of Angolans have lost their limbs "because of the indiscriminate use of landmines by both sides of the conflict." Angola's small and impoverished population could not have perpetuated such carnage were it not for decades of external interference in the nation's internal affairs. The United States, the former Soviet Union, South Africa, Cuba, Zaire, and many others helped to create and sustain this tragedy.

Since 1991, with the end of the cold war and the demise of South Africa's apartheid regime, there has been an almost complete cutoff of outside support for the conflict. An agreement in April 1991 between the MPLA and UNITA to participate in United Nation-sponsored elections led to a dramatic decline in violence during 16 months of "phony peace." The successful holding of elections in September 1992 further raised hopes of a new beginning for Angola. While the MPLA appeared to have topped the poll, UNITA and the smaller National Front for the Liberation of Angola (FNLA) secured a considerable vote. But hopes for a new beginning under an all-party government of national unity were quickly dashed by UNITA's rejection of the election result. As a result, the country was plunged into renewed civil war.

THE COLONIAL LEGACY

The roots of Angola's long suffering lie in the area's colonial underdevelopment. The Portuguese first made contact with the peoples of the region in 1483. They initially established peaceful trading contact with the powerful Kongo kingdom and other coastal peoples, some of whom were converted to Catholicism by Jesuit missionaries. But from the sixteenth to the mid-nineteenth centuries, the outsiders primarily saw the area as a source of slaves. Angola has been called the "mother of Brazil" because up to 4 million Angolans were carried away from its shores to that country, chained in the holds of slave ships. With the possible exception of Nigeria, no African territory lost more of its people to the trans-Atlantic slave trade.

Following the nineteenth-century suppression of the slave trade, the Portuguese introduced internal systems of exploitation that very often amounted to slavery in all but name. Large numbers of Angolans were pressed into working on coffee plantations owned by a growing community of white settlers. Others were forced to labor in other sectors, such as diamond mines or public-works projects.

Although the Portuguese claimed that they encouraged Angolans to learn Portuguese and practice Catholicism, thus becoming "assimilated" into the world of the colonizers, they actually made little effort to provide education. No more than 2 percent of the population ever achieved the legal status of *assimilado*. The *assimilados,* many of whom were of mixed race, were concentrated in the coastal towns. Of the few interior Angolans who became literate, a large proportion were the products of Protestant, non-Portuguese, mission schools. Because each mission tended to operate in a particular region and teach from its own syllabus, usually in the local language, an unfortunate by-product of these schools was the reinforcement (the creation, some would argue) of ethnic rivalries among the territory's educated elite.

In the late colonial period, the FNLA, MPLA, and UNITA emerged as the three major liberation movements challenging Portuguese rule. Although all three sought a national following, each built up an ethnoregional core of support by 1975. The FNLA grew out of a movement whose original focus was limited to the northern Kongo-speaking population, while UNITA's principal stronghold has been the largely Ovimbundu-speaking south-central plateaux. The MPLA has its strongest following among *assimilados* and Kimbundu speakers, who are predominant in Luanda, the capital, and the interior to the west of the city. From the beginning, all three movements have cultivated separate sources of external support.

The armed struggle against the Portuguese began in 1961, with a massive FNLA–inspired uprising in the north and MPLA–led unrest in Luanda. To counter the northern rebellion, the Portuguese resorted to the saturation bombing of villages, which, in the first year of fighting, left an estimated 50,000 dead (about half the total number killed throughout the anticolonial struggle). The liberation forces were as much hampered by their own disunity as by the brutality of Portugal's counterinsurgency tactics. Undisciplined rebels associated with the FNLA, for example, were known to massacre not only Portuguese plantation owners but many of their southern workers as well. Such incidents contributed to UNITA's split from the FNLA in 1966. There is also evidence of UNITA forces cooperating with the Portuguese in attacks on the MPLA. Besides competition with its two rivals, the MPLA also encountered some difficulty in keeping its urban and rural factions united.

(United Nations photo by J. P. Laffont)
Angola's war for independence from Portugal led to the creation of a one-party state.

The Kongo state develops
1400

The Kongo state is contacted by the Portuguese
1483

Queen Nzinga defends the Mbundu kingdom against the Portuguese
1640

The MPLA is founded in Luanda
1956

The national war of liberation begins
1961

Angola gains independence of Portugal
1975

South African–initiated air and ground incursions into Angola
1976

President Agostinho Neto dies; José dos Santos becomes president
1979

Jonas Savimbi visits the United States; U.S. "material and moral" support for UNITA resumes
1986

1990s

Savimbi and dos Santos shake hands in Zaire, opening the door to direct peace negotiations; but the war continues

Efforts for national reconciliation; multiparty elections

UNITA may be the Africa's first armed faction to have an Internet address: http://www.sfiedi. fr/kup/kup@ worldnet

CIVIL WAR

The overthrow of Portugal's Fascist government in 1974 led to Angola's rapid decolonization. Attempts to create a transitional government of national unity among the three major nationalist movements failed. The MPLA succeeded in seizing Luanda, which led to a loose alliance between the FNLA and UNITA. As fighting between the groups escalated, so did the involvement of their foreign backers. Meanwhile, most of Angola's 300,000 or more white settlers fled the country, triggering the collapse of much of the local economy. With the notable exception of Angola's offshore oil industry, most economic sectors have since failed to recover their preindependence output as a result of the war.

While the chronology of outside intervention in the Angolan conflict is a matter of dispute, it is nonetheless clear that, by October 1975, up to 2,000 South African troops were assisting the FNLA–UNITA forces in the south. In response, Cuba dispatched a force of 18,000 to 20,000 to assist the MPLA, which earlier had gained control of Luanda. These events proved decisive during the war's first phase. On the one hand, collaboration with South Africa led to the withdrawal of Chinese and much of the African support for the FNLA–UNITA cause. It also contributed to the U.S. Congress' passage of the Clarke Amendment, which abruptly terminated the United States' direct involvement. On the other hand, the arrival of the Cubans allowed the MPLA quickly to gain the upper hand on the battlefield. Not wishing to fight a conventional war against the Cubans by themselves, the South Africans withdrew their conventional forces in March 1976.

By 1977, the MPLA's "People's Republic" had established itself in all of Angola's provinces. It was recognized by the United Nations and most of its membership as the nation's sole legitimate government, the United States numbering among the few that continued to withhold recognition. However, the MPLA's apparent victory did not bring an end to the hostilities. Although the remaining pockets of FNLA resistance were overcome following an Angola–Zaire rapprochement in 1978, UNITA maintained its largely guerrilla struggle. Until 1989, UNITA's major supporter was South Africa, whose destabilization of the Luanda government was motivated by its desire to keep the Benguela railway closed (thus diverting traffic to its own system) and harass Angola-based SWAPO forces. Besides supplying UNITA with logistical support, the South Africans repeatedly invaded southern Angola and on occasion infiltrated sabotage units into other areas of the country. South African aggression in turn justified Cuba's maintenance (by 1988) of some 50,000 troops in support of the government. In 1986, the U.S. Congress approved the resumption of "covert" U.S. material assistance to UNITA via Zaire.

An escalation of the fighting in 1987 and 1988 was accompanied by a revival of negotiations for a peace settlement among representatives of the Angolan government, Cuba, South Africa, and the United States. In 1988, South African forces were checked in a battle at the Angolan town of Cuito Cuanavale. South Africa agreed to withdraw from Namibia and end its involvement in the Angolan conflict. It was further agreed that Cuba would complete a phased withdrawal of its forces from the region by mid-1991.

The scaling back of external support, in the context of a relaxation of cold war tensions around the world, provided a basis for further contacts between the warring parties themselves. An agreement in April 1991 between the MPLA president, Eduardo dos Santos, and the UNITA leader, Jonas Savimbi, led to the establishment of a UN–supervised cease-fire and a national reconciliation process. This process culminated in the September 1992 elections. After initially fierce fighting, the renewed civil war degenerated into a bloody stalemate.

UNITA currently occupies up to 75 percent of the countryside, but most of the population is crowded into government-controlled areas. A series of meetings between MPLA and UNITA resulted in a fragile peace in late 1994. The United Nations hoped to inaugurate a new peacekeeping operation in Angola, but the prospects for a lasting peace remain uncertain.

DEVELOPMENT

Most of Angola's export revenues currently come from oil. There are important diamond and iron mines, but their output has suffered due to the war, which has also prevented the exploitation of the country's considerable reserves of other minerals. Angola has enormous agricultural potential, but currently only about 2% of its arable land is under cultivation.

FREEDOM

Despite new constitutional guarantees, pessimists note that neither UNITA nor MPLA has demonstrated a strong commitment to democracy and human rights in the past. Within UNITA, Jonas Savimbi's word has been law; he has been known to have critics within his movement burned as "witches."

HEALTH/WELFARE

Civil war has caused a serious deterioration of Angola's health service, resulting in lower life expectancy and one of the highest infant mortality rates in the world.

ACHIEVEMENTS

Between 1975 and 1980, the Angolan government claimed that it had tripled the nation's primary school enrollment, to 76%. That figure subsequently dropped as a result of war.

Botswana

GEOGRAPHY

Area in Square Kilometers (Miles):
600,372 (231,804) (about the size of Texas)
Capital (Population): Gaborone (133,000)
Climate: arid to semiarid

PEOPLE

Population
Total: 1,477,700
Annual Growth Rate: 2.36%
Rural/Urban Population Ratio: 74/26
Major Languages: (Se)Tswana; English; Khoisan dialects; Kalanga; Herero
Ethnic Makeup: Tswana; Kalanga; others

Health
Life Expectancy at Birth: 61 years (male); 67 years (female)
Infant Mortality Rate (Ratio): 38/1,000
Average Caloric Intake: 90% of FAO minimum
Physicians Available (Ratio): 1/5,417

KURU ARTISTS

Botswana's small but lively arts scene has been enriched in recent years by the international and domestic success of the Kuru Art and Cultural Project. The project was begun in 1990 by a group of local Khoisan speakers (often labeled as "Bushmen" by outsiders) who were inspired by their community's ancient rock paintings at the Tshodilo Hills. *Kuru* is a Khoisan word meaning "do it/create it." Through their abstract works, the Kuru artists have affirmed their community's dynamic cultural identity, overturning stereotypes of Bushman culture as being primitive and stagnant. Initially they began to paint on textiles, but they quickly branched out into other media. Kuru paintings have been exhibited throughout Europe and Southern Africa, winning growing critical acclaim. The emergence of the Kuru artists has coincided with growing social and political activism on the part of Botswana's Khoisan.

Religions
75% Christian

Education
Adult Literacy Rate: 50%–76% (est.)

COMMUNICATION

Telephones: 26,000
Newspapers: 6

TRANSPORTATION

Highways—Kilometers (Miles): 11,514 (11,098)
Railroads—Kilometers (Miles): 888 (554)
Usable Airfields: 100

GOVERNMENT

Type: parliamentary republic
Independence Date: September 30, 1966
Head of State: President Sir Ketumile Masire
Political Parties: Botswana Democratic Party; Botswana National Front; Botswana People's Party; Independence Freedom Party; others
Suffrage: universal at 21

MILITARY

Number of Armed Forces: 6,100
Military Expenditures (% of Central Government Expenditures): 5.2%
Current Hostilities: none

ECONOMY

Currency ($ U.S. Equivalent): 1.71 pulas = $1
Per Capita Income/GDP: $3,130/$4.3 billion
Inflation Rate: 10%
Natural Resources: diamonds; copper; nickel; salt; soda ash; potash; coal
Agriculture: livestock; sorghum; corn; millet; cowpeas; beans
Industry: diamonds; copper; nickel; salt; soda ash; potash; frozen beef; tourism

FOREIGN TRADE

Exports: $1.8 billion
Imports: $1.8 billion

Botswana

⊗ Capital
● City
〰 River
- - - Road

0   100   kilometers
0   100   miles

BOTSWANA

Botswana has been the Cinderella story of postcolonial Africa. In 1966, the country emerged from 80 years of British colonialism as one of the 10 poorest countries in the world, with an annual per capita income of $69. Yet over the past 3 decades, the nation's economy has grown at an average annual rate of 11 percent, one of the world's highest. Infrastructure has been created and social services expanded. Whereas at independence the country had no paved roads, major settlements have become increasingly interlinked by ribbons of asphalt and tarmac. A vibrant city has emerged at Gaborone, the nation's capital. New schools, hospitals, and businesses dot the landscape. Such growth has translated into improved standards of living for most Botswana citizens. However, the gap between the small but growing middle class (and the few truly wealthy) and the majority who remain poor is also widening, resulting in social tension.

Botswana's economic success has come in the context of its unbroken postindependence commitment to political pluralism, respect for human rights, and racial and ethnic tolerance. Freedom of speech and association has been upheld. In October 1994, the nation held its seventh successive multiparty elections. The Botswana Democratic Party, which has ruled since independence, won with a greatly reduced majority. As a result, a genuine two-party competition has now emerged, with the left-leaning opposition Botswana National Front taking on the role of an alternative government-in-waiting.

Most of Botswana's people share (Se)Tswana as their mother tongue, a language that is also commonly spoken in much of South Africa. There also exist a number of sizable minority communities—Kalanga, Herero, Khalagari, Khoisan groups, and others—but contemporary ethnic conflict is relatively modest. In the nineteenth century, most of Botswana was incorporated into five Tswana states, each centering around a large settlement of 10,000 people or more. These states, which incorporated non-Tswana communities, survived through agropastoralism, hunting, and their control of trade routes linking Southern and Central Africa.

Lucrative dealing in ivory and ostrich feathers allowed local rulers to build up their arsenals and thus deter the aggressive designs of South African whites. An attempt by white settlers to seize control of southeastern Botswana was defeated in an 1852–1853 war. However, European missionaries and traders were welcomed, leading to a growth of Christian education and the consumption of industrial goods.

A radical transformation took place after the imposition of British overrule in 1885. Colonial taxes and economic decline stimulated the growth of migrant labor to the mines and industries of South Africa. (In some regions, migrant earnings remain the major source of income.) Although colonial rule brought much hardship and little benefit, the twentieth-century relationship between the peoples of Botswana and the British was complicated by local fears of being incorporated into South Africa. For many decades, leading nationalists championed continued rule from London as a shield against their powerful, racially oppressive neighbor.

ECONOMIC DEVELOPMENT

Economic growth since independence has been largely fueled by the rapid expansion of mining activity. Botswana has become one of the world's leading producers of

(United Nations photo by E. Darroch)

Botswana, like many other African nations, is susceptible to periodic drought. The country, however, has a good supply of underground water and the governmental competence to utilize this resource. In this photograph, antelopes drink from a hole dug to allow water seepage.

Emergence of the Tswana trading center at Toutswemogala **700**	Kololo and Ndebele invaders devastate the countryside **1820s**	Tswana begin to acquire guns through trade in ivory and other game products **1830s**	Batswana defeat Boer invaders **1852–1853**	The British establish colonial rule over Botswana **1885**	Botswana regains its independence **1966**	Elections in 1984 and 1989 result in landslide victories for the Democratic Party; the National Front is major opposition party **1980s**

1990s

South African raids kill Botswana citizens and South African exiles; new security laws are passed

The Ruling Democratic Party wins the 1994 elections, but the opposition National Front makes significant gains amid charges of official corruption and increasing concern about unemployment

diamonds, which typically account for 80 percent of its export earnings. Local production is managed by Debswana Corporation, an even partnership between the Botswana government and DeBeers, a South African-based global corporation; DeBeers' Central Selling Organization has a near monopoly on diamond sales worldwide. The Botswana government has a good record of maximizing the local benefits of Debswana's production.

The nickel/copper/cobalt mining complex at Selibi-Pikwe is the largest nongovernment employer in Botswana. Falling metal prices and high development costs have reduced the mine's profitability, but high operating efficiency has assured its survival.

Given that mining can make only a modest contribution to local employment and the potential vulnerability of the diamond market, Botswana is seeking to expand its small manufacturing and service sectors. Meat processing is currently the largest industrial activity outside minerals, but efforts are under way to attract overseas investment in both private and parastatal production. Botswana already has a liberal foreign exchange policy and has established an Export Processing Zone at Selibi-Pikwe. Small-scale production is encouraged through government subsidies.

Tourism is of growing importance. Northern Botswana is particularly noted for its bountiful wildlife and stunning scenery. The region includes the Okavango Delta, a vast and uniquely beautiful swamp area, and the Chobe National Park, home of the world's largest elephant herds.

Agriculture is still the leading economic activity for most Botswana citizens. The

standard Tswana greeting, Pula ("Rain"), reflects the significance attached to water in a society prone to its periodic scarcity. Botswana suffered severe droughts between 1980 and 1987 and again in 1991–1992, which—despite the availability of underground water supplies—had a devastating effect on both crops and livestock. Up to 1 million cattle are believed to have perished. Small-scale agropastoralists, who make up the largest segment of the population, have been particularly hard hit. However, government relief measures have prevented famine. The government also provides generous subsidies to farmers, but environmental constraints hamper efforts to achieve food self-sufficiency even in nondrought years.

Commercial agriculture is dominated by livestock. The Lobatse abbatoir, opened in 1954, stimulated the growth of the cattle industry. Despite periodic challenges from disease and drought, beef exports have become relatively stable. Much of the output of the Botswana Meat Commission has preferential access to the European Union. There is some concern about the potential for future reductions in the European quota. Because most of Botswana's herds are grazed in communal lands, questions about the allocation of pasture are a source of local debate. There is also a growing, but largely misinformed, international concern that wildlife are being threatened by overgrazing livestock.

SOUTH AFRICA

Until recently, Botswana's progress has taken place against a backdrop of political

hostility on the part of its powerful neighbor, South Africa. Since the nineteenth century, Botswana has sheltered refugees from racist oppression elsewhere in the region. This led to periodic acts of aggression against the country, especially during the 1980s, when Botswana became the repeated victim of overt military raids and covert terrorist operations. The establishment of a nonracial democracy in South Africa has led to a normalization of relations. In 1992, the two countries established formal diplomatic ties for the first time. Botswana has, nonetheless, continued to increase its military spending in recent years, stirring public controversy.

Gaborone is the headquarters of the Southern African Development Community, which was originally conceived to reduce the economic dependence of its 10 member nations on the apartheid state. SADC now plans to transform itself into a common market that could eventually include a democratic South Africa. Despite their political differences, Botswana has maintained a customs union with South Africa that dates back to the colonial era.

DEVELOPMENT

Primary education has become nearly universal since independence. In 1991 more than 70% of those leaving primary school gained access to secondary education. A university, several other tertiary institutions, and 70 vocational centers have also been established.

FREEDOM

Democratic pluralism has been strengthened by the growth of a strong civil society and an independent press. Concern has been voiced about social and economic discrimination against Khoisan-speaking communities living in remote areas of the Kalahari, who are known to many outsiders as "Bushmen."

HEALTH/WELFARE

The national health service provides medical, dental, and optical care for all Botswana residents. More than 90% of the population live within 10 miles of a health care facility. Efforts are now being made to upgrade facilities and staff. Malnutrition remains a major concern, automobile fatalities a growing one.

ACHIEVEMENTS

The UN's 1990 Human Development Report singles out Botswana among the nations of Africa for significantly improving the living conditions of its people. In 1989, President Masire was awarded the Hunger Project's leadership prize, based on Botswana's record of improving rural nutritional levels during the 1980s despite 7 years of severe drought.

Lesotho (Kingdom of Lesotho)

GEOGRAPHY

Area in Square Kilometers (Miles): 30,344 (11,716) (about the size of Maryland)
Capital (Population): Maseru (367,000)
Climate: temperate

PEOPLE

Population
Total: 1,971,000
Annual Growth Rate: 2.44%
Rural/Urban Population Ratio: 80/20
Major Languages: English; Sesotho
Ethnic Makeup: 99% Sotho

Health
Life Expectancy at Birth: 61 years (male); 64 years (female)
Infant Mortality Rate (Ratio): 69/1,000
Average Caloric Intake: 107% of FAO minimum
Physicians Available (Ratio): 1/14,306

Religions
80% Christian; 20% traditional indigenous

THE SESOTHO LANGUAGE

Sesotho has been a leading literary language in Africa since the mid-nineteenth century. Basotho writers have produced a wealth of prose, poetry, and nonfiction in their vernacular. The *Leselinyane La Lesotho*, first published in 1863, is sub-Saharan Africa's oldest continuous vernacular newspaper. Thomas Mofolo's play *Chaka* and Paulas Mopeli's novel *Blanket Boy* are among the many works that have been translated for international audiences. Sesotho also continues to be a major medium in music, journalism, and broadcasting. The South African government has promoted a separate Sesotho alphabet for use among Sotho peoples living in South Africa; this has created one more barrier for South Africans who have tried to encourage reconvergence among various regional dialects.

Education
Adult Literacy Rate: 59%

COMMUNICATION

Telephones: 5,920
Newspapers: 3

TRANSPORTATION

Highways—Kilometers (Miles): 7,215 (4,480)
Railroads—Kilometers (Miles): 2.6 (1.61)
Usable Airfields: 29

GOVERNMENT

Type: constitutional monarchy
Independence Date: October 4, 1966
Head of State/Government: King Letsie; Prime Minister Ntsu Mokhehle
Political Parties: Basotho National Party; Basutoland Congress Party; National Independence Party; others
Suffrage: universal at 21

MILITARY

Number of Armed Forces: 2,000
Military Expenditures (% of Central Government Expenditures): 13%
Current Hostilities: none

ECONOMY

Currency ($ U.S. Equivalent): 3.54 malotis = $1
Per Capita Income/GDP: $1,340/$2.6 billion
Inflation Rate: 14%
Natural Resources: diamonds; water; agricultural and grazing land
Agriculture: mohair; corn; wheat; sorghum; peas; beans; potatoes; asparagus; sheep; cattle
Industry: carpets; woolen apparel; candle making; pottery; jewelry; tapestries; tourism; mining

FOREIGN TRADE

Exports: $109 million
Imports: $964 million

Lesotho emerges
as a leading
state in Southern
Africa
1820s

Afrikaners annex
half of Lesotho
1866

The Sotho
successfully fight
to preserve local
autonomy under
the British
1870–1881

Independence
is restored
1966

The elections
and Constitution
are declared void
by Leabua
Jonathan
1970

An uprising
against the
government
fails
1974

The Lesotho
Liberation Army
begins a
sabotage
campaign
1979

South African
destabilization
leads to the
overthrow of
Jonathan by the
military
1986

1990s

The BCP returns
to power in
multiparty
elections

Restored King
Moshoeshoe II
dies in an auto
accident

The Army
crushes police
mutiny

LESOTHO

Listed by the United Nations as one of the world's least developed countries, each year the lack of opportunity at home causes up to half of Lesotho's adult males to seek employment in South Africa. Increasing retrenchment of Basotho mine workers has reduced this flow in recent years, giving rise to a 40 percent unemployment rate. Chronic political instability has also plagued the country, despite the restoration of multiparty democracy in 1993.

Lesotho is one of the most ethnically homogeneous nations in Africa. Almost all its citizens are Sotho. The country's emergence and survival were largely the product of the diplomatic and military prowess of its nineteenth-century rulers, especially its great founder, King Moshoeshoe I. In the 1860s, warfare with South African whites led to the loss of land and people as well as an acceptance of British overrule. For nearly a century, the British preserved the country but also taxed the inhabitants and generally neglected their interests. Consequently, Lesotho remained dependent on its neighbor, South Africa. However, despite South African attempts to incorporate the country politically as well as economically, Lesotho's independence was restored by the British in 1966.

Lesotho's politicians were bitterly divided at independence. The conservative Basotho National Party (BNP) had won an upset victory in preindependence elections, with strong backing from the South African government and the local Roman Catholic Church, Lesotho's largest Christian denomination. The opposition, which walked out of the independence talks, was polarized between a pro-royalist faction, the Marema-Tlou Freedom Party (whose regional sympathies largely lay with the African National Congress of South Africa), and the Basotho Congress Party (or BCP, which was allied to the rival Pan-Africanist Congress).

Soon after independence, the BNP prime minister, Leabua Jonathan, placed the king, Moshoeshoe II, under house arrest. Later, the king was temporarily exiled. The BCP won the 1970 elections, but Jonathan, possibly at the behest of South Africa, declared a state of emergency and nullified the results.

In the early 1980s, armed resistance to Jonathan's dictatorship was carried out by the Lesotho Liberation Army (LLA), an armed faction of the BCP. The Lesotho government maintained that the LLA was aided and abetted by South Africa as part of that country's regional destabilization efforts. By 1983, both the South African government and the Catholic hierarchy were becoming nervous about Jonathan's establishment of diplomatic ties with various Communist-ruled countries and the growing sympathy within the BNP, in particular its increasingly radical youth wing, for the ANC. South African military raids and terrorist attacks targeting anti-apartheid refugees in Lesotho became increasingly common. Finally, a South African blockade of Lesotho in 1986 directly led to Jonathan's ouster by his military.

Lesotho's new ruling Military Council, initially led by Major General Justinus Lekhanya, was closely linked to South Africa. In 1990, Lekhanya had Moshoeshoe II exiled (for the second time), after he refused to agree to the dismissals of several senior officers. Moshoeshoe's son Letsie was installed in his place. In 1991 Lekhanya was himself toppled by the army. The new leader, General Elias Rameama, promised to hold multiparty elections. In July 1992, Moshoeshoe returned, to a hero's welcome, but he was prevented from resuming his role as monarch. His status was uncertain after elections in March 1993 brought the BCP back to power.

Under its aging leader, Prime Minister Ntsu Mokhehle, the BCP has been unable to govern effectively in the face of continued opposition to its rule by elements of the military. An outbreak of internal fighting within the army in January 1994 was followed, in April, by the assassination of the deputy prime minister and the kidnapping of other ministers by mutinous soldiers. In August, King Letsie attempted to dismiss the government and suspend sections of the Constitution. His action was rejected by Mokhele and led to violent clashes between BCP supporters and the military. With other countries in the region also refusing to recognize the coup, in September 1994, Letsie accepted a joint mediation effort by the presidents of Botswana, South Africa, and Zimbabwe. This resulted in Mokhehle's restoration and the return of Moshoeshoe II as king. Moshoeshoe died in a January 1996 auto accident and was succeeded by Letsie. Lesotho's political situation remains unsettled, as does the question of its continuing independence from a postapartheid South Africa.

DEVELOPMENT

Despite an infusion of international aid, Lesotho's economic dependence on South Africa has not decreased since independence; indeed, it has been calculated that the majority of outside funds have actually ended up paying for South African services.

FREEDOM

Basic freedoms are compromised by continuing political instability. Basotho journalists have come out against proposed measures that they say will gag Lesotho's vigorous independent press.

HEALTH/WELFARE

With many of Lesotho's young men working in the mines of South Africa, much of the resident population relies on subsistence agriculture. Despite efforts to boost production, malnutrition, aggravated by drought, is a serious problem.

ACHIEVEMENTS

Lesotho has long been known for the high quality of its schools, which for more than a century and a half have trained many of the leading citizens of Southern Africa.

Malawi (Republic of Malawi)

GEOGRAPHY

Area in Square Kilometers (Miles): 118,484 (45,747) (about the size of Pennsylvania)
Capital (Population): Lilongwe (268,000)
Climate: subtropical

PEOPLE

Population
Total: 9,453,000
Annual Growth Rate: 2.6%
Rural/Urban Population Ratio: 83/17
Major Languages: Chichewa; English; Nyanja; Yao; Sena; Tumbuka; others
Ethnic Makeup: 90% Chewa; 10% Nyanja, Lomwe, other Bantu groups

Health
Life Expectancy at Birth: 38 years (male); 40 years (female)
Infant Mortality Rate (Ratio): 141/1,000
Average Caloric Intake: 97% of FAO minimum
Physicians Available (Ratio): 1/47,634

Religions
75% Christian; 20% Muslim; 5% traditional indigenous

Education
Adult Literacy Rate: 22%

JOHN CHILEMBWE

In 1915, John Chilembwe of Nyasaland (now Malawi) struck a blow against British colonialism and died in the attempt. Chilembwe was a Christian minister who had studied in South Africa as well as in the United States. He had returned home to establish the Providence Industrial Mission and to build a great church. His feelings against the British settlers developed from the injustices he had seen—European takeover of lands for plantations, poor working conditions for laborers, increased taxation, and, especially, the recruitment of Africans to fight and die in World War I. He rallied a few followers and planned an uprising, which led to the deaths of three settlers and the imprisonment or deaths of the Africans involved or suspected of involvement. Chilembwe appears to have planned his martyrdom. This uprising was the first effort in Southern Africa to resist colonialism and yet maintain many of the aspects of society that had developed from its influence.

COMMUNICATION

Telephones: 42,250
Newspapers: 5

TRANSPORTATION

Highways—Kilometers (Miles): 13,135 (8,143)
Railroads—Kilometers (Miles): 789 (489)
Usable Airfields: 47

GOVERNMENT

Type: multiparty democracy
Independence Date: July 6, 1964
Head of State: President Bakili Muluzi
Political Parties: United Democratic Front; Malawi Congress Party; Alliance for Democracy; others
Suffrage: universal at 21

MILITARY

Number of Armed Forces: 10,400
Military Expenditures (% of Central Government Expenditures): 0.7%
Current Hostilities: none

ECONOMY

Currency ($ U.S. Equivalent): 7.84 kwachas = $1
Per Capita Income/GDP: $750/$7.3 billion
Inflation Rate: 30%
Natural Resources: limestone; uranium potential
Agriculture: tobacco; tea; sugar; corn; peanuts
Industry: food; beverages; tobacco; textiles; footwear

FOREIGN TRADE

Exports: $311 million
Imports: $308 million

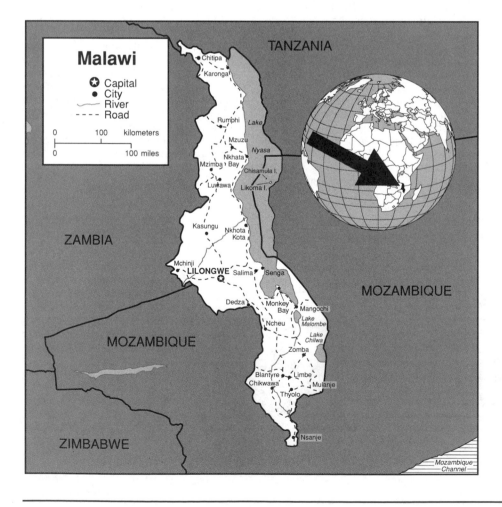

Malawi trading kingdoms develop **1500s**

Explorer David Livingstone arrives along Lake Malawi; missionaries follow **1859**

The British protectorate of Nyasaland (present-day Malawi) is declared **1891**

Reverend John Chilembwe and followers rise against settlers and are suppressed **1915**

The Nyasaland African Congress, the first nationalist movement, is formed **1944**

Independence, under the leadership of Hastings Banda **1964**

Diplomatic ties are established with South Africa **1967**

"Ngwazi" Hastings Kamuzu Banda becomes president-for-life **1971**

1990s

The influx of Mozambican refugees is accompanied by drought and food shortages

Bakili Muluzi is elected president, ending Banda's 30-year dictatorship

Banda and key associates tried and aquitted of political murders.

MALAWI

Despite official attempts to restrict the number of voters, on May 17, 1994, Malawians turned out in overwhelming numbers to cast their ballots in their country's first multiparty elections since independence. The result was a victory for United Democratic Front (UDF) candidate Bakili Muluzi, who succeeded 96-year-old Dr. Kamuzu Banda to become Malawi's second president. Banda's ouster brought an end to what had been one of Africa's most repressive regimes.

Since the early months of independence in 1964, when he purged his cabinet and ruling Malawi Congress Party (MCP) of most of the young politicians who had promoted him to leadership in the nationalist struggle, Banda had ruthlessly used his secret police and MPC's militia, the Malawi Young Pioneers (MYP), to eliminate potential alternatives of his highly personalized dictatorship. Generations of Malawians, including those living abroad, have grown up with the knowledge that voicing critical thoughts about the self-proclaimed "Life President," or "Ngwazi" ("Great Lion"), could prove fatal. Only senior army officers, Banda's long-time "official state hostess" Tamanda Kadzamira, and her uncle John Tembo, the powerful minister of state, survived Ngwazi's jealous exercise of power.

In 1992, Banda's grip began to weaken. Unprecedented antigovernment unrest gave rise to an internal opposition, spearheaded by clergy, underground trade unionists, and a new generation of dissident politicians. By 1993, this opposition had coalesced into two major movements: the southern-based UDF, and the northern-based Alliance for Democracy (AFORD). The detention of AFORD's leader, Chakufwa Chihana, and others failed to stem the tide of opposition. A referendum in June showed two-to-one support for a return to multiparty politics. In November, while Banda was hospitalized in South Africa, young army officers seized the initiative by launching a crackdown against the MYP while purging a number of senior officers from their own ranks. Thereafter, the army played a neutral role in assuring the success of the election.

While the ruthless efficiency of its security apparatus contributed to past perceptions of Malawi's stability, Banda did not survive by mere repression. A few greatly benefited from the regime. Until 1979, the country enjoyed an economic growth rate averaging 6 percent per year. Almost all this growth came from increased agricultural production. The postindependence government favored large estates specializing in exported cash crops. While in the past the estates were almost exclusively the preserve of a few hundred white settlers, today many are controlled by either the state or local individuals.

In the 1970s, the prosperity of the estates helped to fuel a boom in industries involved in agricultural processing. Malawi's limited economic success prior to the 1980s came at the expense of the vast majority of its citizens, who survive as small landholders growing food crops. By 1985, some 86 percent of rural households farmed on less than 5 acres. Overcrowding has contributed to serious soil depletion while marginalizing most farmers to the point where they can have little hope of generating a significant surplus. In addition to land shortage, peasant production has suffered from low official produce prices and lack of other inputs. The northern half of the country, which has almost no estate production, has been relatively neglected in terms of government expenditure on transport and other forms of infrastructure. Many Malawian peasants have for generations turned to migrant labor as a means of coping with their poverty, but there have been far fewer opportunities for them in South Africa and Zimbabwe in recent years.

Under pressure from the World Bank, the Malawian government has since 1981 modestly increased its incentives to the small landholders. Yet these reforms have been insufficient to overcome the continuing impoverishment of rural households, which has been aggravated in recent decades by a decline in migrant-labor remittances. The maldistribution of land in many areas remains a major challenge. On a more positive note, peace in Mozambique has reopened Malawi's access to the Indian Ocean ports of Beira and Nacala while reducing the burden of dealing with what once numbered 600,000 refugees. Communications infrastructure to the ports, damaged by war, is now being repaired.

DEVELOPMENT

As in other parts of Africa, there is increasing recognition that rural development in Malawi must be addressed from a perspective that recognizes the key role of women, especially in arable agriculture. Securing property rights for women has become an important development as well as human-rights issue.

FREEDOM

The end of Banda's one-party dictatorship has opened a new chapter for human rights in Malawi. Political prisoners have been freed, and independent associations and press have emerged. The once-feared Malawi Young Pioneers have been disbanded.

HEALTH/WELFARE

Malawi's health service is considered expectionally poor even for an impoverished country. The country has one of the highest child mortality rates in the world, and more than half its children under age 5 are stunted by malnutrition.

ACHIEVEMENTS

Although it is the poorest, most overcrowded country in the region, Malawi's response to the influx of Mozambican refugees was described by the U.S. Committee for Refugees as "no less than heroic."

Mozambique (People's Republic of Mozambique)

GEOGRAPHY

Area in Square Kilometers (Miles):
786,762 (303,769) (about twice the size of California)
Capital (Population): Maputo (931,000)
Climate: tropical to subtropical

PEOPLE

Population

Total: 17,878,000
Annual Growth Rate: 2.87%
Rural/Urban Population Ratio: 91/9
Major Languages: Portuguese; Yao; Tubbuka; Batonga; Makua; Shona
Ethnic Makeup: Bantu groups

Health

Life Expectancy at Birth: 47 years (male); 51 years (female)
Infant Mortality Rate (Ratio): 126/1,000
Average Caloric Intake: 78% of FAO minimum
Physicians Available (Ratio): 1/43,536

Religions

60% traditional indigenous; 30% Christian; 10% Muslim and others

Education

Adult Literacy Rate: 33%

COMMUNICATION

Telephones: 59,000
Newspapers: 2

MOZAMBICAN WOMEN: PROGRESS AND PERIL

Women played an important role as both fighters and support personnel during Frelimo's struggle against the Portuguese, and they have become increasingly prominent in social areas since independence. In general, the party and, more particularly, its affiliate the Organization of Mozambican Women have actively sought to end gender discrimination. Education and job opportunities have been opened up for working women. A Family Law has given women protection in areas of divorce, desertion, and child custody; and rules against sexual harassment have been vigorously enforced. For most Mozambican women, such progress was overshadowed by the struggle for survival in the drought-plagued countryside during the civil war. In Renamo-held areas, women, along with their children, were commonly enslaved and raped. Some escaped children testified that they were forced to kill their own mothers when they became too weak.

TRANSPORTATION

Highways—Kilometers (Miles):
26,498 (16,465)
Railroads—Kilometers (Miles): 3,288 (2,038)
Usable Airfields: 192

GOVERNMENT

Type: republic
Independence Date: June 25, 1975
Head of State: President Joaquim Chissano
Political Parties: Mozambique Liberation Front (Frelimo); Mozambique National Resistance Party; Democratic Union Party
Suffrage: universal at 18

MILITARY

Number of Armed Forces: 49,800
Military Expenditures (% of Central Government Expenditures): 7.3%
Current Hostilities: civil war

ECONOMY

Currency ($ U.S. Equivalent): 5,220 meticais = $1
Per Capita Income/GDP: $610/$10.6 billion
Inflation Rate: 50%
Natural Resources: coal; iron ore; tantalite; flourite; timber
Agriculture: cotton; tobacco; cashews; sugar; tea; copra; sisal; subsistence crops
Industry: processed foods; textiles; beverages; refined oil; chemicals; tobacco; cement; glass

FOREIGN TRADE

Exports: $150 million
Imports: $1.14 billion

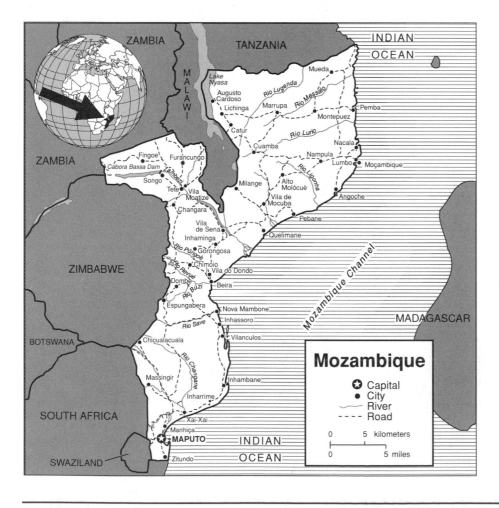

Mozambique
- ⊗ Capital
- • City
- River
- --- Road

0   5 kilometers
0   5 miles

MOZAMBIQUE

One of the world's poorest countries, for 3 decades Mozambique was bled by war. But a 1992 cease-fire agreement, followed by multiparty elections in 1994 have gone some way toward restoring the hope that Mozambicans can look forward to a better future.

The economic, political, and social challenges facing the country, however, remain immense. Since the 1994 elections, the long-ruling Mizambique Liberation Front, or Frelimo Party, of President Joaquim Chissano has faced a large opposition bloc in Parliament, where its old civil-war adversary—the Mozambique National Resistance (MNR, or Renamo) movement—controls 112 out of the 250 seats, with nine remaining seats belong to the Democratic Union Party.

A now peaceful Renamo is, arguably, less of a challenge to the government than the dictates of international donors, whose funding it now depends upon. While the government must be concerned about improving the dismal living conditions faced by the majority of its people, the donors have insisted on fiscal austerity and a privatization program that has led to retrenchments as well as a loss of government influence.

Frelimo originally came to power as a result of a liberation war. Between 1964 and 1974, it struggled against Portuguese colonial rule. At a cost of some 30,000 lives, Mozambique gained its independence in 1975 under Frelimo's leadership. Although the new nation was one of the least developed countries in the world, many were optimistic that the lessons learned in the struggle could be applied to the task of building a dynamic new society based on Marxist-Leninist principles.

Unfortunately, hopes for any sort of postindependence progress were quickly dashed by the Mozambique National Resistance Movement (MNR, or Renamo), which was originally established as a counterrevolutionary fifth column by the Rhodesian Central Intelligence Organization (refer to the country report on Zimbabwe). More than 1 million people died due to the rebellion, a large proportion murdered in cold blood by Renamo. It is further estimated that, out of a total population of 17 million, some 5 million people were internally displaced, and about 2 million others fled to neighboring states. No African nation paid a higher price in its resistance against white supremacy.

Although some parts of Mozambique were occupied by the Portuguese for more than 400 years, most of the country came under colonial control only in the early twentieth century. The territory was developed as a dependency of neighboring colonial economies rather than that of Portugal itself. Mozambican ports were linked by rail to South Africa and the interior colonies of British Central Africa—that is, modern Malawi, Zambia, and Zimbabwe. In the southern provinces, most men, and many women, spent time as migrant laborers in South Africa. The majority of the males worked in the gold mines.

Most of northern Mozambique was granted to three predominantly British concessions companies, whose abusive policies led many to flee the colony. For decades, the colonial state and many local enterprises also relied on forced labor. After World War II, new demands were put on Mozambicans by a growing influx of Portuguese settlers, whose numbers swelled during the 1960s, from 90,000 to more than 200,000. Meanwhile, even by the dismal standards of European colonialism in Africa, there continued to be a notable lack of concern for human development. At independence, 93 percent of the African population in Mozambique were illiterate. Furthermore, most of those who had acquired literacy or other skills had done so despite the Portuguese presence.

Although a welcome event in itself, the sudden nature of the Portuguese empire's collapse contributed to the destabilization of postindependence Mozambique. Because Frelimo had succeeded in establishing itself as a unified nationalist front, Mozambique

(United Nations photo by Kate Truscott)

Mozambique was in a bitter civil war for 3 decades. The resulting drain on natural resources, the displacement of approximately one fifth of the population, and the persistent drought led to the need to import food to stave off famine.

Portuguese explorers land in Mozambique
1497

The Northern Nguni of Shosagaane invade southern Mozambique, establishing the Gaza kingdom
1820s

The Frelimo liberation movement officially launched
1962

Frelimo's leader, Eduardo Mondlane, is killed by a parcel bomb
1969

The liberation struggle is successful when the Portuguese revolution brings independence
1975

Increased Renamo attacks on civilian and military targets
1980s

President Samora Machel is killed in a mysterious airplane crash; Joaquim Chissano becomes president

1990s

Renamo agrees to end fighting, participate in multiparty elections

Multiparty elections

was spared an immediate descent into civil conflict, such as that which engulfed Angola, Portugal's other major African possession. However, the economy was already bankrupt due to the Portuguese policy of running Mozambique on a non-convertible local currency. The rapid transition to independence compounded this problem by encouraging the sudden exodus of almost all the Portuguese settlers.

Perhaps even more costly to Mozambique in the long term was the polarization between Frelimo and African supporters of the former regime, who included about 100,000 who had been active in its security forces. The rapid Portuguese withdrawal was not conducive to the difficult task of reconciliation. While the "compromised ones" were not subjected by Frelimo to bloody reprisals, their rights were circumscribed, and many were sent, along with prostitutes and other "antisocial" elements, to "reeducation camps." While the historically pro-Portuguese stance of the local Catholic hierarchy would have complicated its relations with the new state under any circumstance, Frelimo's Marxist rejection of religion initially alienated it from broader numbers of believers.

A TROUBLED INDEPENDENCE

Frelimo assumed power without the benefit or burden of a strong sense of administrative continuity. While it had begun to create alternative social structures in its "liberated zones" during the anticolonial struggle, these areas had encompassed only a small percentage of Mozambique's population and infrastructure. But Frelimo was initially able to fill the vacuum and launch aggressive development efforts. Health care and education were expanded, worker committees

successfully ran many of the enterprises abandoned by the settlers, and communal villages coordinated rural development. However, efforts to promote agricultural collectivization as the foundation of a command economy generally led to peasant resistance and economic failure. Frelimo's ability to adapt and implement many of its programs under trying conditions was due largely to its disciplined mass base (the party's 1990 membership stood at about 200,000).

No sooner had Mozambique begun to stabilize itself from the immediate dislocations of its decolonization process than it became embroiled in the Rhodesian conflict. Mozambique was the only neighboring state to impose fully the "mandatory" United Nations economic sanctions against Rhodesia. Between 1976 and 1980, this decision led to the direct loss of half a billion dollars in rail and port revenues. Furthermore, Frelimo's decision to provide bases for the fighters of the Patriotic Front led to a state of undeclared war with Rhodesia as well as its Renamo proxies.

Unfortunately, the fall of Rhodesia did not bring an end to externally sponsored destabilization. Renamo had the support of South Africa. By continuing Renamo's campaign of destabilization, the Pretoria regime gained leverage over its hostile neighbors, for the continued closure of Mozambique's ports meant that most of their traffic had to pass through South Africa. In 1984, Mozambique signed a nonaggression pact with South Africa, which should have put an end to the latter's support of Renamo. However, captured documents and other evidence indicate that official South African support for Renamo continued at least until 1989, while South African supplies were still

reaching the rebels under mysterious circumstances. In response, Zimbabwe, and to a lesser extent Malawi and Tanzania, contributed troops to assist in the defense of Mozambique.

In its 1989 Congress, Frelimo formally abandoned its commitment to the primacy of Marxist-Leninist ideology and opened the door to further political and economic reforms. Multipartyism was formally embraced in 1991. With the help of the Catholic Church and international mediators, the government opened talks with Renamo. In October 1992, Renamo's leader, Alfonso Dlakama, signed a peace accord that called for UN-supervised elections. The cease-fire finally came into actual effect in the early months of 1993, by which time the UN personnel on the ground reported that some 3 million Mozambicans were suffering from famine.

Besides their mutual distrust, reconciliation between Renamo and Frelimo was troubled by their leaderships' inability to control their armed supporters. With neither movement able to pay its troops, apolitical banditry by former fighters for both sides increased. International financial and military support, mobilized through the United Nations, was inadequate to meet this challenge. In June and July 1994, a number of UN personnel, along with foreign-aid workers, were seized as hostages. The near-complete collapse of the country, however, has so far encouraged Mozambique's political leaders to sustain the peace drive.

DEVELOPMENT

To maintain minimum services and to recover from wartime destruction, Mozambique relies on the commitment of its citizens and international assistance. Western churches have sent relief supplies, food aid, and vehicles.

FREEDOM

Ongoing constitutional changes have liberalized the political climate. Many Mozambicans, however, still live at the mercy of local armed gangs who often recognize no authority.

HEALTH/WELFARE

Civil strife, widespread Renamo attacks on health units, and food shortages drastically curtailed health care goals and led to Mozambique's astronomical infant mortality rate.

ACHIEVEMENTS

Between 1975 and 1980, the illiteracy rate in Mozambique declined from 93% to 72% while classroom attendance more than doubled. However, progress slowed during the 1980s due to Renamo attacks.

Namibia

GEOGRAPHY

Area in Square Kilometers (Miles):
824,292 (318,261) (twice the size of California)
Capital (Population): Windhoek (161,000)
Climate: arid; semiarid

PEOPLE

Population

Total: 1,677,000
Annual Growth Rate: 3.45%
Rural/Urban Population Ratio: 67/33
Major Languages: English; Ovambo; Kavango; Nama/Damara; Herero; Khiosan; German; Afrikaans
Ethnic Makeup: 50% Ovambo; 9% Kavango; 7% Herero; 7% Damara; 27% others

Health

Life Expectancy at Birth: 59 years (male); 65 years (female)
Infant Mortality Rate (Ratio): 54.8/1,000
Average Caloric Intake: n/a
Physicians Available (Ratio): 1/4,594

Religions

70% Christian; 30% traditional indigenous

Education

Adult Literacy Rate: 38%

COMMUNICATION

Telephones: 62,800
Newspapers: 11

NAMIBIA'S FISHING INDUSTRY

Namibia's fishing sector has made an impressive recovery after years of decline. The country's coastal waters had long supported exceptionally high concentrations of sea life due to the upwelling of nutrients by the cold offshore current. But, in the years before independence, in 1990, overfishing, mostly by foreign vessels, had nearly wiped out many species. Since then, the government has established a 200-nautical-mile Exclusive Economic Zone along Namibia's coast and passed a Sea Fisheries Act designed to promote the conservation and controlled exploitation of the country's marine resources. These measures have been backed up by effective monitoring on the part of the new Ministry of Fisheries and Marine Resources and the creation of a National Fisheries Research and Information Centre. A rapid recovery in fish stocks has led to an annual growth of 35 percent in the sector's value.

TRANSPORTATION

Highways—Kilometers (Miles): 54,500 (33,866)
Railroads—Kilometers (Miles): 2,340 (1,454)
Usable Airfields: 135

GOVERNMENT

Type: republic
Independence Date: March 21, 1990
Head of State: President Sam Nujoma
Political Parties: South West Africa People's Organization; DTA of Namibia; United Democratic Front; Action Christian National; others
Suffrage: universal at 18

MILITARY

Number of Armed Forces: 8,000
Military Expenditures (% of Central Government Expenditures): 2.0%
Current Hostilities: border dispute with Botswana

ECONOMY

Currency ($ U.S. Equivalent): 3.54 Namibian dollars = $1
Per Capita Income/GDP: $3,600/$5.8 billion
Inflation Rate: 11%
Natural Resources: diamonds; copper; lead; zinc; uranium; silver; cadmium; lithium; coal; possible oil reserves; fish
Agriculture: corn; millet; sorghum; livestock
Industry: meat canning; dairy products; leather tanning; textiles; clothing; mineral concentrates

FOREIGN TRADE

Exports: $1.3 billion
Imports: $1.1 billion

NAMIBIA

Namibia became independent in 1990 after a long liberation struggle. Its transition from the continent's last colony to a developing nation-state marked the end of a century of often brutal colonization, first by Germany and later South Africa. The German colonial period (1884–1917) was marked by the annihilation of more than 60 percent of the African population in the southern two thirds of the country during the uprising of 1904–1907. The South African period (1917–1990) saw the imposition of apartheid as well as a bitter 26-year war for independence between the South African Army (SADF) and the South West Africa People's Organization (SWAPO). During that war, countless civilians, especially in the northern areas of the country, were harassed, detained, and abused by South African–created death squads, such as the Koevoet (the Afrikaans word for "crowbar").

Namibia's final liberation was the result of South African military misadventures and U.S.–Soviet cooperation in reducing tensions in the region. In 1987, as it had done many times before, South Africa invaded Angola to assist Jonas Savimbi's UNITA movement. Its objective was Cuito Cuanavale, a small town in southeastern Angola where the Luanda government had set up an air-defense installation to keep South African aircraft from supplying UNITA troops. The SADF met with fierce resistance from the Angolan Army and eventually committed thousands of its own troops to the battle. In addition, black Namibian soldiers were recruited and given UNITA uniforms to fight on the side of the SADF. Many of these proxy UNITA troops later mutinied because of the poor treatment at the hands of white South African soldiers.

South Africa failed to capture Cuito Cuanavale, and its forces were eventually surrounded. Faced with military disaster, the Pretoria government bowed to decades of international pressure and agreed to withdraw from its illegal occupation of Namibia. In return, Angola and its ally Cuba agreed to send home troops sent by Havana in 1974 after South Africa invaded Angola for the first time. Key brokers of the cease-fire, negotiations, and implementation of this agreement were the United States and the Soviet Union. This was the first instance of their post–cold war cooperation.

A plebiscite was held in Namibia in November 1989. Under United Nations supervision, more than 97 percent of eligible voters cast their ballots—a remarkable achievement given the vast distances that many had to travel to reach polling stations. SWAPO emerged as the clear winner, with 57 percent of the votes cast. The party's share of the vote increased to 73 percent in the subsequent December 1995 elections, while support for its main political rival, the Democratic Turnhalle Alliance was reduced to 15 percent.

CHALLENGES AND PROSPECTS

Namibia is a sparsely populated land. More than half its nearly 1.6 million resi-

(United Nations photo by J. Isaac)

The importance of developing agricultural production in arable parts of the country is key to the economic future of Namibia. The sanctions that applied before independence have been lifted, and Namibia is now free to enter the potentially profitable markets of Europe and North America. This man working in a cornfield near Grootfontein is part of the agricultural economy.

Germany is given rights to colonize Namibia at the Conference of Berlin **1884–1885**	Herero, Nama, and Damara rebellions against German rule **1904–1907**	The UN General Assembly revokes a 1920 South African mandate; SWAPO begins war for independence **1966**	Bantustans, or "homelands," are created by South Africa **1968**	A massive strike paralyzes the economy **1971**	An internal government is formed by South Africa **1978**	Defeat at Cuito Cuanavale leads to a South African agreement to withdraw from Namibia **1980s**	SWAPO wins UN-supervised elections; a new Constitution is approved **1990s**

SWAPO wins increased majority in 1994 national elections

In face of international conservationist pressure, Namibia authorizes the culling of 17,000 out of its seal population of 500,000

Namibia and Botswana agree to take their border dispute to the International Court of Justice.

dents live in the northern region known as Ovamboland. Rich in minerals, Namibia is a major producer of diamonds, uranium, copper, silver, tin, and lithium. A large gold mine recently began production, and the end of hostilities has opened up northern parts of the country to further mineral explorations.

Much of Namibia is arid. Until recently, pastoral farming was the primary agricultural activity, with beef, mutton, and goat meat the main products. Independence brought an end to international sanctions applied when South Africa ruled the country, giving Namibian agricultural goods access to the world market. Although some new investment has been attracted to the relatively well-watered but historically neglected northern border regions, most of Namibia's rural majority, including many relatively well-educated former exiles, are barely able to eke out a living, even in nondrought years.

Despite the economic promise, the fledgling government of Namibia faces severe economic problems. It inherits an economy structurally perverted by apartheid to favor the tiny white minority. With a glaring division between fabulously wealthy whites and the oppressively poor black majority, the government is faced with the daunting problem of promoting economic development while at the same time encouraging the redistribution of wealth. Apartheid ensured that managerial positions were filled by whites, leaving a dearth of qualified and experienced nonwhite executives in the country. This past pattern of discrimination has contributed to extremely high levels of black unemployment today. The hardest hit have been the youth and those living in the north.

The demobilization of 53,000 former SWAPO and South African combatants and the return of 44,000 exiles aggravated this problem. A few former soldiers—notably the Botsotsos, made up of former Koevoet members—turned to organized crime. Having already inherited a civil service bloated by too many white sinecures, the SWAPO administration resisted the temptation of trying to hire its way out of the problem. In 1991–1992, several thousand ex-combatants received vocational training in Development Brigades, modeled after similar initiatives in Botswana and Zimbabwe, but inadequate funding and preparation limited the program's success. Namibia's overall unemployment rate is estimated to be 40 to 50 percent on average.

Another major problem lies in Namibia's economic dependence on South Africa. Before independence, Namibia had been developed as a captive market for South African goods, while its resources had been depleted by overexploitation on the part of South African firms. In 1990, all rail and most road links between Namibia and the rest of the world ran through South Africa. But South Africa's March 1, 1994, return of Walvis Bay, Namibia's only port, has greatly reduced this dependence. The port has now been declared a free trade area. Namibia has also been linked to South Africa through a Common Monetary Area. In 1994, a new Namibian dollar was introduced, replacing the South African rand. But, at least for the time being, its value remains tied to the rand.

The government of President Sam Nujoma has taken a hard look at these and other economic problems and embarked on a program to solve them. SWAPO surprised everyone during the election campaign by modifying its previously strident socialist rhetoric and calling for a market-oriented economy. Since taking power, it has joined the International Monetary Fund and proposed a code for foreign investors that includes protection against undue nationalizations. Since independence, the Ministry of Finance has pursued conservative policies, which have calmed the country's largely white business community but have been criticized as insufficient to transform the economy for the greater benefit of the impoverished masses.

The government recognizes the need to attract significant foreign investment to overcome the colonial legacy of underdevelopment. In 1993, a generous package of manufacturing incentives was introduced by the Ministry of Trade and Industry. In the same year, the Namibia National Development Corporation was established to channel public investment into the economy. It is too early to assess the success of these initiatives.

DEVELOPMENT

The Nujoma government has instituted English as the medium of instruction in all schools. (Before independence, English was discouraged for African schoolchildren, a means of controlling their access to skills necessary to compete in the modern world.) This effort requires new curricula and textbooks for the entire country.

FREEDOM

The Namibian Constitution is considered a model of democratic government. Universal suffrage and a strong emphasis on human rights are prominent throughout the document. Freedom of the press, freedom of speech, an independent judiciary, and provisions against discrimination in any form are constitutional guarantees.

HEALTH/WELFARE

The social-service delivery system of Namibia must be rebuilt to eliminate the structural inequities of apartheid. Health care for the black majority, especially those in remote rural areas, will require significant improvements. Public-health programs for blacks, nonexistent prior to independence, must be created.

ACHIEVEMENTS

The government of President Sam Nujoma has received high praise for its efforts at racial and political reconciliation after a bitter 26-year war for independence. Nujoma has led these efforts and has impressed many observers with his exceptional political and consensus-building skills.

South Africa (Republic of South Africa)*

GEOGRAPHY
Area in Square Kilometers (Miles):
1,222,480 (437,872) (about twice the size of Texas)
Capital (Population): Pretoria (administrative) (1,000,000); Cape Town (legislative) (1,911,500); Bloemfontein (judicial) (232,900)
Climate: temperate; semiarid; arid

PEOPLE

Population
Total: 45,096,000 (includes the 10 so-called homelands, which are not recognized by the United States)
Annual Growth Rate: 2.6%
Rural/Urban Population Ratio: 43/57
Major Languages: Afrikaans; English; Ndebele; Pedi; Sotho; Swati; Tsonga; Tswana; Venda; Xhosa; Zulu
Ethnic Makeup: 75% black; 14% white; 9% Colored; 2% Indian

Health
Life Expectancy at Birth: 63 years (male); 68 years (female)
Infant Mortality Rate (Ratio): 46/1,000
Average Caloric Intake: 116% of FAO minimum
Physicians Available (Ratio): 1/1,529

Religions
81% Christian; 19% Hindu and Muslim

Education
Adult Literacy Rate: 76%

COMMUNICATION
Telephones: 4,500,000
Newspapers: 42

TRANSPORTATION
Highways—Kilometers (Miles):
188,309 (116,751)

Railroads—Kilometers (Miles):
20,638 (12,796)
Usable Airfields: 853

GOVERNMENT
Type: republic
Independence Date: May 31, 1910
Head of State: President Nelson Mandela
Political Parties: African National Congress; National Party; Inkatha Freedom Party; Freedom Front; Democratic Party; Pan Africanist Congress; others
Suffrage: universal at 18

MILITARY
Number of Armed Forces: 61,500 standing; 135,000 ready reserves; 140,000 paramilitary commando volunteers; 37,000 police
Military Expenditures (% of Central Government Expenditures): 2.8%
Current Hostilities: civil unrest

ECONOMY
Currency ($ U.S. Equivalent): 4.42 rands = $1
Per Capita Income/GDP: $4,420/$194.3 billion
Inflation Rate: 9%
Natural Resources: gold; diamonds; mineral ores; uranium; fish
Agriculture: corn; wool; wheat; sugarcane; tobacco; citrus fruits; dairy products
Industry: mining; automobile assembly; metal working; machinery; textiles; iron and steel; chemicals; fertilizer; fishing

FOREIGN TRADE
Exports: $25.3 billion
Imports: $21.4 billion

*When separated, figures for blacks and whites vary greatly.

THE AFRICAN NATIONAL CONGRESS

The African National Congress (ANC) was founded in 1912, in response to the taking of land from Africans and the introduction of "pass laws" controlling their employment and movement. For 50 years, members carried on peaceful resistance to apartheid by organizing protest marches, supporting workers' demands and strike actions, and creating independent schools and services. ANC goals were expressed in the Freedom Charter, which stated that "South Africa belongs to all who live in it, black and white . . ." and called for "one man, one vote" and the abolition of the color bar. These beliefs caused the arrest of thousands and the trial of ANC leaders for treason. The ANC went underground in the 1960s, planning sabotage against military and political targets. The ANC and Nelson Mandela, who since his release in 1990 has acted as the movement's leader, gained supporters and stature as internal resistance against the apartheid state grew during the 1980s. In 1994, the ANC attracted 63 percent of the national vote, becoming the major party in the new Government of National Unity, and Mandela became the country's president.

South Africa
⊛ Capital
● City
〜 River
- - - - Road

0   200 kilometers
0   200 miles

SOUTH AFRICA

In April 1994, millions of South Africans turned out to vote in their country's first nonracial elections. Most waited patiently for hours to cast their ballots for the first time. The result was a landslide victory for the African National Congress (ANC), which, under the new interim Constitution, would nonetheless cooperate with two of its long-standing rivals, the National Party (NP) and the Inkatha Freedom Party (IFP), in a Government of National Unity (GNU). On May 10, the ANC's leader, Nelson Mandela, was sworn in as South Africa's first black president. Despite the history of often violent animosity between its components, the GNU survived for 2 years, facilitating national reconciliation. In July 1996, the NP pulled out of the GNU, giving the ANC a freer hand to pursue its ambitious but largely unrealized program of "Reconstruction and Development."

With the emergence of an elected nonracial government, South Africa has decisively turned away from its long, tragic history of racism. For nearly 3½ centuries, the territory's white minority expanded and entrenched its racial hegemony over the nonwhite majority. After 1948, successive NP governments consolidated white supremacy into a governing system known as *apartheid* ("separatehood"). But in a dramatic political about-face, the NP government, under the new leadership of F. W. De Klerk, committed itself in 1990 to a negotiated end to apartheid. Political restrictions inside the country were significantly relaxed through the unbanning of anti-apartheid resistance organizations, most notably the ANC, the Pan Africanist Congress (PAC), and the South African Communist Party (SACP). Thereafter, 3 years of on-again, off-again negotiations, incorporating virtually all sections of public opinion, resulted in a 1993 consensus in favor of a 5-year, nonracial, interim Constitution.

Notwithstanding its remarkable political progress in recent years, South Africa remains a deeply divided country. In general, whites continue to enjoy relatively affluent, comfortable lives, while the vast majority of nonwhites survive in a state of impoverished deprivation. The boundary between these two worlds remains deep. Under the pre-1990 apartheid system, nonwhites were legally divided as members of three officially subordinate race classifications: "Bantu" (black African), "Coloureds" (people of mixed race), or "Asians." (*Note:* Many members of these three groups prefer the common label of "Black," which the government now commonly uses in place of Bantu as an exclusive term for black Africans, hereafter referred to in this text as *blacks*.)

THE ROOTS OF APARTHEID

White supremacy in South Africa began with the Dutch settlement at Cape Town in 1652. For 1½ centuries, the domestic economy of the Dutch Cape Colony, which gradually expanded to include the southern third of modern South Africa, rested on a foundation of slavery and servitude. Much like the American South before the Civil War, Cape Colonial society was racially divided between free white settlers and nonwhite slaves and servants. Most of the slaves were Africans imported from outside the local region, although a minority were taken from Asia. The local blacks, who spoke various Khiosan languages, were not enslaved. However, they were robbed by the Europeans of their land and herds. Many were also killed either by European bullets or diseases. As a result, most of the Cape's Khiosan were reduced to a status of servitude. Gradually, the servant and slave populations, with a considerable admixture of European blood,

(United Nations photo)

The system of apartheid made it impossible for most black South Africans to share in South Africa's economic prosperity.

merged to form the core of the so-called Coloured group.

At the beginning of the nineteenth century, the Cape Colony reverted to British control. In the 1830s, the British abolished slavery and extended legal rights to servants. But, as with the American South, emancipation did not end racial barriers to the political and economic advancement of nonwhites. Nonetheless, even the limited reforms that were introduced upset many of the white "Cape Dutch" (or "Boers"), whose society was evolving its own "Afrikaner" identity. (Today, some 60 percent of the whites and 90 percent of the Coloureds in South Africa speak the Dutch-derived Afrikaans language.) In the mid-nineteenth century, thousands of Afrikaners, accompanied by their Coloured clients, escaped British rule by migrating into the interior. They established two independent republics, the Transvaal and the Orange Free State, whose Constitutions recognized only whites as having any civil rights.

The Afrikaners, and the British who followed them, did not settle an empty land. Then, as now, most of the people living in the area beyond the borders of the old Dutch Cape Colony were blacks who spoke languages linguistically classified as Bantu. While there are nine officially recognized Bantu languages in South Africa, all but two (Tsonga and Venda) belong to either the Sotho-Tswana (Pedi, Sotho, Tswana) or Nguni (Ndebele, Swati, Xhosa, and Zulu) subgroupings of closely related dialects.

Throughout the 1700s and 1800s, the indigenous populations of the interior and the eastern coast offered strong resistance to the white invaders. Unlike the Khiosan of the Cape, these communities were able to preserve their ethnolinguistic identities. However, the settlers eventually robbed them of most of their land as well as their independence. Black subjugation served the economic interests of white farmers, and later industrialists, who were able to coerce the conquered communities into providing cheap and forced labor. After 1860, many Asians, mostly from what was then British-ruled India, were also brought into South Africa to work for next to nothing on sugar plantations. As with the blacks and Coloureds, the Asians were denied civil rights.

The lines of racial stratification were already well entrenched at the turn of the twentieth century, when the British waged a war of conquest against the Afrikaner republics. During this South African, or Boer, War, tens of thousands of Afrikaners, blacks, and Coloureds died while interned in British concentration camps. The camps helped to defeat the Afrikaner resistance but left bitter divisions between the resistance and pro-British English-speaking whites. However, it was the non-whites who were the war's greatest losers. A compromise peace between the Afrikaners and the British Empire paved the way for the emergence, in 1910, of a self-governing Union of South Africa, made up of the former British colonies and Afrikaner republics. In this new state, political power remained in the hands of the white minority.

"GRAND APARTHEID"

In 1948, the Afrikaner-dominated Nationalist Party was voted into office by the white electorate on a platform promising apartheid. Under this system, existing patterns of segregation were reinforced by a vast array of new laws. "Pass laws," which had long limited the movement of blacks in many areas, were extended throughout the country. Black men and women were required to carry "passbooks" at all times to prove their right to be residing in a particular area. Under the Group Areas Act, more than 80 percent of South Africa was reserved for whites (who now make up no more than 15 percent of the population). In this area, blacks were confined to townships or white-owned farms, where, until recently, they were considered to be temporary residents. If they lacked a properly registered job, they were subject to deportation to one of the 10 "homelands."

Under apartheid, the homelands—poor, noncontiguous rural territories that together account for less than 13 percent of South Africa's land—were the designated "nations" of South Africa's blacks, who make up more than 70 percent of the population. Each black was assigned membership in a particular homeland, in accordance with ethnolinguistic criteria invented by the white government. Thus, in apartheid theory, there was no majority in South Africa but, rather, a single white nation, which in reality remained divided between speakers of Afrikaans, English, and other languages, and 10 separate black nations. The Coloureds and the Asians were consigned a never clearly defined intermediate position as powerless communities associated with, but segregated from, white South Africa. The apartheid "ideal" was that each black homeland would eventually become "independent," leaving white South Africa without the "burden" of a black majority. Of course, black "immigrants" could still work for the "white economy," which would remain reliant on black labor. To assure that racial stratification was maintained at the workplace, a system of job classification was created that reserved the best positions for whites, certain middle-level employments for Asians and Coloureds, and unskilled labor for blacks.

Before 1990, the NP ruthlessly pursued its ultimate goal of legislating away South Africa's black majority. Four homelands—Bophutatswana, Ciskei, Transkei, and Venda—were declared independent. The 9 million blacks who were assigned as citizens of these pseudo-states (which were not recognized by any outside country) did not appear in the 1989 South African Census, even though most lived outside of the homelands. Indeed, despite generations of forced removals and influx control, today there is not a single magistrate's district (the equivalent of a U.S. county) that has a white majority.

While for whites apartheid was an ideology of mass delusion, for blacks it meant continuous suffering. In the 1970s alone, some 3.5 million blacks were forcibly relocated because they were living in "black spots" within white areas. Many more at some point in their lives fell victim to the pass laws. Within the townships and squatter camps that ringed the white cities, families survived from day to day not knowing when the police might burst into their homes to discover that their passbooks were not in order.

Under apartheid, blacks were as much divided by their residential status as by their assigned ethnicity. In a relative sense, the most privileged were those who had established their right to reside legally within a township like Soweto. Township dwellers had the advantage of being able to live with their families and seek work in a nearby white urban center. Many of their coworkers lived much farther away, in the peri-urban areas of the homelands. Some in this less fortunate category spent as much as one third of their lives on Putco buses, traveling to and from their places of employment. Still, the peri-urban homeland workers were in many ways better off than their male colleagues, who were confined to crowded worker hostels for months at a time while their families remained in distant rural homelands. There were also millions of female domestics who generally earned next to nothing while living away from their children in the servant quarters of white households. Many of these conditions still persist in South Africa.

Further down the black social ladder were those living in the illegal squatter camps that existed outside the urban areas. Without secure homes or steady jobs, the squatters were frequent victims of night-time police raids. When caught, they were generally transported back to their homelands, from whence they would usually try once more to escape. The relaxation of influx control regulations eased the tribulations of many squatters, but their lives remained insecure.

Yet even the violent destruction of squatter settlements by the state did not stem their explosive growth. For many blacks, living without permanent employment in a cardboard house was preferable to the hardships of the rural homelands. Nearly half of all blacks live in these areas today. Unemployment there tops 80 percent, and agricultural production is limited by marginal, overcrowded environments.

Economic changes in the 1970s and 1980s tended further to accentuate the importance of these residential patterns. Although their wages on average remain only a fraction of those enjoyed by whites, many township dwellers have seen their wages rise over the past decade, partially due to their own success in organizing strong labor federations. At the same time, however, life in the homelands has become more desperate as their populations have mushroomed.

Apartheid was a totalitarian system. Before 1994, an array of security legislation gave the state vast powers over individual citizens, even in the absence of a state of emergency, such as existed throughout much of the country between 1985 and 1990. Control was more subtly exercised through the schools and other public institutions. An important element of apartheid was "Bantu Education." Beyond being segregated and unequal, black educational curricula were specifically designed to assure underachievement, by preparing most students for only semi-skilled and unskilled occupations. The schools were also divided by language and ethnicity. A student who was classified as Zulu was taught in the Zulu language to be loyal to the Zulu nation, while his or her playmates might be receiving similar instruction in Tsonga or Sotho. Ethnic divisions were also often encouraged at the workplace. (At the mines, even today, ethnicity generally determines the job and hostel to which one is assigned.)

LIMITED REFORMS

In 1982 and 1983, there was much official publicity about reforming apartheid. Yet the Nationalist Party's moves to liberalize the system were limited and were accompanied by increased repression. Some changes were simply semantic. In official publications, the term "apartheid" was replaced by "separate development," which was subsequently dropped in favor of "plural democracy."

A bill passed in the white Parliament in 1983 brought Asian and Coloured representatives into the South African government—but only in their own separate chambers, which remained completely subordinate to the white chamber. The bill also concentrated power in the office of the presidency, which eroded the oversight prerogatives of white parliamentarians. Significantly, the new dispensation completely excluded blacks. Seeing the new Constitution as another transparent attempt at divide-and-rule while offering them nothing in the way of genuine empowerment, most Asians and Coloureds refused to participate in the new political order. Instead, many joined together with blacks and a handful of progressive whites in creating a new organization, the United Democratic Front (UDF), which opposed the Constitution.

In other moves, the NP gradually did away with many examples of "petty" apartheid. In many areas, signs announcing separate facilities were removed from public places; but, very often, new, more

(United Nations photo)

Millions of black South Africans were forcibly resettled in villages. The formation of these so-called black homelands represented the largest forced movement of people in peacetime history.

				Shaka develops the Zulu nation and sets in motion the wars and migrations known as the Mfecane	
Migration of Bantu speakers into Southern Africa 1000–1500 ●	The first settlement of Dutch people in the Cape of Good Hope area 1652 ●	The first Khiosan attempt to resist white encroachment 1659 ●	The British gain possession of the Cape Colony 1815 ●	1820s ●	The Boer War: the British fight the Afrikaners (Boers) 1899–1902 ●

subtle signs were put up to assure continued segregation. Many gas stations in the Transvaal, for example, still have their facilities marked with blue and white figures to assure that everyone continues to know his or her place. Another example of purely cosmetic reform was the legalization of interracial marriage—although it was no longer a crime for a man and a woman belonging to different racial classifications to be wed, before 1992 it remained an offense for such a couple to live in the same house. In 1986, the hated passbooks were replaced with new "identity cards." Unions were legalized in the 1980s, but in the Orwellian world of apartheid, their leaders were regularly arrested. The UDF was not banned but, rather, was forbidden from holding meetings. Although such reforms were meaningless to most nonwhites living within South Africa, some outsiders, including the Reagan administration, were impressed by the "progress."

BLACK RESISTANCE

Resistance to white domination dates back to 1659, when the Khiosan first attempted to counter Dutch encroachments on their pastures. In the first half of the twentieth century, the African National Congress (founded in 1912 to unify what until then had been regionally based black associations) and other political and labor organizations attempted to wage a peaceful civil-rights struggle. An early leader within the Asian community was Mohandas (Mahatma) Gandhi, who pioneered his strategy of passive resistance in South Africa while resisting the pass laws. In the 1950s, the ANC and associated organizations adopted Gandhian tactics on a massive scale, in a vain attempt to block the enactment of apartheid legislation. Although ANC president Albert Luthuli was awarded a Nobel Peace Prize, the NP regime remained unmoved.

The year 1960 was a turning point. Police massacred more than 60 persons when they fired on a passbook-burning demonstration at Sharpeville. Thereafter, the government assumed emergency powers, banning the ANC and the more recently formed Pan Africanist Congress. As underground movements, both turned to armed struggle. The ANC's guerrilla organization, the Umkonto we Sizwe ("Spear of the Nation"), attempted to avoid taking human lives in its attacks.

Poqo ("Ourselves Alone"), the PAC's armed wing, was less constrained in its choice of targets but proved less able to sustain its struggle. By the mid-1960s, with the capture of such figures as Umkonto leader Nelson Mandela, active resistance had been all but fully suppressed.

A new generation of resistance emerged in the 1970s. Many nonwhite youths were attracted to the teachings of the Black Consciousness Movement (BMC), led by Steve Biko. The BMC and like-minded organizations rejected the racial and ethnic classifications of apartheid by insisting on the fundamental unity of all oppressed black peoples (that is, all nonwhites) against the white power structure. Black consciousness also rejected all forms of collaboration with the apartheid state, which brought the movement into direct opposition with homeland leaders like Gatsha Buthelezi, whom they looked upon as sellouts. In the aftermath of student demonstrations in Soweto, which sparked months of unrest across the country, the government suppressed the BMC. Biko was subsequently murdered while in detention. During the crackdown, thousands of young people fled South Africa. Many joined the exiled ANC, helping to reinvigorate its exiled ranks.

Despite heavyhanded repression, internal resistance to apartheid continued to grow. Hundreds of new and revitalized organizations—community groups, labor unions, and religious bodies—emerged to contribute to the struggle. Many became affiliated through coordinating bodies such as the United Democratic Front, the Congress of South African Trade Unions (COSATU), and the South African Council of Churches (SACC). SACC leader Archbishop Desmond Tutu became the second black South African to be awarded a Nobel Peace Prize for his nonviolent efforts to bring about change. But in the face of continued oppression, black youths, in particular, became increasingly willing to use whatever means necessary to overthrow the oppressors.

The year 1985 was another turning point. Arrests and bannings of black leaders led to calls to make the townships "ungovernable." A state of emergency was proclaimed by the government in July, which allowed for the increased use of detention without trial. By March 1990,

(United Nations photo)

Resistance groups gained international recognition in their struggle against the South African apartheid regime.

The Union of South Africa gives rights of self-government to whites
1910

The African National Congress is founded
1912

The Nationalist Party comes to power on an apartheid platform
1948

The Sharpeville Massacre: police fire on demonstration; more than 60 deaths result
1960

Soweto riots are sparked off by student protests
1976

Unrest in the black townships leads to the declaration of a state of emergency
1980s

Thousands are detained while violence escalates

F. W. de Klerk replaces P. W. Botha as president

Anti-apartheid movements are unbanned; political prisoners are released
1990s

Negotiations for a nonracial interim Constitution begin

Nonracial elections in May 1994 result in an ANC-led Government of National Unity; Nelson Mandela becomes president

The National Party pulls out of the GNU

some 53,000 people, including an estimated 10,000 children, had been arrested. Many detainees have been tortured while in custody. Stone-throwing youths nonetheless continued to challenge the heavily armed security forces sent into the townships to restore order. By 1993, more than 10,000 people had died during the unrest.

TOWARD A NEW SOUTH AFRICA

Despite the Nationalist Party's ability to marshall the resources of a sophisticated military–industrial complex to maintain its totalitarian control, it was forced to abandon apartheid along with its 4-decade-long monopoly of power. Throughout the 1980s, South Africa's advanced economy was in a state of crisis due to the effects of unrest and, to a lesser extent, of sanctions and other forms of international pressure. Under President P. W. Botha, the NP regime stubbornly refused to offer any openings to genuine reform. However, Botha's replacement in 1989 by F. W. de Klerk opened up new possibilities. The unbanning of the ANC, PAC, and SACP was accompanied by the release of many political prisoners. As many had anticipated, after gaining his freedom in March 1990, ANC leader Nelson Mandela emerged as the leading advocate for change. More surprising was the de Klerk government's willingness to engage in serious negotiations with Mandela and others. By August 1990, the ANC felt that the progress being made justified the formal suspension of its armed struggle.

Many obstacles blocked the transition to a postapartheid state. The NP initially advocated a form of power sharing that fell short of the concept of one person, one vote in a unified state. The ANC, UDF (disbanded in 1991), Cosatu, and SACP, which were associated as the Mass Democratic Movement (MDM), however, remained steadfast in their loyalty to the nonracial principles of the 1955 Freedom Charter. Many members of the PAC and other radical critics of the ANC initially feared that the apartheid regime was not prepared to agree to its dismantlement and that the ongoing talks could only serve to weaken black resistance. On the opposite side of the spectrum were still-powerful elements of the white community who remained openly committed to continued white supremacy. In addition to the Conservative Party, the principal opposition in the old white Parliament, there were a number of militant racist organizations, which resorted to terrorism in an attempt to block reforms. Some within the South African security establishment also sought to sabotage the prospects of peace. In March 1992 these far-right elements suffered a setback when nearly 70 percent of white voters approved continued negotiation for democratic reform.

Another troublesome factor was Mangosuthu Buthelezi's Inkatha Freedom Party and other, smaller black groups that had aligned themselves in the past with the South African state. Prior to the elections, thousands were killed in clashes between Inkatha and ANC/MDM supporters, especially in the Natal/Kwazulu region. As the positions of the ANC and NP began to converge in 1993, the IFP delegation walked out of the negotiations and formed a "Free-

dom Alliance" with white conservatives and the leaders of the Bophutatswana and Ciskei homelands. It collapsed in March 1994, following the violent overthrow of the Bophutatswana regime and the defeat of groups of armed white right-wingers that rallied to its defense. Following this debacle the IFP and more moderate white conservatives—the "Freedom Front"—agreed to participate in national elections. Attempts by more extreme right-wingers to disrupt the elections through a terrorist bombing campaign were crushed in a belated security crackdown.

The elections and the subsequent installation of the GNU were remarkably peaceful, despite organizational difficulties and instances of voting irregularities. In the end, all major parties accepted the result in which the ANC (incorporating MDM) attracted 63 percent of the vote, the NP 20 percent, IFP 10 percent, the Freedom Front 2.2 percent, and the PAC a disappointing 1.2 percent. Although the Government of National Unity, has gotten off to a good start, it still faces many challenges. Under even the best of circumstances, it will not be easy for South Africans to dismantle the legacies of apartheid.

DEVELOPMENT

The Government of National Unity's major priority has been the implementation of the comprehensive Reconstruction and Development Plan. A major aspect of the plan is a government commitment annually to build 1 million low-cost houses over a 5-year period.

FREEDOM

South Africa has been transformed into a model democracy. The current interim Constitution contains a bill of rights guaranteeing basic freedoms. The judicial branch has been empowered to safeguard these constitutional guarantees. Political violence has declined dramatically.

HEALTH/WELFARE

Public health and educational facilities are being desegregated. In its first 100 days, the new government introduced free child health-care and AIDS-prevention programs. A 10-year program of schooling is to be free to all pupils. Students have returned to school in large numbers. Crime remains a major problem, with a recent study concluding that South Africa is the most murderous country in the world.

ACHIEVEMENTS

With the end of international cultural and sporting boycotts, South African artists and athletes have become increasingly prominent. In 1993, Nelson Mandela and F. W. de Klerk were awarded the Nobel Peace Prize, following in the footsteps of their countrymen Albert Lethuli and Desmond Tutu.

Swaziland (Kingdom of Swaziland)

GEOGRAPHY

Area in Square Kilometers (Miles):
17,366 (6,704) (slightly smaller than
New Jersey)
Capital (Population): Mbabane
(administrative) (46,000); Lobanta
(legislative)
Climate: temperate; subtropical;
semiarid

PEOPLE

Population
Total: 998,800
Annual Growth Rate: 3.23%
Rural/Urban Population Ratio: 77/23
Major Languages: English; Siswati
Ethnic Makeup: predominantly African

Health
Life Expectancy at Birth: 53 years
(male); 61 years (female)
Infant Mortality Rate (Ratio):
90.7/1,000
Average Caloric Intake: 97% of FAO
minimum
Physicians Available (Ratio): 1/9,731

Religions
60% Christian; 40% traditional
indigenous

Education
Adult Literacy Rate: 67%

COMMUNICATION

Telephones: 17,000
Newspapers: 6

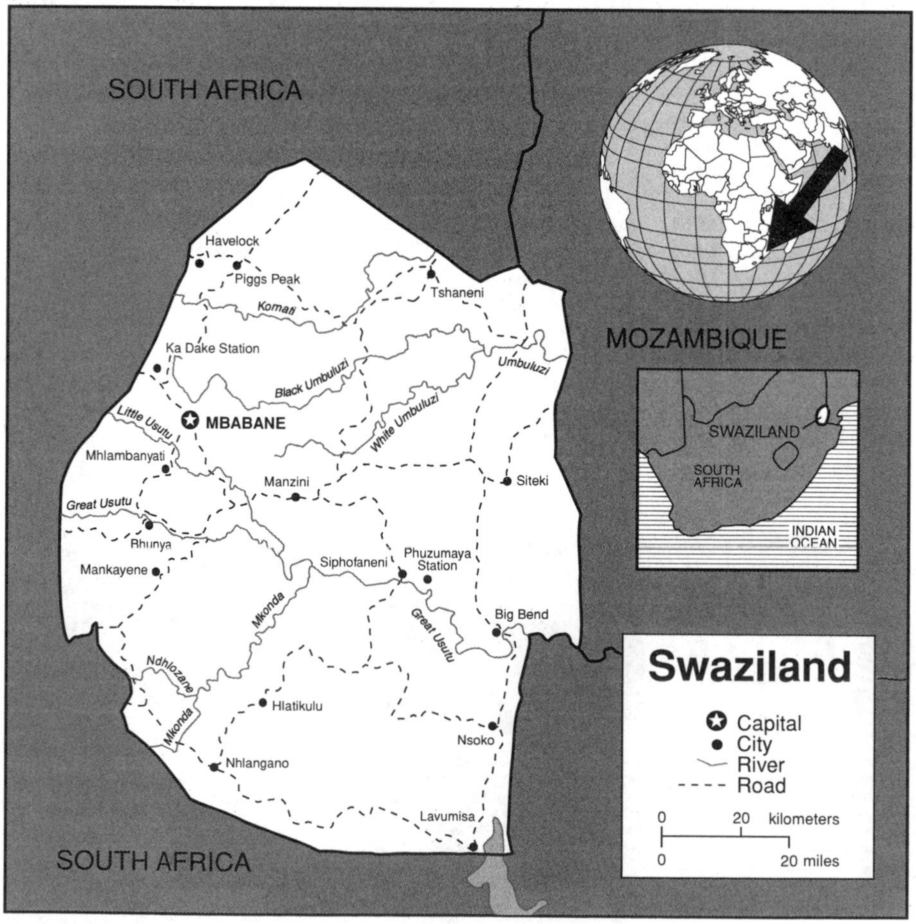

NCWALA

Visitors to Swaziland are frequently impressed by the pageantry associated with many of its state occasions. The most important ceremonies take place during the lunar *Ncwala* month, in December and January. This is a time when the nation reaffirms its bonds with the royal house. As the month begins, runners are sent to collect water from the ocean and various rivers, thus reestablishing their historic association with the Swazi. The main festival lasts for 6 days and includes the king's tasting of the first fruits, blessings to the ancestors, and prayers for rain. There is ritual dancing during the entire period, the most important of which is performed on the fourth day by the king and other members of royalty.

TRANSPORTATION

Highways—Kilometers (Miles): 2,853
(1,769)
Railroads—Kilometers (Miles): 297
(184)
Usable Airfields: 18

GOVERNMENT

Type: monarchy
Independence Date: September 6, 1968
Head of State/Government: King
Mswati III; Prime Minister Prince
Jameson Mbilini Olamini
Political Parties: banned; several
illegal parties exist
Suffrage: none

MILITARY

Number of Armed Forces: n/a
*Military Expenditures (% of Central
Government Expenditures):* n/a
Current Hostilities: none

ECONOMY

Currency ($ U.S. Equivalent): 3.54
emalangenis = $1
Per Capita Income/GDP: $3,490/$3.3
billion
Inflation Rate: 11.3%
Natural Resources: iron ore;
asbestos; coal; timber
Agriculture: corn; livestock;
sugarcane; citrus fruits; cotton; rice;
pineapples
Industry: milled sugar; cotton;
processed meat and wood; tourism;
chemicals; machinery; beverages;
consumer goods; paper milling;
mining

FOREIGN TRADE

Exports: $632 million
Imports: $734 billion

Swaziland

- ✪ Capital
- ● City
- ⌇ River
- --- Road

| Zulu and South African whites encroach on Swazi territory **1800s** | A protectorate is established by the British **1900** | Britain assumes control over Swaziland **1903** | Independence is restored **1968** | Parliament is dissolved and political parties are banned **1973** | King Sobuza dies **1982** | King Mswati III is crowned, ending the regency period marked by political instability **1986** | **1990s** |

The ban on political parties is defied

Swaziland's relationship with South Africa shifts

SWAZILAND

Swaziland is a small, landlocked kingdom sandwiched between the much larger states of Mozambique and South Africa. Casual observers have tended to look upon the country as a peaceful island of traditional Africa that has been immune to the continent's contemporary conflicts. This image is a product of the country's status as the only precolonial monarchy in sub-Saharan Africa to have survived into the modern era. Swazi sociopolitical organization is ostensibly governed in accordance with age-old structures and norms. But below this veneer of timelessness lies a dynamic society that has been subject to internal and external pressures.

The holding of restricted, nonparty elections in 1993 did not quell the debate over the country's political future between defenders of the status quo and those demanding a restoration of multiparty politics. A stay-away campaign in favor of reform at the beginning of the year, coupled with quiet diplomacy by Swaziland's neighbors, helped push the Swazi government toward dialogue on the issue. In July 1996, King Mswati announced the appointment of a committee of 30 to draw up a new constitution, but one of its members, Mario Masuku, of the People's United Democratic Movement (PUDEMO), withdrew, demanding the immediate repeal of a 1973 law banning parties.

From 1903 until the restoration of independence in 1968, the country remained a British colonial protectorate, despite sustained pressure for its incorporation into South Africa. Throughout the colonial period, the ruling Dlamini dynasty, which was led by the energetic Sobuza II after 1921, served successfully as a rallying point for national self-assertion on the key issues of

regaining control of alienated land and opposing union with South Africa. Sobuza's personal leadership in both struggles contributed to the overwhelming popularity of his royalist Imbokodvo Party in the elections of 1964, 1967, and 1972. In 1973, faced with a modest but articulate opposition party, the Ngwane National Liberatory Congress, Sobuza dissolved Parliament and repealed the Westminster-style Constitution, characterizing it as "un-Swazi." In 1979, a new, nonpartisan Parliament was chosen; but authority remained with the king, assisted by his advisory council, the Liqoqo.

Sobuza's death in 1982 left many wondering if Swaziland's unique monarchist institutions would survive. A prolonged power struggle increased tensions within the ruling order. Members of the Liqoqo seized effective power and appointed a new "Queen Regent," Ntombi. However, palace intrigue continued until Prince Makhosetive, Ntombi's teenage son, was installed as King Mswati III in 1986, at age 18. The new king approved the demotion of the Liqoqo back to its advisory status and has ruled through his appointed prime minister and cabinet.

One of the major challenges facing any Swazi government is its relationship with South Africa. Under Sobuza, Swaziland managed to maintain its political autonomy while accepting its economic dependence on its powerful neighbor. The king also maintained a delicate balance between the apartheid state and the forces opposing it. In the 1980s, this balance became tilted, with a greater degree of cooperation between the two countries' security forces in curbing suspected African National Congress activists. In an abrupt reversal of fortunes, Swaziland's prodemocracy activists now look to

the new ANC–led government in South Africa for support.

Swaziland's economy, like its politics, is the product of both internal and external initiatives. Since independence, the nation has enjoyed a high rate of economic growth, led by the expansion and diversification of its agriculture. Success in agriculture has promoted the development of secondary industries, such as a sugar refinery and a paper mill. There has also been increased exploitation of coal and asbestos. Another important source of revenue is tourism, which depends on weekend traffic from South Africa.

Swazi development has relied on capital-intensive, rather than labor-intensive, projects. As a result, disparities in local wealth and dependence on South African investment have increased. Only 16 percent of the Swazi population, including migrant workers in South Africa, were in formal-sector employment by 1989. Until recently the economy was boosted by international investors looking for a politically preferable window to the South African market. An example is Coca Cola's decision to move its regional headquarters and concentrate plant from South Africa to Swaziland; the plant employs only about 100 workers but accounts for 20 percent of all foreign-exchange earnings. The current reform process in South Africa, however, is reducing Swaziland's attraction as a center for corporate relocation and sanctions-busting. It has also increased pressure for greater democracy.

DEVELOPMENT

Much of Swaziland's economy is managed by the Tibiyo TakaNgwana, a royally controlled institution established in 1968 by Sobuza. It is responsible for the financial assets of the communal lands (upon which most Swazi farm) and mining operations.

FREEDOM

The current political order restricts many forms of opposition, although its defenders claim that local councils, *Tikhudlas*, allow for popular participation in decision making. The leading opposition group is the People's United Democratic Movement.

HEALTH/WELFARE

Swaziland's low life expectancy and high infant mortality rates have resulted in greater public health allocations. There has also been a greater emphasis placed on preventive medicine.

ACHIEVEMENTS

The University of Swaziland was established in the 1970s and now offers a full range of degree and diploma programs.

Zambia (Republic of Zambia)

GEOGRAPHY

Area in Square Kilometers (Miles):
752,972 (290,724) (slightly larger
than Texas)
Capital (Population): Lusaka
(982,000)
Climate: tropical to subtropical

PEOPLE

Population

Total: 9,159,000
Annual Growth Rate: 2.7%
Rural/Urban Population Ratio: 51/49
Major Lanugages: English; Bemba;
Nyanja; Ila-Tonga; Lozi; others
Ethnic Makeup: predominantly Bantu

Health

Life Expectancy at Birth: 43 years
(male); 43 years (female)
Infant Mortality Rate (Ratio):
86/1,000
Average Caloric Intake: 90% of FAO
minimum
Physicians Available (Ratio): 1/6,959

Religions

50% Christian; 48% traditional
indigenous; 2% Hindu, Muslim, and
others

Education

Adult Literacy Rate: 73%

COMMUNICATION

Telephones: 81,000 *Newspapers:* 3

THE H-P WOMAN'S DEVELOPMENT CORPORATION

The H-P Woman's Corporation is an entirely female-owned and -run
company aimed at helping women to get ahead by starting self-sustaining small businesses. Named after its founder, women's-rights lawyer
Tsitsi Himuyanga-Phiri, it loans small amounts of money to women
who lack the necessary collateral or male permission to get ordinary
bank loans. In addition to money, H-P provides facilities for project
assessment, accounting, market research, legal, and record keeping. Its
Mother's Aid program provides such services as child care, house
cleaning, and home nursing to allow its loan recipients to devote
themselves to their businesses. Successful entrepreneurs have become
shareholders; H-P has survived since 1989 without any government or
donor-agency assistance. With only 350,000 jobs currently available in
Zambia's unproductive formal sector, innovative grassroots initiatives
like the H-P Development Corporation could play a key role in the
nation's economic reconstruction.

TRANSPORTATION

Highways—Kilometers (Miles):
36,370 (22,549)
Railroads—Kilometers (Miles): 1,266
(785)
Usable Airfields: 113

GOVERNMENT

Type: multiparty republic
Independence Date: October 24, 1964
Head of State: President Frederick
Chiluba
Political Parties: Movement for
Multiparty Democracy; United
National Independence Party;
National Party
Suffrage: universal at 18

MILITARY

Number of Armed Forces: 24,400
*Military Expenditures (% of Central
Government Expenditures):* 1.4%
Current Hostilities: none

ECONOMY

Currency ($ U.S. Equivalent): 672.8
kwachas = $1
Per Capita Income/GDP: $860/$7.9
billion
Inflation Rate: above 200% (est.)
Natural Resources: copper; zinc;
lead; cobalt; coal
Agriculture: corn; tobacco; cotton;
peanuts; sugarcane
Industry: foodstuffs; beverages;
chemicals; textiles; fertilizer

FOREIGN TRADE

Exports: $1.01 billion
Imports: $1.13 billion

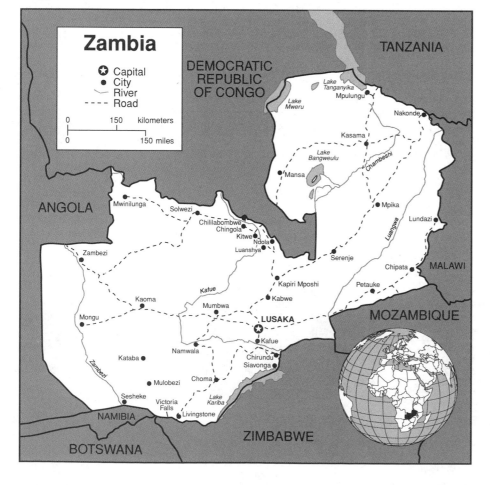

Rhodes' South
African Company
is chartered by
the British
government
1889
●

Development of
the Copperbelt
1924–1934
●

Federation of
Northern
Rhodesia,
Southern
Rhodesia, and
Nyasaland is
formed; still part
of British Empire
1953–1963
●

Zambia gains
independence
1964
●

Nationalization of
51% of all
industries
1969
●

Zambia becomes
a one-party state
under the United
National
Independence
Party
1972
●

South African
military raids on
Zambia
1980s
●

1990s

In the face of
mounting unrest,
President
Kenneth Kaunda
agrees to
internationally
observed
multiparty
elections

Kaunda is
defeated; victor
Frederick Chiluba
is immediately
sworn in as the
nation's second
president

Foreign Minister
Vernon
Mwaanga
resigns over
allegations of
drug trafficking,
the 11th minister
to resign from
Chiluba's cabinet

ZAMBIA

In November 1996, President Frederick Chiluba and his Movement for Multiparty Democracy (MMD) were reelected in a poll boycotted by much of the opposition amidst widespread reports of voter registration irregularities. The election was preceded by the enactment of a new constitution that barred former president Kenneth Kaunda and others from running. A brief bombing campaign in March by a shadowy group called the "Black Mamba" (after an especially poisonous snake species) led to treason charges being brought against nine leading members of Kenneth Kaunda's United National Independence Party (UNIP). Growing political discontent was accompanied by continued economic decline, which had been a factor in the 1991 defeat of UNIP. An unquestioned landslide victory by Chiluba's MMD gave hope that Zambia's "hour has come."

But Chiluba's government has since been plagued by annual inflation above 200 percent, shrinking GDP, exposures of high-level corruption including drug trafficking, and desertions from the MMD to the new National Party. As a result, thousands of educated Zambians have left their country in search of opportunities elsewhere.

The roots of Zambia's woes lie in Kaunda's 27-year rule. During much of this period, the nation's economy, along with the well-being of its citizenry, steadily declined. Kaunda consistently blamed his country's setbacks on external forces rather than on his government's failings. There was some justification for his position. The high rate of return on exported copper made the nation one of the most prosperous in Africa until 1975. Since then, fluctuating, but generally depressed, prices for the metal—and the disruption of landlocked Zambia's traditional sea outlets as a result of strife in neighboring states—have had disastrous economic consequences. Nonetheless, it has long been apparent that internal factors have also contributed to Zambia's decay and have created barriers to its recovery.

From the early years of independence, Kaunda and UNIP showed little tolerance for political opposition. In 1972, the country was legally transformed into a one-party state in which power was concentrated in the hands of Kaunda and his fellow members of UNIP's Central Committee. After 1976, the government ruled with state-of-emergency powers. Although Zambia was never as repressive as such neighboring states as Malawi and Zaire, torture and political detention without trial were common.

In its rule, UNIP was supposedly guided by the philosophy of "humanism," a term that became synonymous with the thoughts of Kaunda. The party also claimed adherence to socialism. Although it was once a mass party that spearheaded Zambia's struggle for majority rule and independence, UNIP came to stand for little other than the perpetuation of its own power.

An underlying economic problem has been the decline of rural production, despite Zambia's considerable agricultural potential. The underdevelopment of farming is rooted in the colonial policies that favored mining to the exclusion of other sectors. Since independence, the rural areas have continued to be neglected in terms of infrastructural investment. Until recently Zambian farmers were paid little for their produce, while the urban diet was maintained through government subsidization of imported food. The result has been a continuous influx of individuals into the towns, despite a lack of jobs, and falling food production.

Zambia's rural decline has severely constrained the government's ability to meet the challenge imposed by the depressed international price of copper. Falling prices have resulted in severe shortages of foreign exchange and mounting indebtedness. After years of relative inertia, the government, during the 1980s, devoted greater attention to rural development. Agricultural production rose modestly in response to increased incentives. But the size and desperate condition of the urban population discouraged the government from decontrolling prices altogether; rising maize prices in 1986 set off riots that left at least 30 people dead. The new MMD government ended the subsidies.

By 1990, the government's continuing economic crisis had dovetailed with rising agitation for a return to multiparty democracy. Despite the president's attempts to label multiparty advocates as "misfits, malcontents, drug-peddlers and dissidents," the movement grew, with the support of Zambia's major labor federation, its powerful Catholic Church, and a number of prominent UNIP backbenchers. In June–July 1990, severe riots culminated in a coup attempt, which, although unsuccessful, exposed the weakness of Kaunda's regime, forcing it finally to agree to free and fair elections.

DEVELOPMENT

Higher producer prices for agriculture, technical assistance, and rural-resettlement schemes are part of government efforts to raise agricultural production. The agricultural sector has shown growth. However, financial inputs are needed, and much maize is smuggled over the border to Zaire, reducing Zambia's potential for recovery.

FREEDOM

The MMD's victory has been seen as a great victory for democracy. But some, fearing a continuation or revival of the bad habits of its predecessor, are demanding that the new government honor its election commitments to privatize the media and reform the security services.

HEALTH/WELFARE

Life expectancy rates have increased in Zambia since independence, as a result of improved health-care facilities. In 1986, some 80% of primary-age children attended school; about 1 out of 4 went on to at least some secondary education. AIDS increasingly looms as a critical problem in Zambia.

ACHIEVEMENTS

Zambia has long played a major role in the fight against white supremacy in Southern Africa. From 1964 until 1980, it was a major base for Zimbabwe nationalists. Namibia's SWAPO and South Africa's ANC have also had headquarters in Zambia's capital of Lusaka.

Zimbabwe (Republic of Zimbabwe)

GEOGRAPHY

Area in Square Kilometers (Miles): 390,759 (150,873) (slightly smaller than Montana)
Capital (Population): Harare (1,200,000)
Climate: subtropical

PEOPLE

Population
Total: 11,272,000
Annual Growth Rate: 1.78%
Rural/Urban Population Ratio: 73/27
Major Languages: English; (Chi)Shona; (Si)Ndebele; others
Ethnic Makeup: 71% Shona; 16% Ndebele; 13% others

Health
Life Expectancy at Birth: 40 years (male); 43 years (female)
Infant Mortality Rate (Ratio): 72.7/1,000
Average Caloric Intake: 86% of FAO minimum
Physicians Available (Ratio): 1/6,900

Religion(s)
50% syncretic (part Christian, part indigenous beliefs) 25% Christian;
24% traditional indigenous; 1% Muslim

Education
Adult Literacy Rate: 67%

COMMUNICATION

Telephones: 247,000
Newspapers: 2

AGRICULTURAL SURPLUSES AND FOOD SECURITY

During Zimbabwe's first decade of independence, farmers on both small communal farms and large commercial estates enjoyed great success in improving local food production. Peasant farmers boosted their marketed maize surpluses by as much as 1,000 percent, while their statistical share of agricultural production rose from 8 to 64 percent. Large-scale commercial farmers were able to triple their output. Government loans and investment in infrastructure, an end to wartime dislocations, and the modest efforts to resettle landless Zimbabweans contributed to this growth in productivity.

Unfortunately, the very success of Zimbabwean agriculture encouraged complacency regarding the need to assure food security. Allegedly encouraged by international financiers, record agricultural exports in 1990 and 1991 left Zimbabwe without adequate emergency stocks to cope with the severe 1992 drought, a painful lesson.

TRANSPORTATION

Highways—Kilometers (Miles): 85,237 (52,964)
Railroads—Kilometers (Miles): 2,743 (1,704)
Usable Airfields: 471

GOVERNMENT

Type: paramilitary democracy
Independence Date: April 18, 1980
Head of State: Executive President Robert Mugabe
Political Parties: Zimbabwe African National Union–Patriotic Front; Zimbabwe African National Union–Sithole; Zimbabwe Unity Movement; Democratic Party; Forum Party
Suffrage: universal over 18

MILITARY

Number of Armed Forces: 70,000
Military Expenditures (% of Central Government Expenditures): 6.0%
Current Hostilities: none

ECONOMY

Currency ($ U.S. Equivalent): 8.38 Zimbabwe dollars = $1
Per Capita Income/GDP: $1,580/$17.4 billion
Inflation Rate: 22%
Natural Resources: gold; chrome ore; coal; copper; nickel; iron ore; silver; asbestos
Agriculture: tobacco; corn; sugar; cotton; livestock
Industry: mining; steel; textiles

FOREIGN TRADE

Exports: $1.7 billion
Imports: $1.8 billion

Zimbabwe
- ✪ Capital
- ● City
- River
- - - - Road

0 ___ 75 kilometers
0 ___ 75 miles

ZIMBABWE

Zimbabwe achieved its formal independence in April 1980, after a 14-year armed struggle by its disenfranchised black African majority. Before 1980, the country had been called Southern Rhodesia—a name that honored Cecil Rhodes, the British imperialist who had masterminded the colonial occupation of the territory in the late nineteenth century. For its black African majority, Rhodesia's name was thus an expression of their subordination to a small minority of privileged white settlers whose racial hegemony was the product of Rhodes' conquest. The new name, *Zimbabwe,* was symbolic of the greatness of the nation's precolonial roots.

THE PRECOLONIAL PAST

By the fifteenth century, Zimbabwe had become the center of a series of states that prospered through their trade in gold and other goods with Indian Ocean merchants. These civilizations left as their architectural legacy the remains of stone settlements known as *zimbabwes.* The largest of these, the so-called Great Zimbabwe, lies near the modern town of Masvingo. Within its massive walls are dozens of stella, topped with distinctive carved birds whose likeness has become a symbol of the modern state. Unfortunately, early European fortuneseekers and archaeologists destroyed much of the archaeological evidence of this site, but what survives confirms that the state had trading contacts as far afield as China.

From the sixteenth century, the Zimbabwean civilizations seem to have declined, possibly as a result of the disruption of the East African trading networks by the Portuguese. Nevertheless, the states themselves survived until the nineteenth century, while their cultural legacy is very much alive today, especially among the approximately 80 percent of Zimbabwe's population who speak (Chi)Shona.

Zimbabwe's other major ethnolinguistic community are the (Si)Ndebele speakers, who today account for about 16 percent of the population. This group traces its local origin to the mid-nineteenth-century conquest of much of modern Zimbabwe by invaders from the south under the leadership of Umzilagazi, who established a militarily strong Ndebele kingdom, which subsequently was ruled by his son.

WHITE RULE

Zimbabwe's colonial history is unique in that it was never under the direct rule of a European power. In 1890, the lands of the Ndebele and Shona were invaded by agents of Rhodes's British South Africa Company (BSACO). In the 1890s, both groups put up stiff resistance to the encroachments of the BSACO settlers, but eventually they succumbed to the invaders. In 1924, the BSACO administration was dissolved and Southern Rhodesia became a self-governing British Crown colony. "Self-government" was, in fact, confined to the white-settler community, which grew rapidly but never numbered more than 5 percent of the population.

In 1953, Southern Rhodesia was federated with the British colonial territories of Northern Rhodesia (Zambia) and Nyasaland (Malawi). This Central African Federation was supposed to evolve into a "multiracial" dominion; but from the beginning, it was perceived by the black majority in all three territories as a vehicle for continued white domination. As the Federation's first prime minister put it, the partnership of blacks and whites in building the new state would be analogous to a horse and its rider—no one had any illusions as to which race group would continue to be the beast of burden.

In 1963, the Federation collapsed as a result of local resistance. Black nationalists established the independent "nonracial" states of Malawi and Zambia. For a while, it appeared that majority rule would also come to Southern Rhodesia. The local black community was increasingly well organized and militant in demanding full citizenship rights. However, in 1962, the white electorate responded to this challenge by voting into office the Rhodesia Front (RF), a party determined to uphold white supremacy at any cost. Using already-existing emergency powers, the new government moved to suppress the two major black nationalist movements: the Zimbabwe African People's Union (ZAPU) and the Zimbabwe African National Union (ZANU).

RHODESIA DECLARES INDEPENDENCE

In a bid to consolidate white power along the lines of the neighboring apartheid regime of South Africa, the RF, now led by Ian Smith, made its 1965 Unilateral Declaration of Independence (UDI) of any ties to the British Crown. Great Britain, along with the United Nations, refused to recognize this move. In 1967, the UN imposed mandatory economic sanctions against the "illegal" RF regime. But the sanctions were not fully effective, largely due to the fact that they were flouted by South Africa and the Portuguese authorities who controlled most of Mozambique until 1974. The United States continued openly to purchase Rhodesian chrome for a number of years, while many states and individuals engaged in more covert forms of sanctions-busting. The Rhodesian economy initially benefited from the porous blockade, which encouraged the development of a wide range of import-substitution industries.

With the sanctions having only a limited effect and Great Britain and the rest of the international community unwilling to engage in more active measures, it soon became clear that the burden of overthrowing the RF regime would be borne by the local population. ZANU and ZAPU, as underground movements, began to engage in armed struggle beginning in 1966. The success of their attacks initially was limited; but from 1972, the Rhodesian Security Forces were increasingly besieged by the nationalists' guerrilla campaign. The 1974 liberation of Mozambique from the Portuguese greatly increased the effectiveness of the ZANU forces, who were allowed to infiltrate into Rhodesia from Mozambican territory. Meanwhile, their ZAPU comrades launched attacks from bases in Zambia. In 1976, the two groups became loosely affiliated as the Patriotic Front.

Unable to stop the military advance of the Patriotic Front, which was resulting in a massive white exodus, the RF attempted to forge a power-sharing arrangement that preserved major elements of settler privilege. Although rejected by ZANU or ZAPU, this "internal settlement" was implemented in 1978–1979. A predominantly black government took office, but real power remained in white hands, and the fighting only intensified. Finally, in 1979, all the belligerent parties, meeting at Lancaster House in London, agreed to a compromise peace, which opened the door to majority rule while containing a number of constitutional provisions designed to reassure the white minority. In the subsequent elections, held in 1980, ZANU captured 57 and ZAPU 20 out of the 80 seats elected by the "common roll." Another 20 seats, which were reserved for whites for 7 years as a result of the Lancaster House agreement, were captured by the Conservative Alliance (the new name for the RF). ZANU leader Robert Mugabe became independent Zimbabwe's first prime minister.

THE RHODESIAN LEGACY

The political, economic, and social problems inherited by the Mugabe government were formidable. Rhodesia had essentially been divided into "two nations": one black, the other white. Segregation prevailed in virtually all areas of life, with those facilities open to blacks being vastly inferior to those open to whites. The better half of the national territory had also been reserved for white ownership. Large commercial farms prospered in this white area, growing maize and tobacco for export as well as a diversified mix of crops for domestic consumption. In contrast, the black areas, formally known as Tribal Trust Lands, suffered from inferior soil and rainfall, overcrowding, and poor infrastructure. Most black adults had little choice but to obtain seasonal work in the white areas. Black workers on white plantations, together with the large number of domestic servants, were particularly impoverished. But until the 1970s, there were also few opportunities for skilled blacks as a result of a de facto "color bar," which reserved the best jobs for whites.

Despite its stated commitment to revolutionary socialist objectives, since 1980, the Mugabe government has taken an evolutionary approach in dismantling the socioeconomic structures of old Rhodesia. This cautious policy is, in part, based on an appreciation that these same structures support what, by regional standards, is a relatively prosperous and self-sufficient economy. Until 1990, the government's hands were also partially tied by the Lancaster House accords, wherein private property, including the large settler estates, could not be confiscated without compensation. In its first years, the government nevertheless made impressive progress in improving the livelihoods of the Zimbabwean majority by redistributing some of the surplus of the still white-dominated private sector. With the lifting of sanctions, mineral, maize, and tobacco exports expanded and import restrictions eased. Work-

ers' incomes rose, and a minimum wage, which notably covered farm employees, was introduced. Rising consumer purchasing power initially benefited local manufacturers. Health and educational facilities were expanded, while a growing number of blacks began to occupy management positions in the civil service and, to a lesser extent, in businesses.

Zimbabwe had hoped that foreign investment and aid would pay for an ambitious scheme to buy out many white farmers and to settle African peasants on their land. However, funding shortfalls have resulted in only modest resettlement. Approximately 4,000 white farmers own more than one third of the land. In 1992, the government passed a bill that allows for the involuntary purchase of up to 50 percent of this land at an officially set price. While enjoying overwhelming domestic support, this land-redistribution measure has come under considerable external criticism for violating the private-property and judicial "rights" of the large-scale farmers. Others have pointed out that, besides producing large surpluses of food in nondrought years, many jobs are tied to the commercial estates. Revelations in 1993–1994 that some confiscated properties had been turned over to leading ZANU politicians gave rise to further controversy.

While gradually abandoning its professed desire to build a socialist society, the Zimbabwean government has continued to face a classic dilemma of all industrializing societies: whether to continue to use tight import controls to protect its existing manufacturing base or to open up its economy in the hopes of

enjoying a takeoff based on export-oriented growth. While many Zimbabwean manufacturers would be vulnerable to greater foreign competition, there is now a widespread consensus that limits of the local market have contributed to stagnating output and physical depreciation of local industry in recent years.

POLITICAL DEVELOPMENT

The Mugabe government has promoted reconciliation across the racial divide. Although the reserved seats for whites were abolished in 1987, the white minority, who now make up less than 2 percent of the population, are well represented within government as well as business. Unfortunately, Mugabe's ZANU administration has shown less tolerance of its political opponents, especially ZAPU. ZANU was originally a breakaway faction of ZAPU. At the time of this split, in 1963, the differences between the two movements had largely been over tactics. But elections in 1980 and 1985 confirmed that the followings of both movements have become ethnically based, with most Shona supporting ZANU and Ndebele supporting ZAPU.

Initially, ZANU agreed to share power with ZAPU. However, in 1982, the alleged discoveries of secret arms caches, which ZANU claimed ZAPU was stockpiling for a coup, led to the dismissal of the ZAPU ministers. Some leading ZAPU figures were also detained. The confrontation led to violence that very nearly degenerated into a full-scale civil war. From 1982 to 1984, the Zimbabwean Army,

(Oxfam America photo)

As in many African institutions, decisions in Zimbabwean organizations are often made by consensus, arrived at after long discussions.

Heyday of the gold trade and Great Zimbabwe **1400s–1500s**	The Ndebele state emerges in Zimbabwe **1840s**	The Pioneer Column: arrival of the white settlers **1890**	Chimurenga: rising against the white intruders, ending in repression by whites **1895–1897**	Local government in Southern Rhodesia is placed in the hands of white settlers **1924**	Unilateral Declaration of Independence **1965**	Armed struggle begins **1966**	ZANU leader Robert Mugabe becomes Zimbabwe's first prime minister **1980**

1990s

ZANU and ZAPU merge and win the 1990 elections	Severe drought in 1992 leads to widespread suffering and economic depression	Elections in 1995 result in a landslide victory for ruling ZANU-PF; Mugabe is reelected in 1996; both elections were boycotted by the opposition

dominated by former ZANU and Rhodesian units, carried out a brutal counterinsurgency campaign against supposed ZAPU dissidents in the largely Ndebele areas of western Zimbabwe. Thousands of civilians were killed—especially by the notorious Fifth Brigade, which operated outside the normal military command structure. Many more fled to Botswana, including, for a period, the ZAPU leader, Joshua Nkomo.

Until 1991, Mugabe's stated intention was to create a one-party state in Zimbabwe. With his other black and white opponents compromised by their past association with the RF and its internal settlement, this largely meant coercing ZAPU into dissolving itself into ZANU. However, the increased support for ZAPU in its core Ndebele constituencies during the 1985 elections led to a renewed emphasis on the carrot over the stick in bringing about the union. In 1987, ZAPU formally merged into ZANU, but their shotgun wedding has made for an uneasy marriage.

With the demise of ZAPU, new forces have emerged in opposition to Mugabe and the drive for a one-party state. Principal among these is the Zimbabwe Unity Movement (ZUM), led by former ZANU member Edger Tekere. In the 1990 elections, ZUM received about 20 percent of the vote, in a poll that saw a sharp drop in voter participation. The election was also marred by serious restrictions on opposition activity and blatant voter intimidation. The deaths of ZUM supporters in the period before the election reinforced the message of the government-controlled media that a vote for the

opposition was an act of suicide. A senior member of the Central Intelligence Organization and a ZANU activist were subsequently convicted of the murder of ZUM organizing secretary Patrick Kombayi. However, they were pardoned by Mugabe.

Mugabe initially claimed that his 1990 victory was a mandate to establish a one-party state. But in 1991, the changing international climate, the continuing strength of the opposition, and growing opposition within ZANU itself caused him to shelve the project. Under 1992 election law, however, ZANU alone was made eligible for state funding.

The survival of political pluralism in Zimbabwe reflects the emergence of a civil society that is increasingly resistant to the concentration of power. Independent nongovernmental organizations have successfully taken up many social human-rights issues. Less successful have been attempts to promote an independent press, which has remained almost entirely in government/ZANU hands.

In 1992, the Forum Party, a new opposition movement, was launched, under the leadership of former chief justice Enoch Dumbutshena. But it failed to break the mold of Zimbabwean politics due to its own internal splits and failure to unite with other groups. As a result, Mugabe was easily reelected in March 1996 in a low voter turnout (it was ultimately boycotted by the entire opposition).

Notwithstanding its continuing electoral success, public confidence in the ZANU government has been greatly eroded by its

relative failure in handling the 1992 drought crisis. Despite warning signs of the impending catastrophe, little attempt was made to stockpile food. This failure resulted in widespread hunger and dependence on expensive food imports. Long-neglected waterworks, especially those serving Bulawayo, the country's second-largest city, proved to be inadequate. The government also lost support due to its seeming insensitivity to the plight of ordinary Zimbabweans suffering from high rates of unemployment and inflation. With inflation at 22 percent, a civil servants strike was sparked in August 1996 by an across-the-board 6 percent raise for ordinary workers as compared to a 130 percent raise for members of Parliament.

Notwithstanding such controversies and a still weak economy, the welfare of most Zimbabwean has improved since 1980, and the prospects for future growth are good. Nonracial policies are helping to overcome the legacy of the "two nations."

DEVELOPMENT

Peasant production has increased dramatically since independence, creating grain reserves and providing exports for the region. The work of communal farmers has been recognized both within Zimbabwe and internationally.

FREEDOM

Since the 1990 lifting of the state of emergency that had been in effect since the days of the Federation, Zimbabwe's human-rights record has generally improved. Institutions of government, however, especially the Central Intelligence Organization, are still accused of extrajudicial abuses.

HEALTH/WELFARE

Public expenditure on health and education has risen dramatically since independence. Most Zimbabweans now enjoy access to medical facilities, while primary-school enrollment has multiplied fourfold. Higher education has also been greatly expanded. But the advances are threatened by downturns in the economy, and school fees have been reintroduced.

ACHIEVEMENTS

Zimbabwe's capital city of Harare has become an arts and communications center for Southern Africa. Many regional as well as local filmmakers, musicians, and writers based in the city enjoy international reputations. And the distinctive malachite carvings of Zimbabwean sculptors are highly valued in the international art market.

Annotated Table of Contents

Articles from the World Press

Topic Guide to Articles

TOPIC AREA	TREATED IN	TOPIC AREA	TREATED IN
Agriculture	1. Sub-Saharan Africa 7. Africa's Oldest Survivors	Economy	2. False Hope 7. Africa's Oldest Survivors 10. Botswana: One African Success Story 11. An African Star? 18. South Africa's Promise
AIDS	1. Sub-Saharan Africa		
Apartheid	17. Afrikaners after Apartheid	Environment	12. An African Forest Harbors Vast Wealth
Arts	1. Sub-Saharan Africa 16. A Nation of Poets	Exports	3. Waiting to Export 11. An African Star?
Athletes	9. Africa's Quest for Gold	Foreign Aid	1. Sub-Saharan Africa 13. Kenya: A Tarnished Jewel
Beliefs	5. In the Shadows 6. Voodoo Nation 20. African Tradition of Polygamy	Foreign Investment	2. False Hope 3. Waiting to Export
Civil War	19. A Divided Country	Foreign Relations	13. Kenya: A Tarnished Jewel
Class	7. Africa's Oldest Survivors	History	1. Sub-Saharan Africa 4. Who Was Responsible? 7. Africa's Oldest Survivors 13. Kenya: A Tarnished Jewel 14. A Life of Bare Essentials 15. Nigeria: Inside the Dismal Tunnel 17. Afrikaners after Apartheid
Conservation	1. Sub-Saharan Africa 12. An African Forest Harvests Vast Wealth		
Crime	18. South Africa's Promise		
Cultural Roots	4. Who Was Responsible? 5. In the Shadows 7. Africa's Oldest Survivors 16. A Nation of Poets	HIV/AIDS	1. Sub-Saharan Africa
		Human Rights	18. South Africa's Promise
Current Leaders	1. Sub-Saharan Africa 10. Botswana: One African Success Story 13. Kenya: A Tarnished Jewel 18. South Africa's Promise	Independence	13. Kenya: A Tarnished Jewel
		Medicine	5. In the Shadows
Debt	2. False Hope 3. Waiting to Export	Militarism	15. Nigeria: Inside the Dismal Tunnel
Democracy	1. Sub-Saharan Africa 10. Botswana: One African Success Story 11. An African Star? 13. Kenya: A Tarnished Jewel 18. South Africa's Promise	Mining	1. Sub-Saharan Africa
		Muslims	19. A Divided Country
		Natives	7. Africa's Oldest Survivors 14. A Life of Bare Essentials
Economic Development	1. Sub-Saharan Africa 2. False Hope 3. Waiting to Export 7. Africa's Oldest Survivors 10. Botswana: One African Success Story 11. An African Star? 12. African Forest Harbors Vast Wealth 18. South Africa's Promise	Natural Resources	1. Sub-Saharan Africa 7. Africa's Oldest Survivors 12. An African Forest Harbors Vast Wealth
		Nomadic Life	14. A Life of Bare Essentials
		Olympics	9. Africa's Quest for Gold
Economic Reform	10. Botswana: One African Success Story 11. An African Star? 18. South Africa's Promise	Peacekeeping	1. Sub-Saharan Africa

TOPIC AREA	TREATED IN	TOPIC AREA	TREATED IN
Political Reform	1. Sub-Saharan Africa 18. South Africa's Promise	Slavery	4. Who Was Responsible?
Political Unrest	15. Nigeria: Inside the Dismal Tunnel	Tourism	1. Sub-Saharan Africa
Politics	10. Botswana: One African Success Story 15. Nigeria: Inside the Dismal Tunnel 18. South Africa's Promise	Tribalism	1. Sub-Saharan Africa
		Turmoil	19. A Divided Country
Railroads	11. An African Star?	Violence	15. Nigeria: Inside the Dismal Tunnel 19. A Divided Country
Regional Integration	1. Sub-Saharan Africa	Voodoo	5. In the Shadows
Religion	5. In the Shadows 6. Voodoo Nation 19. A Divided Country	Wildlife	1. Sub-Saharan Africa
		Witchcraft	5. In the Shadows
Safari	1. Sub-Saharan Africa	Women	8. I Am Not Just an African Woman 11. An African Star? 20. African Tradition of Polygamy

Articles from the World Press

Article 1   *The Economist,* September 7th 1996

SUB-SAHARAN AFRICA

So Little Done, So Much to Do

*The world is washing its hands of sub-Saharan Africa, leaving its 700m people
to save themselves. They might yet succeed if, like the new South Africans,
they can work together, writes Tony Thomas*

Tony Thomas

TUCKED away beside the museum in Bulawayo is a statue of Cecil Rhodes. It used to bestride Main Street, facing north to symbolise his dream that a swathe of British territory, coloured imperial red on the map, would stretch from the Cape to Cairo. Until a few years ago, the empire builder's likeness also appeared in the watermark of Rhodesia's pound note, ringed with these words from a poem by Rudyard Kipling:

The immense and brooding spirit still
Shall quicken and control.
Living he was the land, and dead,
His soul shall be her soul.

The vision has gone with the wind. The European powers which formalised their scramble for Africa at the Conference of Berlin in 1884–85 have all departed. So have the white minority governments that Rhodes's imperial Britain planted and then, somewhat deviously, helped uproot—starting with Kenya after the Mau Mau rebellion, moving on to the Central African Federation of Rhodesia and Nyasaland (now Zambia, Zimbabwe and Malawi) and ending, eventually, with a democratic election in South Africa in 1994.

The process of European disengaged began in earnest with Kwame Nkrumah, the antithesis of Rhodes, whose Gold Coast (renamed Ghana) in 1957 became the first black African colony to achieve independence. As it happens, his statue, too, is tucked away beside a museum, in Accra. With a rusting right foot, it looks even more forlorn than Rhodes's. A notice explains that it used to stand in front of Parliament House until it was attacked by a mob after a military coup in 1966.

Like Rhodes, Nkrumah had his own pan-African dream: an Africa united against what he saw as the neo-colonial machinations of its former masters, and especially the multinational corporations of the United States.

A few leading African nationalists shared part of his vision, among them Patrice Lumumba in the Belgian Congo (later Zaire), Julius Nyerere in Tanganyika (Tanzania) and Kenneth Kaunda in Northern Rhodesia (Zambia). In many more African countries, radical rhetoric about the wickedness of neo-colonialism was little more than a cover for tribal struggles to fill the power vacuum left by the voluntary or forced withdrawal of the colonial powers.

In the cold-war era, outsiders largely disregarded the African origins and complexities of these conflicts. They grotesquely oversimplified the problems by imposing an east-west perspective on everything. If the Soviet Union supported nationalist x (eg, in Angola, Agostinho Neto), then America would support nationalist anti-x (first Holden Roberto and then Jonas Savimbi).

The outside powers provided some of the world's most unpleasant regimes with arms and aid. President Reagan welcomed Mobutu Sese Seko, the predatory boss of the Zairean kleptocracy, to the White House as "a voice of good sense and goodwill", and decided to "Go with Doe" after Master-Sergeant Samuel K. Doe had stolen a spectacularly corrupt election in Liberia. France sent soldiers to sustain incumbent dictators in francophone Africa. Britain's Margaret Thatcher played footsie with the white supremacist government in Pretoria, even after apartheid started to crumble, and dismissed Nelson Mandela's African National Congress as "a typical terrorist organisation". Russia's protégés in Mozambique, Angola and Ethiopia converted already poor lands into just about the most wretched places on earth.

But with the cold war over, both Nkrumah's dream and his nightmare have vanished. The implosion of the Soviet Union and its communist empire in Eastern Europe has discredited his authoritarian brand of African socialism; yet at the same time, his "neo-colonial" powers and their multinational corporations, far from exploiting Africa, have quite lost interest in the place.

Not, of course, in the Arab states that border on the Mediterranean. These are too close to Europe's soft un-

| Measuring Misery United Nations Human Development Index,* 1993 ||||
Country	Rank	Country	Rank
Mauritius	54	Central African Rep.	148
Seychelles	60	Mauritania	149
Boswana	71	Madagascar	150
South Africa	100	Rwanda	152
Swaziland	110	Senegal	153
Namibia	116	Benin	154
Gabon	120	Uganda	155
Cape Verde	122	Malawi	157
Zimbabwe	124	Liberia	158
Congo	125	Guinea	160
Cameroon	127	Guinea-Bissau	161
Kenya	128	Gambia	162
Ghana	129	Chad	163
Lesotho	130	Djibouti	164
Equatorial Guinea	131	Angola	165
São Tomé & Príncipe	132	Burundi	166
Zambia	136	Mozambique	167
Nigeria	137	Ethiopia	168
Comoros	139	Burkina Faso	170
Togo	140	Mali	171
Zaire	141	Somalia	172
Tanzania	144	Sierra Leone	173
Sudan	146	Niger	174
Côte D'Ivoire	147		

colony in Africa. The United States Institute for National Strategic Studies, a Washington-based research centre, could not have spelled out the message more clearly than it did in its strategic assessment for 1995: "The US has essentially no serious military/geostrategic interests in Africa any more, other than the inescapable fact that its vastness poses an obstacle to deployment in the Middle East and South Asia, whether by sea or air."

Among the European nations, France alone seems willing to go on providing military and financial aid at current levels to its former possessions, which account for one-third of its population. This French commitment will, however, come under strain if the Chirac government achieves its ambition to streamline France's armed forces and abolish conscription. And it is hard to see how the franc of the Communauté Financière Africaine (CFA) can survive if France becomes part of a European Monetary Union.

The outside world's dismay is understandable. In the past 30 years or so, Africa has averaged a couple of coups a year, and more than two dozen presidents and prime ministers have lost their lives through political violence. Four of Africa's potentially richest and most powerful states—Angola, Nigeria, Sudan and Zaire—are in desperate straits. Somalia has disintegrated, and Liberia, Rwanda and Burundi are heading that way.

These depredations are reflected in the global development ratings drawn up by the United Nations Development Programme (UNDP), which seeks to measure human progress on such things as longevity, education and living standards. As the accompanying table shows, most African countries cluster near the bottom end of the scale. Of the world's poorest three dozen countries, two dozen are in sub-Saharan Africa. Worse, during the 1980s the area's GNP per head declined by more than 1% a year as its population soared. Two-fifths of all Africans are aged under 16, compared with only one-fifth in the developed world.

In the past couple of years, the World Bank and the IMF have hailed an improvement in Africa's economic performance. But sustained economic development is impossible without greater political stability. Is that in prospect?

derbelly and too influential in the Islamic and oil-rich Arab worlds to be ignored. But the rest of the continent—the 47 countries of sub-Saharan Africa that this survey will be examining—has dismayed the outside world with its post-colonial performance. Last year, these countries attracted a mere 3% of the flow of foreign direct investment into the developing world. Latin America and the Caribbean got 20%; East Asia and the Pacific region as much as 59%.

Goodbye to All That

Nearly all the former colonial powers now regard Africa as marginal to their own well-being and security. So does Russia. America has all but disengaged. It resolutely refused to lift a finger to help the West African peace-keeping effort in Liberia, the nearest thing it ever had to a

The Democratic Habit

Hard to learn, easy to break

PEOPLE will never comprehend Africa's crisis so long as they continue to assume that it is mainly an economic one, says Adebayo Adedeji, a Nigerian economist: "What we confront in Africa is primarily a

political crisis, albeit with devastating economic consequences." Mr. Adedeji, who for many years was executive secretary of the UN Economic Commission for Africa, knows from experience that Africans cannot

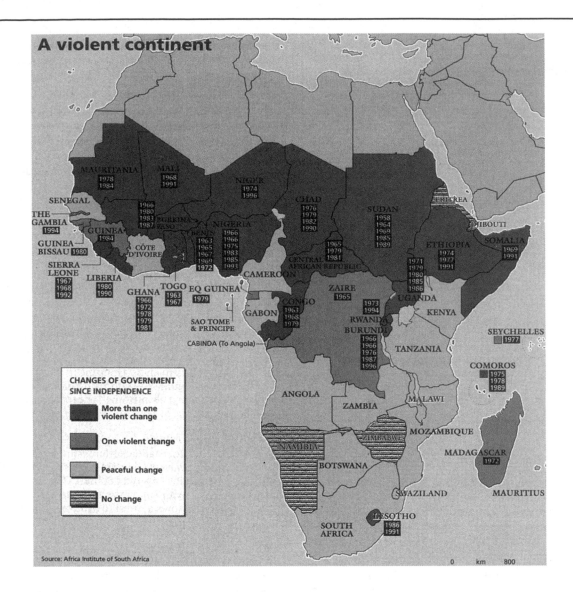

A violent continent

CHANGES OF GOVERNMENT
SINCE INDEPENDENCE

- More than one violent change
- One violent change
- Peaceful change
- No change

Source: Africa Institute of South Africa

0   km   800

hope for sustained economic progress until they achieve good governance.

The right to liberty, personal security and participation in the political process; freedom from torture and from cruel, inhumane or degrading punishment; the right to recognition and equal treatment under the law and to effective judicial remedy; freedom from arbitrary interference, and freedom of association and assembly: all these, as Mr. Adedeji says, are essential requirements for a civilised political system, yet in many African countries they cannot be taken for granted. Nor, add businessmen, can a competent, uncorrupt civil service or the absence of bribery in public contracts.

Sadly, these indictments remain true, but at least political repression and corruption have stopped advancing further, and even started receding. The one-party states that became widespread from the mid-1960s reached their apogee in 1989, when only four countries in sub-Saharan Africa had a multi-party political system. A re-

port published in mid-1995 by the Africa Institute of South Africa was able to cite instances of elective institutions and/or elections and/or political parties in 33 states in the area.

From Bullet to Ballot

Removing leaders by the ballot rather than the bullet is no longer inconceivable. When Benin in 1991 became the first country in mainland Africa to vote a ruling party and president out of office in free elections, it set a trend. Later that year, Kenneth Kaunda, who had ruled Zambia with well-meaning incompetence since that once copper-rich land had achieved independence in 1964, was defeated in a presidential election by Frederick Chiluba. In 1994, Hastings Banda, Malawi's president for life, discovered that life was full of little disappointments when he lost the presidential election to Bakili Muluzi. And in March of this year, in another first, Mathieu Kérékou, a former Marxist-Leninist now converted to caring Christianity, won 52% of the vote in Benin to turn the tables on Nicéphore Soglo, who had trounced him in 1991.

Still more surprising, and encouraging, have been the elections this year in African countries that used to be bywords for darkest depravity. Sierra Leonians managed to hold a reasonably democratic election in February and March in the midst of a civil war. Against all the odds, the victorious candidate, Ahmed Tejan Kabba, succeeded in consolidating civilian rule, albeit with a lot of help from disciplined mercenaries from South Africa.

Yoweri Museveni's triumph in the presidential election in Uganda in May was even more heartening. The campaign was cramped by the government's insistence on a "no-party contest", and by fanatical terrorists in the north parading under the name of the Lord's Resistance Army. But even if the election was flawed, it is wonderful to think that Uganda has become a quasi-democracy. More than most African countries, the country is riven by conflicts over ethnicity, religion, language, income and class. Between 1971 and 1985, first under Idi Amin and then under Milton Obote, around 750,000 Ugandans were murdered.

Yet Mr Museveni's Uganda today is among the less threatening countries in Africa. Its city streets and country roads are relatively safe. Asians expelled by Idi Amin have been welcomed back, and have had their confiscated (and dilapidated) property returned to them. And when Mr Museveni talks about the need for forcing investors, privatisation, an uncorrupt civil service and sound public finances, he sounds as though he really means it.

However, these few African democratic successes are both fragile and exceptional. Elections where the incumbent president secures 97.85% of the vote, as Teodoro Obiang Nguema Mbasogo did in Equatorial Guinea in February, are still embarrassingly common. So are soldiers ready to remove elected politicians, as happened in Niger in January, and nearly happened in the Central African Republic in May, when President Ange-Félix Patassé had to call in French troops to restore order.

Nonetheless, the very holding of elections is an advance. They may not be as free or as fair as elections in today's western democracies, but they make the point that African leaders are accountable to the publics they rule. People can perfect democracy only by practising it, and with each election, even when it is little more than a tribal head-count, the democratic habit becomes more ingrained.

The new South Africa, too, is making a big difference for the better. After casting a shadow on the rest of the continent for so long, it is now a beacon. No tribe there is strong enough to dominate, and Nelson Mandela seems genuinely committed to building a nation where everybody—white and coloured, Indian brown and Negroid black, Xhosa and even Zulu—counts as equally South African, with no nonsense about this or that group being more indigenous than the rest. That ideal will come under pressure when Mr Mandela retires, especially if the economy falters, but it provides a sound starting point for a newly democratic nation.

It helps that civil society is deeply rooted in South Africa. A black intelligentsia started to emerge there in the mid-19th century. The rule of law prevailed until the last, cruel days of P. W. Botha's institutionalised terrorism. Voluntary associations—church groups, round tables, masonic lodges, women's institutes, parent-teacher associations—are vigorously independent of party politics.

Equally important, South Africa possesses the stature and the confidence to think not just nationally but regionally. In world terms it is small, with an economy the size of Thailand's, but in its neighbourhood it is a giant, with a manufacturing sector seven times as large as second-place Nigeria's and two-fifths of the GNP of sub-Saharan Africa.

On balance, South Africa looks like using its muscle constructively within the Southern African Development Community (SADC), a 12-country grouping that also includes Angola, Botswana, Lesotho, Malawi, Mauritius, Mozambique, Namibia, Swaziland, Tanzania, Zambia and Zimbabwe, Now that the cold war is over and South Africa no longer has a government intent on destabilising its neighbours, all of these countries—with palpitations in Angola—are enjoying something approaching peace for the first time in 30 years.

Reluctant Regional Leader

South Africa, with understandable doubts and hesitations, is exploring ways of maintaining this stability through SADC'S new Organ for Politics, Defence and Security. Along with Zimbabwe and Botswana, it has already faced down a threat to democracy in Lesotho, where it reinstated the

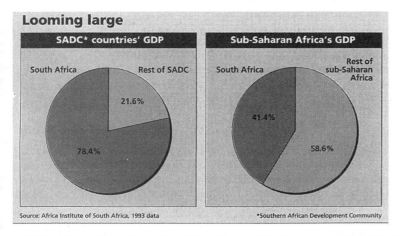

Looming large

SADC* countries' GDP		Sub-Saharan Africa's GDP	
South Africa	Rest of SADC	South Africa	Rest of sub-Saharan Africa
78.4%	21.6%	58.6%	41.4%

Source: Africa Institute of South Africa, 1993 data   *Southern African Development Community

government of Ntsu Mokhehle. Although anxious not to be seen as the regional bully, it has also tried, less successfully, to dissuade Mr Chiluba from rigging the constitution in Zambia to relegate Mr Kaunda permanently to the political sidelines.

The Americans in particular would dearly like South Africa to take the lead in creating a pan-African peacekeeping force under the aegis of the Organisation of African unity (OAU). The South African government is leery of this idea, arguing that it has neither the military power nor the inclination to undertake the sort of tasks that defeated Operation Restore Hope, the UN's American-led peacekeepers in Somalia, and West Africa's ill-disciplined peacekeepers in Liberia.

On the economic front, South Africa is less inhibited. Although its protectionist trade policies and capital controls, both legacies of the apartheid era, irk other SADC members, it could eventually play a constructive role. Africa has two dozen stock exchanges, but only Johannesburg's counts for much. It is the world's tenth biggest by market capitalisation and could raise substantial capital from African (albeit mainly white African) investors, who know the continent and are keen, unlike risk-averse foreigners, to back enterprises in its hinterland. This opportunity must not be fluffed. Africa sorely needs private investment to reduce its over-dependence on aid, which often comes with strings attached—and may not come at all.

A Dying Industry?

The wrongs and rights of aid

THE pendulum has swung so decisively that even people on the left wing of South Africa's African National Congress now agree that foreign aid alone is not enough and private capital from abroad is essential. Leading African economists such as Anthony Hawkins go so far as to call aid a dying industry. Donor fatigue is spreading even to such exemplary givers as the Canadians, the Dutch and the Scandinavians.

In these disillusioned times, it is important that the miracles the foreign benefactors sometimes perform should not go unrecognised. One such miracle was their response to the 1992 drought in Malawi, Mozambique, Zambia and Zimbabwe, which followed the worst failure of the rains in a century.

Unlike the earlier shrivelled harvests in northeast Africa, this natural disaster did not generate television footage of children with swollen bellies, of wizened old people lying down in the dirt to die, and of dog-tired paramedics trying to get fortified fluids into starving babies. Yet the southern African drought destroyed three-quarters of the staple crop of maize and much of the more drought-resistant millet and sorghum. Peasants had to kill their cattle or watch them die for want of fodder.

What made the difference between this drought and those in Ethiopia, Somalia and Sudan was an effective international and regional relief effort backed by interest-free loans from the World Bank's International Development Association (IDA). Ernie Rice, a member of the World Bank team that went out to help, says the supplementary feeding programmes worked especially well. Children were too weak to walk to school and fainted in the classroom until aid agencies helped to ensure that

they got at least one meal a day. At one typical school they were fed with barley gruel and bread with peanut butter. In Zimbabwe, Mr. Rice was flabbergasted by the behaviour of famished people.

> Once, in a high-density suburb of Harare, a truck pulled up to a store, and a crowd thronged around and climbed up on it. It seemed there was going to be some sort of riot. People grabbed bags of maize. But then they went round to the front, paid the driver, and walked away with their purchases. That level of social cohesion and social contract helped Zimbabweans to succeed.

For the following rainy season, the IDA financed the purchase of seed and fertiliser for peasant farmers. Without this they could not have replanted and their families would have gone hungry again.

The Miracle Workers

Miracles are also performed regularly by the people at the UN'S much-derided Food and Agriculture Organisation (FAO) who launch sorties against the swarms of locusts that threaten the crops of the Sahel and East Africa. If nobody hears about them, it is because averted plagues tend to go unreported.

Such efforts, though, come under the heading of emergency relief, and nobody much takes issue with them. By contrast, aid classified as long-term development assistance is contentious. Its critics have put the international development agencies on the defensive. The World

Bank tried to answer back with a research report entitled "Adjustment in Africa", published in 1994, but some of its many African critics remained unimpressed. They argued that the World Bank had doctored the evidence to be able to reach the conclusion that those countries which had done as they were told (such as Ghana and Tanzania) had performed much better than those countries which had not (such as Cameroon and Congo).

Yet the critics are being unduly rough. The World Bank, having prescribed such sensible remedies as balanced budgets, monetary discipline, the privatisation of state assets, financial deregulation, trade liberalisation and the abolition of price controls, can take some of the credit for recent economic upturns in "adjusting" African countries. However, the improvements are modest. Growth rates per head of 1–2% in the past couple of years are nothing to brag about in countries that gained from temporary surges in the price of coffee, cocoa and other commodities. As Jeffrey Sachs, director of the Harvard Institute for International Development, noted in a broadside against the World Bank's and the IMF'S African policy recently published in *The Economist*, many low- and middle-income countries in Asia and Latin America achieve growth per head of more than 5% a year. Only three of the 47 African countries—Botswana, Mauritius and Uganda—have come anywhere near that.

The common African retort, that Asian countries in particular benefited from much greater government intervention in the economy than the World Bank is willing to acknowledge, has some force. But it is also irrelevant. African countries simply do not yet possess the human capital—the impartial civil service, the skilled professionals, the technical experts—for their governments to intervene in the way that, say, the Japanese did in the 1950s and 1960s or the South Koreans in the 1970s and 1980s.

Tribal Trouble

Tribalism holds Africa back. Although ethnic loyalties are gradually diminishing in the cities, where many people are Namibians, Kenyans or Nigerians before they are Ovambos, Kikuyus or Ibos, they remain strong in the rural areas, where most Africans live. Even in relatively advanced South Africa, the tribally based Inkatha Freedom Party continues to enjoy the powerful support of Zulus living outside the urban areas of KwaZulu-Natal. In Kenya, President Daniel arap Moi owes his political longevity to crafty tribal coalition building. The vertical solidarities of tribalism or, at least, of the extended family, remain intact almost everywhere in Africa, sustaining nepotism and favouritism in bureaucracies. That makes governments ill-qualified to act as economic agents and arbitrators.

Africans are on stronger ground in their other criticisms of the Bretton Woods institutions. Excessively severe terms have indeed put unbearable strains on politically and socially fragile societies. Budget cuts demanded have been too crude, and spending restrictions on infrastructure, education and health have handicapped future development (which is why radicals sometimes call the IMF the Infant Mortality Fund).

Africans also have a point when they say that the IMF, the World Bank and other donors have in the past paid insufficient attention to regional development, regional trade and regional infrastructure, and treated landlocked African states as if they were islands. Africa is the only continent where regional trade has declined, from around 10% of the total in the 1920s to about 6% today. Critics also have good reason to worry that donors, in their anxiety to come up with success stories, will heap more aid on promising countries that can usefully be absorbed. It happened in Madagascar and Ghana yesterday, may be happening in Uganda today, and could happen in Eritrea tomorrow.

But the worst example of economic mismanagement, by donors and governments alike, is being neglected: the horrible mess made of Africa's great natural resources. The continent's comparative advantage lies in its natural beauty and wildlife, its metals and minerals, and its agriculture—its greatest asset, and the one most squandered.

Withering Indictment

African farm policies too often fail to produce the food

FARMING is the one area in which South Africa has more to gain from the rest of the continent than the other way round. Long-term changes in the climate appear to be moving the rain belt northwards, up from South Africa and Zimbabwe to the land on the other side of the Zambezi river. Southern Africa may depend on countries such as Zaire and Zambia to provide it with food in the next century—a change that would require their farmers to become vastly more competent.

For, unbelievable though it seems, per capita food production in Africa between 1961 and 1995 actually dropped by 12%, whereas it advanced by leaps and

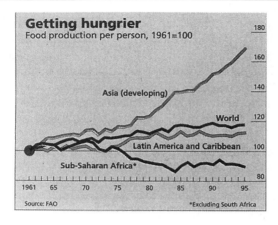

Getting hungrier
Food production per person, 1961=100

Asia (developing)

World

Latin America and Caribbean

Sub-Saharan Africa*

1961 65   70   75   80   85   90   95

Source: FAO   *Excluding South Africa

bounds in developing countries in Asia (see chart). Zaire, which used to export food when it was the Belgian Congo, now cannot even feed itself. The same is true of post-colonial Zambia.

The decline in African agriculture is partly self-induced, but can also partly be blamed on the rich industrial countries. North America, Western Europe and Japan practise freeish trade in the manufactured goods and services in which they have a comparative advantage, but remain determinedly protectionist about food, a sector in which African countries offer competitive products at attractive prices. Their battery of tariff and non-tariff barriers to agricultural trade includes duties, quotas, subsidies to domestic producers and calculatedly complicated health-and-safety regulations.

The United States protects its sugar, tobacco and groundnut growers, its ranchers and its dairymen. The European Union will not allow free trade in agricultural products that compete with those of its member states, notably wine, citrus fruits, tobacco, vegetable oils and tomatoes. Japan so cossets its beef farmers and rice growers that Japanese shoppers have to pay a multiple of the world price for their products. The periodic dumping on African markets of milk powder, wheat, beef and other European and American food surpluses ruins prices for local farmers.

How Not to Do It

The agencies and consultancies that advise African governments too often make things worse by arrogantly assuming that traditional African ways are useless and western methods are invariably superior. In the Sahel, the FAO bullied farmers into growing potatoes. They produced a bumper crop, which then rotted unsold in city markets where potatoes looked as exotic as bush rats or kinkilaba would in a western supermarket.

The foreign foresters who persuaded West Africans to clear their acacias and plant non-indigenous trees instead also ended up apologising. Within a few years

it had become obvious that the native acacias were vastly more suitable than the imported substitutes. They needed less water and less attention and, crucially, sprouted leaves for goats and sheep to browse on during the dry season.

In southern Africa, western experts have spent much of this century wiping out wildlife in the low veld in an effort to eradicate the tsetse fly, which kills horses and cattle, and so open up the area to livestock farming. Only now have they become persuaded that the land is too marginal to support domesticated animals and that it has been seriously degraded by over-grazing. The wild animals which had once been ruthlessly pursued because they acted as hosts for the tsetse fly are now being reintroduced for their value as game.

In East Africa, horror stories circulate about fisheries projects such as the one at Lake Rudolf (now Lake Turkana), where Norwegian experts persuaded 20,000 nomadic Turkana cattlemen to give up their cows and take up fishing for tilapia and Nile perch instead, only to find that the cost of chilling the fish far exceeded the price it fetched in the markets. Millions of dollars-worth of fishing equipment was written off and the Turkana, minus their cattle, were left dependent on food aid.

Unpalatable Ideology

Africa's capacity to feed itself has been further damaged by an intellectual bias in the industrial countries against subsistence agriculture. Advisers from the old Soviet Union were particularly guilty of this. Following Marx, himself an urban intellectual, they regarded the peasantry with near-contempt, and urged African leaders to create an industrial base on the back of primary commodities.

Kwame Nkrumah turned a listening ear. One of the sugar factories he commissioned went bust in the mid-1980s. It is now an immense, eerie hulk, rusting in the Ghanaian bush about two hours' drive north of Accra. Only a small part of it, a gin-making plant, is still in working order. Around it cluster the devalued plots of the former sugar growers. But this story may yet have a happy ending: F. C. Schaffer, an intrepid agricultural company based in Baton Rouge, Louisiana, has high hopes of bringing the sugar factory back into production.

The Maoist Chinese, who were especially influential in Julius Nyerere's Tanzania, had more respect for the peasantry than the Soviet communists did, but that respect was contingent on collectivisation. In Tanzania, the peasants were herded off their scattered smallholdings into Ujama'a (self-help villages) and told by bureaucrats from Dar-es-Salaam to work together on large communal plots, sharing draught animals, ploughs, seeds, fertilisers and pesticides. They failed to flourish, as did President Nyerere's political fortunes.

The sins of western economists have been those of omission more than commission. In advising governments to try to add value to agricultural commodities and to give priority to agricultural exports, they tended to overlook the fact that more than two-thirds of Africans still live on the land, most of them on subsistence farms.

As western economists admitted in "Aid to African Agriculture", a World Bank report in 1992 on the lessons to be learnt from "two decades of donors' experience", the consequences of that oversight could be dire. Because all eyes were focused on macroeconomic statistics, Hastings Banda's Malaw, for instance, was praised for setting an example of how to achieve agriculture-led economic growth. It was not until the second half of the 1980s that "pervasive malnutrition, high infant mortality and other manifestations of the extreme poverty of most Malawians came to the attention of policymakers and donors".

Malawi made it hard for its smallholders to profit from growing the most lucrative crops. It required them to sell their tobacco to a state-owned agricultural marketing board which paid them only a third of the price it obtained from auctioning their output. Such state-owned marketing companies have long been the bane of African agriculture. Bloated by bureaucracy, they habitually pay farmers below-market prices for their produce and often charge them above-market prices for sub-standard seeds, fertilisers, pesticides and other inputs.

Ghana's cocoa board is a notorious case in point. In the old colonial days, under the redoubtable Eric Tansley, the board was a law unto itself, and practically ran the Gold Coast. In the early years of independence its staff of 50,000 efficiently handled annual cocoa crops of more than 500,000 tonnes. But 20 years later the government of Jerry Rawlings lost its temper with the board: its staff had doubled, the crop had halved and the Ghanaians were being left behind by the better organised Ivoirean cocoa growers next door.

Such inefficiencies in agriculture are more intolerable than ever. So are overvalued exchange rates which, in effect, subsidise farm inputs and handicap exports. So are export taxes on agricultural commodities. So are price controls on food, which keep urban consumers' grocery bills low by depressing the prices paid to rural producers.

Governments can no longer count on a world food surplus to shield them from the consequences of policy mistakes and bureaucratic bungles. The demand for food is set to soar in the next generation, not so much because of population growth as because of changes in diet. Rising living standards are whetting the world's appetite for meat, which is a less efficient source of food than crops. In the past, the world's breadbasket, the United States, could meet any shortfall by bringing idle land into production. But this reserve capacity is disappearing.

Some of the further reforms that would change African farming for the better would require fundamental shifts in attitudes that may not come about for a generation or more. Male dominance remains entrenched. Women working on the land produce 70% of the food (more in Muslim areas), yet they remain all but invisible as policymakers. Farm ministries and marketing boards remain male bastions and continue to hire city boys, including those who studied agriculture only after failing to get into law or economics or accountancy courses.

From Acorns to Oaks

But even within the constraints of deeply traditional societies, where men tend the animals and women grow the crops, it is possible to make big improvements. Hybrid seeds can bring spectacular productivity gains. So can the use of fertiliser when companies can be persuaded to pack and market it in the five-pound bags that peasant farmers might be prepared to try. Draught oxen can bring into production land that is too hard to be broken by women's hoe-power.

Better rural roads are another priority. Many today can be used only by four-wheel-drive vehicles, so surplus crops rot while only a few hundred miles away people go hungry. The Great Lakes area provides a demonstration of just such a transport failure. Uganda is so fertile that people say a walking stick stuck in the ground will sprout bananas the next morning. But Ugandan peasant farmers, who produce more food than their families can eat, find it hard to deliver the food to people who want it and need it in eastern Zaire, Rwanda and Burundi. Up to 40% of African crops are lost to poor transport and poor storage.

Low-value bulk commodities cause the biggest problems. Mark Wood, a Zimbabwean who heads a project called Investment in Developing Export Agriculture (IDEA) along with a Ugandan called Martin Wamaniala, is trying to offer Ugandan farmers an alternative. Behind the long name is a simple but excellent programme that aims to persuade peasant farmers to grow non-traditional crops with export potential. Some, such as roses and vanilla, depend entirely on sales abroad. Others, such as white and kidney beans, can be eaten by the farmers themselves if they remain unsold. Similar efforts are under way in West Africa, where the non-traditional crops now being promoted include pineapples, green beans and varieties of okra.

These schemes are no substitute for increasing the production of traditional crops and adding value to them, but they are just the kind of thing African peasant farmers need to break out of their poverty trap. The cut flowers that Kenya and Zimbabwe now air-freight to European supermarkets are an innovation that shows the way.

How to Dig Yourself Out of a Hole

In mining, it helps to be African

LIKE its agriculture above the ground, Africa's great natural resources below the ground are mismanaged. Not everywhere, of course. South Africa's gold industry has entered its mature phase: output last year declined by more than 10% to 522 tonnes, the lowest level in almost 40 years, but gold still accounts for nearly 5% of the country's GNP and 20% of its export earnings.

Botswana is another bright spot. As the Bechuanaland Protectorate, it used to be an imperial slum where thin, small boys clad only in loin cloths begged for food at railway sidings. The Debswana Diamond Company's three big mines—Orapa, Lethakane and Jwaneng—and three decades of relatively stable, relatively democratic government have transformed the fortunes of this former sub-Saharan Cinderella.

Black Spots

Unfortunately, South Africa and Botswana are exceptions. In neighbouring Zimbabwe, Australia's Broken Hill Proprietary still fumes over the delay in the development of its platinum mine at Hartley, outside Harare, where the immigration visas of expatriates were scrutinised first by the ministry of mines, next by the immigration service and then by a cabinet committee representing seven different ministries. Of the Angolan diamond lands, where unruly bands of *garimpeiros*—amateur diggers—run wild, a mine manager says "It's the Wild West up here, it's Dodge city, it's Chicago, it's gangster-land." In Zaire and Zambia, great copper wealth is simply squandered.

It is much the same story in the oil-producing states of Central and West Africa, with Nigeria doing worst. The country's GNP per head has halved since 1983, and the military government of Sani Abacha was named as the most corrupt in the world in a survey recently published in London's *Financial Times*. Ken Saro-Wiwa, an Ogoni dissident executed last November after the most perfunctory of trials, described it thus:

> Of all the countries with black gold, Nigeria was the only one that had succeeded in doing absolutely nothing with it. The Arabs had used their oil very well indeed; not only had they given their people education and a lot else that conduced to good living, they also had invested nothing, absolutely nothing. They had spent all their money buying foreign food which they consumed or even

threw away; in paying for ships waiting on the high seas to deliver food. Sometimes, they paid out hundreds of millions of dollars for goods and services not delivered.

Against this gloomy backdrop, it is good to be able to report that a West African mining company has emerged to compete today, and probably collaborate tomorrow, with the great South African mining houses in responsibly exploiting the continent's underground treasure. Ashanti Goldfields, which this year became the first African company to be fully listed on the New York Stock Exchange, keeps finding more gold in the ground than it takes out. Since 1985, it has increased production at its Obuasi mine in Ghana more than fourfold, from around 220,000 ounces a year to more than 900,000, while cutting its labour force from 15,000 to 10,000. These output gains have been made despite the raids by 1,000–2,000 illegal miners on open-cast pits at Obuasi. Company security guards have had to fight them off with cattle prods, and skirmishes with the police in July this year left three people dead. Imagine the world outcry if this had happened in the oilfields of Ogoniland, where Shell is viewed as a multinational rather than an African company.

Mining for Africa

Ashanti Goldfields has been unusual in that it has expanded through acquisition, something more generally associated with European and American multinationals than with an African company led by a black chief executive (Sam Jonah) and a black chairman (Richard Peprah). It has a bid in for Australia's Golden Shamrock and has recently taken over Canada's International Gold Resources and, joy of joys, Cluff Resources, a British company that turned from oil extraction in the North Sea and oil exploration in the South China Sea to gold mining in Africa. For some the symbolic flavour of the Cluff acquisition could not have been sweeter. It delivered to Ashanti Goldfields the Freda Rebecca Mine in Zimbabwe that had been opened by Margaret Thatcher, the woman who had striven to prevent South Africa's ANC "terrorists" coming to power.

Ashanti Goldfields usually divests itself of the non-African properties that come with its acquisitions. It sees and presents itself as an African company run by Africans, of all colours, for the benefit of Africa. There is calculation as well as idealism in this. Ashanti Goldfields

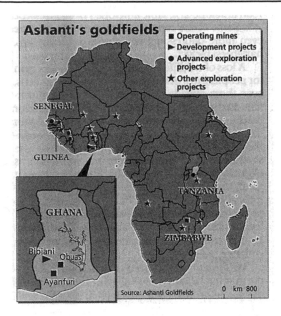

Ashanti's goldfields
- ■ Operating mines
- ► Development projects
- ● Advanced exploration projects
- ★ Other exploration projects

Source: Ashanti Goldfields
0 km 800

maintaining Ashanti Goldfields' authentic African character. It is this authenticity that gives the company its competitive edge. Mr Jonah was speaking from the head as well as from the heart when he told the *Wall Street Transcript*:

> We consider Africa very much our constituency. . . . We are Africa's favourite son and that is reflected in the kind of responses and welcomes that we get wherever we go in Africa. We have been inundated with requests from African governments for us to go in as an African company—a truly authentic African company—and join them as partners in the development of their gold mining industry. We are quite proud and privileged to be called upon to do this.

The company is putting its money where Mr Jonah's mouth is. It is an active prospector or miner in Senegal, Guinea, Mali, Niger, Burkina Faso, Eritrea, Ethiopia, Tanzania, Angola and Zimbabwe as well as in Ghana (see map), where its antecedents go back to the 1890s. And its three-pronged strategy seems clear and sensible: develop Obuasi as a large, long-lived, low-cost producer; build a high-quality exploration portfolio of gold properties in Africa; and take on board projects or companies with which Ashanti Goldfields can achieve synergies.

In such a volatile continent things can always go dreadfully wrong, but everybody must hope that Ashanti Goldfields goes from strength to strength. Africa needs a roaring new corporate success story, and nowhere more so than in the mining industry. If Ashanti Goldfields realises its ambitions, other African companies will find it a bit easier to raise money on reasonable terms on the world's capital markets. Just as important, the face of capitalism will become more acceptable to the African on the overcrowded rural omnibus.

is well aware that many African governments are leery of foreign multinationals, and especially of multinational mining companies, which they suspect of exploiting African labour and African natural resources for the benefit of already affluent overseas shareholders.

Rivals are nonetheless wide of the mark when they question the authenticity of Ashanti Goldfields' Africanism and point to a mid-year shareholder register showing Lonrho holding 38% of the stock, almost twice as much as the Ghanaian government, the second largest shareholder. They skate over three inconvenient facts: the Ghanaian government's ownership of a golden share which allows it to block any deal it opposes; the dethronement of Lonrho's controversial founder, Tiny Rowland; and the interest all shareholders, including Lonrho and (via Lonrho) Anglo American, ought to have in

Safari-bound

Why Africa needs its elephants

AFRICA'S third great natural resource, after agriculture and mineral wealth, is scenic grandeur and unrivalled wildlife. The continent's potential for tourism is impressive, but it certainly does not lie in its increasingly anarchic cities.

In Abidjan pushy youths manhandle you and your luggage as you leave the airport. In Nairobi it is not unknown for the police to demand money with menaces. In Johannesburg hotels advise guests not even to think of stepping outside after dark. And the Lonely Planet

Guide to West Africa rightly says that travellers detest Lagos, where "taxi drivers seem to be involved in most of the thefts involving foreigners". Those foreigners are warned to "avoid taxis where there is a second person riding for some inexplicable reason".

The sunshine and the beaches are indeed wonderful, but other places too can offer those. Africa's unique attraction for the traveller is its hinterland—the veld of Southern Africa, the grasslands of East Africa and (for the most adventurous) the bush and the forests of Central Africa.

West Africa is in a somewhat different category. Animal life there is relatively thin on the ground, though bird life is marvellous. But what black visitors from other continents, particularly America, come for in their thousands is to discover their roots. They want to experience the life of the people, to make friends and to eat and sing and dance (though not quite to live) as the cheerful West Africans do. Just as Irish-, Italian- and other hyphenated white Americans who visit the old migrant processing shed on Ellis Island in New York harbour weep as they imagine the sufferings of their immigrant great-grandparents, so African-Americans grow tearful on visits to the slave castles along the Guinea coast, or to the still-dreadful Maison des Esclaves on Ile de Gorée, off Dakar.

Other visitors to Africa are less interested in the people than in the big five: elephant, rhinoceros, buffalo, lion and leopard. Some, though by no means all, African governments are now committed to wildlife conservation, at least in designated game reserves and national parks, which cover about 185,000 square miles (480,000 square kilometres). This is a bigger proportion of the land area than in other continents—a fact worth remembering before criticising African governments for not doing enough.

This does not mean, however, that the future in the wild of Africa's dangerous animals, and with it that of the tourist industry, is assured. Governments have neither the money nor the manpower to prevent big game animals from being shot, trapped or poisoned by poachers. "Living with Wildlife", an intelligent World Bank working paper, points out that legislation and the designation of special areas cannot protect wildlife in the long term without the acquiescence of its human neighbours.

Survival of the Fittest

This acquiescence cannot be taken for granted. About two-thirds of the original wildlife habitat has already been lost to logging, farming, urban settlement and other causes. This, together with the ivory trade, has reduced the continent's elephant population from 10m 500 years ago to below 700,000 now. But at least the elephant is not yet an endangered species—in some areas it is actually overabundant—whereas the black rhinoceros could soon follow the bluebuck and the quagga into extinction. Over the past 20 years the number of black rhinos, although largely confined to protected areas, has declined from over 60,000 to under 3,000, as rich Chinese and other East Asians have paid ever higher prices for ground rhino horn as a remedy for fever (not as the aphrodisiac of popular mythology).

A census of wildlife published in the early 1990s by the Department of Wildlife and National Parks in Botswana provided a grim snapshot of what is happening to animals in too many parts of Africa. It revealed that over the previous five years Cape buffalo had fallen in number by 46%, zebra 27%, roan antelope 21%, sable antelope 13% and tsessebe 17%. Some of the comparisons over ten years were even more depressing: wildebeest down by 90%, hartebeest by 88%.

A loss of wildlife does not even constitute a gain for people. Most of the remaining wilderness areas, even those outside the national parks, are unsuitable for intensive agriculture because of low or patchy rainfall, tsetse-fly infestation, poor and thin soil or difficult gradients. If the animals are exterminated or driven off, the land supports crops or livestock for only a few years before it is eroded and, as often as not, turns into desert. But that does not mean rural people will leave the land and the animals alone. Elephant and buffalo, along with hippopotamus and baboon, devastate crops. Lion and leopard carry off livestock and pets. And like elephant, buffalo and crocodile, big cats sometimes endanger people's lives.

Wildlife managers need to persuade rural people that the benefits they will gain from tolerating dangerous animals will outweigh the costs. This in turn requires a better balance to be struck between the main aims of wildlife conservation. Foreign visitors are keen to see wild animals, and especially endangered species, preserved for future generations. African governments want to extract as much revenue as possible from the increasingly lucrative safari and big-game hunting business. People living near big game expect jobs as game guides and trackers, and want to be allowed to eat or sell the meat of game culled or hunted in the parks.

Most economists accept that it is much better to give local people an incentive to protect game, and to report poachers, than to rely on sanctions to enforce conservation. They can also see the force of the "Living with Wildlife" argument that the terms of trade are moving against cattle-raising (the main alternative in the wildlife areas) and in favour of tourism. That trend seems likely to continue. The kind of tourism Africa has to offer is the sort of luxury which fast-rising incomes in the industrial countries will make increasingly attainable.

Romantics v Pragmatists

But many well-meaning supporters of wildlife charities in the West remain implacably opposed to such commercial uses. As Graham Child writes in "Wildlife and People" (Wisdom Foundation, 1995), a book in which scholarship and years of practical experience are woven seamlessly together:

> It is important to recognise the inherent contradiction in human nature between the desire to protect game and the desire to use it. The conflict often

occurs in the same person who both protects wildlife for aesthetic reasons, but enjoys hunting or dining on a haunch of venison. Polarised attitudes in modern, crowded and highly competitive societies tend to be intolerant of this ancient dichotomy within the human spirit, although its antiquity is well illustrated by the beauty of the rock art left by our Stone Age forebears. Many of the paintings are of these hunter-gatherers and the large animals that they preyed on but also respected, much as the Bushmen of the Kalahari and the Inuits of the Arctic still do.

Fundamentalists in the conservation movement disagree: they will not accept any use of wild animals. Through the Convention on International Trade in Endangered Species (CITES), they are putting intense pressure on African governments to safeguard each and every elephant, even though southern African countries with sound wildlife management systems argue that in some areas elephant numbers far exceed the land's capacity, and unless culled will destroy the habitats of other animals, such as the bushbuck. Zimbabwe, for example, has produced figures showing that its elephant population has increased from 4,000 when the white pioneers arrived in the 1890s to more than 70,000 today, though the land cannot support more than 35,000 to 40,000 of them.

The fundamentalists' closed-mindedness creates difficulties for the more sophisticated western conservation organisations. Their experts on the ground accept the case for exploiting wildlife, but are loth to say so too plainly or too publicly for fear of losing donations. David Cumming of the Worldwide Fund for Nature is a forthright exception. The African wilderness cannot, he says, survive in competition against cattle ranching unless the landholders are able to offer a whole range of activities, including killing game for meat and sport. "There are", he adds, "no strong feelings against safari hunting in Africa. Only in Britain and America do people mistake animal welfare for conservation. To force western values on African culture is cultural imperialism."

No End of Plagues

Can AIDS be contained?

AFRICA is struggling against being overwhelmed by the worst plague in modern times—in addition to all the other plagues it already has. AIDS is by far the most serious threat to life, but there are plenty of others. Travelling to Africa today can seem as hazardous as in the days of Stanley, Speke, Burton and Moffat, especially for visitors to the tropics.

A smallpox vaccination is no longer needed, but doctors advise immunisation against yellow fever, typhoid, tetanus, hepatitis A, meningitis, polio and, for the risk-averse, rabies. Cholera jabs are not recommended only because they are not much use and induce a false sense of security.

In much of the continent, water from the tap has to be boiled before being drunk, or even used for cleaning teeth. The water in lakes and slow-moving rivers is also dangerous. Bilharzia, a water-borne parasitic disease, invades the bodies of anglers, swimmers and even paddlers. It is usually curable but can do terrible damage to vital organs.

Malarial mosquitoes are roaming wider. Civil wars and shortage of money have interrupted the spraying of waters where the insects breed, so malaria is now a hazard in parts of South Africa where it had been conquered decades ago. In other places, mosquitoes have developed resistance to the usual anti-malaria pills. Visitors to those parts of Central and West Africa that were once known as "the white man's grave" are now advised to take mefloquine, a powerful new treatment marketed under the trade name Lariam, the possible side effects of which include dizziness, vertigo, loss of balance, headache, sleep problems, diarrhoea, stomach ache and, more rarely, hallucinations, ringing in the ears and forgetfulness.

But the worst scourge is AIDS. When significant numbers of cases were first detected in Africa in the early 1980s, the disease was thought to be confined mainly to white homosexuals. Victims received scant sympathy in a continent where homosexuality is widely regarded as a disgusting perversion. Even when HIV/AIDS spread into the general population in Central and East Africa, it was at first considered to be no more serious than other diseases. Governments had a vested interest in encouraging that belief to protect their tourist industries.

The Multiplier Effect

Nobody is complacent now. The HIV/AIDS epidemic is more virulent in Africa than anywhere else on earth. Hiroshi Nakajima, director-general of the World Health Organisation, reckons that if present infection rates continue, by 2000 some 24m in Africa south of the Sahara

Too Crafty

ART galleries all over Africa worry about "airport art". Commercial exploitation, they claim, is devaluing the work of Africa's creative painters, potters, carvers and sculptors. A visit to any gift shop shows what they are up against: winsomely naive carvings of animals, West African figurines engaging in grotesque sexual contortions, stridently decorated ostrich eggs parodying the subtle designs of the Kalahari Bushmen.

In essence, it is much the same kind of stuff that is displayed for sale on park railings in the rich world. The big difference, say the African galleries, is that in Africa, unlike in Paris, London and New York, there is no critical mass of knowledgeable commentators and collectors to sustain a market for creative work. The African market is dominated by foreigners. Because few local people can afford their prices, African artists are cut off from the people who understand their spiritual, cultural and political influences and themes.

The argument is put most persuasively by a foreigner: Olivier Sultan, the French founder of the Pierre Gallery in Harare. In his book, "Life in Stone" (Baobab Books), he says that when Zimbabwean sculpture won international acclaim and an international market, hundreds of "artists of lesser class" were drawn in by the prospect of financial gain. "The slow, rigorous process of work, the perfection in the finish of the pieces, the communion with stone—all those things which constituted the strength of the best artists—were progressively replaced with a type of sculpture closer to craft, produced quickly and in a series: 'airport art' rather than authentic creation."

Businesses can help, by commissioning work from African artists rather than from foreigners. Churches and missions have Africanised their liturgy and such devotional aids as stained-glass windows. But businesses remain stubbornly Eurocentric. The English hunting scenes that appear on many an African corporate wall look out of place, as do the Churchilliana in the Best Western hotel in Bulawayo, the pictures of Mediterranean fishing boats at the Grand Imperial Hotel in Kampala and the books about the Windsors and English country houses in the library of the Muthaiga Club in Nairobi, among many similar solecisms.

Governments, too, could help, starting with more authentic architecture. The soggy American wedding cakes they commission for their ministries and state-owned companies seem sadly inappropriate. And inside the building, the only African picture is often a flattering mugshot of the president.

will be infected with HIV. In Malawi, one in eight of the sexually active population is already HIV-positive, and in urban areas one-third of the women attending antenatal clinics carry the virus. In Kenya, by the end of this year 300,000 children will have been orphaned by the epidemic. Economists reckon that by 2005 the country's GNP will be 15% smaller than it would have been without the virus. In Zaire, official figures suggest that only 3–6% of the population are HIV-positive, but everybody reckons they are rigged.

The epidemic is now spreading fast through South Africa. KwaZulu-Natal is in the front line. It borders on Mozambique, the poorest country on earth with an annual GNP per head of under $100, and is on a truck route to the rest of South Africa. Over 18% of the women attending antenatal clinics there tested HIV-positive last year, compared with under 2% in the Western Province, at the southwestern tip of the continent.

But, according to a paper by Norman Miller and Robert Yeager in "AIDS Analysis Africa", military men are even more susceptible to HIV. "They are generally young and sexually active, are often away from home . . . imbued with feelings of invincibility and an inclination towards risk-taking, and are always surrounded by ready opportunities for casual sex."

Officers in some flying units and armoured units are reported to be 100% HIV-positive, which, as the paper notes, raises hard questions. At what point should such patients be discharged and sent home? Should they be selected for advanced training courses and promotion? Should they serve in other countries? Should the armed forces pay for funeral expenses and dependents' medical costs? And what sort of pension should they provide for the family if the soldier dies at a young age?

In Africa, hopes that AIDS might become a chronic but manageable disease such as diabetes are forlorn. Health services there cannot afford the cost of AZT, let alone of the newer, more expensive treatments now available. Even generic drugs used for treating common diseases and injuries are beyond the budget of many African hospitals: the patients' families have to buy them from a pharmacy.

Do Something

Yet the fight against AIDS goes on. South Africa, with a tradition of academic medicine, and doctors and nurses

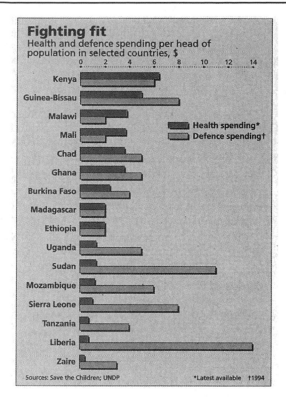

Fighting fit
Health and defence spending per head of population in selected countries, $

Countries (top to bottom): Kenya, Guinea-Bissau, Malawi, Mali, Chad, Ghana, Burkina Faso, Madagascar, Ethiopia, Uganda, Sudan, Mozambique, Sierra Leone, Tanzania, Liberia, Zaire

Health spending*
Defence spending†

Sources: Save the Children; UNDP   *Latest available †1994

• Mass communication, including billboard campaigns, advertisements on taxis, tapes mixing music with AIDS messages, even calendars using some of the slang words for condoms: goalkeepers, cool Johnnies, rain-coats, gloves and copper hats.
• Increasing access to barrier methods. In the past financial year, 17m condoms were distributed free in South Africa and more will be given away this year, many of them in shebeens, night clubs, bazaars and other non-traditional outlets. Meanwhile, a female condom is being distributed in a pilot project to test its acceptability.
• Appropriate care and support, including different guidelines for the treatment of men, women and children.

But even in South Africa much remains to be done. The churches, which led the fight against apartheid, have been strangely diffident about tackling AIDS (though this is not true in the rest of the continent, where the mission hospitals are the only alternative to chronically ailing national health services). Yet their help is desperately needed. They have unrivalled access to poor people in rural areas and are a liberating force for women in a continent where non-Christian men customarily have several wives and treat them as chattels.

Dr. Rosemary Coleman, who has worked at a hospital in rural KwaZulu-Natal, notes in another paper in "AIDS Analysis Africa" that there is also a role for the traditional medical practitioners in relieving pain and easing suffering. They include, in Zulu terminology, *izi-nyanga* (herbalists), *izan-goma* (spirit mediums) and *abathandazi* (faith healers). These traditional practitioners are available for consultation 24 hours a day, are often within easy reach of a patient's home, share a common language, and outnumber western-trained doctors by ten to one even in South Africa.

trained to international standards, has an anti-AIDS programme which could serve as a model for the rest of the continent. It includes:

• Sexual education targeted at young people, both in and out of school, integrated into the teaching of life skills.
• Appropriate treatment for patients with other sexually-transmitted diseases which may make them more vulnerable to HIV/AIDS. Instead of treating the patient specifically for gonorrhoea, say, medical practitioners use a cocktail of the antibiotics used to combat a variety of venereal diseases, saving money and time.

A New Beginning

Where South Africa leads, others may follow

ALAN PATON, the author of "Cry the Beloved Country", an African classic, could not have put it better when he said: "I think the Americans broke the Red Indians' heart. We have never been able to break the heart of the blacks. We haven't come close to it." Africans' ebullience, their zest for life, their friendly smiles and their belly laughs astonish visitors who think of Africa as a continent of civil wars and starving children.

But even the Africans' resilience would be tested by another decade as awful as the 1980s, during which living standards fell relentlessly. In the shanty towns that sprawl

around the big cities, people lack the most basic necessities of life: weatherproof shelter, clean water, enough food to keep body and soul together. It does not bear thinking about that there might be an even greater rush of people from failed farms into the cities, where the number of new workers far outstrips the number of new jobs and where violent crime often spirals out of control.

It may not happen. South Africa's economic and political reintegration has given the whole continent the chance of a new beginning. The first-ever non-racial elections held in that country in April 1994, marking the end of apartheid, were as fair as any held in Africa. The country has a manufacturing sector seven times the size of second-place Nigeria's and its economy, which accounts for two-fifths of the GNP of all sub-Saharan Africa, is large and advanced enough to help a marginalised continent recover.

The timing of prodigal South Africa's return—soon after the collapse of communism in Europe—was serendipitous. The exposure of the deep unpopularity and economic bankruptcy of the one-party regimes of Eastern Europe (especially that of the unspeakable yet influential Nicolae Ceausescu in Romania) helped to discredit those on the radical wing of the African National Congress who hankered after an authoritarian one-party black nationalist government.

Instead, Nelson Mandela's government has made multiracial democracy respectable in a continent where white Africans had previously been disparaged as "settlers", even if their families had arrived in the 17th century with Jan van Riebeeck and Simon van der Stel. The Mandela government now has the ability, and shows some signs of having the will, to help create a prosperous 12-country regional grouping in Southern Africa, committed to liberalising trade, promoting private investment and realising the area's vast potential for farming, mining and tourism.

Success in Southern Africa would inspire renewed efforts at regional integration in East, Central and West Africa, where political and economic policies are converging. Prodded by the IMF, the World Bank and other donors, many African countries are already trying simultaneously to introduce free (or, at least, freer) elections and free (or, at least, freeish) economic systems.

In West Africa, Ghana, Mali, Burkina Faso and Côte d'Ivoire, among others, have done relatively well, but all of them are aware that converting national into regional progress will remain impossible so long as Nigeria is run by a military regime as incompetent as it is corrupt. France's strong continuing influence in the area, which serves to keep francophone Africans aloof from other Africans, is further impediment to getting together. So is the CFA currency zone, which tends to sustain old colonial patterns of trade, aid and investment and to cut off the economies of francophone Africa from their neighbours.

The immediate prospects for greater regional integration are more promising in East Africa. Relations between Uganda, Tanzania and Kenya are better now than they have been at any time since the collapse of the East African community after these three colonial territories achieved independence from Britain in the early 1960s. More important, in a continent where personal ties count for a lot, so are relations between their leaders.

Although Mr Museveni's Uganda is keener than Daniel arap Moi's more nervous Kenya, all three East African countries are more open than ever before to the idea of stronger trade links with South Africa, and to welcoming South African investment. Their eyes are also turning to Central and West Africa, and there is even talk about dusting off long-moribund plans for a trans-African highway linking the Indian and the Atlantic Oceans. So it is not impossible that some time in the next century the dream of African unity will be revived—though, thank goodness, it will bear little resemblance to that of either Kwame Nkrumah or Cecil Rhodes.

Article 2   *Harvard International Review*, Fall 1996

False Hope

Structural Adjustment and Growth in Africa

Kaniaru Wacieni

Kaniaru Wacieni is a Staff Writer for the Harvard International Review.

FOR MANY COUNTRIES IN AFRICA, the last decade has been marred by widespread economic despair. Despite an influx of World Bank and International Monetary Fund (IMF) aid, programs intended to spur sustainable long-term economic growth have failed. This failure is evident in a litany of statistics.

According to the World Debt Tables of 1989 to 1990, the per capita Gross National Product (GNF) of Sub-Saharan nations stood at US$365 while per capita debt averaged US$334, a staggering debt to GNP ratio of 91 percent. Between 1986 and 1989, growth of per capita real GNP in Sub-Saharan Africa was negative 1.7 percent. Though completely disaggregating the causes of this stagnation may not be possible, strong evidence indicates that some of the IMF- and World Bank-sponsored policies have, in fact, inhibited growth. Furthermore, evidence suggests that even if the IMF and World Bank were to change their policies now, they would no longer be able to carry them out effectively.

Structure of Donor Lending

The IMF and World Bank differ in the types of loans that they provide. IMF lending is principally geared towards alleviating a balance of payments deficit, a deficit that results from a nation's imports exceeding its exports. Imports are usually paid for with a hard currency such as the US dollar, and governments rely heavily on exports for inflow of these hard currencies. Therefore, when there is a shortage of foreign exchange, a government may become unable to meet its financial obligations. Such countries negotiate with the IMF for standby credit agreements, usually involving the disbursement of several credit payments subject to attached policy conditions. These policy conditions seek to promote fiscal discipline by closely monitoring tax revenue, public expenditure, and inflation rates.

World Bank loans, on the other hand, focus on supply-side reforms such as improving terms of trade through currency devaluations and trade policy liberalization. The World Bank introduced Structural Adjustment Programs (SAPs) in 1979 to help developing countries, especially in Africa, cope with increasingly difficult economic situations. According to 1981 World Bank report entitled "Accelerated Development of Sub-Saharan Africa," SAPs had three main objectives: to make trade and exchange rate policies more suitable for export-led growth, to increase efficiency of resource use in the public sector, and to improve agricultural policies to facilitate production and distribution.

Theoretically, disbursement of SAPs should be preceded by an IMF standby credit agreement, so the efficacy of these SAPs hinges in part on the stabilizing role of the precursor IMF policies. In practice, this discrete sequencing has not occurred. Paul Mosley, in his book *Aid and Power: The World Bank and Policy-based Lending*, asserts that "the recipient government [often] found itself implementing structural adjustment, not on a firm basis of financial stability, but in the midst of stabilization." One of the major problems of this breakdown in the sequencing of IMF and World Bank policies was the conflict that arose between their respective policy conditions. IMF conditions generally tended toward quantitative targets such as credit ceilings on government expenditure or attainment of particular interest rates. However, World Bank conditionality is phrased in more qualitative terms that may not be met when an IMF condition is fulfilled. For example, the IMF may require a half percentage point increase in real interest rates while the World Bank asks for a substantive increase in real interest rates. The problem that arises is whether a half percentage point can be considered substantive. Therefore, the simultaneous implementation of IMF loan agreements and SAPs creates ambiguous policy targets for the borrower nation and often results in conflicts between the IMF, the World Bank, and the borrower nation itself.

Moreover, the lack of loan conditionality coordination between the two agencies has resulted in the phenomenon of "paper conditionality," conditions that exist in principle but are not enforceable in practice. Because of this lack of coordination, nations have managed to avoid making the substantive reforms required by loan conditions. Inflow of new aid has typically just softened budget constraints of recipient governments, which continue to spend in an undisciplined manner.

Despite these difficulties, SAPs have become a leitmotif in the recent economic history of Sub-Saharan Africa. Kenya provides a valuable example of how this happened. In the early 1970s, the growth of real GDP in Kenya was approximately six percent. This economic expansion was fueled by a rise in world coffee prices. During this coffee boom, the government rapidly increased its social expenditure through a larger number of health and education programs. Unfortunately, it also indulged in politically motivated state largesse. The oil shocks of 1979 and falling export earnings forced an increasingly undisciplined government to resort to deficit borrowing. That year, the Kenyan government signed a SAP agreement with the World Bank,

and a loan of US$55 million was disbursed in March of 1980.

Similar stories occurred throughout Sub-Saharan Africa. In the early 1970s, the average regional growth rate of real GDP was about 3.7 percent. After the 1979 oil shocks, nations such as Malawi, Ghana, Ivory Coast, and Tanzania signed SAPs. The number of countries in the region resorting to these policies increased dramatically, and by 1985 Sub-Saharan Africa comprised 45 percent of all SAPs made out by the World Bank.

These SAPs have achieved marked success in reducing the black market premium on foreign exchange, introducing competitive markets, and reducing the role of the state in economic planning. However, despite gains on these fronts, SAPs have achieved very little in terms of economic growth. The real GDP growth rate in the region averaged 1.4 percent between 1982 and 1985, and according to the World Bank, the investment to GDP ratio fell from 21.5 percent between 1973 and 1981 to 17.1 percent between 1986 and 1989.

Aid, Debt, and Exports

The debt burden that accompanies SAPs has hindered investment and exports. According to the 1995 World Development Report, 38 percent of Africa's external debt is owed to multilateral institutions such as the IMF and the World Bank. The funds used for servicing this debt are drawn from capital inflow, which consists of foreign direct investment, exports, new aid, and reinvestment of "capital flight"—money held abroad by nationals. Given the relatively small capital inflow from capital flight and the absence of new foreign aid, the burden of debt service is largely borne by exports and investment. Between 1986 and 1989, the amount of required debt servicing stood at approximately 26 percent of export revenues, with scheduled debt payments even higher. Projected net present values of debt service to export ratios show that the legacy of unsustainable debt will persist into the future for many countries, implying that new resources will be used to service debt at the expense of boosting growth. High debt distorts incentives for foreign investment because it implies a high future tax liability. If only one person invests, then this investor will have to pay the debt from his returns. High debt also implies an unstable government, and this engenders uncertainty concerning the repatriation of returns, making foreign investors even more hesitant. Furthermore, the high demand for foreign capital inflow, especially in the transition economies of Eastern Europe that do not have such serious debt problems, could effectively crowd out the heavily indebted nations of Africa from the international pool of funds. The nations that face these problems find themselves in a low investment equilibrium, where more debt leads to progressively less investment and slower growth.

High debt hinders exports in many ways. It creates an implicit export tax and a disincentive for export-led growth because a greater proportion of export earnings is channeled toward debt payments. The poor design and sequencing of policy reforms required by adjustment programs also hinder exports. Malawi provides a valuable case in point. A loan condition requiring devaluation of the local currency was intended to boost exports by making the prices of Malawi's agricultural commodities internationally competitive. Before the devaluation, nominal tariff rates on imports had been very low due to an overvalued local currency, and this boosted the nation's ability to purchase imports. Devaluation greatly increased the effective tariff rate, making the price of imported factors of production, such as tobacco plant fertilizer, go up. A devaluation intended to reduce the price of Malawian tobacco on the world market and thus increase exports was annulled by the high costs of fertilizer that resulted from higher import prices.

The case of Kenya illustrates another way in which debt hinders exports. Though the volume of exports rose in absolute terms between 1979 and 1985, the level of exports in 1985 in real terms was only 93 percent of the 1979 level. In this period, the Kenyan shilling had been devalued by 47 percent against the US dollar without any appreciable increase in exports. At an artificially strong exchange rate, exports are too expensive on international markets and little foreign exchange is accrued. Therefore, export growth accounts only marginally for the slight growth (1.1 percent) achieved in Sub-Saharan Africa between 1987 and 1991. Finally, high debt is a barrier to sustainable, export-led growth. Increased foreign aid allows a nation to grow, but it does so by providing scarce hard currency for the import of intermediate inputs, especially in the manufacturing sector and export crop sector. Growth resulting from an increased ability to import will disappear as soon as the aid supporting these imports is terminated. Therefore, such growth is inherently unsustainable.

Defensive Lending

Besides the economic constraints on growth, there have also been political constraints. Many nations have balked at restructuring their markets, especially in light of the fact that continued aid and policy reform have not been closely correlated. Kenya provides a particularly egregious example. In 1982, the Kenyan government signed an agreement with the World Bank for its second SAP. Among the attached conditions was the privatization of the maize marketing sector. The National Cereals and Produce Board (NCPB), a vestige of Kenya's long legacy of colonial settler farming, was the targeted government body as it was the sole buyer and seller of maize in the country. Only the NCPB and those that it licensed were allowed to distribute maize. Therefore the NCPB was also able to determine producer and consumer maize prices. Enormous political pressure and government intransigence assured that little was done to change this system or to privatize maize markets. However, despite this lack of significant reform, the loan was disbursed and followed by a similar loan in 1986.

The lack of correlation between policy reform and aid disbursement can be seen in international comparisons as well. Ghana implemented 58 percent of the World Bank's conditions but received less aid than Kenya, which implemented only 38 percent of the conditions. A recent World Bank report entitled "Adjustment in Africa: Reforms, Results, and the Road Ahead" surveyed 26 nations undergoing structural adjustment and found that net transfers increased to eight nations that recorded poorer macroeconomic performance than their peers with less aid. The same report also notes that for these countries, "there was no clear relationship between change in net external transfers and change in macroeconomic policies."

The reason behind this is that much of Sub-Saharan Africa faces a debt overhang, a situation in which a nation's expected present value of potential future resources is less than its debt. Paul Krugman, an economist at Stanford University, argues that a country in such a situation must seek new funds just to avoid a liquidity crisis. Furthermore, it is in the interests of existing creditors to re-lend enough funds to avoid immediate default on the part of the country. In such cases, new aid is essentially a support for debtor nations' balances of payments. This poses great difficulties for conditionality. Krugman asserts that attempts to impose conditions on loans will flounder due to a lack of credible threats. Creditors must continue to lend money to debtor nations in order to avoid default on their previous loans. Where this defensive lending has superseded economic restructuring as the driving force behind new loans, non-adherence to stipulated conditions is likely.

Nevertheless, increasing loans required to service increasing debt often lead to greater conditionality as creditors desperately try to engender reform. However, greater conditionality increases the risk of default and reduces investment. The reforms that are mandated by the more stringent conditions inevitably become bogged down by political obstacles, increasingly lethargic government machinery, and reduced institutional capacity to carry out change. When a nation has difficulty meeting loan conditions, foreigners become hesitant about investing. Without the hard currency from foreign investment, the nation has trouble making debt service payments. Then, if a liquidity crisis is to be avoided, creditors make more loans, thus completing a vicious circle of debt.

Once again, Kenya provides an illustrative example. Tighter loan conditions called for the restructuring of moribund state-owned firms and huge cutbacks in the bloated civil service agencies. Furthermore, there was increased pressure to reform the NCPB and to crack down on corruption. Unfortunately, prominent political figures were involved, and there were numerous conflicts with strong vested political interests. All these issues culminated in the government announcing its intention to repeal earlier reforms in March 1993. Subsequently, investment levels decreased as the uncertainty over government commitment to reform hindered foreign direct investment. As a result, there was a need for more loans.

The Path to Growth

Addressing the debt problem is obviously integral to encouraging long-term growth in Africa. Paul Krugman has suggested that debt repayment be proportional to export revenues, where higher export revenues could lead to less debt repayment. This would reduce the debilitating effects of new debt on export performance. However, determining whether the level of exports is due to sound economic planning or unforeseen global market shifts is difficult.

Debt forgiveness is another option for solving Sub-Saharan Africa's problems. Some have suggested that the IMF auction its gold reserves to fund such a project. However, this may not be politically feasible. Debt forgiveness on World Bank loans may also be difficult because the World Bank raises money in financial markets. A high default risk would

make it harder for the World Bank to raise future funds. Furthermore, World Bank debt forgiveness to countries in Sub-Saharan Africa would pose questions of fairness since other debtors would still have to pay their debts.

While these problems must be solved before growth can occur in Sub-Saharan Africa, other factors must also be considered. Debt reduction alone cannot spur growth. It is equally important that

policies designed to boost growth approach the issue with a long-term outlook and provide safety nets to those nations that are most vulnerable to falling into a debt circle. The mutually self-negating policies of the last 15 years must be avoided. Adjustment policies, as they stand, are doing nothing more than providing a false sense of hope for many African nations plagued by economic despair.

Article 3   *Multinational Monitor,* July/August *1996*

Waiting to Export

Africa Embraces Export Processing Zones

Robert Weissman

NAIROBI, KENYA—History is repeating itself in Africa, as a mixture of both tragedy and farce.

Having abandoned efforts to build economies designed to serve local needs as well as attempts to develop meaningful intra-continental economic linkages, impoverished African countries are now desperately seeking foreign investment and export earnings. With little to offer outside of the resource sector, African nations from Tunisia in the north to Zimbabwe in the south have embraced export processing zones (EPZs) as a device to attract foreign investment.

Following the advice of international aid agencies including the World Bank and the United Nations Conference on Trade and Development (UNCTAD), these countries hope EPZs—enclaves providing special incentives to exporting businesses—will enable them to emulate the success of Asian nations which achieved rapid economic growth significantly through an export-led strategy.

But there is little evidence that African nations are aware of the special circumstances which made possible the success of the Asian Tigers (Taiwan, South Korea, Hong Kong and Singapore, with Malaysia and Thailand now poised to join the pack).

Nor is there any apparent awareness of the general failure of EPZs to spark sustained growth in Latin America, the Caribbean and in Asian countries such as the Philippines and Sri Lanka. The African countries appear

equally oblivious to the widespread labor rights violations which have characterized EPZ activity across the globe.

Caution and reflection have been thrown to the wind as countries rush to jump on the EPZ bandwagon. Even Burundi, before it recently devolved one step closer to complete chaos and national breakdown, was eager to develop an EPZ program, according to an UNCTAD official in Addis Ababa, Ethiopia. That was too much even for an EPZ proponent such as this official to take, however; he urged the country to concentrate on ensuring political stability as a prerequisite to attracting foreign investors to EPZs or any undertaking in the country.

Low Wages, Lower Taxes

The logic of EPZs, also known as free trade zones and the equivalent of zones for what are called *maquiladoras* in Latin America, is to attract export-oriented manufacturing investment by setting aside a physical area where investors will be given a range of incentives. These include benefits such as tax breaks, waivers of industry regulations, exemptions from import and export duties, suspension of rules requiring foreign investors to make investments in conjunction with local partners, strict guarantees against expropriation, assurances of physical security and access to efficient communications and transportation networks.

Well over a dozen African countries now offer most or all of these regulatory waivers and exemptions. And as they strive to attract foreign investors to EPZs, African countries are also offering them a full panoply of tax exemptions:

- Kenya provides EPZ investors with a 10-year tax holiday.
- Egypt offers entities operating in "free zones" a life-long exemption from all taxes.
- Cameroon's "industrial free zones" give investors a 100 percent tax exemption for 10 years followed by a 15 percent tax thereafter and free repatriation of profits; the country also gives industrial free zone investors "flexibility in hiring/firing workers," according to a promotional brochure, and an exemption from the nation's standard wage classification scheme.
- Mauritius' export processing zones offer a flat 15 percent corporate tax rate and dividends tax free for 20 years.

Senegal, Morocco, Zimbabwe, Tunisia, Ghana, Namibia, Mozambique and the Ivory Coast are among the other nations offering similar EPZ incentive packages.

In the vast majority of the African countries now infatuated with the concept, EPZs are only in their infancy. Most countries have only a few EPZ sites developed, if that, and typically very few investors.

As important as tax exemptions may be, however, and while basic infrastructure networks are a prerequisite to foreign investors considering a site, in practice one of the chief attractions of EPZs is a cheap, brutalized and controlled workforce.

EPZ investors tend to be smaller concerns in labor-intensive industries, especially garments. Increasingly, they are Asian investors on the run from escalating wages in their home countries. With labor costs a high proportion of production expenses, a few pennies an hour difference in wages matters to these companies' managers.

Wages in EPZs are almost always rock bottom, and conditions are typically, though not always, oppressive. EPZ workers—overwhelmingly women—commonly work in unsafe, dirty factories, and are forced to work at high speeds with supervisors who abuse them. Workers in Chinese and Thai factories in EPZs or their local equivalent have perished in major industrial fires [see "China's Toy Industry Tinderbox," *Multinational Monitor,* September 1994]. In El Salvador, Haiti and Guatemala, women workers report being beaten, sexually harassed and cursed at by supervisors [see "The U.S.-Haiti Connection: Rich Companies, Poor Workers," *Multinational Monitor,* April 1996; "Zones of Exploitation: Korean Investment in Guatemala, *Multinational Monitor,* December 1992].

In country after country, from Sri Lanka to El Salvador to the Philippines, workers who have tried to organize to improve conditions in EPZs have met with brutal repression—firings, jailings, police attacks, assassination by death squad [see "Organizing and Repression," *Multinational Monitor,* June 1995; "Busting Labor in Sri Lanka," *Multinational Monitor,* January/February 1995; "Repression to Cooptation: Challenges for Women Workers in Southeast Asia," *Multinational Monitor,* November 1993]. In a March 1996 report, the International Confederation of Free Trade Unions concludes, "Anti-union repression is an integral part of the export processing zone concept. Potential investors see the absence of trade unions as a major advantage of the zones, and their preference for women workers is a deliberate part of their anti-union policy."

Examining the Tigers

It is not the disturbing record of labor repression that has led to the EPZ fad sweeping the continent. It is the desire to imitate some of the magic that enabled the Asian Tigers to transform themselves from very poor to relatively well off countries in a manner of decades.

The World Bank and neoliberal theorists take from the Asian experience a single lesson: while inward-oriented development fails, export-oriented economies succeed. African nations have now bought this interpretation.

But those who have examined the Asian Tigers' experience carefully—commentators such as Walden Bello and Alice Amsden—have convincingly shown that the Tigers succeeded for a range of reasons which EPZ promoters such as the World Bank ignore.

Part of the Tigers' success can be traced to unique historical circumstances: the Tigers began their export drive at a time when the United States economy was growing rapidly, and when hot and cold war battlefields in Asia made the United States a huge regional consumer. The Tigers also began their export push at a time when other Third World nations were focusing on producing for domestic markets, meaning the the Tigers did not face the ruinous competition that awaits those who now undertake low-wage, export-oriented strategies.

More generally, the Tigers' achievements followed from critical policy choices that are antithetical to World Bank economic orthodoxy. First, major land reforms preceded the industrialization of the large Tigers, Taiwan and South Korea, as well as Japan. Land reforms helped jumpstart the domestic market by creating a significant market of rural consumers for both agricultural inputs and some consumer goods; reduced the pressure on the rural poor to migrate to the cities by giving them a base to support themselves; strengthened the bargaining position of factory workers for whom the option of returning to the countryside became more viable; and created the basis for relatively economically egalitarian societies. Second, governments in the Tiger countries intervened heavily in the economy, protecting and subsidizing local enterprises in a variety of ways.

In the absence of these historical happenstances and decisive policy decisions, there are strong reasons to believe the Tigers' export-led strategies would have failed.

For skeptics who raise doubts about the likely success of the African EPZ strategy, however, proponents have a single-word answer: Mauritius.

The Mauritius Miracle

The small island-nation of Mauritius, located far off of Africa's southeast coast, to the east of Madagascar in the Indian Ocean, has successfully relied on EPZs to fuel its development since 1970. The country has turned the entire island into an EPZ, offering EPZ status and benefits to exporters wherever they locate.

According to a July 1995 UNCTAD report, per capita income in Mauritius has risen by approximately 500 percent in the last 25 years, from $600 to $3,000; EPZs employ nearly 90,000 workers, one third of the country's workforce; unemployment has fallen from 20 percent to almost nil; and EPZs have successfully enabled Mauritius to diversity away from sugar exports, which accounted for more than 90 percent of the country's export earnings in 1971 but have now been surpassed by EPZ revenue.

"The credit arguably goes to the progressive contribution of the export processing zone for the elevation of Mauritius from the ranks of low income to middle income economies in a span of less than 20 years, in sharp contrast with regressive welfare loss in most African countries during the same period," concludes the UNCTAD report.

Mauritius' EPZ sector grew rapidly by producing or assembling the normal set of labor-intensive goods—apparel (accounting for 80 percent of the jobs created by foreign EPZ investors), watches, jewellery. But as wages have risen, the country has lost its wage competitiveness in low-end textile and garment manufacturing to countries such as China, Bangladesh, Vietnam and Madagascar, according to the UNCTAD report. Since 1993, Mauritius has adopted an explicit policy of promoting more technologically advanced production in EPZs; whether initially promising results ultimately prove successful remains to be seen.

Foreign investors in Mauritius EPZs come from across the globe, but the large plurality—30 percent—are Hong Kong-based.

Nearly three-quarters of the exports from Mauritius are shipped to the European Union; most of the rest go to the United States.

As successful as the Mauritius EPZ experience has been, it, like the Asian Tigers, has benefitted from unique factors, and is unlikely to be replicated in Africa, argues Dr. Godfrey Kanyenze, chief economist for the Zimbabwe Confederation of Trade Unions. As a country with strong cultural ties to Hong Kong, Mauritius was uniquely well positioned to attract Hong Kong investment, Kanyenze explains. Mauritius also benefitted from Hong Kong investors' nervousness about staying in Hong Kong once China and Britain agreed to transfer Hong Kong to Chinese control in 1997.

Maybe even more importantly, foreign investors used Mauritius as a platform from which trade rules could be manipulated. Investors took advantage of Mauritius' membership in the Lomé Convention, a special trading arrangement which gives former European colonies preferential access to the European market. The country also enabled investors from Hong Kong and other Asian Tigers to place "made in Mauritius" labels in their goods, and thus circumvent the textile quotas established by the Multi-Fiber Agreement. The new General Agreement on Tariffs and Trade (GATT), however, is phasing out the textile quota system, and reducing tariffs so that preferential treatment will be far less important.

Finally, Mauritius was lucky. Like the Asian Tigers, it pursued an export-oriented strategy at a time when most other nations were looking inward. In contrast, a couple dozen African nations are now planning to participate in a global competition for foreign investment. Mauritius was also able to turn its isolation and small size to advantage; the creation of 90,000 jobs absorbed all of its excess labor—but similar-sized job creation would barely make a dent in the unemployment situation in a large country like Kenya.

Kenya Joins the Craze

Kenyan authorities, mesmerized with the Mauritius success story, are forging ahead with an EPZ plan. While

EPZs in Ghana: A Dismal "Success Story"

ACCRA, GHANA—The firing of more than 50 garment workers at a Volta Garments factory housed here in Ghana's capital city's export processing zone (EPZ) stands as a potent rejoinder to those who praise the proliferation of African EPZs and to those citing Ghana as an African free-market success story.

The Hong Kong-based Volta fired a first group of workers in June 1995 for refusing to work seven days a week at below the minimum wage; it suspended a second group which took legal action following blocked attempts to form a union.

The first group complained to Ghana's Commission on Human Rights and Administrative Justice (CHRAJ), and recently attained a favorable settlement. But although the settlement requires Volta Garments to pay the employees six-and-one-half months of salaries each, the workers remain bitter about their experience with Accra's EPZ.

The second group of workers challenged in court Volta's attack on their right to unionize and still await a final verdict.

Before the labor conflict and firings, Volta Garments' regular work week was eight hours a day, seven days a week. It paid the workers 800 cedis a day, about 50 U.S. cents, only two thirds of the minimum wage of 1,200 cedis. Even the minimum wage barely pays for a loaf of bread, which costs 1,000 cedis.

The Volta Garment workers were entitled to premium pay for overtime and weekend work, but the company refused to comply with the law. Former Volta worker Freda Sasu says her manager "said that he would add it to the monthly pay, but he never did." According to Sasu, any extra pay was at less than the standard rate, not more.

Workers complained to the government labor minister when he visited the factory in early 1995, but, according to Sasu, "He said that there was no work in Ghana and that we should just keep quiet."

Eventually, the Volta workers decided to challenge the company directly. On June 11, 1995, more than 100 members of the 550 mainly female workforce refused to go to work. "We were tired," says Sasu, "and when we come in they don't pay us."

"When we reported to work on Monday, the gate was locked up. They made people sign a form to agree to come to work every day." Fifty-one workers refused; the company then fired them.

After the first round of firings, workers tried to improve conditions at the plant by setting up a union. Volta Garments responded harshly. When five workers applied to the High Court for a proclamation that they had the right to join a union, they were suspended by the company. The five have since won the right to return to work, but final disposition of their complaint against the company is still pending in the courts.

The Illusion of Success

EPZs are an important part of Ghana's firm and ongoing embrace of the International Monetary Fund (IMF) and World Bank's structural adjustment program that emphasizes exports and deregulation.

Under the leadership of J. J. Rawlings, who first seized power in a 1979 coup and was elected president in 1992, Ghana has carefully adhered to World Bank/IMF-approved policies. It has formally pursued structural adjustment since 1983.

In the eyes of the World Bank, Ghana is a structural adjustment success story, registering growth rates of about 5 percent during much of the reform period, high above most other African countries.

Critics, however, say that the need to create a "success story" ensured that aid flowed disproportionately into Ghana; that despite 13 years of structural adjustment programs the economy is still structurally dependent on primary commodities (cocoa, gold and timber account for 80 percent of total export earnings); and that dependency on, and vulnerability to, foreign interests has increased, not decreased, with debt rising from $1.4 billion in 1982 to $5 billion in 1994.

More immediately, ordinary Ghanaians say that they've not seen the results of the growth. Christian Agyei, secretary general of the Ghanaian Trade Union Congress says: "We think that growth must transfer into development. . . . To us, [Ghana] is not a success story." More bluntly, Kwarteng Ofosuhene, a student from the University of Ghana, says, "The growth is always on paper and never in our pockets."

Ordinary Ghanaians have much to complain about:

The minimum wage is approximately a quarter of its level of 15 years ago, in dollar-denominated terms;

Massive devaluation of the currency (from 2.75 cedis to US$1 in 1983 to a 1,600-to-1 ratio today) has fueled high inflation, which rose to over 70 percent earlier in the year.

The government has axed at least 100,000 public-sector jobs, and many more have been lost in the private sector.

The World Bank and IMF claim that Ghana's pioneering PAMSCAD (the Programs to Mitigate the Social Costs of Adjustment) has cushioned the blow of the free market reforms. But Agyei says the very existence of PAMSCAD is "an admittance that the programs didn't go well." PAMSCAD is underfunded, he says, and has made little impact on the lives of ordinary Ghanaians.

The statistics support Agyei's claims, with an array of social indicators worsening: the country now has a worse under-5 mortality rate then it did in 1975; it enrolls fewer children in primary and secondary school than it did in 1980; and has fewer doctors per person than it had in the 1960s and 1970s.

Winners and losers

The case of the Volta workers illustrates clearly the winners and losers in Ghana after 13 years of World Bank/IMF-induced free market "adjustments." The formal sector has shrunk and now employs fewer people than it did in 1960—when the population was less than half its present level. Informal work makes up 80 percent of all jobs in cities like Accra. Unemployment has reached an estimated 30 percent. The result: an enormous surplus of workers desperate for a job—and rich pickings for the sweatshops.

When Ghana passed its Free Zone Act in 1995, opening the way for the establishment of EPZs, EPZ investors immediately saw the enormous bargaining leverage they would possess. Although Ghanaian unions pressed the government to guarantee that national labor laws would be applied in the EPZs, reports Harry Mbiah, administrative secretary of the Trade Union Congress, the government refused, agreeing only to a reference that certain International Labor Organization standards would be upheld.

With minimal protection for organizing and a workforce that, the investors believed, would work for anything—as well as tax and other incentives offered to EPZ investors—companies like Volta Garments were sure to prosper—and they have.

The Volta Garments workers have tried to stand up to the overwhelming power of one of the beneficiaries of Ghana's structural adjustment program, but even their partial victory in winning compensation has brought them little solace. Even though publicity has forced management to improve conditions, many workers say that things have not improved enough and that they will not go back to work for the company.

Samuel Asane, one of the leaders of the first group of employees, says sadly, "We are slaves in our own country."

—*Mark Hunter*

approximately 97 percent of African EPZ workers are in Mauritius, Tunisia or Egypt, according to Kanyenze, of those countries which have recently embraced EPZs, Kenya is one of the furthest along.

The Kenyan EPZ Authority, created by the EPZ Act of 1990, has certified 13 zones in four cities including Nairobi. So far, more than 20 companies employing more than 3,000 workers are active and exporting from EPZs. Currently, Kenyan EPZ jobs are predominantly in textiles; the government would like to see a diversification to include leather goods, electronics and telecommunications products, solar products and horticulture processing, says the EPZ Authority's promotions executive, Jonathan Chifallu. In 10 to 15 years, Chifallu says, the government hopes to see 30,000 jobs in the EPZ sector.

The broad goals of the Kenyan EPZ program, says Chifallu, are creating jobs, expanding the country's export base and eventually promoting training and technology transfer. He also hopes local, African-owned and

-operated companies will eventually take advantage of the EPZ benefits. For now, most EPZ investors are foreign, from Hong Kong, Korea, Germany, Ireland and elsewhere.

As in other countries, investors in Kenyan EPZs are exempted from a wide range of taxes and regulations. In addition to a 10-year tax holiday, investors receive a waiver of import and export duties and of value-added taxes (VAT). They are exempt from the country's Factories and Statistics Acts, which subject factories to a number of inspection and reporting requirements.

All licensing and other bureaucratic requirements are handled not through normal government agencies, but through the EPZ Authority, which provides streamlined, "one-stop" service for EPZ investors. EPZ Authority officials also provide "aftercare" once new facilities are operating; they will speed the unloading of goods or oversee utility connections, if there is any bureaucratic delay, and otherwise intervene to overcome bureaucratic obstacles, says Chifallu.

The streamlined assistance from the EPZ Authority is particularly important in overcoming Kenya's legendary corruption, says James Gatigi, manager of the Sameer Industrial Park, an EPZ in Nairobi. "Within the EPZ program, companies are sort of protected," says Gatigi. "The framework does not allow for corruption." The one-stop EPZ shop for business licenses enables investors to avoid paying the normal bribes to government officials. Companies "don't have to bribe those guys; they are trying to bring [the companies] here," says Gatigi.

The Sameer Industrial Park is the largest currently operating EPZ in Kenya, housing nine companies which employ 1,300 workers. Investors are from Korea, Hong Kong, Malaysia, Germany and five other countries. Four of the facilities at the site make or assemble garments.

The EPZ is a wholly owned subsidiary of Firestone East Africa, a publicly traded company which itself is 20 percent owned by Firestone/Bridgestone USA. Firestone decided to develop the site for light industry before adoption of Kenya's EPZ Act, quickly turning the industrial park into an EPZ after passage of the Act. Sameer provides perimeter security, general maintenance, and optional support services ranging from secretarial support to forklifts to recruitment.

Firestone insists that EPZ companies tolerate unions; and Gatigi says all companies at the EPZ will be unionized. Although some employers prefer not to have unions, Gatigi says, in fact it is easier to manage with negotiated contracts.

In Kenya, where the labor movement is exceedingly weak—as it is in almost all African countries outside of South Africa and to a lesser extent Zimbabwe—unionization poses little threat to employer prerogatives. "Kenyan labor has not been disruptive," Gatigi explains, adding that the country "does not have a militant type" of labor movement.

Agrees Chifallu, "Kenya has a non-militant workforce—and that is our strength."

EPZs: A Bad Debt

An obvious concern with the EPZs in Kenya and elsewhere is why investors in EPZs, usually foreigners, deserve preferential treatment over other businesses. Certainly the most beneficial components of the Kenyan EPZ program—avoidance of excessive bureaucratic licensing requirements, freedom from corruption and the provision of sound infrastructure—are benefits that should be provided to all investors in the country, most particularly Kenyans producing for the local market, the business group most disfavored by the EPZ program.

The Kenyan officials supporting EPZs say EPZs are just a beachhead in an eventual transformation of the entire national economy. "The reality of globalization is hitting" African governments, says Chifallu. "EPZs are very useful in bringing reforms into the economy. . . . If they prove effective, they can be extended to the whole economy." But in referring to reforms, Chifallu refers only partially to streamlining the bureaucracy. More generally, he says, EPZs can spur Kenya to adopt a more liberalized, deregulated and export-oriented economic strategy.

In that sense, EPZs pose a major threat not only to workers but to Kenya and African nations' economic well-being. As governments spend resources on EPZs, they forsake the opportunity, as the ZCTU's Kanyenze points out, to create more jobs for the same amount of money by investing in and supporting small enterprises serving the local market. Even more dangerously, they adopt economic policies that tie their countries ever tighter into the globalized economy but which are likely to discriminate against and harm local businesses producing to meet local needs.

The winnings and losses of the African countries' heavy wagers that they will be able to grow and prosper in the global casino economy will be totaled in the years and decades to come. For now, it can be said that they are betting against the odds.

Article 4   The UNESCO Courier, October 1994

Who Was Responsible?

Africans were above all victims of the slave trade, but some of them were partners in it.

Elikia M'Bokolo

Elikia M'Bokolo, Zairean historian, is director of studies at the Ecole des Hautes Etudes en Sciences Sociales in Paris. He is the author of many works on African history, cultures and development problems, including L'Afrique au 20ᵉ siècle, le continent convoité *(1985) and* Afrique noire, Histoire et civilisations, 19–20ᵉ siècles *(1992).*

To judge from the number of countries taking part in it, the slave trade must have been for Europeans both a profitable business and, considering the number of years it lasted, a familiar fact of life. Even so, in some of the ports involved in the trade, like Nantes, the slave-traders themselves were reluctant to call it by its name and instead spoke of it in more veiled terms as the "matter".

What about the Africans? Were they merely its victims or were they conscious and consenting partners in a business arrangement with whose terms they were perfectly familiar?

A controversial question

There has always been heated debate over the part played by Africans in the slave trade. For a long time, the slave-traders took refuge behind what they saw as the irrefutable argument that the Africans made a regular practice of selling their fellow Africans, and that if the Europeans refused to buy slaves from them, other people—meaning the Arabs, who also used black slaves, among others—would hasten to do so. Nowadays, African intellectuals and statesmen contend that these exchanges were always unequal (in that human beings were bought with baubles) and that the Europeans always resorted to violence to get the Africans to co-operate against their will.

For historians the story is not quite as simple as that, in the first place because our criteria are not the same as those of 500 or even 150 years ago. We believe that if only one slave had been shipped across the Atlantic, it would have been one too many. But did Africans think like this in the past? Secondly, the slave trade, which

went on for almost four centuries, was a very complex process involving a very wide variety of power relationships and participants whose interests and responses were bound to have changed with the course of time. This has prompted the British historian Basil Davidson to say that the "notion that Europe altogether imposed the slave trade on Africa is without any foundation in history. . . . [it] is as baseless as the European notion that institutions of bondage were in some way peculiar to Africa."*

From slave-raiding to slave-trading

The first method by which the Europeans acquired African slaves was through straightforward abduction. Striking examples of this can be found in the celebrated *Crónica dos Feitos da Guiné (Chronicle of the Discovery and Conquest of Guinea)*, written by the Portuguese Gomes Eanes de Zurara in the mid-fifteenth century. When the Europeans landed on the coasts of Africa, they stopped at random at places they thought might be suitable for their purpose and set out on man-hunts. This was not without its risks, however, as evidenced by the massacre in 1446 of almost all the members of the expedition led by Nuno Tristao near the Cap Vert peninsula in present-day Senegal. This was not the only such massacre, but it certainly shows that the Africans were determined to fight against enslavement.

The drawbacks of slave-raiding were that its outcome was uncertain and it was incapable of catering for the constantly growing demand, when the plantations and mines of the Americas had to be supplied with slave labour. The Portuguese were the first to switch from merely seizing captives to actually trading in slaves, following a suggestion made by Prince Henry the Navigator in 1444 and subsequently followed by Portuguese sovereigns until the end of the fifteenth century. However, even after this trade had become a routine matter,

*Basil Davidson, *Black Mother, The Years of the African Slave Trade*, Boston/Toronto, Little, Brown and Company, 1961.

raiding continued to provide slave-traders with an additional source of supply. The so-called "roving" trade—in which slaving ships sailed along the coast and captured slaves at various places until they had a full consignment—often took the form of armed incursions against villages situated near to the coast. When countries engaged in the slave trade, they often began by organizing raiding expeditions, as did the first vessels hailing from the "twelve colonies" (the future United States of America) in the first half of the seventeenth century.

By that time, however, the leading European nations had imposed a code of ethics of a kind on the slave trade. The English, Portuguese and French agreed to make a joint declaration to the effect that the slave trade was justified only when it involved slaves duly sold by Africans. Forts were built along the coastline in order to organize the trade and at the same time to instill a healthy sense of fear among the Africans. The message they conveyed was perfectly clear: "Sell us slaves—and we shall leave it to you to choose them as you see fit—or else we shall take the slaves we need at random."

The slave trade was therefore a one-sided relationship, founded and maintained on the threat of force. We once again have to agree with Basil Davidson when he says, "Africa and Europe were jointly involved. . . . Europe dominated the connection, shaped and promoted the slave trade, and continually turned it to European advantage and to African loss."

Affairs of state and lineage societies

At its height, the slave trade was regarded by Africans as a kind of diabolical plot in which they had to be accomplices or perish. Hence almost all the lineage or state societies of the African seaboard were compelled to become involved in it. They did this in ways and under conditions which differed significantly from one region to another and from one period to another.

The social history of pre-colonial Africa shows that slavery was a widespread institution in states where, in some instances, a domestic trade in slaves already existed for military or economic reasons. However, a distinction has to be made between those states which maintained relations with the outside world and those which did not. The former were quicker and more ready to join in the slave-trade cycle. This was true of the states bordering the Sahel, which were already in the practice of selling slaves, among other goods, to their Arab and Berber partners, who actually went on to sell some of them to the Europeans. The chronicler Alvise de Ca' da Mósto, who took part in a Portuguese expedition to Senegambia in 1455–1456, reported that the local sovereigns were skilled at taking advantage of the new competition that was growing up between the trans-Saharan

trade and the Atlantic trade by selling slaves to the Arabs and Berbers in exchange for horses, and other slaves to the Portuguese in exchange for European goods.

The situation was by no means the same in those states which had no trading links with the outside world. The part these played in the slave trade is a pointer to the ambiguous and contradictory attitudes they displayed and the difficulties they faced when they came to take decisions, often under duress. The kingdom of Kongo, one of the most powerful in Africa at the time of its encounter with the Portuguese at the end of the fifteenth century, is a typical example. In the view of contemporary historians, its economic, political and social standing was on a par with that of Portugal. From the time of the very first contacts, the Kongo nobility became converts to Christianity and the king saw fit to address the Portuguese sovereign as "my brother". Yet the fact was that the slave trade had already started, in violation of the agreements, both tacit and formal, concluded between the two states. A number of letters, in which the king of Kongo protested against the seizure of slaves, including members of noble families, have survived to the present day. There is still some controversy as to what was really the motive behind these protestations. Some historians regard them as being an outburst of nationalist sentiment, but others look upon them more as a sign of the concern of the country's aristocracy not to allow so lucrative a business to slip through their hands. In any event, the kingdom did not survive the impact of the slave trade for very long. The same drama was to be played out to varying degrees elsewhere in Africa.

The kingdom of Dahomey was also exposed to the bitter experience of the slave trade. In the mid-eighteenth century, it took over the port of Ouidah, one of the main centres of the trade in the Gulf of Guinea. The king of Dahomey regarded the port—where there was a growing buildup of firearms—as posing a threat to the security of his possessions, since the slave trade gave it a tactical advantage over its neighbours. Once they took control of Ouidah, the rulers of Dahomey were caught in a vicious circle: in order to maintain a strong state, they needed rifles and gunpowder, but to obtain these they had to sell slaves to the Europeans. The answer was really very straightforward: since the sale of the kingdom's own subjects was strictly forbidden, powerful armies were raised to raid neighbouring peoples and make war on them for the purpose of taking slaves.

Unlike states, lineage societies did not have any means of obtaining slaves by force. In such cases, servitude was based on complex practices in which various categories of social outcasts, such as criminals, misfits, sorcerers and victims of natural or economic disasters, were relegated to being slaves. Even so, this would not have been sufficient to turn the slave trade into the vast and lasting business it became. Other means were therefore found of meeting the Europeans' demands. For example, in the city of Arochukwu ("the voice of Chukwu", the supreme deity), in the Niger delta, a celebrated oracle whose authority was respected by all the population was called on to designate those who, for whatever reason, were condemned to be sold into slavery. This practice continued until the beginning of the nineteenth century.

In other regions, especially in central Africa, trading networks were gradually established, extending from the coast deep into the interior. All the goods exported or imported via these networks—predominantly slaves—transited through the heads of the lineages. In Gabon and Loango in particular, the coastal societies forming the key links in these trading networks had a highly developed ranking social order based on the extent to which their members were involved in the slave trade. Kinship relations, which are fundamental in lineage societies, gradually gave way to relations based on fortunes made in the trade, which came to dictate people's standing in society.

Africans and the abolition of the slave trade

On the African side, however, the basis of the slave trade was very precariously balanced. The part played by Africans in the trade cannot be discussed without reference to the part they played in its abolition. In a one-sided view of history, the role of Europeans—philosophers, thinkers, men of religion and businessmen—is too often stressed, while that played by the Africans is left in the shade. Some people have even gone so far as to tax the Africans with being the main impediment to the phasing-out of the trade in the nineteenth century. Nothing could be further from the truth.

Outside Africa, the resistance of the victims of the slave trade—which took a variety of forms, including the "Back to Africa" movement, the founding of "Maroon" communities and even armed insurrection, like that in San Domingo in 1791—was primarily instrumental in calling the whole institution of slavery into question. Those who had managed to escape its clutches took a very active but often unacknowledged part in the campaign for abolition. They included people like Ottobah Cuguano, who had been born in Fantiland, in present-day Ghana, had been a slave in the West Indies, and published his *Thoughts and Sentiments on the Evil and Wicked Traffic of Slavery* in London in 1787. In 1789, another African, Olaudah Equiano, alias Gustavus Vassa, a native of Iboland, in Nigeria, published, again in London, *The Interesting Narrative of the Life of Olaudah Equiano, or Gustavus Vassa the African, written by himself.* These books played a significant role in the movement of opinion which led to the abolition of the slave trade.

In Africa itself, all through the "years of trial" of the slave trade, along with slaves, blacks continued to sell the produce of their soil and subsoil, such as timber, ivory, spices, gold, vegetable oils, and others besides. Changing European demand was sufficient for the Africans to turn to a more "legal" form of commerce.

Article 5

The World & I, March 1996

In the Shadows

The Persistence of Witchcraft in Africa

*Muiva Ndambuki was bewitched in January 1994. He is certain of it,
because that's when the headaches and stomach troubles the forty-year-old Kenyan
father of eight had been experiencing suddenly got worse. "It felt as if a metal rod
was being turned around in my brain. I kept vomiting."*

Sinikka Kahl

Sinikka Kahl is a free-lance writer based in Nairobi.

"I couldn't sleep. I went to the hospital, and the pills they gave me did not help. Then I knew it was witchcraft."

Ndambuki knows the perpetrator. "It was a fellow worker on the construction site where I work near Machakos. He was jealous, because the boss preferred me and I was a better carpenter."

Ndambuki describes the man who allegedly made him so sick as a typical witch, a weird character whom nobody liked. "He was solitary. An outsider. He did not come from our area but from farther away, from Kitui," says Ndambuki.

In sub-Saharan Africa, an experience like this is nothing exceptional. Millions of people in eastern, southern, and western Africa believe that there are witches, both male and female. In the shadows of skyscrapers and among computers and fax machines, people maintain that their slow career progress is due to a colleague's witchcraft. Worldly politicians suspect opponents of using witchcraft when they lose an election. Wealthy businessmen have their products "protected" by diviners in case a competitor resorts to witchcraft. Religious people of every faith take care when cutting hair or nails not to leave the remains lying around, so that they will not be taken by a witch for use in a spell.

Witchcraft beliefs are said to be typical of prescientific, low-technology societies, where there are few rational explanations for illness and misfortune. Why then, have they persisted even in cities, where the alternative of Western rationalism is available to many? These age-old beliefs, some researchers argue, give an answer to the fundamental problem of evil. And to many Africans, they do so more convincingly than the Western worldview.

Reversing Human Norms

In contemporary Africa, witchcraft beliefs are considered primitive, and both church and state have tried to eradicate or discourage their practice. Nevertheless, all sorts of bad luck—from a traffic accident to a woman's inability to conceive children, a student's exam failure to difficulties in finding a marriage partner, a crop failure to an epidemic—are still attributed to witchcraft. Though few people will openly discuss witchcraft beliefs, anecdotal evidence suggests they are still widely held.

In Busia, western Kenya, a courtroom was stunned into terrified silence when the tools of a suspected witch were dumped on the table: the claws of an animal, rags, human hair, shirt buttons, horns, ashes, coins, and herbs. In South Africa's Northern Transvaal Province, an old man was recently stoned and burned to death, accused of causing lightning to strike and kill a schoolboy. In Kitwe, Zambia, street battles erupted between local residents and police, who were trying to protect a woman accused of killing a boy in order to transfer his intelligence to her son. On their arrival in Zaire, members of the Kenyan soccer team Gor Mania were thoroughly searched because the competing team had claimed they were carrying amulets that would enable them to win the game. In Sierra Leone's civil war, soldiers known as the Tamas, allied with the government, declared that they had conquered a town by turning into lions and leopards and tearing their enemies into pieces.

Though witchcraft beliefs are thought to be stronger in Africa than on other continents, they are not specifically African. Witchcraft beliefs exist "from Africa to the South Seas and from Asia to America," notes Philip Mayer in *Witchcraft and Sorcery*. In Europe, an estimated nine million women were burned as witches in witchhunts that lasted for centuries; the last burning of a witch in Europe took place as late as 1782, in Switzerland. Even apparently unrelated phenomena, such as

Freed from Sorcery

In the center of Nairobi, businessmen walk briskly before shop windows offering everything from designer clothes to computers. Secretaries meet for lunch in pizzerias or Japanese restaurants, while international organizations hold meetings in modern skyscrapers. In the same city center, on the more run-down streets, signs advertise *mgangas*, diviners who offer help against witchcraft and other problems. And only a short distance away, in the slums, their business is booming.

The "clinic" of Issa Namanda Lusambu, known as "Professor Issa," is in one of the better slums, where drab concrete houses dot narrow, stony paths of reddish dust, even as the sweet smell of rot floats from a pile of garbage.

In the waiting room, a man is sitting on a comfortable armchair covered with hand-knit white lace. He is not looking at the assortment of pictures on the dull gray walls; his mind seems far away. Suddenly, he collapses on the floor with a loud thump and lets out a wail of pain.

"He's almost dead," Issa says. "We have to act quickly." An assistant helps him carry the unconscious man into a small, windowless room wall-papered with red cloths. Gourds, fly whisks, bags covered with cowrie shells, and other magic objects form a dark, musty smelling pile in one corner. The assistant forces the man's mouth open, and Issa pours in an herbal concoction. A protective talisman—a small, square leather bag filled with secret substances—is placed on the man's chest.

Suddenly, it's completely dark, and the rattling sound of the gourd calls forth the ancestors. Then, a loud knocking and thumping fills the room, as if someone—or something—were walking all over the walls. Eerie, almost inhuman, voices come from all over the room and at the same time from far away. Issa's ancestors, who had promised to help him with this difficult case of bewitchment, have allegedly returned.

Later, when the lights are back on, the small room is filled with bitter smoke as the patient is revived by burning herbs. Issa displays a clay pot which he says was brought by his ancestors from the place from which the witch "remote-controlled" the victim. "Don't come near it." he warns. "It's lethal." The pot, he says, contains the witchcraft that killed the man's four children, make him lose his land, made him impotent, and almost killed him.

Talismans, animal skulls, insects, and other unidentifiable objects sit in a muddle of reddish sand. The patient, who has sat up, recoils in fear. Issa, a thoroughly modern-looking man in his white shirt and stylish yellow trousers, pokes at a small bone. "Could be a human bone," he says. "Bad stuff. It has to be neutralized by pouring blood over it. We'll sacrifice a chicken."

—S.K.

McCarthyism in the United States, have been likened to witch-hunts.

Beliefs in places thousands of miles apart present so many similarities that it has been suggested that witchcraft beliefs have a common prehistoric origin. Images of witches show resemblances between peoples as diverse as the Pueblo Indians of Mexico and the Gusii people of Kenya. Some aspects of African tales of witches are reminiscent of our own folktales and horror movies.

What are witches like? According to the beliefs of various African peoples, witches can fly. They dig out corpses, eat the flesh, and dance naked on graves at night. They copulate with animals, commit incest, and eat their own children. They may come at night, take a victim's head, use it as a ball in a game, and return it in the morning without the aggrieved's noticing anything. They may walk backward and on their hands, eat salt when thirsty, and hang by their feet from a tree when resting.

Witches, in short, reverse human norms. They are everything a human being is not, must not be. They are a society's collective nightmare, a personification of its fears and forbidden desires.

But in real life, those accused of being witches are not the terrifying, other-worldly creatures of nightmares. In Africa, as elsewhere, people are most likely to accuse each other of witchcraft in small, close-knit communities, where jealousies and tensions abound. The witch is hardly ever a stranger; he is, on the contrary, someone familiar, someone close to you, someone who knows you well and wishes you ill. It may be a colleague, as in Ndambuki's case, or a neighbor, or even a family member.

The strongest kind of witchcraft, it is whispered, requires human body parts. "The most popular body parts used in magic are genitals, the heart, the brain, and the finger," reports Chris Erasmus, the correspondent of the Kenyan daily *Nation* in Johannesburg. In countries such as South Africa, Zambia, and Botswana, there have been reports of murders being committed to obtain body parts for witchcraft rituals. In South Africa, a small boy was found almost dead, his genitals and thumbs cut off. Evidence of such horrors is, however, extremely rare.

Among some peoples, such as the Tswana of Botswana, witches are believed to use a very concrete tool: poison. But usually, a witch manipulates someone through his fears. Even Westerners living in Africa may find the surface layer of their rational consciousness suddenly wearing thin.

"I come from a dysfunctional family, and a lot of fear was planted in me during my childhood," says a European woman living in Nairobi. "Then, in Kenya, I fired a maid. She left with a threat that I would not live another five years. Then I found this ugly black piece of cloth on my daughter's doll; it looked like something that had been put there for witchcraft. I told myself that it was just superstition, but after that, every time something bad happened—the child got sick, strange animals soiled our laundry—I could not help thinking that it was working."

Western doctors have seen cases where people died of fear of witchcraft. A person who believed himself to be bewitched simply gave up hope, though there was no observable physical cause of death.

Fear of Doing Well

Do Africans, then, live in constant fear, as many Westerners believe? No more than a U.S. citizen might live in fear of a traffic accident. According to anthropologist Lucy Mair, "Most people begin to think seriously of witchcraft after disaster has struck." But do people really try to bewitch each other, or is it just imagination?

In Kenya, a woman found that her business had started failing: Her trucks had accidents, and her bank started sending her notices about overdrafts. Suddenly everything was going wrong. A friend advised her that she had probably been bewitched. "You remove a thorn in the flesh with another thorn. Fight witchcraft with witchcraft," the friend said.

The woman consulted a diviner, who offered not only to lift the spell but to send the evil spirits back to the jealous acquaintance who had bewitched her. "The facts in a given case can always be interpreted in opposite ways," explains Mayer. "Each party can say that his own sufferings are due to his enemy's witchcraft and that his enemy's sufferings are due to his own *mosira* [protective magic]." There is no doubt that people do try to put spells on each other—but who is the witch and who the victim depends on your point of view.

In the African countryside, a stranger may experience a hospitality and human warmth that are becoming increasingly rare in the Western world. Land may be collectively used by a clan, and equality and sharing are still important values—but they also have the negative side of holding back development. Here, it would seem almost indecent if someone did too well. The individualistic, achieving Western hero could easily be suspected of being a witch.

Often, people accused of witchcraft are marginal and poor; they may be deformed; they may make others feel guilty and therefore angry at them. But the supposed witch can also be the opposite of a loser. He may be someone too beautiful, too clever, too successful.

"There is usually a great fear of displaying one's ability to build a remarkable house, dress smartly or do well in school," one inhabitant explains in a witch-fearing village near Voi, Kenya. Research by students in the Lands Institute of Dar-es-Salaam showed that witchcraft beliefs were an obstacle to development in the northern district of Handeni in Tanzania. People fear that if they do well, they will be accused of witchcraft, or bewitched out of jealousy. Though he is the operator of a Nairobi clinic and a high school-educated diviner, Issa Namanda Lusambu echoes the opinion of many when he says, "It is witchcraft that is keeping Africa poor."

Solutions to Evil

Why did Ndambuki fall ill? In the West, it would be said that he had caught a virus, or that there was some other medical explanation. But why was it just Ndambuki who had to suffer? Westerners would give vague answers about coincidence or evil as God's way of testing man's free will. But the traditional African, while he also believes in God, has clear, more immediate answers as to why bad things happen. Perhaps the spirits of your ancestors are responsible, maybe some other spirits caused the problem—or maybe it was witchcraft.

"When something goes wrong, the individual immediately wonders who has caused it to happen," writes professor John Mbiti, a specialist on African religions.

Witchcraft beliefs not only explain negative events but also provide solutions to evil. Unlike in Christianity, part of the answer is not relegated to the afterlife. Evil is dealt with here and now.

In various African countries, the evil caused by witches and spirits is handled by specialists such as priests of the traditional religions, mediums, prophets, or diviners. The "cleansing" of Ndambuki, for instance, was performed by Moki Mutwota, an experienced diviner near Machakos.

Having nothing better to do, some children have gathered to watch as Mutwota, wearing a black dress and colorful beads, receives Ndambuki at her "clinic," an empty, bare-walled concrete room. In her matter-of-fact, methodical way, Mutwota makes Ndambuki sit or stand, aligns her limbs to his, and encloses them both in circles that she makes in the air with the movements of her magic horn. This is done to remove the witchcraft from Ndambuki's body and transfer it onto Mutwota, who is resistant to the witchcraft.

In another phase of the complex ceremony, Mutwota makes small cuts in Ndambuki's forehead, hands, and feet, and rubs in curative powders. Then, in silence, the diviner throws magic objects—nuts, seashells, and glass pearls given to her by her grandmother—on the ground. All through the treatment, the man plays his part patiently, as if he was receiving aspirin in a hospital. The ceremony costs him an entire month's salary.

In the end, the oracle of the gourd promises Ndambuki health and prosperity. The worried, downcast expression has disappeared from his face as he smiles with relief. "The last time I was bewitched, her remedies kept me healthy for a long time," he says.

Traditional healers such as Mutwota are often skillful herbalists and sensitive psychologists. If they sometimes resort to tricks, that does not mean they lack a deep belief in the traditional theology and their craft. The relief that they bring, many observers have seen, may be worth the help brought by Western medicine in many cases.

Diviners treat the witches' victims, but they often cannot rid a community of witchcraft. This is done by witch-hunters. One such, the Kenyan Juma Tsume Washe, known as Kajiwe, even became a national celebrity. Kajiwe died in 1993, but the legend lives on.

Kajiwe was called when witchcraft was suspected in a homestead. He started by pointing at places, and when they were dug out, charms would often be found. Kajiwe pointed to the person who had been doing the bewitching, paraded him, and urinated on him to neutralize him. "Many people, however, were of the opinion that the complainants tipped Kajiwe beforehand about the person they suspected to be the witch," the daily *Standard* remarked.

Nevertheless, hundreds of people would flock to his home to seek help against witchcraft. Kajiwe operated in large areas of Kenya and became so prosperous that he married fifty-three wives. He had some two hundred children, for whom he built a school. At one time, the government was so wary of his possible political influence that he spent two years in prison.

Kajiwe's son and successor, Suleiman Tsuma, has developed a witch-detection ordeal that resembles those of many African peoples. He gives the suspects a magically treated piece of bread and makes them swallow it in the presence of other people. The suspect who has trouble swallowing it is said to be the witch.

Other witch-detection ordeals are more cruel and dangerous. In Zambia recently, a poisonous concoction of herbs administered by a witch-hunter left fifteen suspects dead.

The veracity of the results of witch-detection ordeals is hard to check. But many observers have testified to the efficiency of similar methods in other contexts. "One of my staff was stealing," relates a Western diplomat who used to work in Liberia. "A diviner was called. Once he had started the ceremony, with people drumming and him eyeing the suspects, the guilty one got so scared he confessed." Just as the witch gets to a victim, the witch-hunter gets to the witch through his fear.

Between Old and New

Not all supposed witches get away with confessing and repenting. Traditionally, the punishment for witchcraft in many communities would be expulsion or death. Today, there are reports of increases in witch-hunts and of lynchings of suspects in some African countries.

In Kenya in 1992, over three hundred people accused of witchcraft were lynched, often by torching their houses. In Zambia, the government tried to stop a wave of witch-hunts by ordering witch-hunters and people suspected of witchcraft to pay high fees. South Africa reported an increase in ritual killings in 1992.

The increases in witch-hunts are, no doubt, a sign of the times. Witch crazes are known to be symptomatic of increased social tensions and rapid change. In Europe, preoccupations with witchcraft became epidemic during the transition from the Middle Ages to the Renaissance and the Reformation. With the advent of urbanism, the imposition of Western values, and problems ranging from civil wars to galloping population growth, Africa is also going through tumultuous times.

In Europe, however, witchcraft accusations were official affairs, dealt with by the church and the Inquisition. The judiciaries of modern Africa usually lack laws for such cases. For instance, under Kenyan law, witchcraft is not considered a crime; people accused of being witches can only be prosecuted for intentions to cause fear, annoyance, and harm. Traditional ways of dealing with witchcraft accusations, such as mediation by village elders or witch-detection ordeals, have declined or been abolished. In the vacuum, mobs take the law into their own hands and lynch suspects.

Attitudes toward witchcraft are symptomatic of the way many Africans are caught between the old and the new. "A friend of mine, a westernized university professor, quarrelled with someone in his village of origin," says a Catholic missionary well versed in African cultures. "He was told that he would be bewitched and would not arrive back at his home in Nairobi alive. He laughed, said he didn't believe in witchcraft, and started driving toward Nairobi. But throughout the trip, he kept looking over his shoulder, paralyzed with fear. For many Africans, it's like speaking two languages, the Western and the African. You can speak both but not at the same time. Between the Western and African value systems, there is no synthesis."

Article 6

BENIN

BBC Focus on Africa, April–June 1996

Voodoo Nation

Beninoise have a new public holiday to enjoy—Voodoo Day. In January, President Soglo not only established this new date in the calendar, he declared voodoo an official religion, as Karim Okanla reports.

Karim Okanla

Karim Okanla reports for the BBC from Cotonou.

With the vast majority of Beninoise adhering to voodoo in some shape or form, the decision by President Soglo to celebrate Voodoo National Day on January 10th has met with widespread acclaim. But it has also cast a doubt over his genuine commitment to Christian values.

Until recently, President Nicephore Dieudonne Soglo was seen by many outside Benin as a modern, new-breed technocrat who had adhered to western values. The president's middle name, Dieudonne, means "God Given", and he regularly attended Sunday prayers.

In fact Soglo has been currying favour with voodoo priests since early 1992. It is said that he was saved from death a year earlier thanks to the spiritual powers of two voodoo chiefs, Daagbo Hounon and Sossa Guedehoungue. The president was then suffering from a strange combination of apparently incurable diseases which his French doctor was unable to diagnose. Some government ministers called on the two voodoo chiefs, and their medicine worked like magic. Soglo quickly recovered, and his French doctor privately confessed that there was something unfathomable about his recovery.

Thereafter voodoo became a personal issue for the president. Not only did he want to pay a moral debt and express his gratitude; above all, he was determined to restore the religious practices that had been driven underground during the previous Marxist regime of Mathieu Kerekou.

When Kerekou became president following a military coup in October 1972, he and his officers declared voodoo an evil practice, and moved to destroy sacred temples all over the nation.

What is Voodoo?

In understanding voodoo, it is important to know what voodoo is not. It is not black magic, juju, witchcraft or sorcery. It is, in fact, a complex religion, practised worldwide by 40 million people. It has an oral history spanning hundreds of years, and a loosely organised priesthood.

The word voodoo can be traced to "vodu", which in the language of the Fon people of Benin means "spirit". There are hundreds of spirits in the voodoo pantheon, representing either figures from the past or elements from the natural world.

These spirits can be found in everything, from trees and rivers, to the living and the dead, and can be summoned by voodoo priests for good or bad.

It is believed that when invoked, these spirits descend to earth to possess a worshipper, using his or her body and voice to chastise and advise the people.

Voodoo originated in Benin, (formerly Dahomey) in West Africa, and spread with the slave trade to Latin America and the Caribbean, especially Haiti.

Although Kerekou himself was born in Kouarfa, a notorious fetish village located the northern part of Benin, his government declared war on "witchcraft" which in official parlance was synonymous with voodoo.

However Kerekou's mother, Yokossi, a much feared fetish priestess, was left entirely alone, with no one daring to destroy her fetish temple. Later it was discovered that Kerekou himself had sought the services of a Mali-born soothsayer to help him stay in power. Some claim this soothsayer used his mystical powers to hypnotise and trick the military ruler and fleece Benin's public coffers.

Kerekou was voted out of power in 1991, and replaced by Soglo who took a much more liberal approach towards voodoo. But there are various explanations for his softly-softly approach, other than simple gratitude to voodoo priests for his miraculous recovery.

The president's wife, Rosie Vieyra Soglo, was born in Ouidah, a former slave port famous for voodoo practices. According to reliable sources, Daagbo Hounon, one of Benin's voodoo chiefs, is a close relative of the president's wife and has sought to increase his power under Soglo's presidency. But Hounon's wishes to be seen as Benin's supreme voodoo leader have been frustrated by the ambitions of another charismatic voodoo chief, Sossa Guedehoungue, who claims to have been democratically elected by his peers across the nation.

An open feud, nurtured by a strong mutual animosity between the voodoo chiefs still lingers on. And so far, Soglo has refrained from officially siding with either one. When Voodoo Day was celebrated in January, the two priests held separate ceremonies in Cotonou and Ouidah. The president made sure that he was represented at both celebrations by some of his cabinet ministers.

Although voodoo is generally popular, Soglo's decision to lend it official support has provoked anger in some quarters. Some Beninoise, especially those in political parties opposed to Soglo, resent what they see as the president's attempts at politicising voodoo. As one voodoo follower told me recently, "Voodoo is voodoo, not an electoral device to be used by politicians seeking top posts in government." The move has also been unpopular in the mainly Muslim north, the home of Kerekou, and it has gone down just as badly with the southern Catholic community, who see voodoo as regressive, and little more than a tourist attraction.

Monseigneur Isidore de Souza, Archbishop of Cotonou, believes that Christianity and voodoo do not mix. Asked how he felt about Soglo's move to officially recognise voodoo, de Souza merely replied, "True Christians go to church, not voodoo rituals. You cannot have it both ways. Either you accept the word of God, or you believe in obscure practices."

While the Catholic church takes a hard line, Benin's Protestants have an apparently liberal view towards voodoo. Reverend Henri Harry, a retired leader of the Protestant church, once said he did not see anything wrong with Christians visiting voodoo temples. For a pragmatic Harry, all ways lead to God. "The Christian church in Africa will survive only if it integrates with local cultures and customs."

Article 7   *World Monitor, April 1993*

Africa's Oldest Survivors

*The continent's newest nation is home to its oldest indigenous culture—
which was on the brink of extinction after 40,000 years. How did the Bushmen
of Namibia win a rare second chance to survive?*

David Goodman

David Goodman is a freelance journalist who has written widely on southern Africa. Among other publications, his work has appeared in The Boston Globe, Village Voice, and The Nation.

The long flat dusty road known locally as "the white road," becomes a luminescent ribbon weaving through the gray landscape in the late afternoon light.

I take in the endless expanse of sand and gnarled brush. No other vehicles pass me during several hours and more than a hundred miles on my way to the edge of the Kalahari Desert in eastern Namibia.

I am traveling to meet Namibia's only famous Bushman—and to spend several weeks moving around his far-flung community. Twelve years ago he starred in the hit comedy "The Gods Must Be Crazy." The movie grossed $65 million; its Bushman star returned to the desert with $1,300. Ironically, just as the film was presenting an idyllic image of Bushmen and their farcical encounter with modern civilization, the real Namibian Bushmen were losing a deadly battle for survival. Only recently—owing partly to the changing whims of international politics—has the tide of that battle been turning.

As I continue driving, slowly I see that the inhospitable terrain is abounding with life. The gemsbok dart in and out along the edges of the road. The brilliant plumage of lilac-breasted rollers, starlings, and black-and-white hornbills splashes color across a vast palette of earth tones.

This wildlife is the first clue to what sustained the Bushmen—said to be Africa's first inhabitants and last hunter-gatherers—for some 40,000 years. Their

(Photo © David Goodman)

Civilization in Transit: "Gods Must Be Crazy" star G/aqo/'hana and family cook the old way.

(Dave Herring-Staff)

decline, and potential restoration, provide a remarkable model for the UN's current International Year for the World's Indigenous People ("Return of the Natives," WM, March).

The road winds on to what was officially called Bushmanland, one of 11 apartheid homelands created in Namibia in the early 1970s. The homeland system was the brainchild of the South African authorities who ruled this sparsely populated southwest African nation from just after World War I until Namibian independence in 1990. The creation of Bushmanland resulted in the loss of 90% of the Bushmen's traditional lands. Their celebrated survival skills began to fade into myth and they quickly became the poorest stratum of Namibian society. Anthropologists warned that the continent's oldest culture might vanish within a generation.

"Bushmen" is the familiar—some say pejorative or colonial—name still widely accepted among anthropologists and the people themselves. Namibia is home to four distinct language groupings of Bushmen. The Kalahari Bushmen are the Ju/'hoansi, which translates as "the correct, or proper, people"; they are also known as the Kung or San. "Ju/'hoansi" is the plural of "Ju/'hoan" (pronounced "zhu-twa"). Their language is full of clicks and pops, indicated in transliteration by, for example, slashes and exclamation marks.

The Bushmen's plight poses a dilemma for Africa's newest nation: how to integrate this struggling ancient culture into the nascent economic and political order? The unpredicted twist is that Bushmen, who had been politically invisible, seized the political opportunity offered by Namibia's independence. They are now organizing and fighting for a last chance at

survival. In response, the Namibian government has shown unexpected interest in raising their economic and social status. It is providing development assistance and, most important, negotiating with the Bushmen over legal recognition of their land rights.

After about 130 miles, the road I am traveling ends abruptly in Tjum!kui, the drab administrative center of Bushmanland. Cement shacks with metal roofs stand at the edge of town. They were built to house the Ju/'hoansi after they were kicked off their land in the early 1970s. They are still crowded with families living on government food handouts and welfare. Young children dressed in tattered Western clothing run about, while adults stare lazily as I pass through. Liquor bottles litter the sand between the shacks. I understand better why older Ju/'hoansi dubbed Tjum!kui "the place of death."

Tjum!kui today resembles a ghost town from the North American West. The nearest telephone and post office are almost 200 miles away. The gas station occasionally has gas. There is a school, a police station, and a medical clinic that sees few patients. At the end of the town's lone dirt road, a small jail sits vacant.

Repression of Bushmen began long before apartheid. Early German and South African settlers viewed Bushmen as little more than vermin, and they were hunted, hanged, and shot for sport at the turn of the century. The result was their extermination in South Africa proper, where as late as 1941 a minister of native affairs told parliament, "We look upon them as part of the fauna of the country."

By the time of "The Gods Must Be Crazy" many younger Bushmen had grown up in settlements such as

Tjum!kui, and they had few or no traditional hunting skills. Yet in 1978 the South African Defense Force (SADF) set up two "Bushmen Battalions" consisting of about 1,000 troops, supposedly utilizing skills Bushmen had honed in the bush—only this time they were tracking down Namibian guerrillas of the South-West Africa People's Organization. Dispossessed Bushmen became easy targets for recruitment. By the time of Namibian independence, 9,000 Bushmen—over a quarter of the Bushman population in Namibia—were dependent on SADF salaries. When the South Africans left Namibia, so too did the only paying jobs many Bushmen had ever known.

Today Namibia has about 33,000 Bushmen out of a total 87,000 who live in Namibia, Botswana, and Angola. Most of those in Namibia work as migrant laborers on white-owned commercial farms, or simply live in poverty as wards of the state. Only the 2,000 Ju/'hoan Bushmen who live in the former Bushmanland have retained access to some of their ancestral hunting grounds and water holes.

I drive 17 miles past Tjum!kui on a dirt track to a newly settled Bushman village. A dozen grass huts are clustered around a tall baobab tree in the sand. Cattle huddle in a kraal, a frail defense against prowling lions. A young man sits beneath a tree playing a plaintive melody on a guitar made from a metal can and a piece of wood. A woman intently puts together a necklace from ostrich eggshells. Some people sleep in the hot midday sun. A few are munching marula nuts foraged in the wild. I wait for something to happen; nothing does. The changing intensity of the sun seems the main determinant of the activity level.

How did these isolated people become so well known in the West? For one thing, they are among the world's most intensively studied ethnic groups—especially by American anthropologists. Scientists have long had keen interest in their ability to subsist peacefully for thousands of years in the harsh desert environment.

But there is another reason why the Bushmen have become well known. It is the small, muscular man whose graceful movements barely disturb the sand as he strides through the village to greet me. His skin is tan and weathered, his high cheekbones accentuated by the gold evening light. He carries a bow and arrows, having just returned from hunting. The middle-aged man introduces himself through an interpreter as G/aqo /'hana (pronounced roughly "gow kana").

(Photo © David Goodman)

G/aqo /'hana is barefoot and wearing a ripped T-shirt and patched pants. He does not look the part of an international movie star. But then "The Gods Must Be Crazy" did not resemble the real life of G/aqo /'hana either.

He left his job as a janitor in a local school to play the lead part of a "primitive Bushman" in the 1979 hit film. He returned to the bush afterwards and has lived there ever since. He flashes his trademark broad smile when I ask how his hunt went. He spotted a porcupine but was unable to catch it, he says in the flurry of clicks that characterize his language: "There were more fruits and animals when I was younger."

G/aqo /'hana continues, "For the past years the life for the Ju/'hoansi was very low." He cites his experience with "The Gods Must Be Crazy." He says he was paid about $1,300 for the first film and $2,100 for the sequel by the films' South African director, Jamie Uys. "I spent the money to feed my family and buy some cows. Now there is nothing left."

American documentary filmmaker John Marshall, who first met and filmed the Bushmen in the 1950s, returned to Bushmanland in the late '70s and was shocked by the social decay he witnessed. He wrote: "For Ju/'hoansi the lessons . . . [are] simple and grim: No land means no subsistence; no subsistence means no mixed economy; no mixed economy means dependence on the lowest paying jobs, or mealie-meal welfare, or on begging and prostitution.

Extreme or abject poverty means illness, despair, and a high death rate."

By the early '70s the death rate among Bushmen exceeded the birthrate. Marshall decided that the only hope for the Ju/'hoansi was to reclaim their traditional lands in the Nyae Nyae region on the Namibia-Botswana border. He formed what is now called the Nyae Nyae Development Foundation to help Ju/'hoansi create a mixed economy of hunting and gathering, small farming, and livestock raising. The idea was for Bushmen to return to a place where they could break free of the spiraling cycle of dependency.

In 1981 three Bushman families went back to their n!ore—literally "the place to which you belong" (rhymes with

211

"story")—where natural water sources support life in the harsh veld. Since then the back-to-the-land movement has grown steadily. By Namibian independence, nearly 2,000 Ju/'hoansi had resettled more than 25 n!ores; today some 30 n!ores have been resettled.

The Nyae Nyae Farmers' Cooperative—formed in 1986 with the help of the Nyae Nyae Development Foundation—filled a political vacuum and has emerged as the collective voice for Bushmen. They are now negotiating with the government for their place in the new Namibia. Their central demand is that they be granted title to their ancestral lands. If this happened, it would be the first time since white men came to southern Africa that Bushman land rights in Namibia would be ensured by law.

Namibian President Sam Nujoma has visited Bushmanland three times since taking office in March 1990, the first top official of any government to meet with Namibia's Bushmen. The cordial working relationship that has evolved is especially surprising in the light of history: Many of today's elected leaders were guerrillas who were recently stalked by Bushman soldiers whom the government is now helping.

Granting special privileges to ensure land rights presents a thorny dilemma for Namibia. "Namibia has emerged from an apartheid history which has systematically Balkanized the entire country into ethnic homelands," said Wolfgang Werner, a top official in Namibia's Ministry of Lands, Resettlement, and Rehabilitation who oversees land policy. "On the political level there is considerable resistance against this concept of enshrining certain exclusive rights in law based on ethnicity." Werner

is opposed to "reintroducing a different version of apartheid."

It now appears that Namibian leaders will honor the spirit, if not the letter, of the Bushmen's demands. At a 1991 government conference on land reform an ambiguous resolution was adopted to provide "special protection" to Bushmen in recognition of their long history of exploitation. President Nujoma endorsed the resolution and indicated what this protection would mean when he backed the recent removal of neighboring Herero cattle herders who had encroached on Bushman lands.

A national land reform program has yet to be implemented in Namibia. Werner expects land policies to be introduced this year. Until then, and perhaps even after, Bushmen will have to rely on the good will of government leaders as they continue resettling their old n!ores.

"Guaranteed land rights is the critical issue facing Ju/'hoansi in independent Namibia," says Namibian-born anthropologist Robert Gordon of University of Vermont. "That means having land which they call their own, [on which they] do their own thing—be it cattle farming or whatever—and not having bloody outsiders imposing their will on them."

But land will not solve all the Bushmen's problems. The Ju/'hoansi of Bushmanland comprise only 2,000 of Namibia's total Bushman population, and they've been the focus of an extraordinary development program. The plight of some 30,000 other Namibian Bushmen gets little attention. Also, the Ju/'hoansi's effort to develop a mixed economy has met with limited success. Hungry Bushmen have sometimes slaughtered their own dairy cattle for

food, and other livestock have been killed by lions.

Dependency and poverty, the legacies of dispossession, have become entrenched in Bushman culture. I saw it often in my travels. Long lines of people formed for government food handouts in Tjum!kui. People routinely asked me for food and goods, and the co-op must continually decline demands by Bushmen for handouts. Professor Gordon cautions that "even well-intentioned development work runs a similar risk of fostering dependency."

Despite the complex problems and lingering questions, many anthropologists take heart in the gains the Bushmen have made. "I would say that the situation of the Namibian Kung is a sign of hope in a worldwide situation for indigenous peoples that is otherwise very bleak," says Richard Lee, a University of Toronto anthropologist and former co-leader of the Harvard Kalahari Research Group.

I left Bushmanland on the lone road that links it with the rest of Namibia. The determination of many Bushmen to forge a place for their people was inspiring. But the harshness of their isolation, poverty, and cultural wounds inflicted over the past 40 years makes their battle for a secure place in Africa's newest nation daunting.

Bushman leaders are prepared for their struggle back from the brink to be a long one. As former co-op leader Tsamkxao ≠ Oma told anthropologist Megan Biesele: "We who are representatives of the Nyae Nyae Farmers' Cooperative are like people planting a tree. We should realize that we are not just one small thing but are starting something big. The work will go on, even beyond our deaths."

Article 8   *The Christian Science Monitor,* July 1, 1996

I Am Not Just an African Woman

BEFORE my emigration to the United States five years ago, I was known as a Nigerian of the Yoruba ethnic group. I was also a Western-educated woman with certain privileges and high expectations.

Since coming here, though, my identity has changed. I am now an "African woman." My culture, attitude, and experience are presumed to reflect all of Africa, a continent of 55 countries, 400 million people, and thousands of ethnic and linguistic groups. By definition, I am supposed to be poor, uneducated, and ridden with disease.

My first jolt came one evening in 1991, when I was a new immigrant. I was watching a public-television documentary about little children's first day at school in such countries as Japan, the United Kingdom, the United States, and of course, "Africa."

"Africa is not a country," was my first thought. But what followed was even more distressing. While parents in other countries were shown engaging in different rituals of sending children to school, in "Africa," children were seen climbing trees in the forest. This, the narrator said, is something they learn from older children. I could not believe my eyes.

I grew up in a rural town in Nigeria. We had five primary schools and a high school. There was a post office and a small clinic. All these facilities have since expanded as Nigeria grew rich from its oil.

I remember my first day at school. My father took me, and I was so proud to be wearing a school uniform, carrying my black slate and chalk. I recall the elegance of my teacher: I wanted to dress and walk just like her. I persuaded my father to buy hair ornaments for me, even though my hair was closely cropped, as is the hair of all little children.

My primary school, run by the Anglican mission, had many flower gardens that were carefully cultivated and tended by the pupils under the supervision of the teachers.

In high school, we studied Shakespeare, George Eliot, Jonathan Swift, the Brontë sisters, and Charles Dickens. Under British colonial rule, generations of Nigerians studied such writers to the exclusion of African authors.

My teenage idol was Nancy Drew, an American teenage detective I discovered in my father's library one vacation. I read the books many times over.

The TV documentary didn't show any of this. I can understand such misconceptions from the average person. But in December 1993, Sen. Ernest Hollings (D) of South Carolina, returning from trade talks in Switzerland, jokingly implied that African leaders were cannibals.

I was shocked to read this, not only because of the insult, but also because of what it implied about the great ignorance of the realities of our lives.

Some of the worst riots in Nigeria have their roots in the disparity between the opulent lifestyles of the elite—the privileged diplomats who traveled to Geneva—and the austere lives forced on the rest of the population by the government. While a large percentage of the population is suffering, the elites are driving BMWs, Mercedes-Benzes, and Alfa Romeos. Their opulent houses are built with tall fences and staffed with servants, guards, and dogs.

Since the supply of electricity and water is erratic, the elites have generators and water pumps. Their children go to schools and colleges abroad. Their conspicuous consumption generates so much anger and resentment among the underprivileged that they sometimes take to the streets to vent their anger.

These rulers were the same ones characterized as starving cannibals. This could be said with impunity, because this is what being an African seems to mean in America.

It does not matter that some of these "cannibals" are products of the world's best universities; neither does it seem to matter that they belong to the class that controls and distributes the resources of their countries.

I am beginning to understand the differences between the myth of the African that I am in America and the Nigerian I consider myself to be. I spoke to my first Kenyan and tasted my first dish from Sierra Leone in this country. It was a dinner given by an American friend who worried all evening that she had not prepared it the authentic way. I doubt I convinced her that I wouldn't know an authentic Sierra Leonean dish from her version. Both were as foreign to my palate as pizza.

EVEN as I become accustomed to what Americans expect from me—do I know their friend in Mombasa, Kenya? or perhaps an acquaintance in Ghana?—their stereotype of the silent and voiceless African woman remains alien to me. The women I grew up with were anything but silent.

Yoruba women of southwestern Nigeria have a long history of organization and prosperity. Many of our grandmothers put our parents through college. Many own real estate and farms. They employ workers and commute home at the end of the day in luxury cars after they've closed their shops. In fact, women dominate the retail segment in southern Nigeria.

And in 1939, the disturbances known later as the Aba riots began when women in southeastern Nigeria organized a peaceful protest against taxes levied by the British rulers. Women were killed as the demonstrations were violently put down. That was many decades before the current tide of Western feminism. This is a part of my history.

To become an African woman is to struggle against the myths and misconceptions of African womanhood. Yes, I am an African, but I am a Nigerian first. That is the only honest claim I can make. I cannot speak for a continent.

Call me Nigerian, and I won't tell you any tall African tales.

Bunmi Fatoye-Matory

Article 9

BBC Focus on Africa, July–September 1996

OLYMPICS

Africa's Quest for Gold

This year's Olympic Games in Atlanta, USA, could see more Africans than ever before mounting the winners' podium. But the road to success has been a long and arduous one, as Phil Minshull reports.

Phil Minshull

In 1904, in the US state of Missouri, two Zulus dressed in longsleeved shirts and trousers cut off at the knees ran in the Olympic Games. That was Africa's first Olympic involvement. Len Taunyne and Jan Mashiani were in St Louis, the American host city, as part of a Boer War exhibition patronisingly entitled "How Natives and Savages Would Fare at Olympic Events". In fact they fared quite well in the marathon, considering their limited preparation and the perilous hot and dusty conditions which saw temperatures soar above 90 degrees.

> *"In 1904 two Zulus ran the marathon. One managed to finish ninth, despite being chased off the course by two large dogs!"*

Taunyne managed to finish a very creditable ninth, despite being chased off the course and through a cornfield by two large dogs at one point!

Mashiani followed his compatriot home three places further back in a race notable for the fact that fewer than half of the 32 starters made it to the finish.

Fifty-six years later, in 1960, it was the marathon which heralded Africa's arrival as a true Olympic power when Ethiopia's Abebe Bikila triumphed in Rome. Racing barefoot, Bikila (a member of Haile Selassie's Imperial Guard) broke clear just before the halfway point with Morocco's Rhadi Ben Abdesselem. The pair stayed together until just over a mile from the finish, when Bikila moved ahead at the Arch of Constantine. He was never caught. Looking over the course a few days before, Bikila and his Finnish

THE MEDALS

Country	Gold	Silver	Bronze	Total
South Africa	16	17	20	53
Kenya	13	13	13	39
Egypt	6	6	6	18
Ethiopia	6	1	6	13
Morocco	4	2	3	9
Nigeria	—	4	4	8
Uganda	1	3	1	5
Tunisia	1	2	2	5
Algeria	1	—	3	4
Ghana	—	1	3	4
Namibia	—	2	—	2
Tanzania	—	2	—	2
Cameroon	—	1	1	2
Zimbabwe	1	—	—	1
Ivory Coast	—	1	—	1
Senegal	—	1	—	1
Dijbouti	—	—	1	1
Niger	—	—	1	1
Zambia	—	—	1	1

coach, Omni Niskanen, had noticed that alongside the Arch was the obelisk of Axum, which had been taken from Ethiopia by Italian troops in the 1930s. They decided it would be an appropriate point to put in the decisive effort which led to Bikila becoming the first-ever black African Olympic gold medallist.

Rome also witnessed the last appearance of apartheid South Africa at the Olympics. South Africa first sent an official team to the 1908 Games in London, and until their suspension from the Olympics just prior to the 1964 Games, they won 51 medals across the sporting spectrum, including 16 golds. Unfortu-nately the South African teams were white-only. Several genuine medal contenders, particularly in boxing and weightlifting, were excluded solely because of their country's racist politics.

But South Africa was not the only villain in those days. In the pre-independence era, most colonial powers were reluctant to include sportsmen from their African territories and often denied them the opportunity to qualify for the Games.

However several Algerians did manage to defy the odds and appear in French colours. One such example was Bourghera El Ouafi who won the 1928 marathon. El Ouafi might have been a winner at the Olympics but he was a loser in life. His feat was barely recognised by the French government, and was generally ignored by the French public which preferred their heroes home-grown. He soon returned to his former job as a car mechanic.

In 1956, when expatriate Algerian Alain Mimoun trod a similar path, winning the Olympic marathon for France, journalists tracked down El Ouafi who was then virtually destitute and living in a Parisian suburb. His last few years were made a bit more comfortable after French sportsmen raised some funds for him. But three years later, as an innocent

---

DID YOU KNOW?

Madagascar's Jean-Louis Ravelomanatsoa and Greece's Vasilios Papageorgopoulous contributed to the ultimate TV commentator's nightmare when they were drawn in the same 100m heat at the 1972 Olympics. American and British commentators just referred to them as the men in lanes six and eight.

bystander, he was tragically shot dead when a dispute broke out in a café.

A notable exception to the African absence from the medals in the early years were the Egyptian strong men. A host of weightlifting medals were won during two golden decades between 1928 and 1948. Egypt's finest hour came at the infamous "Nazi Olympics" in Berlin in 1936 when Khadr Sayed el-Thouni won the middleweight title. However since 1948, Egypt has not had a single Olympic champion.

Ghana and Nigeria followed South Africa and Egypt into the Olympic arena in 1952 at the Helsinki Games, and four years later Kenya and Ethiopia followed suit in Melbourne. Ironically this was the same year that Egypt chose to boycott the Olympics in protest at the Israeli-led takeover of the Suez Canal.

"Bikila finished more than four minutes clear of his nearest challenger; whilst waiting for the rest to finish he entertained the crowd by lying on his back and doing some cycling exercises"

While the Rome Olympics in 1960 will forever be associated with Ethiopia's Bikila, Ghana did have the spotlight for a day. Boxer Clement 'Ike' Quartey, the elder brother of the then WBA welter-

---

DID YOU KNOW?

John Akii-bua, the 1972 400m hurdles gold medallist, spent a month in a Kenyan prison in 1979, after fleeing Uganda following the overthrow of Idi Amin, without anyone recognising him or believing who he was! He now runs a sportswear shop in Uganda.

HOT PROSPECTS FOR ATLANTA

• The 800m has a habit of throwing up surprises. Remember Paul Ereng in 1988? Watch out for **Uganda's** Julius Achon and **Zimbabwe's** Savieri Nghidi who have both been making waves on the US collegiate circuit recently.

• **Burundi** will make its first-ever appearance at an Olympics in Atlanta, but will not be going to the USA simply to make up the numbers. In Arthemon Hatungimana and Venuste Niyangabo, medallists at the 1995 world championships, Burundi has two ready-made and very serious contenders over 800m and 1,500m respectively.

• Over the longer distance of 10,000m, Mattias Ntawalikura is hoping to notch up **Rwanda's** first-ever Olympic medal so that his war-torn country can unite behind a common cause for celebration.

• *Zambia* also have a pair of young talents, Charles Mulinga and Godfrey Siamusiye, who might challenge the established powers from **Ethiopia, Kenya** and **Morocco.**

• **Nigeria** is still searching for its first gold medal, after only four silvers and four bronzes since 1964. The best bet to end their drought might be sprinter Davidson Ezinwa who made the 100m final in Bar-

celona. Ezinwa, 24, has just returned to action after a three-month ban for taking an illegal cough remedy. But before his misdemeanour he put in one of the fastest indoor times this year.

• What of the women? **Mozambique's** Maria Mutola is hardly an unknown and she has already been to two Olympics. Even so, the 1993 world 800m gold medallist will still be only 23 in Atlanta, and Mozambique has never won an Olympic medal of any description.

• On the soccer pitch, Africa's three qualifiers, **Ghana, Nigeria, and Tunisia,** are all experienced campaigners, but after the travails of the Nigerians in the wake of their senior side's ban from international action, Ghana's Black Meteors look to be Africa's strongest side. In 1992 the Ghanaian bronze medal squad contained the likes of Yaw Acheampong, Maxwell Konadu and Nii Odartey Lamptey, who all went on to become European-based professionals. Stephen Baidoo, Ebenezer Hagan and Prince Amoaku, the three scorers in the 3–0 final qualifying round win over Cameroon, are among those expected to impress, and Ghana's changes could be enhanced with some careful selection of the three players over the age of 23 that they are allowed.

---

weight world champion with the same name, won the light welterweight silver medal and beat Bikila by a day to the accolade of being the first-ever black African medallist—though it was Bikila who got the gold.

In Tokyo in 1964, Bikila was again the man of the moment. He had undergone an operation to remove his appendix less than two months previously, but any suggestion that he was destined to be an also-ran was soon dismissed. Running this time in shoes and socks, he finished in 2:12:11, a world best by more than a minute, and more than four min-

utes clear of his nearest challenger. Whilst waiting for the rest of the field to finish he entertained the 75,000 crowd by lying on his back and doing some cycling exercises.

But sadly, there was no happy ending for the man who is, arguably, Africa's greatest sporting hero. A leg injury meant that Bikila failed to finish in Mexico City in 1968, his last ever marathon. In 1969 he crashed his Volkswagen, a present from Haile Selassie after his Tokyo triumph, and was left paralysed below the waist. Confined to a wheelchair, he returned to international competition the same year, competing in the archery competition at the Paraplegic Games. In 1973 Bikila died of a brain haemorrhage at the tragically early age of 41.

His compatriot, Mamo Wolde, inherited Bikila's marathon mantle in Mexico in 1968, but it had been a long haul. In Melbourne in 1956, Wolde had been part of the first-ever Ethiopian Olympic team, but had finished last in his heats of the 800m and 1,500m. He did not go to Rome in 1960, but by 1964 he was back—this time finishing fourth over the 10,000m. Four years later in Mexico City he stepped up to take the silver medal in the 10,000m, behind Kenya's Naftali Temu. Seven days later though there was no denying him, and almost as impressively as Bikila, he finished more than three minutes ahead of the rest of the marathon field.

Mexico also witnessed the start of the Kenyan gold rush thanks to Temu, Amos Biwott and Kip Keino. With these Games being staged at altitude, western observers initially belittled the African successes, attributing them to the natural altitude advantages many East Africans had. But as history has demonstrated, it was no fluke.

In the boxing ring of Mexico, Cameroon and Uganda joined the growing list of African countries with medals to their name.

Not even the massacre of Israeli athletes by Palestinian terrorists overshadowed John Akii-bua's run at the 1972 Munich Olympics. The Ugandan police instructor won the 400m hurdles in a world record time of 47.82 seconds, coming home more than half a second ahead of his nearest rival. Kip Keino added to his Mexico 1,500m gold and his increasingly legendary status by winning the steeplechase in an Olympic record time, whilst Niger's Issaka Daborg

DID YOU KNOW?

Sudan's Mohammed Hammed made one of the quickest exits in Olympic boxing history. On the bell of his opening bout at the 1988 Olympic in Seoul, he took three steps forward, only to find that the referee had stopped the fight. His coach had thrown in the towel to protest at an earlier decision when another Sudanese fighter had apparently been felled with an illegal kidney punch.

Country	Gold	Silver	Bronze	Total

All figures up to and including the Los Angeles Olympics, 1992
List of the 1996 Medalists

Marathon, men's	Josia Thugwane, South Africa	gold
" "	Eric Wainana, Kenya	bronze
Marathon, women's	Fatuma Roba, Ethiopia	gold
100m breaststroke	Penelope Heyns, South Africa	gold
200m breaststroke	Penelope Heyns, South Africa	gold
800m	Hezekiah, South Africa	silver
200m race	Mary Onyaii, Nigeria	bronze
400m race	Falilat Ogunkoya, Nigeria	bronze
4X400m race	Nigeria	silver
women's long jump	Chioma Ajunwa, Nigeria	gold
women's 10,000m	Gete Wami, Ethiopia	bronze
men's 10,000m	Haile Gebrselassie, Ethiopia	gold
" "	Paul Tergat, Kenya	silver
" "	Hissuoh, Morocco	bronze
3,000m steeplechase	Joseph Keter, Kenya	gold
" "	Moses Kiptanui, Kenya	silver
100m, men's	Frankie Fredricks, Namibia	silver
200m, men's	Frankie Fredricks, Namibia	silver
800m, women's	Maria Mutola, Mozambique	bronze
5,000m, men's	Venuste Niyongabo, Burundi	gold
" "	Paul Bitok, Kenya	silver
" "	Khalid Boulami, Morocco	bronze
400m, men's	Davis Kamoga, Uganda	bronze
400m hurdles	Samuel Mtete, Zambia	silver
super-heavyweight boxing	Duncan Dokwari, Nigeria	bronze

earned a small place in boxing history with a light welterweight bronze, his country's only medal to date.

The 1976 Montreal Olympics were something of a low point for Africa as New Zealand's rugby tour of apartheid South Africa, led to a boycott by many African countries.

The International Olympic Committee claimed, with some justification, that since rugby was not an Olympic sport it was outside its authority to act against New Zealand. Tanzania was the only country to stay at home completely but many other Olympic ambitions were frustrated as governments, one by one, brought their teams home from Canada.

Most of Africa, although not Kenya, returned in 1980 at the Moscow Games, and it was there that Ethiopia's Miruts Yifter fulfilled dreams which had been thwarted four years previously, by winning both the 5,000m and 10,000m with devastating bursts of speed over the final lap. Zimbabwe's women's hockey team were the only other African winners in Moscow, even after the US-led boycott following the Soviet invasion of Afghanistan had decimated the competition. The International Olympic Committee invited the newly independent Zimbabwe to compete only five weeks before the Games were due to start. But

much to everyone's amazement, the women's hockey team went through the tournament undefeated.

Tanzania's Filbert Bayi had been the 1,500m world record holder and favourite for the event when his country decided to stay away from Montreal. By 1980 he was past his best but got some compensation when he won his country's first-ever medal with a silver in the steeplechase.

At the 1984 Los Angeles Games, all three of Africa's gold medals came on the track. Julius Korir revived Kenyan fortunes after an eight-year absence by winning the steeplechase, and the incomparable Moroccan, Said Aouita, comfortably won the 5,000m. Aouita's countrywoman, Nawal el-Moutawakel, who broke new ground with her victory in the 400m hurdles, was the first woman from an Islamic nation and the first African woman, other than a white South African, to win a solo Olympic medal. The final was televised live, at 2am local time, in her home town of Casablanca and the celebrations carried on all night.

In Los Angeles, sportsmen from Algeria, Ivory Coast and Zambia also climbed the medal podium for the first time.

Kenya was without question the African star of the 1988 Olympics in Seoul

DID YOU KNOW?

Sportsmen from Cameroon, Egypt, Morocco and Tunisia all competed in the 1976 Games before their governments joined the Tanzania-led boycott.

with her tally of five gold medals. Paul Ereng, Peter Rono, John Ngugi and Julius Kariuki were all triumphant on the athletics track, but it was Robert Wangila in the boxing ring who arguably stole the show, becoming the first black African boxer to strike gold by stopping his French opponent, in less than two rounds. Sadly he never found the same success as a professional; struggling to be anything more than a journeyman, he died tragically in 1994 from boxing injuries.

Africa's only other gold at the Seoul Games went back to Morocco, though not in the luggage of Said Aouita as had been expected. Hamstring injury ruined his chances and the glory went instead to his 21-year-old compatriot, Brahim Boutaib, who won the 10,000m.

In Barcelona in 1992 it was the turn of African women to grab the headlines. In a titanic duel over the 10,000m, Ethiopia's Derartu Tulu triumphed over Elana Meyer, the major hope for a South African team that was participating at the Olympics for the first time since 1960. The pair then embarked together on a symbolic lap of honour in celebration of the 'new' South Africa's acceptance by the rest of Africa.

Noureddine Morceli was expected to earn gold for Algeria in the 1,500m, but after his unexpected failure to produce the goods, it was Hassiba Boulmerka who triumphed in the women's event over the same distance.

The most controversial moment of the last Olympics also involved Americans. Morocco's Khalid Skah and Kenya's Richard Chelimo were clear of the chasing pack in the 10,000m and disputing the ownership of the gold medal when, with three-and-a-half laps to go, another Moroccan, Hammou Boutayeb, entered the fray. Boutayeb was about to be lapped by the leaders when he upped his tempo. As he came abreast of the leading pair he started talking to Skah, trying to pace his compatriot along. Eventually, with a lap to go, Skah and Chelimo shrugged off their unwanted companion to finish the real race, which was won by Skah. The result was greeted with whistles and hissing, one of the most hostile receptions ever for an Olympic champion. The Kenyans immediately put in a protest which was initially upheld. For fourteen hours Chelimo was Olympic champion, but then the Jury of Appeal adjudged that Boutayeb had been as much a hindrance as a help to Skah and had obstructed his team-mate as much as Chelimo. The gold medal was then hung around the Moroccan's neck and this was accepted by most people as the right result, even if it was achieved in a far-from-ideal manner.

Kenya did get some satisfaction from other track events. Matthew Birir led home a clean sweep of the steeplechase medals while William Tanui took gold in the 800m. For Namibia's Frankie Fredericks gold would have been great, but silver was also special. He finished second in both the sprints to give a huge amount of sporting pride to a country that had been independent for only two years. Ghana's Black Meteors also got Africa's first soccer medals, winning 1–0 in a tense bronze medal play-off against Australia.

DID YOU KNOW?

Kenya's Peter Rono became the youngest-ever 1,500m gold medallist when he won in 1988 at the age of 21. However after that he didn't win another race for five years!

Expectations will be high for the latest Games in Atlanta. Athletes from all points of the compass such as Noureddine Morceli, Moses Kiptanui, Haile Gebresilassie and Maria Mutola will start as overwhelming favourites for their events. Boxers from the continent are also expected to have an impact and African soccer players will be feared after their successes in recent World Cups, particularly at junior level.

It promises to be Africa's most successful Olympics yet.

Article 10   *Current History*, May 1994

Botswana: One African Success Story

"The Botswana model is but one option available to African states. In Asia, more authoritarian regimes have promoted economic growth and then had their power challenged by new social groups arising as their economies prospered. In Europe and North America, bourgeois groups used economic independence from the state to create new wealth and then promote democratization. The most compelling aspect of the Botswana model is that it has already worked in an African environment and has allowed democracy and economic growth to emerge concomitantly."

John D. Holm

John D. Holm is a professor of political science at Cleveland State University and associate dean of the Ohio School of International Business. He has conducted field research and written on political development in Botswana since 1970. He is a cofounder of the University of Botswana's Democracy Project. The author wishes to thank Rodger Govea for commenting on an earlier version of this essay.

Botswana is often considered "exceptional" among African states. For more than two decades, this southern African country has enjoyed one of the highest rates of economic growth in the world. At the same time, the government has maintained the only uninterrupted liberal democracy in postcolonial Africa.

Botswana's economic and political successes raise two questions: How were economic growth and democratic development achieved at the same time? And, are there any lessons from Botswana's experience that other African countries can learn from?

Economic Growth

In the last 25 years Botswana's economy has grown in real per capita terms at an annual rate of around 8 percent. In contrast, the rest of sub-Saharan Africa managed marginal increases up to 1980 and subsequently showed a slight economic decline, although the last few years have seen some increase.

The economic miracle is easily explained in terms of sectoral performance. The discovery of diamonds in the late 1960s led to the development of three mines over the next decade and a half that have made Botswana the world's foremost producer of diamonds. Including a copper-nickel complex, mining now encompasses just over half of GDP; at independence this sector did not exist. The massive surge in income has spurred rapid infrastructure expansion, new mining projects, and an impressive growth in government services.

This growth did not occur spontaneously. The government, especially the Ministry of Finance and Development Planning, has designed and managed the process through seven development plans. Each plan sets new directions based on development achieved and problems encountered in the previous period. Political intervention is minimal because Seretse Khama, the country's first president, and his successor, Quett Masire, have protected the independence of the planning bureaucracy. To be sure there are occasional exceptions. In the 1970s, for example, government veterinarians with the support of elected politicians managed to obtain funds for a foot-and-mouth vaccine research center despite the fact that this project was not in the current plan. In this case President Khama, who was himself a major cattle owner, decided to side with the vets. But such cases are the exception rather than the rule.

Presidential protection has given the planners in the Ministry of Finance exceptional control over the economy. They set goals for almost all areas, from mining to services, and regulate wages and salaries for the public and private sectors, keeping them relatively equal. The planners also control consumption, particularly by keeping foreign exchange rates low and thus the price of imported goods high. To reduce the inflationary effect of the massive diamond income, they insist on maintaining substantial foreign exchange reserves. Still another tool the planners use to control prices, especially for food and housing, are government-owned enterprises.

The government relies on private and semiprivate corporations to implement certain projects. It engages in cooperative ventures with foreign private capital on major investments. For instance, Debeers, the international diamond marketing cartel, has managed and helped finance the diamond mines. Rhone Selection Trust, a mining multinational, does the same for a copper-nickel operation. The government allocates large infrastructure projects to foreign construction companies through a competitive bidding process. Government-owned companies operate the major utilities, the country's airline, and the railroad. They also run the slaughterhouses that process beef for export and a housing corporation that caters to the middle class.

In contrast to many African countries, state-economy relations are encumbered with a minimum of patrimonial connections. In part this derives from the legalistic character of the culture of the Tswana, the country's largest ethnic group, which tends to support rule-oriented, bureaucratic decision making. Most government-owned enterprises receive subsidies, but the Ministry of Finance launches periodic campaigns to lower the amount. Recently it has been campaigning to make them financially independent. Corruption is a recurrent problem; however, newspaper reports and government investigations have brought punishment to wrongdoers and the reorganization of management systems to establish better controls. A current example of this self-correcting process is the National Development Bank, where losses have been skyrocketing. The Ministry of Finance is forcing the bank to reduce its staff by half, including some of those at the top, and mandating a reorganization designed to increase financial controls. At the same time, opposition groups and newspapers are demanding that the bank deal with large uncollected loans to politicians, even some held by President Masire.

Another impressive part of Botswana's planned development system are the social justice objectives that have governed its evolution. Ninety percent of children primary school age attend school. Extensive social services have reached remote areas. While there are many deficiencies in these services, it is not unusual for villages of a thousand people to have a primary school, health clinic, post office, police station, water affairs specialist, community development officer, agricultural officer, and livestock adviser.

During the periodic droughts the country experiences (Botswana is located in the eastern half of the Kalahari Desert), the government activates a far-reaching relief structure to provide jobs and deliver food, water, and other supplies to rural areas. The result is that almost no deaths from malnutrition were reported during droughts

in the 1980s and early 1990s. In the cities the government operates a low-cost housing program that has prevented the squatter communities so evident in other parts of Africa. Probably most important for both urban and rural areas, planners have focused on expanding formal employment as quickly as possible. In many cases labor-intensive approaches have been used rather than those that are capital intensive. As a result, employment has grown at three times the rate of expansion of the economically active population.[1]

The success of this welfare-oriented development strategy is evident in evaluations of Botswana's economic performance relative to other African countries. A good example is Botswana's ranking on the Human Development Index (HDI) which the United Nations Development Program has created to measure the changing material living conditions of a nation's citizenry. Botswana ranks higher on this scale than any other country in black-ruled sub-Saharan Africa. In terms of change on the HDI scale between 1970 and 1990, only six other countries in the world and one in Africa (Tunisia) have advanced a greater distance on the scale than Botswana.

Economic performance alone is sufficient to make Botswana exceptional. However, the fact that it is also an evolving liberal democracy makes it even more remarkable on a continent where similar examples are hard to find.

Political Development

Botswana's government is headed by a strong presidency that operates in conjunction with a parliamentary system. Parliament consists of a National Assembly and a House of Chiefs, with the latter having only an advisory role on selected issues. The assembly has 34 elected members chosen from single-member districts. These elected MPs select the president, who since independence in 1966 has been the candidate from the Botswana Democratic party (BDP), which has won all national elections.

The president has considerable power in his relations with the assembly. A no-confidence vote dissolves the assembly rather than allowing the assembly to select a new executive. The president appoints his cabinet from among members of the assembly, but the appointments do not require the assembly's approval. Neither of the two presidents since independence has consulted with assembly members before announcing a new cabinet.

Political rights and liberties are generally guaranteed. In terms of the former, most adults enjoy the right to vote; there are few restraints that restrict running for office; and election laws and regulations are enforced in a nonpartisan fashion. Political liberty is evident in that citizens are free to oppose government policies or officials in public assemblies; the mass media faces minimal censorship; and private newspapers disseminate a variety of opinions.

This is not to say that Botswana is a model liberal democracy. There are a number of legal constraints benefiting the ruling party. With respect to elections, the law prohibits chiefs from running for office. The minimum voting age is 21. No provision is made for absentee ballots (20 percent of the adult population are migrant workers). And the constitution allows the rural-based BDP to gerrymander constituencies to the disadvantage of urban areas (in 1989, urban assembly constituencies were 70 percent larger than rural ones).

In terms of political liberty, the BDP government also does not have an unblemished record. It has enacted a law that limits the ability of unions to organize and negotiate (the government has not ratified most International Labor Organization conventions). It threatens newspaper editors with lawsuits from time to time over unfavorable articles. In 1986 the assembly passed a law that classifies almost all information concerning the Botswana Defense Force.

While the foregoing reduce opportunities for political competition, the BDP and the three opposition parties have considerable opportunity to debate one another. The public follows these political discussions in the private newspapers and in "freedom squares." The latter are critical for the illiterate. Political parties can hold freedom squares on public property as long as police permission is obtained, which is rarely a problem. At these meetings local and national party officials promote their party's platform and attack their opponents, often in incredibly vicious and personal terms. In the weeks before an election, each party holds freedom squares in almost all small villages and in the neighborhoods of larger towns. The high point of a meeting is the question and answer period as members from other parties attempt to belittle the opposing speakers.

Three or four hours may be consumed on a hot weekend afternoon by a freedom square. The atmosphere is festive but competitive. Surveys indicate that freedom squares are the primary source of information on political parties for the attentive public.[2] Newspapers sometimes treat freedom squares in large cities as major events, featuring them on the front page.

Some analysts contend that Botswana is not a democracy because the BDP has swept every election since 1965, winning at least two-thirds of the vote. But there are a number of reasons for the BDP's one-party dominance. Without question, opposition parties, which draw their support more from cities, the youth, and migrant laborers, are constrained by the electoral restrictions. Moreover, some chiefs would like to be more active in opposing the government, but would have to resign their positions to do so.

Selected average annual growth rate in GDP (in percent)		
Country	1970–1980	1980–1991
Botswana	14.5	9.8
South Africa	3.0	1.3
Ghana	−0.1	3.2
Nigeria	4.6	1.9
Hong Kong	9.2	6.9
Singapore	8.3	6.6
Taiwan	n/a	7.7
South Korea	9.6	9.6
China	5.2	9.4
Chile	1.4	3.6
Mexico	6.3	1.2
Venezuela	3.5	1.5
United States	2.8	2.6
Germany	2.6	2.3
Japan	4.3	4.2

Sources: World Bank, *World Development Report 1993* (New York: Oxford University Press, 1993) and *Taiwan Statistical Databook* (Taipei: Council for Economic Planning and Development, 1992)

Other factors limit the opposition vote as well. The three largest opposition parties could win more seats if they united behind a single ticket. In 1989 they might have picked up as many as five seats this way. The major opposition party, the Botswana National Front (BNF), often exacerbates opposition divisions by kicking out one or more internal factions in the year before an election. The resulting conflict then leads to loss of at least one assembly seat.

The most serious barrier to a competitive party system is the ethnic basis of voting in rural areas. There is strong evidence that each of Botswana's ethnic groups tends to vote on the basis of its ties to a party. These ties were defined at the time of independence or shortly thereafter. Thus, the entire Bamangwato area, which includes one-fourth of the population, votes for the BDP in overwhelming (between 80 percent and 90 percent) proportions. The original impetus for this association was that the Bamangwato perceived Seretse Khama, the leader of the BDP in the first election, as the true heir to their chieftaincy.[3] A number of the leading royals among the Bakwena, another large Tswana group, used their prestige to foster BDP loyalty among their people.

In some cases, the parties take advantage of subethnic conflicts. Thus among the Bakgatla people, opposition parties have been able to win the major village of Mochudi, which has close to half the district's population, by playing on the Mochudi populace's fear of domination by their less sophisticated rural tribesmen, who vote for the BDP.

The major area of electoral change is the cities. While ethnic considerations are still important, every election has brought a larger number of votes to the opposition parties based on their class and interest appeals. For instance, since 1984 the BNF has won the Gaborone (Botswana's capital city) council and the city's two National Assembly seats by rallying the working class vote. In 1988 the BNF almost won the assembly seat for Selebi Phikwe, a mining city in the heart of Bamangwato. It is very likely the BNF will take this seat in the elections scheduled for October.

UCLA political scientist Richard Sklar has emphasized that democracy in Africa should be looked at from a developmental point of view, and not as something that emulates existing Western political systems. This makes sense with respect to Botswana. A system of accountability to the public is emerging in part as the political elite establishes structures that fit with the existing culture. Thus freedom squares are modeled after the traditional *kgotla*, in which Tswana communities gathered to hear about and react to proposals from their traditional leaders. The support citizens give to political parties on the basis of ethnicity is another example. In their minds the bond of ethnicity is the best insurance that political authorities will listen to them.

Part of this development process, however, is that new social forces are challenging traditional ways by supporting practices that are found in more progressive democracies. Youth and women are demanding access to politics and leadership roles, something that was unheard of in the past. Social class and occupational interests are overriding ethnic identity as a basis for political action in the cities. None of these changes is happening overnight. Rather this widening of the democratic process is proceeding through debates on the advisability and feasibility of making even the smallest reform in reaction to these new social forces. Thus, political change will continue to be more glacial and syncretistic than its economic change.

The Duality of Economics

A striking aspect of Botswana's developing democracy are the minimal linkages between economics and politics. The state bureaucracy attempts to keep economic policy decisions out of the political arena. Equally important, political parties have not organized to give direction to the bureaucracy on policy questions.

This separation stems from a number of sources. Most critical is the role of the president. Both Khama and Masire have insisted that connections between the civil service and politicians be minimized. To this end, almost all civil servants are rotated every three or four years to different parts of the country. The result is that networks between local politicians and government officials do not have time to form. Augmenting this separation is the fact that top civil servants control advancement through an annual evaluation process. Political interference is rare. This further reduces the motivation for state officials to seek support from politicians. Also isolating the state is an elitist attitude that is widespread in the civil service. Over the last two and a half decades, government has recruited into its ranks the best graduates from secondary and postsecondary schools. This has led government employees to believe they are the only ones who know what is best for society.

Politicians are markedly less well trained. Most MPs have finished secondary school at best. Most local councilors do not even have a primary education. Civil servants regularly take advantage of their advanced training to intimidate elected officials through public displays of literary and analytic skills. They sometimes openly suggest to politicians that the latter's main function is to serve as messengers from a knowing government to an unknowing people.

Further reducing the power politicians hold with the bureaucracy is the fact that political parties have not mobilized existing social organizations to support elected officials. One example of this is the opposition BNF's relation with trade unions. Thus far the party leadership has made no attempt to work with union leaders to mobilize votes, even though the party represents itself as speaking for the workers. Likewise, the BDP makes little attempt to use various rural women's groups such as the Red Cross, the YMCA, and the Botswana Council of Women to gain votes. Both parties prefer to set up their own organizations for social groups they claim to represent. However, these auxiliary party wings tend to sustain the party organizations (the BDP women's wing provides food at local meetings, for example), but do little to articulate societal political demands. In effect, Botswana's political parties are stalling the development of civil society.

The civil service has taken advantage of the parties' lack of contact with civil society to develop its own linkages with citizen groups. The bureaucracy has created a series of advisory councils composed of representatives of various segments of society. These councils deal with topics such as income, education, sports, and women's affairs. Ministries also probe public opinion by using survey research concerned with various policy options. Most important, local implementation of government policies does not occur until a specific program has been approved in the appropriate *kgotla* presided over by a traditional authority. In effect, the bureaucracy has various means to give legitimacy to its policies, which is particularly useful in the face of politician opposition.

A major advantage of this separation of elected politicians from policymaking is that Tswana democracy does not provide the temptation for corruption so endemic in other African countries. It has given top planners the opportunity to invest the state's resources in productive economic activities. But, increasingly tension is mounting between elected officials and top bureaucrats. At recent BDP congresses ministers and, by implication, the president, have been criticized for their failure to give direction to government policy. In the forthcoming BDP primaries in preparation for this year's election, almost every contest will pit those supporting the bureaucracy against those who believe there should be more political control.

One important exception to the forgoing should be noted. Elected politicians do give direction to the bureaucracy when it formulates polices that could do serious political damage to the BDP's rural constituency. Thus, a rural development program to commercialize large cattle herds has been modified to allow the continuation of traditional management practices. Recently, the Department of Water Affairs shelved a proposal to dredge parts of the Okavango Swamps and channel the water into neighboring villages after the project met with vehement opposition from local politicians. In effect, elected officials veto projects that threaten their reelection.

An African Model of Development?

The tendency to treat Botswana as an exceptional state on the African continent misses an important point. If African states are to develop economically and democratize politically, they must confront the problems Botswana has faced. They must mobilize capital, invest it efficiently, make public officials responsible to others for their decisions, and allow open policy debate. In so doing African leaders would do well to consider Botswana's overall approach, although not the actual implementation.

Botswana's economic and political success has resulted in part from some unique factors. Its economy grew exceptionally fast because of the high value the world economy places on diamonds. Patrimonialism has been less a problem than in other parts of Africa because of Tswana legalism. Some African countries suffer from much more intense ethnic conflict than Botswana does. However, these exceptions do not mean that the basic

Botswana strategy of development is not worth considering, particularly if the state is to play a dominant role in mobilizing resources for economic growth.

Four generalizations about Botswana's strategy are most relevant to an African statist approach to development:
- The bureaucratic state should be staffed by a trained mandarin class with a firm commitment to developing the economy. In this context, the state's isolation from society ensures that savings are invested in productive endeavors.
- In the early stages of economic development, democratic institutions should reduce abuse of public power rather than establish policy directions. In this regard, it is more important that elected officials and the media review policy decisions rather than be involved in making policy.
- Political rights and liberty should exist, but citizen demands should not be allowed to undermine the state's capacity to promote economic growth. In the transition to democracy it is important that some form of elections and political freedom exist, but at the same time calls for social and economic justice need to be limited.
- Democratic institutions should both arise from traditional structures and challenge those structures. Democracy and African tradition need be neither mutually exclusive nor synonymous.

The Botswana model is but one option available to African states. In Asia, more authoritarian regimes have promoted economic growth and then had their power challenged by new social groups arising as their economies prospered. In Europe and North America, bourgeois groups used economic independence from the state to create new wealth and then promote democratization. The most compelling aspect of the Botswana model is that it has already worked in an African environment and has allowed democracy and economic growth to emerge concomitantly.

Notes

1. Stephen R. Lewis, "Policy Making and Economic Performance: Botswana in Comparative Perspective," in *Botswana: The Political Economy of Democratic Development*, Stephen John Stedman, ed. (Boulder, Colo.: Lynne Rienner Publishers, 1993), p. 11.
2. Mogopodi H. Lekorwe, "The *Kgotla* and Freedom Square: One-way or Two-way Communication?" in *Democracy in Botswana*, John Holm and Patrick Molutsi, eds. (Athens, Ohio: Ohio University Press, 1989), p. 225.
3. Khama did not become Bamangwato chief because the British refused to allow him to do so, fearing that the newly elected Afrikaner government in South Africa would be offended.

Article 11   *Multinational Monitor*, July/August 1996

An African Star?

Free Eritrea Faces the Challenges Ahead

Robert Weissman

ASMARA, ERITREA—The winding railway which descends 7,000 feet in 70 miles from Eritrea's highlands capital of Asmara to the Red Sea coastal city of Massawa is emblematic of this recently liberated country.

Originally built by Italian colonizers, the railway, which runs parallel to a narrow road connecting Eritrea's two most important commercial centers, is operational for only about two-and-a-half miles inland from Massawa. Those couple miles of rail, along with an additional 18 miles of track not currently in use, have been rebuilt in the five years since the Eritrean People's Liberation Front (EPLF) freed the country from Ethiopian occupying forces.

Ethiopia took control of Eritrea in the period after World War II; after Haile Mariam Mengistu and a junta known as the Dergue seized control of Ethiopia in 1974, Ethiopian rule in Eritrea was characterized by brutality and plunder. Facing a well-disciplined national liberation movement which was led by the EPLF and enjoyed the virtually complete support of Eritreans, the Ethiopian military pulled up the railway track, using the metal to line foxholes and for other military purposes.

Foreign contractors have estimated the cost of rebuilding the railway at between $200 million and $400 million, and foreign governments have offered to lend Eritrea the money to employ the contractors. But the Eritrean government, led by the EPLF—now renamed the Peoples' Front for Democracy and Justice (PFDJ)—has refused. The desperately poor country cannot afford such an expenditure, government officials reason; and besides, they believe, Eritreans will acquire useful skills in rebuilding the railway themselves.

Now Eritreans are building the railway on their own—as well as widening the parallel road—using labor intensive techniques. As part of a mandatory national service program, old men who once managed the railway are helping oversee construction, and young men are laying the ties.

The decision to build the railroad without foreign assistance reflects the PFDJ's fierce commitment to self-reliance. PFDJ leaders' emphasis on self-reliance is rooted in their war experience, when the EPLF received no aid from either of the Cold War superpowers, nor from China in its battle against an Ethiopian regime backed first by the United States and then by the Soviet Union, and when the EPLF created makeshift underground factories in the territory it controlled to produce everything from munitions to pharmaceuticals to sandals.

"We stood alone for 30 years against the mighty," says Eden Fassil, legal adviser to the Eritrean government. "Self-reliance has taught us a lot and we strongly believe in it."

But the stripped railway also signifies the enormous devastation wreaked upon this already poor country by a bloody war of liberation that lasted 30 years, the last two decades of which were characterized by World War I-style trench warfare. Much of the country's physical infrastructure has been destroyed; and what was not destroyed was allowed to deteriorate during the years of rule by the Dergue. As it became clear that the EPLF would win the war, in a final paroxysm of violence the Ethiopian military heavily bombed Massawa, destroying most of the port facilities and a great deal of the town itself.

Finally, the effort to rebuild the railroad as part of a national service ethic symbolizes the national determination to reconstruct the country, and the enormous credibility the government maintains with the population as a result of having led a truly unified, nationwide movement against

© Robert Weissman

A bombed mosque in Massawa.

the Ethiopian occupation. The sense of shared national purpose, and willingness to contribute to its achievement, may constitute the country's biggest asset.

At the same time, the government's top-down mobilizational approach to reconstructing the country, while appropriate for the war effort and likely for the building of a railroad, may ultimately interfere with the country's effort to create a sustainable economy.

The Daunting Tasks Ahead

There is no disputing that the new Eritrean government faces extraordinary challenges in countless areas, including confronting sheer poverty, dealing with the aftermath of the war and combatting oppression of women:

- The country is among the poorest in the world. Its annual per capita income is under $200, well below the sub-Saharan Africa average of $350.

While many Eritreans largely live outside of the cash economy, a variety of social indicators suggest the country's poverty is as severe as the per capita income suggests. Infant mortality is 135 per thousand lives births; 203 of every 1000 children die before the age of five. The average life expectancy is 46. The adult literacy rate is 20 percent, probably half that for women. Daily caloric intake is one-sixth lower than the sub-Saharan African average.

- Eritrea has suffered from chronic food shortages. It was Eritrea, then considered in most of the world's eyes part of Ethiopia, that suffered the brunt of the mid-1980s famine that seared images of starving Ethiopian children in Western eyes. As estimated two thirds of the population relies on some form of food aid.

The country has been subjected to frequent droughts, a particularly serious condition given the fact that most farming is rain-fed. Only 20 percent of the nation's farms are irrigated. The government estimates that the nation's farmers could supply only 60 percent of the country's food needs even with good weather conditions.

- In addition to leaving much of the port of Massawa in ruins and resulting in the destruction of the railroad, the war left Eritrea with a legacy of undetonated, buried land mines, disabled veterans and displaced refugees.

Eritrea now stands among the dozen countries in the world with the worst land mine problems. Farming or herding in much of the countryside has become a dangerous activity.

Worse still is the enormous toll of disabled war veterans. Many thousands of the 3 million to 3.5 million Eritreans were disabled by the war.

Even the combatants who survived the war without incurring permanent casualties pose a major problem.

Many of them spent all of their adult lives experiencing the excitement and camaraderie of wartime. More than 50,000 soldiers have been discharged since 1993. Now they must integrate into civilian society, a task made all the more difficult by the fact that many have few skills.

Also facing the challenge for reintegration into society are the approximately 400,000 Eritreans who took refuge in the Sudan in the war.

- Eritrean women in Christian and Muslim communities (Eritrea is approximately 40 percent Christian, 40 percent Muslim nd 20 percent animist) live in some of the most patriarchal societies in the world. These women do backbreaking agricultural work, have virtually no control over family economic decisions, do not own land, are subjected to painful and dangerous circumcisions, do not have access to birth control and are often viewed as property.

During the war, the EPLF adopted a strictly egalitarian approach to gender relations. Thirty percent of combatants were women, and women were treated as equals in EPLF-controlled territory, with the traditional gender hierarchy suppressed. While in government, the PFDJ has maintained its firm commitment to promoting non-sexist social relations, but with the military demobilization, many traditional gender roles, especially in the countryside, have resurfaced.

Given the depth of patriarchal structures in rural Eritrea, there is little doubt that, even with enlightened government policies, change will come slowly. "We cannot just do away with attitudes," says Mehret Iyob, a member of Eritrea's constitution commission and a former combatant. "What makes us optimistic," she says, "is that the 30 years of struggle was not just a military struggle; social transformation took place in liberated areas," a social transformation she hopes to see continued and spread across the country.

An Independent Drive

The Eritrean government has no illusions about the depth of the challenges it faces. But government officials are ready to confront these difficulties with a unique drive and purpose.

A small country in a continent largely ignored in the Western media, Eritrea has not received much media attention, but the press coverage it has received has been overwhelmingly positive. Even World Bank officials talk about the Eritreans with a different voice, one that considers them almost equals in promoting development, a sharp contrast to Bank officers' attitude toward other African countries, which are often characterized as if they were children.

The Eritreans themselves are quick to distinguish themselves from African nations, even as they consider

©Robert Weissman

Scrapped Ethiopian military equipment.

numerous forms of cooperative arrangements with regional neighbors. "Thirty years ago when we went to the bushes, most African countries were getting their independence," says Eden Fassil. "Thirty years later, we look around, and not a single African country is a success story."

Integral to PFDJ leaders' notion of how they will differentiate themselves from other African countries is their attitude toward foreign aid.

Although the country has no choice but to accept food aid for the time being, government officials insist the aid is transitional only, and will be phased out as the country develops its agricultural base.

The government's rules covering foreign non-governmental organizations (NGOs) are strict, limiting the NGOs to a single foreign staff person, and requiring the NGOs to work on projects only in collaboration with government agencies. These restrictions, according to Eden Fassil, are motivated by concerns about inappropriate NGO use of resources and especially by the government's desire to promote self-reliance.

Regarding official aid, the country has declined not only loans for the railroad, but assistance offerings ranging from UN offers to develop technical classifications of occupational categories to World Bank loans. It has kicked numerous aid officials and agencies out of the country for interfering in national policy making.

The government has maintained a policy of flatly refusing aid or loans that are conditioned on adopting certain policies. On this principle it has turned down conditional World Bank loans—even though the government intended on its own to implement the World Bank-demanded policies.

"We are doing adjustment, so why do we need conditions?" Teame Tewolde-Berhaw, head of macro-policy

and international economic cooperation for the government, asks impatiently.

"We cannot surrender the managing of our economy to others," he says. "We have to [gain experience]—that is how our development can be sustainable."

In its selective approach to accepting aid, Eritrea does have a single, important advantage over other developing nations: it started life as an independent country free of foreign debt. The country inherited none of the massive debt the Dergue accumulated in waging war against Eritrea and Ethiopian liberation fighters. Thus despite its extreme poverty, Eritrea, unlike virtually every other developing country, does not need foreign loans to pay off old foreign debts.

Striving To Be Singapore

In a country where everything needs to be done, the government has adopted what it terms a two-pronged strategy to revitalize the economy and alleviate social problems. Within this framework, says Teame Tewolde-Berhaw, "the development rehabilitation effort is so large, the challenge so huge, it is hard to say [a single element] is a 'priority.'" He speaks of the government adopting "an interactive, rather than a sequential view of development."

The government defines the first prong of its strategy as a program of recovery and rehabilitation. This prong has relied heavily on the use of mandatory national service on behalf of what the government, in a November 1994 paper on macro-policy, calls "a multi-sector program that covered the restoration of essential agricultural and industrial activities, the repair and rehabilitation of infrastructure, the restoration of community assets, such as schools, clinics, water systems, agricultural tools, livestock, etc., and the building and strengthening of institutional capacity."

Pursuant to this prong, the large armed force of the EPLF continued to serve, but transferred its attention to rebuilding the country. Government employees—from the lowest-level worker to President Isaias Afewerki—served without salary, working only for minimal subsistence allowance, from liberation in 1991 until early 1995.

The government is also emphasizing human resource development, training Eritreans in skills ranging from plumbing to building construction. In this area, the government is especially focusing on ex-combatants, in an effort to integrate them into civil society.

The second prong of the economic program involves the more complicated problem of energizing the economy and setting it on the path to sustained growth. Failing to discover any attractive models in Africa, leaders of the once self-defined Marxist-Leninist EPLF, now entrenched in top government positions, have set for the country the goal of becoming the "Singapore of the twenty-first century," in the words of Eden Fassil.

Despite its emphasis on self-reliance, the PFDJ intends to create an export-oriented, outward-focused economy. The government hopes to promote tourism, especially on the Red Sea coast; mineral and oil exports, assuming projections of oil deposits in the Red Sea are correct; fish exports; and eventually labor-intensive manufacturing exports. Ultimately, it hopes to be an international financial center.

The government is proceeding cautiously in its dealings with multinationals, but it has adopted a liberal foreign investment code and is relying on multinationals to exploit the country's mineral deposits and is open to other forms of foreign investment as well. So far, the government has awarded mining permits to a handful of foreign firms: the Western Mining Corporation of Australia, the Canadian Golden Star Resources and Rift Resources, a Canadian company in which another Canadian corporation, Echo Bay, owns a 12.2 percent share, and Ghana's Ashanti Goldfields. The U.S.-based Anadarko Petroleum Corporation has signed an oil exploration and production sharing agreement covering a 6.7 million acre area in the Red Sea.

Internally, the government says in its macro-policy paper, "the private sector [will be] the lead actor in the economic activities of Eritrea."

But the government is approaching the issue of state involvement in the economy in characteristic pragmatic fashion. The Eritrean economy is overwhelmingly state-dominated. As a result of far-reaching nationalization policies of the Dergue, the state owns not only every major factory in the country, but the hotels and even many houses.

Eritrea does not have a domestic capacity to absorb sudden, massive privatizations, so the government is approaching the privatization issue cautiously. (The private sector is so weak that the Minister of Labor worries about the possibility that the country's small labor movement is strong enough to overwhelm the tiny, weak business class.) The macro-policy paper says, "In view of the present dearth of a capable business community in Eritrea, there is a clear need for a pioneering and catalytic role to be played by the government."

The government recently announced plans to privatize 23 companies, including metal work and shoe factories and a dairy products plant, in its first major round of privatizations; other privatizations will proceed even more slowly. Privatization will proceed "in a manner and pace that will be useful for the economy and the people who work in those enterprises," says Teame Tewolde-Berhaw.

Despite their commitment to privatization, government officials are not averse to state involvement in the economy. Where the private sector cannot perform necessary functions, they say, the state will step in. "We will

©Robert Weissman

A street scene in Asmara.

intervene," says Teame Tewolde-Berhaw, pointing to the example of electricity as a case where the private sector is too tiny to be able to command the large loans needed to invest in upgrading the electric system. Ultimately, Eritrea is likely to wind up with a mixed economy, albeit one in which the private sector plays a leading role.

Democracy and Development

Paralleling the country's economic-building project is an effort to construct a viable state machinery and a working democracy.

The central element of democracy building is the constitution-drafting process. A constitution commission is drafting a short constitution intended to articulate foundational principles for the new country, and undertaking a systematic and wide-ranging popular consultative process. Among the bedrock rights which will be guaranteed in the final version of the constitution, says Paulos Tesfa Giorgis, a member of the commission's executive committee, are free speech, free association, freedom of movement and other liberal democratic rights. The finalized constitution is expected to be adopted in April 1997.

In the interim period, however, democratic rights have an uncertain position. Eritrea is certainly not a totalitarian state. Indeed, one of the PFDJ's most stunning accomplishments has been to disarm the civil society while maintaining order. In a country in the throes of a full-fledged war half a decade ago, there are fewer signs of an armed police presence than in a comparably sized U.S. city. At the same time, there is virtually no street crime.

But Eritrea is not a particularly tolerant country, either. The government clamped down on the only effort so far to create an independent NGO, a proposed human rights group. The government owns the media, which does voice some criticism of government policies. In a political culture in which public criticism of the government is expected to remain within certain bounds and in which almost no one wishes to undermine the government, however, self-censorship is prevalent.

More broadly, and perhaps more worrisome for the ultimate development of a democratic culture, there remains a top-down orientation to government policy and program implementation. By all accounts, the EPLF governed the territory it controlled and ran its military operations in as democratic a fashion as possible in wartime, relying on citizen committees and assemblies to establish some policies and carry out administrative responsibilities. But out of necessity, wartime organization relies on a mobilizational model that is ultimately top down in approach. That top-down approach continues to characterize free Eritrea, and it may ultimately impact not only the political culture but the nation's economic rebuilding efforts.

Consider the issue of land tenureship, for example. In much of Eritrean society, land had been held communally, subject to frequent redistribution, as often as every seven years. In the eyes of government officials, this traditional land holding system poses two problems. First, they believe it discourages investment, because investors do not have time to recoup the benefits of their investment. "Ultimately, we believe unless land is converted to a commodity, you can't have economic development," says Eden Fassil. Second, the traditional land system has generally denied women ownership rights, and thus been a critical way in which traditional cultures have subordinated women.

The government's solution was to move quickly to nationalize all the land. For now, that has had little concrete effect in most rural areas, but ultimately the government hopes to move to a private holding system.

The government has such immense credibility with Eritrean citizens that its dramatic restructuring of land rights did not generate any popular outcry.

But the move was undertaken without consultation with, or the meaningful participation of, rural communities. Over time, the remaking of land ownership patterns is likely to alter significantly the country's society, culture and economy—in very uncertain ways, possibly including the fraying of Eritrean communities' strong bonds and the creation of a new rural elite.

"It is very important to have strong communities," says one Eritrean intellectual who is very sympathetic to the government. "Change things, yes, but these are things that sustain the culture, and to a large extent are the culture," says the intellectual, who worries also that making land into a commodity may promote undesirable urbanization, especially in the outskirts of Asmara.

©Robert Weissman

A storefront in Asmara.

"It worries me a lot," says the intellectual, adding that there are no "tools to combat the current legislation." But, noting the legitimate issues raised by government critics of the current land tenure system, he also asks, "You can raise all sorts of questions, but how can you say it is not right, especially without a counter proposal?"

Somewhat harsher criticism comes from Karin De Jonge, an Oxfam United Kingdom and Ireland representative in Eritrea who supports many of the government's restrictions on foreign NGOs. The government has carried over its top-down approach from the war era to the current period, she says, with deleterious effects. Throughout the government, she says, there is a "blueprint approach. [Development] programs are designed for people, rather than with people, and that is not very effective."

De Jonge cites the example of reforestation, a critical issue in Eritrea, which has seen its forest and woodlands cover plunge from 30 percent in the 1920s to less than 3 percent today. The government and before it the EPLF have mobilized young people for many years to plant trees, she says, but the overall forest cover has not increased. Villagers continue to cut trees unsustainably, primarily for firewood purposes. De Jonge and Oxfam advocate a different approach to tree planting; De Jonge proposes that communities be encouraged to plant trees on their own, and be given ownership of, and responsibility for maintaining, the trees. Community members will harvest the forest sustainably, she argues, if they are given stewardship responsibilities. "But those things are very difficult to discuss with the government," she says.

"As long as [the government] does not allow people to take over, they won't be very effective" in implementing rural development projects, she says.

But emphasizing their honesty, efficiency and good faith, she predicts that "it is probably a matter of time" before the government turns to more participatory approaches.

Stepping on to a Growth Path?

Other observers of the Eritrean scene who wish the government placed a higher value on democratic participation believe the country will succeed economically whether or not it becomes as open and participatory as it might.

"Eritrea will not be a democratic model," says one prominent Eritrean, "but it will be an economic model."

The experience of the Asian Tigers (the high-growth East Asian countries of Taiwan, South Korea, Singapore, Hong Kong) suggest that economic gains can be achieved independent of democratic ones. To the extent that honesty, determination, a willingness to sacrifice, independence, pragmatism and efficiency make a difference in achieving economic development, desperately poor Eritrea may be starting on a steady growth path. Whether political will is enough, whether Eritrean officials are making astute policy choices, particularly in their decision to emphasize exports, and whether a top-down orientation impedes the country's economic development will be seen in the years ahead, as Eritrea attempts to traverse that road.

Article 12

The New York Times, April 3, 1996

An African Forest Harbors Vast Wealth and Peril

Howard W. French

EVELA, Gabon—The forest grows so thick at the ends of this tiny settlement that even the N'tem River, a sizable Central African waterway, is completely obscured in the riotous greenery. Asked what lies beyond, a Fang villager shrugs and says "nothing."

From time immemorial, for the Fang—one of the Bantu peoples who make up the bulk of Central Africa's population—this area has been known as the edge of the world. But in fact, the land beyond this point has always been home to others: small groups of Pygmies, whose hunting-and-gathering livelihood had until recently changed little in a millennium.

The equatorial forest inhabited by Gabon's Pygmies, an area about the size of New York state, is at the heart of Africa's last intact belt of rain forest. It is still peopled by fewer than 40,000 inhabitants. But now it is facing changes of a pace and magnitude far greater than anyone here, Fang or Pygmy, has yet grasped.

Only a few dozen miles from this village, convoys of lumber trucks filled with stone are bringing material to French-led crews laying the paved roads that will open up this area as never before. In the capital, Libreville, and in the headquarters of European logging companies, plans are already being laid for the forest's exploitation.

At the same time, groups from the World Wildlife Fund to the World Bank are racing to mount efforts to inventory the huge catalogue of plant and animal species that live here and to identify areas for strict conservation on Gabon's last frontier for commercial forestry.

With its sparse human population and its dense canopy still intact, international environmental experts say that what happens to this jungle in Gabon will be an important bellwether for Africa's last major belt of relatively pristine rain forest, a vast area that stretches from the continent's equatorial coast across Gabon and well into the Congo River basin deep in Zaire.

"A lot of money is being spent in places like Brazil, in areas trying to rescue forests that have already been devastated," said Kathryn Simons, an

The New York Times

Residents and experts see signs of danger to the Minkébé forest.

American environmentalist who is studying conservation efforts in Gabon. "In Central Africa, where relatively little has been done so far, we have a unique opportunity to save a major tropical forest before it is destroyed."

It was in this forest, too, that the Ebola virus appeared in humans last year, killing some people in Gabon before it swept into Zaire and killed 244 others. Some experts warn that opening the forest, where unidentified animals are believed to harbor the disease, could unleash more epidemics.

If northern Gabon still boasts some of Central Africa's densest remaining woodlands, in particular the Minkébé forest, both experts and residents of this area can point to signs of an endangered future. Major logging companies and sawmills have not yet reached this forest, but already to the south and east of here, small operators have begun chipping away at this habitat in search of Okoumé, the most readily exploitable tree species, which is used mostly for plywood.

Wildcat gold miners, too, have been reported operating deep in the forest, where they fell trees and dig deep pits, dumping mercury and other highly toxic chemicals in the ground or in streams.

An arduous two-week hike away from Evela, along ancient footpaths traversed by thick columns of army ants and spied upon by tree leopards, live Pygmies who have never set eyes on Westerners. But already, around the fringes of the Minkébé forest, more and more Pygmies are being drawn into the life of modern Africa and its cash economy.

Throughout Gabon, wild game is considered choice dining. And in towns like this and in nearby Minvoul, Pygmies wait for city folk or Bantu agriculturists to hire their services as master hunters of the prized forest elephants.

Setting out armed with old 12-gauge shotguns and a few shells each, the hunters can spend weeks in the forest, wandering a landscape teeming with wildlife. The forest's estimated 65,000 elephants, along with Zaire's elephant population the largest in Africa, are the most prized game, but the array of potential targets is mind-boggling.

Pygmy hunters say their prizes include 30-foot boa constrictors, antelopes, gorillas, porcupines, boars and monkeys of all kinds. But if the variety is rich, the Pygmies themselves say that their search for game becomes more difficult each year as the hunting parties multiply.

"When we were young men, the hunt was done with arrows," said Omer Amaya, a 58-year-old Pygmy hunter whose settlement lies in a forest clearing at the edge of Minvoul. "We could go out for eight or nine hours and come home with a big catch. Nowadays you must walk at least three days before you can count on even seeing anything interesting."

For the hunters, the reasons for this increasing scarcity seem simple: their hunting has thinned game populations. "Wherever the barrel of the gun belches, the animals will try to avoid," said Hilarion Mikou. "After a time, if all is quiet, the animals will come back."

For environmental experts, however, the picture is more complex. "These forests are still primary forests in their structure, but already they are being exploited," said Marc Languy, a forest expert with the World Wildlife Fund. "We have noted a decrease of 80 percent in chimpanzee populations. If it is true that they can rebound, this is a process that might take 15 or 20 years."

The recent outbreak of the deadly Ebola virus in the town of Mayibout, another small Bantu outpost in the forest 130 miles to the southeast of here, has reminded many of another possible consequence of the forest encroachment. The outbreak killed less than 20 people in Gabon, but swept through the Zairian town of Kikwit with devastating effects last year, quickly killing 244 people.

The origins of the virus are not known, but it is presumed to have a natural host somewhere in the forest, from which it infects primates. Those who died in Gabon had recently feasted on chimpanzee meat.

Scientists at a major international conference on Ebola held in Kinshasa, Zaire, earlier this month theorized that environmental damage to previously pristine forest areas brought about the emergence of Ebola as a major health threat.

"In Gabon, gold prospectors went deep into the forest, they cut down trees in all directions, they dug up and destroyed a part of this environment" said Jean-Jacques Muyembé, a Zairian Ebola researcher. "This gave rise to the emergence of the virus." His theory is that the virus was dormant until its environment was so severely disrupted.

Pygmy hunters, meanwhile, say that in recent months they have encountered increasing numbers of dead gorillas and chimpanzees in the forest, where they have been felled by a mysterious affliction.

"You can hardly find any live gorillas anymore," said Mr. Mikou. "We've never seen this before. A big game animal that fears nothing is just dropping dead."

If conservation groups are beginning to marshal an effort to save Gabon's northern forests from the heavy logging that has taken place almost everywhere else in this country, tropical wood interests would seem to have the early upper hand.

A Dutch concern known as Wijima has already secured rights to just over one million acres of the Minkébé forest. And Gabon's President, Omar Bongo, has roped off another 542,000 acres of virgin forest for logging, just to the south of Minkébé.

"This is the last place that good supplies of wood are left in the country," said Pierre Mezui M'Eyié, a Government forest inspector based in the provincial capital of Oyem. "Right now, no one seems to know what kind of wealth there is here, but once the first commercial permits are issued, you will see a flood of applications.

"Then [it] is only a matter of time before the Minkébé is destroyed."

Article 13   *The National Interest*, Winter 1995/1996

Kenya: A Tarnished Jewel

Smith Hempstone

Smith Hempstone was U.S. ambassador to Kenya during 1989–93. Before that he was at various times editor of the Washington Star *and editor-in-chief of the* Washington Times. *His book dealing with his time in Kenya,* Rogue Ambassador, *will be published next year.*

From the beginning, Kenya was the jewel in Britain's African crown, an idyllic, wife-swapping, polo-playing, lion-shooting place in the sun for the restless, titled, but often impecunious younger sons of empire. The viscounts and the baronets were followed by men whose blood was not so blue but whose hearts were stout, chance-takers to whom neckties and offices were anathema, who wanted nothing so much as to turn a corner of "bloody Africa" into a little slice of Devon or Sussex. Some brought their women with them, intending to stay. And of course there were among them miscreants whose previous lives could not bear close scrutiny, adventurers looking for a fresh start in a country where there were no police records. Nineteenth-century Africa held small appeal for plump and comfortable men.

In the 1890s, British strategic thinkers wanted Kenya not for itself, but to guard the backdoor to Uganda and the source of the Nile, the key, so it was thought, to the control of Egypt, which secured the Suez Canal (completed in 1869) and the route to the treasures of India. To provide the capability of moving troops quickly from Mombasa on the Indian Ocean to Lake Victoria, a railway—dubbed the "Lunatic Line" because of the difficulties in building it (lions insisted on eating the Indian construction workers)—was completed in 1901. Both to guard the tracks and to provide the freight and passengers to pay for the railroad, London wanted white settlers along the right-of-way. So land was free, or nearly so.

But land was worthless if you couldn't survive on it. Everyone knew that West Africa was the white man's grave ("Beware and take heed of the Bight of Benin, for few come out although many go in", went the ditty). The third Baron Delamere, father of white settlement in Kenya, might claim that, while he farmed on the Equator, he did not live in an equatorial country. But what did that mean? It meant that a mile-high altitude in the highlands moderated the heat of the tropical sun, producing green forests of conifers and cold trout streams in the shadow of snow-capped Mount Kenya. Kenya, Delamere said, would prove to be "a white man's country." And indeed it did draw nearly one hundred thousand white settlers in its pre-independence salad days. Today, only about four thousand remain.

In addition to dirt-cheap land and an equitable climate, Kenya boasted then (and now) the largest congeries of wildlife in the world. There was money to be made from ivory, rhino horn, hides, and skins. You could (they said) shoot a lion before your breakfast of antelope chops. Some sportsmen called it Eden, and it was very nearly that.

Americans too came to know and love Kenya, this ravishingly beautiful land of white mischief and black magic. Teddy Roosevelt went there on safari in 1909, Hemingway wrote about it in the 1930s, Clark Gable, Stewart Granger, Humphrey Bogart, Grace Kelly, and Ava Gardner made movies there in the 1950s and 1960s. Americans who didn't know Bamako from Bangui could tell you that Nairobi was the capital of Kenya. A few even settled there.

I first came to Kenya in 1957, lived there during 1960–4 as a foreign correspondent, and visited there many times subsequently. In the early years I found it a quiet, pleasant place. If Africans had few political rights, at least they had enough to eat, education was good by continental standards, medical services were adequate, and the three races—whites, Africans, and people of the Indian subcontinent—lived together in relative amity. The country, with an economy based on coffee, tea, and tourism, was doing rather well.

Today, all that has changed. Foreign investment is flat, foreign aid—the United States put almost one billion dollars, more than half of it in outright grants, into Kenya between 1953 and the present—is falling, tourism is off, and the country is riven with tribal animosity that has cost the lives of more than one thousand Kenyans since 1991. Eden has become a hungry land where ragged urchins beg for pennies, the police beat grandmothers with truncheons, magazines are padlocked, dissent is equated with treason, and where bishops, ambassadors, publishers, foreign correspondents, and lawyers are vilified by the government of President Daniel arap Moi. What went wrong? What, if anything, can be done about it?

A Thin Veneer

Kenya, like most African countries, came half-baked from history's oven. It had slept through the Renaissance and the Reformation, missed the American, French, and industrial revolutions, was still fixated on bride-price and circumcision rites (male and female) when the nuclear age dawned. Somehow, it had occurred to nobody to invent the wheel.

Its institutions were few and weak, its people had virtually no experience with democracy—tribal or colonial—and its leaders tended to be demagogues rather than men who understood governance. Largely absent was any sense of nationhood or commonweal. Kenya inherited from Britain the facade of parliamentary democracy—wigs, woolsacks, and maces—but not the substance. Well-documented atrocities in the former Belgian Congo (now Zaire) in 1961 showed just how thin and fragile the Western veneer was throughout the continent.

Small wonder: democracy, while it clearly has global applicability from Costa Rica to Japan, evolved over generations in Northern Europe to meet the needs of that society at a specific point in time. It rested on certain facts and assumptions largely absent in Africa, a large proportion of whose peoples still lived in Bronze Age tribal cultures. Conformity and obedience, not innovation and initiative, were prized by both tribal chiefs and colonial governors. Literacy, industrialization, and decent per capita incomes, the glue of democracy, were low. The notions of constitutional checks and balances and respect for the rule of law were alien concepts. While some would argue that it was a good thing, Kenya could boast exactly one African lawyer when independence came in 1963.

Weakened by World War II and under heavy pressure from the United States, which had forced the British, French, and Israelis from Suez in 1956, Britain and Belgium were eager to throw down the burden of empire. And perhaps wisely: France would fight for Indochina and Algeria, Portugal for Angola and Mozambique, and its white settlers for Rhodesia, but the eventual outcome would be the same. In the case of Kenya, British disillusionment was hastened by the particularly nasty Mau Mau insurgency of the 1950s, which took thousands of lives. With faded pomp and circumstance, designed in part to conceal the abandonment of Kenya, the British in 1963 turned the country over to the Kikuyu leader, Jomo Kenyatta, who had been earlier vilified as the inspirer of terror.

The first decade of independence did not go badly, and there was hope for the future. while Kenya lacked oil, minerals, and navigable rivers, and was far from its major markets, it had certain assets. While Kenyatta was no democrat, he enjoyed the solid political support of all the tribes with the exception of the Luos, the Somalis, and the small pastoral groups. He had lived in England for many years—his first wife had been English—and was a pro-Western capitalist. Although Kenyatta inherited many parastatal organizations—government-run

corporations—from the British and created more (146 still exist, despite the admonitions of the World Bank and the International Monetary Fund), he always understood that socialism, far from creating wealth, only distributed poverty. Until they drifted away into politics or the private sector, the country boasted a small but well-trained cadre of civil servants. It had a small but vigorous entrepreneurial class drawn mainly from Kenyatta's Kikuyu tribe. It had a university and would soon have four more, although Kenyans continued to send their brightest sons (and, later, their daughters) to England, America, and India for higher education. (An "underground railroad" carried dissident Luo students down the Nile to Cairo and on to the Soviet Union and Eastern Europe for their training.) It had a teachable, industrious work force and reasonable internal communications. Kenya could claim sub-Saharan Africa's third largest economy, after heavily-industrialized South Africa and oil-rich Nigeria.

Inevitably, after any successful revolution (including our own) the have-nots are in a hurry to acquire the goods and chattels of the haves, and are not unduly fastidious as to the means they employ to do so. Kenya proved no exception, and blacks who wielded political power became millionaires almost overnight. As one white lawyer who later became a Kenyan judge told me, "If I can emerge from a revolution on the losing side with the loss of only 25 percent of my net worth—and I have—I'm fortunate."

Perhaps the real rot set in with the alienation of the two hundred thousand Somalis who roam across the northeastern fifth of Kenya's territory. Between 1960 and Kenya's independence in 1963, the Somalis almost to a man made it abundantly clear to a series of visiting British commissions that they wanted to be reunited with their kinsmen and Islamic co-religionists in Somalia (independent since 1960) rather than becoming part of an independent, ostensibly Christian Kenya. Once before, the British had played fast and loose with Kenya's territory, ceding to Somalia (then an Italian colony) a hunk of land west of the Juba River, including the port of Kismayu, as the price of bringing Italy into World War I on the allied side. This time, the British—who wanted a peaceful departure from Kenya—simply ignored the findings of their own commissions.

This triggered the so-called *Shifta* (bandit) War, with independent Somalia supporting Kenya's irridentist Somalis against the Nairobi government. This war, like most others, produced profiteering. The costly conflict lasted five years, and at least three thousand people lost their lives. Although Kenyatta was able in 1968 to negotiate a settlement, Kenya was flooded with automatic weapons in the hands of disaffected men who knew how to use them.

Kenya's Somali rebels turned poachers, slaughtering 80 percent of Kenya's one hundred thousand elephants (for ivory figurines, piano keys, cue balls and Japanese name-stamps), and virtually eradicating the country's ten thousand rhinos (whose horns are prized by Arabian dandies for dagger-handles and by the Chinese as an aphrodisiac). Members of the Kenyatta family, far from trying to stamp out the poaching, muscled in on this bloody racket and became its principal beneficiaries.

The lawlessness of the poaching plague reached its apogee in 1977, a year before Kenyatta's death. But since at least 1975 the increasingly senile president had reigned rather than ruled, with the country being run by a kitchen cabinet that included his Kenyan third wife, the powerful Attorney General Charles Njonjo, and other Kikuyu power-brokers. Sensing the approaching end of the Kenyatta era and the Kikuyu ascendancy, these klep-tocrats began the systematic looting of the state's coffers.

L'État, C'est Moi

Daniel arap Moi's political weakness is the second major cause of the cancer of corruption that is eating Kenya alive today. Nobody, possibly not even he, expected the long-time vice president to become a power in his own right on Kenyatta's death, or to remain long in the State House. He was neither sophisticated nor intellectual. His private sector credentials were negligible: he had been a grade school principal, and had only a high school diploma himself. He was the leader of no powerful tribe. His Tugen tribe was one of Kenya's smallest and most disadvantaged, and the Kalenjin-speaking linguistic group of which it was a member accounted for only 14 percent of Kenya's population (the four big tribes, accounting together for more than half the country's population, are the Kikuyu, Luhya, Luo, and Kamba).

It was precisely the personal and demographic weakness of Moi's position that had led Njonjo to commend him to Kenyatta as vice president in the first place: He would be a threat neither to the president nor to other powerful political barons. (This is a phenomenon not entirely unknown in our own politics.) But if Moi lacked a national reputation and popular support, he soon got it the old-fashioned way: He bought it. Scores of briefcases stuffed with money poured into the State House every week, tribute from the countryside, and part of it went back out to Moi's favored minions. Everybody was encouraged to get in on the game—when you're a passenger on the train, you don't blow the whistle—and soon bribes had to be paid for everything: to get (and keep) a job, to acquire a driver's license, to obtain medicine or a bed pan in a hospital, to get your child promoted in school. They called giving a bribe "pouring *chai*

(tea)" and the tea party was crowded. The culture of corruption was fired by the world's highest birth rate, a 4 percent annual increase that doubled Kenya's population in seventeen years. With one million Kenyans trying to enter the work force every year, there were jobs for only three hundred thousand.

Once in office, Moi quickly proved he had the shrewdness to stay there, by manipulating and vastly expanding the system of corruption. True, Kikuyu rule, too, had been corrupt. But the corruption until the end of the Kenyatta era had been kept within bounds, and the administration at least had been relatively efficient. Kalenjin rule brought both unbridled corruption *and* gross mismanagement (most of the parastatals were headed by Kalenjins and few of them showed a profit, even in good years).

Within four years, some of the Kikuyu, Luo, and Kamba had had enough. In 1982, the air force staged a coup that might have succeeded had the freedom-loving rebels not stopped to rape Asian girls and loot Nairobi's stores. The attempted coup changed Moi, who was already showing signs of clinical paranoia. Where before he had been avuncular and generous with the carrot, he became more and more inclined to use the stick against those whom he could not buy, or at least rent. The old Kikuyu elite (including Njonjo) were forced out of the cabinet, detentions and arrests increased, journalists were harassed and Kenya was declared a *de jure* one-party state, which meant that those ousted from the ruling Kenya African National Union (KANU) for insufficient fervor for Moi became political non-persons, ineligible to run for public office.

When I arrived in Kenya as ambassador in December of 1989, the Berlin Wall had been toppled, the Cold War was over, and African urban elites from Dakar to Djibouti were demanding a new political dispensation, a "second liberation" that would free their people from corrupt, authoritarian, single-party, or military rule. Washington, which historically in Africa had followed the lead of the former colonial powers, felt that the time had come to devise a new policy more in keeping with American ideas and ideals. President George Bush and Secretary of State James Baker went on record to the effect that, in the future, the United States would give its warmest support (and most of its economic assistance) to those states that cherished human rights, respected the rule of law, and expanded democracy. Kenya was doing none of these things, and I determined to do something about it. (So did a few others among forty-four U.S. ambassadors in Africa, forty of them career professionals, but many gave only lip-service to the cause of freedom.)

Moi was no stranger to me. I had met him in 1957 when he became one of the first eight Africans admitted to the colonial legislature. Moi was no Caligula. If his fingers were sticky, he was not alone among African Big Men to have difficulty in differentiating between public funds and their private fortunes. He had killed fewer political opponents than Idi Amin, embezzled less money than Mobuto Sese Seko, mismanaged the economy no more than Kwame Nkrumah. While minister of the interior during his vice presidency, he had also done some service for the anti-communist cause.

Recognizing that Kenya's "second liberation" could take place more peacefully with him than against him—there is, after all, something to be said for continuity—I was perfectly prepared to see Moi lead that "liberation" and benefit from it. In 1989, he still enjoyed a measure of national respect and prestige. He had only to turn the revolution against the most vicious, venal, and backward elements within KANU, legalize multi-party politics, and move with all deliberate speed toward free and fair elections. To do so would have made himself a hero at home and abroad. What I failed to see in those early days was that Moi was too deeply and intimately involved with the thug wing of KANU to move against those within it; either that or he was too lacking in courage or imagination to try.

With the brutal murder of Foreign Minister Robert John Ouko less than three months after my arrival in Nairobi—there was obvious high-level government involvement—I began to understand the nature of the black mafia with which I had to deal. In a May 1990 speech to a highly revolutionary group (the Rotary Club of Nairobi), I said publicly what I had been saying privately for some weeks: That if it wanted the present high level of U.S. aid to continue, Kenya would have to put its political and economic house in order.

Moi hit the roof, the more so when eight prominent Kenyan politicians (three of them former cabinet ministers) chose the day of my speech to announce the formation of the Forum for the Restoration of Democracy (FORD), a pressure group that called for the legalization of multi-party politics, free and fresh elections (elections were not due until 1993), and a two-term limit on presidential tenure. During May and June, I continued to expand my contracts with the opposition, which further enraged Moi and caused some consternation among the more timid souls at the State Department and elsewhere. (The Central Intelligence Agency traditionally had enjoyed a cozy relationship with Moi, who had a regular late-night checkers game with at least one station chief.) KANU launched a vitriolic press campaign against me. This reached an unprecedented height of hysteria when Kenya's old war-horse and first vice president, the octogenarian Luo leader Oginga Odinga, came to a party to which I had invited him in Kisumu. For nearly thirty years, Odinga had been a non-person: his movements were restricted, nothing he said or wrote could be reported in Kenya, and his son Raila frequently was held

as a hostage for his father's good behavior. He was one of the founders of FORD and its first interim chairman (Odinga died in 1994).

Two other dissident former cabinet ministers, the Kikuyus Kenneth Matiba and Charles Rubia, applied for a permit to hold a FORD rally on July 7,1990. It was denied, and they publicly canceled the meeting. Nevertheless, the police swooped down on FORD on July 4 and 5, detaining the entire leadership with the exception of the charismatic young Kikuyu lawyer, Paul Muite, who went underground. On July 7 (*Saba Saba:* the seventh day of the seventh month), wild rioting broke out in Nairobi and other Kenyan cities. The General Services Unit, the tough, paramilitary riot police, was called out, shots were fired and the police repeatedly charged the crowds, beating men, women, and children alike with truncheons. During the melee, Gibson Kamau Kuria, a well-known Kikuyu human rights lawyer who had previously been imprisoned and tortured, took refuge in my embassy and asked for political asylum, which I granted. Moi was not pleased that Kuria had escaped his net.

When the smoke of *Saba Saba* had cleared, at least twenty-nine civilians were dead, hundreds injured, and more than one thousand arrested. I issued a public statement deploring the arson and looting by the rioters, but protesting the severity and indiscriminate brutality of the government's reaction. Three of the detainees—Matiba, Rubia, and Raila Odinga—were held under harsh conditions for nearly a year, despite my protests. The health of the first two was permanently impaired by their ordeal. As Moi had boasted, it looked like multi-party politics would come to Kenya only over his dead body.

FORD's high-water mark came on June 18, 1992, when more than one hundred thousand dissidents rallied at the Kamukunji fairgrounds. I did not attend the rally, to which I had been invited, but sent embassy officers to report on events. A score of heads were broken, but only one person was killed. I was accused by KANU of masterminding the opposition, and Foreign Minister Wilson Adolo Ayah publicly called me a racist "with a slave-owner mentality", a violent man who had provided drugs and liquor for young demonstrators. Later, parliament devoted an entire afternoon to debating my shortcomings, and unanimously demanded that I be recalled. Both the White House and the State Department supported me strongly at this critical juncture. Scarcely had the FORD leaders arrested at Kamukunji been released than the opposition began to splinter, a destructive process that continues to this day. FORD split into two, with the elder Odinga and Muite leading what came to be known as FORD-Kenya. Matiba and the Luhya populist, Martin Shikuku, hived off to form FORD-Asili ("the original"). Later, when the opportunistic former vice president Mwai Kibaki resigned from the government, he further divided the opposition by forming the Democratic Party (DP), an elitist group whose membership is overwhelmingly Kikuyu.

Since the British covertly continued to support Moi, it became clear that the United States, while it enjoyed great prestige, lacked the economic clout to force Moi to expand democracy. Accordingly, the United States and its allies—Germany, Denmark, Sweden, Canada, and Finland—began lobbying in Nairobi and elsewhere for the support of the other donor nations in reducing foreign aid.

Moi was obviously shaken when the donors (ten industrialized nations, plus the World Bank and IMF), meeting in Paris in November of 1991, froze $350 million of the $1 billion in aid earmarked for Kenya. Within a month, Moi had ordered his rubber-stamp parliament to revoke Article 2(A) of the constitution, thus permitting multi-party politics. New presidential, parliamentary, and local elections eventually were set for December 29, 1992.

Dirty Tricks

Having agreed reluctantly to hold multi-party elections, Moi promply did everything possible—and that was a great deal—to skew them in his direction. It was made as difficult as possible for opposition parties to register and organize, although five splinter groups did take the field, denying the three major anti-Moi parties new recruits. Presidential candidates such as Matiba, Kibaki, and Odinga were restricted in their movements and denied access to the state-owned electronic media. Opposition organizers were warned they would be "burned alive" if they entered certain "KANU zones." Most opposition candidates were harassed, and some were physically prevented from registering. KANU thugs launched a reign of terror in Western Kenya, driving two hundred and fifty thousand opposition tribesmen from their homes and ballot boxes. The registration period was shortened, denying at least one million eligible young Kenyans the right to vote. Meanwhile, the presses worked overtime printing money to finance KANU candidates.

In a free and fair election against a unified opposition, Moi and KANU would have lost decisively. But dirty tricks, personal ambition, and tribal rivalries gave Moi and KANU a tarnished victory. Moi led the presidential field, but polled only 1.9 million votes, 36 percent of the total. Matiba polled 1.4 million votes, Kibaki 1 million, and Odinga 944,000. In the parliamentary balloting, KANU polled only 30 percent of the vote, but gerrymandering, constituency-loading, and the absence of a single opposition slate gave KANU 100 of the 188 seats at stake. Nearly half of Moi's cabinet lost their seats, and little more than a quarter of the KANU incumbents won new parliamentary terms. The opposition managed to win control of most of the largely powerless local councils.

Moi's behavior since the 1992 election has, if anything, been worse than it was before the balloting. He has appointed to parliament discredited quislings defeated decisively at the polls. He has denied development funds and humanitarian relief to districts that voted massively against him, as in Kikuyuland, where he polled exactly 2 percent of the vote. Of the eighty-eight opposition parliamentarians elected in 1992, more than half have spent time in jail since then. Others have been bribed to defect to KANU. At least three independent publications have been padlocked, firebombed, or driven out of business. Moi has accused the country's eighteen Catholic bishops of being in league with guerrillas because they described Kenya as "very sick" in a pastoral letter. The world-renowned paleontologist, Richard Leakey, who headed the Kenya Wildlife Service until he was forced out of office by Moi in 1994—and is now secretary-general of the unregistered SAFINA (Noah's ark) opposition party—has been beaten by KANU thugs while the police looked on, and made the target of a campaign of vituperation. Leakey, a Kenyan citizen, lost both his legs below the knees after a suspicious plane crash in 1993.

Of the diplomatic corps, only the recently departed German ambassador, Bernd Mutzelburg, and his Scandinavian colleagues have openly criticized Moi's most blatant acts of repression, and only their countries have significantly reduced aid. Kenya had tried without success to have Mutzelburg recalled before completion of his four-year term.

Kenya's Population: 25 million

Tribal Groups:

Kikuyu—5.3 million

Luhya—3.4 million

Luo—3.2 million

Kamba—2.8 million

Kalenjin—2.7 million

Kisii—1.5 million

22 other tribes—4 million

other—500,000

from *Kenya: Africa's Real Test* by James Capel & Co. Limited of London (1992)

Although by 1994, Paul Muite, the young Kikuyu lawyer, had described the American embassy in Nairobi as "irrelevant" to the fight for democracy, Moi has accused the current business-as-usual American ambassador, Aurelia Brazeal, and at least four other envoys of "meddling" in Kenyan politics. The defense pact that kept a battalion of British troops in Kenya more or less continuously since independence has been allowed to lapse. Moi has threatened to renege on Kenya's agreements with the World Bank and the IMF. Things are going from bad to worse.

What, if anything, can be done to restore the luster to what was once the jewel in Britain's African crown?

Clearly there is not much profit or purpose in reasoning with Moi. Most opposition leaders are on record as favoring a complete cut-off of Western aid. But that probably is not in the cards; having just resumed aid a year ago, the donors would feel silly refreezing it. But it could be, and to a certain extent has been, "refrigerated"—not formally cut off but slowed to a snail's pace. U.S. aid could be further reduced from its present level of $29 million (down from a high of about $80 million). Ambassador Brazeal could be recalled to Washington for prolonged consultations and instructed to take a more critical view of the KANU government, if and when she returned to Nairobi. Kenya's most-favored-nation economic status might be reviewed—if need be, we can buy our coffee, tea, insecticide, and cut flowers elsewhere. After Moi's recent insults to Baroness Lynda Chalker, British minister for overseas development, during her visit to Nairobi, it is even possible that Britain might come to the conclusion that Moi is not a client who reflects much credit on London.

At the end of the day, there is not a great deal the West can do to prevent Moi from turning Kenya into another Haiti if he is determined to do so. But the withholding of nearly $1 billion in foreign aid might well bring to the fore Kenyans who would see to it that Moi modifies his ways, or is replaced by someone who will.

There will be those who will say that what happens in Kenya is none of our business. But America can only be true to itself when it opposes repression and stands up for decency and democracy. That said, however, we should be under no illusion that the United States can on its own install stable democracy. In the end, Kenya's fate will be determined by Kenyans.

Article 14   *The Washington Post National Weekly Edition*, January 6, 1997

A Life of Bare Essentials

Nomads still live the way they have for thousands of years

Stephen Buckley

Washington Post Foreign Service

NORTH OF TIMBUKTU, MALI

Sididi Ag Inaka has never used a television, toilet or telephone. He has never read a newspaper. He has never heard of a facsimile machine. He has never seen an American dollar. He is entirely disconnected from the global economy and its ever-rippling waves. And he does not care.

"My father was a nomad, his father was a nomad, I am a nomad, my children will be nomads," says Inaka, who was not sure of his age but looked to be in his fifties. "This is the life of my ancestors. This is the life that we know. We like it."

Thousands of nomads pepper this western expanse of the Sahara desert, and most share Inaka's perspective.

For centuries, they have subjected themselves to the oft-bitter whims of nature, without real connections to society. They have lived off their camels, goats and sheep, depending upon them for everything from food to transportation. And they have survived.

But they have paid a price for their conscious disconnection. They are among the world's poorest people, unable to educate and provide health care for their children, continually scratching to make it through one more day, always one drought away from seeing their animals and families wiped out.

In many ways, their lives mirror those of Africans who live in the villages, towns and cities of the world's poorest continent. The difference is that many of those Africans long for an economic escape from a torturous existence. Most nomads here say they do not.

They are content in this land of thorn trees and murderous heat, where the ground is sprinkled with the bones of burros. Brutal sandstorms rise up in seconds.

Squealing children, hungry for play, tumble over sand dunes at sunset.

They follow water and grass, sometimes travel with another family member and generally move every couple of weeks. A month in one area is an eternity.

Years ago these nomads, most of whom come from an ethnic group known as the Tuaregs, were wealthy by African standards. Many piled up hundreds of camels for annual caravan treks to the salt miens in Mali's far north. Many owned thousands of goats and sheep. They owned slaves.

But over decades, annual rainfall has diminished, drying precious lakes, reducing grazing area for animals, decimating grain-rich areas and ultimately squeezing the livable territory available for nomads. Historically, the Tuaregs have ranged principally across the northern deserts of Mali and Niger.

A failed rebellion by the Tuaregs also have wreaked havoc with their economic lives since 1990. The fighting, which killed thousands before a peace agreement was reached last year, has forced at least 100,000 nomads to flee to Algeria, Burkina Faso and Mauritania.

"Today a nomad is considered very lucky if he has 300 camels," says McKinley Posely, Mali director of Africare, an aid group that has worked extensively with nomads. "They are a lot poorer than they used to be."

He pulls a map from his office wall and points to several lakes in north-central Mali. "You can now drive across what used to be the middle of this lake," he says, noting Lake Faguibine, one of Mali's largest. Gesturing to others, he continues: "This one is totally dry, and this one here has lost at least 80 percent of its water."

One outcome of their sharpening poverty is that some nomads take advantage of special areas developed by aid groups that offer water, food and other relief for them and their animals.

More also now travel and settle, albeit briefly, near towns to shop at markets and be closer to some semblance of stability.

Every Saturday, Inaka trudges five miles to the village of Ber, 40 miles east of Timbuktu, to buy and trade goods at the market. One recent day, he brought with him slices of goat cheese his wife had made earlier in the week. He hoped that selling the cheese would help him buy sugar, tea, tobacco and a gerba, a water container made from a goat carcass.

As he tried to sell the cheese, Inaka ran into other nomads, some seeking to sell animals, others in the village to restock rice and millet and other staples. They hugged and chatted and laughed. And, eventually, Inaka sold his cheese.

Then Inaka returned to where he had camped for more than a week. The nomad's camp—two tents made of camel hide—was strewn with all that he owned: torn clothes, a metal bowl, a goatskin sack, a straw cradle, three leather pillows, four straw mats, four gerbas, a small burner filled with charcoal, a teapot, a bag of sugar, a can of tea.

Inaka had come to this spot with his wife and three children nearly two weeks earlier. Within walking distance stood three other tents belonging to two of Inaka's brothers and a family friend. Nomads often travel together, then set up tents several hundred yards apart. In desperate times, they share grain and care for one another's animals.

Dozens of Inaka's animals roamed near his tent. He owns 5 donkeys, 25 sheep and 4 goats. He has no camels. Goats supply milk and cheese. Sheepskin provides, among other things, warm coverings on chilly desert nights. Donkeys, the cheap substitute for camels, are long-distance transportation.

"The animals are my life," says Inaka, a sharp-featured man with caramel-brown eyes, bronze skin, gray chin stubble and deep wrinkles rippling out from his eyes. "If the animals die, we die."

During the past year, it has rained little in parts of Mali's north, and nomads have suffered. The conditions revived wrenching memories of 1973, when a drought killed thousands of animals, forcing some nomads to abandon life in the desert.

Inaka has lost about 20 animals since 1995. In mid-September, one of his sheep, sick for days, died. The nomad slit its throat and, in the late afternoon light, knelt 15 yards from his camp, used two hands to scoop a shallow sandy grave and buried his animal.

"This costs [$33], so it's very painful for me," he says, still kneeling. "If it had grown bigger than this, I could have gotten [$50] for it." If animals continue to die, and he cannot feed his family, Inaka will likely find help from several relief agencies that work with nomads.

The Tuaregs have received more attention from such aid groups in recent years—some camps use buckets that sport faded U.N. insignia—but still have virtually no contact with the Malian government.

Some nomads have Malian identity cards, usually long-expired, but they generally have never used the government bureaucracy. Most have never traveled to Bamako, the capital. Most do not know that Alpha Oumar Konare is Mali's president.

They shun government services, unless desperate. The nomads near Timbuktu venture to the government hospital there only as a last resort. Women give birth in their tents. Men heal headaches with a spike of tobacco. Medicinal plants and aspirin donated by tourists and aid workers take care of most other ailments.

There are no schools in the desert. Children learn to read the Koran, the Muslim holy scripture, but receive no other education. From an early age, their lives revolve around caring for their families' animals.

Every morning, minutes after bowing in prayer toward the burst of white light that signals sunrise, Ahmid Mohamed takes his family's sheep, goats and camels grazing. Then he brings back the camels and takes them to the well to drink. Eventually, he gathers the sheep and goats. The next day, he starts again.

He is 15 years old. He knows nothing else.

"I enjoy my life," says Ahmid, whose family was camped about 15 miles north of Timbuktu. "I like taking care of the camels. I don't know the world. The world is where I am."

But Ahmid, with slim, serious features and a shadow of a mustache, has dreams. He wondered what school

would be like. He wondered about the airplane that split the sky as he spoke. He wondered what it would be like to drive a car.

"I would like to see if driving a car is different from riding a camel," he said.

Later that day, some 50 miles to the east, Inaka and his 10-year-old son Mohamed, ramble together down a hill near their camp, about to gather the family's sheep, goats and donkeys. The sky, a breathtaking blue, holds up a crescent moon, though the sun has not yet set.

The father carries a staff in his right hand and drapes his left arm over this slightly built son. Inaka says something, and they laugh. Then, at the bottom of the hill, the father hands his staff to his son, who scampers away to find the animals.

Article 15 *Current History*, May 1996

Nigeria:
Inside the Dismal Tunnel

"Nigeria first entered . . . 'the dismal tunnel' on January 15, 1966, when the military overthrew all the institutions of a democratically elected government. . . . If there is light at the end of [this] tunnel, it is imperceptible to anyone not paid to see it."

Richard Joseph

Richard Joseph, a visiting professor of political science at the Massachusetts Institute of Technology, has written extensively on Nigerian politics. His books include Democracy and Prebendal Politics in Nigeria: The Rise and Fall of the Second Republic *(Cambridge: Cambridge University Press, 1987). This article is based on a paper presented at a conference on the "Dilemmas of Democracy in Nigeria" at the University of Wisconsin at Madison, November 10–12, 1995.*

The November 10, 1995, execution of Ken Saro-Wiwa and eight other activists from the Movement for the Survival of the Ogoni People by the military government of General Sani Abacha quickly earned worldwide condemnation. It also led to greater international awareness of the regime's repressive policies and highlighted the fact

that, although Nigerians have been governed longer by soldiers than by elected politicians since independence in October 1960, the legitimacy and efficacy of military rule have always been vigorously contested.

One month after the regime of General Yakubu Gowon was overthrown in a palace coup in July 1975, Obafemi Awolowo published a set of recommendations to the new rulers. Awolowo had been a civilian member of the Gowon government, but left once the Biafran war ended. Although it promised to return power to civilians in a measured manner, the Gowon government had begun implementing a vast number of far-reaching policies—a pattern that would be followed by all its military successors. Awolowo's admonitions are as relevant today as they were two decades ago: the military administration should serve as "an essentially corrective regime, and not a reconstructing administration with ready and lasting answers to all our political and economic ills. . . . It would be too much of a task for it to attempt the massive and neverending task of rebuilding or reconstructing the body politic."

> *Nigeria has become a rogue state, and as such refuses to abide by prevailing international ethical and legal norms in the conduct of public affairs.*

This advice has never been heeded by Nigeria's military rulers. Although General Ibrahim Babangida spent eight futile years between 1985 and 1993 directing a large number of structural reforms, including a complicated transition to civilian rule, the Sani Abacha regime has unveiled a similar set of initiatives to justify remaining in power. Awolowo had his own motives in counseling the armed forces to limit its political agenda. However, in this and other matters, his comments went to the heart of the Nigerian dilemma.

Nigeria first entered what Awolowo labeled "the dismal tunnel" on January 15, 1966, when the military overthrew all the institutions of a democratically elected government. That date echoed in the decision of the constitutional conference, established by Abacha after he seized power on November 17, 1993, to set January 1996 as the date his regime would return power to elected civilians. It took considerable effort and persistence to obtain such a declaration from a conference packed with Abacha appointees and subject to all forms of inducements, co-optation, and coercion. But in April 1995 the conference reversed itself and left the termination date open. On October 1, 1995, Abacha demonstrated his dominance over all internal political forces and his disregard for international opinion by declaring that he would remain in power until 1998. The execution of the Ogoni activists a month later was a clear signal that only extraordinary measures will loosen the military's grip on power.

Although Nigeria has seen the arrival of an entirely new generation of political, military, and civilian elites and has undergone several regime changes, purges, dismissals, and detentions of members of the political class,

the criticisms of Major Kaduna Nzeogwu, who led the seizure of power in northern Nigeria in the January 1966 coup, are as pertinent today as they were 30 years ago. Nzeogwu identified Nigeria's main "enemies" as "the political profiteers, the swindlers, the men in high and low places . . . those who seek to keep the country divided permanently so that they can remain in office as ministers or VIPs at least; the tribalists, the nepotists, those who make the country look big for nothing before international circles, those who have corrupted our society and put the Nigerian political calendar back by their words and deeds."

There is little dispute about what Nigeria has become. The economy is in shambles, kept afloat only by the continued production and export of petroleum. All major public institutions are in a state of advanced decay; social services have deteriorated steadily for over a decade. Once described as kleptocratic, the conduct of public officials merits a stronger designation as the society has become increasingly criminalized. Nigeria is now a major transit point in international drug trafficking and in the laundering of illicit fortunes. Although it has been a major oil producer for over two decades, Nigeria is now included among the debt-distressed nations. Moreover, it lacks the governing capacity even to manage the effective servicing of its estimated international debt of $37 billion.

Even more troubling, Nigeria has become a rogue state, and as such refuses to abide by prevailing international ethical and legal norms in the conduct of public affairs. There are many indications of this new status: suspension of Nigeria's membership by the Commonwealth of States; universal criticism of the continued detention of president-elect Moshood Abiola along with scores of journalists, lawyers, human rights monitors, and political activists; condemnation of the June 1995 secret trials and subsequent sentences imposed on accused coup plotters, including the former president, General Olusegun Obasanjo, and his former deputy, General Shehu Yar'Adua; decertification by the United States government because of drug trafficking (which excludes Nigeria from most forms of assistance); designation, together with Burma, as one of the worst human rights abusers in the United States State Department March 1996 annual report; cancellation of sporting events, including an international soccer tournament scheduled to take place in Nigeria in 1995; tight restrictions on the issuance of visas to Nigerian public officials and their families seeking visas to visit Western nations; and suspension of new loans and investments by multilateral agencies.

Although Nigeria's status has fallen internationally, it is still being given every chance to "return to the fold" before more drastic measures are imposed, such as a ban on arms sales and purchases of Nigerian crude oil. Even the Commonwealth chose to suspend Nigeria for two years rather than expel it after the November 1995 executions.

How did this state of affairs come to pass? Why has Nigeria, which has conducted perhaps the most extensive attempts of any developing nation to construct a constitutional democracy, failed so abysmally? Why has the Nigerian military, after governing the country during much of the post-civil war decade in a manner that permitted a wide degree of openness and autonomy in civil society, produced one of the few regimes on the continent still characterized today as "authoritarian"? How did a country that had a deserved reputation as a principled leader of the continent on international matters, especially the struggle against the racist regimes of Rhodesia and South Africa, come to be described by a British foreign minister as a place of "growing cruelty"?

The Prebendal Republic

The current crisis in Nigeria can be seen as the outcome of a number of forces whose interactions have pushed the nation down a particular path. One of the elements that should not be overlooked is the repeated failure of civilian politics. As General T. Danjuma, the chief of the army staff under Obasanjo, pointed out with some exasperation in the 1970s, "It is now fashionable in Nigeria to talk about a military regime being an aberration, and that a return to civilian rule means a return to democracy. This is a fallacy because we never had a democracy in Nigeria."

The state was a national cake to be divided and subdivided among officeholders.

A critical moment came in 1979, following a careful attempt to lay the basis for a stable democracy, that masked a deep flaw that would undermine the new system. That flaw was the relationship between the administration of public office and the acquisition and distribution of material benefits. These practices had also become central to the processes of party building and the making of political alliances. The party that won power in the elections did so for a number of reasons, including its willingness to capitalize on this logic. These

well-established practices in Nigerian sociopolitical life can yield short-term gains but also contribute to the sapping of the authority, legitimacy, capacity, and finances of the state.

According to the theory of prebendalism, state offices are regarded as prebends that can be appropriated by officeholders, who use them to generate material benefits for themselves and their constituents and kin groups. In Nigeria, the statutory purposes of such offices became a matter of secondary concern. With the National Party of Nigeria (NPN)—which regarded itself as Nigeria's natural party of government—leading the way in entrenching these practices at the federal level, and all other parties doing likewise in the state and local governments they controlled, Nigeria during the Second Republic between 1979 and 1983, evolved into a full-fledged "prebendal republic."[1] The state was a national cake to be divided and subdivided among officeholders. Politics degenerated, as the scholar Claude Ake has pointed out, into an unrelenting war to acquire, defend, or gain access to state offices.

Although civilians had fashioned this system while Nigeria was under colonial rule, the Nigerian military contributed to its extension. There was little difference between the final years of the Gowon administration and those of the Second Republic in this regard. In fact, the members of every Nigerian government, from the regional administrations under colonial rule in the 1950s to the Abacha regime, have demonstrated an increasing propensity to divert public funds for their personal use. Justice Akinola Aguda stated it quite simply when he remarked in the late 1970s that the one achievement of every Nigerian government is that it has created more millionaires than its predecessor. Today, with the emergence of "pharaonic" in place of the milder "prebendal" corruption, that comment should be amended to "multimillionaires."

Babangida's Bogus Transition

Despite these failings, Nigeria has usually remained a place of hope. It was, and still is, the greatest agglomeration of African peoples within the boundaries of a single nation-state, and it still possesses considerable natural resources. Nevertheless, in 1989 there came a moment when it became evident that the country was lost in the "dismal tunnel." General Babangida, having already postponed the promised date for the handover of power to civilians from 1990 to 1992, allowed political

---

[1]The first independent civilian government, between 1960 and 1966, is often referred to as the First Republic. The Third Republic, constructed under Babangida, was stillborn.

associations being formed to seek registration as political parties. However, the requirements were grossly unreasonable. The number of offices that associations had to open, the lists and photographs of supporters that had to be provided, and the timetable imposed on them—everything had to be done in a matter of only a few months. The regime set the rules and it could impose any criteria it wished.

After the mountains of materials were delivered to the Electoral Commission in Lagos, the verdict soon followed: none of the associations had met the test and the government would create its own political parties, name them, write their manifestos, and oversee their development. The military regime had embarked on what Awolowo and others had long cautioned against as "the massive and neverending task of rebuilding or reconstructing the body politic"; it was assuming full responsibility for establishing the instruments by which Nigerian civil society would be allowed to pursue its political and social objectives. Little wonder that Nigerian critics dismissed the new parties as parastatals (state-financed enterprises).

As was revealed to participants in an August 1990 conference, the two-party system imposed by the Babangida regime after it dismissed all political associations in 1989 was a preconceived plan. All the political aspirants and entrepreneurs who took part in these exercises have been dupes to one extent or another, since the regime had no intention of ceding power. The transition to democracy became a game in which the rules were changed as soon as the civilian politicians felt they had mastered them. In the hope of inheriting power, or some parcel of it, many Nigerians—soldiers, trade unionists, established politicians, traditional rulers, intellectuals, businesspersons—had been led by Babangida further into the dismal tunnel.

In the election of June 12, 1993, Babangida finally allowed two affluent businessmen—who considered themselves his cronies—to contest the presidency. They were only the last of the many individuals who had been led to believe that Babangida supported their candidacies only to find themselves dismissed as they reached for the brass ring. On the very eve of his June 23 annulment of the elections, some of Babangida's advisers left a meeting with him reassured that the next day he would announce the winner and next president of the nation.

After 1989 it seemed that there was little new to be said about Nigerian politics. The prebendal character of the state and political life generally had been repeatedly confirmed. Rather than changing what had become fundamental to Nigerian political life, the major developments under the Babangida regime—the considerable growth of the powers of the presidency, Babangida's domination over all aspects of political and social life, the colossal sums pri-

vately appropriated (especially by senior members of the regime), the minute stage managing of an elusive transition process—only deepened the contradictions that had been identified by many analysts.

[T]he military was an unaccountable body that could not restrain the inevitable abuses of office.

Throughout this period, concerned Nigerians were unable to arouse awareness of the direction Babangida was leading Nigeria as long as the regime repeated its promise to transfer power to an elected government. Following a byzantine series of developments, Babangida was induced by the military hierarchy to leave office on August 26, 1993, clearing the way for Sani Abacha to brush aside Ernest Shonekan's "Interim Civilian Government" less than three months later. Abacha, a man Obasanjo has described as Babangida's "eminent disciple, faithful supporter, and beneficiary," proceeded to take the nation deeper into the dismal tunnel after seizing power on November 17, 1993.

The Military-Civilian Revolving Door

Although Awolowo claimed that military rule was an abnormality in Nigeria, it is also the case that civilian rule has not left a commendable record. The violence and mayhem, especially in western Nigeria at the time of the 1983 elections, were reminiscent of the carnage and confusion during the final years of the First Republic. The corrupt behavior of public officials and the gross mismanagement and increasing repressiveness of the federal and state governments during the Shehu Shagari era raised fears that Nigeria would experience a severe crisis if it continued to be inefficiently and corruptly governed while becoming increasingly impoverished. When the armed forces stepped in on December 31, 1983, the ease of their takeover reflected the extent to which the civilian government had lost legitimacy in the eyes of the demoralized and anxious population. Even the embryonic Third Republic, in the form of elected governments at the local, state, and federal levels under Babangida, showed signs of continuing this pattern. As Obasanjo has noted, "In very few states were cases of corruption and obscene malpractice and abuse of office not the order of the day. At the national level, the scale of corruption was monumental."

But Nigeria has also known peace, some economic progress, and a sense of hopefulness during certain periods of military rule. This was the case during the first years following the Biafran war, for much of the Murtala Muhammed-Obasanjo regime, between 1975 and 1979, and for the early years of the Babangida administration. During each of these episodes a distinctly Nigerian military system of governance was in evidence. This system, beginning with Gowon, was refined by each subsequent military administration. In both federal and state governments, a relatively small group of military officers were assisted by civilian appointees, who included well-known politicians as well as private citizens from the professions and the business world. The effective sharing of power took place between the higher military and civil bureaucracies.

This system allowed considerable freedom and autonomy within civil society. Indeed, Nigeria had a freer press during these episodes and a more active, autonomous, and effective array of interest and professional groups than most African countries. Moreover, the balancing of representation of Nigeria's major ethnic groups in the government and in the major public institutions was also handled reasonably well by this system.

Each military government, however, was subject to decay because the military was an unaccountable body that could not restrain the inevitable abuses of office and, except for the Obasanjo regime, was unable to arrange a smooth succession. It thereby increasingly invited countercoups. When Sani Abacha seized power in November 1993, even he temporarily aroused hopes that this known system of governance would be reinstalled. Although Abacha dismissed all the elective political institutions, he managed to draw into his government an impressive group of national politicians, including the long-time human rights lawyer Olu Onagoruwa, who became his minister of justice. By this time, however, such gestures no longer had any substantive meaning; they were merely rituals aimed at obtaining compliance with continued military rule.

When Babangida came to power in August 1985, it seemed that Nigeria was returning to the familiar conciliar system of governance. As Babangida stated in criticizing his predecessors, "A diverse polity like Nigeria required recognition and the appreciation of differences in both cultural and individual perceptions." In fact, the first year of Babangida's rule, characterized by his wide degree of consultation and an open style, kept at bay criticisms of his self-described "military democracy."

By the end of his eight years in power, what the country had experienced, in the words of one of its erstwhile agents, was "organized confusion." Babangida's government claimed to be laying the basis for a "stable liberal democracy" and in its early years pushed through reforms intended to create the foundation for a more market-oriented economy. The Political Bureau appointed by Babangida shortly after he came to power recommended the construction of a socialist republic, a goal the regime rejected while accepting the need for extensive social and ethical mobilization of the population and the creation of a costly bureaucracy to fulfill that role. It initially adopted the conciliar mode of interest accommodation, but gradually supplanted it with a corporatist propensity to charter new institutions and make formerly autonomous bodies dependent on presidential largesse. And after promoting a vigorous human rights policy, it moved to harassing and imprisoning the country's leading human rights lawyers and activists, detaining journalists and banning publications.

Another Replay?

At the end of the 1980s the Campaign for Democracy and its affiliates had called for a national conference to lay the basis for a genuine transition process in place of Babangida's manipulations. In the neighboring francophone countries of Benin, Congo, and Niger, this approach had brought an end to military regimes, but it had been stoutly resisted or derailed in others, such as Cameroon and Zaire. Nigeria needed a new basis for civilian politics that would emerge from an "ingathering" of all political and social forces rather than a renewed top-down crafting by a military regime.

In addition to the need for a transitional process that would mobilize the broad forces of Nigerian society, another issue needed to be addressed: that these transitions were largely phases in the circulation of powerful elites. Since civilians have held government posts under military as well as civilian regimes, they have tended to become involved in promoting changes within military systems, or even military coups (as in 1983 and 1993), that benefit their own material interests.

The idea of a period of nonpartisan civilian government as a kind of "probationary" exercise has regularly surfaced in Nigerian political discourse. One flaw in the transition to the Second Republic was the absence of such an experience at the national level. Indeed, three of the regime's four years in power were devoted to the making of the constitution and only one year to legalized party building, campaigning, and elections.

What was required was a bridge between the system of governance established by the military and the reestablishment of a fully open system of competitive party politics. Such a "bridge" was also advocated in 1975 by Awolowo, who suggested that Nigeria should not move directly to a winner-take-all system. He therefore revived a recommendation put forward earlier by Aminu Kano, a populist opposition leader, that any "political probationary period" should last five years, during which a sharing of all government positions would be proportional to the votes won by parties in the elections—a proposal remarkably similar to the transitional arrangements put into effect in South Africa two decades later. Such an idea, if adopted in Nigeria, should not be introduced as another superficial exercise in political engineering but should be anchored to a broader institutional process, such as a national conference or its equivalent.

The Abacha regime has unveiled a new draft constitution whose most striking feature is the introduction of a rotational presidency in which the position of head of state will revolve among the country's major ethnolinguistic groups. And on October 1, 1995, Abacha announced a new three-year "transition program." Already, Nigerian political aspirants have begun creating political associations, anticipating the starting pistol for the formation of political parties and renewed competition for electoral office. But as long as a Nigerian military regime maintains effective control of the security forces, it can dictate any "transition" program it wants with the knowledge that politically ambitious Nigerians will dance to the new tune. Despite the country's economic shambles, oil production continues and there will always be major fortunes to be made by holding state office.

What, therefore, are Nigeria's options three years after the Babangida regime was forced out? The most likely is another replay of the Babangida scenario: a supposedly democratizing regime that uses its leverage to keep revising the "transition program," thereby prolonging its stay in power until it is forced out. A second option is a different transition program based on a national conference or power-sharing framework, as suggested earlier. This option would depend on the termination of Sani Abacha's rule and its replacement by a military regime committed to a genuine transition. A third option was taking shape within the Babangida "transition" and was blocked by a preemptive military coup by Babangida himself against an incipient "citizens' republic" when he canceled the elections of June 12, 1993.

A fourth option has always been rumored within the country but has never been carried out—a radical military coup comparable to the second seizure of power by Jerry Rawlings in Ghana in 1981, with the intention of establishing a revolutionary government and sidelining the established military and civilian political class. Although junior officers have often played a significant role in coups in Nigeria, once successful, they have usually ceded place to more senior officers. The threat of the dire actions the "Young Turks" would unleash once in power has often been used to justify a preemptive move by

more conservative senior officers. The bloodbath at the time of the attempted overthrow of the Babangida regime in April 1990 is an indication of the carnage that would ensue if a military faction tried to seize power without having firm control of core units of the army.

Democracy Deferred

Pini Jason, a Nigerian journalist, contends that "General Babangida annulled Nigeria's best chance to enter the 21st century as a modern democracy." Something unusual did take place in Nigeria on June 12, 1993, and the report by Peter Lewis, who was present for the occasion, is instructive. He notes that the party-building process up to the presidential elections had replicated the misconduct normally associated with civilian politics in Nigeria; "aspiring political factions employed fraud, financial inducement, and violence in the bid for advantage."[2] It seemed that hardly a week went by when one party official or another was not suspending a colleague, or defecting to the opposition. In 1992 the regime had canceled the presidential primaries on the basis of alleged irregularities and substituted an even more complicated system. When the day of the presidential elections arrived in 1993, however, Nigerians performed a collective and national act that made these elections one of the most peaceful to take place in Africa during the current wave of democratic transitions.

Lewis's report confirms one issued by the Nigerian Center for Democratic Studies, which had organized its own election-monitoring exercise. The election campaign was conducted with "unprecedented decorum; [it] was marked by little of the political violence and electoral manipulation of the past; there was limited evidence of fraud and vote-rigging; polling was generally conducted in a peaceful and orderly manner" and the results were promptly collated by the [National Electoral Commission]."

Any observer of previous Nigerian elections—even the Babangida "transition"—is likely to blink on reading these words. Something very remarkable had happened in Nigeria. The unannounced results of the election, which would have shown a 58 percent majority for Moshood Abiola, were also noteworthy both for the size of his plurality and for the fact that he drew significant support from all areas of the country, including several major northern precincts.

The deliberately contrived judicial pronouncements canceling the elections, then blocking the announcement of the returns, and the bizarre exertions of Arthur Nzeribe's Association for Better Nigeria to get the gov-

[2] "Endgame in Nigeria: The Politics of a Failed Democratic Transition," *African Affairs*, vol. 93 (1994), p. 324.

ernment to scuttle the entire process, reflect the panic within government circles and among some of its constituencies that, despite all the roadblocks and "organized confusion," the Nigerian people were going to elect a president who could not be relied on, once in office, to do the bidding of the outgoing regime.

Moshood Abiola is no paragon of democratic accountability; he has become fabulously wealthy by mastering the strategies for acquiring power and wealth in Nigerian society. However, only someone with his wide networks of political and business associates could have reached the end-point in Babangida's "transition." But the Nigerian electorate was voting for much more than a man. After all the delays, it had been granted one final chance to get the military out of power and restart the Nigerian "political calendar"—and it made the most of it. As Lewis points out, "the combined influences of apathy, apprehension and confusion kept many away from the polls." The resulting 35 percent turnout was subsequently used by the regime's supporters in its campaign to weaken Abiola's claims. In view of all that Nigerians had experienced since the "transition" began eight years earlier, it is remarkable that so many were still prepared to go to the polls.

> *With each reshuffling of Nigerian military rulers, the risk of an unbridled tyranny grew.*

June 12, 1993, should not be seen in isolation. The argument can be made that it represents one of several elements of a citizens' republic whose emergence has been stymied by the misconduct of civilian politicians as well as the deliberate interference of a politicized military. Thus, during the First Republic a political system with two broad political groupings evolved. A similar process was in evidence during the Second Republic. Both trends were halted by the irresponsible behavior of the political class and the military's arrogation of the absolute right to rule. Rather than the military rushing in to "save" the Nigerian nation, it is Nigerian civilian politicians who will have to experience, and surmount, the deepest challenges to the nation, whether they take the form of economic difficulties, internal discord, or external threats to the nation's security.

Chief Adisa Akinloye, a leading politician in the National Party of Nigeria during the Second Republic, made the observation that "there are really two parties in Nigeria: the military and the civilians." Only the latter can still give rise to a sustainable democracy in Nigeria. When Babangida rounded up a number of politicians and detained them for violating the ban on political activities in 1991, another remarkable event occurred that presaged what took place in June 1993. Although these politicians came from different parts of the country and belonged to different political formations, they discovered that they shared much common ground. When they were released they put forward a set of common positions on the political process, much to the chagrin of the Babangida administration. This is an indication of the kind of experience that a national conference or its equivalent could force Nigeria's senior politicians to undergo, similar to the transition proceedings in South Africa. It could also lead to the fashioning of a common political program, together with a commitment to overcome the country's regional, ethnic, and religious divisions and make possible the national concord that could sustain an extended period of civilian rule.

Beyond the Rogue State

It is in the behavior of the ruthless security services, which proliferated under the Babangida regime, that the embryonic rogue state may be discerned. When the dynamic journalist and publisher Dele Giwa was blown apart in October 1986 by a parcel bomb while he was investigating the connections between the criminal and military networks, a signal was sent of what could be in store for other Nigerians who threatened the consolidation of mafia-style governance. With each reshuffling of Nigerian military rulers, the risk of an unbridled tyranny grew. As a private citizen commented with chilling prescience just before Babangida stepped down: "Unless we say never again, we will wake up one day and a psychopath in uniform will usurp authority, use and abuse power to plunder the nation, and dare us speak."

Less than a year after he had handed power to civilians, General Obasanjo took part in a debate with a law lecturer on the campus of the University of Ibadan. That confrontation can now be seen as having taken place across the fault line in the construction of the Nigerian polity. Rejecting the argument that the Nigerian military undermined the rule of law, Obasanjo contended that the military invoked an alternate and equally authoritative legal system whenever it dismissed civilians and suspended the constitution. As a consequence, he argued, the "ability, competence, and authority" of the Nigerian military "to make law that is valid and binding on all citizens should not be in doubt or questioned once they are effectively in political power." He also extended such authority to include the right to disregard not just constitutional procedures but such fundamental principles as the inadmissibility of retroactive laws; "when occasions do call for such laws to save the nation from political or economic destruction, the governing majority must be able to act in defense of the nation."

Fifteen years later Obasanjo has been arrested, tried, and imprisoned on the basis of the very alternate "legal system" he once defended. A spokesperson for the Abacha regime brushed off criticisms of the 1995 secret trials by arguing that "this is not the first time we have had this type of trial" in Nigeria, and wondered why "past secret coup trials in Nigeria did not attract this kind of attention." In the kafkaesque world that Nigeria has become since the Babangida era, Emeka Ojukwu, who led an armed struggle against the Nigerian nation between 1967 and 1970, can rebuke Olusegun Obasanjo, who defended the nation in that civil war: "If there is any punishment that comes, should he be found guilty of whatever it is, it will be prescribed by no other person than himself."

As any passing knowledge of the speeches and writings of Obasanjo would indicate, the former military ruler has come a long way from his defense of the military's right to disregard fundamental rules of jurisprudence in "the defense of the nation." When the Abacha regime declared in 1994 that it was suspending habeas corpus, and when it detains lawyers who try to defend their clients, what exists is no longer a "militarized Leviathan" that seeks to preserve organized society but a rogue state whose motivations cannot be predicted, and whose boundaries for irrational behavior are unknown.

In exiting this tunnel, Nigeria cannot just go back to the "good old days" of the prebendal republic, whether in its military or civilian form. It must go further back to a citizens' republic. This republic can only be brought into being incrementally and through an extended period of accommodation and power-sharing among civilian groups in an open and accountable national unity government.

The June 1993 elections demonstrated that the Nigerian people may be ready for such an exercise. In 1975 they believed that Murtala Muhammad would create such an opportunity; in 1985 and 1986, Ibrahim Babangida sparked similar hopes. In the various regions of Nigeria other civilian politicians have also emerged from time to time to rekindle that vision. But the solemn fact is that, by the end of this century, Nigerians will have experienced nearly 50 years of political experimentation, beginning with the formation of the first major political parties around 1950, followed by elected regional administrations. These experiments, many inspired by the finest democratic ideals, have resulted in a ravaged economy, a poorly functioning state, and recurrent social upheavals.

The Abacha regime has shown little sign of veering from its determination to undertake its own reconstruction of the body politic. Commissions have been established to supervise a new "transition," to oversee elections from the local to the national level, and to review the number and composition of states and local governments. In the meantime, sporadic bombings and attacks on individuals continue, as well as arrests and harassment of political opponents.

The United States government is calling for increasing international sanctions on Nigeria, but the discovery of new oil deposits and major foreign investments in natural gas production are enhancing the leverage of the regime. Despite an aggressive public relations campaign, the transition program lacks international legitimacy. Nevertheless, a new set of Nigerian politicians, and some old ones, will be induced to take part as long as there is hope of reaching the political trough that the state now exclusively represents. If there is light at the end of the dismal tunnel, it is imperceptible to anyone not paid to see it.

Article 16   *Africa News*, December 21, 1992—January 3, 1993

A Nation of Poets

Tami Hultman

Africa News Service

Americans know Somalia as a land of gaunt children and marauding gunmen. But for centuries, those familiar with the wedge-shaped piece of land jutting into the Indian Ocean have called it "A Nation of Poets."

Somalia's poetic tradition differs markedly from Western practice. Somali scholar Said Sheikh Samatar, in an essay to accompany a 1986 exhibit at the Smithsonian's Museum of African Art, wrote that it is difficult for Westerners to appreciate the role of poetry in Somali culture. "Whereas in the industrialized West, poetry—and especially what is regarded as serious poetry—seems to be increasingly relegated to a marginal place in society," he said, "Somali oral verse is central to Somali life."

Samatar wrote that "even a casual observation" of Somali society reveals "the remarkable influence of the poetic in the Somali cultural and political scene."

English explorer Richard Burton, who traveled through Somalia in 1854, noted the prevalence of the art. "The country teems," he wrote, "with 'poets, poetasters, poetitoes, poetaccios': every man has his recognized position in literature as accurately defined as though he had been reviewed in a century of magazines—the fine ear of this people causing them to take the greatest pleasure in harmonious sounds and poetical expressions, whereas a false quantity or a prosaic phrase excite their violent indignation."

Somali poetry has been the country's chief means of mass communication, substituting for history books, broadcasting and newspapers. In recent decades, after the Somali language was written for the first time, and cheap radios and tape recorders began to spread into rural as well as urban areas, there was an expectation that oral poetry might decline as a societal force.

In fact, modern communications and transportation have spread the art more efficiently from one area to another. Distinguished poets began to travel from area to area, leaving behind tapes of their work to be passed around and evaluated. After World War II, literary productions on Somali national radio and the Africa Service of the BBC attracted huge audiences.

"Thus, it is a common, if amusing, thing," Samatar wrote, "to come upon a group of nomads huddled excitedly over a short-wave transistor, engaged in a heated discussion of the literary merits of poems that have just been broadcast while they keep watch over their camel herds grazing nearby."

But to say that poetry permeates Somali society is not to say that everyone is a poet. Somalia is no exception to the rule that artistic genius is a scarce commodity anywhere. There is keen competition among talented poets, and a nation of poetry connoisseurs demands a high level of skill and persuasiveness from its practitioners.

Poets who win public favor are a privileged class, socially and politically. At the same time, though, they assume the burden and responsibility of preserving history and shaping current events. Historically, Somali bards have mobilized public opinion in support of war or peace, as they saw the need.

Sayyid Muhammad Abdille Hasan—who was immortalized in British history as the "Mad Mullah"—used his verse to unify Somalis in the fight against British colonialism.

And the Somali Dervish Movement, a religious-based resistance to foreign domination in the first two decades of this century, produced a body of work that pitted the Dervishes not only against the European powers who were carving up the country, but also against their Somali collaborators. Since the Somalis on both sides were skilled poetic gladiators, the verse of the period is filled with appeals to opponents to change sides and with pleas to neutrals to join the battle.

"Although most of the poets, on both sides of the conflict, were concerned mainly with the conduct of the war," writes B. W. Andrzejewski in an essay for the Smithsonian exhibit, "they remained faithful to their calling as artists." The formal skills and devises, such as poetic diction and figurative language, continued to be cultivated. Even the most practical of poems, such as those designed to communicate military strategy, were full of lyrical passages.

Dervish leader Sayid Maxamed Cabdulle Xasan, whose rise to power depended heavily on his talent as an epic poet, was a master of the genre. In a poem warning his followers about the perfidy of an ally who changed sides when threatened by enemy reprisals, there is a preamble about the loyalty and bravery of the Dervish "reciter," who carries the poetic message and transmits it to others. Although the alliteration—a key component of Somali verse—is lost in translation, the evocative images remain.

> You did not leave me when the ignorant stampeded...
>
> You loaded your camels and came over to me when they defected to the British generals...
>
> And I count on you during the dry season of the year.
>
> A rosy cloud, a scud of white vapor, precipices of cloud flashing with lightning,
>
> Resounding thunder, flood water running over the parched earth,
>
> The past night's repeated showers, noisy as the jibin bird
>
> The heavy rain which fell, the longed-for rain of the spring,
>
> Ponds brimming over, old campsites luxuriant,
>
> Thorns become as tall as grass, thick undergrowth crackling—
>
> I shall satisfy your needs as when one pours out salty water for a she-camel
>
> And I shall entertain you with a poem as precious as a jewel.

The poetry of Salaan Arrabay, on the other hand, became an anti-war weapon. His best-known work, "O Kinsman, Stop the War," was an appeal to end a long-standing feud between two rival sections of the Isaaq clan in northern Somalia. "Tradition has it," says Samatar, "that the poet on his horse stood between the massed opposing forces and, with a voice charged with drama and emotion, chanted the better part of the day until the men, smitten with force of his delivery, dropped their arms and embraced one another."

The collapse of the Dervish resistance in 1921 set the stage for Somalia's current tragedy. The legacy of the conflict was poverty and destruction among the vanquished Somalis. "The situation was made worse," says Andrzejewski, "by the fact that large quantities of firearms had found their way into the nomadic interior and were now used in fratricidal warfare devoid of any ideological aspect." Poetry again played a role, whether in-

Pierce the Sky

Somalis have long debated the merits of a nomadic, pastoral existence versus those of a settled agricultural community. In this excerpt from a Somali poem, a nomad explains his decision to return to his herd after a brief try at farming:

It is said that one cannot pierce the sky to get rain for one's garden,

Nor can one drive the farm, as one drives animals, to the place where the rain is falling.

Worst of all, one cannot abandon one's farm, even though barren, because all one's efforts are invested in it.

The farmer, in counter argument, replies:

A man with no fixed place in this world cannot claim one in heaven.

citing local feuds, "or counseling peace and appealing to the sentiments of a common culture and religion."

The colonial and post-colonial period saw a change in Somali poetic traditions. The 1940s gave birth to a romantic species of verse that avoided the hazards of political and social commentary. But politics continued to intrude, sometimes covertly. "The metaphoric and allusive language," says Andrzejewski, "was well suited to fooling the foreign censors who at that time were trying to check the activities of those Somalis who were working toward independence, and it sometimes happened that an apparently harmless love lyric was easily decoded by Somali listeners into an attack on the authorities."

During the two-decade dictatorship of Mohamed Siad Barre, who ruled Somalia from 1970 to 1991, poetry became a tool of an authoritarian regime. While verse helped mobilize the population for such social programs as national immunization and literacy campaigns, it also was employed to consolidate Siad Barre's power.

At the same time, Somali writers began to explore prose fiction. But the poetic tradition infused the new form, as in a 1981 serialized story by Cismaan Caliguul. The tale of two young lovers, whose relationship is opposed by their families, glows with poetic imagery in the heroine's accounts of her elopement.

We rode on and on through the night in complete darkness—darkness which knew nothing of our

troubles. I turned my head and there was the dawn pursuing us. We listened and the birds were chirping and twittering—they were pleased with the new day that was running toward them. How different was their situation from ours! They wanted the dawn to break quickly so that they could begin picking berries, and we wanted the dawn to linger behind so that we could escape beyond the territory of my clan under the cover of night. . . .

The grass on which the rain had fallen the night before now spread its blades towards the sun for which it had been waiting, and the dew resting on the leaves of the trees took on the color of gold. The trees were pleased with the growing warmth and the sunshine, but all this was of no benefit to us, travelers who were passing by.

Now, in a break with centuries of history, Somalia's poets have fallen silent. Before Siad Barre's overthrow last year in a mass uprising, oral traditions were already in decline. The combined pressures of increasing poverty and political repression sapped energies, dampened creativity and curbed the free expression upon which poetry had thrived.

Andrzejewski predicts that in the future, poetry as a living art will be confined mainly to texts of work and dance songs, anecdotal narratives, and children's lore. But in a more optimistic mood, he believes that an improvement in Somalia's material situation will permit a flowering of written literature, including poems, short stories, novels and literary scholarship.

For the moment, though, Somalia's rich civilization is obscured by images of human suffering. In the language of modern media, Somalis are either victims or thugs, passive or drug-crazed. And the exquisite sound of poetry has been drowned by the vulgar thunder of guns.

For more information about Somalia's verbal and visual arts, see *Somalia in Word and Image,* a 1986 publication of Indiana University Press. Prepared for an exhibition mounted by the Foundation for Cross Cultural Understanding, the book is available at the National Museum of African Art of the Smithsonian Institution, Washington, DC.

Article 17

Current History, May 1996

The Afrikaners after Apartheid

"So far the Afrikaners traditional deference to authority has dominated public responses to [South Africa's] majority government, but this has been easy because Afrikaner economic interests remain unchallenged even as formal apartheid has given way to legal equality."

Ben Schiff

Ben Schiff, a professor of politics at Oberlin College, is coauthor with June Goodwin of Heart of Whiteness: Afrikaners Face Black Rule in the New South Africa *(New York: Scribner, 1995) and author of* Refugees unto the Third Generation: U.N. Aid to Palestinians *(Syracuse, N.Y.: Syracuse University Press, 1995).*

In April 1994, apartheid, South Africa's unique system of legally imposed racial separation, officially came to an end when the African National Congress (ANC) won the country's first nationwide nonracial elections. The former ruling party, the white Afrikaner National Party, became the junior member of a government of national unity headed by President Nelson Mandela.

Two years later, even as the National Party deteriorates and negotiations over a new constitution promise to lead to majority government in 1999, the Afrikaners retain vast influence. Understanding why they remain a key element in black-ruled South Africa and a potential source of instability requires an examination of postapartheid South Africa in historical context.

Prior to 1994, outsiders usually portrayed white South Africans as divided between the Dutch-descended Afrikaner apartheid rulers and the moderately liberal, antiracialist English speakers of British origin. Within each of these groups there was (and remains) a much broader spectrum than the simple racist-liberal division implies. Of the approximately 5 million whites, Afrikaners number about 3 million; English speakers comprise most of the rest, including a substantial Jewish community. There are also small Portuguese and Greek communities, and a newly arrived contingent of Eastern European immigrants. The African population includes close to 30 million people, and there are approximately 3.5 million Afrikaans speaking people of mixed race or "coloured" background, and several hundred thousand Asians.

Although the Afrikaners bear the onus of apartheid and its crimes, their system evolved from legal structures developed under English rule in the nineteenth and early twentieth centuries. After the Afrikaners took complete control of the South African government following their Nationalist Party's electoral victory in 1948, they fully articulated and legally rationalized a welter of existing restrictions into the codes of official apartheid ideology, policy, and law. The economic effects of apartheid—in its nascent form under British rule, and in full flower under the Nationalists—devastated the African population, and its legacies persist. Although whites currently fear and some are experiencing what they call "falling standards" in personal security, economic opportunities, and educational quality, they remain a highly privileged population.

But the Afrikaners are arrayed along a wide political spectrum. While elements of the old ruling clique still seek to retain power without formal authority, some (particularly younger) Afrikaners reject the old ways and embrace change. Although racial distinctions in South Africa may be subsumed by differences in economic privilege—as in Brazil, where the main axis of conflict is economic and in which privilege is partly identified with color but color is not the dividing element— Afrikaner nationalism could still emerge as a destructive force.

Birth of a Nationalism

Afrikaners trace their origins to Dutch East India Company employee Jan Van Riebeeck, who landed at what became Cape Town in 1652, sent by the company to establish a victualing station. Dutch settlers came from the bottom of society— press-ganged workers, people fleeing prosecution, or those opting for emigration instead of jail. Mostly illiterate farmers, they populated an isolated agricultural colony in which the power of the company and its European technology enabled them to suppress and dominate the indigenous local pastoralist and nomadic peoples.

French Huguenots fleeing religious persecution in the years after 1685 added a small educated elite to the Dutch farming population. Meanwhile, the Dutch East India Company imported slaves and indentured servants from its possessions farther to the east in what are now Indonesia and Malaysia. Despite the myth of racial purity later made the root of Afrikaner nationalism, sexual relations and intermarriage with local women and with those brought from the East Indies were relatively common among the early Dutchmen. The poor Dutch *boere* (farmers) could not afford the time or money required to return to the Netherlands, find a European wife, and then return to the colony.

The end of the Napoleonic period in Europe brought British rule to the colony, and a large tide of English and Scottish people immigrated in the 1820s and 1830s. Generally better educated, wealthier, more in touch with industrializing Europe and often more serious about their (Scottish Presbyterian) Calvinism than the Dutch, the English speakers became the British-controlled Cape Colony's elite. When the British Empire moved to eliminate slavery throughout its possessions, some Afrikaners stayed in the Cape Colony and accepted change. Others embarked on the "Great Trek," striking out to find new land and freedom from British rule in South Africa's interior.

These *Voortrekkers* (pioneers) repeatedly clashed with the Africans they encountered. Confronting the militarily powerful Zulus, the trekkers first suffered a massacre at the hands of Dingaan, a local Zulu chief, and then defeated him on December 16, 1838, in the Battle of Blood River. In Afrikaner history December 16 became the Day of the Covenant because legend had it that the Voortrekkers had promised God they would honor Him if they were victorious in battle. The hardships of the Great Trek became the foundational myth of Afrikaner nationalism. (Those who trekked—and their descendants—still disdain those Afrikaners who stayed in the Cape even as the latter often deem themselves educationally and socially superior to the trekkers).

After diamonds were discovered in 1867 along the Orange River, the British annexed the Boers' fledgling inland republics, the Orange Free State and the Transvaal Republic. Reacting to British efforts to tighten control, the Boers rebelled and defeated the crown in the first Anglo-Boer War (called by Afrikaners the War of Independence) between 1880 and 1881. Afrikaner nationalism burst forth, spurred by anti-British fury. A few elite Afrikaners began efforts to "uplift" *die volk* (the people) and provide them with the trappings of a nation. They began with a language movement based on Dutch, but then focused on standardizing the local creole "kitchen language," combining elements of Dutch, Malay, and African languages into Afrikaans.

After gold was discovered in 1886 near what became Johannesburg, the British again moved to subdue the Boers. In the second Anglo-Boer War (or more commonly, the Boer War) fought between 1899 and 1902, a massive British army used scorched-earth tactics to defeat the Afrikaners. Approximately 26,000 of the roughly 30,000 Afrikaner war fatalities were women and children who died of malnutrition and disease in wretched British camps. The heroism of outgunned Boers and the suffering of their wives and children provided new fuel for Afrikaner nationalist fires.

The conservative British government that conducted the Boer War fell before the war ended, the electorate horrified by stories of the Boers' suffering. The Peace of Vereeniging, negotiated by a new conciliatory British government, aimed to placate Afrikaner nationalism. The comparatively liberal race policies that had been proclaimed as part of British war aims were jettisoned, and dual English-Dutch domination was enshrined in law in 1910.

Out of Unity, Apartheid

Even with peace, Afrikaner leaders rightly perceived the British to be their primary rivals for economic and political power; however, the two groups collaborated against the indigenous population. In the Land Act of 1913, the Union of South Africa restricted African land ownership to "native reserves" that constituted a mere 13 percent of the country's land, crushing the last vestiges of independent African agriculture and relegating the Africans to lives of itinerant, landless wage labor. In the following decade drought and economic depression forced the Afrikaners themselves from the land and into the cities, only to face employment competition from cheap African labor. Its people lacking the skills and education necessary to compete with the British for influence and with the Africans for jobs, the Afrikaner leadership pursued two strategies. It laid the groundwork for creating a new Afrikaner community capable of challenging British domination, and it successfully lobbied the government to reserve jobs for whites.

In 1918 a small group of young Afrikaner clerics and civil servants founded the Afrikaner Broederbond (Union of Brothers) to "uplift" the volk and proclaim Christian values; in 1922 the Broederbond became a secret organization. Throughout the drought and depression years of the 1920s and 1930s, as Afrikaner farmers struggled to survive migration into South Africa's cities, the Broederbond founded hundreds of nationalist educational, social, religious, cultural, economic, and political organizations that were centered around an ideology of

Christian Nationalism developed in the Afrikaans Dutch Reformed Church. Apartheid—separating people in South Africa into their language groups—was a corollary of Christian Nationalist theory.

Broederbonders finally attained political preeminence with the Afrikaner Nationalist Party's 1948 electoral victory over Jan Smuts's ruling South African Unified (English and Afrikaans) Party. Apartheid became the ruling political ideology of the state. Although English capital still dominated business, the state became a giant machine for the enrichment and empowerment of the Afrikaners. Government monopolies in arms, steel, electricity and coal production, telecommunications, transportation, and postal services soaked up Afrikaner workers. South Africa developed one of the largest state sectors of any noncommunist country.

Since the Great Trek, Afrikaners have been a fractious people.

Voortrekkers: The Next Generation

Since the Great Trek, Afrikaners have been a fractious people. Cape Afrikaners largely accommodated British rule while the Free Staters and Transvaal Boers fought against it. From 1910 to 1948 some Afrikaners formed coalition parties and governments with the British, while others developed the exclusivist nationalist ideology that became apartheid.

As the Afrikaner Nationalists came to power in 1948, divisiveness remained, although from the outside the volk appeared monolithic. When National Party ideologists revoked the coloureds' limited franchise in 1956, even though they were Afrikaans speakers and had stood closely with the Boers, the move disgusted a small group of Afrikaners, who quit the party. In the late 1960s, in protest against government permission for some integrated foreign sports teams to tour South Africa, the Herstigte (Purified) Nasionale Party split on the right. As the apartheid system aged, a spectrum developed, ranging from "rigid" to "enlightened" National Party members, divided over tactics to maintain Afrikaner domination. The former sought ideological purity while the latter pursued pragmatism.

In 1982, when President P. W. Botha implemented a new constitution that included legislative assemblies for coloureds and Asians in addition to the white parliament, hard-liners left the National Party to form the Conservative Party. The Nationalists and Broederbond struggled to maintain the image of a monolithic Afrikaner volk while Botha's government responded to escalating African political protests with a thoroughgoing militarization of government.

In the 1980s, international ostracism, sanctions, and global recession broke the long record of economic expansion, and South Africa faced financial crisis.

Even as Botha cracked down, Broederbond moderates in the Dutch Reformed Church laid the groundwork for loosening apartheid, declaring in 1986 that apartheid could no longer be biblically justified. Church conservatives split to form the Afrikaanse Protestante Kerk (Afrikaans Protestant Church, or APK), which claimed more than 33,000 adult adherents in the early 1990s.

In the 1980s, international ostracism, sanctions, and global recession broke the long record of economic expansion, and South Africa faced financial crisis. By the time President Botha suffered a series of strokes in 1988, the National Party was ready to begin major reforms to apartheid. Those changes began with the election of F. W. de Klerk as president in 1989. De Klerk, who had emerged from the hard-line wing of the party, announced on February 2, 1990, an entirely new direction—legalization of the ANC, South African Communist Party (SACP), and other anti-apartheid organizations that had been banned since the 1960s—and indicated that the state's most celebrated political prisoner, Nelson Mandela, would be released. De Klerk had moved to the left of his party, apparently hoping to manage the forces of change. The Broederbond was secretly charting a course that would dispense with apartheid but retain its benefits. In 1992, APK leader Reverend Willi Lubbe charged that because de Klerk no longer embraced apartheid, "He's definitely not an Afrikaner."

In response, the Conservative Party and an ever shifting group of far-right wing parties and paramilitary groups initially called for a return to 1950s apartheid, and then increasingly focused on a *volkstaat* (Afrikaner people's state) as their goal. But the problem with partition was and remains that Afrikaners lack a majority in any significant, geographically compact area of South Africa.

Dissent on the Afrikaner left had already begun to gain momentum from the mid-1980s. An erosion of religious faith reduced church power, and the growing toll of young Afrikaners killed, maimed, and psychologically damaged in the so-called border wars in Namibia, Angola, and Mozambique brought home the price of government ideology. An anti-National Party and Broederbond but pro-Afrikaner, left-wing newspaper, *Vrye Weekblad* (Free Weekly), began in 1988 to attack the government, exposing death squad activities and charging that the Broederbond's definition of Afrikaans culture was destructive.

Among some young Afrikaners, an "alternative" Afrikaans music movement took hold, exposing in microcosm youthful cynicism and countering the squeaky-clean official Afrikaans Federation of Cultural Associations (FAK). The nationwide *Voelvry* (Feel Free) music tour of 1990 was followed by two raucous *Houtstok* (Woodstock) festivals in 1990 and 1992. The *Voelvry* tour rocketed the Gereformeerde Blues Band (as in *Gereformeerde Kerk*, the culturally most conservative of the three Dutch Reformed Churches) to fame as it lampooned the political and cultural establishment. "We're cultural terrorists, we're planting mind bombs," said Theunis Englebrecht, a young writer, poet, and rock band leader. FAK suppressed the *Voelvry* recordings, prevented its stars from performing on Afrikaans university stages, and briefly banned them from the radio airwaves of the South African Broadcasting Company.

Struggling to Keep Power

During the period from de Klerk's February 2, 1990, speech to the April 1994 elections, civil violence escalated in South Africa. Newspaper reports described spiraling "black on black" violence and attributed it to a war between the Zulu Inkatha Freedom Party, led by KwaZulu homeland leader Mangosotho Gatsha Buthelezi, and Mandela's ANC. Massacres in townships and on commuter trains claimed thousands of lives and, according to some commentators, provided a foretaste of life under black majority rule.

A series of reports in the Johannesburg *Weekly Mail* in 1990 (later substantiated in court cases) showed that the government was providing money, weapons, and training to Inkatha. Top KwaZulu police officials who were members of South African intelligence agencies planned and covered up death squad activities. A steady stream of revelations gave increasing credence to charges that a clandestine "Third Force"—was acting at the government's behest to destabilize the transition. De Klerk's brother, Willem, a leading Nationalist strategist, asserted in 1992 in traditional Broederbond-speak, that "authoritative government is almost unavoidable in South Africa."

That applies to the transitional constitution as well as the final constitution." The old white elite had no intention of leaving South Africa's future to the forces of mere democracy or the black majority.

Mounting violence among blacks and threats from the Afrikaner right-wing appeared to strengthen the National Party's hand in transitional constitutional negotiations with the ANC. The Nationalists demanded "group" protections and a collective executive. The ANC rejected these positions, holding out for individual rights and a single president. The Nationalists dropped the "group" protections idea, accepting individual rights and seeking maximum power for provinces to weaken the central government. Federalism became the rallying-cry of de Klerk's Broederbond-elaborated position, while the far right continued to call for a volkstaat. Increasing numbers of Afrikaners on the left openly joined the ANC.

Meanwhile, the Nationalists reached out for new supporters. After 36 years of denying that coloureds were Afrikaners, the National Party suddenly broadened its definition to include all who spoke Afrikaans. The appeal was based on fear: the party claimed the coloureds could not trust the ANC to protect them from the black masses. Then, in 1993, the all-male, all-white Afrikaner Broederbond declared that it had ceased to exist, replaced by an Afrikanerbond open to all Afrikaans speakers who embraced Christian values. Hans Strydom, critic and long-time observer of the Broederbond, argued that it was simply going deeper underground. "They want people to think that they're not powerful. You must never underestimate them. . . If you don't understand the Broederbond, you'll never understand what has happened to the Afrikaner."

The 1994 national election partly vindicated the National Party's strategy. The party won a majority in the Western Cape, where a large coloured population (55 percent of the electorate) enabled it to gain 53.3 percent of the vote. In KwaZulu-Natal, with widespread evidence of electoral fraud, Buthelezi's Inkatha gained 50.3 percent of the vote.

Overall, the ANC garnered 62.7 percent of the vote, the National Party 20.4, Inkatha 10.5, the right-wing Afrikaner Freedom Front about 2.2 percent, the (mostly English) Democratic Party 1.7 percent, and the Pan Africanist Congress 1.3 percent (the remaining 1.2 percent was divided among 13 small parties). Under the transitional constitution, the six largest parties formed a government of national unity, with the ANC's Mandela as president and Thabo Mbeki of the ANC and de Klerk of the National Party as deputy presidents.

The Travails of Unity

To gain agreement with the Nationalists on transition, the ANC made important concessions to Afrikaner concerns, guaranteeing there would be no wholesale layoffs of white civil servants and accepting minority party participation in the cabinet. The ANC backtracked from its socialist economic inclinations and adopted the capitalist model urged on it by the South African business community, Western governments, and international financial institutions.

The government has proved awkward politically for the Nationalists. It has kept de Klerk in the limelight, but he is vastly overshadowed by Mandela and Mbeki. Since the National Party is part of the ruling body, it must mute its criticisms of the ANC dominated government. Thus participation in the national unity government has allowed the Nationalists neither equality of power nor the freedom of loyal opposition.

Ongoing constitutional negotiations—the new constitution is to be completed this May—have revolved around issues of basic individual rights, the division of powers between the provincial and central governments, and the composition of the central government. From 1992 the National Party pursued strong provincial autonomy, sometimes in collaboration with Inkatha. This February the Nationalists finally dropped their demand that the constitution require a national unity government after 1999.

The party's constitutional affairs minister, Roelf Meyer, resigned this March from government to lead the Nationalist's project to "rethink" itself and develop into a broadly based opposition party prepared to contest the 1999 elections. Critics claimed that the party was in disarray, with de Klerk's closest advisers composed of whites unable to abandon apartheid attitudes. To the right, the party appeared to be losing members to the Freedom Front, and to the left, to the ANC. Meanwhile, it was attempting to develop a black constituency by promoting its few African members to highly visible positions in government.

Retention of the massive white (mostly Afrikaner) civil service has led to apparent sabotage and slowdowns that have hamstrung central government action. Major tensions within the police and defense forces continue. During the 1980s, the apartheid regime set up secret intelligence and assassination units, such as the Civil Cooperation Bureau, with front companies initially financed by the government and aimed at becoming self-sustaining. Some of the companies and an unknown number of the secret units' soldiers remain in existence and are possibly connected to "Third Force" operations. It is unclear to what degree criminality and political violence, particularly in KwaZulu-Natal, remains affiliated with the old regime and its functionaries.

Revelations about the apartheid regime's criminal operations have been pouring out of a court case in which a police death-squad commander, Colonel Eugene de

Kock, is standing trial for more than 100 crimes, including several murders. In November 1995, former Defense Minister Magnus Malan and 19 other high-level defense, intelligence, and police officials of the old regime were charged with murder for establishing and financing the training of Inkatha-linked hit squads who subsequently, and with their knowledge, carried out the 1987 massacre of 15 people, mostly women and children, of the family of an anti-apartheid activist in KwaZulu. Freedom Front leader General Constand Viljoen initially called for Mandela to stop the proceedings, threatening Afrikaner mobilization. He later moderated his stand, saying that Afrikaners would watch the court proceedings closely. De Klerk also warned against provoking Afrikaner nationalist sentiment.

On March 11, the Malan trial began. Testimony from survivors of the 1987 attack was followed by that of former special forces soldier J. P. Opperman, who detailed the training and arming by South African Defense Force personnel of the death squad (including himself) that carried out the massacre. The March 8 Johannesburg *Mail and Guardian* reported that secret government documents handed to the court describe how in 1985 the government sought to use Inkatha Freedom Party leader Mangosuthu Buthelezi against the ANC and foment violence among Africans.

In early 1996, a Truth and Reconciliation Commission chaired by Archbishop Desmond Tutu began to deal with apartheid crimes committed from 1960 through December 1993. It remains unclear exactly what the relationship between the commission and the justice system will be; the Malan case appears to show that those who refuse to cooperate may find themselves subject to criminal prosecution.

Under the national unity government, wrenching changes are taking place in South Africa's educational system. In February, after an Afrikaans school in the small town of Potgietersrus refused to accept Africans, a court in the Northern Province (formerly Transvaal) held that schools could not exclude students on the basis of race. When the court forced the school to accept approximately 20 black students, all but approximately 30 of the school's 600 whites stayed away. Many Afrikaners view school integration as the beginning of the destruction of their culture, and government promotion of integration as a direct attack on them.

In October 1995, Ton Vosloo, the executive chairman of the Afrikaner publishing conglomerate Nasionale Pers, called on the ANC not to underestimate "the latent energy of Afrikaner nationalism" that might be unleashed in reaction to what he saw as attacks on Afrikaans. Vosloo argued that "black nationalism will have to accommodate Afrikaner nationalism, and not the other way around." Afrikaner nationalists protested when the

South African Broadcasting Corporation announced a radical reduction in Afrikaans-language broadcasting. Right-wing demonstrators claimed that it was an effort to submerge the volk, and even among mainstream Afrikaners there were rumblings of a reborn nationalism. In turn, President Mandela has been highly sensitive to the language issue, reportedly excoriating ANC members of a parliamentary committee that recommended eliminating the use of Afrikaans in the South African military in favor of English.

Mainstream Afrikanerdom is torn between those wielding the images of nationalism and those pursuing accommodation with the majority. On the fringes, a right-wing rejectionism still simmers, while on the left there are a few Afrikaners in prominent positions in the ANC. So far the Afrikaners' traditional deference to authority has dominated public responses to the majority government, but this has been easy because Afrikaner economic interests remain unchallenged even as formal apartheid has given way to legal equality

Emerging Condominium?

When foreign capital dried up and multinational companies divested holdings in South Africa in the mid- and late 1980s, large Afrikaans economic institutions picked up equity in the manufacturing sector. Embracing the free enterprise ethic that was the ideology of its few remaining international sympathizers, the National Party began privatizing the government's massive holdings, and Afrikaans capital again moved in. Just as the black majority was about to 'gain political power, the white politicians cut state assets loose and steered them into Afrikaner hands.

The national unity government has taken no action to break up the centers of financial power. It has begun to implement a Reconstruction and Development Program of low-interest loans for land and home purchases, mass housing construction, and gradual extension of infrastructure to African residential areas, but it has moved slowly and the program remains tiny. Trapped between a stability-seeking international financial community and demands from the poor for an improvement in living conditions, Mandela and the ANC have chosen to provide stability with the hope that growth will gradually solve problems of poverty. White business interests have been courted, their fears assuaged, and their dominion over the economy maintained. The leadership elite has expanded, enriching former apartheid foes at the top of African society but little has changed for the vast majority of the people.

While the shift in power favors the small African elite, South Africa still appears racially divided. The underclass remains African; however, as in Brazil and the inner cities of the United States, race will tend to coincide with, though no longer be the legally sanctioned source of, huge income and welfare gaps separating the elite from the masses. Even if the political will exists at the top of

the ANC to carry out redistribution, such measures could undermine international support and reignite Afrikaner nationalism sparked by the volk's perception of a deterioration in its quality of life.

Article 18

Foreign Policy, Spring 1996

South Africa's Promise

Princeton N. Lyman

Princeton N. Lyman was the U.S. ambassador to South Africa from 1992 to 1995. The opinions presented here are his own and do not necessarily represent those of the U.S. government.

On May 10,1994, something happened that few people, even those most committed to the struggle against apartheid, ever thought could. Nelson Mandela, flanked by outgoing president F. W. de Klerk and the top generals of the South African Defense Force, took the oath as president of South Africa. Tens of thousands of South Africans, mostly black, but of all races, cheered. At that moment, airplanes of the South African Air Force flew overhead, the colors of the new flag streaming behind. There was an initial moment of apprehension as the planes came into sight. Then the crowd broke into cheers. One black man in the crowd turned to his neighbor and said, "They're ours now."

Thus came to a climax one of the most emotional and important political transitions of our time. Just two weeks earlier, amid fear and uncertainty, voters had gone to the polls in the first fully democratic election in South Africa's history. During the second morning of voting, a bomb exploded at the international airport. People's worst fears seemed to be coming true. But in a matter of hours, the police had arrested the bombers, and for the next three days voting proceeded with hardly any incidence of violence. After 46 years of apartheid, and nearly 350 years of systematic discrimination against nonwhites, South Africa had negotiated a peaceful transfer of power to its majority. The whole nation celebrated.

The euphoria of that successful transition has continued nearly unabated for almost two years. President Mandela's extraordinary emphasis on national reconciliation has calmed white fears. The economy has turned upward after years of stagnation. Political parties have been working together with exceptional harmony. South

Africans of all races feel liberated: whites from the stigma of apartheid, blacks from its horrors.

But as the new government approaches the end of its second year, the celebration is ending. The hard facts and tough decisions of governance have come sharply to the fore. Politics is becoming more "normal"—that is, more fractious. South Africans are beginning to confront the real costs of transformation, and concern over the implications is growing.

As partisanship and criticism increase, it is important to record the significant achievements of the new government in its first two years. President Mandela has ardently fostered a spirit of reconciliation. His use of symbols as well as words has resonated with all elements of the population. After his first year in office, polls showed that Mandela's popularity exceeded that of any other politician by far. When Mandela donned the jersey of South Africa's rugby captain in 1995 and went on the field to encourage South Africa's team in its World Cup championship match—rugby having been the symbol of the country's white-dominated sports—the nearly all-white crowd cheered "Nelson! Nelson!"

The Government of National Unity (GNU) functioned extremely well in its first year, producing landmark policies and legislation. The multiparty negotiations preceding the election had mandated that, until 1999, the Cabinet would be made up proportionally of all parties electing at least 20 seats, which is 5 per cent of the total in the National Assembly. Thus Mandela and the African National Congress (ANC), having received 63 per cent of the vote in the 1994 election, preside over a Cabinet that includes the National Party, or NP (20 per cent), led by Deputy President de Klerk, and the Inkatha Freedom Party (10.5 per cent), led by former KwaZulu homeland leader Mangosuthu Buthelezi.

More significant is that on the last day of negotiations on the operations of a government of national unity, de Klerk conceded his long-sought veto and, alternatively, a weighted voting formula that would give the NP exceptional influence in return for a pledge that the Cabinet would first seek to reach decisions by consensus and would take decisions by vote only if consensus proved unachievable. Some questioned whether this promise from the ANC was but window-dressing to obtain final NP agreement; yet in its first year, the Cabinet made every single decision by consensus save one—the policy on the death penalty.

President Mandela's extraordinary emphasis on national reconciliation has calmed white fears.

These consensus decisions covered an impressive array of issues: overall economic policy; a new budget; a far-reaching social and economic reconstruction and development program (RDP) based on the ANC's election platform; a national health strategy, including free health care for pregnant women and children under six; a land-restitution measure and the establishment of a Land Claims Court; the appointment of judges for the new Constitutional Court; and the establishment of a Human Rights Commission and a Public Protector.

Despite recent criticism of its disorganization and lapses in fairness, the new Parliament's work was equally impressive. Parliament in the apartheid era had served largely as the executive's rubber stamp. The new Parliament, though lacking staff, a library, and basic equipment, was determined to be otherwise. Led by ANC activists, and supported especially by the liberal Democratic party, parliamentary leaders changed the rules to open all committees and plenary sessions, did not hesitate to criticize their own party chiefs for agreements reached in Cabinet, and insisted on revising bills such as that establishing the Truth and Reconciliation Commission. Still, ANC and NP lawmakers together could almost always assure passage of bills crafted in the GNU, and more recently the ANC has used its own majority to push through relatively controversial legislation. Nevertheless, Parliament represents one of the most striking examples of working democracy in the new South Africa.

The adoption of sound economic policies is another notable achievement of the GNU. The first budget of the new government clearly signaled a conservative approach toward spending and borrowing, emphasized economic growth, encouraged the private sector, reduced the deficit, and lowered corporate taxes. For radicals who had hoped for a different philosophy, and others who had feared it, this was a surprise. That this policy was fashioned in complete unity, with the active participation of a communist deputy minister of finance, made it all the more remarkable. The World Bank could not have constructed a more prudent approach. Business has rebounded.

Another significant achievement of the transition from apartheid has been the dramatic drop in political violence throughout the country, with the exception of KwaZulu-Natai (KZN) Province. In Gauteng Province (which includes both Johannesburg and Pretoria), politically related killing dropped nearly 90 per cent in the first year after the election, and more than half of the "political" violence that continues relates to rivalries among taxi associations, not political parties. In the townships east of Johannesburg, long known for their burned homes and dangerous streets, a vigorous redevelopment program is under way, and people are returning to their homes. In a campaign led by the popular Gauteng premier, Tokyo Sexwale, youth groups, once the spearhead of political violence, are being disarmed and their energies channeled in new directions.

Finally, the difficult task of amalgamating the liberation forces of the ANC and the more militant Pan-African Congress (PAC) into the regular defense force, a process that started uneasily, has proceeded with remarkable efficacy. Former ANC and PAC officers are now in key defense positions and should be in commanding roles within a few years. Tens of thousands of liberation fighters have been brought into the defense force, and the government has undertaken to train those not suited for military life, who will be trained for civilian jobs before being demobilized. The all-white draft has been abolished, and the new defense force will rely more on (now integrated) regular units than on all-white reserve forces, as in the past. For the first time, South Africa is creating a civilian defense ministry to oversee its armed forces.

The Realities of Governance

While the new government's achievements are significant, serious problems still impinge on hopes for further progress. First are the problems of administration. At the moment of its elections, South Africa moved from a country of four provinces and 10 homelands, the latter with varying degrees of autonomy, to a country of nine provinces, only two of which have much the same boundaries as before. To avoid chaos, and to soothe white fears, the Interim Constitution guaranteed that every civil servant could keep his or her job. Thus services continued more or less normally after the election. But the new provinces face enormous difficulties. They must consolidate the remnants of provincial and homeland structures into new structures. They must confront vast redundancy, corruption (especially in the former homelands), and bureaucratic resistance—yet they cannot fire anyone. Not surprisingly, the provinces have had difficulty furthering the new RDP and even administering those programs that already existed.

At the national level, other problems slow progress. Ministers of education, health, and welfare have had to integrate numerous race-based ministries. The new minister of education inherited 19 previous ministries of education, the minister of health, a similar number. With few top jobs to award and lacking the authority to fire, the GNU has had trouble eliminating redundancy.

A deeper problem has been the uneasy relationship between the new political leadership and the old bureaucracy it cannot fire. It has taken time for ministers to determine who is trustworthy and who may undermine the new programs. Because of hiring problems, ministers have had to bring in many political appointees as advisers and consultants, aggravating tensions between the new leaders and the bureaucrats. Additionally, all ministers save one are members of Parliament, which meets in Cape Town. Thus ministers spend two to three days per week away from their ministries, which distances them from day-to-day operations.

The RDP goals are ambitious: 1 million houses in five years, improved water facilities in rural areas and improved infrastructure nationwide, vastly improved township services, and equality between whites and nonwhites in standards and resources for education. Not surprisingly, progress has been slow. Some of the difficulty derives from the GNU's conscientious effort to insist on "business plans" for each project, which has placed more responsibility on the weak provincial administrations. In addition, government resources are limited by the sizable deficit (6 per cent) it inherited, obtaining community participation (a strong point of the ANC's ideology) has proved cumbersome, and the time needed to launch such vast efforts has been longer than many expected.

Whatever the reasons, many South Africans and foreign observers worry that frustration will grow into unrest among the vast majority or, at a minimum, create political pressure for more radical policies of redistribution and greater government spending. One long-time observer of South Africa told me before the election, "I am not worried about black expectations and white fears"—the common subject of discussion at the time—"but of white expectations and black fears: white expectations that nothing will change, and black fears that they are right."

It is hard to tell how serious this problem of unmet expectations is. Surveys taken by the Center for Policy Studies and others have found a sophisticated understanding among the majority that the promises of liberation will take a long time to meet. So far, in fact, little

unrest has occurred. Moreover, the November 1995 local elections brought the ANC an increased share of the total vote despite the fact that the opposition sought to turn the ANC's inability to deliver on the reconstruction and development program into a major campaign issue.

Nevertheless, in every black or other nonwhite township one finds evidence of frustration. People are free from governmental harassment, but their lives have not changed much otherwise. In addition, many believe that the real beneficiaries of liberation have so far been the ANC leaders who have received high-paying government jobs and perquisites and a few black businesspeople who have become very rich from highly publicized acts of "black empowerment" in the private sector.

Acts borne of frustration are often fueled by ambitious local politicians or venal exploiters. For example, where plans exist to assist squatters who have long been waiting for housing, the land in question has in some cases been occupied by other squatters who insist that they be given (or have been promised by their leaders in return for a fee) the new houses. Pressure on the land, especially in expectation of redevelopment, is intense. Some informal settlements have tried in vain to limit the number of new entrants in order to facilitate cleanup and improvements but have been unable to stem the crush.

All of these problems further hamper the RDP. The ANC has found itself in the awkward position of forcefully removing squatters who invade designated development areas, a troubling decision given the racially motivated evictions of the apartheid era.

Spurring Economic Growth

Fundamental to the new government's success is accelerating the rate of economic growth. The economy has turned around remarkably in the past two years. Business confidence is at its highest level in 11 years; inflation, which was chronic at double-digit levels for a decade, has dropped to less than 9 per cent, a 23-year low; private gross domestic fixed investment has risen 25 per cent in two years and is reflected in net plant expansion; and gross domestic product (GDP), which fell from 1990 to 1992, is projected to grow by 3.5 per cent in 1995, with a 7 per cent increase in manufacturing alone.

While this is all very good, it is not enough. Official estimates place unemployment in South Africa at 32.6 per cent. Among urban and semi-urban blacks, the rate is much higher. Eighty-seven per cent of those unemployed are black; 66 per cent are under 30 years of age. Some 300,000 people enter the labor market each year— 10 times the number of jobs created in the formal sector annually from 1980 to 1992. Overall, the population grows by about 2.5 per cent each year. In sum, a 3.5 per cent annual rate of growth in the GDP simply will not cut into poverty or unemployment significantly.

Inadequate growth endangers all the goals of the RDP. One of the RDP's prudent aspects is its insistence that the government cannot deliver housing, electricity, water, and other services free of charge. Thus it has embarked on something called the *Masakhane* campaign (meaning "Let's build together"), the goal of which is to have all residents pay for these goods and services. This effort counters the years of nonpayment promoted by the ANC in its "ungovernability" campaign of the 1980s, which made nonpayment a part of the culture. Yet, as more and more self-financed services are introduced, the government will run up against the limits created by unemployment and poverty. The vast majority will simply not have the money to pay.

To move from an economic growth rate of 3.5 per cent to one of 6 or 7 per cent, which most believe is necessary, will require adjustments much greater than South Africa has undertaken so far. South Africa's economy has been highly protected and capital intensive. While the new leadership agreed to tariff reductions under the Uruguay Round Agreements of the General Agreement on Tariffs and Trade, many analysts feel the timetable for implementation is too slow. However, both business and labor are reluctant to accept faster liberalization, since protection is considered essential to preserving jobs in the textile, automobile, and allied industries, where much of organized labor is concentrated. Organized labor opposes establishing export-processing zones, which have been successful elsewhere, because it fears the zones would undo many of labor's hard-won rights.

Deeper structural problems plague the economy. A poor education system for the majority of South Africans leaves people without the skills necessary for entrepreneurship or employment in technical jobs. Antiquated management systems fail to engage labor as a partner in productivity programs. A large part of the formal private sector is in the hands of six or seven conglomerates, while the government itself owns more than 100 corporations. Few well-managed venture capital funds exist that could target small- and medium-size manufacturing firms and attract foreign investment to this sector. And the government has been reluctant to provide special incentives to foreign investors.

The GNU recognizes that breaking through to stronger growth is critical. A recent Cabinet decision set up a high-level committee on just this problem. But the painful adjustments that might be necessary could strain the unity not only within the GNU but among the ANC and its allies—the Congress of South African Trade Unions (COSATU) and the South African Communist Party. A good example of this strain occurred following the government's decision on December 7, 1995, to partially pri-

vatize some of the government-owned companies, such as Telkom (communications) and South African Airways; COSATU took immediate exception.

Crime, Education, and Kwazulu-Natal

Political violence has declined, but criminal violence is becoming a national horror. The murder rate in South Africa is six or seven times that of the United States. In the first 11 months of 1995, police reported 8,170 car hijackings, during which 43 people were killed and 87 were wounded. Almost every South African has either been a victim or is close to one. While crime can be hyped for political purposes (and surveys show that it is higher on the list of concerns for whites than for blacks), it is already harming perceptions of South Africa's future and its ability to attract foreign investment.

Crime is a problem that defies easy solution. As Mandela has pointed out, the police under apartheid were neither structured nor deployed to control crime. Their role in the nonwhite communities was to suppress political activity, and their deployment for protection was focused overwhelmingly on the white communities. Thus far, only the upper levels of police departments have been restructured. Corruption, past abuses, and the lack of trust within the community continue to hamper most of the police force. Moreover, investigative techniques are so poor that many suspects, including murder suspects, are perforce released on bail or acquitted, further angering the population.

Much of the crime is organized, and it is increasingly linked to drug trafficking. South Africa under sanctions was isolated from not only legitimate commerce but also much of the international narcotics trade. With an explosion of airline connections and a police force inadequate to the task, drug syndicates—the police estimate their number at nearly 200—have moved in with a vengeance. Youth gangs, particularly in the Western Cape, are financed by drug sales and are becoming more violent. Crack cocaine has arrived in South Africa, along with heroin, speed, and many other drugs.

Drugs threaten not only the fabric of society, but democracy itself. Organized crime thrives on violence and corruption. Other countries, like Colombia and Nigeria, have seen drug syndicates eat away at the very heart of their political systems. That has not yet happened in South Africa, but the country is in a race against time.

Yet, of all the legacies of apartheid to be rectified, inequalities in the educational system will perhaps be the most difficult. South Africa built a small, concentrated, first-class education system—from primary school to the university level—previously reserved almost exclusively for whites. The vast majority of South African pupils were restricted to other systems that locked them out of careers in science, math, business, and government. While racial disparities were being reduced in the final years before the transition, expenditures per white pupil remain about four times higher than those for blacks.

Equalizing educational opportunities is a goal that all can support in principle. But as plans and programs are developed, deep emotions are engaged. An increase in average student-to-teacher ratios means that white schools will experience bigger classes. White parents worry that open enrollment means that less-qualified students will be entering their children's schools. At the university level, a different debate rages. World-class institutions like the University of Cape Town, whose student body is rapidly becoming mostly nonwhite, argue that they are now training the new elite in science, math, engineering, and business and that removing resources means cheating the nonwhite students of the quality that only whites previously enjoyed.

On the other hand, many blacks regard these arguments as surrogates for maintaining privilege and exclusivity. The former nonwhite colleges and universities—which still educate the majority of college students—are quick to denounce the claims of the formerly all-white universities that have held a vast advantage in resources. Now, they argue, the tables should be turned.

Clearly the debate will be less productive if carried out in racially loaded invective. But such a tone will not be easy to avoid in the education sector, which was the birthplace of the last great uprising against apartheid and still harbors justified black resentment. On the other hand, South Africa's future may well depend on preserving—while democratizing—its advanced educational institutions. Failing this, South Africa could suffer a significant emigration of skilled white professionals, something Mandela has gone out of his way to discourage, and deny the majority access to the quality of teaching and research that currently gives South Africa its competitive edge. Great statesmanship and sensitivity will be needed on all sides to manage change in this sector. Along with crime, education is becoming a battleground for fractious politics.

The one major political issue unresolved by the election was the fierce rivalry within the province of KZN. It is the one province where political violence persists at a very high level. More than 3,000 people were killed in 1995, though some estimate that less than a third of the murders were "purely political." The rivalry pits the ANC against Buthelezi's Inkatha Freedom Party: This is the contemporary manifestation of violent conflict that has roots in age-old clan disputes, historical factors going back to the British-Zulu Wars, and personal vendettas. Nevertheless, the ANC-Inkatha confrontation determines the tempo and nature of the current violence. A terrible massacre on Christmas Day, 1995, in which 18 people were killed, is indicative of the potential magnitude of this violence. The political conflict is often described as being about Zulu autonomy. But the violence within KZN is Zulu against Zulu: urban versus rural Zulus, traditional leaders versus modern political forces, labor versus government.

Buthelezi claims to be fighting only for federalism, but his version involves almost complete political autonomy for the province. His tactics tend toward the confrontational, such as walking out of the Constituent Assembly to demand international mediation. For their part, many ANC figures dislike federalism in principle. All fear an ethnically based political structure that could stir ethnic strife and run counter to the ANC's historical emphasis on multiracialism. There is little common ground here. The strong personalities involved aggravate the situation. So too do charges that hit squads are encouraged or supported by high-ranking party officials—charges made by both sides.

For the time being, the struggle is largely confined to KZN and is likely to remain so. It may fester for some time, until the strong personalities engaged moderate their behavior and bitterness and fear recede. Meanwhile, houses are being burned, people are being killed, and the RDP remains largely moribund in the province.

Facing The Past, Adapting For The Future

Like many other countries emerging from long periods of oppression, South Africa has had to decide how to address past human rights abuses while effecting national reconciliation. South Africans spent more than a year poring over the experiences of nations in Latin America and Europe, particularly Chile and Germany after reunification. Subsequently, after a long, difficult, and emotional debate, Parliament passed legislation creating a Truth and Reconciliation Commission. The Commission will investigate human rights abuses during apartheid, offer amnesty to those who disclose acts that were politically motivated, and determine compensation for victims. The most controversial part of the legislation, insisted on by the ANC, restricts amnesty to those who make full disclosure of the criminal or abusive acts for which amnesty is requested. The accused who do not disclose such acts are liable for prosecution. Thus the Commission will very likely open old wounds.

More serious, perhaps, is that the accused of lesser rank may defend the political nature of their actions by pointing a finger at those who were much higher-level figures during the era and are prominent in today's South Africa. Already, murder charges brought in November 1995 against senior security officials of the old regime—including a former minister of defense, a former chief of staff of the South African Defense Force, and a former military intelligence chief who is now a senator—have raised alarms from de Klerk and the leader of the conservative Freedom Front party, Constand Viljoen. The trial of a retired police colonel for multiple murders in the late 1980s implicated a former minister of safety and security.

In November 1995, Mandela appointed Nobel laureate Archbishop Desmond Tutu to head the Truth and Reconciliation Commission. The appointment has been widely hailed and has alleviated some of the concerns of those who fear a witch-hunt. Nevertheless, South Africa is just beginning these human rights investigations, and the experience will tear at the GNU and test the limits of South Africa's ability to attain reconciliation with justice.

As South Africa tackles these challenges in the years ahead, political structures will have to adapt. At present, the ANC is a broad movement encompassing elements ranging from the far Left to the growing middle class. Dealing with the challenges of economic adjustment, crime, and education will induce strains within the organization. Deputy President Thabo Mbeki has spoken of an evolution, without specifying a time frame, during which parties will develop along more philosophical lines of Right and Left. But how the ANC, as the leading party, evolves along these lines will say much about the survival of the current pragmatism that informs almost all GNU and ANC policies. The Center's ability to hold will be the key to South Africa's ability to prosper and protect its multiracial harmony.

Over the long run, the question is whether or not South Africa will be able to develop political parties that cut across racial lines.

For the opposition, no less difficult tasks lie ahead. De Klerk predicts that his National Party will one day become the majority party by attracting black voters alienated by radical ANC policies. But the NP cannot avoid being linked with the past; for example, it has had to respond to the indictment of former senior security officials. Also, the NP's nonwhite votes have been so far almost entirely from the colored population, who voted based on fears that the ANC would promote black advancement over theirs. The NP will need to respond more fully to its colored constituency, which accounted

for half of its votes in the 1994 election. This will not likely enhance its appeal to black voters. All the opposition parties will have to work to stay strong enough to be relevant so that South Africa does not become, ipso facto, a one-party state.

Over the long run, the question is whether or not South Africa will be able to develop political parties that cut across racial lines. While the ANC is multiracial, its core constituency is black. The Democratic party and, at the other side of the spectrum, the Freedom Front, are overwhelmingly white, and Inkatha is heavily Zulu-based. The dream of nonracial democracy is at stake.

U.S.-South African Relations

South Africa's relations with the United States are evolving. Before April 1994, the United States maintained a virtually one-dimensional relationship with South Africa, focusing on the domestic oppression and internationally destabilizing effects of apartheid. Bilateral agreements were allowed to lapse, trade and investment were discouraged by sanctions, and American aid was delivered only through nongovernmental organizations. The United States did not consult South Africa on many international issues outside the region.

Since the transition, the U.S.–South African relationship has rapidly become richer and more complex. The United States is in fundamental agreement with the Mandela government on such issues as promoting democracy, human rights, the peaceful resolution of conflicts, and the nonproliferation of weapons of mass destruction. The partnership is important. South Africa under its new government played an indispensable role in negotiations leading to the indefinite extension of the Treaty on the Non-Proliferation of Nuclear Weapons, used its prestige and influence to help bring peace to Mozambique and Angola and to press for a return to democracy in Nigeria, and made efforts to contain ethnic strife in Burundi.

For America's part, President Bill Clinton's pledge to the new government of $600 million over three years makes the United States the largest bilateral donor to the RDP. American companies operating in South Africa are among the leading investors—their number has tripled since the lifting of sanctions. The American role in Angola and Mozambique, and in support of regional development in southern Africa, directly advances South Africa's vital interests. The new Binational Commission, co-chaired by U.S. vice president Al Gore and Deputy President Mbeki, promises to deepen the relationship across a wide spectrum of interests.

Inevitably there are differences. South Africa, for historical reasons related to its liberation struggle, views relations with Cuba, Iran, and Libya much differently than the United States. For example, South Africa does not support the American economic embargo of Iran, and the United States is rightly disappointed. But Mandela's South Africa shows no intention of selling arms to or cooperating on nuclear production with Iran—or any other country that threatens the peace. It has promised to raise human rights, terrorism, and Middle East peace matters in its discussions with Iran.

Trade issues also arise when two countries have, as the United States and South Africa now do, a $4.2 billion trade relationship. These issues need to be addressed since they not only affect trade and investment but are indicative of how rapidly South Africa is moving to liberalize its economy. A more contentious issue relates to indictments in the United States against several South African entities that allegedly violated U.S. arms export control laws.

None of these issues can be ignored despite the euphoria over South Africa's transition. They must be addressed frankly, but with care to preserve the fundamental value and strength of the relationship.

There is much to be gained, including learning new ways of achieving racial harmony in both societies.

In 1986, when South Africa's situation was especially grim, the South African poet and playwright Adam Small was asked his views on the future of the country. He wrote of the violence and anger among the youth, but he concluded with an expression of hope that South Africans could perhaps talk themselves through, "by way of human discourse and decisionmaking, to a future." South Africans did talk themselves through to a future, in four years of intense and extraordinarily difficult negotiations that culminated in the May 10, 1994, inauguration of Nelson Mandela.

One of the principal participants in those negotiations, now a Cabinet minister, told me, "If we can maintain the process we learned there—the process whereby whenever we encountered a problem, we found a solution—we can succeed." So far South Africa has done just that. This process is South Africa's contemporary genius, its gift to the world. It can guarantee the country's future.

Article 19   *The Christian Science Monitor*, March 20, 1996

A Divided Country Where Twain Rarely Meet, Except in War

Sudan's southern rebels have been fighting off the Arab north's attempts to impose an Islamic state on the whole country

Judith Matloff

Staff writer of The Christian Science Monitor

CHOKUDUM, SUDAN

ELECTIONS that took place in the north of Africa's biggest country over the past two weeks were news to Angelica Poni and many other villagers living deep behind rebel lines here in Sudan's southeast corner.

Like many supporters of the insurgent Sudan People's Liberation Army (SPLA), what is decreed by the northern government in Khartoum is of little relevance. The south is another world in this divided country where rarely the twain meet, except in battle. The two have have been fighting for 13 years.

"Elections? I never heard about this," an irritated and bewildered Mrs. Poni said about the two-week poll that ended on March 16 and never reached this small town of thatched mud huts because of the civil war. "It doesn't affect my life."

"These elections are not a democracy, they are a mockery," joins in her friend Elizabeth Achol. "They are dropping bullets, not ballots."

The elections were the first time the Sudanese have voted directly for president, instead of indirectly through parliament, as they did in 1986. The vote was widely regarded as window dressing. The country has been ruled since 1989 by military leader Lieut. Gen. Omar Ahmed al-Bashir, who took over in a coup and is expected to have won the election.

'Elections? I never heard about this. It doesn't affect my life.'
—Angelica Poni

'The elections are a mockery. They drop bullets, not ballots.'
—Elizabeth Achol

Groups in the black animist and Christian south have been sporadically at war with the Islamic north since 1955, when it started trying to forcibly impose upon the whole country its religion and customs.

The differences between the two halves of the country are palpable. In the strict north, women must be covered head to toe in Islamic purist tradition; in the south, they walk around bare-breasted as elsewhere in black Africa. In the south, English or local tribal languages, not Arabic, dominate.

At least here in Chokudum, the only armed people are the rebels—often only boys—who strut through the bush with Russian-made AK-47 assault rifles. The only signs of the government Army are the craters of bombs from aerial strikes.

Various guerrilla movements have come and gone, but the SPLA has been the main one since its formation in 1983 by John Garang.

Since 1991, there have been at least five breakaway movements, most notably one led by Riek Machar that devotes most of its energy to battling Mr. Garang and holds little territory.

This vast arid expanse is also the venue for an ongoing humanitarian morass. Brought back from the brink of mass starvation in 1992–93, when a quarter of a million people died, war and periodic drought continue to wreak havoc.

Aid groups estimate that more than 3 million Sudanese were displaced, 1.3 million died from war or famine, and countless numbers have been tortured since the civil war restarted in 1983 after a brief attempt at democracy.

Some victims have suffered at the hands of the rebels in cases widely documented by London-based Amnesty International and other human rights organizations.

But the repressive Khartoum government has committed its own share of abuses, having outlawed all forms of political, press, and religious freedom, and declared war on the people of the south in a religious crusade.

This has alienated Western nations and Sudan's neighbors, Eritrea, Uganda, and Ethiopia, which accuse Khartoum of promoting terrorism and Islamic militancy across its borders.

The SPLA—once reviled by some Western countries during the cold war for its ties to leftist regimes—is mustering greater support as the international community increasingly rejects Khartoum.

"The elections were a blessing in disguise," says Elijah Malok, shadow public services minister of the political arm of SPLA, the Sudan People's Liberation Movement (SPLM). "They helped reinforce the international view that these people don't know what democracy is." He hopes the questionable elections will move the United Nations closer to sanctions against Khartoum.

Last year the SPLM intensified a diplomatic drive that included Garang's visit to Washington in December and the winning of observer status at the UN.

The desire for legitimacy is nowhere more evident than at SPLM's administrative center in New Cush, a well-fortified village nestled in hills about 100 miles from the border with Kenya. Here, the SPLM's 183-member parliament and 16 "ministers" from around the country meet to plan their political future in a mud hut.

But their political future is linked to military success. In October, the SPLA made its biggest advance in four years, capturing the towns of Parajok, Palatoka, Magwe, and Aswa.

"We are fighting to force Khartoum to negotiate with us," said Chokudum's acting base commander, Samuel Mathiang.

The offensive has stopped for now, but commanders say it will resume when they are better prepared to take Juba, the traditional capital of the south, which has eluded them.

In the meantime, the war is at a stalemate, with the government controlling several key towns like islands in the south and the rebels in control of the vast bush surrounding them.

Numbers may be on the side of the rebels, who claim that one-third of the estimated 10 million people living in the south are involved in the resistance effort, including children gathering water and women cooking for troops.

But the government, which has perhaps as many as 120,000 men in its Army and armed civilian militias, is far better armed.

Isolated Sudan Backs Muslim Militancy

KHARTOUM, SUDAN

FOR nearly three of the last four decades, civil war has engulfed this vast, disparate nation.

Ethnically and culturally, Sudan is two separate countries. Its north is predominantly a blend of Christianity and traditional African religions.

Fighting waxes and wanes in the south, where government and rebel troops are locked in Africa's longest-running civil war.

Sudan's military government came to power in a 1989 coup that overturned the three-year-old elected government of Sadiq al-Mahdi. The new regime transformed the country into a strict Islamic state. Sudan was the first African country to follow the path of Iran's Islamic republic. Its foreign policies and support for Muslim militants from abroad have made the government increasingly isolated from the West and alienated many of its neighbors. Eritrea and Uganda have cut off relations, fearing destabilization and infiltration of armed militants across the porous borders.

Leaders of Sudan's National Islamic Front occupy key posts in the government, military, and business communities. Southern rebels reject the Islamic state, as do some northerners.

Sudan's two most powerful leaders are President Omar al-Bashir and Sheikh Hassan al-Turabi, who heads the National Islamic Front. Dr. Turabi is said to be the real power behind the scenes.

Sudan has one of most repressive, extremist regimes in the region. The secret police are feared. Press freedom is curtailed. Political parties are banned. Foreigners need special government permits to travel beyond the capital, Khartoum.

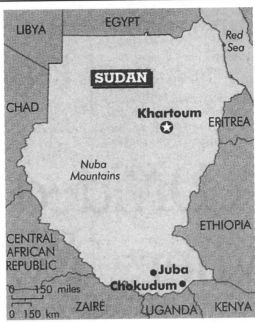

Tom Brown—Staff

FACTS ABOUT SUDAN

Location: Borders on nine countries, including Egypt, and is just across the Red Sea from Saudi Arabia.

Size: 967,500 square miles. Africa's largest country, it takes up a swath of territory as large as the United Sates east of the Mississippi River.

Population: 27 million people. About 80 percent live in rural areas.

Ethnic makeup: About 75 percent are Sunni Muslims. They live mainly in the north. The south is dominated by those who follow a blend of Christianity and African animist religions. The country has many cultures and more than 550 ethnic groups.

Language: Arabic is the official language, but more than 100 other languages are spoken.

Economy: One of Africa's poorest nations, with 40 percent unemployment and periodic famines. Prices rose 70 percent in 1995. Foreign debt is estimated at $16 billion.

But the nation defies stereotypes. In Khartoum, instead of finding a religiously rigid, fanatic populace, visitors encounter an easygoing, intellectually lively society.

—J. M.

Why Are the North and South at War?

THE 13-year civil war is an extension of a centuries-long struggle between the Islamic, Arab north and the black Christian and animist south.

The Sudan People's Liberation Army (SPLA) has been fighting since 1983 to end the domination of the north and to challenge the imposition of strict Islamic law.

The SPLA is led by former Army Col. John Garang and is dominated by the Dinka tribe. The group gained significant ground in an offensive late last year after acquiring substantial new weaponry.

In 1991, another faction, led by Riek Machar's Nuer tribe, broke away from the mainstream SPLA, accusing Colonel Garang of human rights abuses. Garang says Mr. Machar is an agent of Khartoum.

More than 1.3 million people have died in the war and resulting famines. Fighting has driven more than 3 million others from their homes.

One ethnic group, the Nuba people, are suffering greatly, wedged between the government and rebel fronts.

Khartoum: Terrorist Hub?

SUDAN denies Western claims that it shelters international militants. But United States officials claim some 4,000 Islamic radicals receive military training in at least 20 Sudanese camps.

The Palestinian Resistance Group, Hamas, which has claimed responsibility for four suicide bombings in Israel since Feb. 25, has an office and spokesman in Sudan's capital, Khartoum.

US economic aid was blocked in 1993 when the State Department added Sudan to its list of countries supporting terrorism.

Sudan sheltered one of the world's most wanted terrorists, Illich Ramirez Sanchez, better known as "Carlos the Jackal." Facing international pressure, Sudan expelled Mr. Sanchez to France in 1994.

Sudan faces its most damaging charge yet of terrorism with accusations of involvement in the attempted assassination of Egyptian President Hosni Mubarak in June.

Article 20

The Christian Science Monitor, June 12, 1996

African Tradition Of Polygamy Faces Economic, Legal Challenges

Joyce Hackel

Special to The Christian Science Monitor

KAMPALA, UGANDA
BEATRICE intently watches the face of a visitor to her cinder block home, hoping to find a sign of empathy. Finally, she confides: Her husband has had children with five other women, several of whom have become her co-wives. Now Beatrice often has to fend for herself.

"They say a man has the right to marry as many women as possible. But I say, look, the man I'm supposed to be sharing my life with, we're not sharing any happiness, we're not even sharing any sorrow," she says. "I'm running the home almost alone."

Polygamy, the practice of taking more than one wife at the same time, remains the lot of many African women, particularly those in Muslim countries. But the practice is under pressure. Mores are changing. And with the continent's economy in a downswing, even many middle-class men can't support several wives and large families.

Beatrice, who lives in Kampala, Uganda, attended college and has a degree in marketing from a business college. When she married her husband two decades ago, she says, she didn't imagine he would take on more wives.

"Many people think it's just the downtrodden, but women across all classes are in this situation," says Janet Kabeberi Macharia, a law professor at the University of Nairobi and coordinator of a research project called Women in Law in East Africa.

In rural Africa, the practice has been seen as an economic necessity, since multiple wives and their children provide unpaid labor in farm fields. Historically, the first wife helped choose her co-wives, because new brides essentially became her coworkers.

But times are changing. As more Ugandans move to cities, Western ideas about monogamy have gained more influence. Some men still practice polygamy in towns. But now they often resort to hiding their additional marriages from their first wives, says Fabian Byomuhangi, a program officer with the United Nations Population Fund in Kampala.

"When polygamy moves from rural to urban areas it becomes contradictory. In the countryside a man would marry for social status and, more importantly, for economic gains," he says. "Yet most men in urban areas will not take pride moving around with two women and introducing them to their friends as their wives."

Ugandan women are using the legal system to challenge polygamists, demanding that husbands meet their commitments, or make fewer of them.

In Kampala, polygamous men are "feeling the heat," says Jacqueline Asiimwe, an attorney with the Ugandan Association of Women Lawyers. The group, known by its acronym, FIDA, began Kampala's first free legal-aid clinic. Ms. Asiimwe says many Ugandan men fail to appreciate FIDA's role.

"They used to call us 'a bunch of frustrated women.' They'd say 'all the FIDA women are unmarried. They're people who have failed in their marriages. That's why they're going out teaching other women to be rebellious,'" Asiimwe says.

But some women in polygamous marriages endorse the custom. Many African Muslims, as well as some Christians, practice it.

"On the one hand, I feel it should be banned," Ms. Macharia says. "On the other, I ask why I should I impose my monogamous stand on other women?"

FIDA attorneys explain to women that while custom may permit the practice of multiple marriages, husbands are legally bound to provide financial support for all their wives and children.

"Now, when men in Kampala receive a letter on FIDA stationery, it can cause panic," Asiimwe says. "It's not as though we glory in that fact. We're trying to teach men that they should take responsibility."

African societies adhere to a blend of written law and customary or traditional law. The mixture often works to the detriment of women. Beatrice, for instance, was wed in a traditional ceremony that didn't include a trip to the court house or a Christian church. So her customary marriage isn't recognized under statutory law. The arrangement grants her little right to inheritance or a share of her husband's property.

Many African women lawyers advocate legal reform, rather than prohibition of polygamy. They want new laws that recognize all forms of marriage, including customary weddings.

Many women also back laws that call on men to seek their first wife's consent before entering into any other marriages.

The overall objective, FIDA lawyers say, is to ensure that if a woman enters a polygamous relationship, she does so by choice, not because she lacks social or economic clout.

In the Kampala neighborhood of Kamwokya, Helen Elizabeth, a second wife and mother of six, recently ended her multiple marriage.

"For me, there was no happiness in a polygamous home. There was division and discrimination among the children. A man may want to be neutral, but he can't," she says.

"The life I lived in my marriage was a life of competition. I would think, 'What did my co-wife put on? Can I buy something better?' I know I wasted a lot of time that I would have used for constructive and positive things for my children.

"Times are changing," she says. "Many women now stand up bold and say, 'I'm not doing this. I can stand on my own.'"

Credits

Sources for Statistical Reports

U.S. State Department, *Background Notes* (1996).

C.I.A. *World Factbook* (1996–1997).

World Bank, *World Development Report* (1996).

UN *Population and Vital Statistics Report* (January 1997).

World Statistics in Brief (1996).

Statistical Yearbook (1996).

The Statesman's Yearbook (1996–1997).

Population Reference Bureau, *World Population Data Sheet* (1996).

World Almanac (1997).

Demographic Yearbook (1996).

Glossary of Terms and Abbreviations

Acquired Immune Deficiency Syndrome (AIDS) A disease of immune-system dysfunction assumed to be caused by the human immunodeficiency virus (HIV), which allows opportunistic infections to take over the body.

African Development Bank Founded in 1963 under the auspices of the United Nations Economic Commission on Africa, the bank, located in Côte d'Ivoire, makes loans to African countries, although other nations can apply.

African National Congress (ANC) Founded in 1912, the group's goal is to achieve equal rights for blacks in South Africa through nonviolent action. "Spear of the Nation," the ANC wing dedicated to armed struggle, was organized after the Sharpeville massacre in 1960.

African Party for the Independence of Guinea-Bissau and Cape Verde (PAICG) An independence movement that fought during the 1960s and 1970s for the liberation of present-day Guinea-Bissau and Cape Verde from Portuguese rule. The two territories were ruled separately by a united PAIGC until a 1981 coup in Guinea-Bissau caused the party to split along national lines. In 1981 the Cape Verdean PAIGC formally renounced its Guinea links and became the PAICV.

African Socialism A term applied to a variety of ideas (including those of Nkrumah and Senghor) about communal and shared production in Africa's past and present. The concept of African socialism was especially popular in the early 1960s. Adherence to it has not meant governments' exclusion of private-capitalist ventures.

Afrikaners South Africans of European descent who speak Afrikaans and are often referred to as *Boers* (Afrikaans for "farmers").

Algiers Agreement The 1979 peace agreement when Mauritania made peace with the Polisario and abandoned claims to Western Sahara.

Amnesty International A London-based human-rights organization whose members "adopt" political prisoners or prisoners of conscience in many nations of the world. The organization generates political pressure and puts out a well-publicized annual report of human-rights conditions in each country of the world.

Aouzou Strip A barren strip of land between Libya and Chad contested by both countries.

Apartheid Literally, "separatehood," a South African policy that segregated the races socially, legally, and politically.

Arusha Declaration A document issued in 1967 by Tanzanian President Julius Nyerere, committing the country to socialism based on peasant farming, democracy under one party, and self-reliance.

Assimilado The Portuguese term for Africans who became "assimilated" to Western ways. Assimilados enjoyed equal rights under Portuguese law.

Azanian People's Organization (AZAPO) Founded in 1978 at the time of the Black Consciousness Movement and revitalized in the 1980s, the movement works to develop chapters and bring together black organizations in a national forum.

Bantu A major linguistic classification for many Central, Southern, and East African languages.

Bantustans Areas, or "homelands," to which black South Africans are assigned "citizenship" as part of the policy of apartheid.

Basarawa Peoples of Botswana who have historically been hunters and gatherers.

Berber The collective term for the indigenous languages and peoples of North Africa.

Bicameral A government made up of two legislative branches.

Black Consciousness Movement A South African student movement founded by Steve Biko and others in the 1970s to promote pride and empowerment of blacks.

Boers See *Afrikaners*.

Brotherhoods Islamic organizations based on specific religious beliefs and practices. In many areas, brotherhood leaders and their spiritual followers gain political influence.

Cabinda A small, oil-rich portion of Angola separated from the main body of that country by the coastal strip of Zaire.

Caisse de Stabilization A marketing board that stabilizes the uncertain returns to producers of cash crops by offering them less than market prices in good harvest years while assuring them of a steady income in bad years. Funds from these boards are used to develop infrastructure, to promote social welfare, or to maintain a particular regime in power.

Caliphate The office or dominion of a caliph, the spiritual head of Islam.

Cassava A tropical plant with a fleshy, edible rootstock; one of the staples of the African diet. Also known as manioc.

Chimurenga A Shona term meaning "fighting in which everyone joins," used to refer to Zimbabwe's fight for independence.

Committee for the Struggle against Drought in the Sahel (CILSS) A grouping of eight West African countries, formed to fight the effects of drought in the region.

Commonwealth of Nations An association of nations and dependencies loosely joined by the common tie of having been part of the British Empire.

Congress of South African Trade Unions (COSATU) Established in 1985 to form a coalition of trade unions to press for workers' rights and an end to apartheid.

Copperbelt A section of Zambia with a high concentration of copper-mining concessions.

Creole A person or language of mixed African and European descent.

Dergue From the Amheric word for "committee," the ruling body of Ethiopia following the Revolution in 1974 to the 1991 Revolution (it was overthrown by the Ethiopian People's Revolutionary Democratic Front).

East African Community (EAC) Established in 1967, this organization grew out of the East African Common Services Organization begun under British rule. The EAC included Kenya, Tanzania, and Uganda in a customs union and involved common currency and development of infrastructure. It was disbanded in 1977, and the final division of assets was completed in 1983.

Economic Commission for Africa (ECA) Founded in 1958 by the Economic and Social Committee of the United Nations to aid African development through regional centers, field agents, and the encouragement of regional efforts, food self-sufficiency, transport, and communications development.

Economic Community of Central African States (CEEAC, also known as ECCA) An organization of all of the Central African states, as well as Rwanda and Burundi, whose goal is to promote economic and social cooperation among its members.

Economic Community of West Africa (CEAO) An economic organization of former French colonies that was formed to promote trade and regional economic cooperation.

Economic Organization of West African States (ECOWAS) Established in 1975 by the Treaty of Lagos, the organization includes all of the West African states except Western Sahara. The organization's goals are to promote trade, cooperation, and self-reliance among its members.

Enclave Industry An industry run by a foreign company that uses imported technology and machinery and exports the product to industrialized countries; often described as a "state within a state."

Eritrean People's Liberation Front (EPLF) The major group fighting the Ethiopian government for the independence of Eritrea.

European Community See *European Union.*

European Union (EU) Known as the European Community until 1994, this is the collective designation of three organizations with common membership—the European Economic Community, the European Coal and Steel Community, and the European Atomic Energy Community. Sometimes also referred to as the Common Market.

Evolués A term used in colonial Zaire (the Congo) to refer to Western-educated Congolese.

Fokonolas Indigenous village management bodies.

Food and Agricultural Organization of the United Nations (FAO) Established in 1945 to oversee good nutrition and agricultural development.

Franc Zone (Commonly known as the CFA [*le franc des Colonies Françaises d'Afrique*] franc zone.) This organization includes members of the West African Monetary Union and the monetary organizations of Central Africa that have currencies linked to the French franc. Reserves are managed by the French treasury and guaranteed by the French franc.

Free French Conference A 1944 conference of French-speaking territories, which proposed a union of all the territories in which Africans would be represented and their development furthered.

Freedom Charter Established in 1955, this charter proclaimed equal rights for all South Africans and has been a foundation for almost all groups in the resistance against apartheid.

Frelimo See *Mozambique Liberation Front.*

French Equatorial Africa (FEA) The French colonial federation that included present-day Congo, Central African Republic, Chad, and Gabon.

French West Africa The administrative division of the former French colonial empire that included the current independent countries of Senegal, Côte d'Ivoire, Guinea, Mali, Niger, Burkina Faso, Benin, and Mauritania.

Frontline States A caucus supported by the Organization of African Unity (consisting of Tanzania, Zambia, Mozambique, Botswana, Zimbabwe, and Angola) whose goal is to achieve black majority rule in all of Southern Africa.

Green Revolution Use of Western technology and agricultural practices to increase food production and agricultural yields.

Griots Professional bards of West Africa, some of whom tell history and are accompanied by the playing of the kora or harp-lute.

Gross Domestic Product (GDP) The value of production attributable to the factors of production in a given country regardless of their ownership. GDP equals GNP minus the product of a country's residents originating in the rest of the world.

Gross National Product (GNP) The sum of the values of all goods and services produced by a country's residents at home and abroad in any given year, less income earned by foreign residents and remitted abroad.

Guerrilla A member of a small force of irregular soldiers. Generally, guerrilla forces are made up of volunteers who make surprise raids against the incumbent military or political force.

Harmattan In West Africa, the dry wind that blows in from the Sahara Desert during January and February, which now reaches many parts of the West African coast. Its dust and haze are a sign of the new year and of new agricultural problems.

Homelands   See *Bantustans*.

Horn of Africa   A section of northeastern Africa including the countries of Djibouti, Ethiopia, Somalia, and the Sudan.

Hut Tax   Instituted by the colonial governments in Africa, this measure required families to pay taxes on each building in the village.

International Monetary Fund (IMF)   Established in 1945 to promote international monetary cooperation.

Irredentism   An effort to unite certain people and territory in one state with another, on the grounds that they belong together.

Islam   A religious faith started in Arabia during the seventh century A.D. by the Prophet Muhammad and spread in Africa through African Muslim leaders, migrations, and wars.

Jihad   A struggle, or "holy war," waged as a religious duty on behalf of Islam to rid the world of disbelief and error.

Koran   Writings accepted by Muslims as the word of God, as revealed to the Prophet Mohammed.

Lagos Plan of Action   Adopted by the Organization of African Unity in 1980, this agreement calls for self-reliance, regional economic cooperation, and the creation of a pan-African economic community and common market by the year 2000.

League of Nations   Established at the Paris Peace Conference in 1919, this forerunner of the modern-day United Nations had 52 member nations at its peak (the United States never joined the organization) and mediated in international affairs. The league was dissolved in 1945 after the creation of the United Nations.

Least Developed Countries (LDCs)   A term used to refer to the poorest countries of the world, including many African countries.

Maghrib   An Arabic term, meaning "land of the setting sun," that is often used to refer to the former French colonies of Morocco, Algeria, and Tunisia.

Mahdi   The expected messiah of Islamic tradition; or a Muslim leader who plays a messianic role.

Malinke (Mandinka, or Mandinga)   One of the major groups of people speaking Mande languages. The original homeland of the Malinke was Mali, but the people are now found in Mali, Guinea-Bissau, The Gambia, and other areas, where they are sometimes called Mandingoes. Some trading groups are called Dyoula.

Marabout   A dervish Muslim in Africa believed to have supernatural power.

Marxist-Leninism   Sometimes called "scientific socialism," this doctrine derived from the ideas of Karl Marx as modified by Vladimir Lenin; it was the ideology of the Communist Party of the Soviet Union and has been modified in many ways by other persons and groups who still use the term. In Africa, some political parties or movements have claimed to be Marxist-Leninist but have often followed policies that conflict in practice with the ideology; these governments have usually not stressed Marx's philosophy of class struggle.

Mfecane   The movement of people in the nineteenth century in the eastern areas of present-day South Africa to the west and north as the result of wars led by the Zulus.

Movement for the Liberation of Angola (MPLA)   A major Angolan liberation movement that has its strongest following among assimilados and Kimbundu speakers, who are predominant in Luanda, the capital, and the interior to the west of the city.

Mozambique Liberation Front (Frelimo)   Mozambique's single ruling party following a 10-year struggle against Portuguese colonial rule, which ended in 1974.

Mozambique National Resistance   See *Renamo*.

Muslim   A follower of the Islamic faith.

Naam   A traditional work cooperative in Burkina Faso.

National Front for the Liberation of Angola (FNLA)   One of the major Angolan liberation movements; its original focus was limited to the northern Kongo-speaking population.

National Union for the Total Independence of Angola (UNITA)   One of three groups that fought the Portuguese during the colonial period in Angola, later backed by South Africa and the U.S. CIA and fighting the independent government of Angola.

National Youth Service   Service to the state required of youth after completing education, a common practice in many African countries.

Nkomati Accords   An agreement signed in 1984 between South Africa and Mozambique, pledging that both sides would no longer support opponents of the other.

Nonaligned Movement (NAM)   A group of nations that chose not to be politically or militarily associated with either the West or the former communist bloc.

Nongovernmental Organizations (NGO)   A private voluntary organization or agency working in relief and development programs.

Organization for the Development of the Senegal River (OMVS)   A regional grouping of countries bordering the Senegal River that sponsors joint research and projects.

Organization of African Unity (OAU)   An association of all the independent states of Africa (except South Africa) whose goal is to promote peace and security as well as economic and social development.

Organization of Petroleum Exporting Countries (OPEC)   Established in 1960, this association of some of the world's major oil-producing countries seeks to coordinate the petroleum policies of its members.

Pan Africanist Congress (PAC) A liberation organization of black South Africans that broke away from the ANC in the 1950s.

Parastatals Agencies for production or public service that are established by law and that are, in some measure, government organized and controlled. Private enterprise may be involved, and the management of the parastatal may be in private hands.

Pastoralist A person, usually a nomad, who raises livestock for a living.

Polisario Front Originally a liberation group in Western Sahara seeking independence from Spanish rule. Today, it is battling Morocco, which claims control over the Western Sahara (see *SADR*).

Popular Movement for the Liberation of Angola (MPLA) A Marxist liberation movement in Angola during the resistance to Portuguese rule; now the governing party in Angola.

Renamo A South African-backed rebel movement that attacked civilians in an attampt to overthrow the government of Mozambique.

Rinderpest A cattle disease that periodically decimates herds in savanna regions.

Saharawi Arab Democratic Republic (SADR) The Polisario Front name for Western Sahara, declared in 1976 in the struggle for independence from Morocco.

Sahel In West Africa, the borderlands between savanna and desert.

Sanctions Coercive measures, usually economic, adopted by nations acting together against a nation violating international law.

Savanna Tropical or subtropical grassland with scattered trees and undergrowth.

Sharia The Islamic code of law.

Sharpeville Massacre The 1960 pass demonstration in South Africa in which 60 people were killed when police fired into the crowd; it became a rallying point for many antiapartheid forces.

Sorghum A tropical grain that is a traditional staple in the savanna regions.

Southern African Development Community (SADC) (Formerly the Southern African Development Coordination Conference. Its name was changed in 1992.) An organization of nine African states (Angola, Zambia, Malawi, Mozambique, Zimbabwe, Lesotho, Botswana, Swaziland, and Tanzania) whose goal is to free themselves from dependence on South-Africa and to cooperate on projects of economic development.

South-West Africa People's Organization (SWAPO) Angola-based freedom fighters who had been waging guerrilla warfare against the presence of South Africa in Namibia since the 1960s. The United Nations and the Organization of African Unity now recognize SWAPO as the only authentic representative of the Namibian people.

Structural Adjustment Program (SAP) Economic reforms encouraged by the International Monetary Fund which include devaluation of currency, cutting government subsidies on commodities, and reducing government expenditures.

Swahili A trade and government Bantu language that covers much of East Africa and the Congo region.

Tsetse Fly An insect that transmits sleeping sickness to cattle and humans. It is usually found in the scrub-tree and forest regions of Central Africa.

Ujaama In Swahili, "familyhood"; government-sponsored cooperative villages in Tanzania.

Unicameral A political structure with a single legislative branch.

Unilateral Declaration of Independence (UDI) A declaration of white minority settlers in Rhodesia, claiming independence from the United Kingdom in 1965.

United Democratic Front (UDF) A multiracial, black-led group in South Africa that gained prominence during the 1983 campaign to defeat the government's Constitution, which gave only limited political rights to Asians and Coloureds.

United Nations (UN) An international organization established on June 26, 1945, through official approval of the charter by delegates of 50 nations at a conference in San Francisco, California. The charter went into effect on October 24, 1945.

United Nations Development Program (UNDP) Established to create local organizations for increasing wealth through better use of human and natural resources.

United Nations Educational, Scientific, and Cultural Organization (UNESCO) Established on November 4, 1946, to promote international collaboration in education, science, and culture.

United Nations High Commission for Refugees (UNHCR) Established in 1951 to provide international protection for people with refugee status.

Villagization A policy whereby a government relocates rural dwellers to create newer, more concentrated communities.

West African Monetary Union (WAMU) A regional association of member countries in West Africa (Benin, Burkina Faso, Côte d'Ivoire, Mali, Niger, Senegal, and Togo) that have vested authority to conduct monetary policy in a common central bank.

World Bank A closely integrated group of international institutions providing financial and technical assistance to developing countries.

World Health Organization (WHO) Established by the United Nations in 1948, this organization promotes the highest possible state of health in countries throughout the world.

Bibliography

RESOURCE CENTERS

African Studies Centers provide special services for schools, libraries, and community groups. Contact the center nearest you for further information about resources available.

African Studies Center
Boston University
270 Bay State Road
Boston, MA 02215

African Studies Program
Indiana University
Woodburn Hall 221
Bloomington, IN 47405

African Studies Educational Resource Center
100 International Center
Michigan State University
East Lansing, MI 49923

African Studies Program
630 Dartmouth
Northwestern University
Evanston, IL 60201

Africa Project
Lou Henry Hoover Room 223
Stanford University
Stanford, CA 94305

African Studies Center
University of California
Los Angeles, CA 90024

Center for African Studies
470 Grinter Hall
University of Florida
Gainesville, FL 32611

African Studies Program
University of Illinois
1208 W. California, Room 101
Urbana, IL 61801

African Studies Program
1450 Van Hise Hall
University of Wisconsin
Madison, WI 53706

Council on African Studies
Yale University
New Haven, CT 06520

Foreign Area Studies
The American University
5010 Wisconsin Avenue, N.W.
Washington, DC 20016

African Studies Program
Center for Strategic and International Studies
Georgetown University
1800 K Street, N.W.
Washington, D.C. 20006

REFERENCE WORKS, BIBLIOGRAPHIES, AND OTHER SOURCES

Africa South of the Sahara (updated yearly) (Detroit: Gale Research).

Africa Today, An Atlas of Reproductible Pages, rev. ed. (Wellesley: World Eagle, 1990).

Scarecrow Press, Metuchen, NJ, publishes *The African Historical Dictionaries*, a series edited by Jon Woronoff. There are more than 40 dictionaries, each under a specialist editor. They are short works with introductory essays and are useful guides for the beginner, especially for countries on which little has been published in English.

Colin Legum, ed., *Africa Contemporary Record* (New York: Holmes & Meier) (annual). Contains information on each country for the reporting year.

Africa Research Bulletin (Political Series), Africa Research Ltd., Exeter, Devon, England (monthly). Political updates on current issues and events in Africa.

Chris Cook and David Killingray, *African Political Facts Since 1945* (New York: Facts on File, 1990). Chronology of events; chapters on heads of state, ministers, parliaments, parties, armies, trade unions, population, biographies.

MAGAZINES AND PERIODICALS

African Arts, University of California, Los Angeles, CA. Beautifully illustrated articles review Africa's artistic heritage and current creative efforts.

African Concord, 5–15 Cromer Street, London WCIH 8LS, England.

Africa News, P.O. Box 3851, Durham, NC 27702. A weekly with short articles that are impartially written and full of information.

Africa Now, 212 Fifth Avenue, Suite 1409, New York, NY 10010. A monthly publication that gives current coverage and includes sections on art, culture, and business, as well as a special series of interviews.

Africa Recovery, DPI, Room S-1061, United Nations, New York, NY 10017.

Africa Report, African American Institute, 833 UN Plaza, New York, NY 10017. This bimonthly periodical has an update section, but most of each issue is devoted to broad-based articles by authorities giving background on key issues, developments in particular countries, and U.S. policy.

Africa Today, 64 Washburn Ave., Wellesley, MA 02181.

The Economist, 122 E. 42nd St., 14th Floor, New York, NY 10168. A weekly that gives attention to African issues.

Newswatch, 62 Oregun Rd., P.M.B. 21499, Ikeja, Nigeria.

The UNESCO Courier, 31, Rue François Bonvin, 75732, Paris CEDEX 15, France. This periodical includes short and clear articles on Africa, often by African authors, within the framework of the topic to which the monthly issues are devoted.

The Weekly Review, P.O. Box 42271, Nairobi, Kenya.

West Africa, Graybourne House, 52/54 Gray Inn Rd., London WCIX 8LT, England. This weekly is the best source for West Africa, including countries as far south as Angola and Namibia. Continent-wide issues are also discussed.

NOVELS AND AUTOBIOGRAPHICAL WRITINGS

Chinua Achebe, *Things Fall Apart* (Portsmouth: Heinemann, 1965).
This is the story of the life and values of residents of a traditional Igbo village in the nineteenth century and of its first contacts with the West.

___, *No Longer at Ease* (Portsmouth: Heinemann, 1963).
The grandson of the major character of *Things Fall Apart* lives an entirely different life in the modern city of Lagos and faces new problems while remaining committed to some of the traditional ways.

Okot p'Bitek, *Song of Lawino* (Portsmouth: Heinemann, 1983).
A traditional Ugandan wife comments on the practices of her Western-educated husband and reveals her own life-style and values.

Buchi Emecheta, *The Joys of Motherhood* (New York: G. Braziller, 1979).
The story of a Nigerian woman who overcomes great obstacles to raise a large family and then finds that the meaning of motherhood has changed.

Nadine Gordimer, *July's People* (New York: Viking, 1981).
This is a troubling and believable scenario of future revolutionary times in South Africa.

___, *A Soldier's Embrace* (New York: Viking, 1982).
These short stories treat the effects of apartheid on people's relations with each other. Films made from some of these stories are available at the University of Illinois Film Library, Urbana-Champaign, IL and the Boston University Film Library, Boston, MA.

Cheik Amadou Kane, *Ambiguous Adventure* (Portsmouth: Heinemann, 1972).
This autobiographical novel of a young man coming of age in Senegal, in a Muslim society, and, later, in a French school, illuminates changes that have taken place in Africa and raises many questions.

Alex LaGuma, *Time of the Butcherbird* (Portsmouth: Heinemann, 1979).
The people of a long-standing black community in South Africa's countryside are to be removed to a Bantustan.

Camara Laye, *The Dark Child* (Farrar Straus and Giroux, 1954).
This autobiographical novel gives a loving and nostalgic picture of a Malinke family of Guinea.

Ousmane Sembene, *God's Bits of Wood* (Portsmouth: Heinemann, 1970).
The railroad workers' strike of 1947 provides the setting for a novel about the changing consciousness and life of African men and women in Senegal.

Joyce Sikakane, *A Window on Soweto* (London: International Defense and Aid Fund, 1977).

Wole Soyinka, *Ake: The Years of Childhood* (New York: Random House, 1983).
Soyinka's account of his first 11 years is full of the sights, tastes, smells, sounds, and personal encounters of a headmaster's home and a busy Yoruba town.

Ngugi wa Thiong'o, *A Grain of Wheat* (Portsmouth: Heinemann, 1968).
A story of how the Mau-Mau movement and the coming of independence affected several individuals after independence as well as during the struggle that preceded it.

INTRODUCTORY BOOKS

A. E. Afigbo, E. A. Ayandele, R. J. Gavin, J. D. Omer-Cooper, and R. Palmer, *The Making of Modern Africa,* vol. II, *The Twentieth Century,* 2nd ed. (London: Longman, 1986).
An introductory political history of Africa in the twentieth century.

Fredoline O. Anunobi, *International Dimensions of Africa Political Economy: Trends, Challenges, and Realities* (Landham, MD: U Press of America, 1994).

Tony Binns, *People and Environment in Africa* (New York: Wiley, 1995).

Raymond Bonner, *At the Hand of Man: Peril and Hope for Africa's Wildlife* (New York: Random House, 1994).
Reviews the status of Africa's wildlife conservation.

Lynn C. Bowling, *Go Ye into . . . Africa* (Lafayette, LA: Prescott Press, 1993).

Gwendolen Carter and Patrick O'Meara, eds., *African Independence: The First Twenty-Five Years* (Midland Books, 1986).
Collected essays surrounding issues such as political structures, military rule, and economics.

Naomi Chazan et al., *Politics and Society in Contemporary Africa* (Boulder: L. Rienner Publishers, 1992).

John Chiasson, *African Journey* (Upland, CT: Bradbury Press, 1987).
An examination into Africa's social life and customs.

Basil Davidson, *Africa in History* (Macmillan, 1991).
A fine discussion of African history.

___, *The African Genius* (Boston: Little, Brown, 1979). Also published as *The Africans.*
Davidson discusses the complex political, social, and economic systems of traditional African societies, translating scholarly works into a popular mode without distorting complex material.

___, *The Black Man's Burden: Africa and the Curse of the Nation State* (New York: Random House, 1992).
A discussion on Africa's government and the status of the nation state.

___, *A History of Africa,* 2nd ed. (Unwin Hyman, 1989).
A comprehensive look at the historical evolution of Africa.

___, *Let Freedom Come* (Boston: Little, Brown, 1978).
A lively and interesting history of Africa in the twentieth century.

Bill Freund, *The Making of Contemporary Africa: The Development of African Society since 1800* (Bloomington: Indiana University Press, 1984).
Recent African history from an economic-history point of view, with emphasis on forces of production.

Adrian Hastings, *A History of African Christianity, 1950–1975* (Cambridge: Cambridge University Press, 1979).
A good introduction to the impact of Christianity on Africa in recent years.

Goren Hyden, *No Shortcut to Progress: African Development Management in Perspective* (Berkeley: University of California, 1983).
An assessment of development in relation to obstacles, prospects, and progress.

Omari H. Kohole, *Dimensions of Africa's International Relations* (Delmar, NY: Caravan Books, 1993).

Phyllis Martin and Patrick O'Meara, eds., *Africa*, 2nd ed. (Boomington: Indiana University Press, 1986).
This collection of essays covers history, culture, politics, and the economy.

John Mbiti, *African Religions and Philosophy* (Portsmouth: Heinemann, 1982).
This work by a Ugandan scholar is the standard introduction to the rich variety of religious beliefs and rituals of African peoples.

E. Jefferson Murphy, *African Mythology: Old and New* (Storrs, CT: I N Thut World Education Center, 1973).

Joseph M. Murphy, *Working the Spirit: Ceremonies of the African Diaspora* (Boston: Beacon Press, 1994).

J. H. Kwabena Nketia, *The Music of Africa* (New York: Norton, 1974).
The author, a Ghanaian by birth, is Africa's best-known ethnomusicologist.

Robert Ruly, *History of the African People* (New York: Macmillan, 1986).

Chris Searle, *We're Building the New School: Diary of a Teacher in Mozambique* (London: Zed Press, 1981; distributed in the United States by Laurence Hill & Co., Westport).
A lively book that shows that the lives of students and teachers in the nation of Mozambique are both exciting and difficult.

Timothy Shaw and Adebayo Adedeji, *Economic Crisis in Africa: African Perspectives on Development Problems and Potentials* (Boulder: L. Rienner, 1985).

J. B. Webster, A. A. Boahen, and M. Tidy, *The Revolutionary Years: West Africa Since 1800* (London: Longman, 1980).
An interesting, enjoyable, and competent introductory history to the West African region.

Frank Willett, *African Art* (New York: Oxford University Press, 1971).
A work to read for both reference and pleasure, by one of the authorities on Nigeria's early art.

COUNTRY AND REGIONAL STUDIES

Howard Adelman and John Sorenson, eds., *African Refugees* (Boulder: Westview, 1993).

Tony Avirgan and Martha Honey, *War in Uganda: The Legacy of Idi Amin* (Westport: Laurence Hill & Co., 1982).

John E. Bardill and James H. Cobbe, *Lesotho: Dilemmas of Dependence in Southern Africa* (Boulder: Westview Press, 1985).

Gerald Bender, *Angola under the Portuguese: The Myth and the Reality* (Berkeley: University of California Press, 1978).

William Bigelow, *Strangers in Their Own Country* (a curriculum on South Africa), 2nd ed. (Trenton: Africa World Press, 1989).

Allan R. Booth, *Swaziland: Tradition and Change in a Southern African Kingdom* (Boulder: Westview Press, 1984).

Thomas Borstelmann, *Apartheid, Colonialism, and the Cold War: The United States and Southern Africa* (New York: Oxford University Press, 1993).

Louis Brenner, ed., *Muslim Identity and Social Change in Sub-Saharan Africa* (Bloomington: Indiana University Press, 1993).

Mike Brogden and Clifford Shearing, *Policing for a New South Africa* (New York: Routledge, 1993).

Marcia M. Burdette, *Zambia: Between Two Worlds* (Boulder: Westview Press, 1988).

Thomas Callaghy and John Ravenhill, eds., *Hemmed In: Global Responses to Africa's Economic Decline* (New York: Columbia University Press, 1994).

Chazen et al., *Politics and Society in Contemporary Africa* (Boulder: Lynne Rienner, 1992).

T. Terry Childs, ed., *Society, Culture, and Technology in Africa* (Philadelphia: MASCA, University of Pennsylvania, 1994).

Christopher Clapham, *Transformation and Continuity in Revolutionary Ethiopia* (Cambridge: Cambridge University Press, 1988).

Robin Cohen and Harry Goulbourne, eds., *Democracy and Socialism in Africa* (Boulder: Westview Press, 1991).

Maureen Covell, *Madagascar: Politics, Economy, and Society* (London and New York: F. Pinter, 1987).

Toyin Falola and Julius Ihonvbere, *The Rise and Fall of Nigeria's Second Republic, 1979–1984* (London: Zed Press, 1985).

Robert Fatton, *The Making of a Liberal Democracy: Senegal's Passive Revolution, 1975–85* (Boulder: L. Rienner, 1987).

Foreign Area Studies (Washington, D.C.: Government Printing Office). Includes country-study handbooks with chapters on history, politics, culture, and economics, with maps, charts, and bibliographies. There are more than 20 in the series, with new ones added and revised periodically.

Marcus Franda, *The Seychelles: Unquiet Islands* (Boulder: Westview Press, 1982).

Sheldon Gellar, *Senegal: An African Nation between Islam and the West* (Boulder: Westview Press, 1982).

April A. Gordon and Donald L. Gordon, *Understanding Contemporary Africa* (Boulder: L. Rienner Publishers, 1996).

Joseph Hanlon, *Mozambique: The Revolution under Fire* (London: Zed Press, 1984).

Tony Hodges, *Western Sahara: The Roots of a Desert War* (Westport: Laurence Hill & Co., 1983).

Allan and Barbara Isaacman, *Mozambique from Colonialism to Revolution, 1900–1982* (Boulder: Westview Press, 1983).

Richard Joseph, *Democracy and Prebendel Politics in Nigeria: The Rise and Fall of the Second Republic* (Cambridge: Cambridge University Press, 1987).

Michael P. Kelley, *A State in Disarray: Conditions of Chad's Survival* (Boulder: Westview Press, 1986).

Gaim Kibreab, *Refugees and Development in Africa: The Case of Eritrea* (Trenton: Red Sea Press, 1987).

Gerhard Kraus, *Human Development from an African Ancestry* (London: Karnak House, 1990).

David D. Laitin and Said S. Samatar, *Somalia: Nation in Search of a State* (Boulder: Westview Press, 1987).

J. Gus Liebenow, *Liberia: Quest for Democracy* (Bloomington: Indiana University Press, 1987).

David Martin and Phyllis Johnson, *The Struggle for Zimbabwe: The Chimurenga War* (Boston: Faber & Faber, 1981).

Norman N. Miller, *Kenya: The Quest for Prosperity* (Boulder: Westview Press, 1984).

Malyn Newitt, *The Comoro Islands: Struggle against Dependency in the Indian Ocean* (Boulder: Westview Press, 1984).

Roland Anthony Oliver, *The African Experience* (London: Weidenfeld & Nicholson, 1991).

Adebayo O. Olukoshi and Liisa Laakso, *Challenges to the Nation-State in Africa* (Uppsala: Nordiska Afrikainstitutet, in cooperation with Institute of Development Studies, University of Helsinki, 1996).

Thomas O'Toole, *The Central African Republic: The Continent's Hidden Heart* (Boulder: Westview Press, 1986).

Jack Parson, *Botswana: Liberal Democracy and the Labor Resource in Southern Africa* (Boulder: Westview Press, 1984).

Deborah Pellow and Naomi Chazan, *Ghana: Coping with Uncertainty* (Boulder: Westview Press, 1986).

F. Jeffress Ramsay, Barry Morton, and Themba Mgadla, *Building a Nation: A History of Botswana* (Gaborne: Longman Botswana, 1996).

Richard Sandbrook, *The Politics of Africa's Economic Recovery* (Cambridge: Cambridge University Press, 1993).

Alexander Sarris, *Ghana under Structural Adjustment* (New York: New York University Press, 1991).

Bereket Habte Selassie, *Conflict and Intervention in the Horn of Africa* (New York: Monthly Review Press, 1980).

Study Commission on U.S. Policy toward Southern Africa, *South Africa: Time Running Out* (Berkeley and Los Angeles: University of California Press, 1981).

Christopher C. Taylor, *Milk, Honey, and Money: Changing Concepts in Rwandan Healing* (Washington: Smithsonian Institution Press, 1992).

Time-Life Books, ed., *Africa's Glorious Legacy* (Alexandria, VA: Time-Life Books, 1994).

Rachid Tlemcani, *State and Revolution in Algeria* (Boulder: Westview Press, 1987).

Jan Vansina, *Habitat, Economy, and Society in the Central African Rainforest* (Providence: Berg Publishers, 1992).

Margaret A. Vogt, ed., *The Liberian Crisis and ECOMOG, a Bold Attempt at Regional Peacekeeping* (Lagos, Nigeria: Gabumo Publishing Co., 1992).

C. W. Wigwe, *Language, Culture, and Society in West Africa* (Elms Court, UK: Arthur H. Stockwell, 1990).

Michael Wolfers and Jane Bergerol, *Angola in the Frontline* (London: Zed Press, 1983).

Rodger Yeager, *Tanzania: An African Experiment* (Boulder: Westview Press, 1983).

Index